# THE G!DDY LiM!T
## FIFTEENTH ANNIVERSARY BOOK

by Alex Leonard

Published by The Orcadian (Kirkwall Press)
Hell's Half Acre, Hatston, Kirkwall, Orkney, KW15 1GJ
Tel. 01856 879000 • Fax 01856 879001 • www.orcadian.co.uk

Book sales: www.orcadian.co.uk/shop/index.php

Text and Artwork by Alex Leonard © 2020
www.giddy-limit.com

ISBN 978-1-912889-09-9

Printed in Orkney by The Orcadian, Hatston Print Centre, Hell's Half Acre, Hatston, Kirkwall, Orkney, KW15 1GJ

# THE G!DDY LIM!T
## FIFTEENTH ANNIVERSARY BOOK

*Alex*

FOR THEO

# FOREWORD

As my father is a cartoonist, I'm slightly nervous that Alex may have inadvertently approached the wrong McArthur to write this foreword. Certainly, cartooning is a skill that skipped a generation in our family, but here's my take, for what it's worth.

The beauty and true skill of any cartoonist is to be able to convey an often complex message in the simplest of terms. In that sense, it doesn't take an expert to realise that Alex really is a master of his craft. A quick glance through the back catalogue of The Giddy Limit is all the evidence you need - and helpfully that's what lies ahead of you.

As a politician, I'm only too aware of the power of cartoons: they can end careers; bring down governments; even spark violent and murderous protest. But they are an integral part of a living, breathing democracy where the communication of ideas, the right to protest and the challenging of authority are non-negotiables.

The Giddy Limit may not have helped overthrow a Council administration or prompted the citizens of Stromness to take to the streets with pitchforks, but it has observed life in Orkney with a keen and critical eye. Poking fun, revealing truths and engaging a public who may not otherwise have been listening. The gentleness of the humour should not disguise the effectiveness of the message and underscores the talent of the messenger.

Everyone no doubt has their favourite – mine is the fine tribute paid to the Sanday team and supporters after Alex's beloved Stromness beat them in a thrilling Parish Cup final last year. In truth, though, The Giddy Limit is consistently brilliant, as you are about to be reminded….

Liam McArthur MSP
Liberal Democrat, Orkney

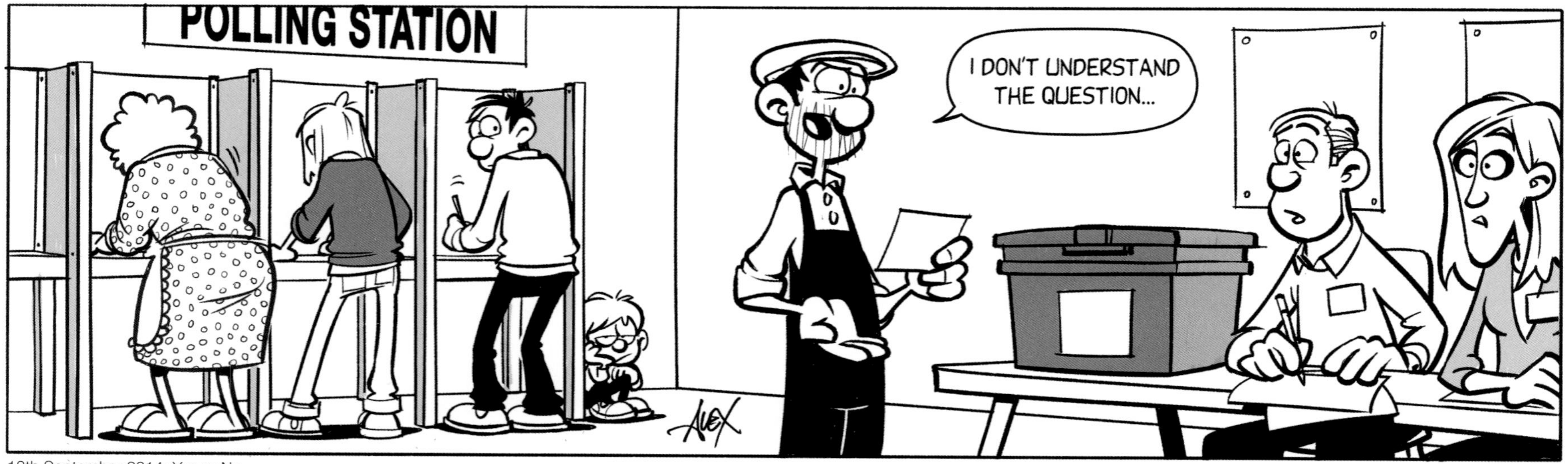
POLLING STATION
I DON'T UNDERSTAND THE QUESTION...

18th September 2014: Yes or No.

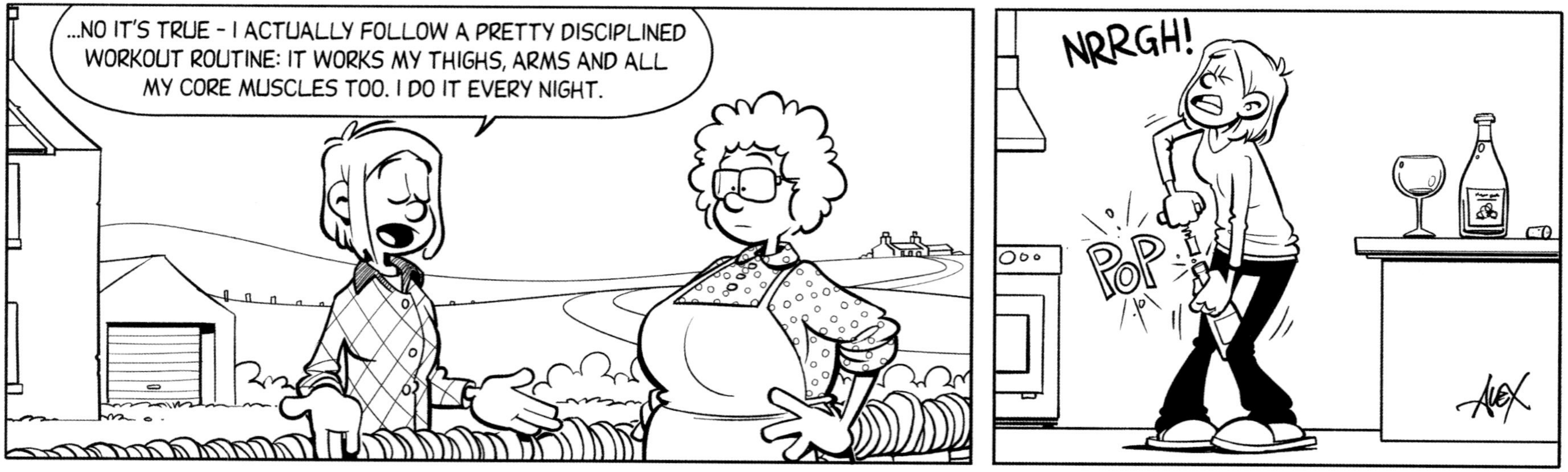
...NO IT'S TRUE - I ACTUALLY FOLLOW A PRETTY DISCIPLINED WORKOUT ROUTINE: IT WORKS MY THIGHS, ARMS AND ALL MY CORE MUSCLES TOO. I DO IT EVERY NIGHT.
NRRGH!
POP

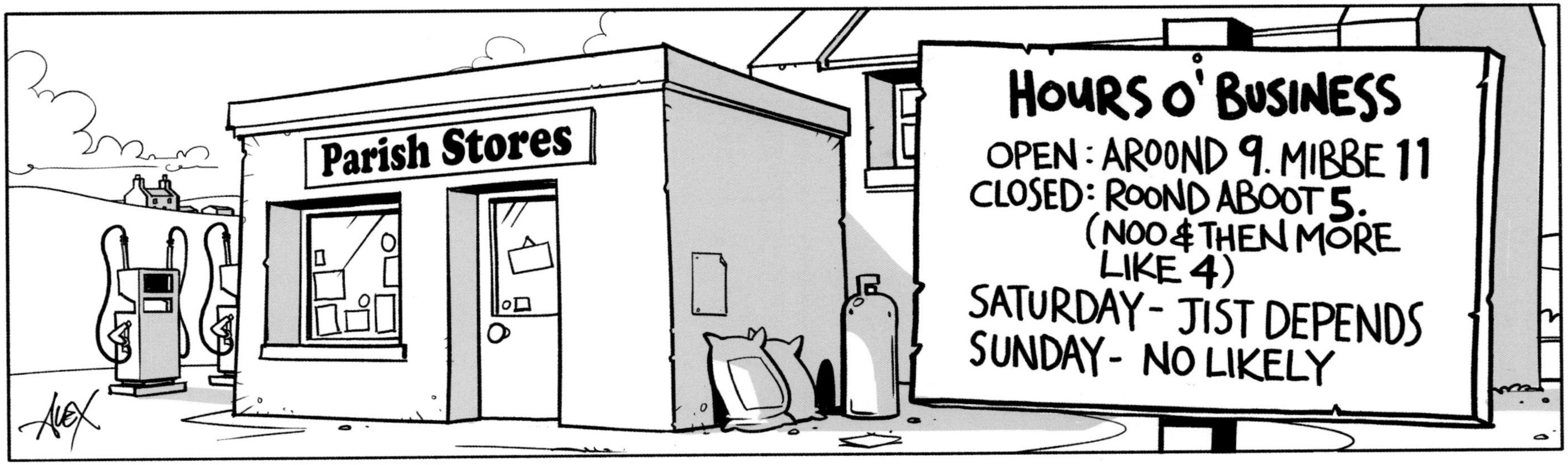
Parish Stores
HOURS O' BUSINESS
OPEN: AROOND 9. MIBBE 11
CLOSED: ROOND ABOOT 5.
(NOO & THEN MORE LIKE 4)
SATURDAY - JIST DEPENDS
SUNDAY - NO LIKELY
ALEX

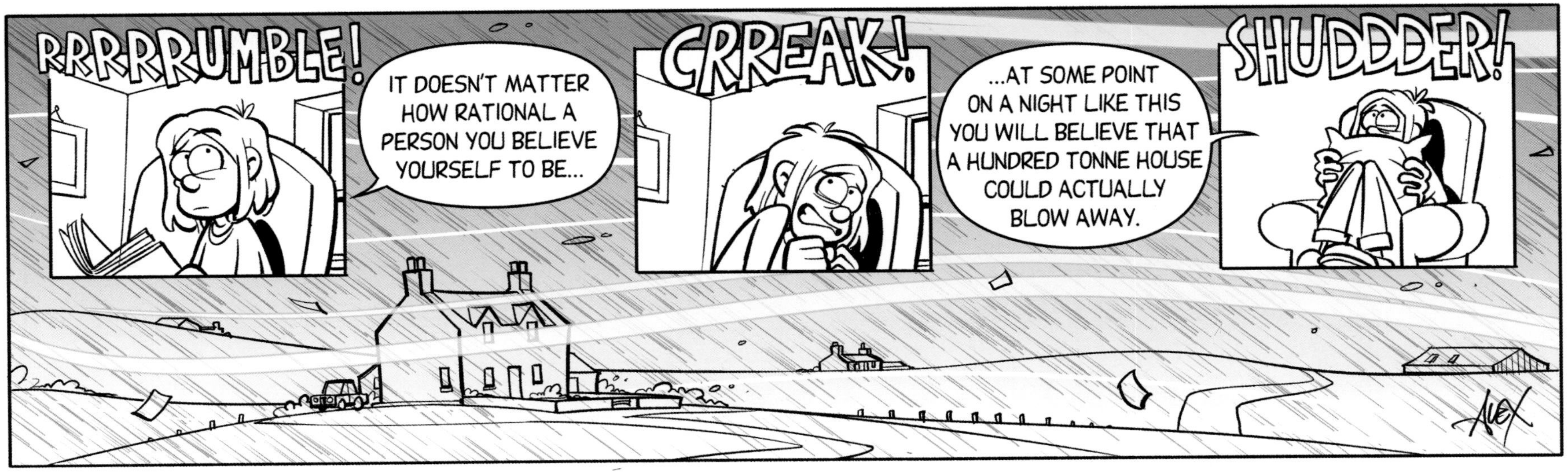
RRRRRUMBLE!
IT DOESN'T MATTER HOW RATIONAL A PERSON YOU BELIEVE YOURSELF TO BE...
CRREAK!
...AT SOME POINT ON A NIGHT LIKE THIS YOU WILL BELIEVE THAT A HUNDRED TONNE HOUSE COULD ACTUALLY BLOW AWAY.
SHUDDDER!
ALEX

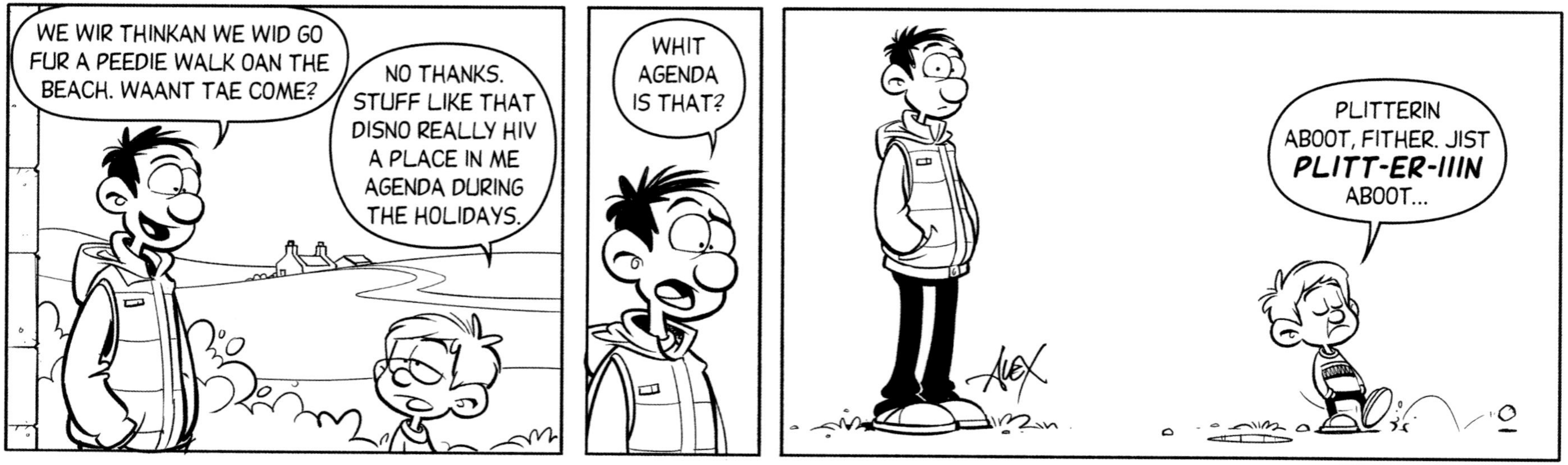
WE WIR THINKAN WE WID GO FUR A PEEDIE WALK OAN THE BEACH. WAANT TAE COME?
NO THANKS. STUFF LIKE THAT DISNO REALLY HIV A PLACE IN ME AGENDA DURING THE HOLIDAYS.
WHIT AGENDA IS THAT?
PLITTERIN ABOOT, FITHER. JIST **PLITT-ER-IIIN** ABOOT...
ALEX

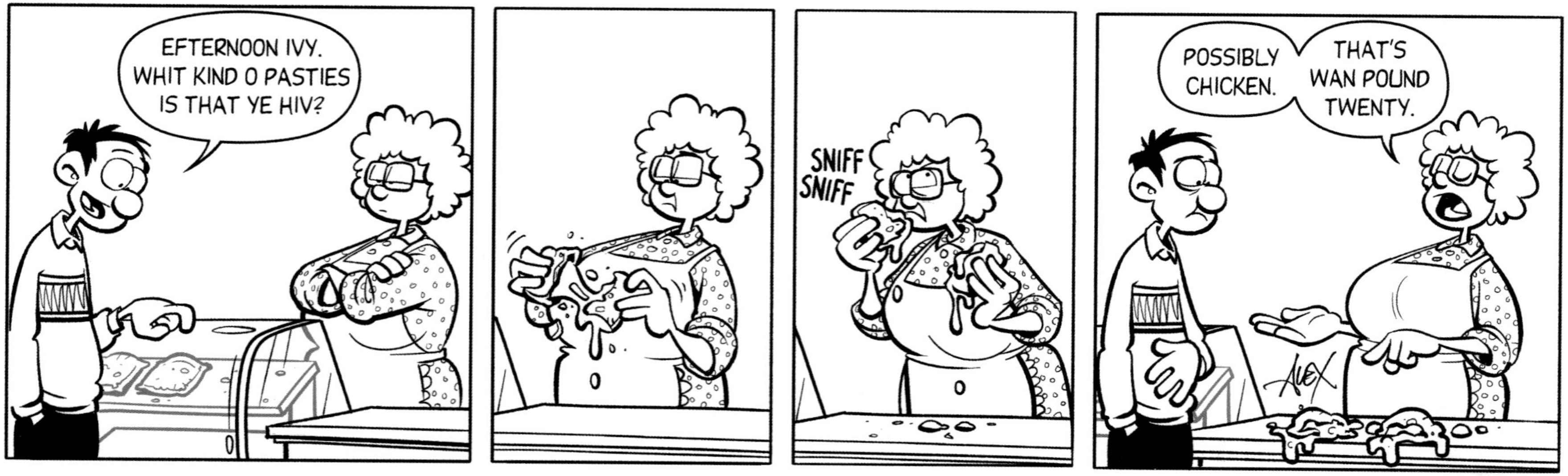
EFTERNOON IVY. WHIT KIND O PASTIES IS THAT YE HIV?
SNIFF SNIFF
POSSIBLY CHICKEN.
THAT'S WAN POUND TWENTY.
ALEX

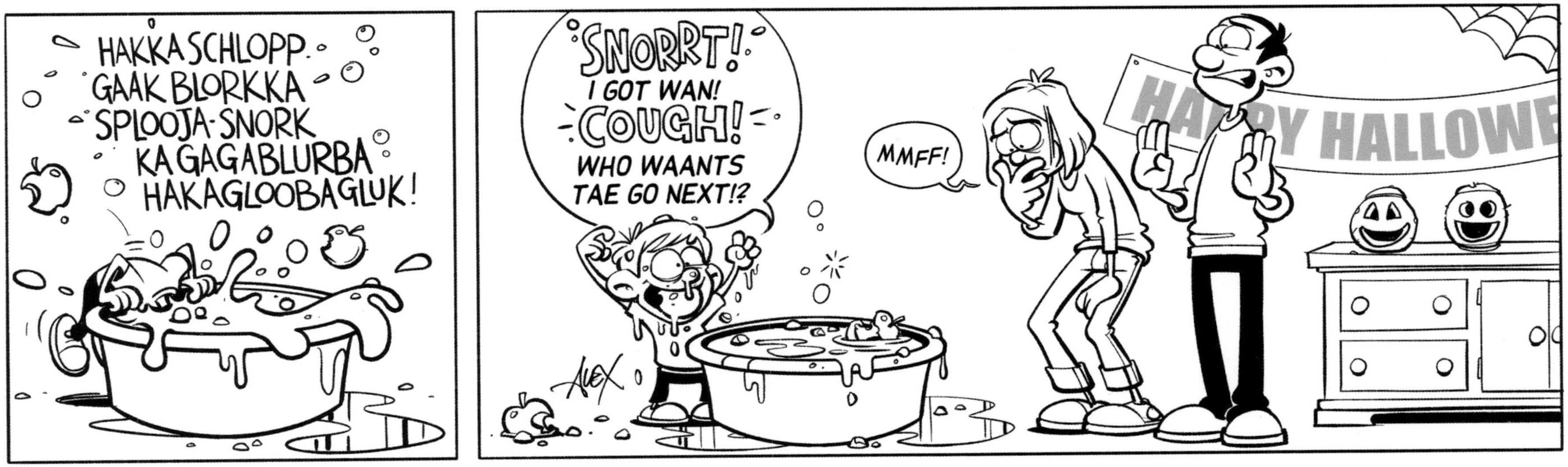
HAKKASCHLOPP GAAK BLORKKA SPLOOJA-SNORK KA GAGABLURBA HAKAGLOOBAGLUK!
SNORRT! I GOT WAN! COUGH! WHO WAANTS TAE GO NEXT!?
MMFF!
ALEX

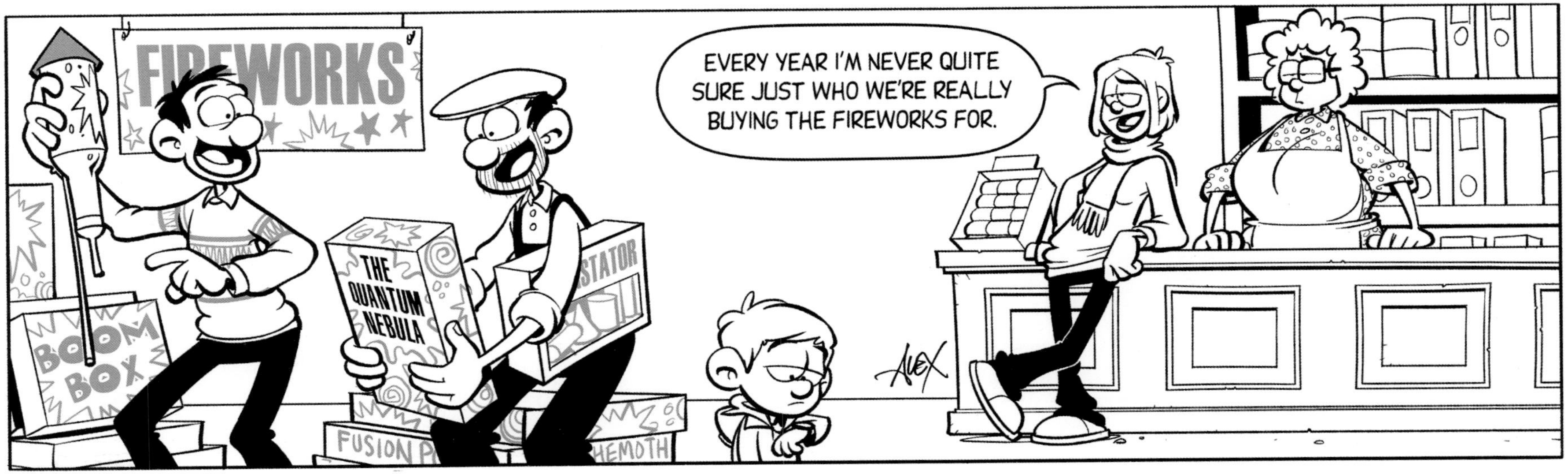
THE QUANTUM NEBULA
BOOM BOX
STATOR
FUSION P
HEMOTH
EVERY YEAR I'M NEVER QUITE SURE JUST WHO WE'RE REALLY BUYING THE FIREWORKS FOR.
ALEX

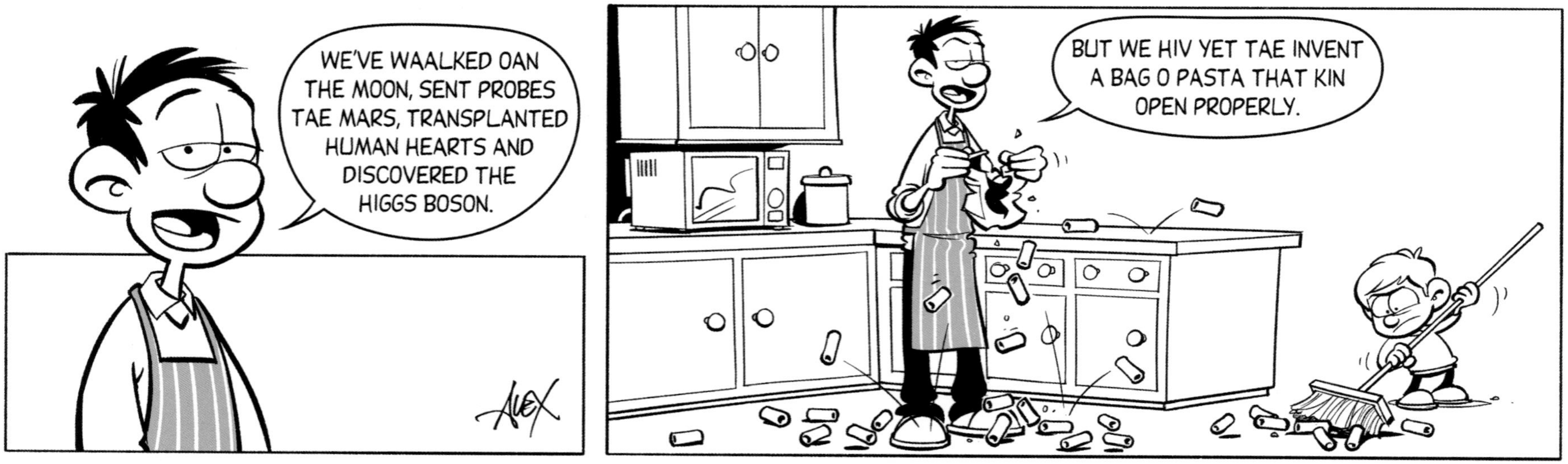
WE'VE WAALKED OAN THE MOON, SENT PROBES TAE MARS, TRANSPLANTED HUMAN HEARTS AND DISCOVERED THE HIGGS BOSON.
ALEX
BUT WE HIV YET TAE INVENT A BAG O PASTA THAT KIN OPEN PROPERLY.

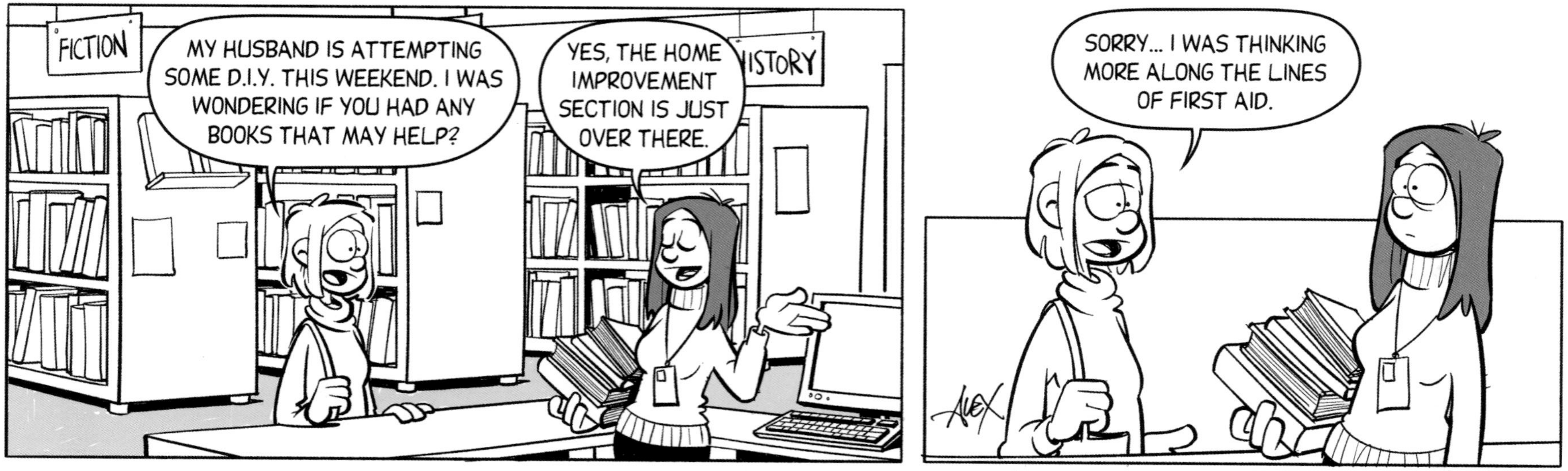
FICTION
HISTORY
MY HUSBAND IS ATTEMPTING SOME D.I.Y. THIS WEEKEND. I WAS WONDERING IF YOU HAD ANY BOOKS THAT MAY HELP?
YES, THE HOME IMPROVEMENT SECTION IS JUST OVER THERE.
SORRY... I WAS THINKING MORE ALONG THE LINES OF FIRST AID.
ALEX

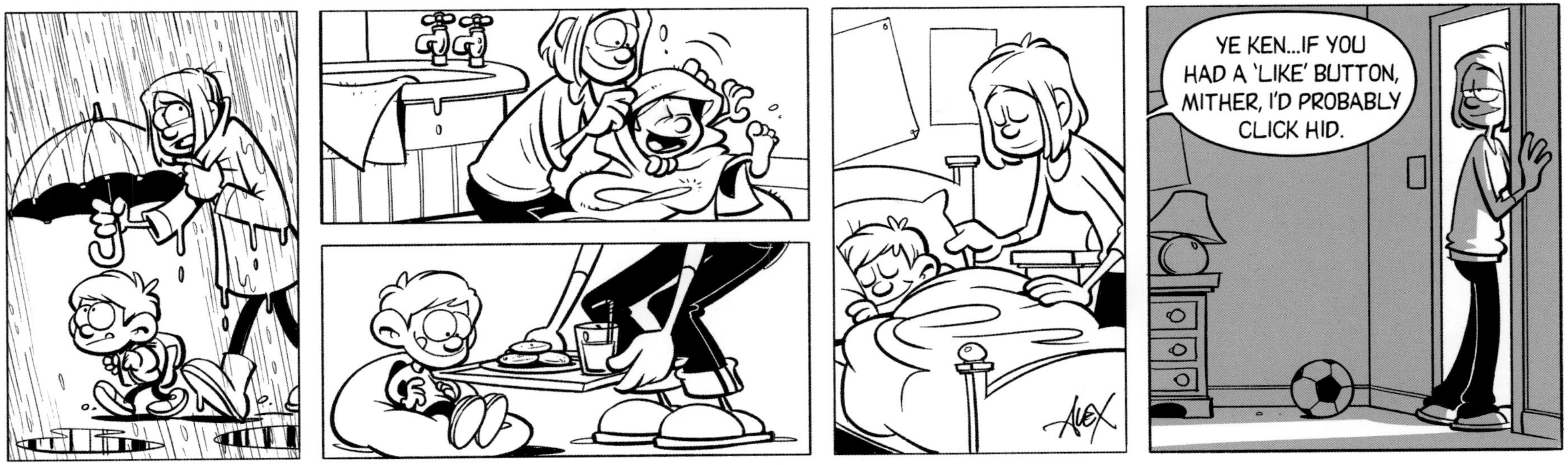
YE KEN...IF YOU HAD A 'LIKE' BUTTON, MITHER, I'D PROBABLY CLICK HID.

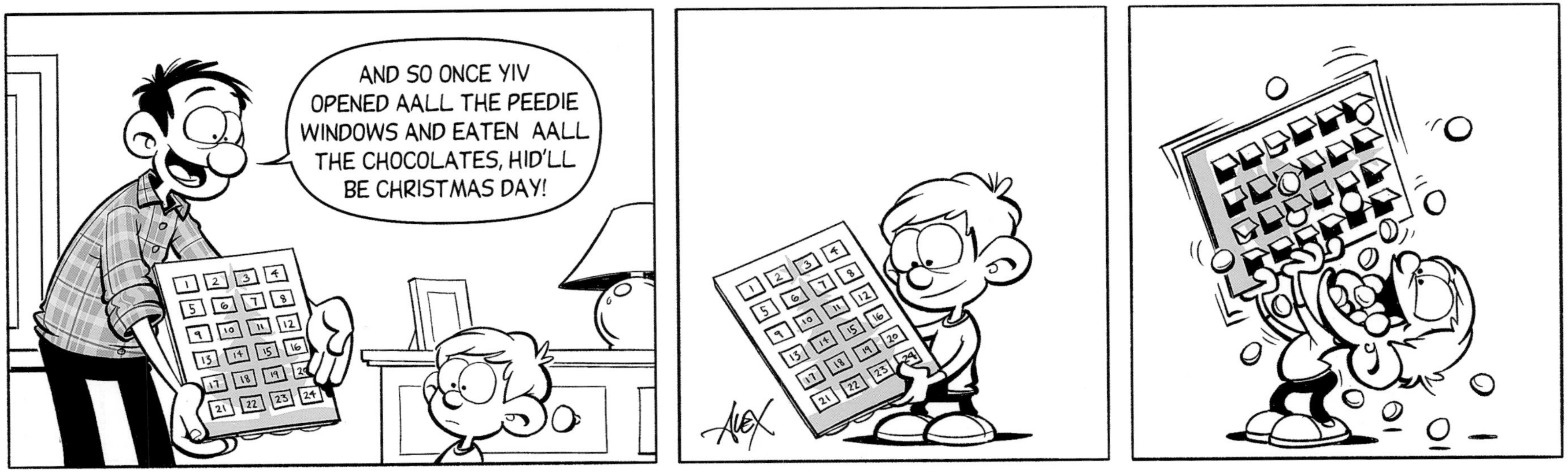
AND SO ONCE YIV OPENED AALL THE PEEDIE WINDOWS AND EATEN AALL THE CHOCOLATES, HID'LL BE CHRISTMAS DAY!

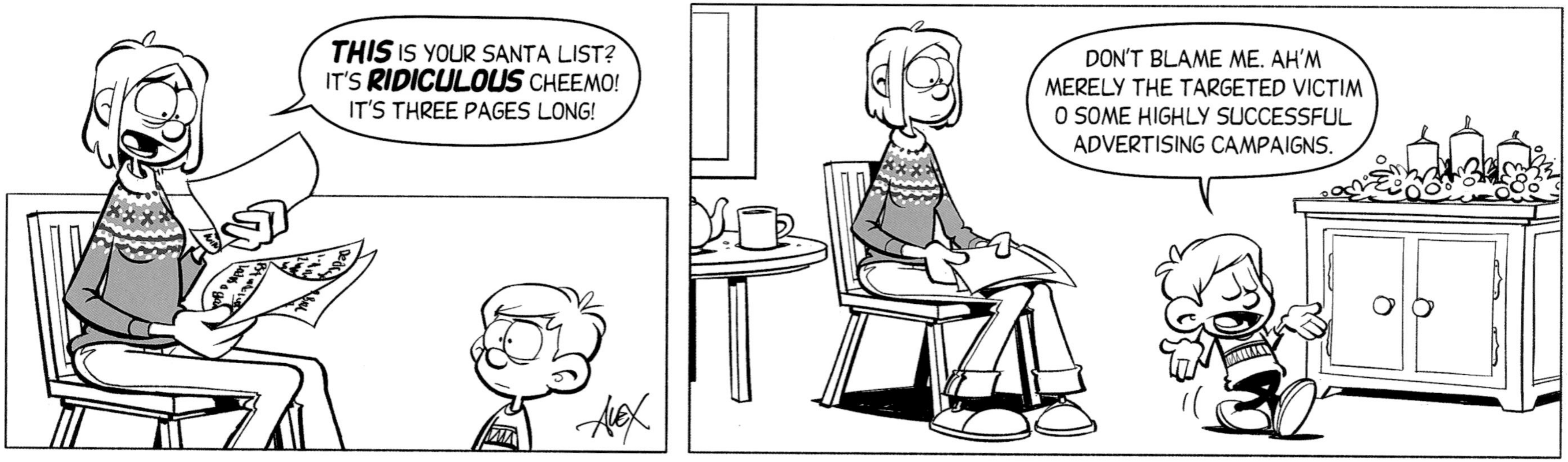
THIS IS YOUR SANTA LIST? IT'S RIDICULOUS CHEEMO! IT'S THREE PAGES LONG!
DON'T BLAME ME. AH'M MERELY THE TARGETED VICTIM O SOME HIGHLY SUCCESSFUL ADVERTISING CAMPAIGNS.
ALEX

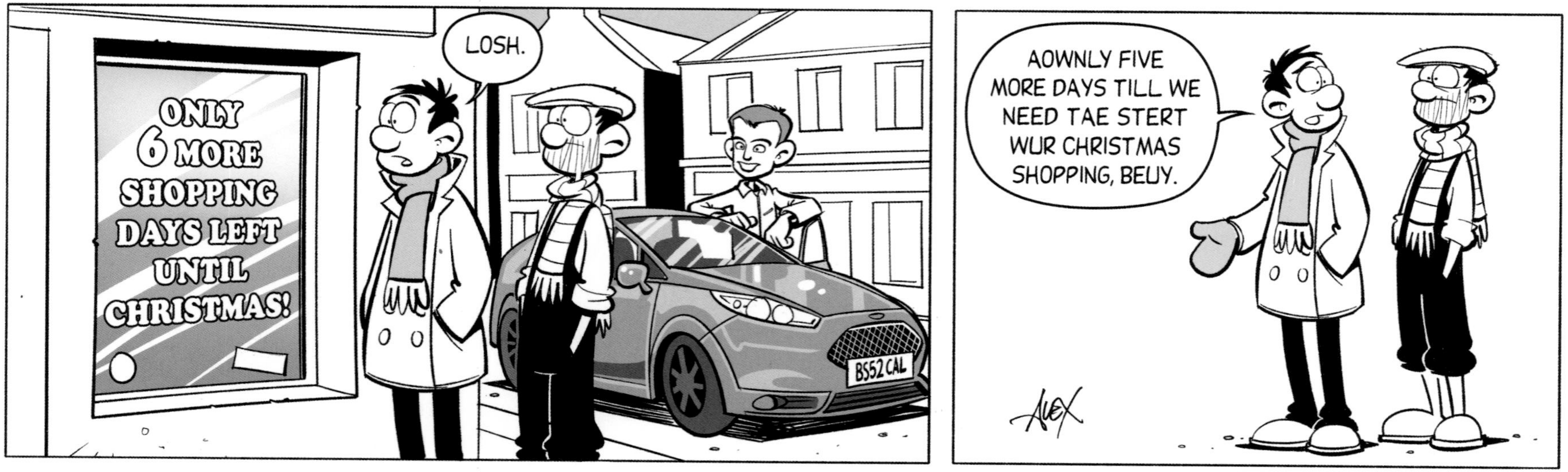
ONLY 6 MORE SHOPPING DAYS LEFT UNTIL CHRISTMAS!
LOSH.
BS52 CAL
AOWNLY FIVE MORE DAYS TILL WE NEED TAE STERT WUR CHRISTMAS SHOPPING, BEUY.
ALEX

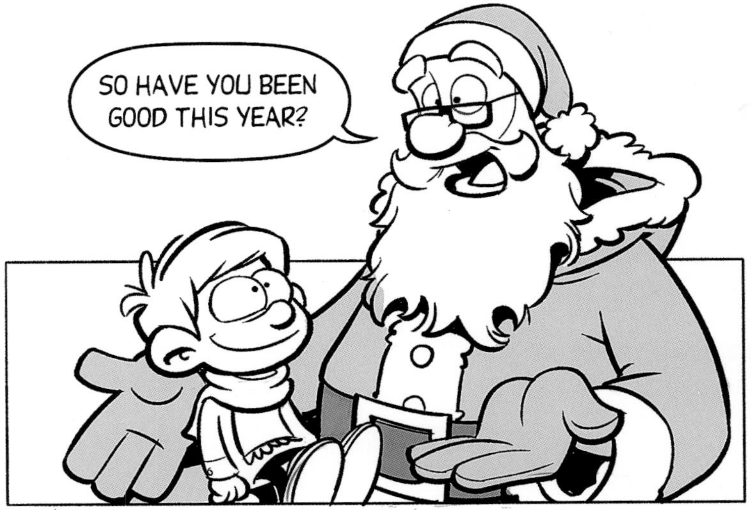
SO HAVE YOU BEEN GOOD THIS YEAR?

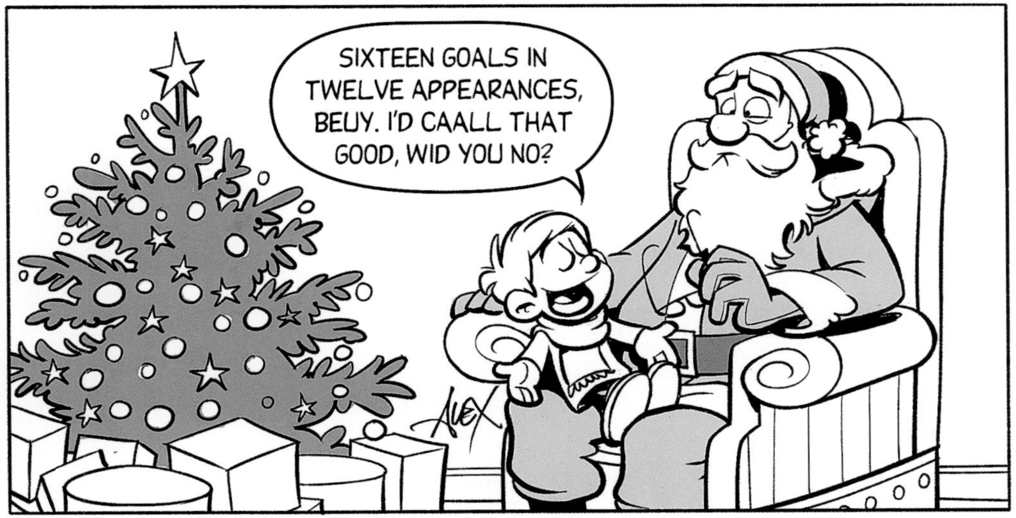
SIXTEEN GOALS IN TWELVE APPEARANCES, BEUY. I'D CAALL THAT GOOD, WID YOU NO?
ALEX

# 2015 CALENDAR

Kye
Oan Demand
THE GIDDY LIMIT
Calendar 2015
Catch Up
Library
Fillums
Kye Store
Showcase
HOLMLAND
PLOUGHING MATCH OF THE DAY
[ spoots ]
modrenfamily
BAND OF BUDDOOS
THE WESTRAY WING
HOY-DE-HOY!
THE WYRE
THE WIRKAN DEAD
ALEX

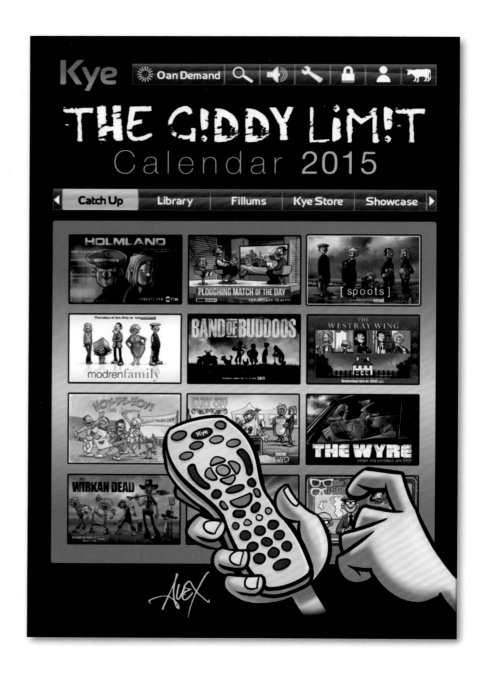

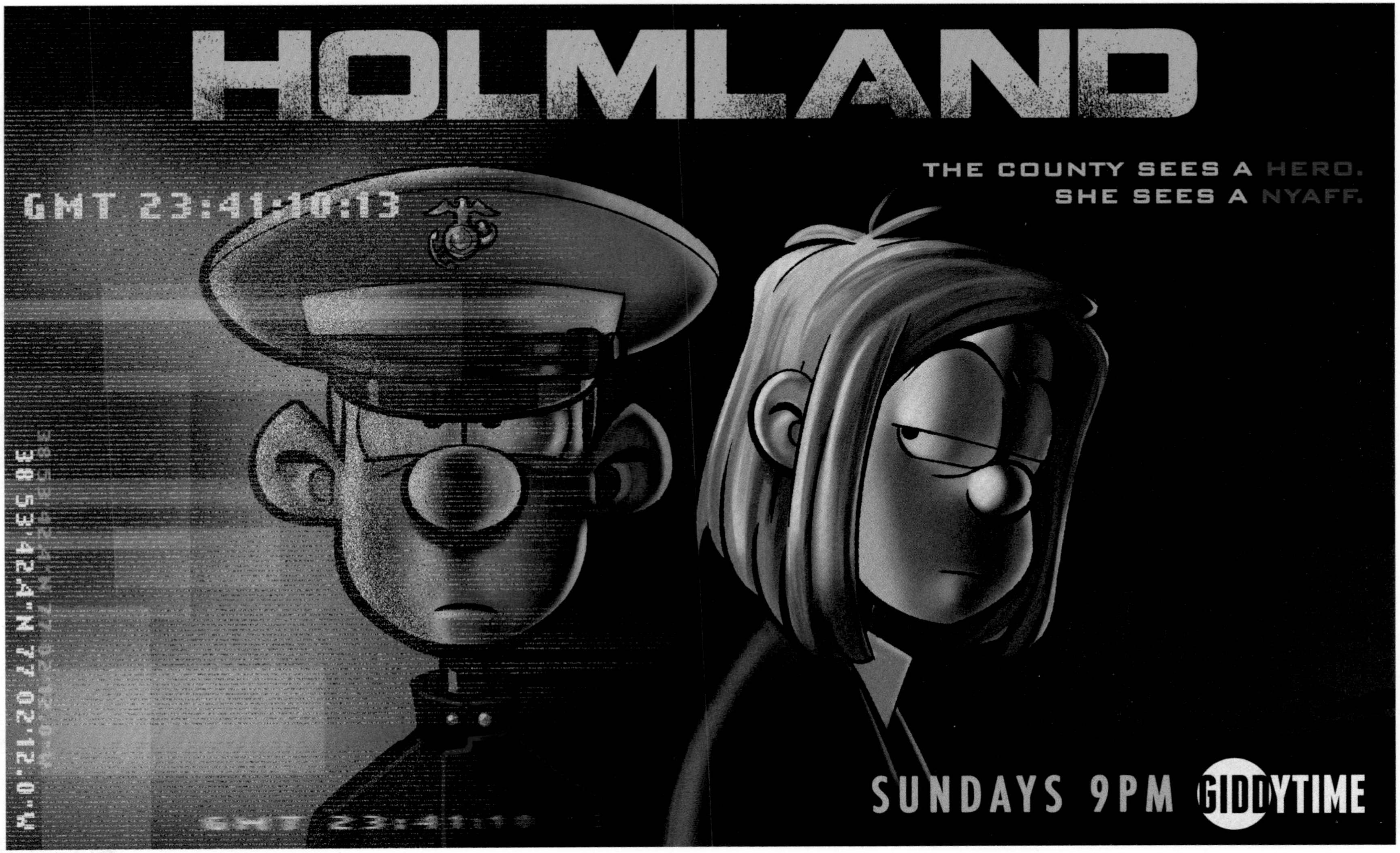
HOLMLAND
THE COUNTY SEES A HERO.
SHE SEES A NYAFF.
GMT 23:41:10:13
38°53'42.4"N 77°02'12.0"W
SUNDAYS 9PM GIDDYTIME

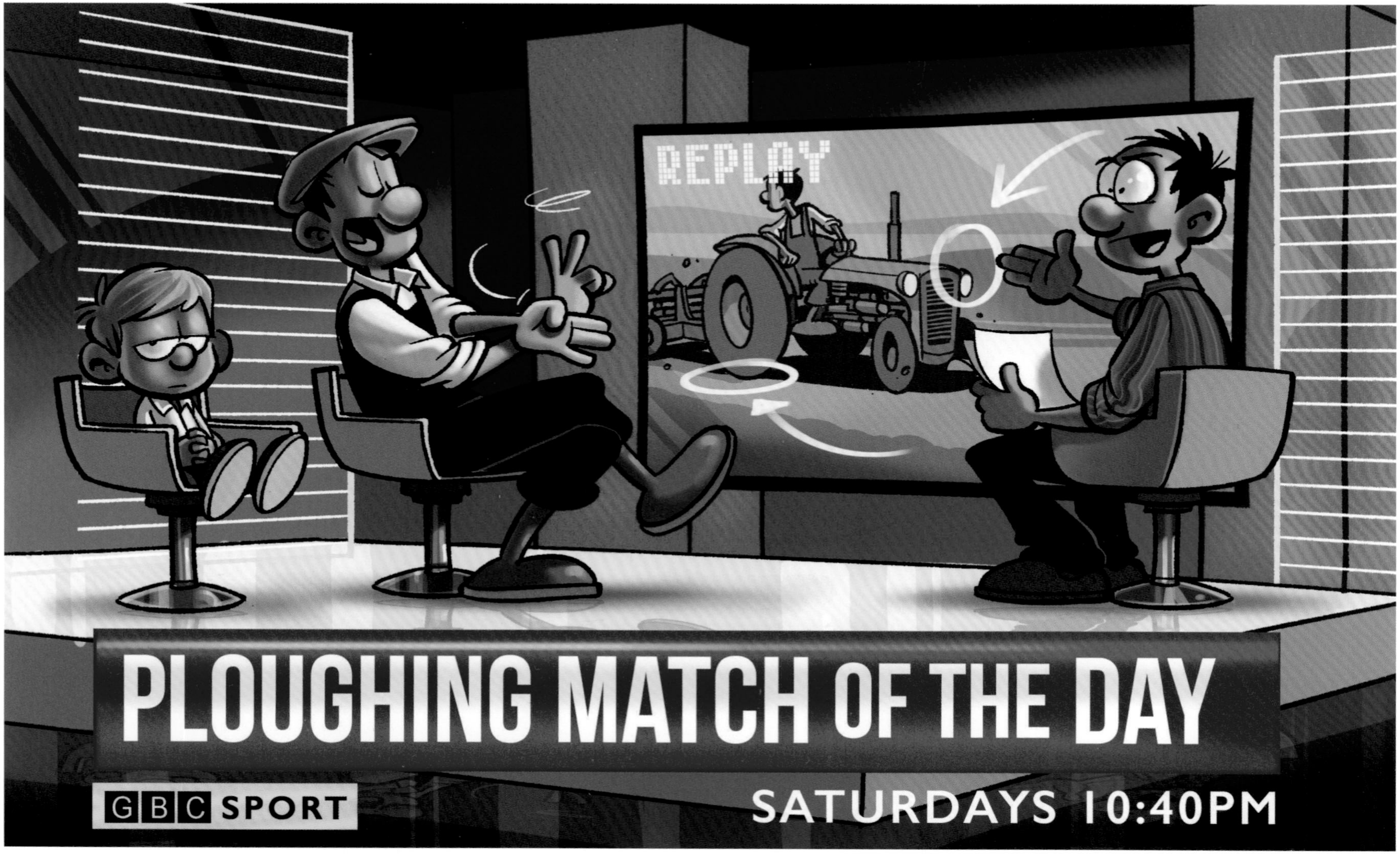

REPLAY
PLOUGHING MATCH OF THE DAY
GBC SPORT
SATURDAYS 10:40PM

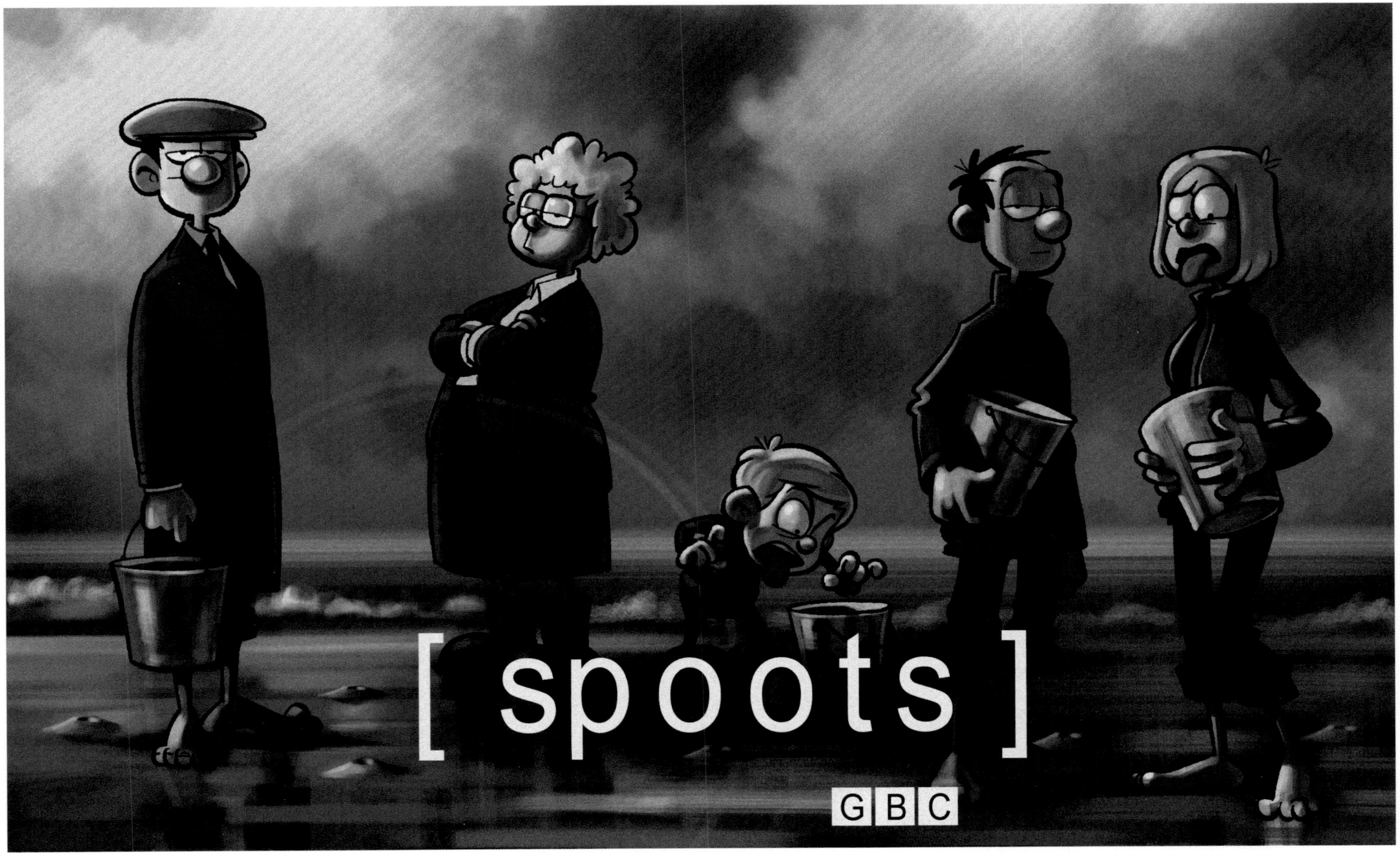
[ spoots ]
GBC

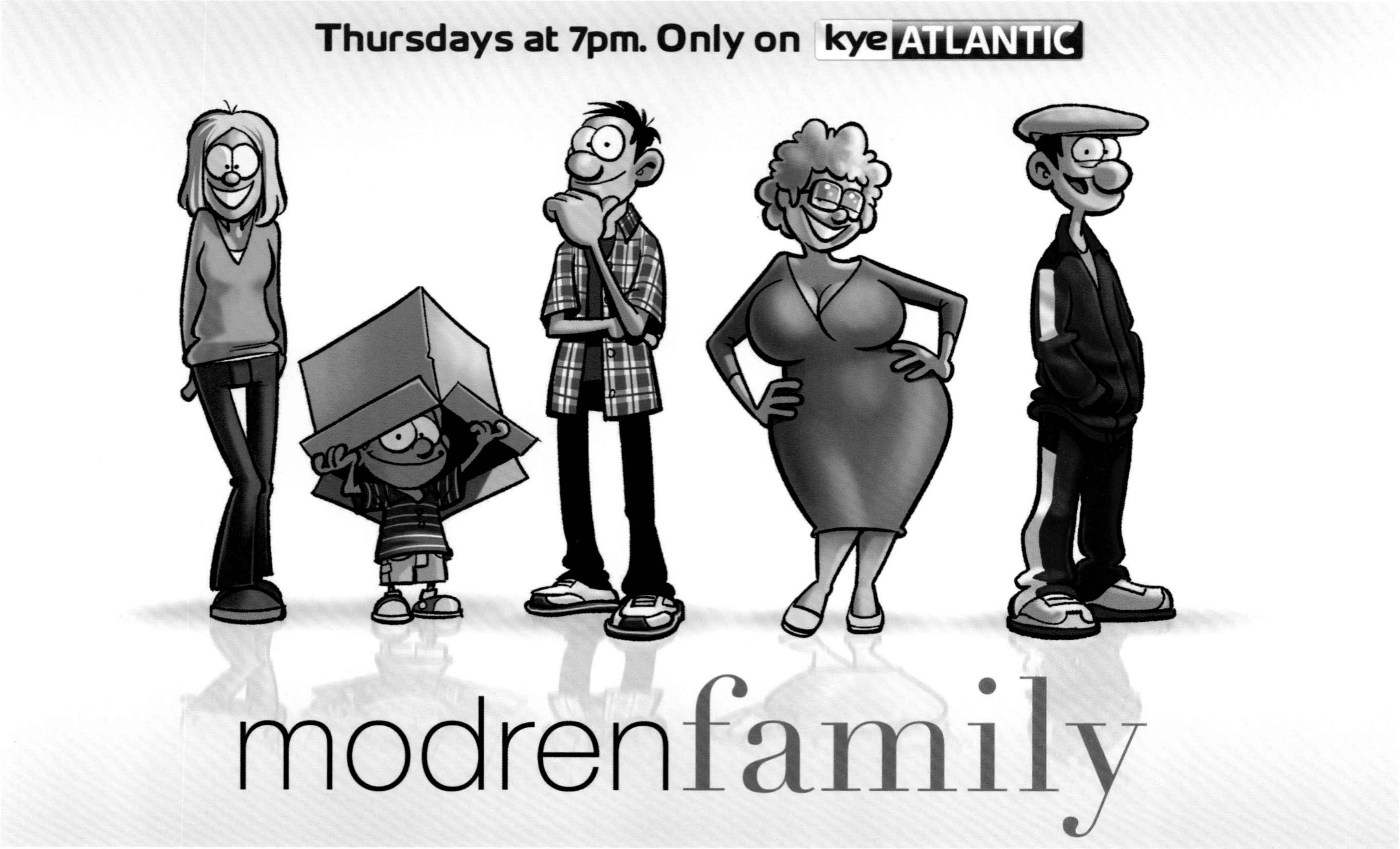
Thursdays at 7pm. Only on kye ATLANTIC
modrenfamily

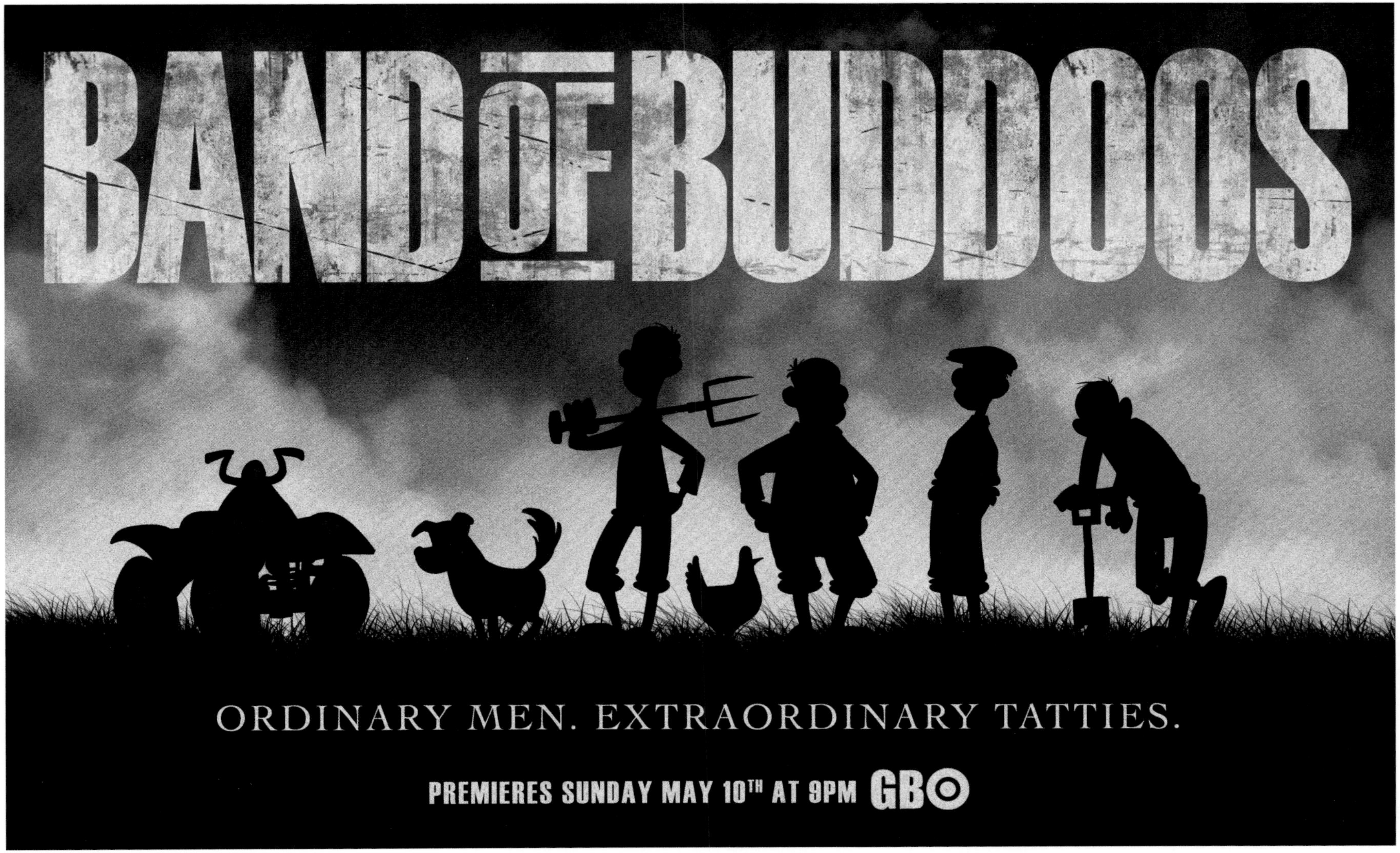
BAND OF BUDDOOS
ORDINARY MEN. EXTRAORDINARY TATTIES.
PREMIERES SUNDAY MAY 10TH AT 9PM GBO

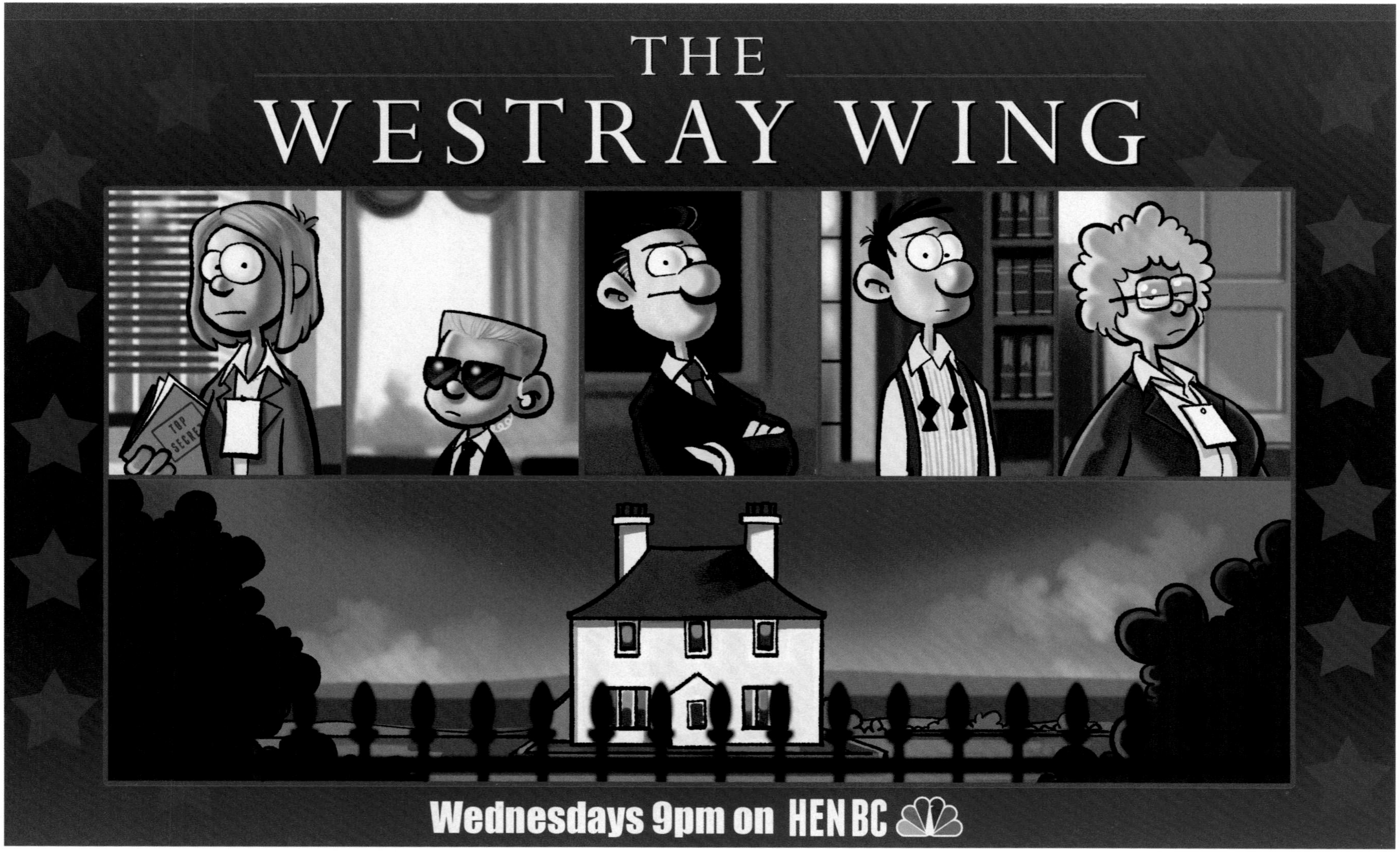
THE
WESTRAY WING
TOP SECRET
Wednesdays 9pm on HENBC

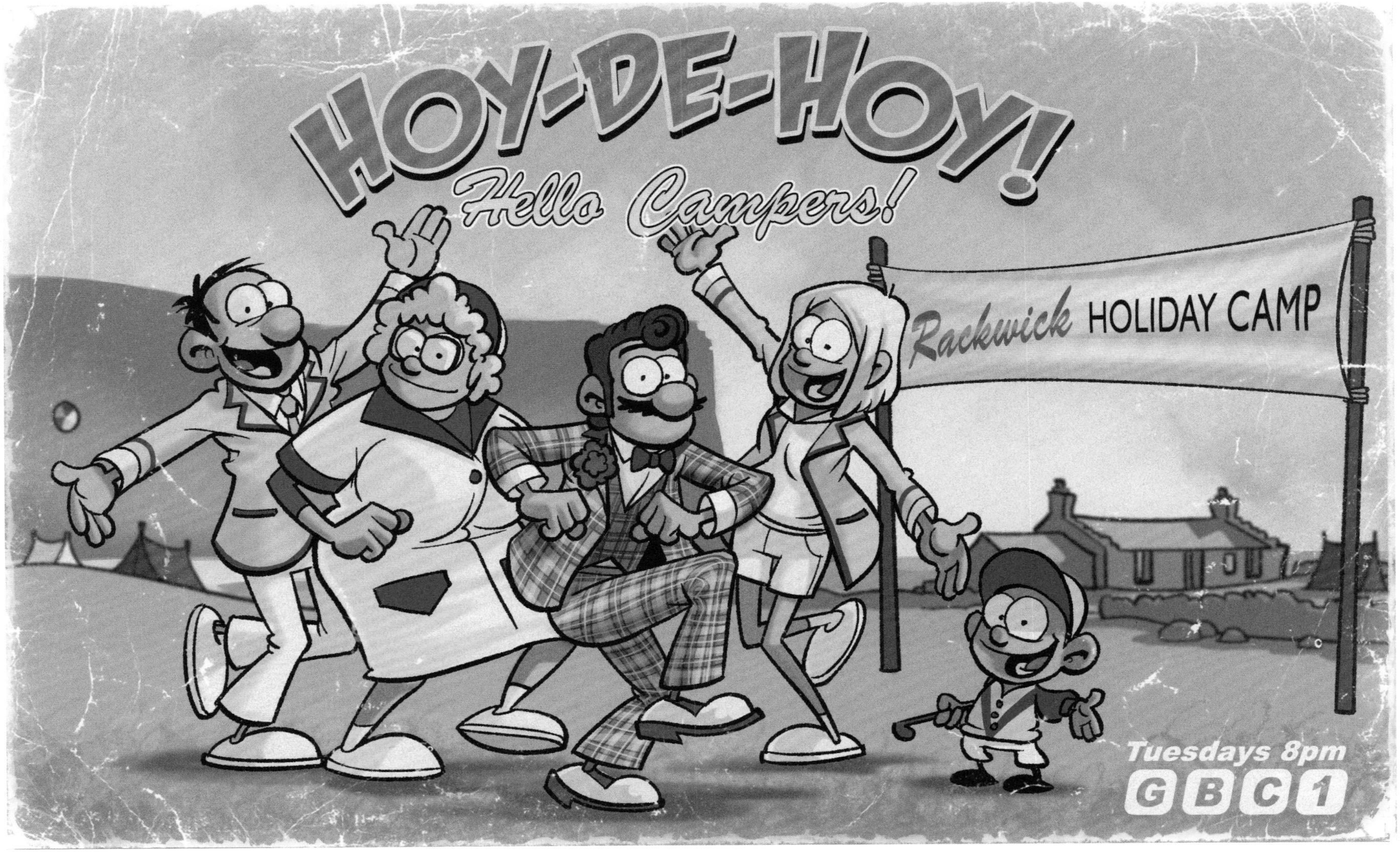
HOY-DE-HOY!
Hello Campers!
Rackwick HOLIDAY CAMP
Tuesdays 8pm
GBC1

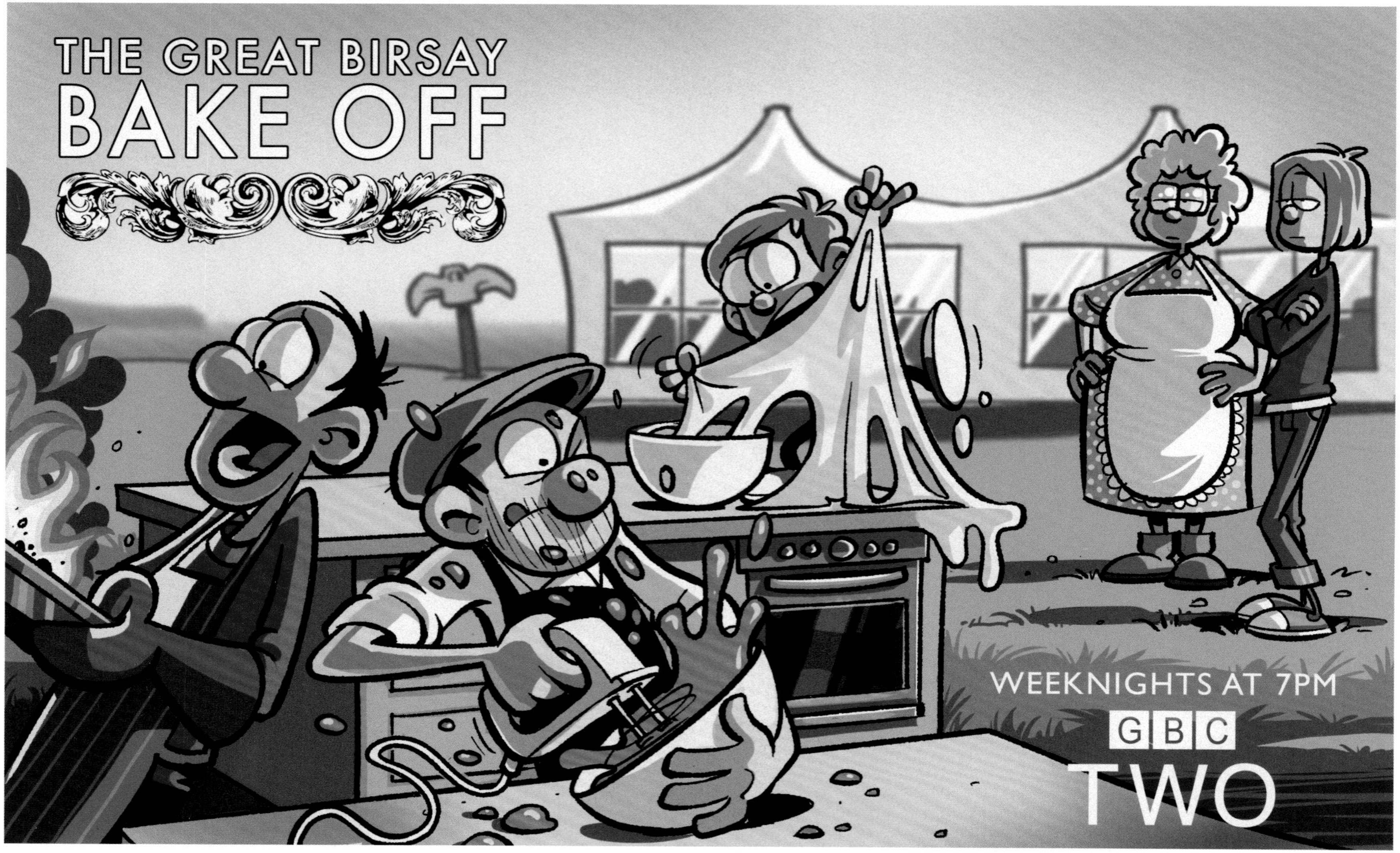
THE GREAT BIRSAY
BAKE OFF
WEEKNIGHTS AT 7PM
GBC
TWO

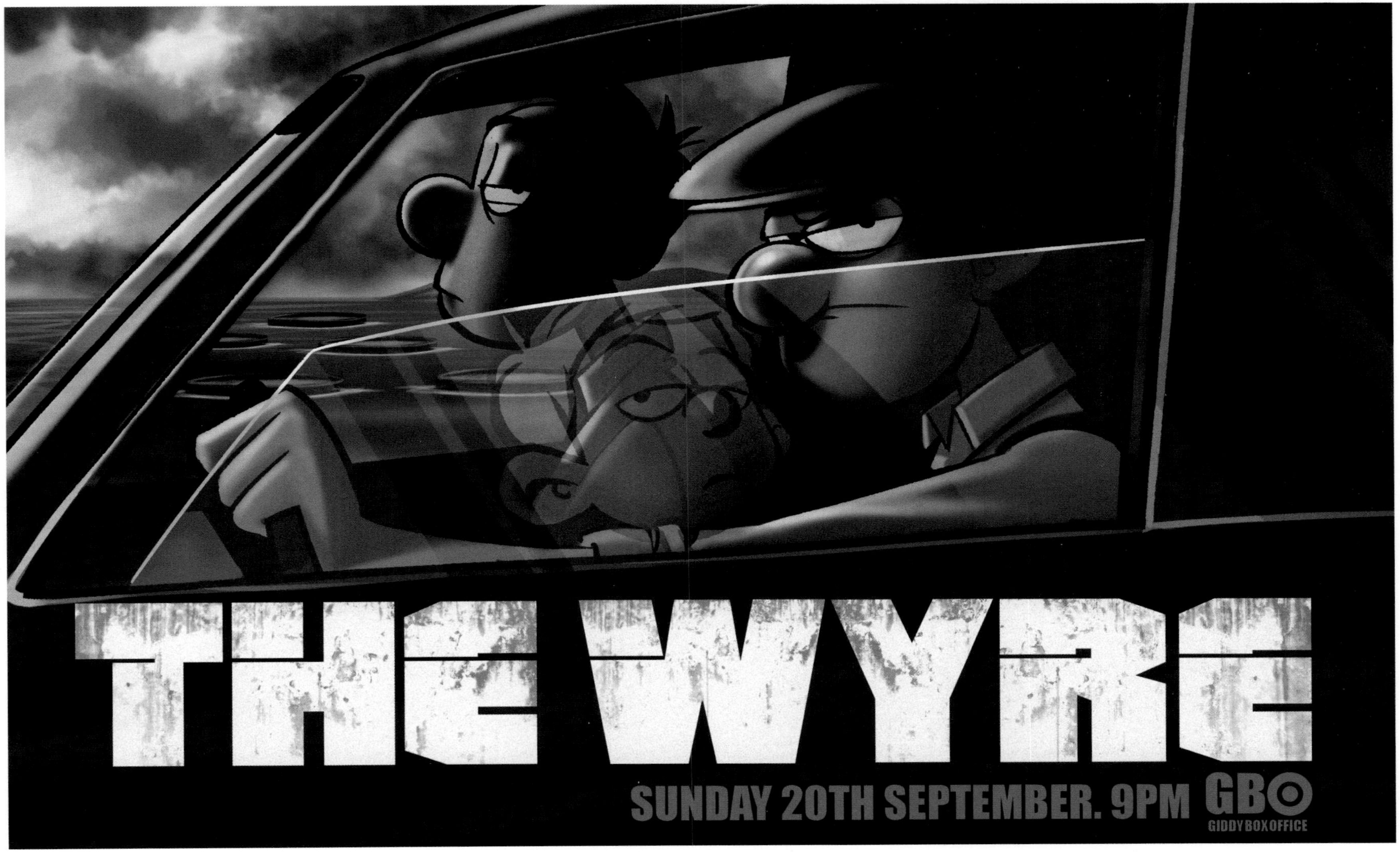
THE WYRE
SUNDAY 20TH SEPTEMBER. 9PM
GBO
GIDDY BOX OFFICE

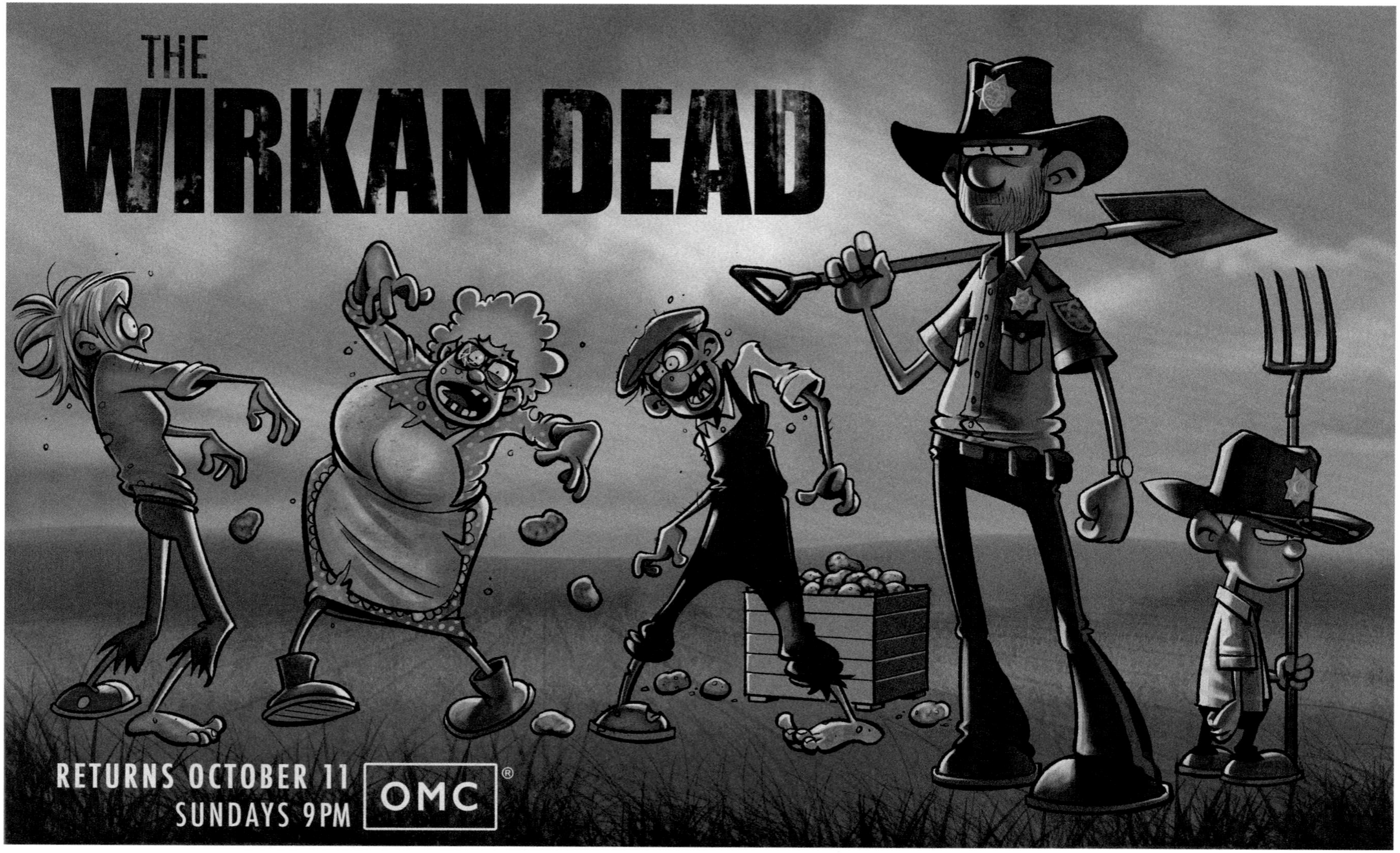
THE
WIRKAN DEAD
RETURNS OCTOBER 11
SUNDAYS 9PM
OMC

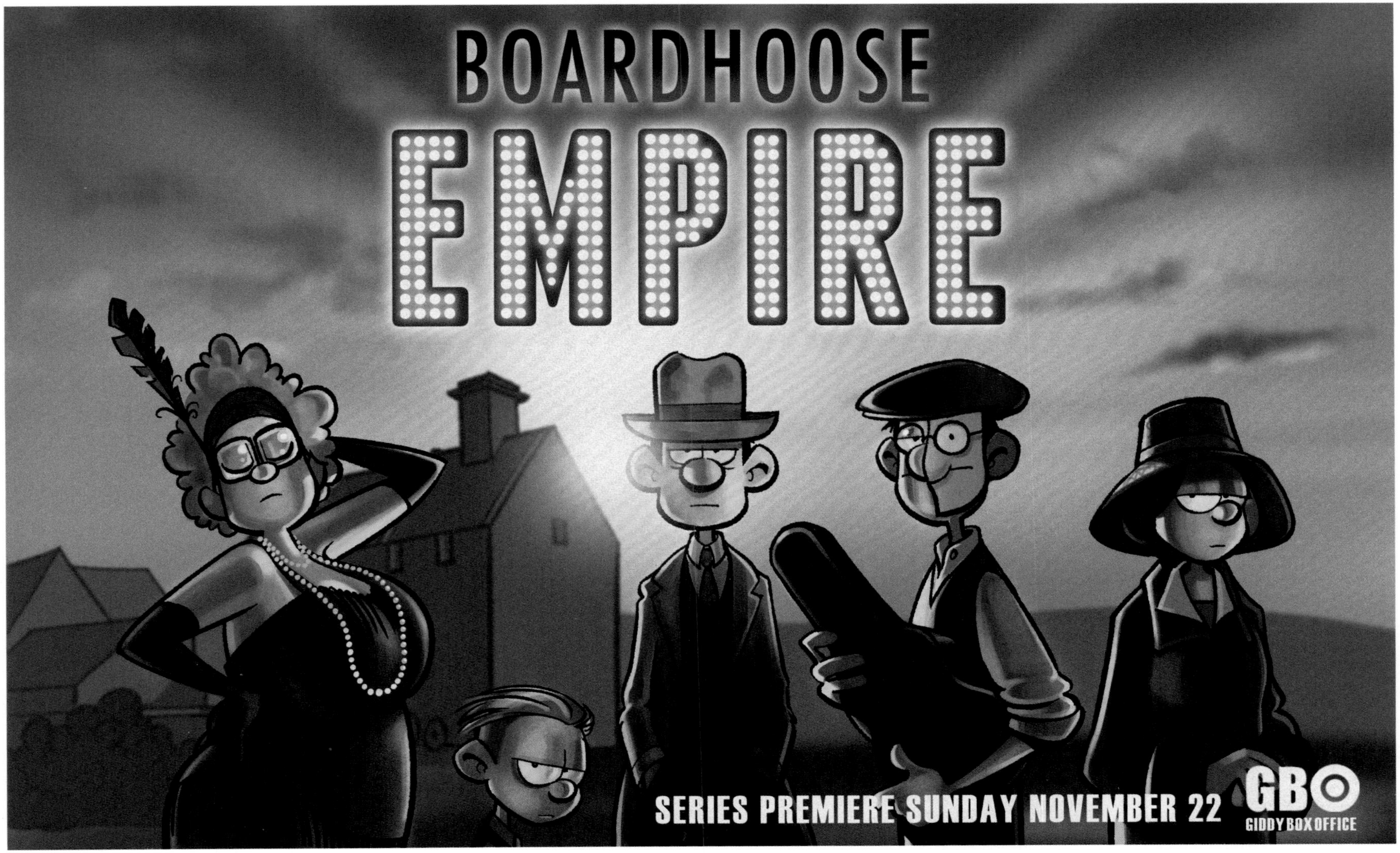
BOARDHOOSE
EMPIRE
SERIES PREMIERE SUNDAY NOVEMBER 22
GBO
GIDDY BOX OFFICE

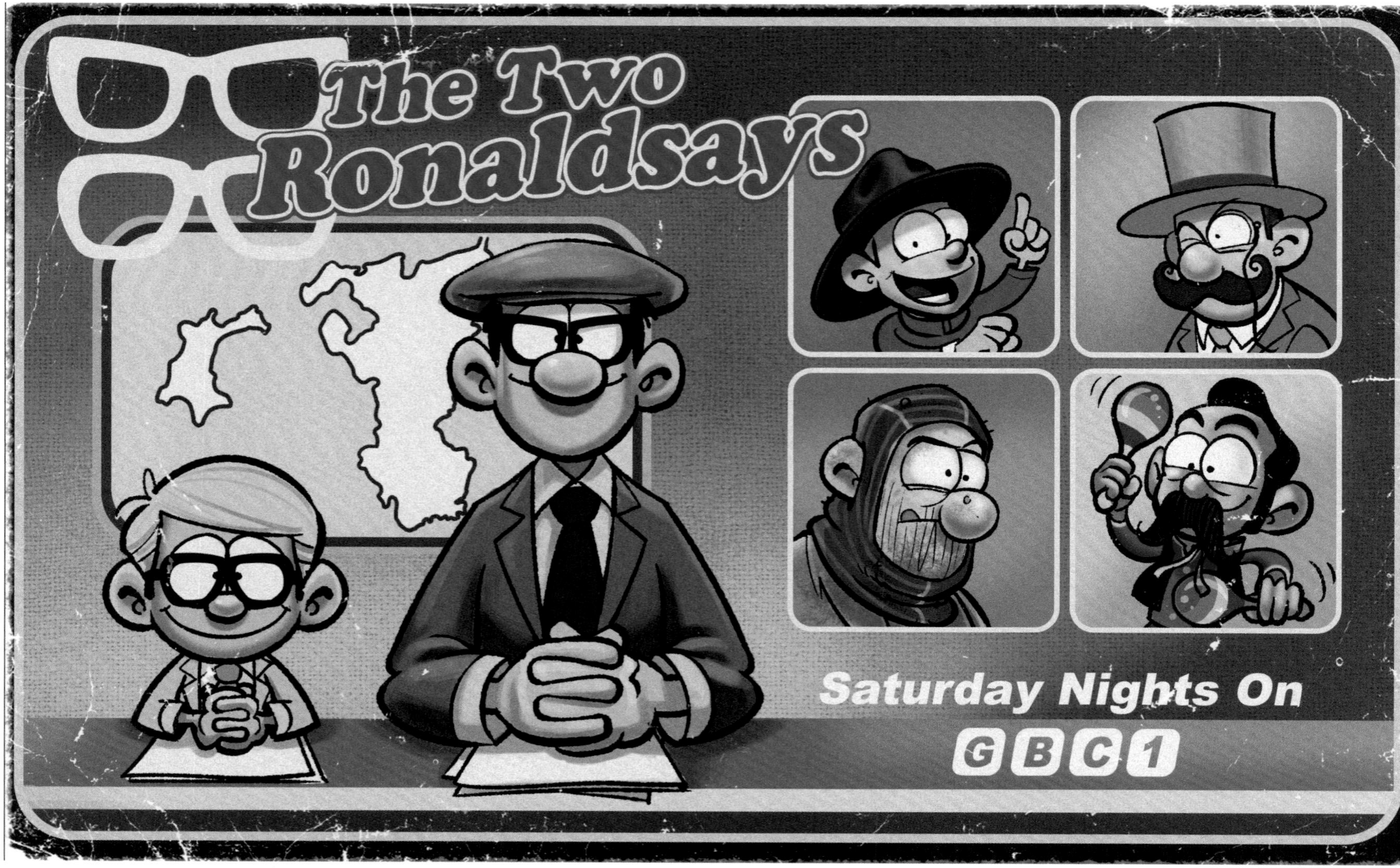
The Two Ronaldsays
Saturday Nights On
GBC1

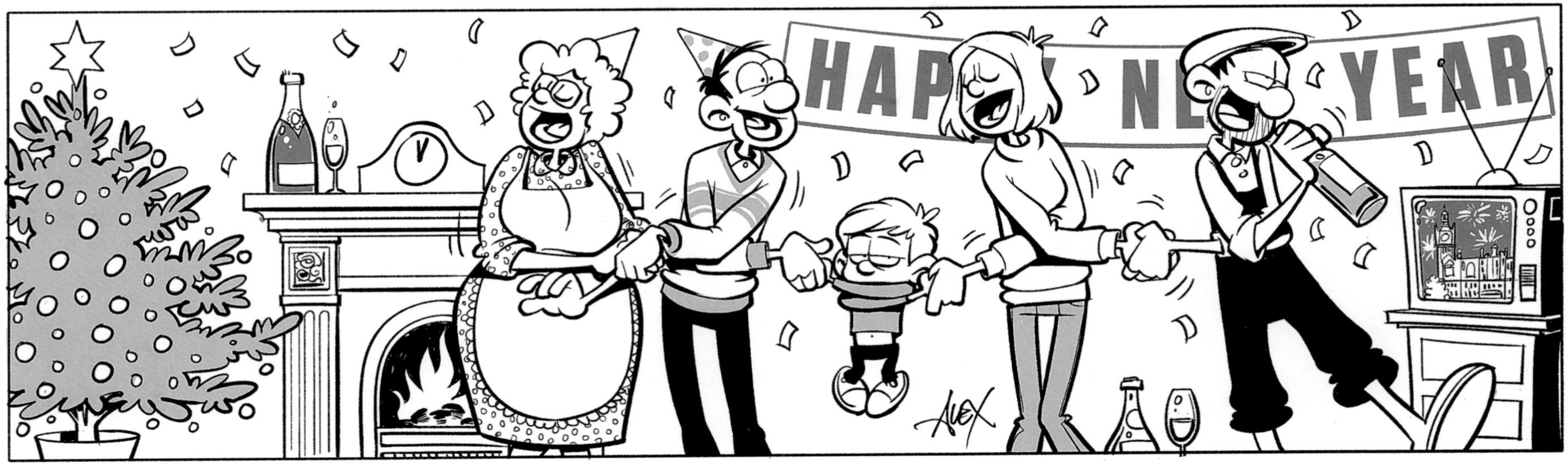
HAP NE YEAR
ALEX

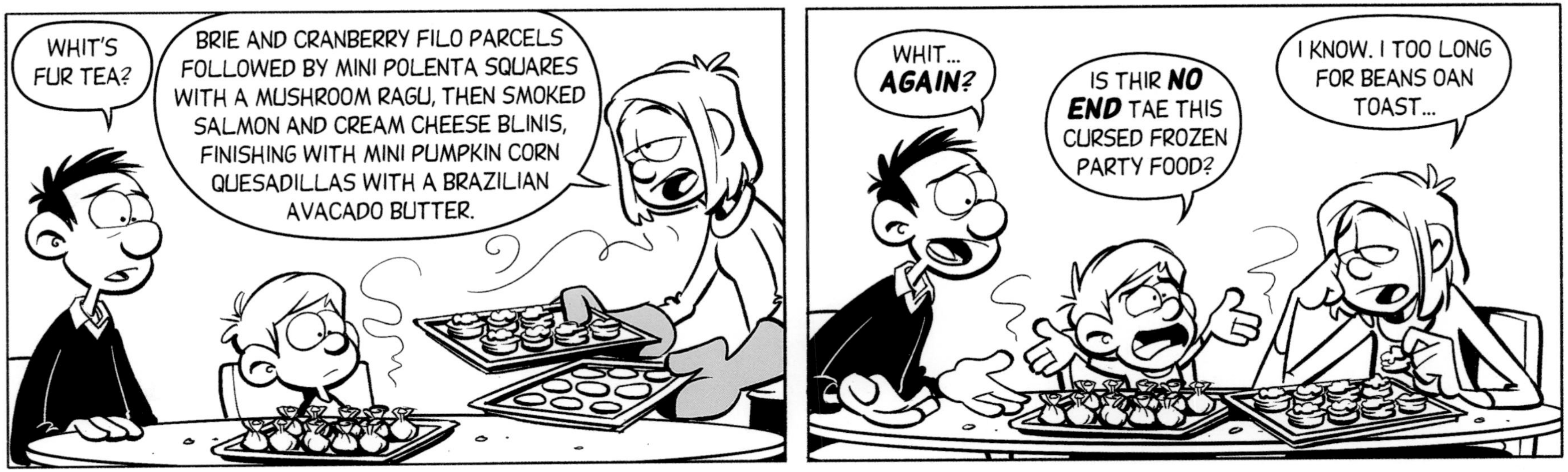
WHIT'S FUR TEA?
BRIE AND CRANBERRY FILO PARCELS FOLLOWED BY MINI POLENTA SQUARES WITH A MUSHROOM RAGU, THEN SMOKED SALMON AND CREAM CHEESE BLINIS, FINISHING WITH MINI PUMPKIN CORN QUESADILLAS WITH A BRAZILIAN AVACADO BUTTER.
WHIT... **AGAIN**?
IS THIR **NO END** TAE THIS CURSED FROZEN PARTY FOOD?
I KNOW. I TOO LONG FOR BEANS OAN TOAST...

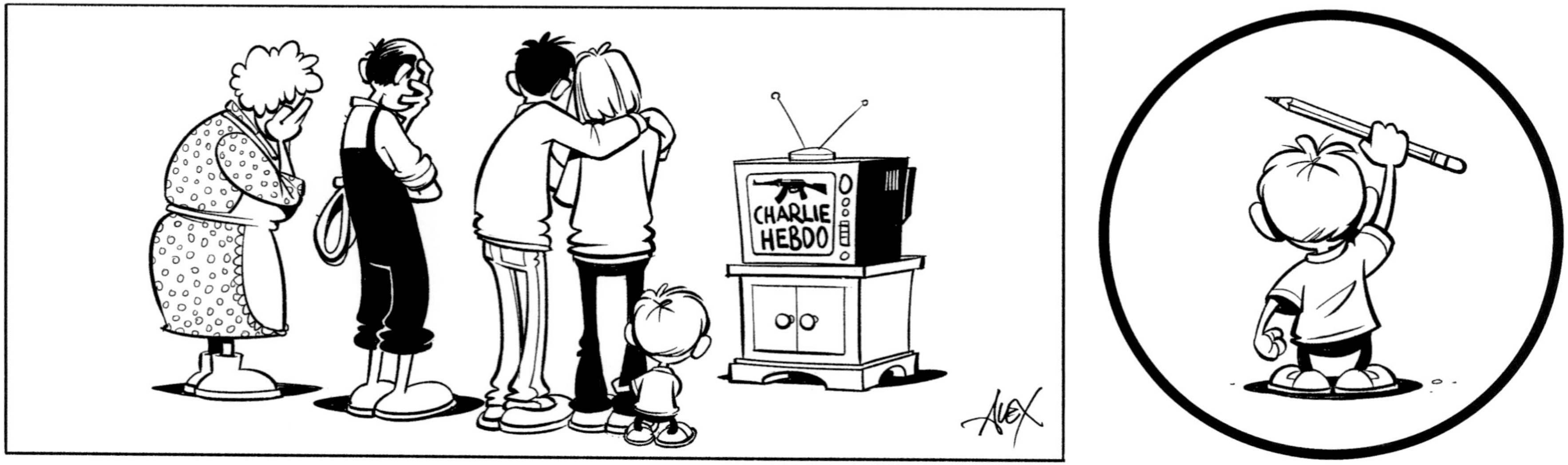
CHARLIE HEBDO
ALEX

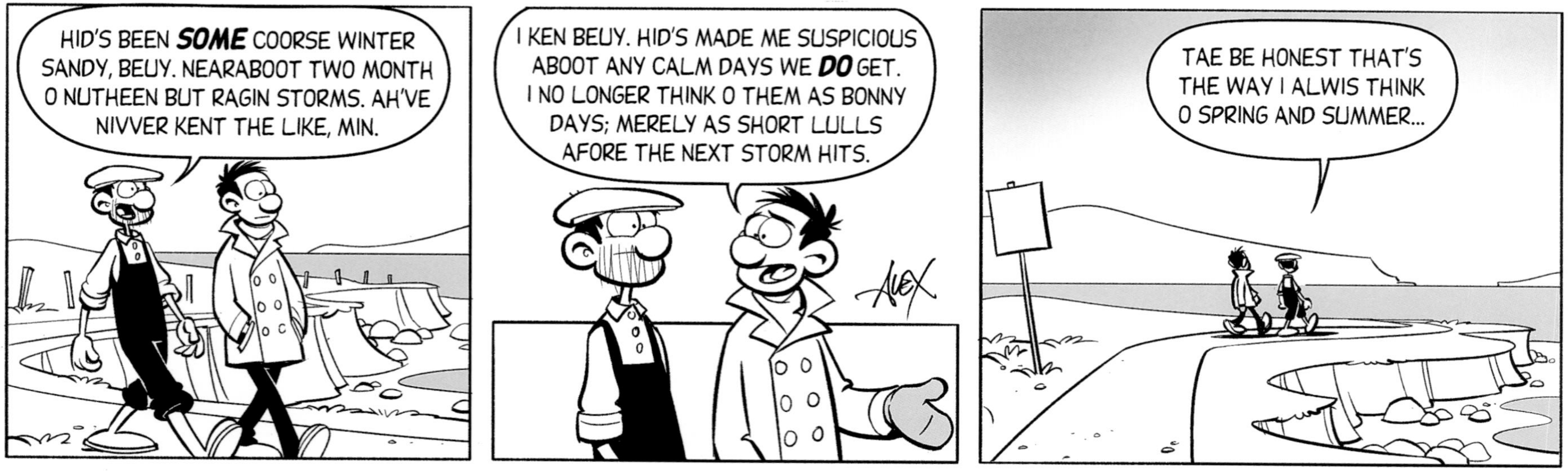
HID'S BEEN **SOME** COORSE WINTER SANDY, BEUY. NEARABOOT TWO MONTH O NUTHEEN BUT RAGIN STORMS. AH'VE NIVVER KENT THE LIKE, MIN.
I KEN BEUY. HID'S MADE ME SUSPICIOUS ABOOT ANY CALM DAYS WE **DO** GET. I NO LONGER THINK O THEM AS BONNY DAYS; MERELY AS SHORT LULLS AFORE THE NEXT STORM HITS.
ALEX
TAE BE HONEST THAT'S THE WAY I ALWIS THINK O SPRING AND SUMMER...

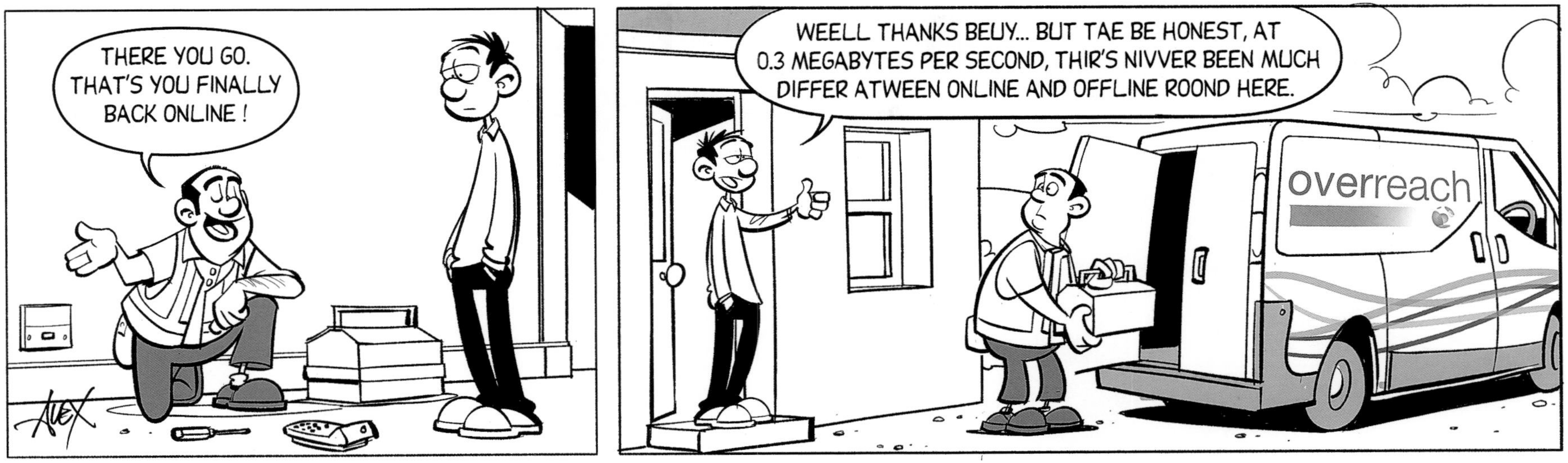
THERE YOU GO. THAT'S YOU FINALLY BACK ONLINE !
WEELL THANKS BEUY... BUT TAE BE HONEST, AT 0.3 MEGABYTES PER SECOND, THIR'S NIVVER BEEN MUCH DIFFER ATWEEN ONLINE AND OFFLINE ROOND HERE.
overreach

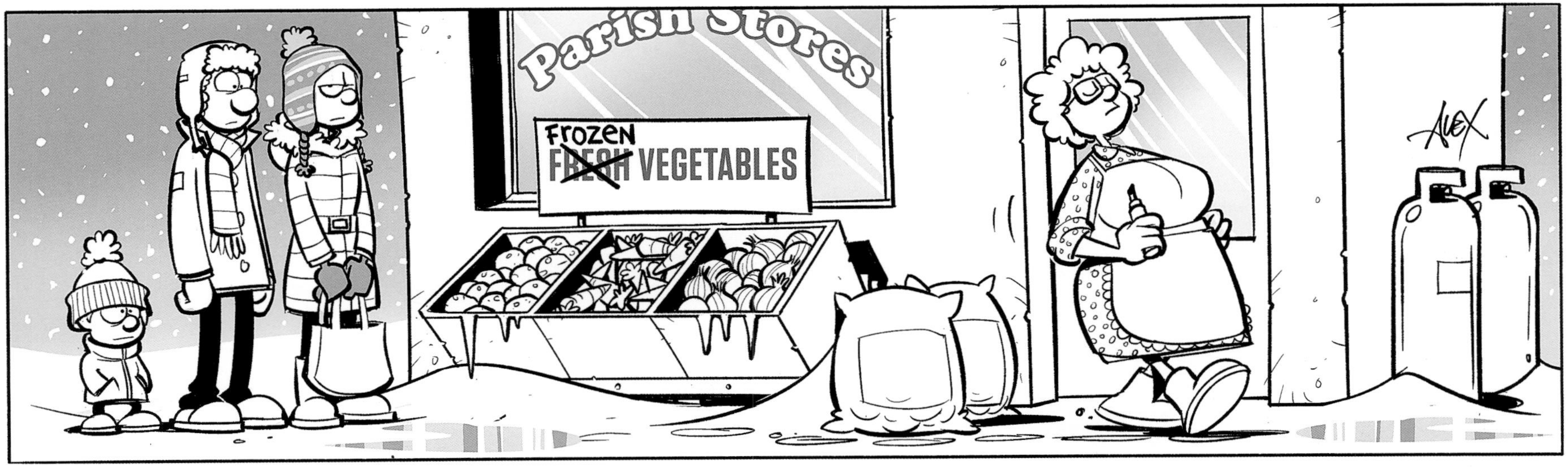
Parish Stores
Frozen
~~FRESH~~ VEGETABLES

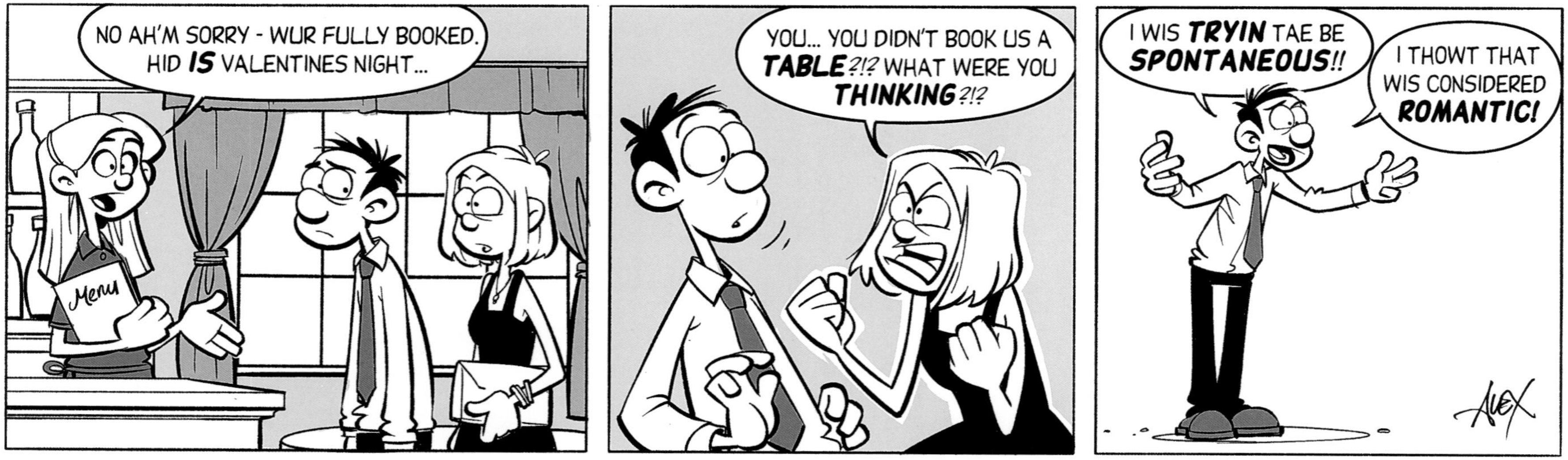
NO AH'M SORRY - WUR FULLY BOOKED. HID IS VALENTINES NIGHT...
Menu
YOU... YOU DIDN'T BOOK US A TABLE?!? WHAT WERE YOU THINKING?!?
I WIS TRYIN TAE BE SPONTANEOUS!!
I THOWT THAT WIS CONSIDERED ROMANTIC!
ALEX

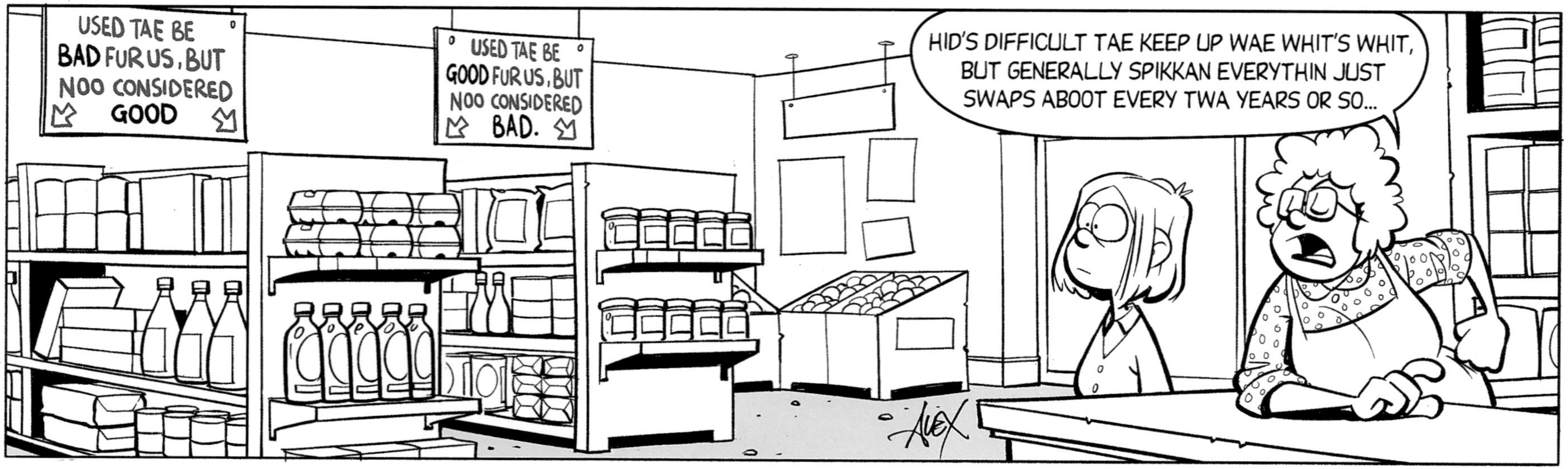
USED TAE BE BAD FUR US, BUT NOO CONSIDERED GOOD
USED TAE BE GOOD FUR US, BUT NOO CONSIDERED BAD.
HID'S DIFFICULT TAE KEEP UP WAE WHIT'S WHIT, BUT GENERALLY SPIKKAN EVERYTHIN JUST SWAPS ABOOT EVERY TWA YEARS OR SO...
ALEX

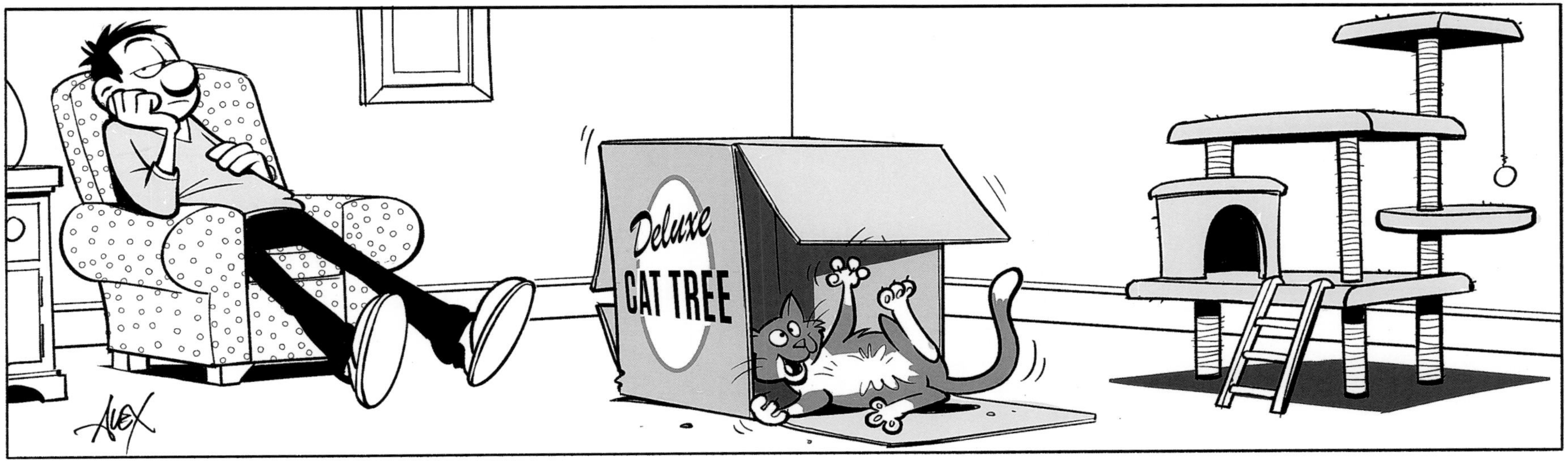
Deluxe
CAT TREE
ALEX

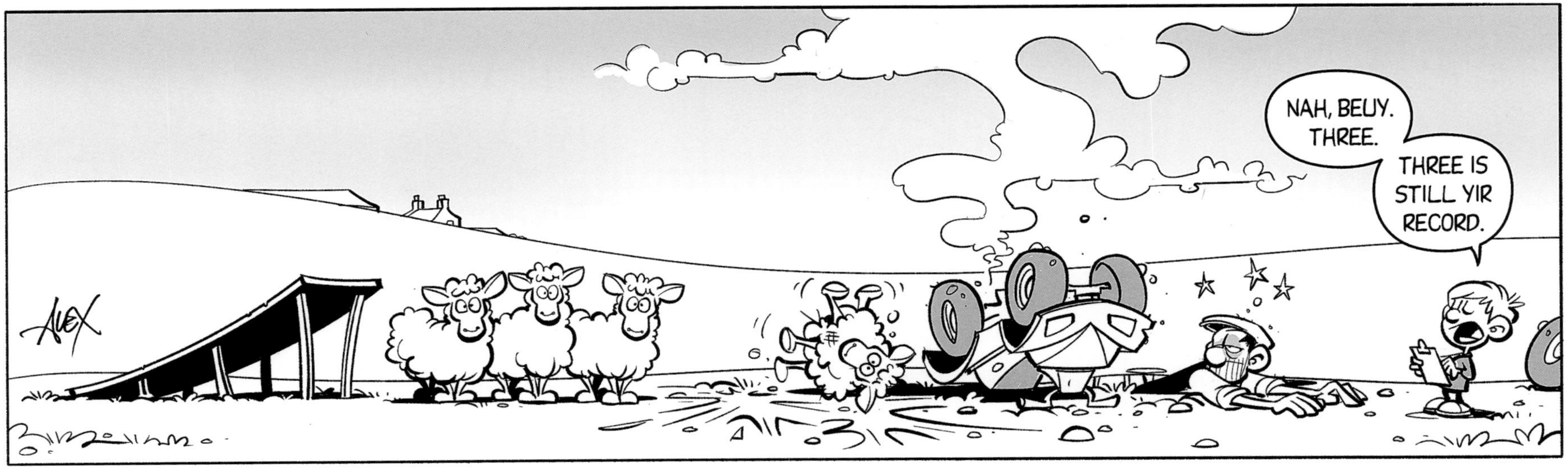
ALEX
NAH, BEUY. THREE.
THREE IS STILL YIR RECORD.

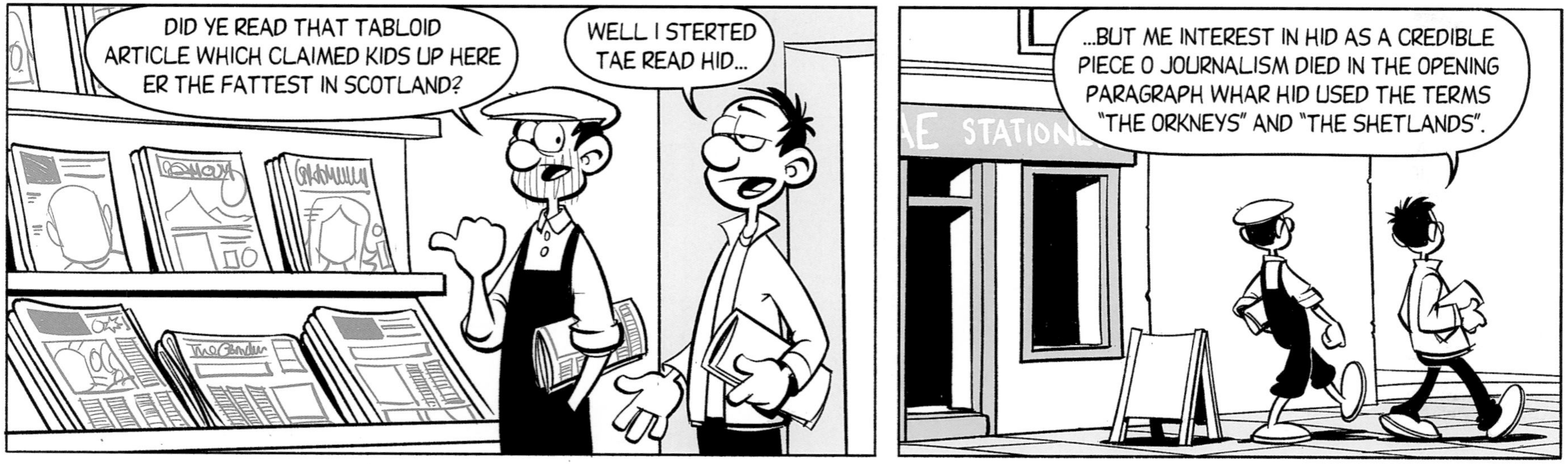
DID YE READ THAT TABLOID ARTICLE WHICH CLAIMED KIDS UP HERE ER THE FATTEST IN SCOTLAND?
WELL I STERTED TAE READ HID...
...BUT ME INTEREST IN HID AS A CREDIBLE PIECE O JOURNALISM DIED IN THE OPENING PARAGRAPH WHAR HID USED THE TERMS "THE ORKNEYS" AND "THE SHETLANDS".

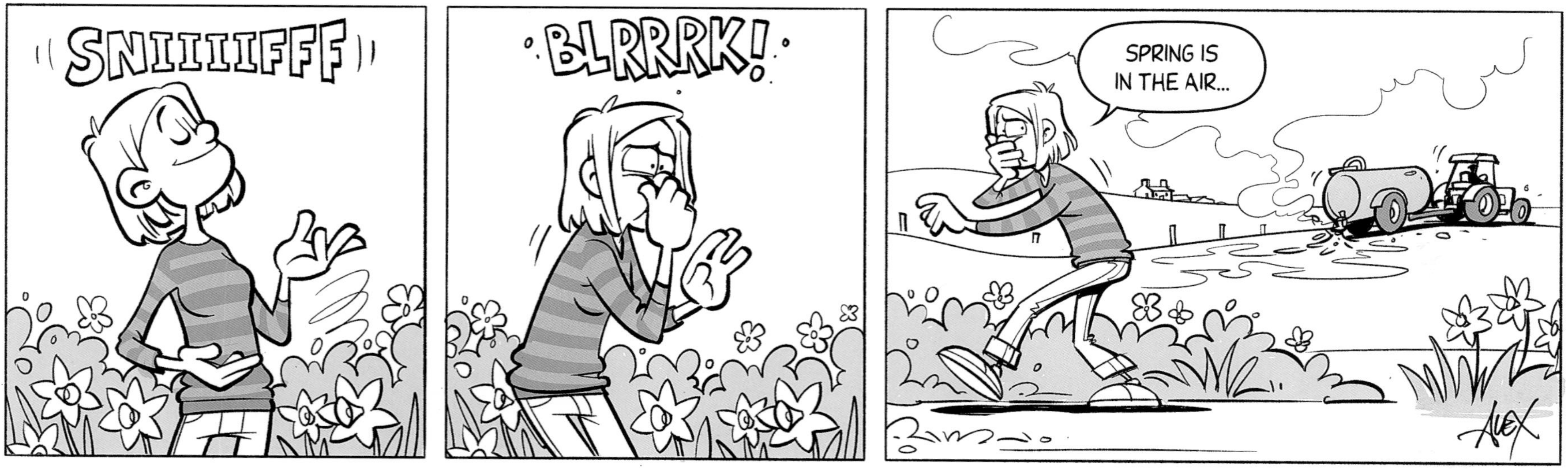
SNIIIIFFF
BLRRRK!
SPRING IS IN THE AIR...
ALEX

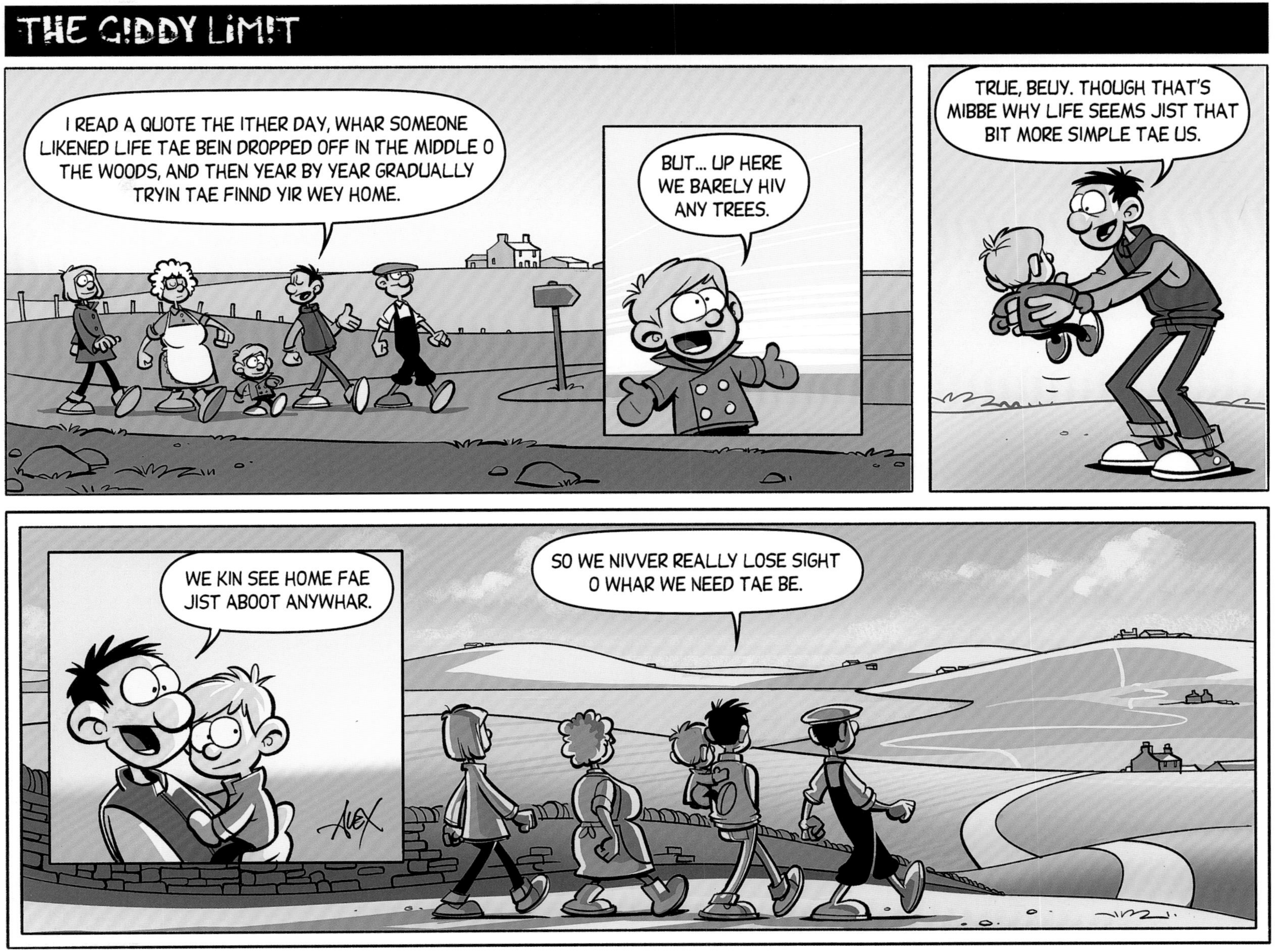
THE GIDDY LIMIT
I READ A QUOTE THE ITHER DAY, WHAR SOMEONE LIKENED LIFE TAE BEIN DROPPED OFF IN THE MIDDLE O THE WOODS, AND THEN YEAR BY YEAR GRADUALLY TRYIN TAE FINND YIR WEY HOME.
BUT... UP HERE WE BARELY HIV ANY TREES.
TRUE, BEUY. THOUGH THAT'S MIBBE WHY LIFE SEEMS JIST THAT BIT MORE SIMPLE TAE US.
WE KIN SEE HOME FAE JIST ABOOT ANYWHAR.
SO WE NIVVER REALLY LOSE SIGHT O WHAR WE NEED TAE BE.
ALEX

The 500th Strip.

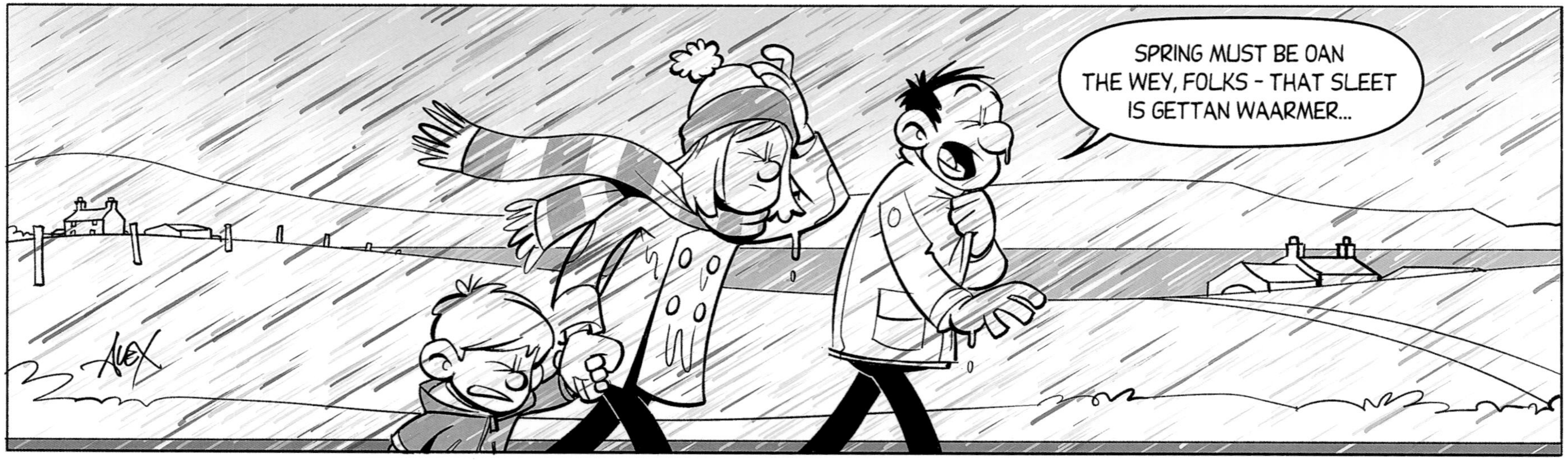

SPRING MUST BE OAN THE WEY, FOLKS - THAT SLEET IS GETTAN WAARMER...


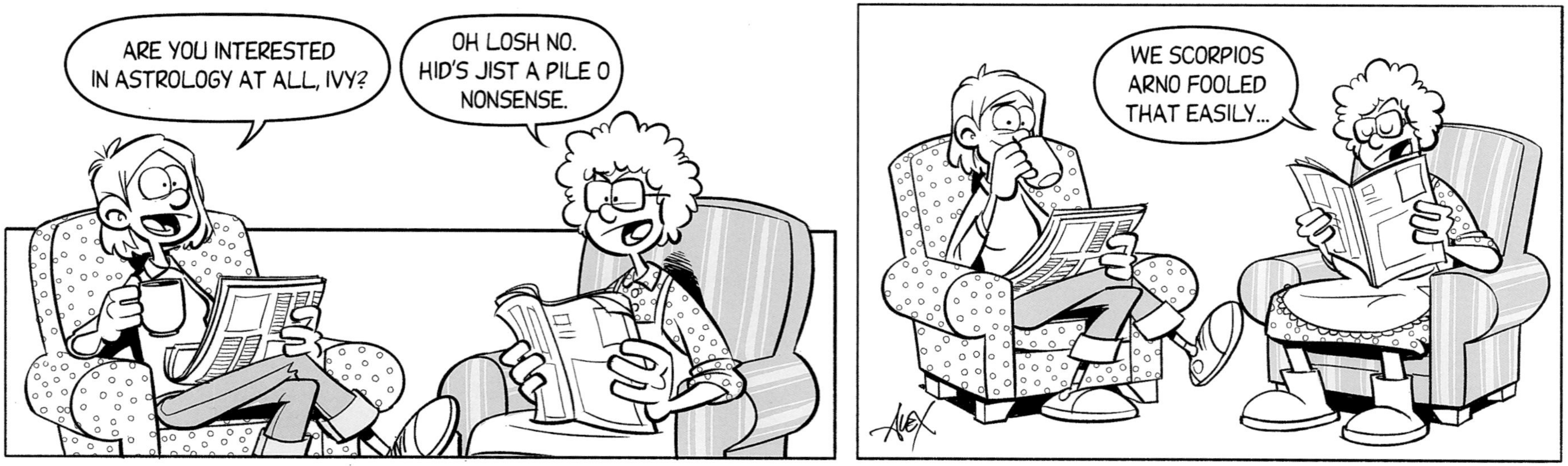

ARE YOU INTERESTED IN ASTROLOGY AT ALL, IVY?
OH LOSH NO. HID'S JIST A PILE O NONSENSE.
WE SCORPIOS ARNO FOOLED THAT EASILY...

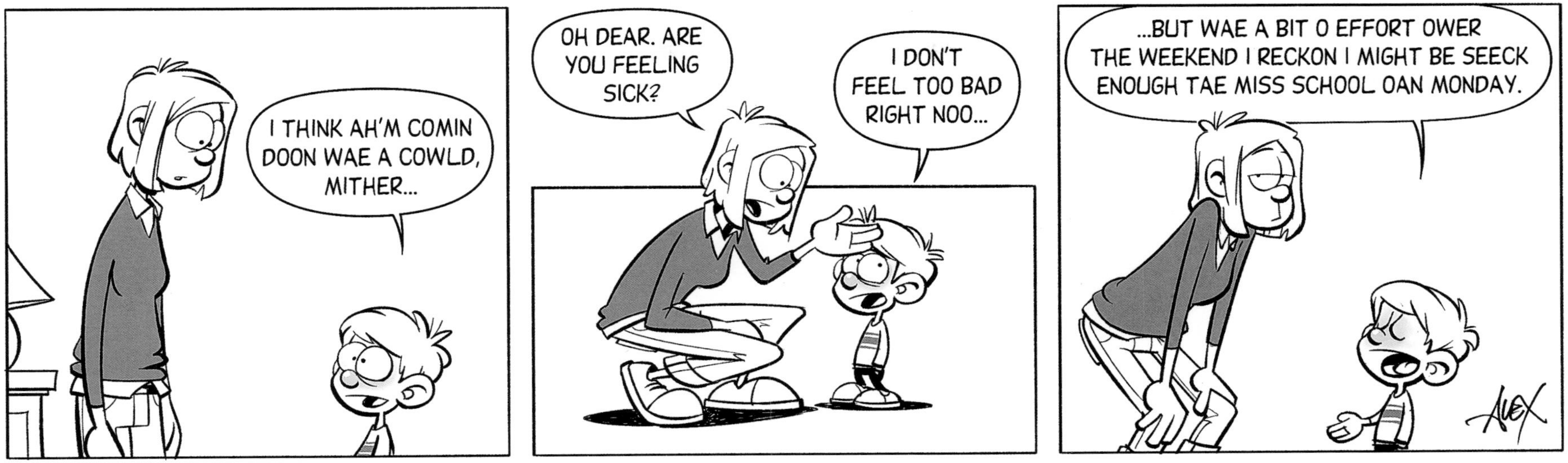
I THINK AH'M COMIN DOON WAE A COWLD, MITHER...
OH DEAR. ARE YOU FEELING SICK?
I DON'T FEEL TOO BAD RIGHT NOO...
...BUT WAE A BIT O EFFORT OWER THE WEEKEND I RECKON I MIGHT BE SEECK ENOUGH TAE MISS SCHOOL OAN MONDAY.
ALEX

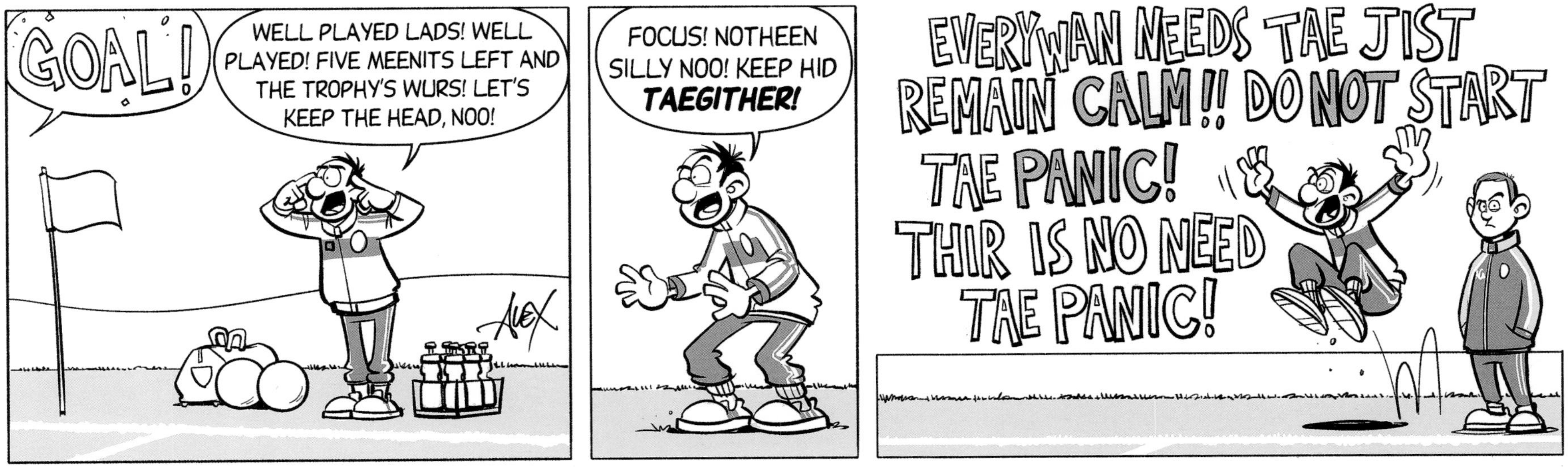
GOAL!
WELL PLAYED LADS! WELL PLAYED! FIVE MEENITS LEFT AND THE TROPHY'S WURS! LET'S KEEP THE HEAD, NOO!
ALEX
FOCUS! NOTHEEN SILLY NOO! KEEP HID **TAEGITHER!**
EVERYWAN NEEDS TAE JIST REMAIN CALM!! DO NOT START TAE PANIC! THIR IS NO NEED TAE PANIC!

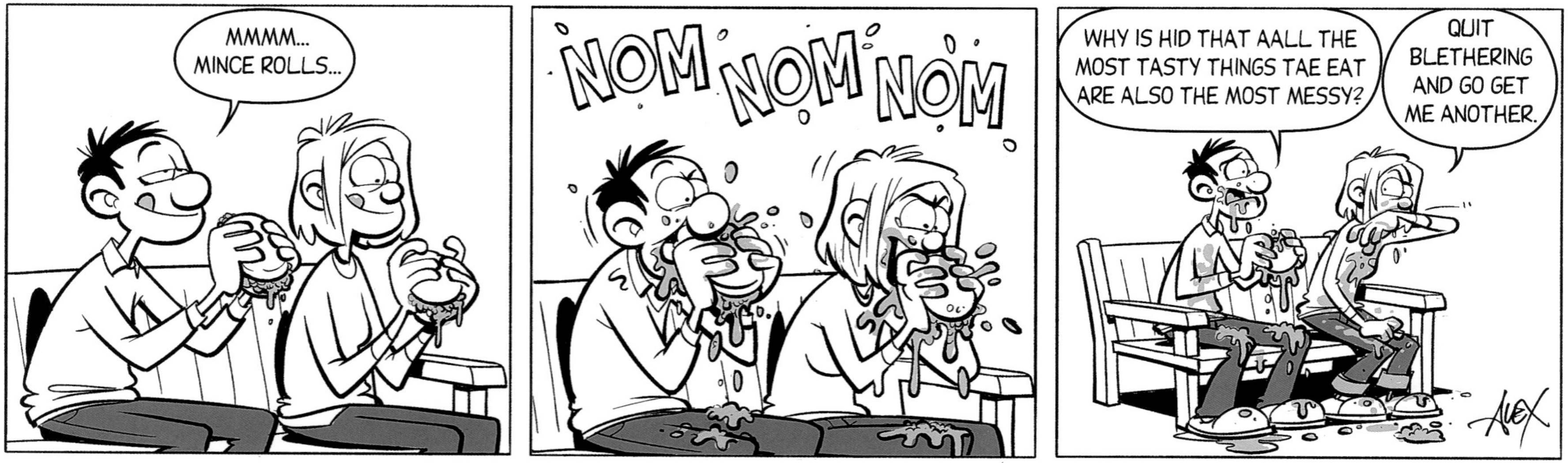
MMMM...
MINCE ROLLS...
NOM NOM NOM
WHY IS HID THAT AALL THE MOST TASTY THINGS TAE EAT ARE ALSO THE MOST MESSY?
QUIT BLETHERING AND GO GET ME ANOTHER.
ALEX

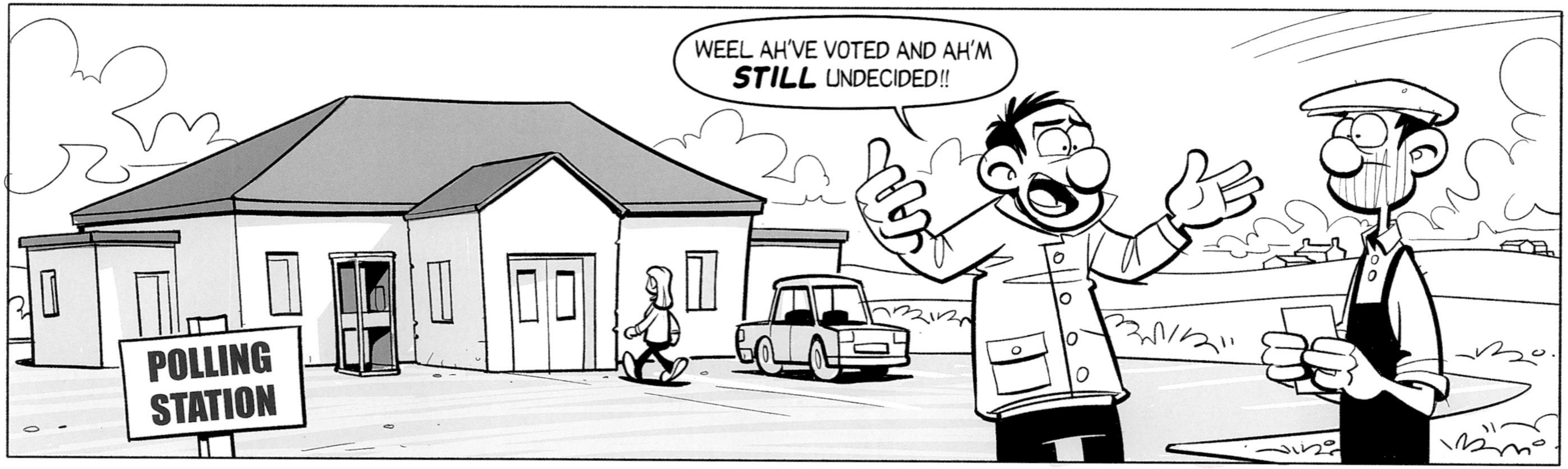
WEEL AH'VE VOTED AND AH'M STILL UNDECIDED!!
POLLING STATION

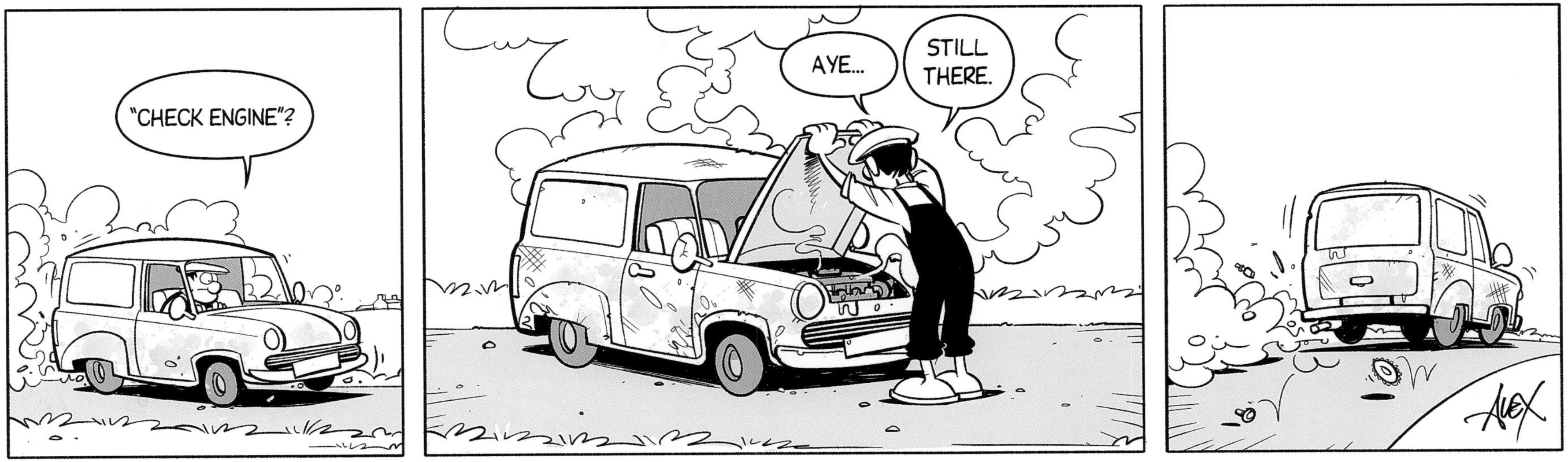
"CHECK ENGINE"?
AYE...
STILL THERE.
ALEX

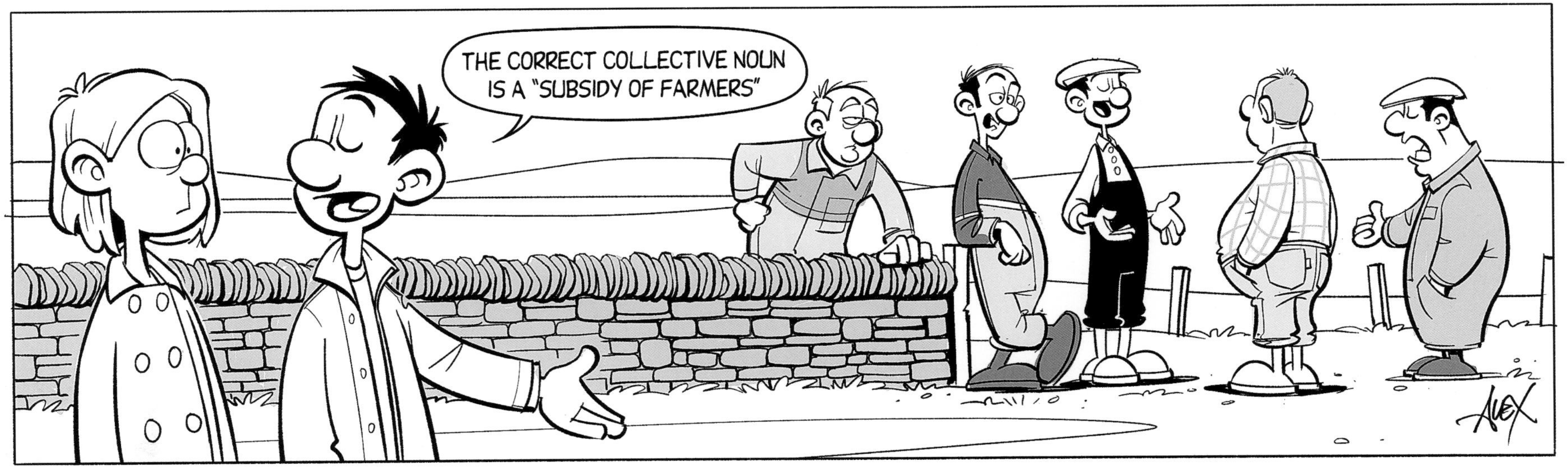
THE CORRECT COLLECTIVE NOUN IS A "SUBSIDY OF FARMERS"
ALEX

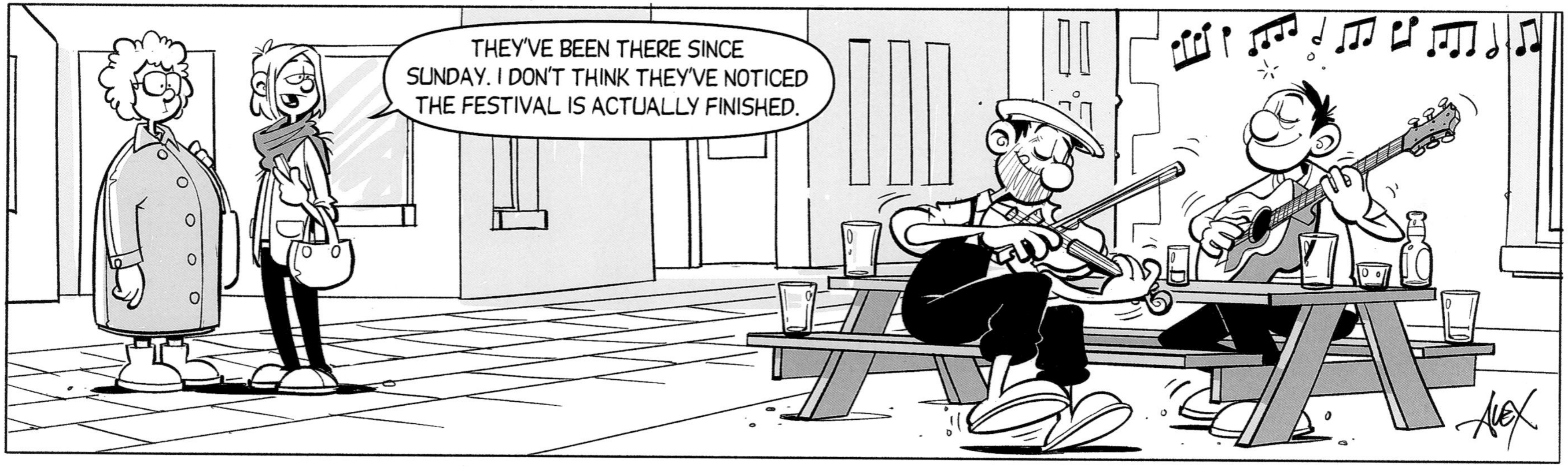
THEY'VE BEEN THERE SINCE SUNDAY. I DON'T THINK THEY'VE NOTICED THE FESTIVAL IS ACTUALLY FINISHED.

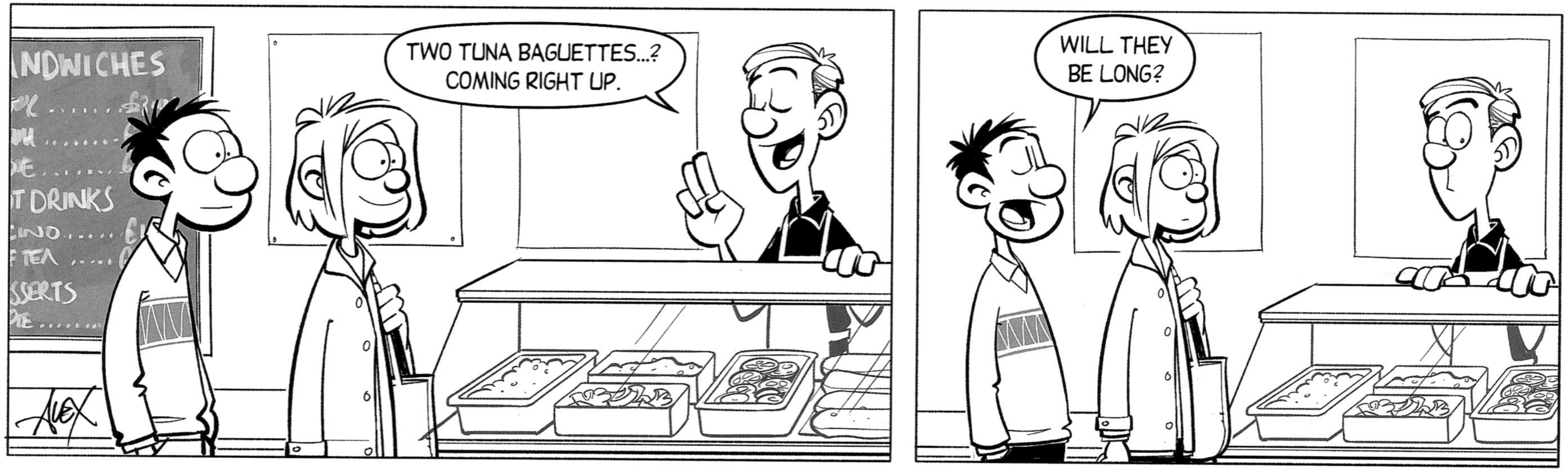
TWO TUNA BAGUETTES...? COMING RIGHT UP.
WILL THEY BE LONG?

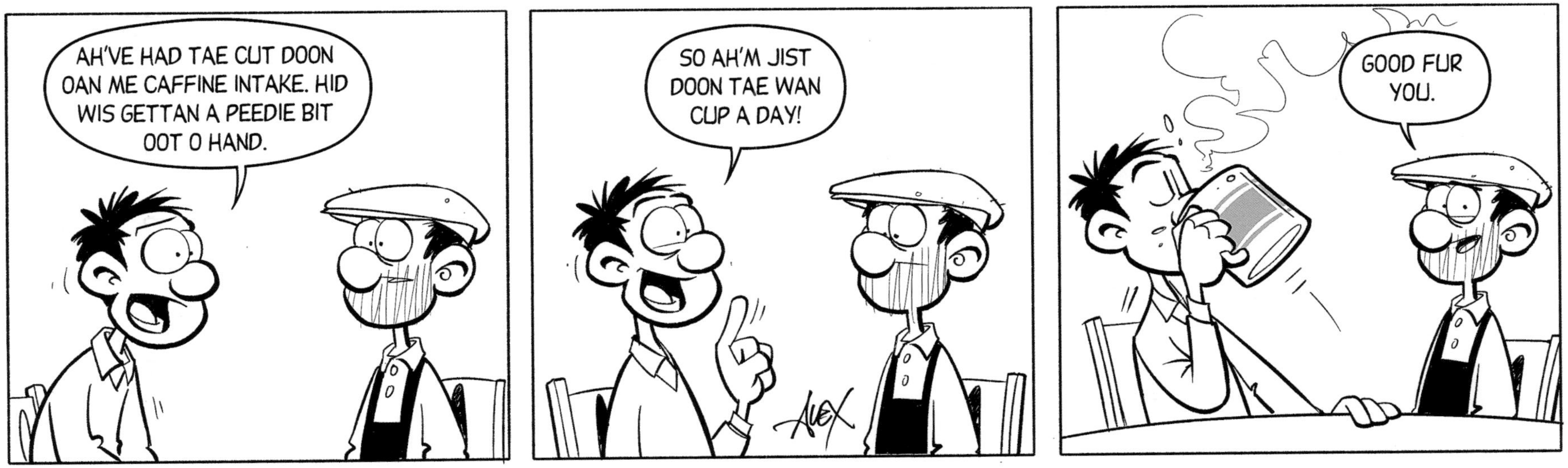
AH'VE HAD TAE CUT DOON OAN ME CAFFINE INTAKE. HID WIS GETTAN A PEEDIE BIT OOT O HAND.
SO AH'M JIST DOON TAE WAN CUP A DAY!
GOOD FUR YOU.

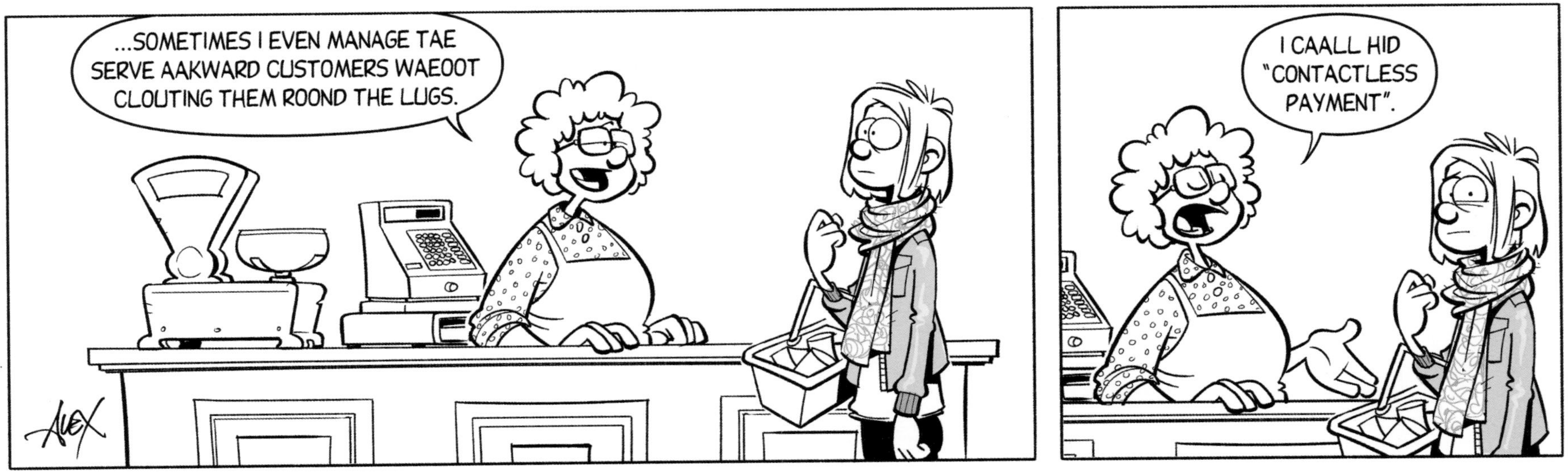
...SOMETIMES I EVEN MANAGE TAE SERVE AAKWARD CUSTOMERS WAEOOT CLOUTING THEM ROOND THE LUGS.
I CAALL HID "CONTACTLESS PAYMENT".

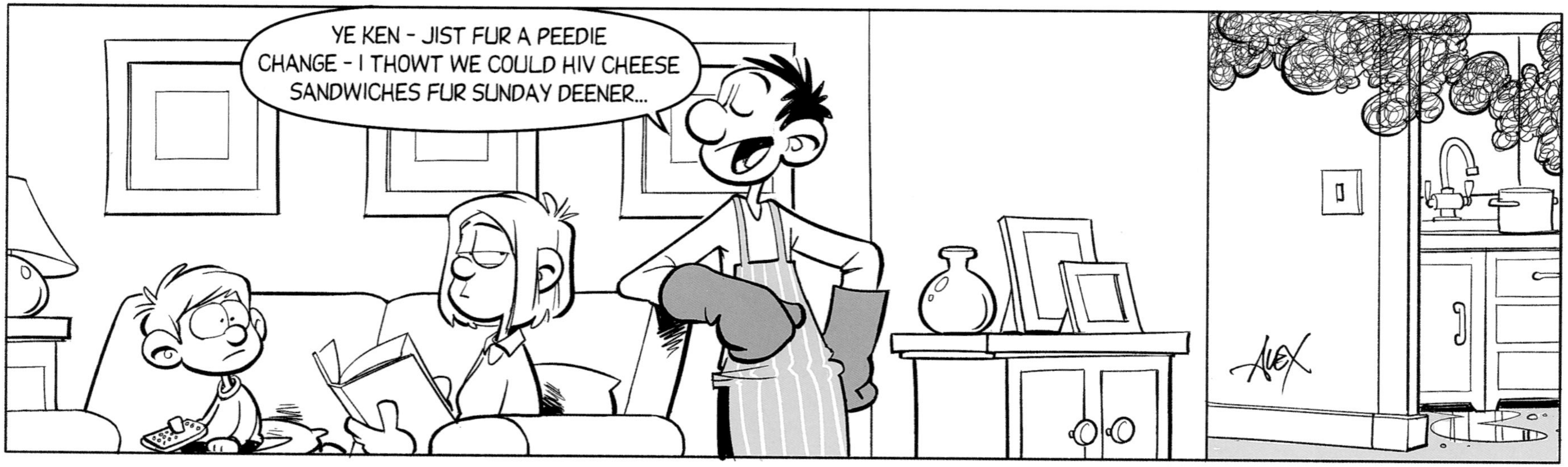
YE KEN - JIST FUR A PEEDIE CHANGE - I THOWT WE COULD HIV CHEESE SANDWICHES FUR SUNDAY DEENER...
ALEX

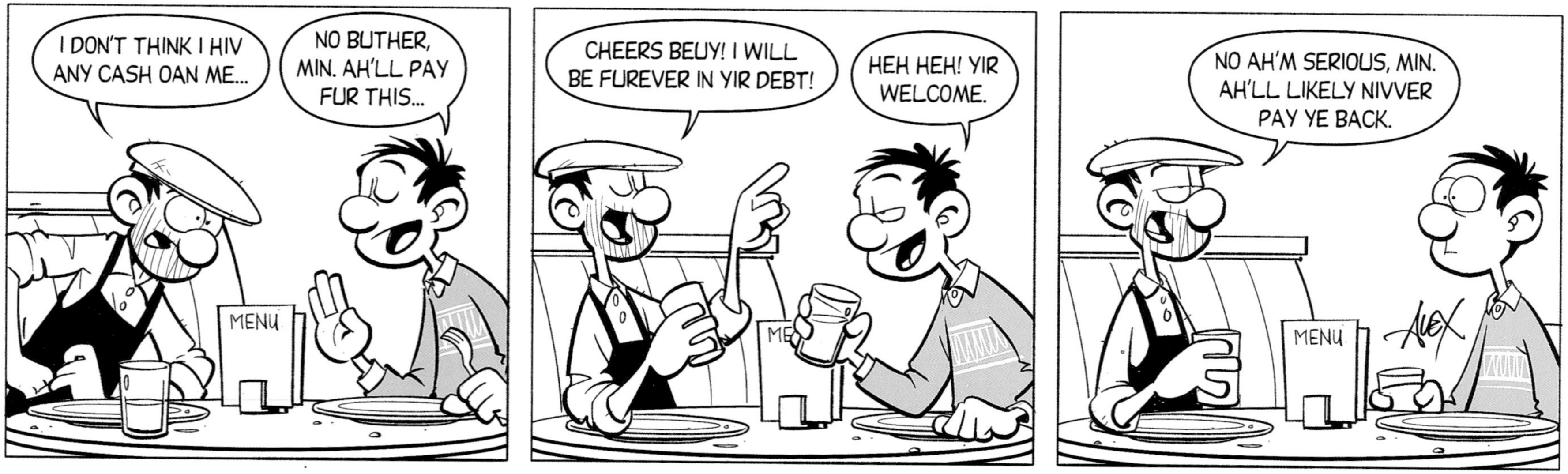
I DON'T THINK I HIV ANY CASH OAN ME...
NO BUTHER, MIN. AH'LL PAY FUR THIS...
MENU
CHEERS BEUY! I WILL BE FUREVER IN YIR DEBT!
HEH HEH! YIR WELCOME.
NO AH'M SERIOUS, MIN. AH'LL LIKELY NIVVER PAY YE BACK.
MENU
ALEX

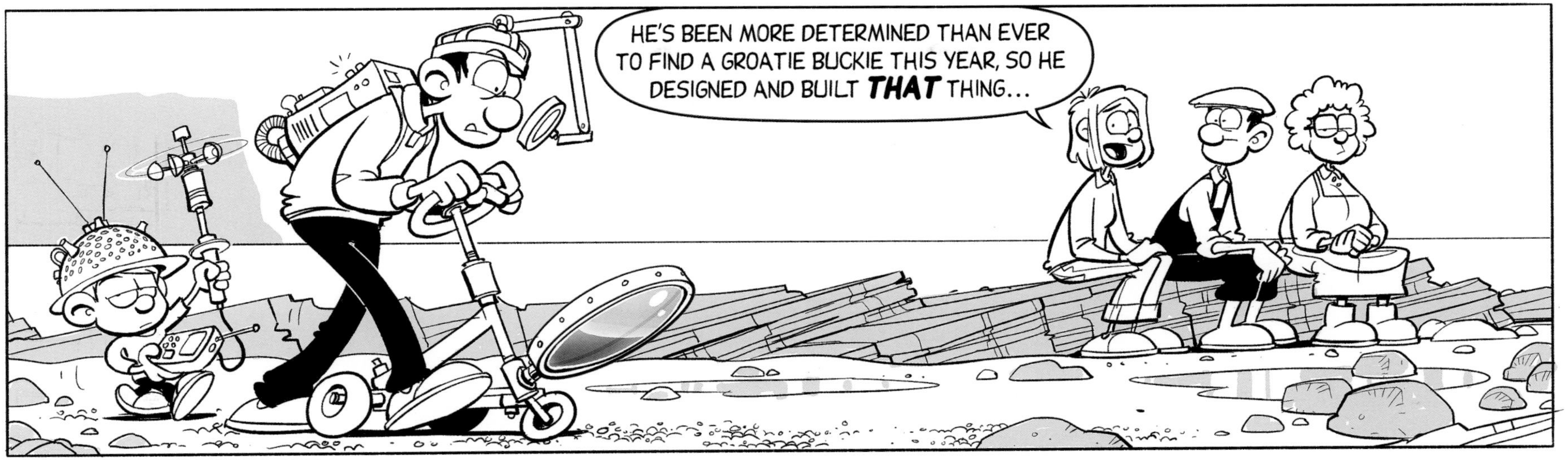
HE'S BEEN MORE DETERMINED THAN EVER TO FIND A GROATIE BUCKIE THIS YEAR, SO HE DESIGNED AND BUILT THAT THING...

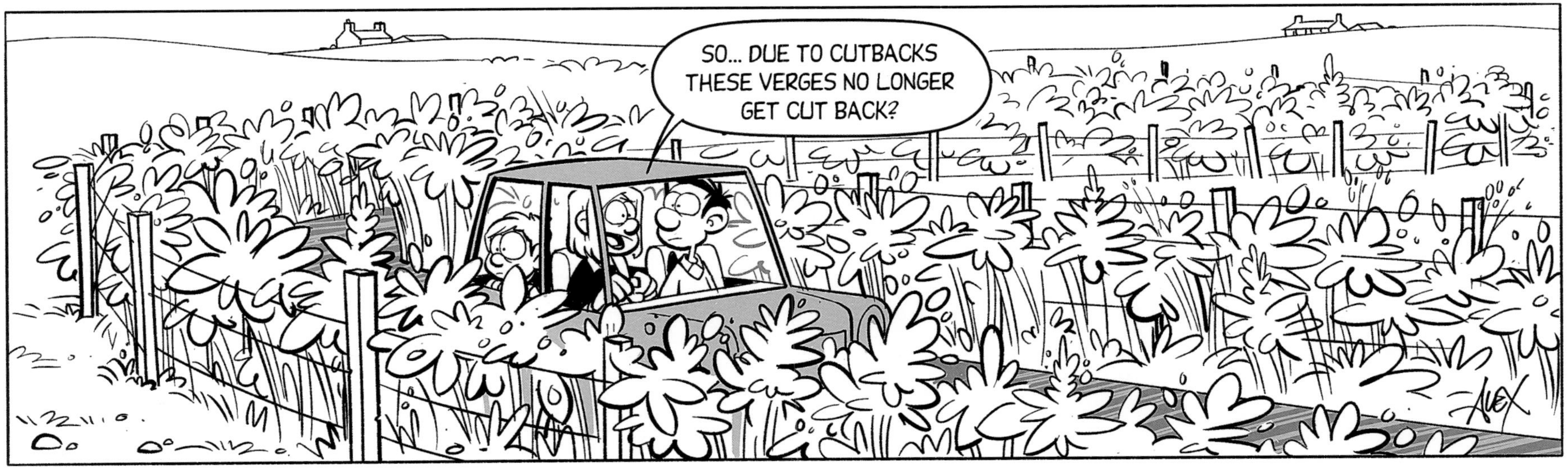
SO... DUE TO CUTBACKS THESE VERGES NO LONGER GET CUT BACK?
ALEX

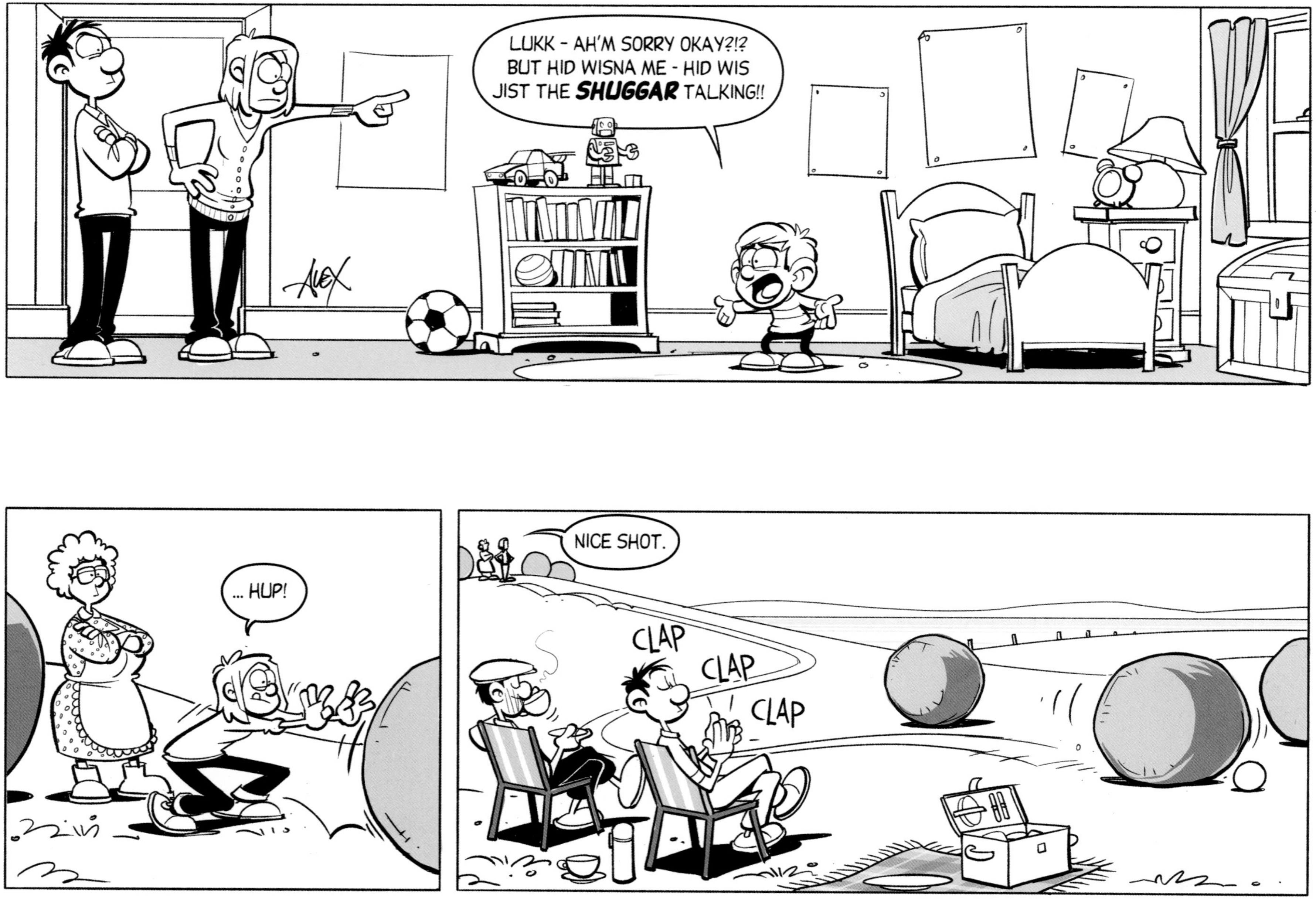

LUKK - AH'M SORRY OKAY?!?
BUT HID WISNA ME - HID WIS
JIST THE SHUGGAR TALKING!!
ALEX
... HUP!
NICE SHOT.
CLAP
CLAP
CLAP

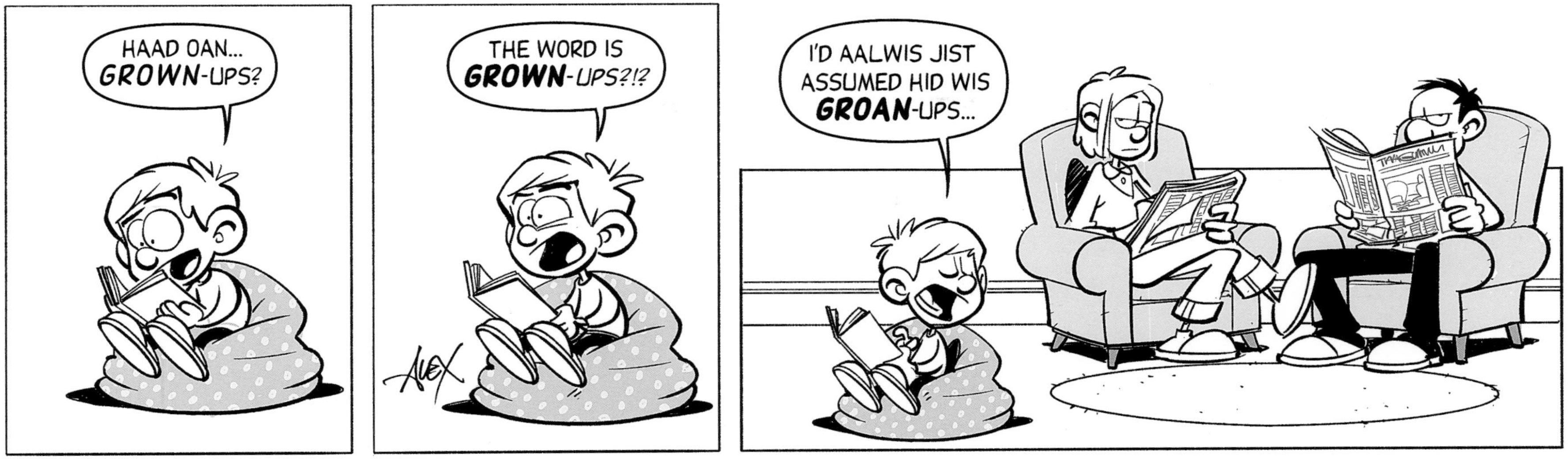
HAAD OAN... GROWN-UPS?
THE WORD IS GROWN-UPS?!?
ALEX
I'D AALWIS JIST ASSUMED HID WIS GROAN-UPS...

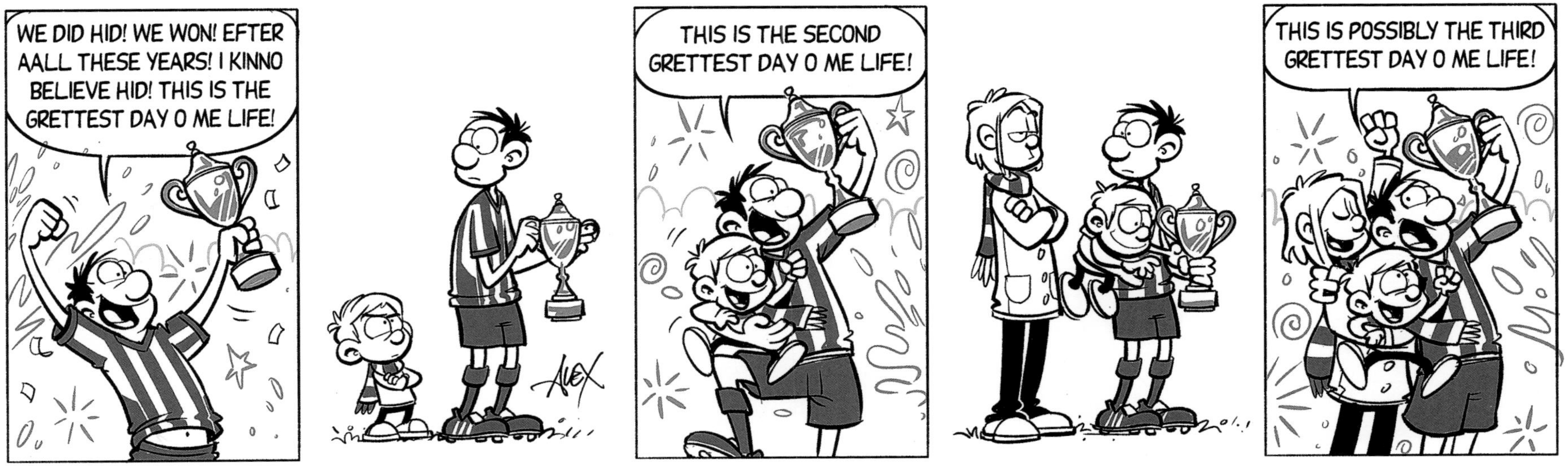
WE DID HID! WE WON! EFTER AALL THESE YEARS! I KINNO BELIEVE HID! THIS IS THE GRETTEST DAY O ME LIFE!
ALEX
THIS IS THE SECOND GRETTEST DAY O ME LIFE!
THIS IS POSSIBLY THE THIRD GRETTEST DAY O ME LIFE!

Parish Cup Final 2015.

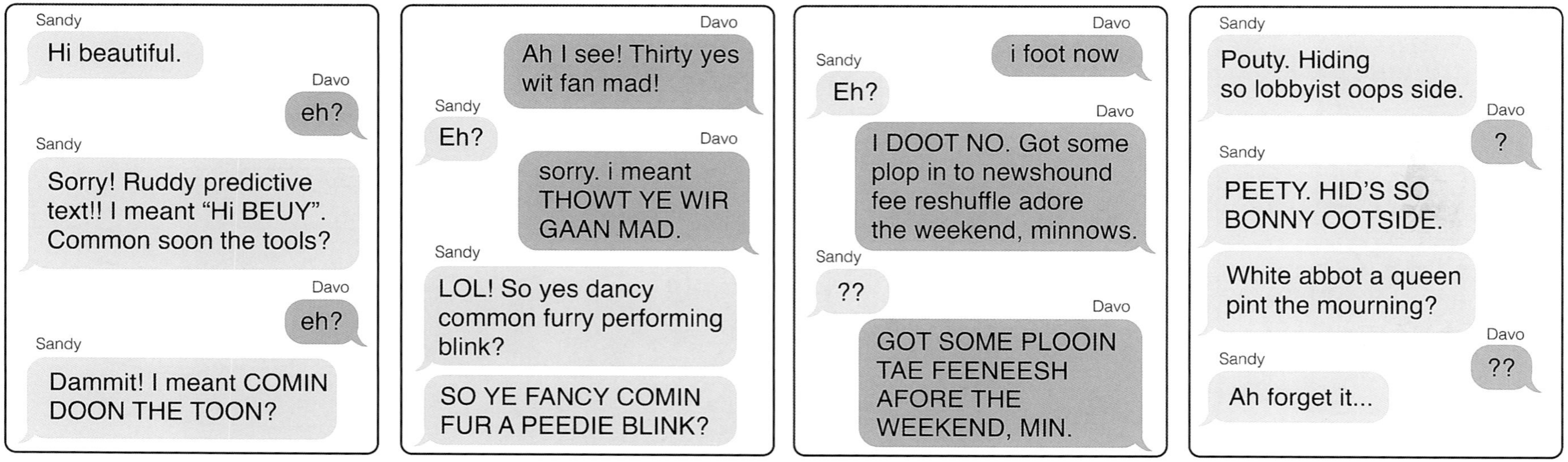
Sandy
Hi beautiful.
Davo
eh?
Sandy
Sorry! Ruddy predictive text!! I meant "Hi BEUY". Common soon the tools?
Davo
eh?
Sandy
Dammit! I meant COMIN DOON THE TOON?
Davo
Ah I see! Thirty yes wit fan mad!
Sandy
Eh?
Davo
sorry. i meant THOWT YE WIR GAAN MAD.
Sandy
LOL! So yes dancy common furry performing blink?
SO YE FANCY COMIN FUR A PEEDIE BLINK?
Davo
i foot now
Sandy
Eh?
Davo
I DOOT NO. Got some plop in to newshound fee reshuffle adore the weekend, minnows.
Sandy
??
Davo
GOT SOME PLOOIN TAE FEENEESH AFORE THE WEEKEND, MIN.
Sandy
Pouty. Hiding so lobbyist oops side.
Davo
?
Sandy
PEETY. HID'S SO BONNY OOTSIDE.
White abbot a queen pint the mourning?
Davo
??
Sandy
Ah forget it...

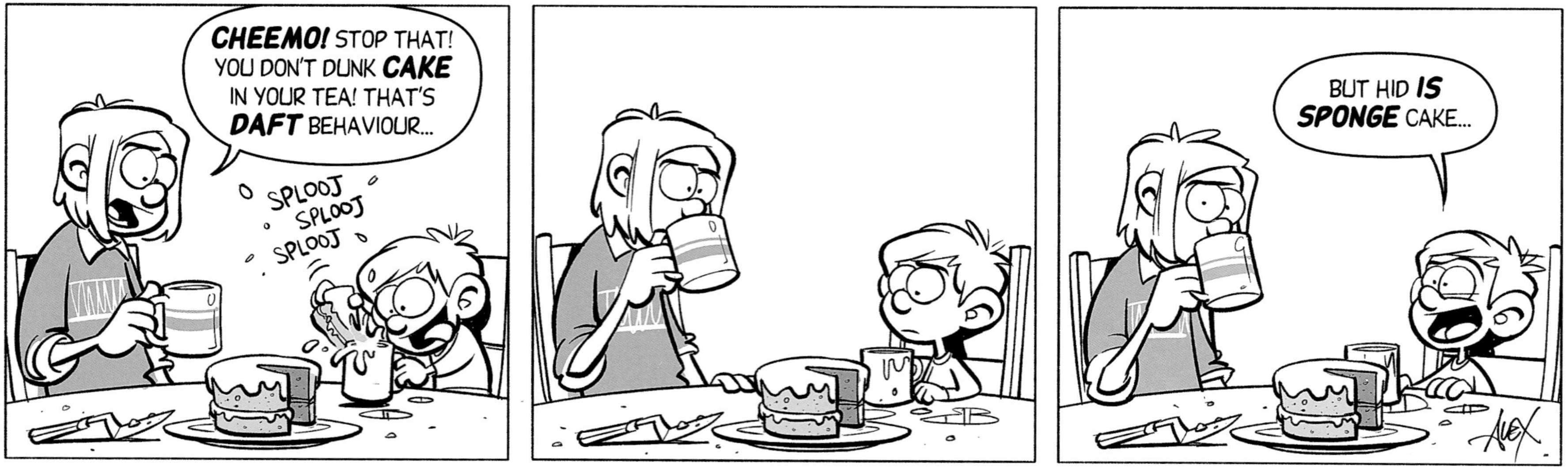
CHEEMO! STOP THAT! YOU DON'T DUNK CAKE IN YOUR TEA! THAT'S DAFT BEHAVIOUR...
SPLOOJ SPLOOJ SPLOOJ
BUT HID IS SPONGE CAKE...
ALEX

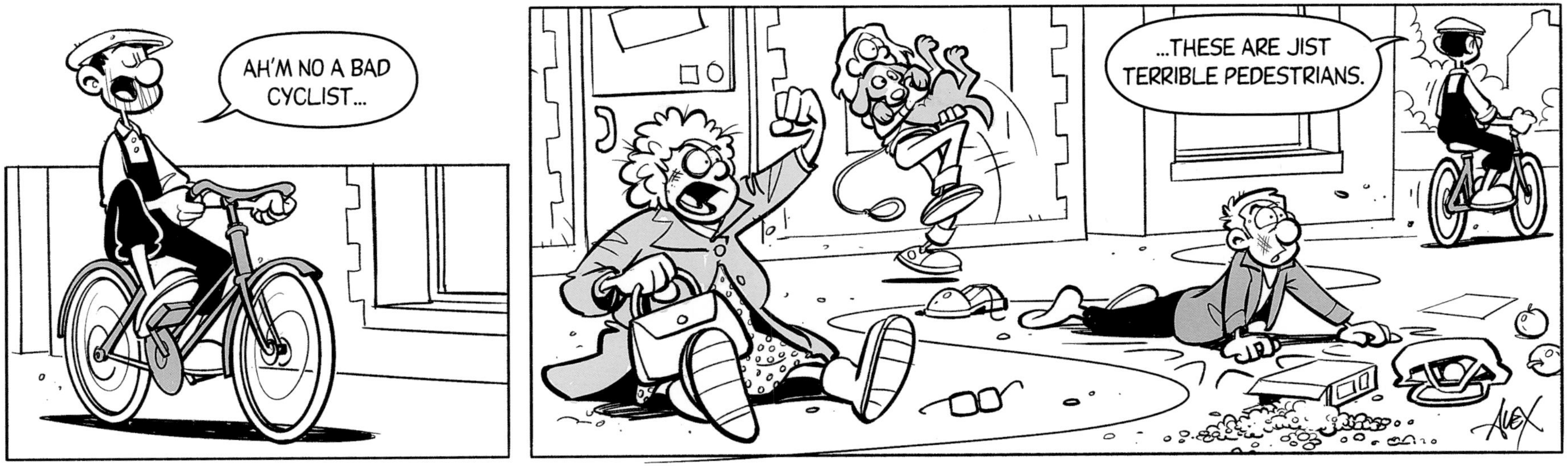
AH'M NO A BAD CYCLIST...
...THESE ARE JIST TERRIBLE PEDESTRIANS.

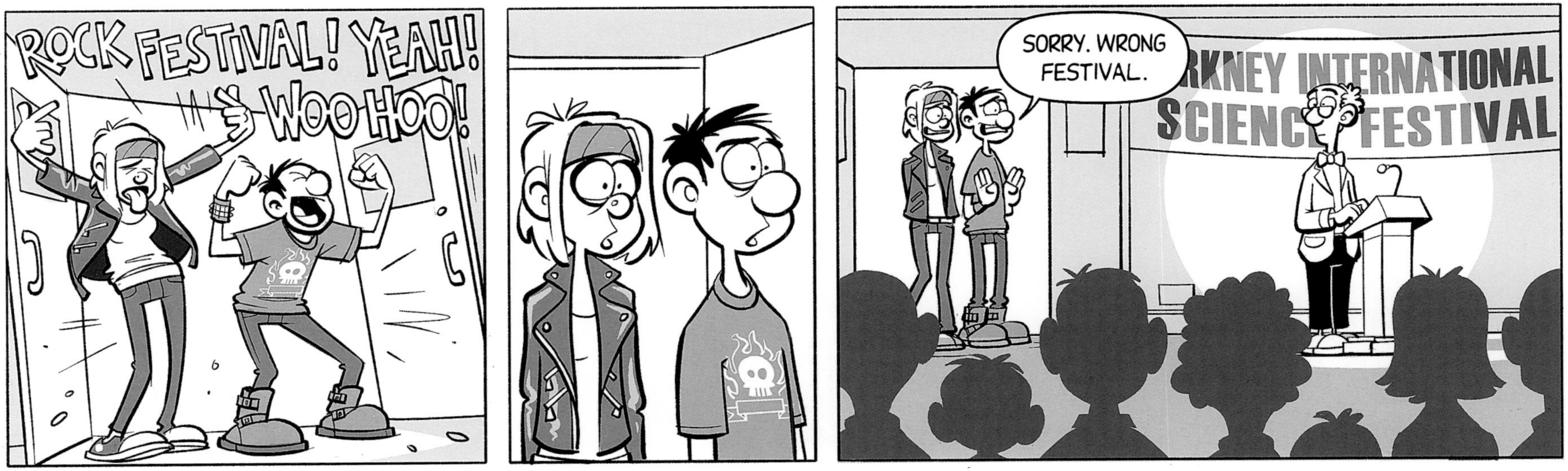
ROCK FESTIVAL! YEAH!
WOO HOO!
SORRY. WRONG FESTIVAL.
RKNEY INTERNATIONAL
SCIENC FESTIVAL

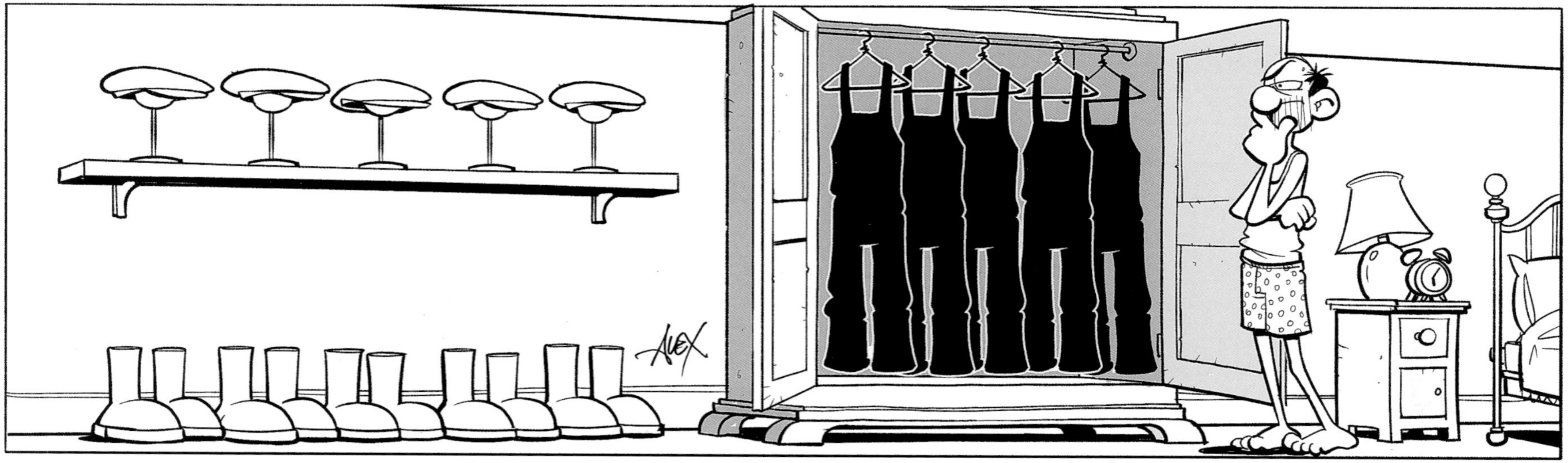
ALEX

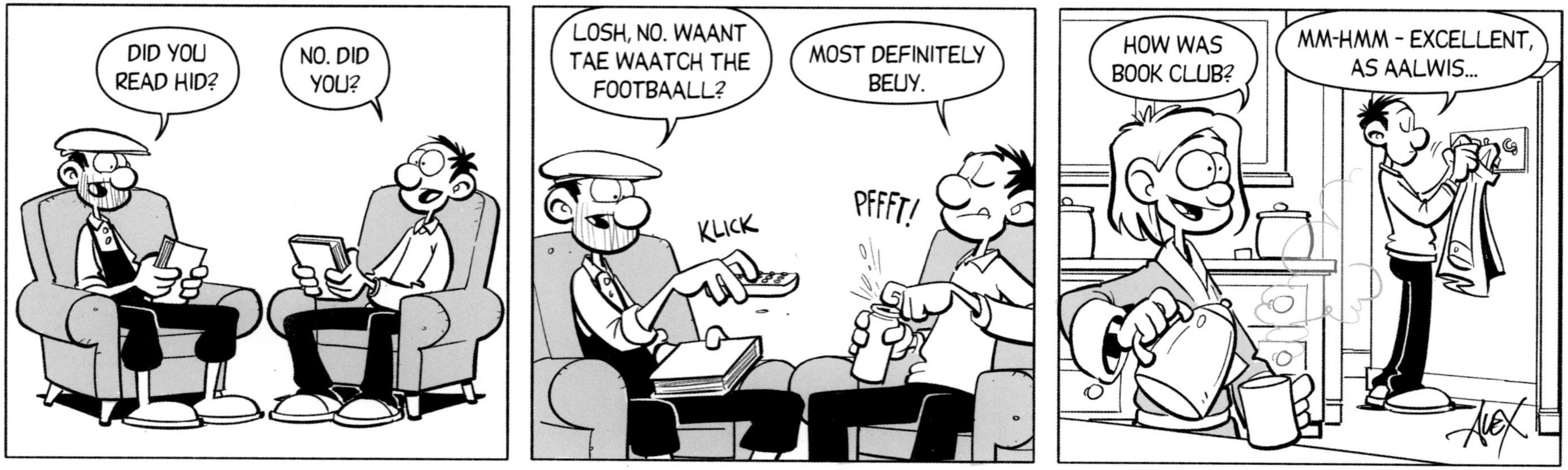
DID YOU READ HID?
NO. DID YOU?
LOSH, NO. WAANT TAE WAATCH THE FOOTBAALL?
MOST DEFINITELY BEUY.
KLICK
PFFFT!
HOW WAS BOOK CLUB?
MM-HMM - EXCELLENT, AS AALWIS...
ALEX

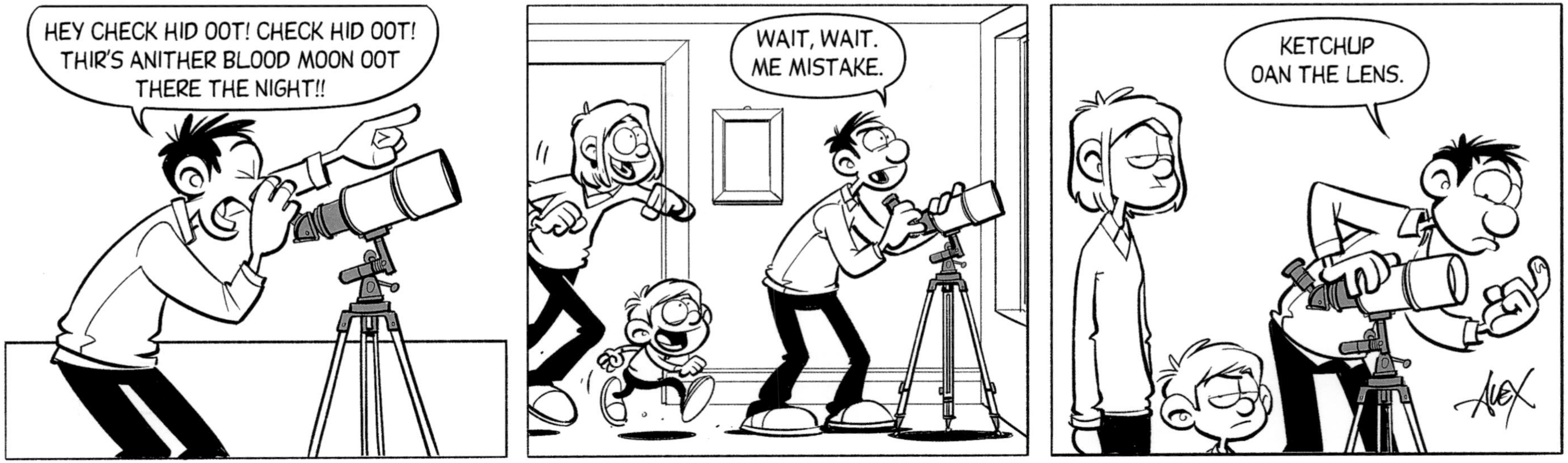
HEY CHECK HID OOT! CHECK HID OOT! THIR'S ANITHER BLOOD MOON OOT THERE THE NIGHT!!
WAIT, WAIT. ME MISTAKE.
KETCHUP OAN THE LENS.

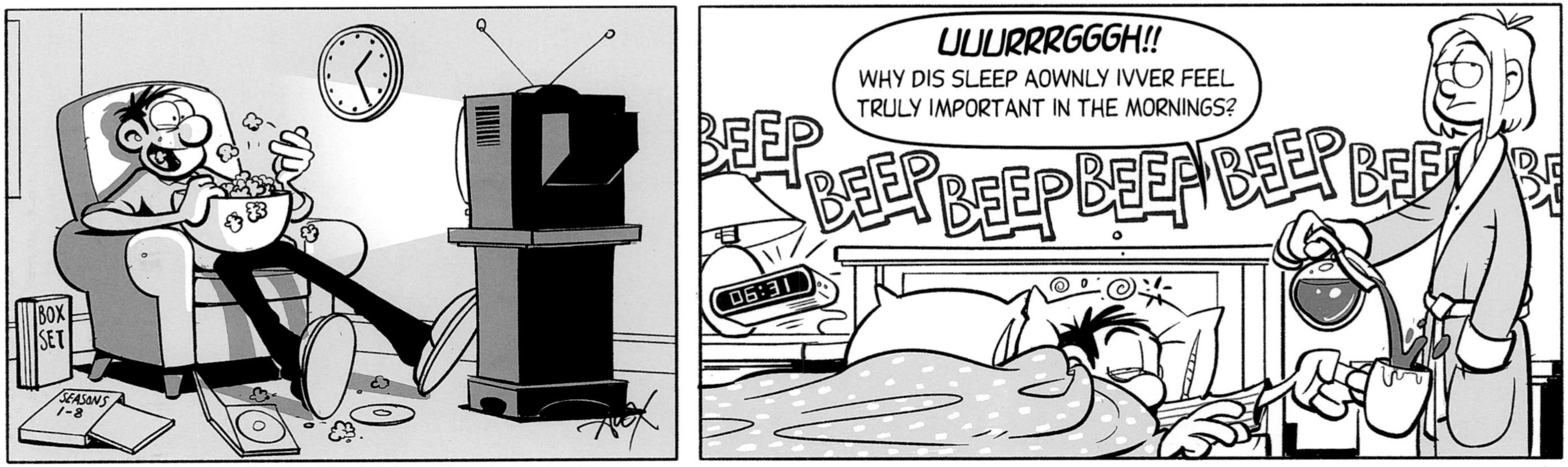
BOX SET
SEASONS 1-8
UUURRRGGGH!!
WHY DIS SLEEP AOWNLY IVVER FEEL TRULY IMPORTANT IN THE MORNINGS?
BEEP BEEP BEEP BEEP BEEP BEEP
06:31

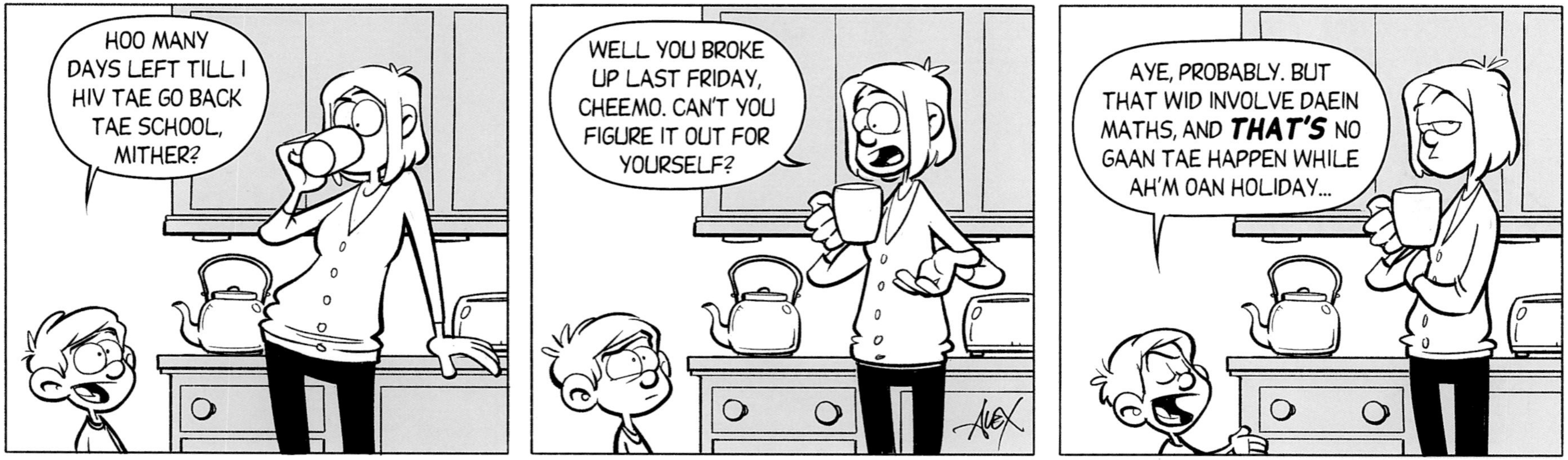
HOO MANY DAYS LEFT TILL I HIV TAE GO BACK TAE SCHOOL, MITHER?
WELL YOU BROKE UP LAST FRIDAY, CHEEMO. CAN'T YOU FIGURE IT OUT FOR YOURSELF?
AYE, PROBABLY. BUT THAT WID INVOLVE DAEIN MATHS, AND **THAT'S** NO GAAN TAE HAPPEN WHILE AH'M OAN HOLIDAY...

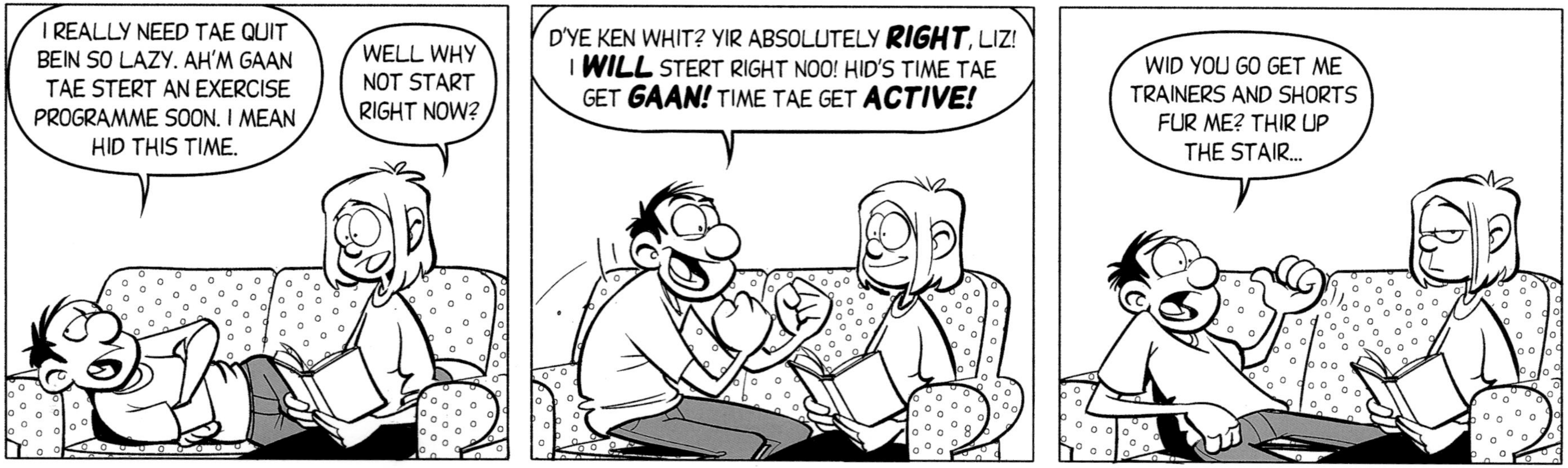
I REALLY NEED TAE QUIT BEIN SO LAZY. AH'M GAAN TAE STERT AN EXERCISE PROGRAMME SOON. I MEAN HID THIS TIME.
WELL WHY NOT START RIGHT NOW?
D'YE KEN WHIT? YIR ABSOLUTELY **RIGHT**, LIZ! I **WILL** STERT RIGHT NOO! HID'S TIME TAE GET **GAAN!** TIME TAE GET **ACTIVE!**
WID YOU GO GET ME TRAINERS AND SHORTS FUR ME? THIR UP THE STAIR...

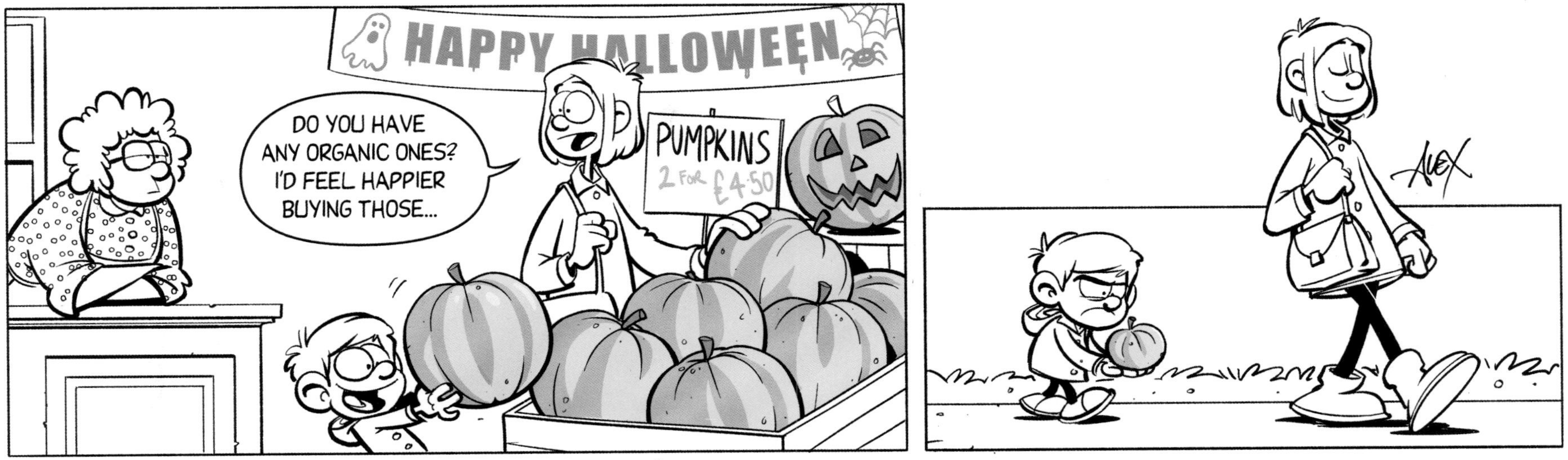
HAPPY HALLOWEEN
DO YOU HAVE ANY ORGANIC ONES? I'D FEEL HAPPIER BUYING THOSE...
PUMPKINS
2 FOR £4.50
ALEX

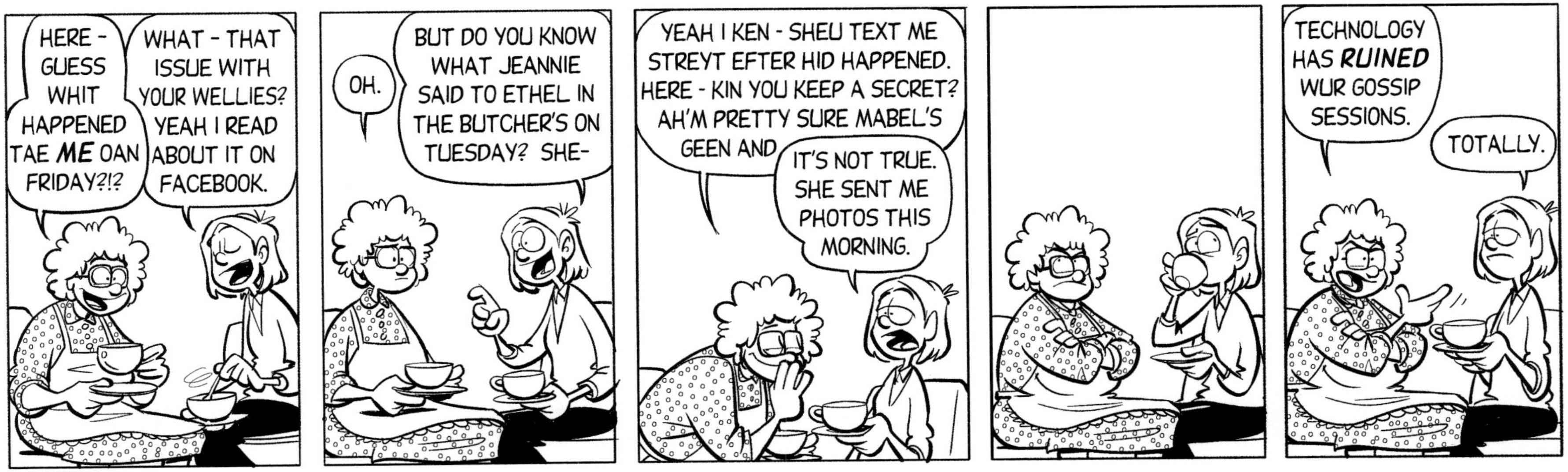
HERE - GUESS WHIT HAPPENED TAE ***ME*** OAN FRIDAY?!?
WHAT - THAT ISSUE WITH YOUR WELLIES? YEAH I READ ABOUT IT ON FACEBOOK.
OH.
BUT DO YOU KNOW WHAT JEANNIE SAID TO ETHEL IN THE BUTCHER'S ON TUESDAY? SHE-
YEAH I KEN - SHEU TEXT ME STREYT EFTER HID HAPPENED. HERE - KIN YOU KEEP A SECRET? AH'M PRETTY SURE MABEL'S GEEN AND
IT'S NOT TRUE. SHE SENT ME PHOTOS THIS MORNING.
TECHNOLOGY HAS ***RUINED*** WUR GOSSIP SESSIONS.
TOTALLY.

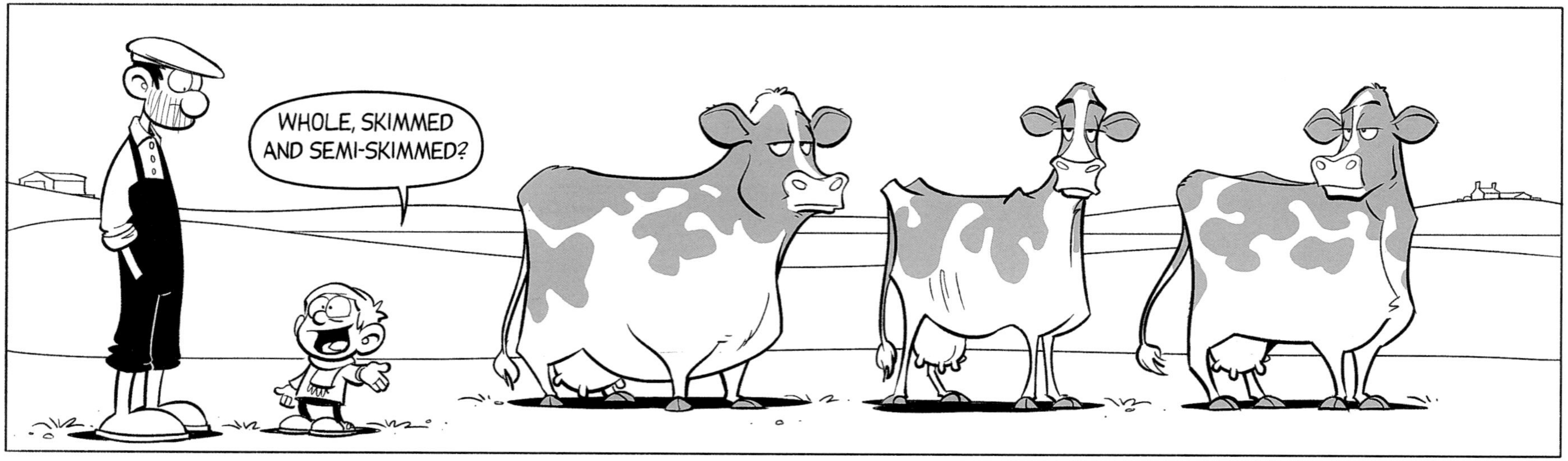
WHOLE, SKIMMED AND SEMI-SKIMMED?

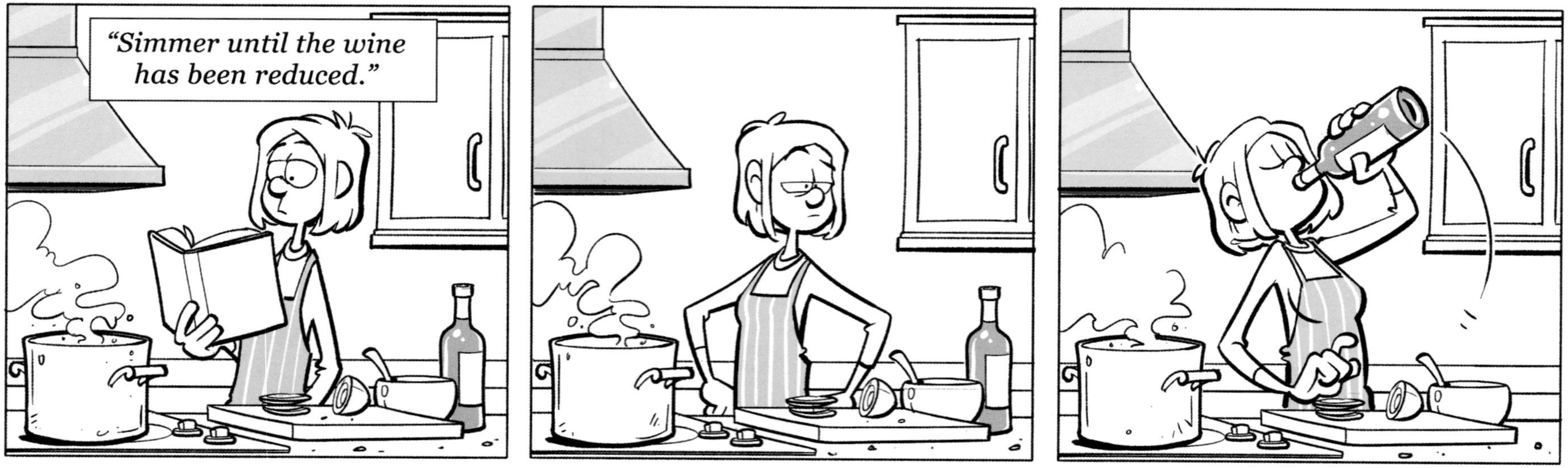
"Simmer until the wine has been reduced."

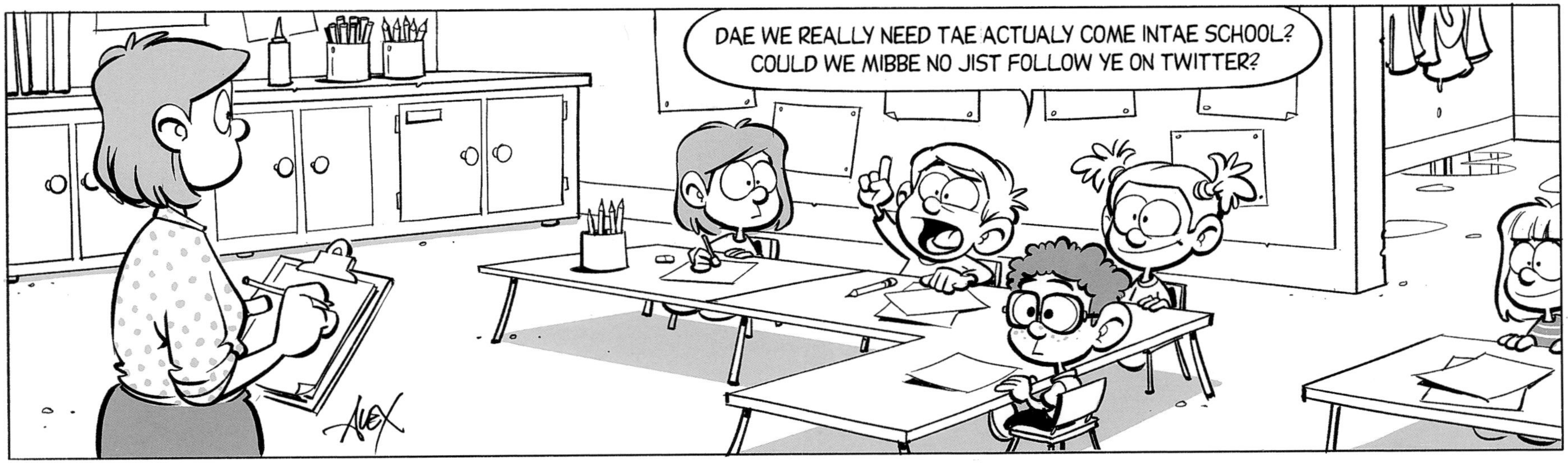
DAE WE REALLY NEED TAE ACTUALY COME INTAE SCHOOL? COULD WE MIBBE NO JIST FOLLOW YE ON TWITTER?

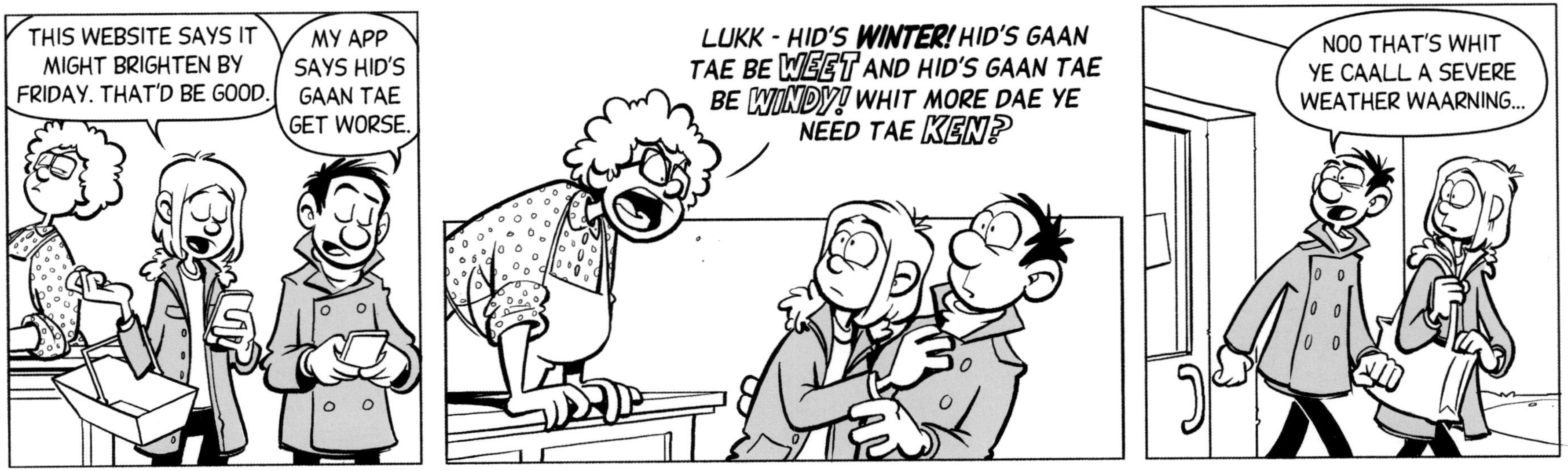
THIS WEBSITE SAYS IT MIGHT BRIGHTEN BY FRIDAY. THAT'D BE GOOD.
MY APP SAYS HID'S GAAN TAE GET WORSE.
LUKK - HID'S WINTER! HID'S GAAN TAE BE WEET AND HID'S GAAN TAE BE WINDY! WHIT MORE DAE YE NEED TAE KEN?
NOO THAT'S WHIT YE CAALL A SEVERE WEATHER WAARNING...

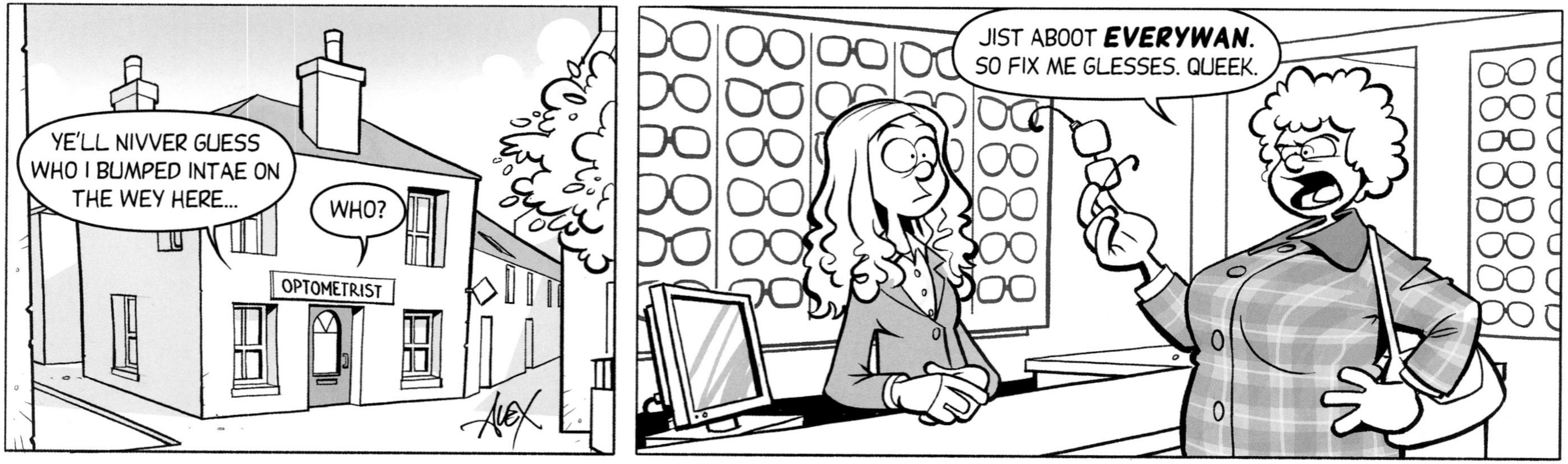
OPTOMETRIST
YE'LL NIVVER GUESS WHO I BUMPED INTAE ON THE WEY HERE...
WHO?
JIST ABOOT **EVERYWAN.** SO FIX ME GLESSES. QUEEK.

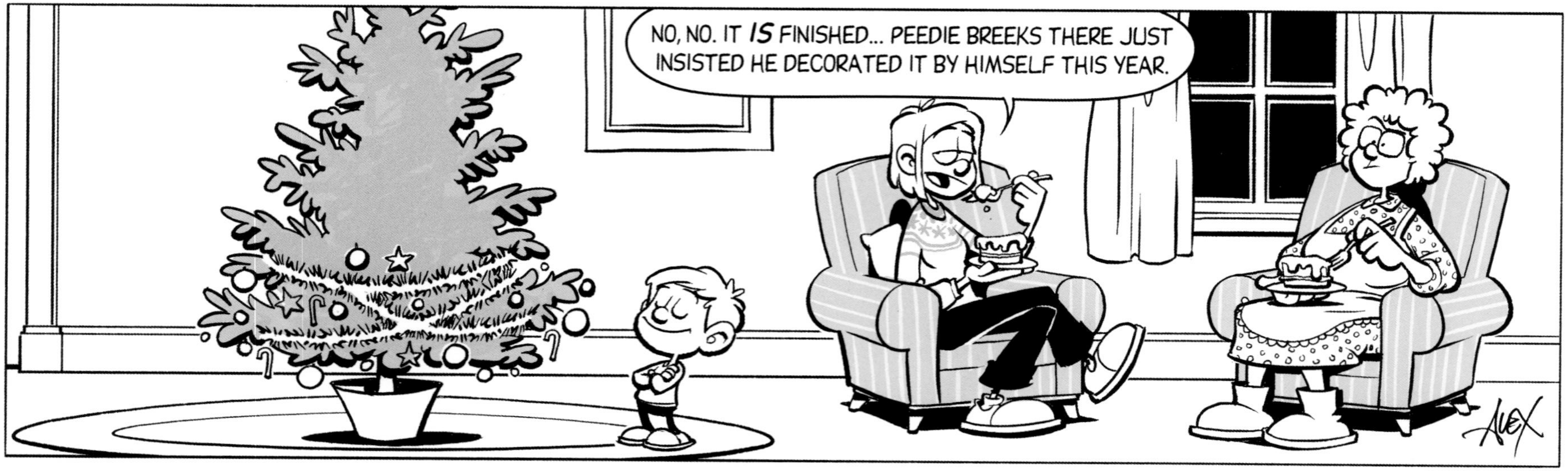
NO, NO. IT *IS* FINISHED... PEEDIE BREEKS THERE JUST INSISTED HE DECORATED IT BY HIMSELF THIS YEAR.

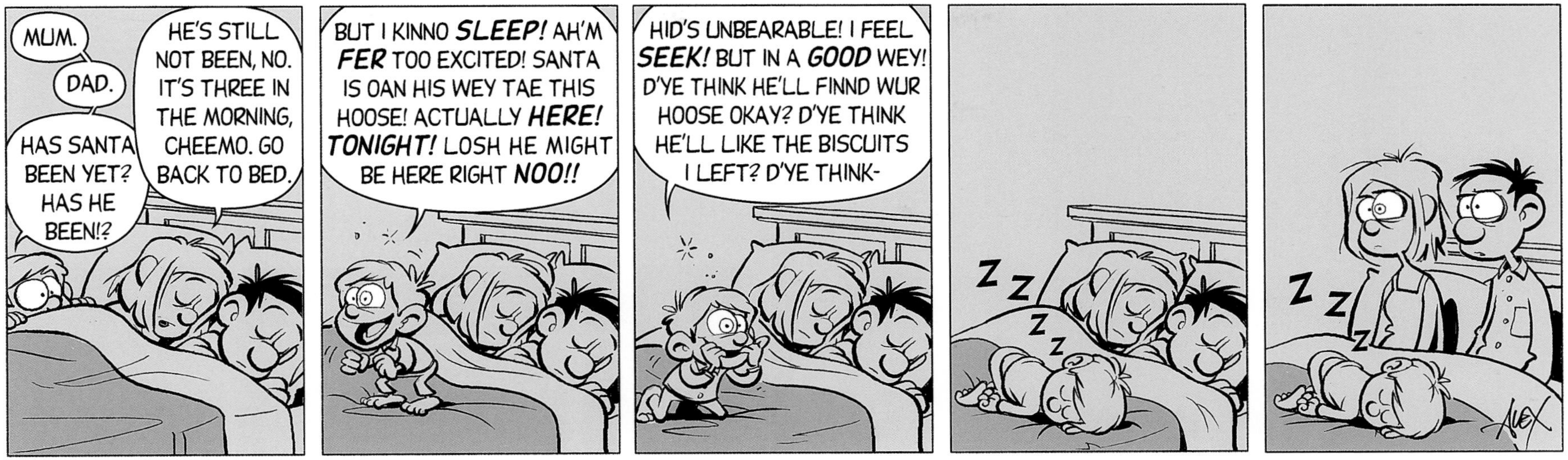
MUM.
DAD.
HAS SANTA BEEN YET? HAS HE BEEN!?
HE'S STILL NOT BEEN, NO. IT'S THREE IN THE MORNING, CHEEMO. GO BACK TO BED.
BUT I KINNO SLEEP! AH'M FER TOO EXCITED! SANTA IS OAN HIS WEY TAE THIS HOOSE! ACTUALLY HERE! TONIGHT! LOSH HE MIGHT BE HERE RIGHT NOO!!
HID'S UNBEARABLE! I FEEL SEEK! BUT IN A GOOD WEY! D'YE THINK HE'LL FINND WUR HOOSE OKAY? D'YE THINK HE'LL LIKE THE BISCUITS I LEFT? D'YE THINK-
Z Z Z Z
Z Z Z
ALEX

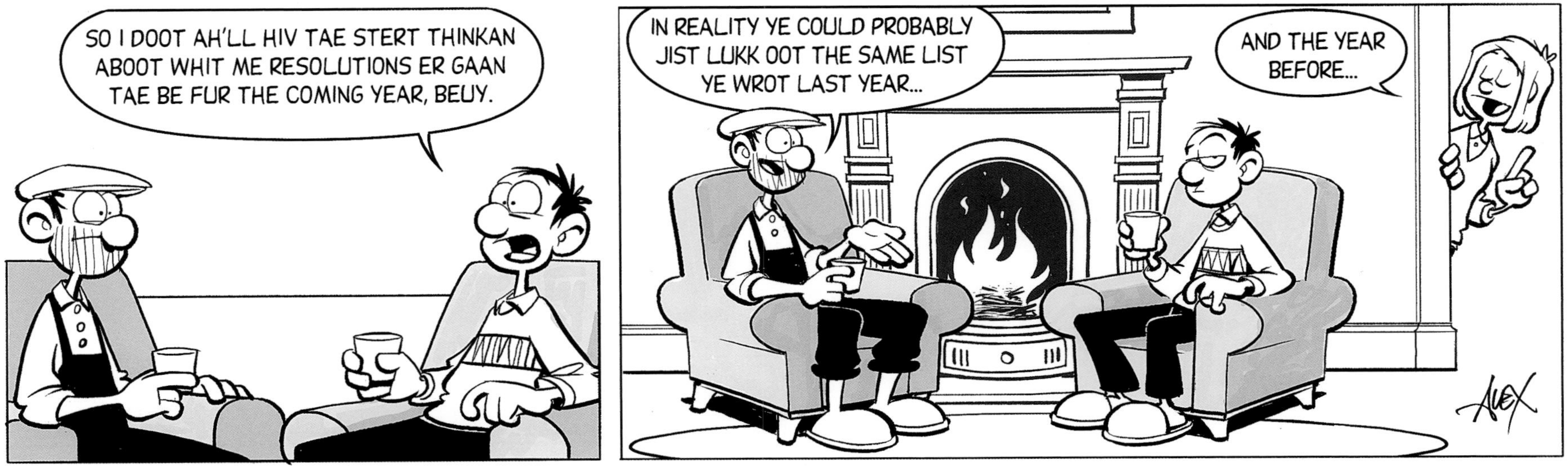
SO I DOOT AH'LL HIV TAE STERT THINKAN ABOOT WHIT ME RESOLUTIONS ER GAAN TAE BE FUR THE COMING YEAR, BEUY.
IN REALITY YE COULD PROBABLY JIST LUKK OOT THE SAME LIST YE WROT LAST YEAR...
AND THE YEAR BEFORE...
ALEX

# 2016 CALENDAR

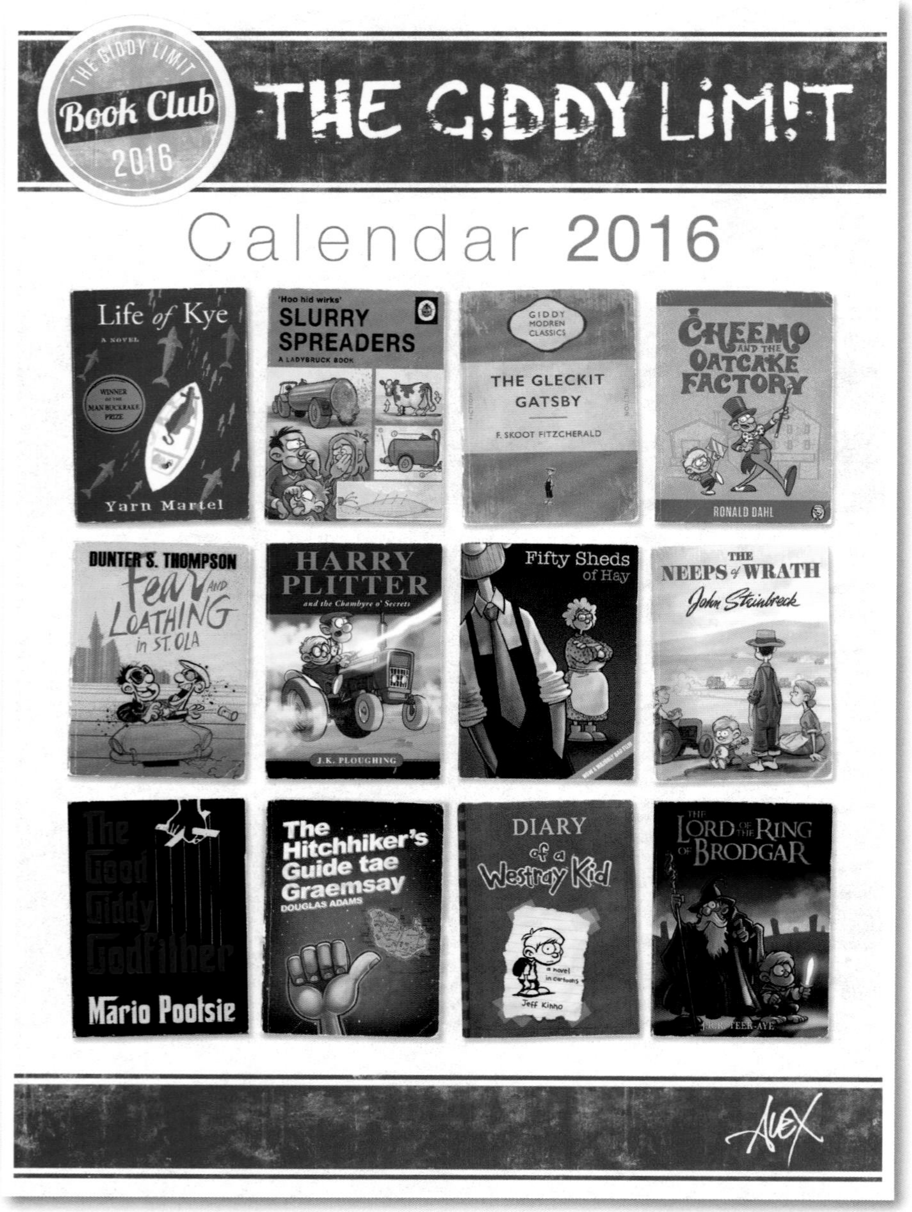
THE GIDDY LIMIT
Book Club
2016
THE GIDDY LIMIT
Calendar 2016
Life of Kye
Yarn Martel
SLURRY SPREADERS
THE GLECKIT GATSBY
F. SKOOT FITZCHERALD
CHEEMO AND THE OATCAKE FACTORY
RONALD DAHL
DUNTER S. THOMPSON
Fear and Loathing in St. Ola
HARRY PLITTER
J.K. PLOUGHING
Fifty Sheds of Hay
THE NEEPS of WRATH
John Steinbreck
The Good Giddy Godfither
Mario Pootsie
The Hitchhiker's Guide tae Graemsay
DOUGLAS ADAMS
DIARY of a Westray Kid
Jeff Kinno
THE LORD OF THE RING OF BRODGAR
ALEX

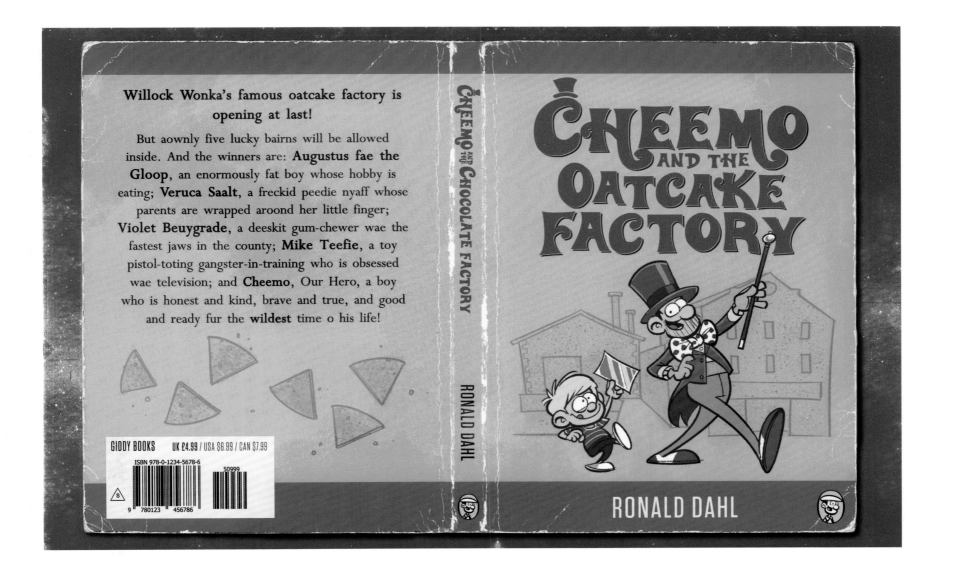

**Willock Wonka's famous oatcake factory is opening at last!**

But aownly five lucky bairns will be allowed inside. And the winners are: **Augustus fae the Gloop**, an enormously fat boy whose hobby is eating; **Veruca Saalt**, a freckid peedie nyaff whose parents are wrapped aroond her little finger; **Violet Beuygrade**, a deeskit gum-chewer wae the fastest jaws in the county; **Mike Teefie**, a toy pistol-toting gangster-in-training who is obsessed wae television; and **Cheemo**, Our Hero, a boy who is honest and kind, brave and true, and good and ready fur the **wildest** time o his life!

GIDDY BOOKS   UK £4.99 / USA $6.99 / CAN $7.99

ISBN 978-0-1234-5678-6

9 780123 456786   50999

CHEEMO AND THE CHOCOLATE FACTORY

**CHEEMO AND THE OATCAKE FACTORY**

**RONALD DAHL**

RONALD DAHL

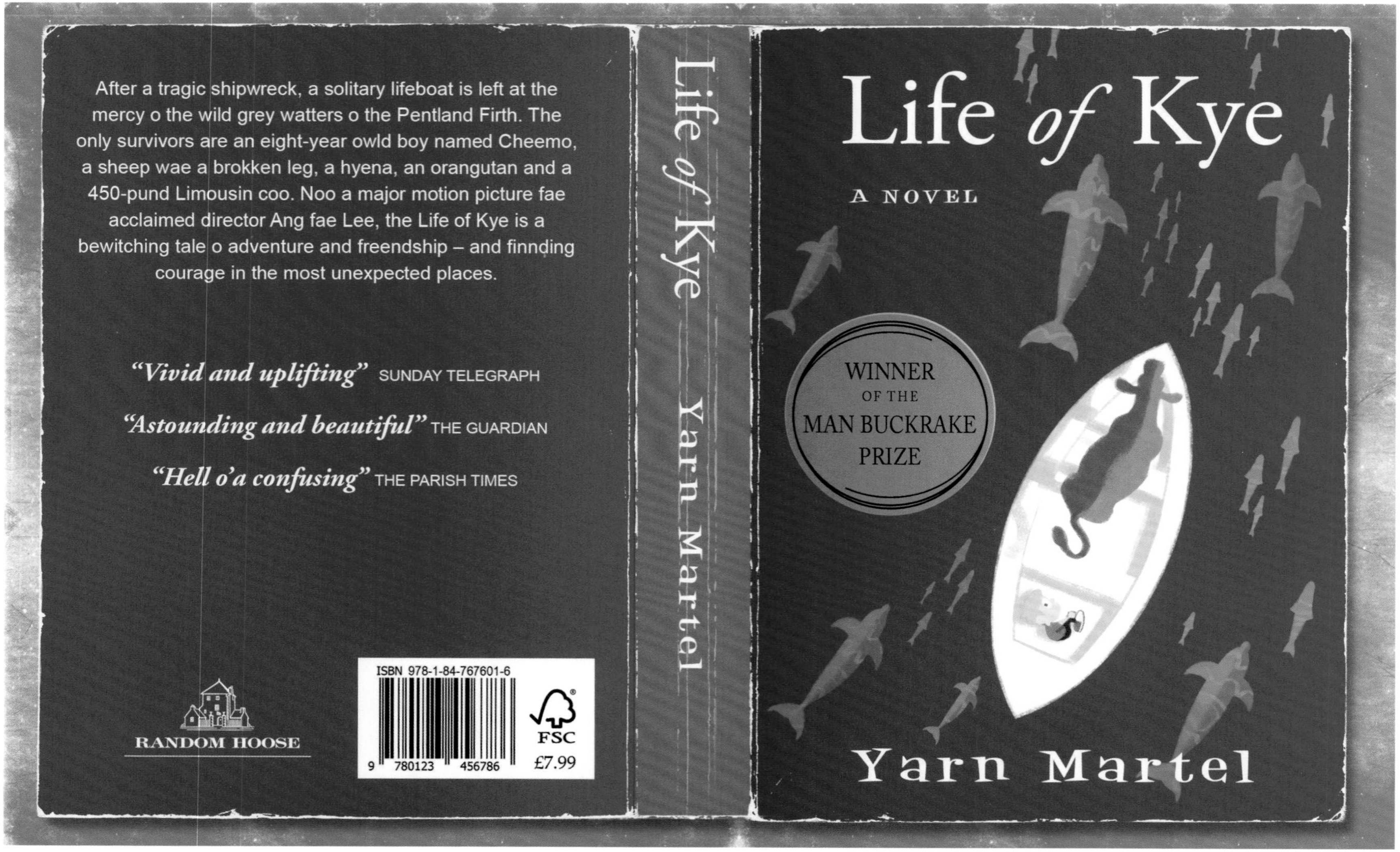
After a tragic shipwreck, a solitary lifeboat is left at the mercy o the wild grey watters o the Pentland Firth. The only survivors are an eight-year owld boy named Cheemo, a sheep wae a brokken leg, a hyena, an orangutan and a 450-pund Limousin coo. Noo a major motion picture fae acclaimed director Ang fae Lee, the Life of Kye is a bewitching tale o adventure and freendship – and finnding courage in the most unexpected places.
"Vivid and uplifting" SUNDAY TELEGRAPH
"Astounding and beautiful" THE GUARDIAN
"Hell o'a confusing" THE PARISH TIMES
RANDOM HOOSE
ISBN 978-1-84-767601-6
9 780123 456786
FSC
£7.99
Life of Kye
Yarn Martel
Life of Kye
A NOVEL
WINNER
OF THE
MAN BUCKRAKE
PRIZE
Yarn Martel

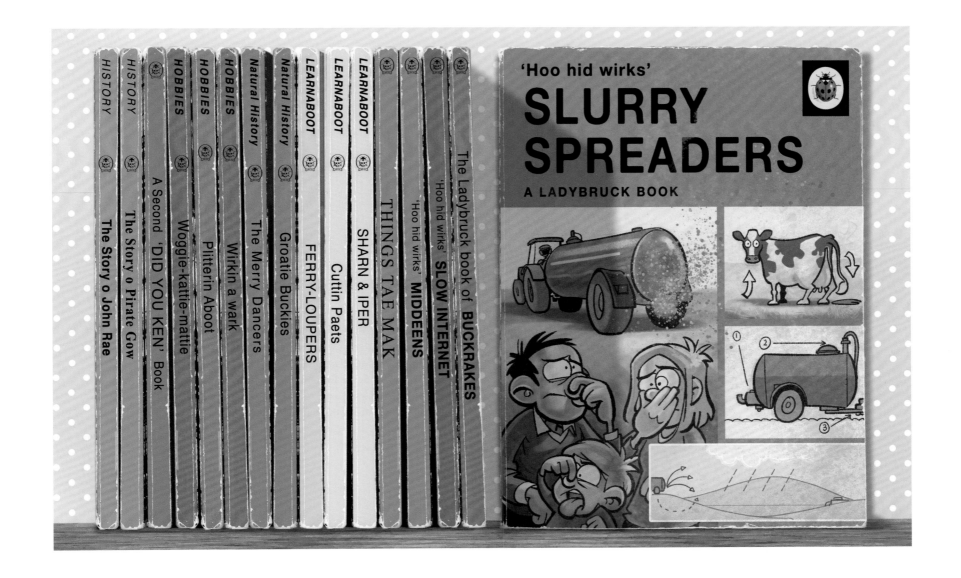

HISTORY

HISTORY

HOBBIES

HOBBIES

HOBBIES

Natural History

Natural History

LEARNABOOT

LEARNABOOT

LEARNABOOT

The Story o John Rae

The Story o Pirate Gow

A Second 'DID YOU KEN' Book

Woggie-kattie-mattie

Plitterin Aboot

Wirkin a wark

The Merry Dancers

Groatie Buckies

FERRY-LOUPERS

Cuttin Paets

SHARN & IPER

THINGS TAE MAK

'Hoo hid wirks' MIDDEENS

'Hoo hid wirks' SLOW INTERNET

The Ladybruck book of BUCKRAKES

'Hoo hid wirks'
# SLURRY SPREADERS
A LADYBRUCK BOOK

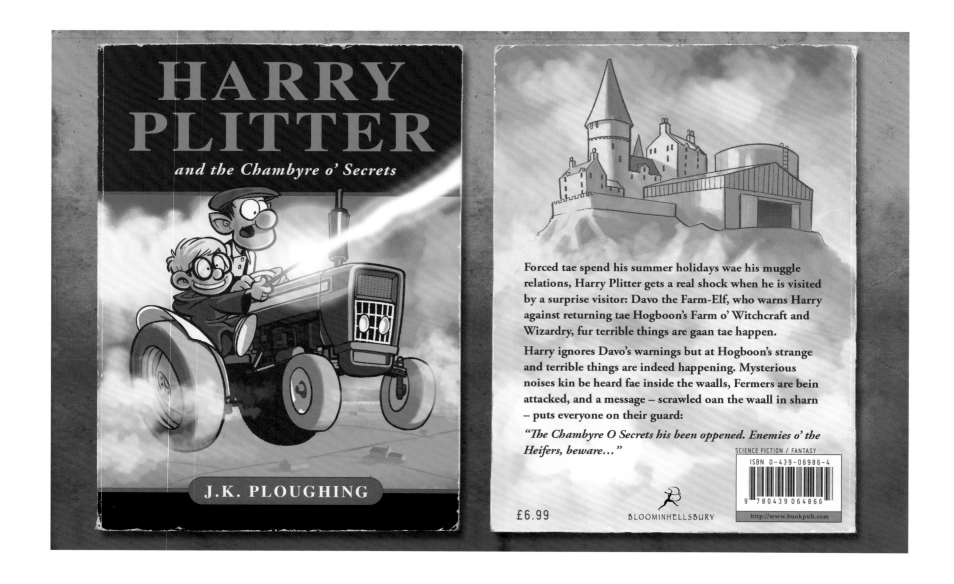

# HARRY PLITTER
### and the Chambyre o' Secrets

**J.K. PLOUGHING**

Forced tae spend his summer holidays wae his muggle relations, Harry Plitter gets a real shock when he is visited by a surprise visitor: Davo the Farm-Elf, who warns Harry against returning tae Hogboon's Farm o' Witchcraft and Wizardry, fur terrible things are gaan tae happen.

Harry ignores Davo's warnings but at Hogboon's strange and terrible things are indeed happening. Mysterious noises kin be heard fae inside the waalls, Fermers are bein attacked, and a message – scrawled oan the waall in sharn – puts everyone on their guard:

*"The Chambyre O Secrets his been oppened. Enemies o' the Heifers, beware..."*

SCIENCE FICTION / FANTASY

ISBN 0-439-06986-4

£6.99

BLOOMINHELLSBURY

http://www.bookpub.com

9 780439 064866

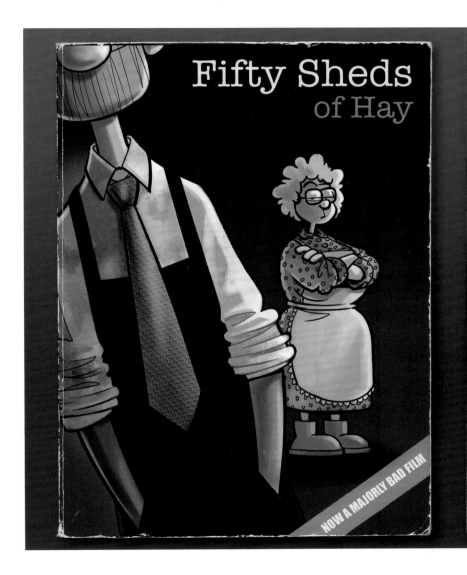

# Fifty Sheds
## of Hay

NOW A MAJORLY BAD FILM

Romantic, liberating and totally addictive, this is a novel that will obsess you, posess you and stay with you forever.

When lokkal shopkeeeper **Ivy** serves successful farmer **Davo o' Clartaquouy**, she finnds him utterly repulsive and deeply annoying. Happy that thir transaction went badly, she manages tae pit him oot o her mind – until he turns up back at the store whar she wirks, and invites her tae the parish dance.

Lugubrious and unsociable, Ivy warns him tae keep his distance, but hid aownly makks him waant her more.

She discovers that Davo is tormented by inner demons and consumed by the need tae makk silage. As they embark oan a totally wan-sided love affair, Ivy discovers much aboot her aown hay-fever allergies, as well as the dark secrets Davo keeps hidden awey fae public view.

ISBN 978-0-09-957994-6

9 780123 456786

FCS

£7.99

Twitter #literaryexcrement  www.fiftysheds.com

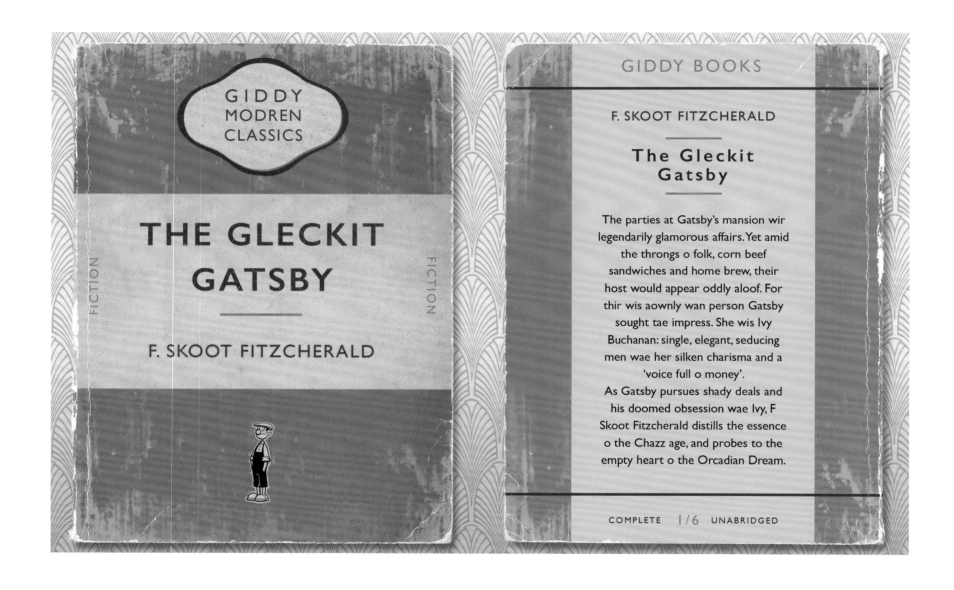

# GIDDY MODREN CLASSICS

## THE GLECKIT GATSBY

FICTION

FICTION

F. SKOOT FITZCHERALD

---

GIDDY BOOKS

F. SKOOT FITZCHERALD

## The Gleckit Gatsby

The parties at Gatsby's mansion wir legendarily glamorous affairs. Yet amid the throngs o folk, corn beef sandwiches and home brew, their host would appear oddly aloof. For thir wis aownly wan person Gatsby sought tae impress. She wis Ivy Buchanan: single, elegant, seducing men wae her silken charisma and a 'voice full o money'.

As Gatsby pursues shady deals and his doomed obsession wae Ivy, F Skoot Fitzcherald distills the essence o the Chazz age, and probes to the empty heart o the Orcadian Dream.

COMPLETE 1/6 UNABRIDGED

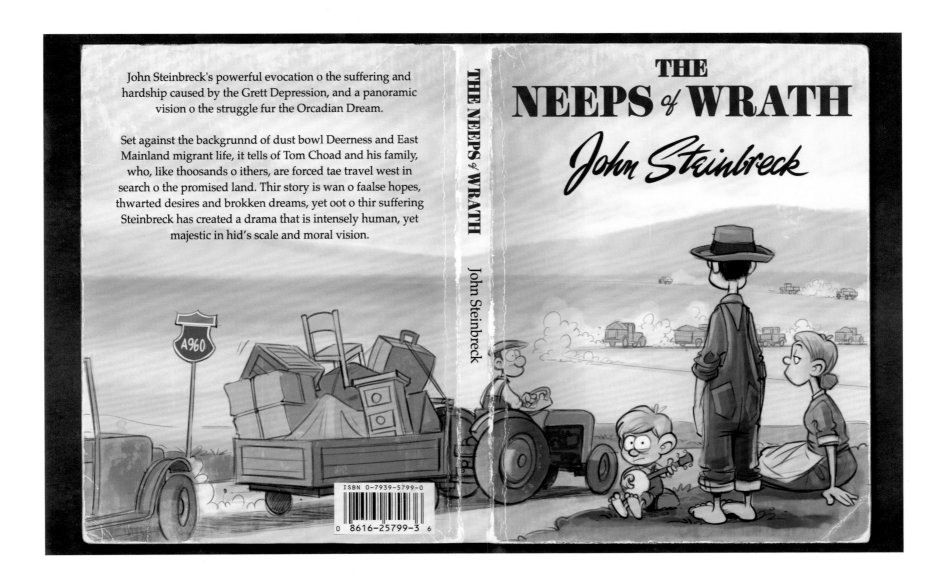

John Steinbreck's powerful evocation o the suffering and hardship caused by the Grett Depression, and a panoramic vision o the struggle fur the Orcadian Dream.

Set against the backgrunnd of dust bowl Deerness and East Mainland migrant life, it tells of Tom Choad and his family, who, like thoosands o ithers, are forced tae travel west in search o the promised land. Thir story is wan o faalse hopes, thwarted desires and brokken dreams, yet oot o thir suffering Steinbreck has created a drama that is intensely human, yet majestic in hid's scale and moral vision.

THE NEEPS of WRATH

John Steinbreck

THE NEEPS of WRATH

John Steinbreck

ISBN 0-7939-5799-0

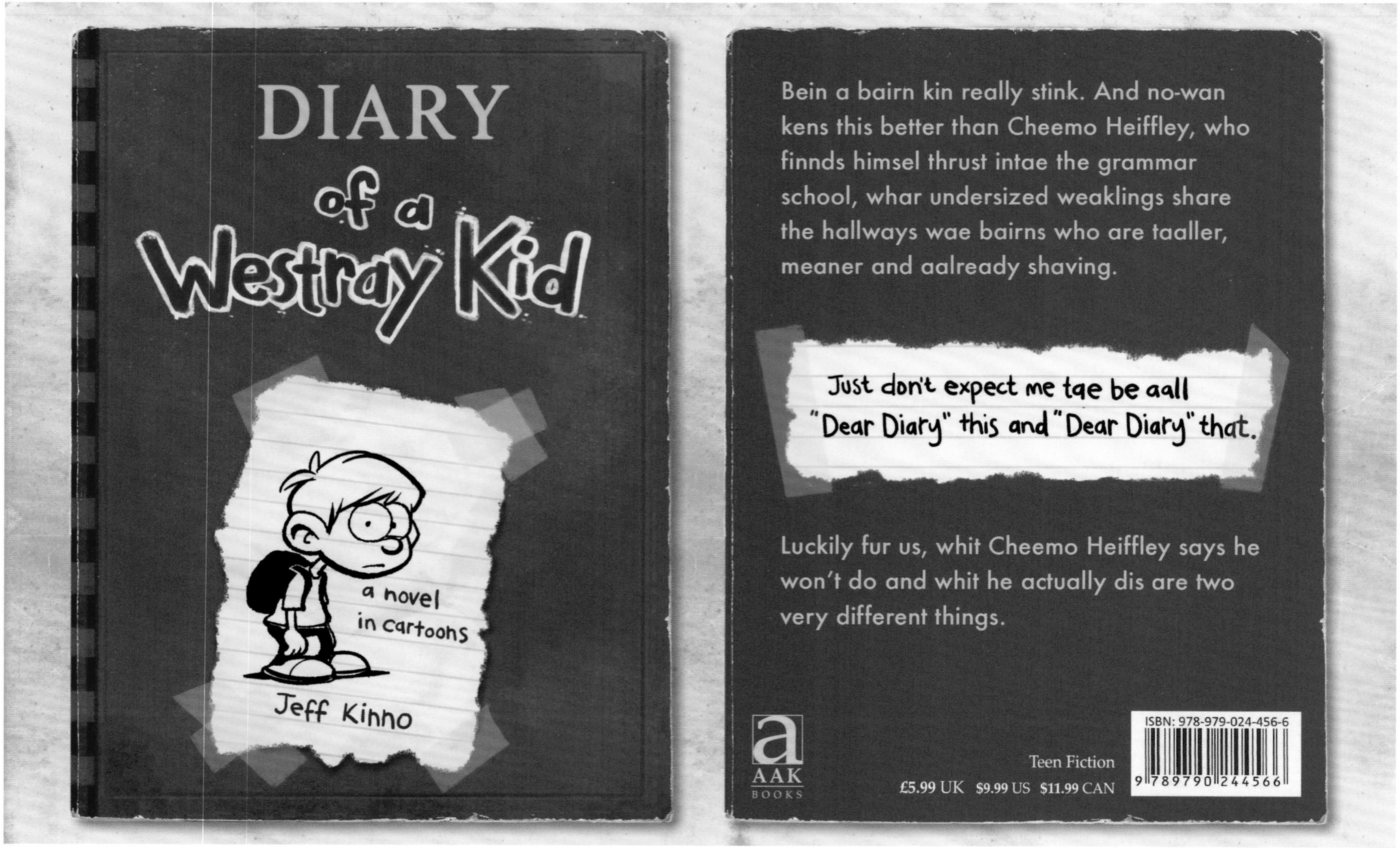
DIARY
of a
Westray Kid
a novel
in cartoons
Jeff Kinno
Bein a bairn kin really stink. And no-wan kens this better than Cheemo Heiffley, who finnds himsel thrust intae the grammar school, whar undersized weaklings share the hallways wae bairns who are taaller, meaner and aalready shaving.
Just don't expect me tae be aall "Dear Diary" this and "Dear Diary" that.
Luckily fur us, whit Cheemo Heiffley says he won't do and whit he actually dis are two very different things.
AAK
BOOKS
Teen Fiction
£5.99 UK $9.99 US $11.99 CAN
ISBN: 978-979-024-456-6
9 789790 244566

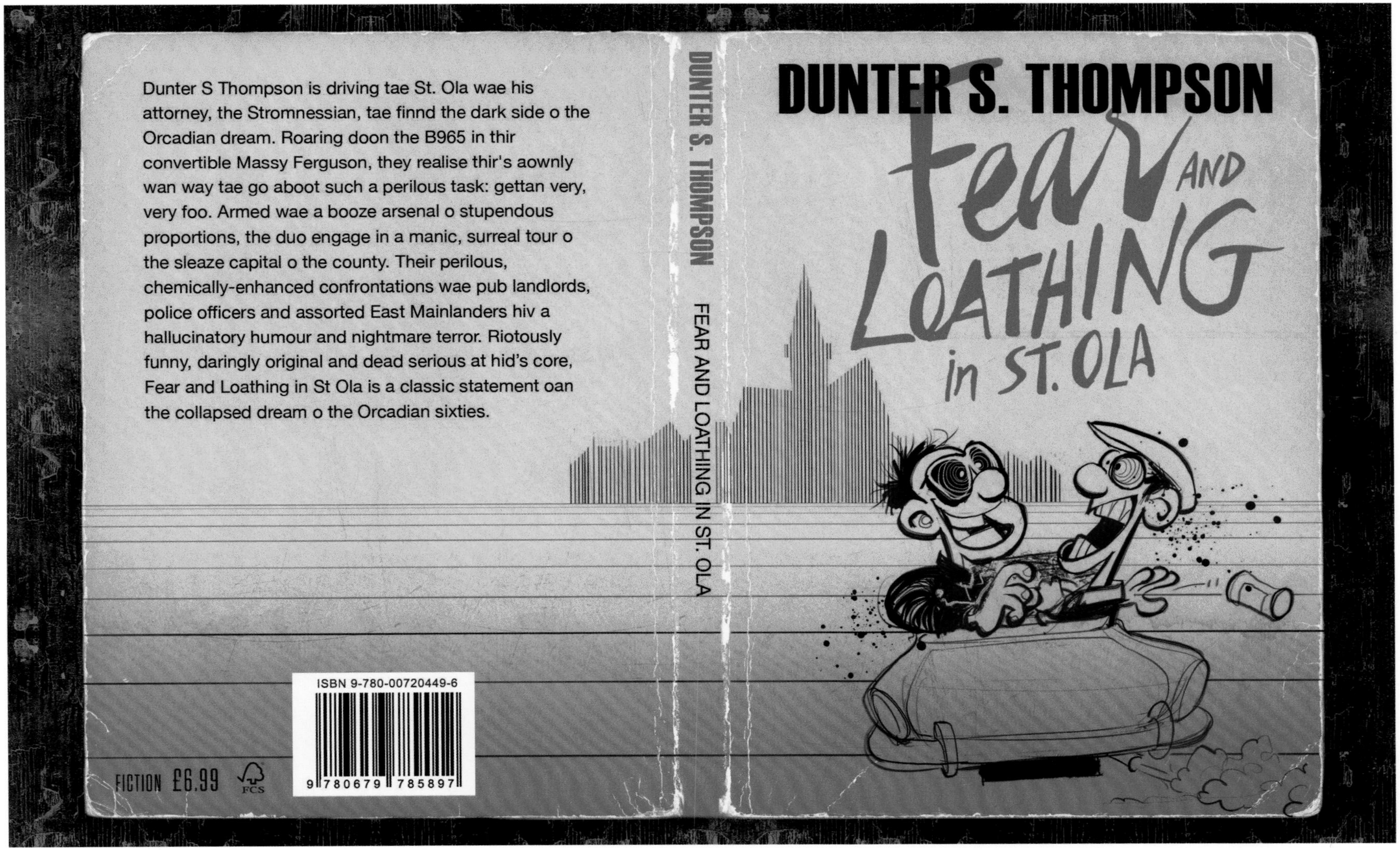
Dunter S Thompson is driving tae St. Ola wae his attorney, the Stromnessian, tae finnd the dark side o the Orcadian dream. Roaring doon the B965 in thir convertible Massy Ferguson, they realise thir's aownly wan way tae go aboot such a perilous task: gettan very, very foo. Armed wae a booze arsenal o stupendous proportions, the duo engage in a manic, surreal tour o the sleaze capital o the county. Their perilous, chemically-enhanced confrontations wae pub landlords, police officers and assorted East Mainlanders hiv a hallucinatory humour and nightmare terror. Riotously funny, daringly original and dead serious at hid's core, Fear and Loathing in St Ola is a classic statement oan the collapsed dream o the Orcadian sixties.
ISBN 9-780-00720449-6
9 780679 785897
FICTION £6.99
FCS
DUNTER S. THOMPSON
FEAR AND LOATHING IN ST. OLA
DUNTER S. THOMPSON
Fear AND LOATHING in ST. OLA

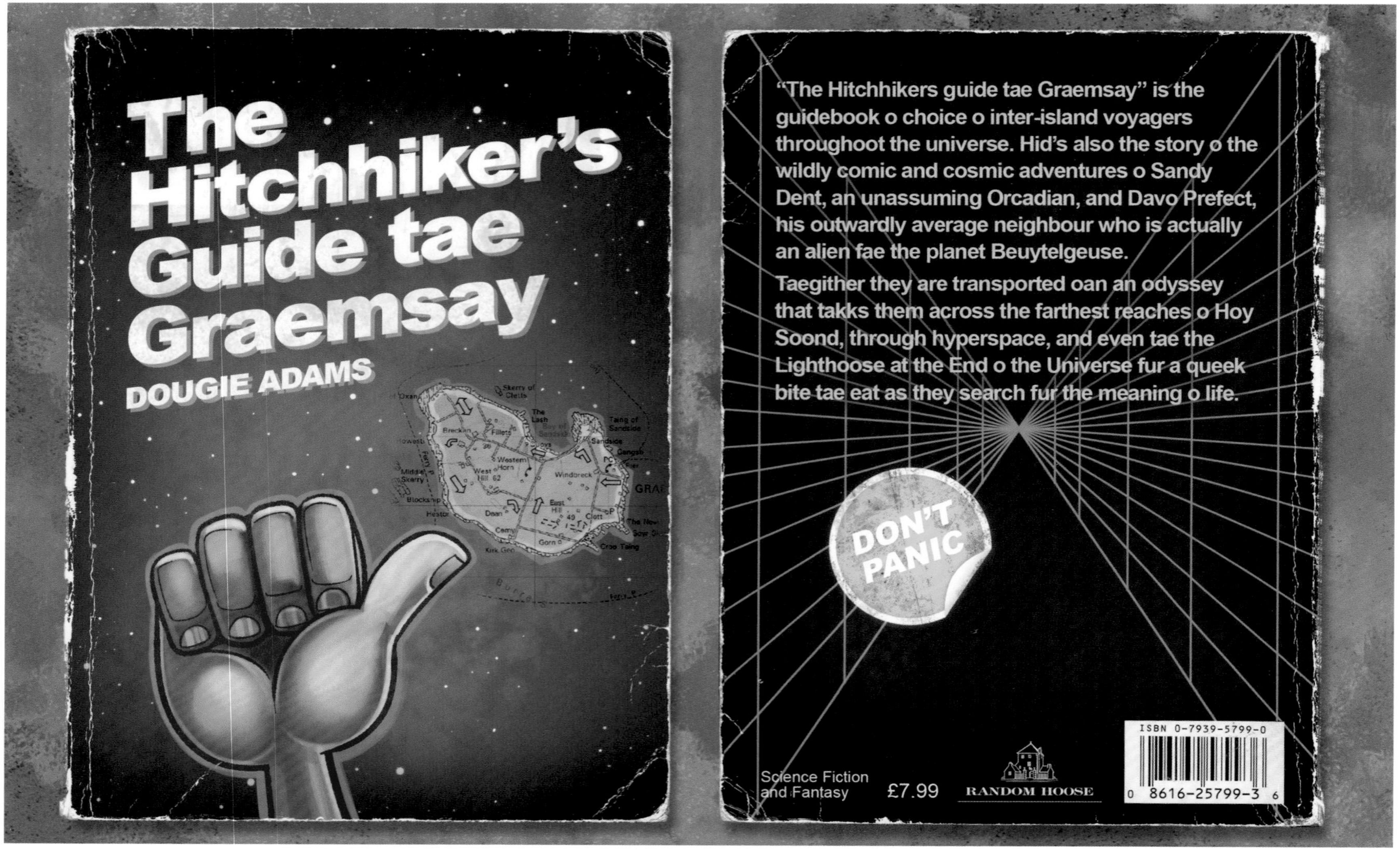
The Hitchhiker's Guide tae Graemsay
DOUGIE ADAMS
"The Hitchhikers guide tae Graemsay" is the guidebook o choice o inter-island voyagers throughoot the universe. Hid's also the story o the wildly comic and cosmic adventures o Sandy Dent, an unassuming Orcadian, and Davo Prefect, his outwardly average neighbour who is actually an alien fae the planet Beuytelgeuse.
Taegither they are transported oan an odyssey that takks them across the farthest reaches o Hoy Soond, through hyperspace, and even tae the Lighthoose at the End o the Universe fur a queek bite tae eat as they search fur the meaning o life.
DON'T PANIC
Science Fiction and Fantasy
£7.99
RANDOM HOOSE
ISBN 0-7939-5799-0
0 8616-25799-3 6

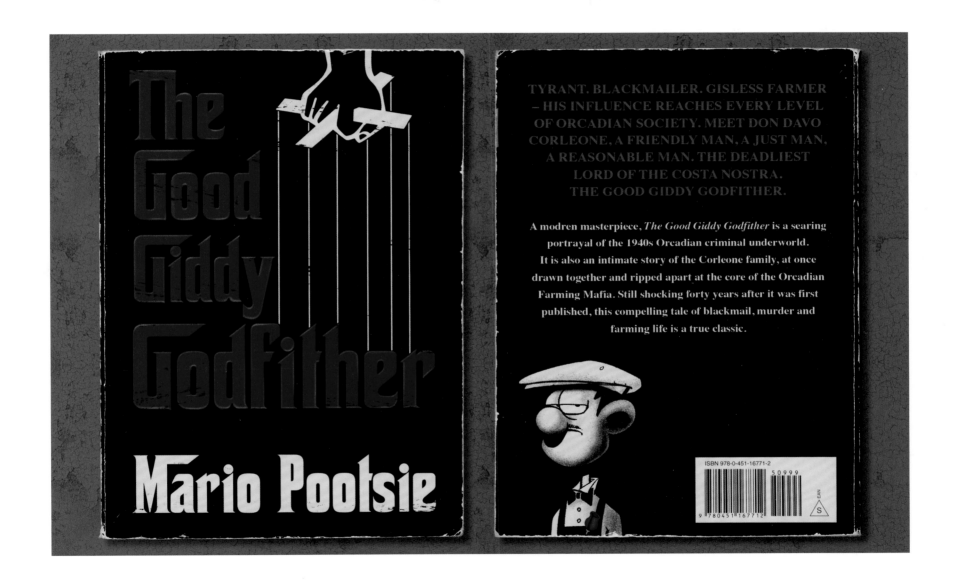

# The Good Giddy Godfither

## Mario Pootsie

TYRANT. BLACKMAILER. GISLESS FARMER – HIS INFLUENCE REACHES EVERY LEVEL OF ORCADIAN SOCIETY. MEET DON DAVO CORLEONE, A FRIENDLY MAN, A JUST MAN, A REASONABLE MAN. THE DEADLIEST LORD OF THE COSTA NOSTRA. THE GOOD GIDDY GODFITHER.

A modren masterpiece, *The Good Giddy Godfither* is a searing portrayal of the 1940s Orcadian criminal underworld. It is also an intimate story of the Corleone family, at once drawn together and ripped apart at the core of the Orcadian Farming Mafia. Still shocking forty years after it was first published, this compelling tale of blackmail, murder and farming life is a true classic.

ISBN 978-0-451-16771-2

50999

9 780451 167712

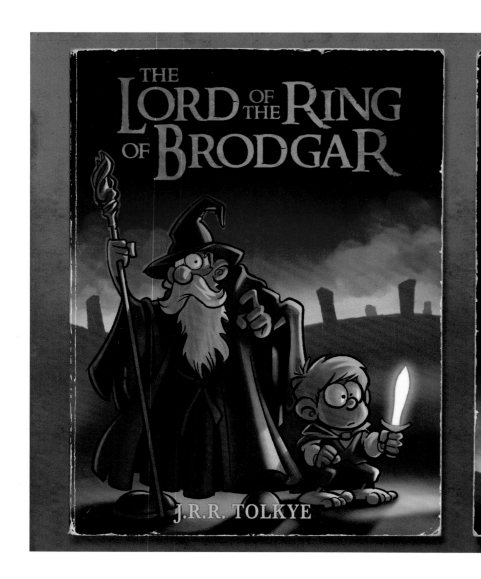

# THE LORD OF THE RING OF BRODGAR

J.R.R. TOLKYE

*Wan Ring tae rule them aall,*
*Wan Ring tae finnd them,*
*Wan ring tae bring them aall,*
*and in the slurry bind them*

When eccentric farmer Bilbeuy Baggins leaves his home in the Parishire, he gives his greatest treasure to his heir Frodo: a magic ring that makes the bearer odourless.

His friend the wizard Graandalf reveals to Frodo that the ring is in fact the Wan Ring, forged by the evil farmer Souron to enable him to enslave and dominate all of Middle-parish.

The ring must be destroyed by throwing it into the fires of Mount Dounby, where it was first created. Despite the hopelessness of the quest, Frodo accepts the burden and resolves to take the ring to the safety of the elven stronghold of Rivrendall…

ISBN-13: 978-0-618-64015-7
ISBN-10: 0-618-64015-0

90000

9 780618 640157

FICTION / £9.99
1005/6-89737

Cover design by Shandy Linnard

BARNS & NOBULL
BOOKSELLERS

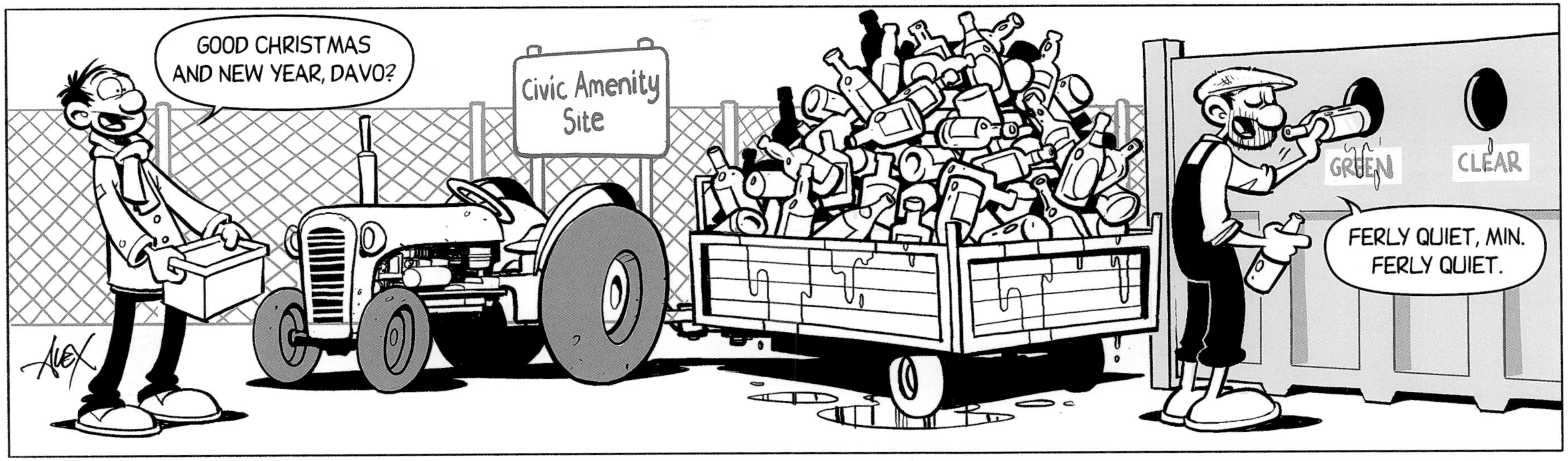
GOOD CHRISTMAS AND NEW YEAR, DAVO?
Civic Amenity Site
GREEN
CLEAR
FERLY QUIET, MIN. FERLY QUIET.
ALEX

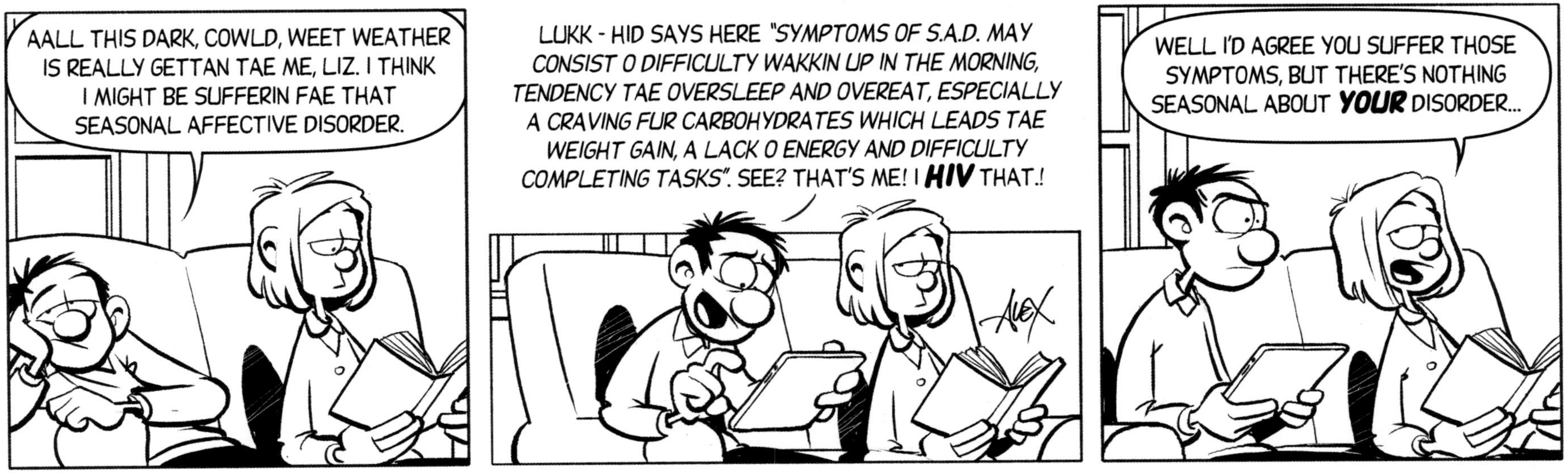
AALL THIS DARK, COWLD, WEET WEATHER IS REALLY GETTAN TAE ME, LIZ. I THINK I MIGHT BE SUFFERIN FAE THAT SEASONAL AFFECTIVE DISORDER.
LUKK - HID SAYS HERE "SYMPTOMS OF S.A.D. MAY CONSIST O DIFFICULTY WAKKIN UP IN THE MORNING, TENDENCY TAE OVERSLEEP AND OVEREAT, ESPECIALLY A CRAVING FUR CARBOHYDRATES WHICH LEADS TAE WEIGHT GAIN, A LACK O ENERGY AND DIFFICULTY COMPLETING TASKS". SEE? THAT'S ME! I HIV THAT.!
ALEX
WELL I'D AGREE YOU SUFFER THOSE SYMPTOMS, BUT THERE'S NOTHING SEASONAL ABOUT YOUR DISORDER...

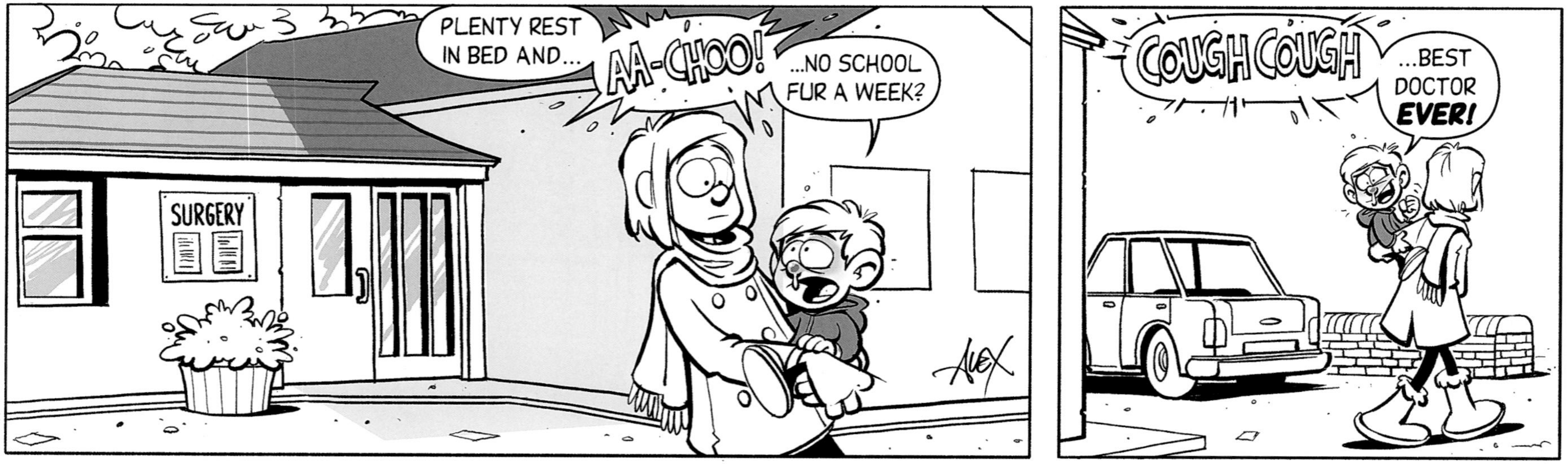
SURGERY
PLENTY REST IN BED AND...
AA-CHOO!
...NO SCHOOL FUR A WEEK?
COUGH COUGH
...BEST DOCTOR **EVER!**

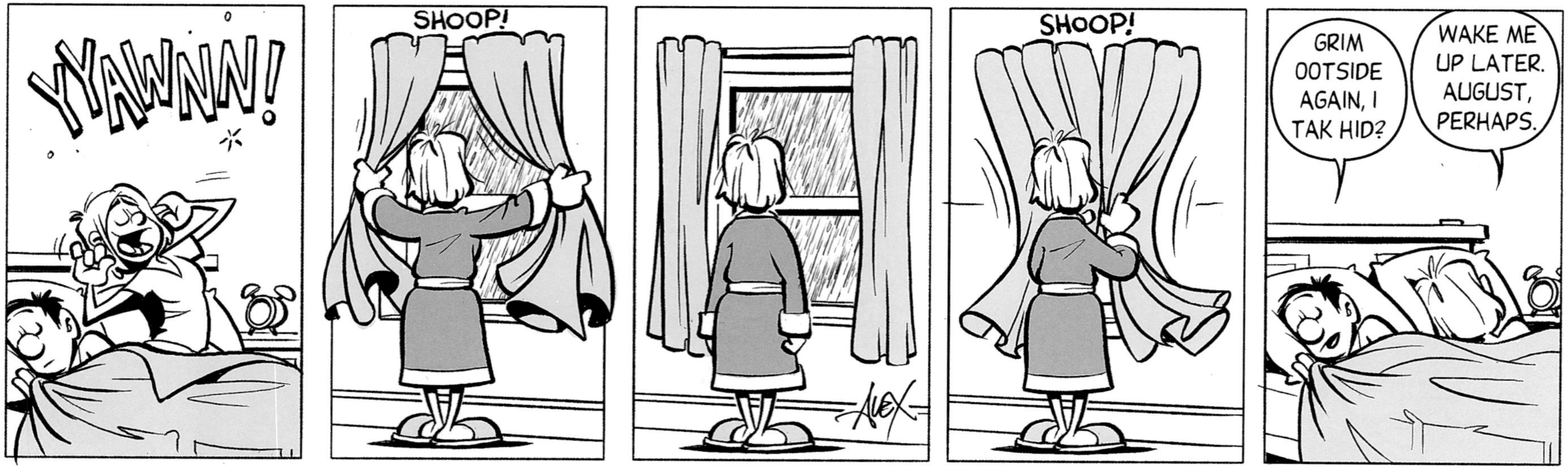
YYAWNN!
SHOOP!
SHOOP!
GRIM OOTSIDE AGAIN, I TAK HID?
WAKE ME UP LATER. AUGUST, PERHAPS.

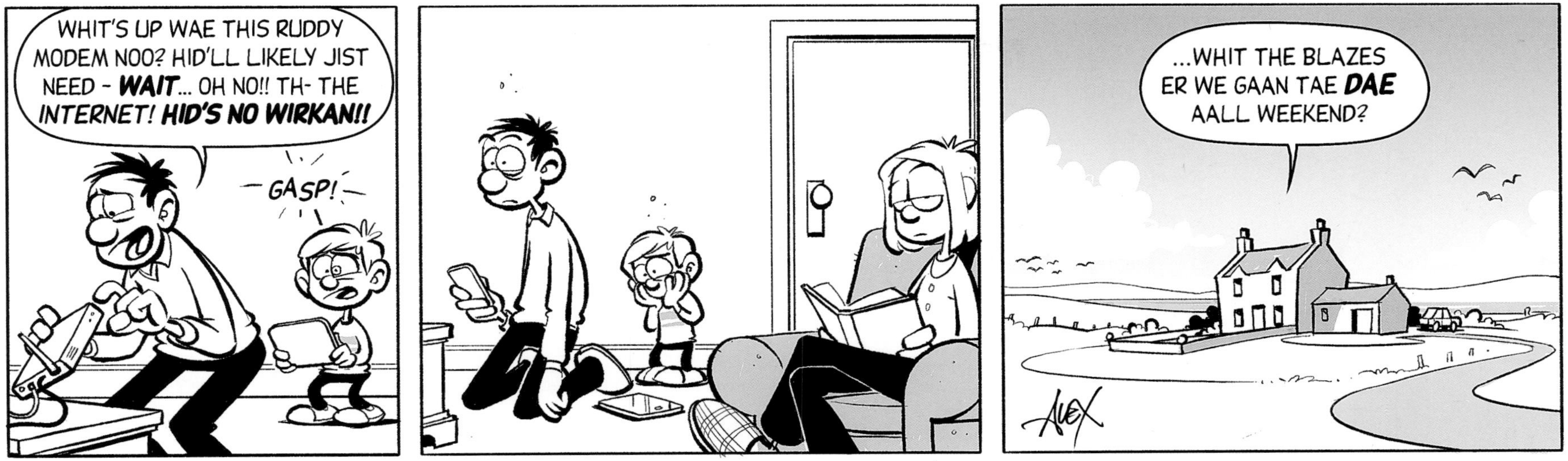
WHIT'S UP WAE THIS RUDDY MODEM NOO? HID'LL LIKELY JIST NEED - **WAIT**... OH NO!! TH- THE INTERNET! **HID'S NO WIRKAN!!**
GASP!
...WHIT THE BLAZES ER WE GAAN TAE **DAE** AALL WEEKEND?
ALEX

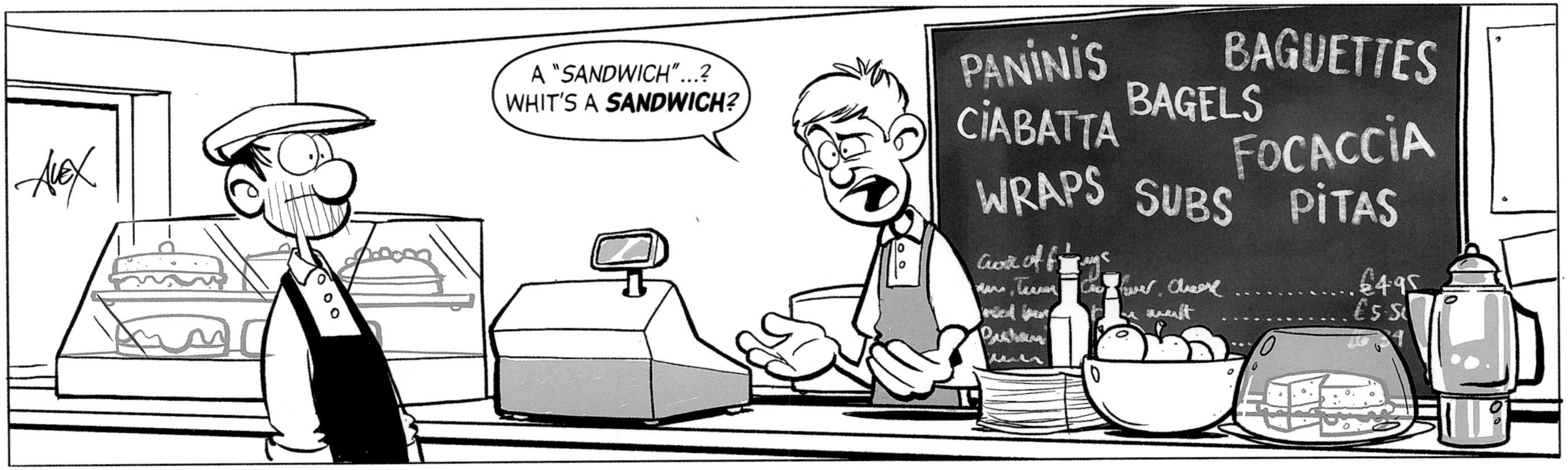
ALEX
A "SANDWICH"...? WHIT'S A **SANDWICH**?
PANINIS
BAGUETTES
CIABATTA
BAGELS
FOCACCIA
WRAPS
SUBS
PITAS

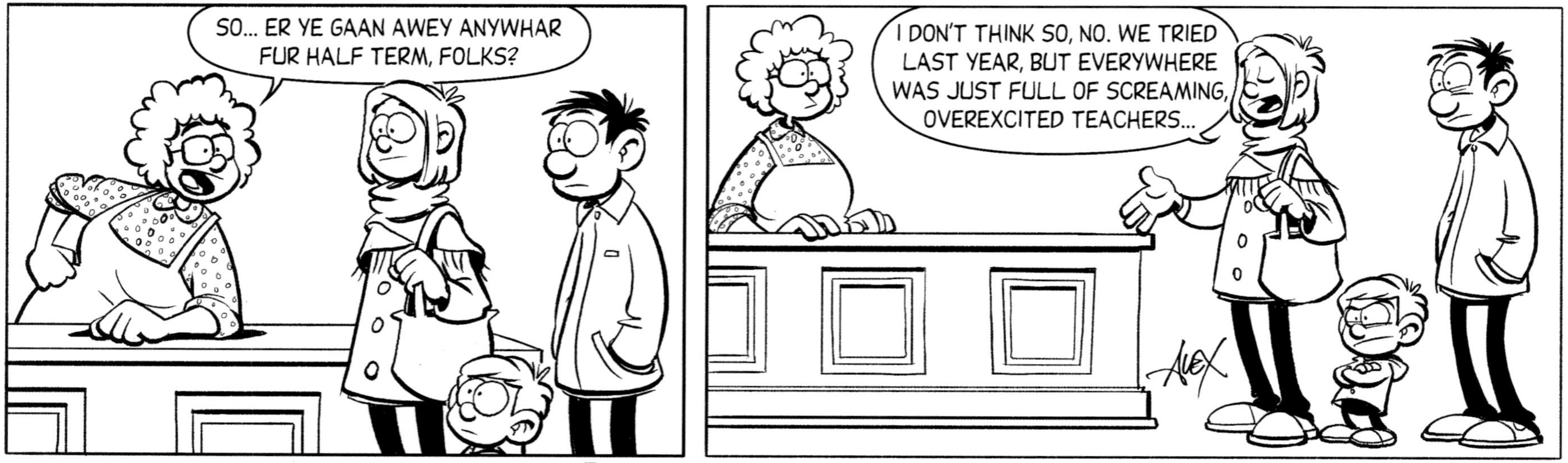
SO... ER YE GAAN AWEY ANYWHAR FUR HALF TERM, FOLKS?
I DON'T THINK SO, NO. WE TRIED LAST YEAR, BUT EVERYWHERE WAS JUST FULL OF SCREAMING, OVEREXCITED TEACHERS...
ALEX

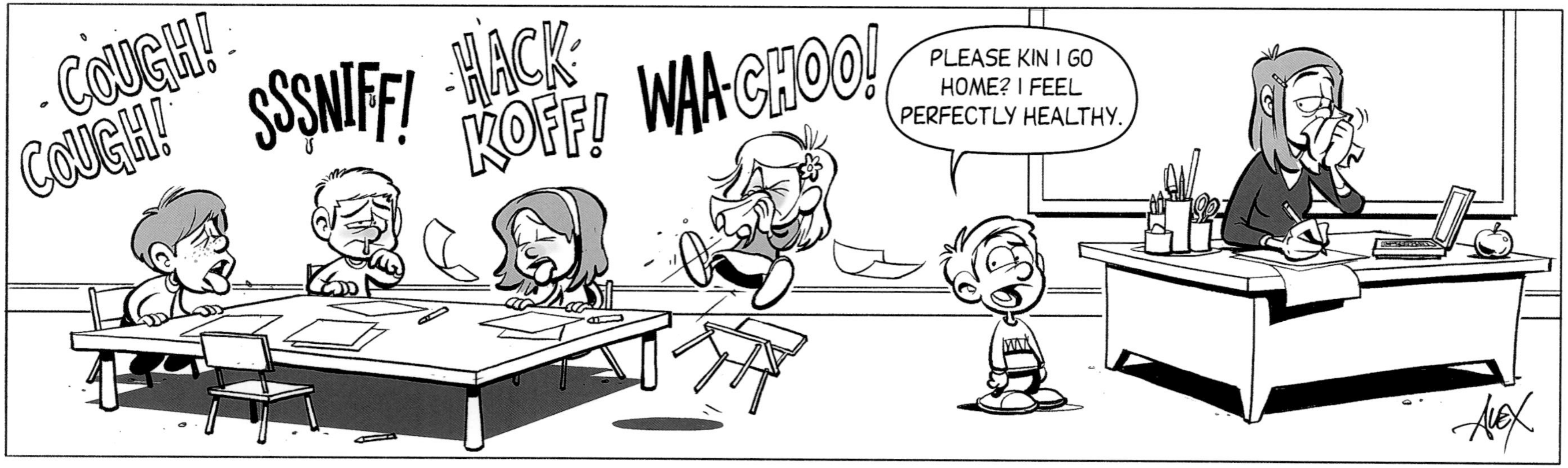
COUGH! COUGH!
SSSNIFF!
HACK KOFF!
WAA-CHOO!
PLEASE KIN I GO HOME? I FEEL PERFECTLY HEALTHY.
ALEX

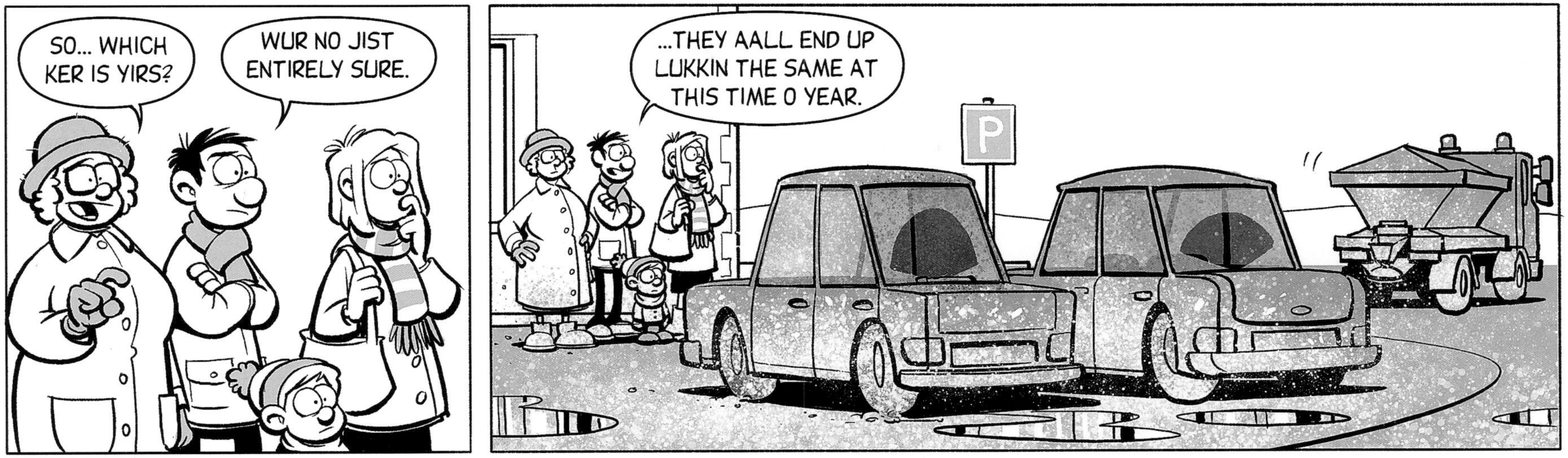
SO... WHICH KER IS YIRS?
WUR NO JIST ENTIRELY SURE.
...THEY AALL END UP LUKKIN THE SAME AT THIS TIME O YEAR.
P

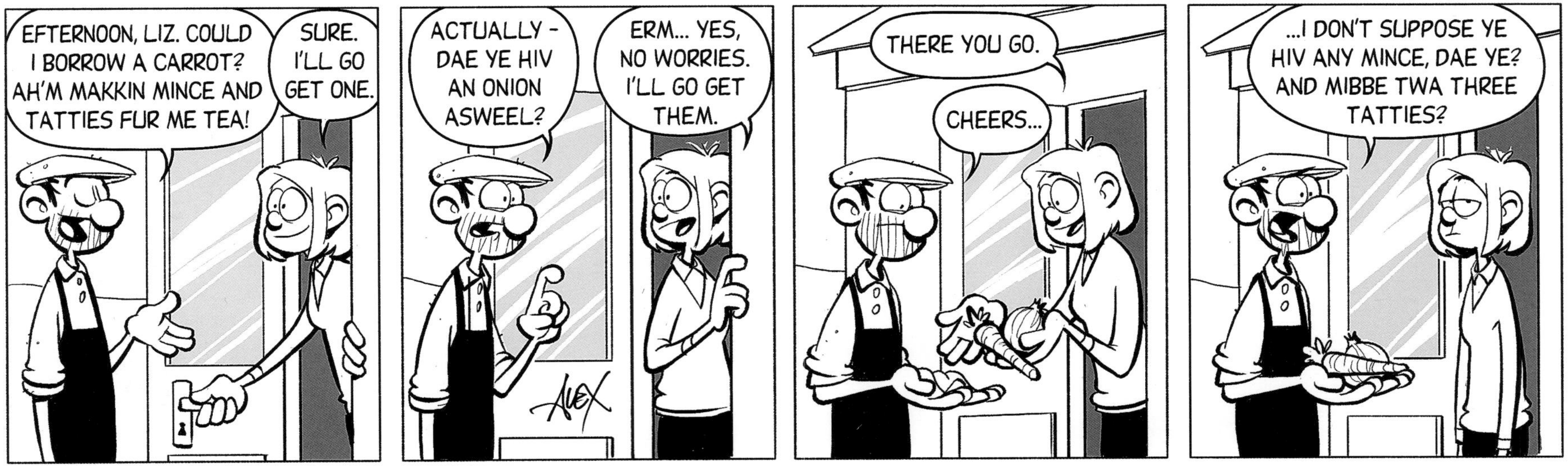
EFTERNOON, LIZ. COULD I BORROW A CARROT? AH'M MAKKIN MINCE AND TATTIES FUR ME TEA!
SURE. I'LL GO GET ONE.
ACTUALLY - DAE YE HIV AN ONION ASWEEL?
ERM... YES, NO WORRIES. I'LL GO GET THEM.
ALEX
THERE YOU GO.
CHEERS...
...I DON'T SUPPOSE YE HIV ANY MINCE, DAE YE? AND MIBBE TWA THREE TATTIES?

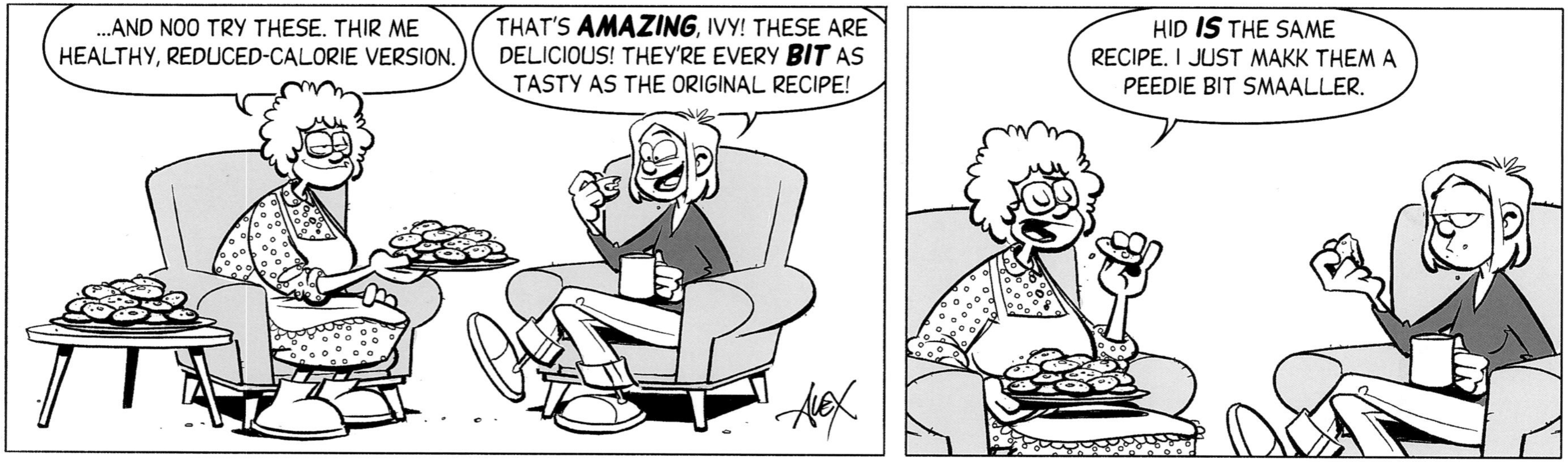
...AND NOO TRY THESE. THIR ME HEALTHY, REDUCED-CALORIE VERSION.
THAT'S AMAZING, IVY! THESE ARE DELICIOUS! THEY'RE EVERY BIT AS TASTY AS THE ORIGINAL RECIPE!
HID IS THE SAME RECIPE. I JUST MAKK THEM A PEEDIE BIT SMAALLER.

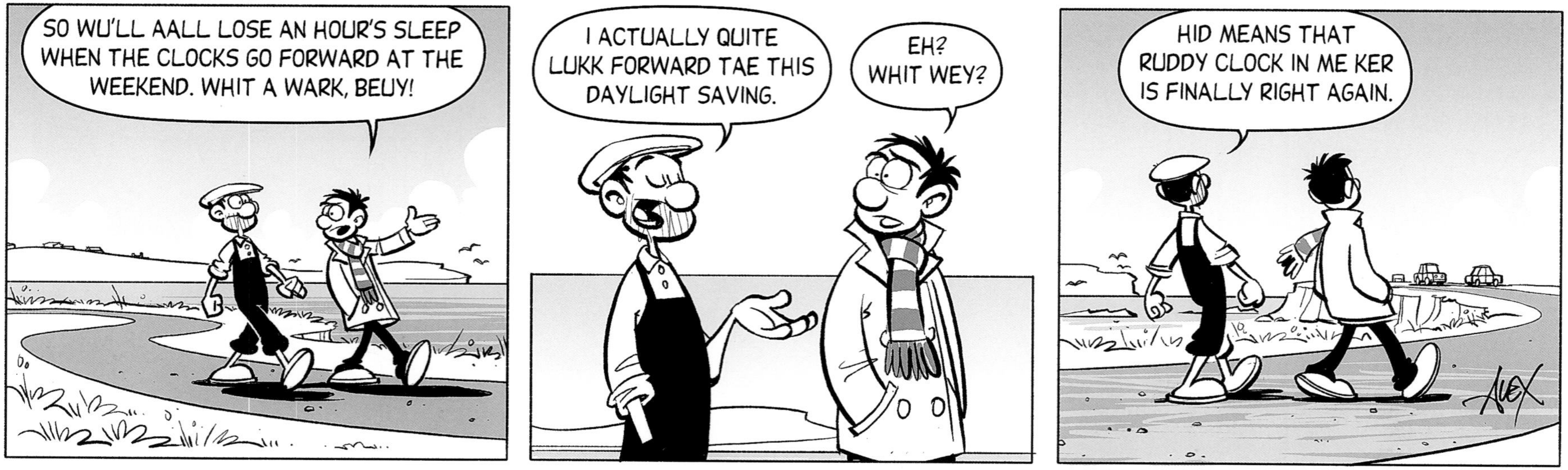
SO WU'LL AALL LOSE AN HOUR'S SLEEP WHEN THE CLOCKS GO FORWARD AT THE WEEKEND. WHIT A WARK, BEUY!
I ACTUALLY QUITE LUKK FORWARD TAE THIS DAYLIGHT SAVING.
EH? WHIT WEY?
HID MEANS THAT RUDDY CLOCK IN ME KER IS FINALLY RIGHT AGAIN.

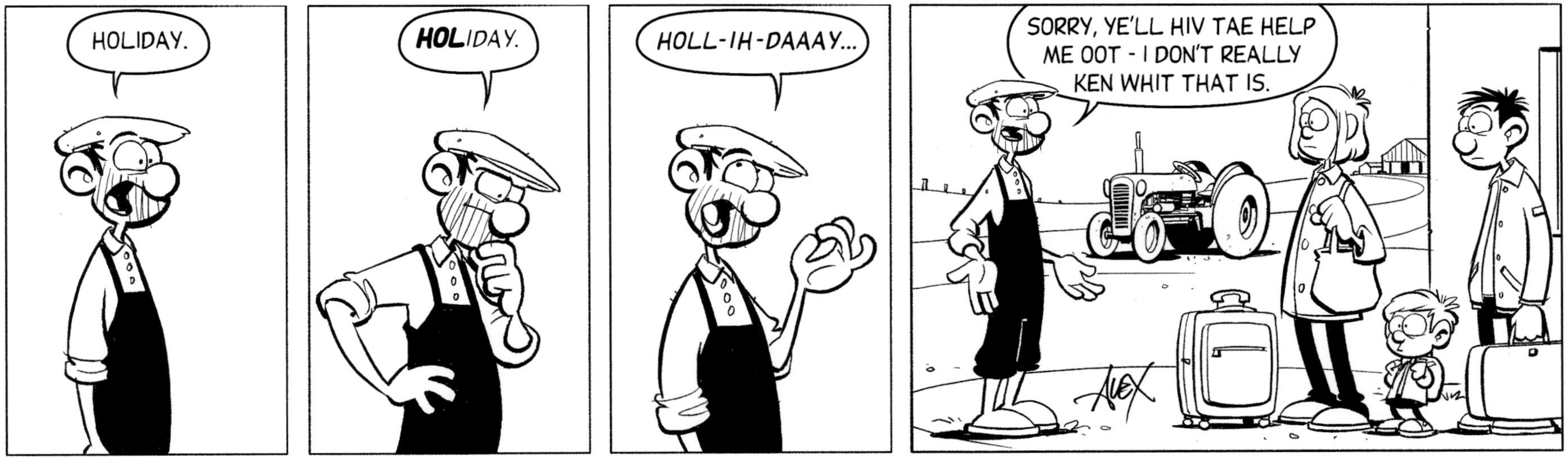
HOLIDAY.
HOLIDAY.
HOLL-IH-DAAAY...
SORRY, YE'LL HIV TAE HELP ME OOT - I DON'T REALLY KEN WHIT THAT IS.
ALEX

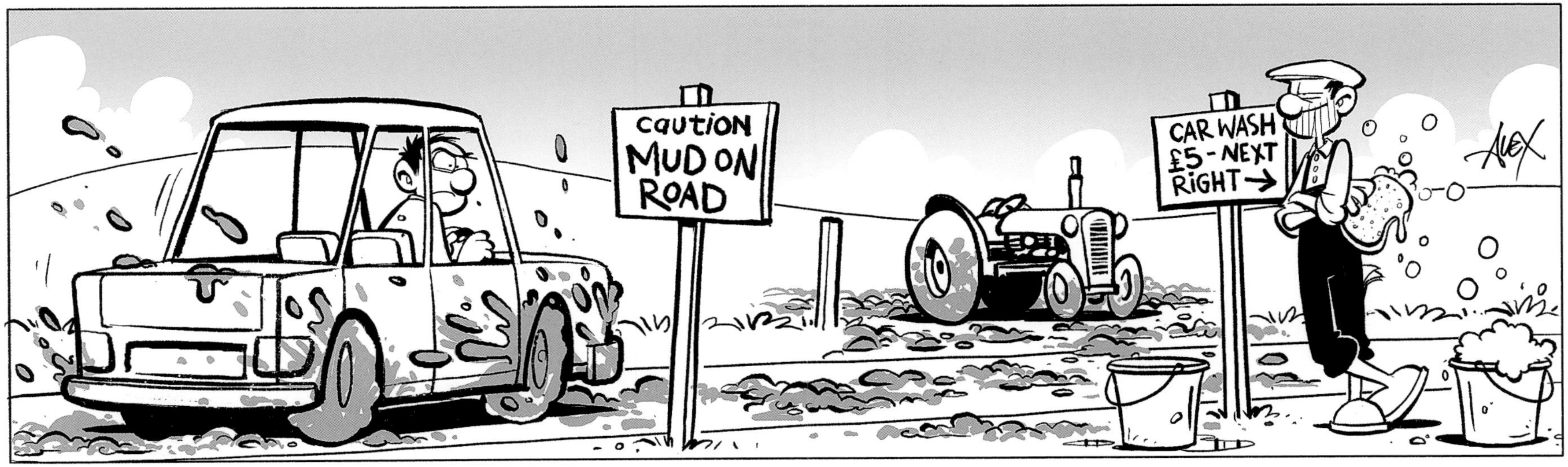
caution MUD ON ROAD
CAR WASH £5 - NEXT RIGHT →
ALEX

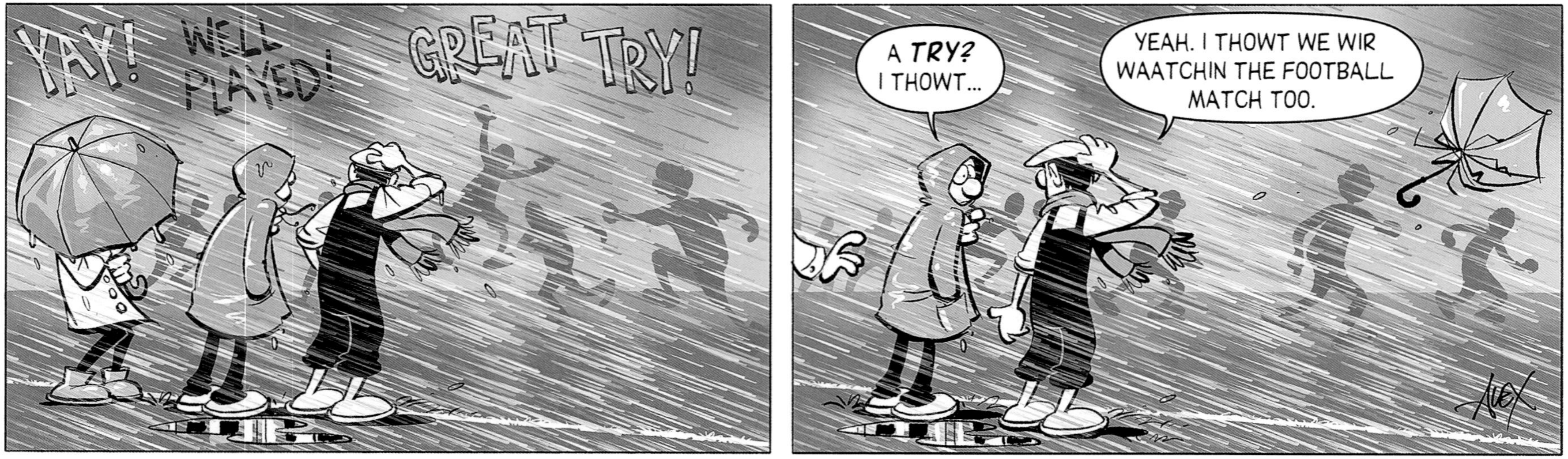
YAY!
WELL PLAYED!
GREAT TRY!
A TRY? I THOWT...
YEAH. I THOWT WE WIR WAATCHIN THE FOOTBALL MATCH TOO.

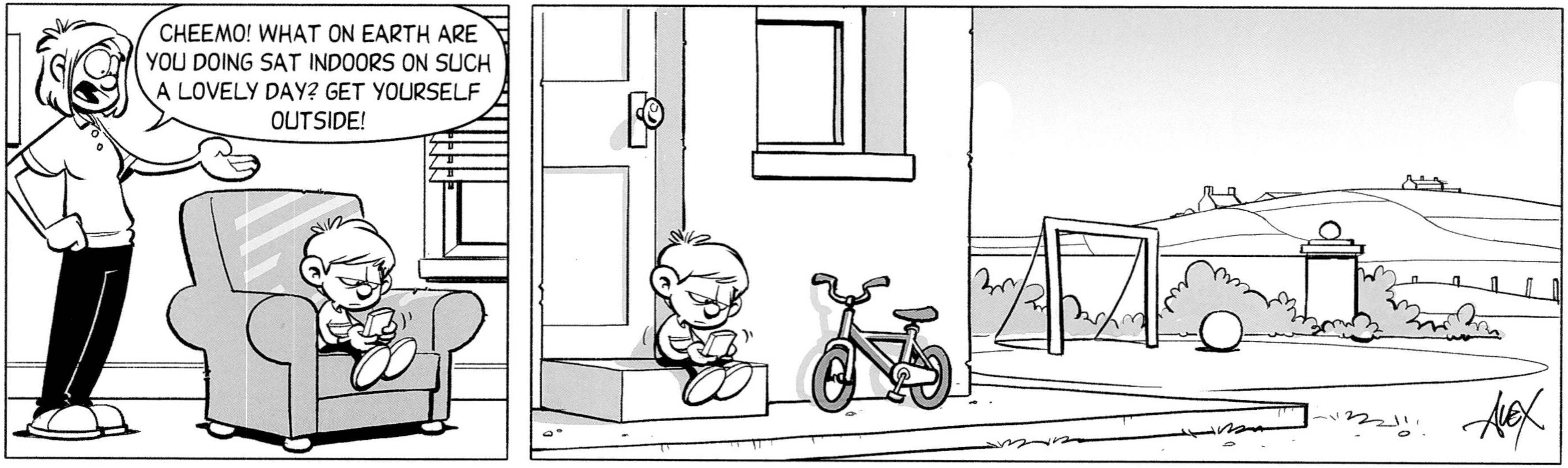
CHEEMO! WHAT ON EARTH ARE YOU DOING SAT INDOORS ON SUCH A LOVELY DAY? GET YOURSELF OUTSIDE!

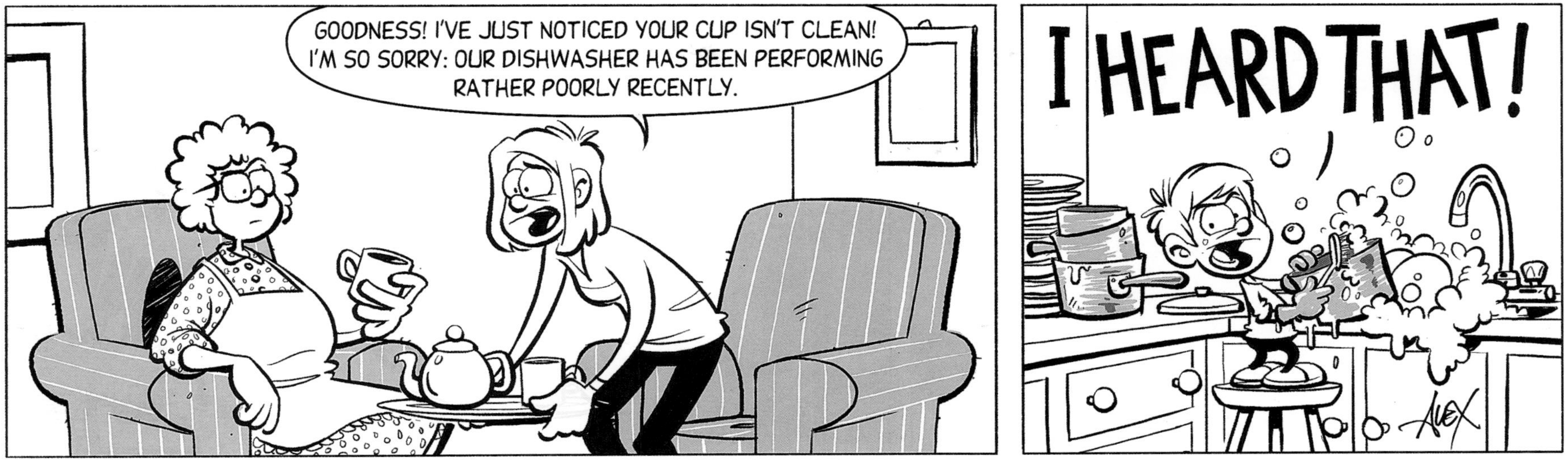
GOODNESS! I'VE JUST NOTICED YOUR CUP ISN'T CLEAN! I'M SO SORRY: OUR DISHWASHER HAS BEEN PERFORMING RATHER POORLY RECENTLY.
I HEARD THAT!
ALEX

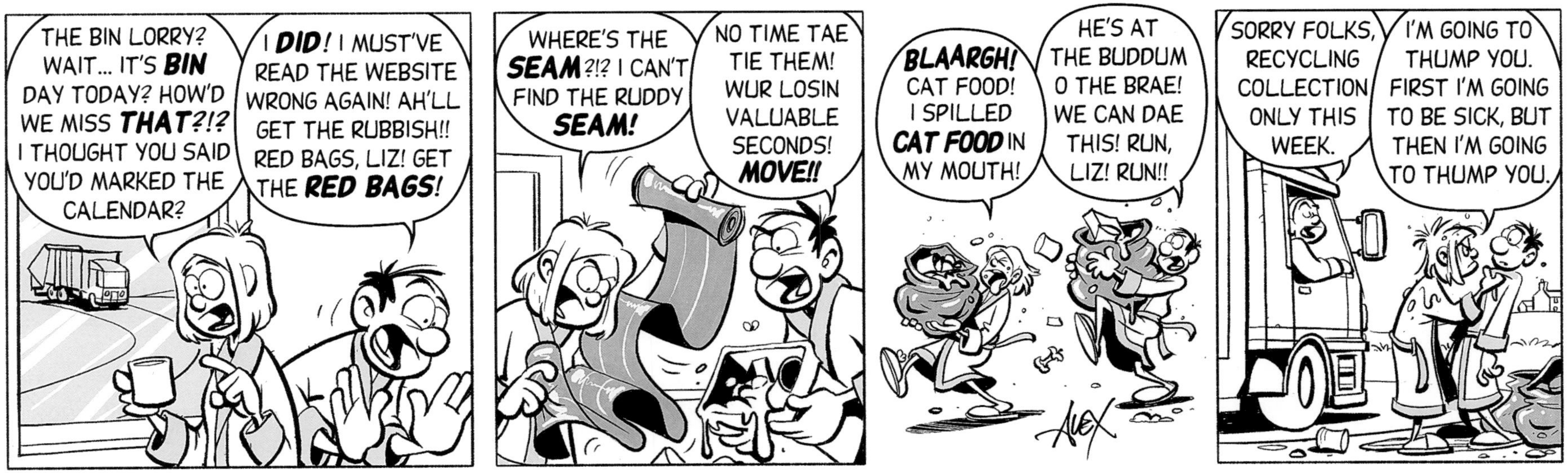
THE BIN LORRY? WAIT... IT'S BIN DAY TODAY? HOW'D WE MISS THAT?!? I THOUGHT YOU SAID YOU'D MARKED THE CALENDAR?
I DID! I MUST'VE READ THE WEBSITE WRONG AGAIN! AH'LL GET THE RUBBISH!! RED BAGS, LIZ! GET THE RED BAGS!
WHERE'S THE SEAM?!? I CAN'T FIND THE RUDDY SEAM!
NO TIME TAE TIE THEM! WUR LOSIN VALUABLE SECONDS! MOVE!!
BLAARGH! CAT FOOD! I SPILLED CAT FOOD IN MY MOUTH!
HE'S AT THE BUDDUM O THE BRAE! WE CAN DAE THIS! RUN, LIZ! RUN!!
ALEX
SORRY FOLKS, RECYCLING COLLECTION ONLY THIS WEEK.
I'M GOING TO THUMP YOU. FIRST I'M GOING TO BE SICK, BUT THEN I'M GOING TO THUMP YOU.

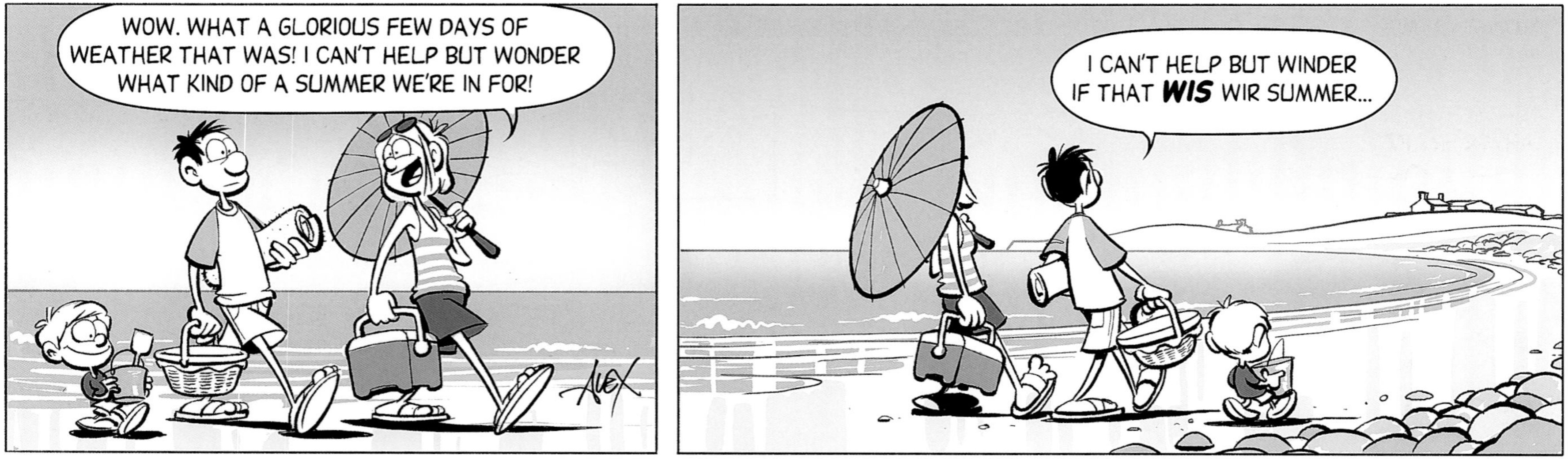
WOW. WHAT A GLORIOUS FEW DAYS OF WEATHER THAT WAS! I CAN'T HELP BUT WONDER WHAT KIND OF A SUMMER WE'RE IN FOR!
I CAN'T HELP BUT WINDER IF THAT **WIS** WIR SUMMER...
ALEX

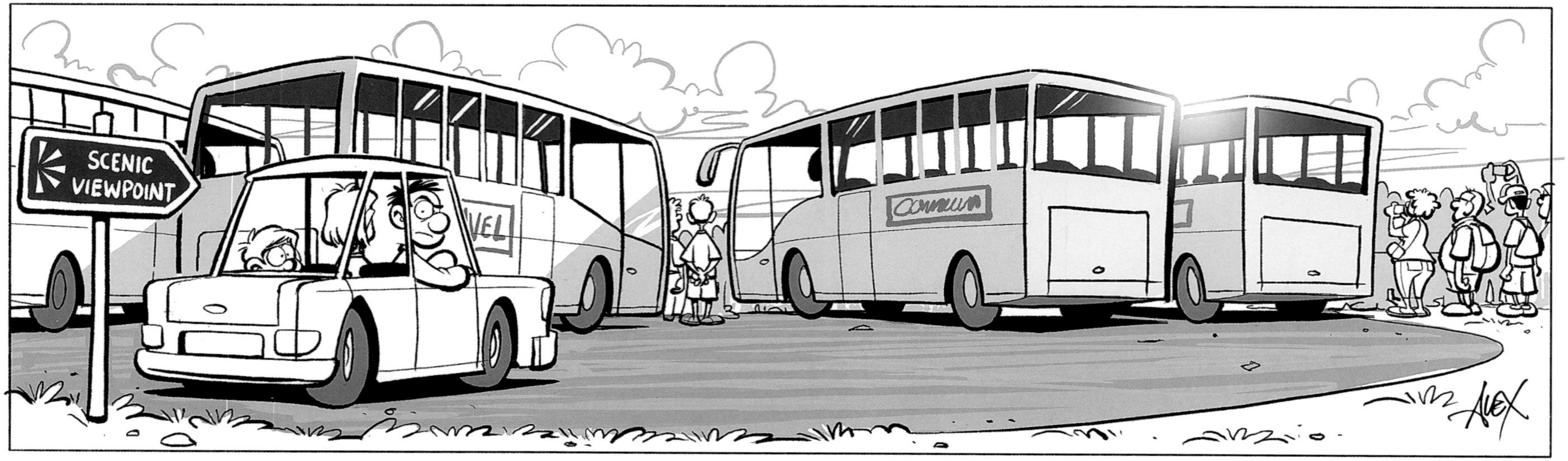
SCENIC VIEWPOINT
ALEX

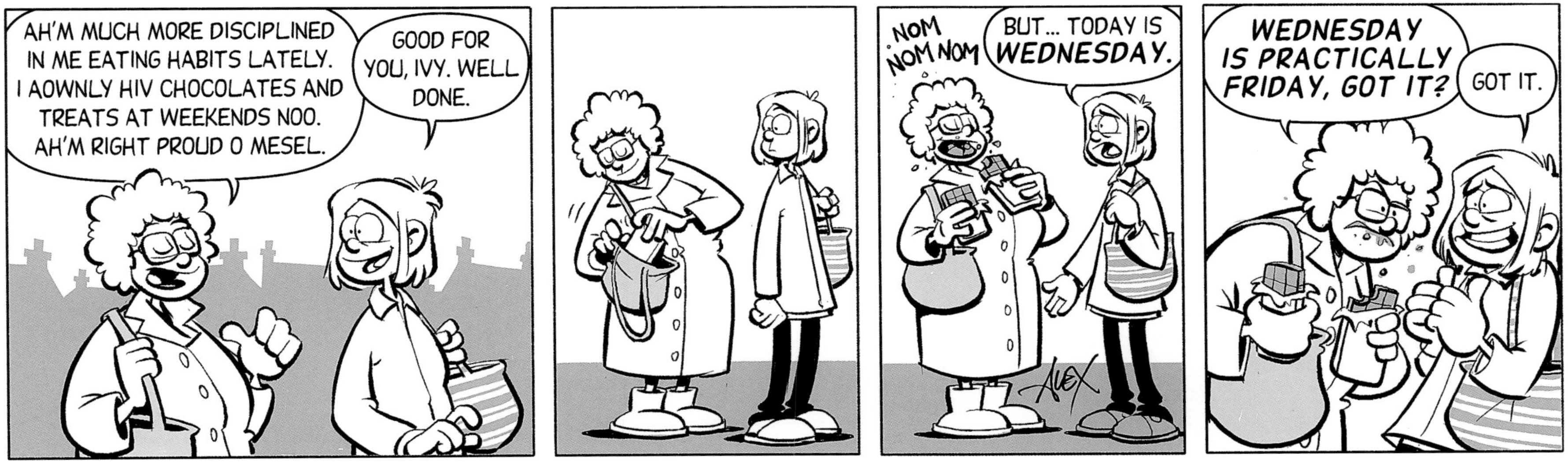
AH'M MUCH MORE DISCIPLINED IN ME EATING HABITS LATELY. I AOWNLY HIV CHOCOLATES AND TREATS AT WEEKENDS NOO. AH'M RIGHT PROUD O MESEL.
GOOD FOR YOU, IVY. WELL DONE.
NOM NOM NOM
BUT... TODAY IS WEDNESDAY.
ALEX
WEDNESDAY IS PRACTICALLY FRIDAY, GOT IT?
GOT IT.

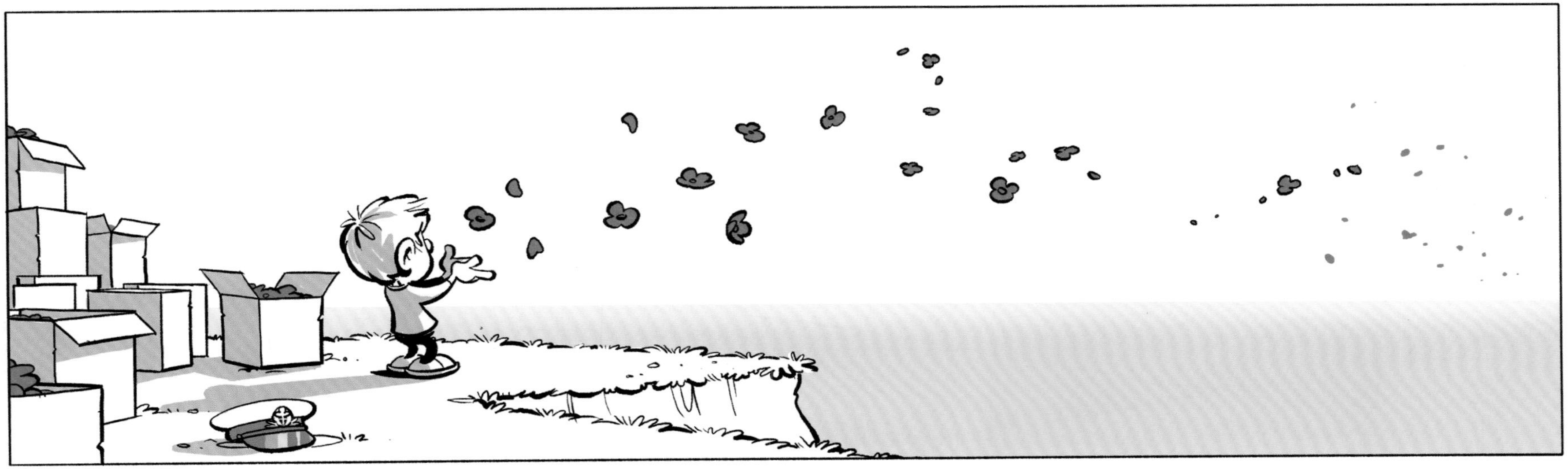

The Jutland 100 Commemorations.

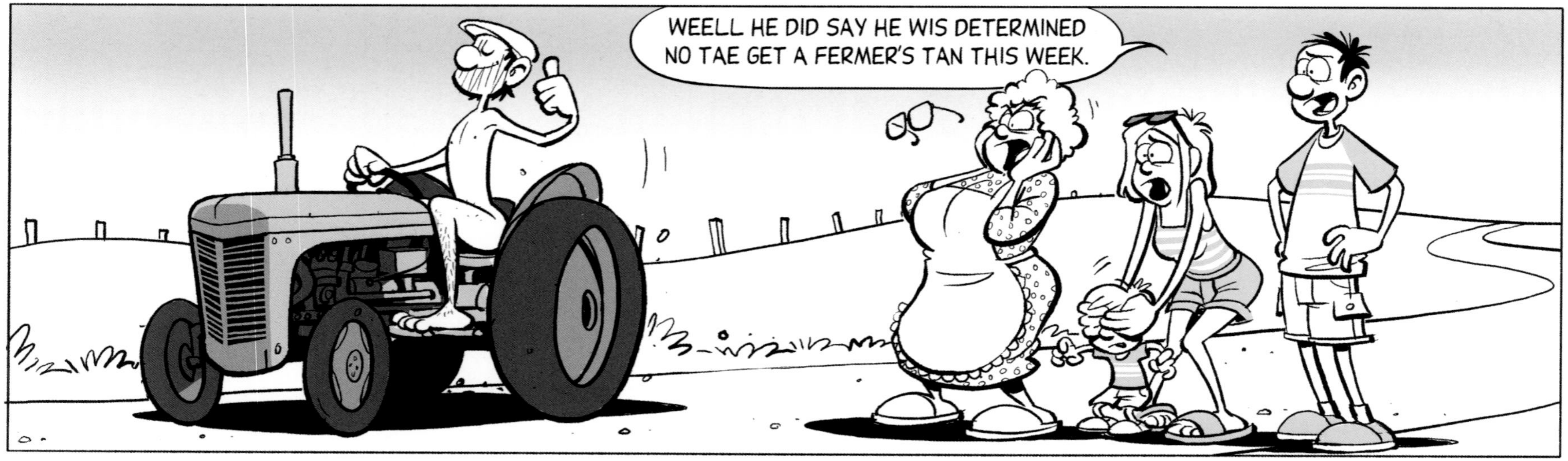
WEELL HE DID SAY HE WIS DETERMINED NO TAE GET A FERMER'S TAN THIS WEEK.

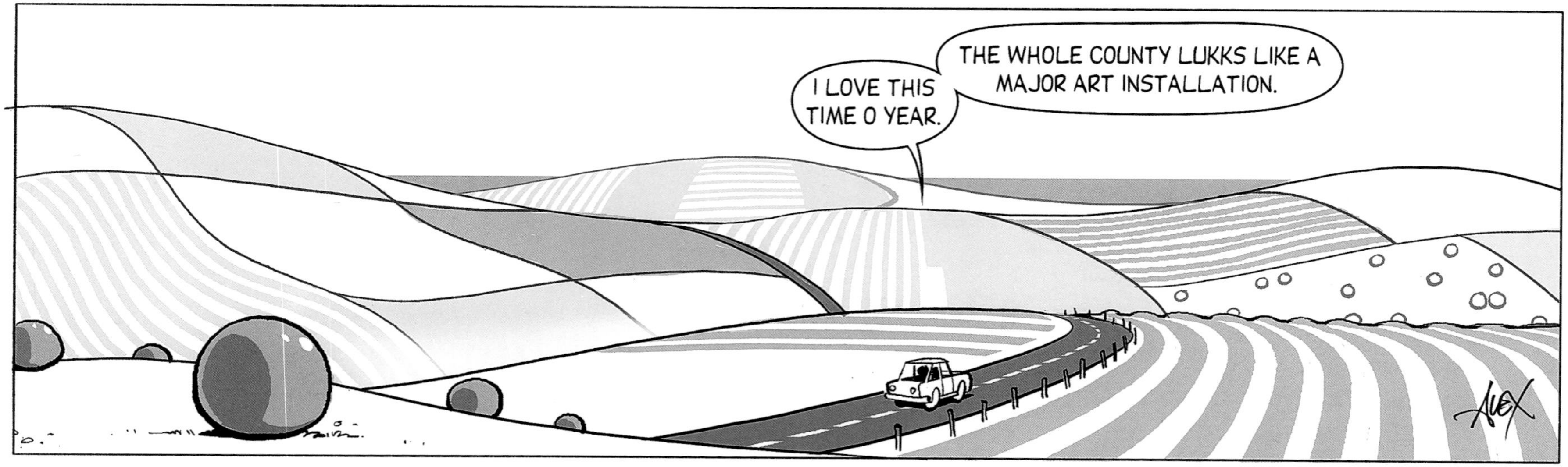
I LOVE THIS TIME O YEAR.
THE WHOLE COUNTY LUKKS LIKE A MAJOR ART INSTALLATION.
ALEX

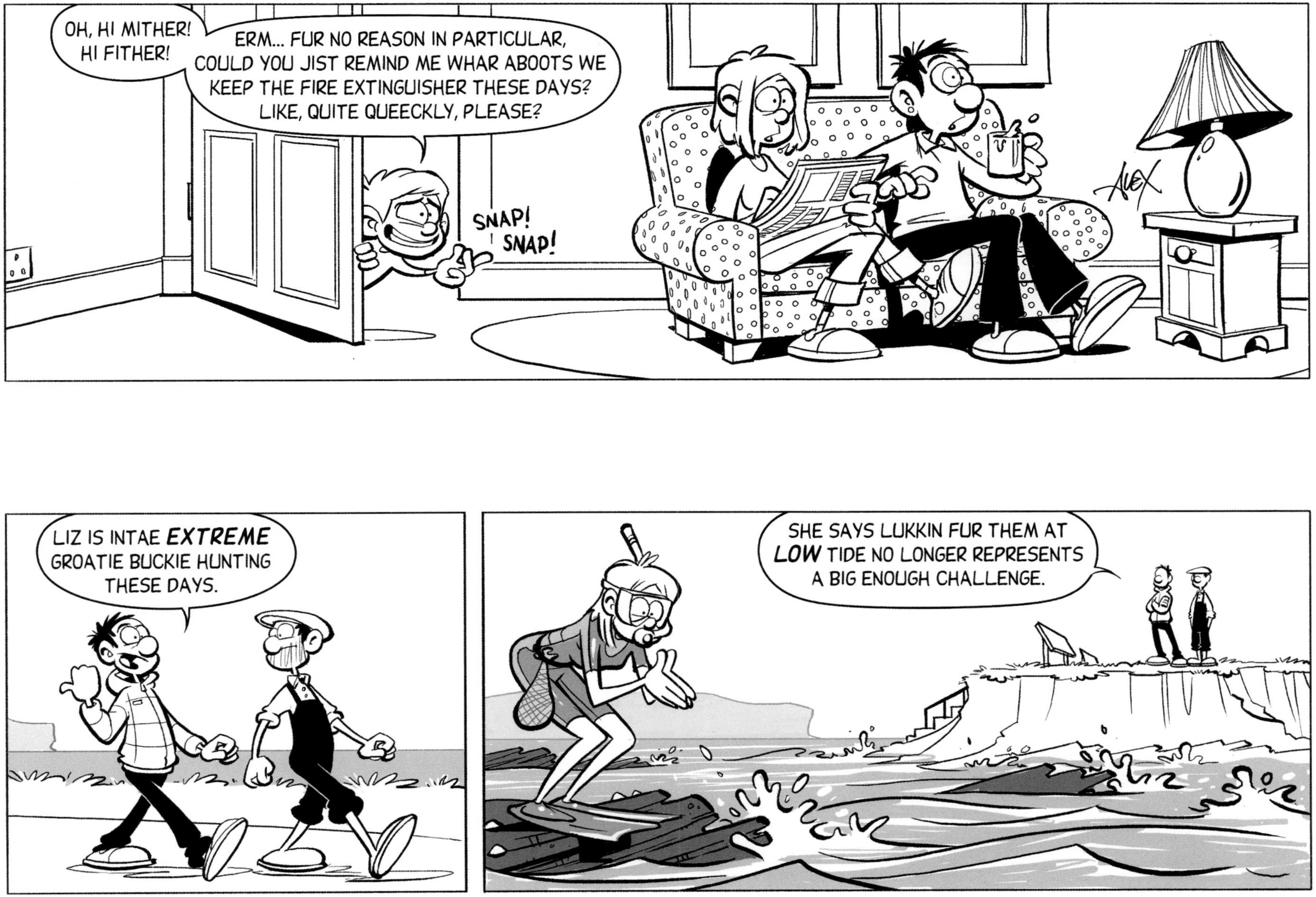
OH, HI MITHER! HI FITHER!
ERM... FUR NO REASON IN PARTICULAR, COULD YOU JIST REMIND ME WHAR ABOOTS WE KEEP THE FIRE EXTINGUISHER THESE DAYS? LIKE, QUITE QUEECKLY, PLEASE?
SNAP! SNAP!
ALEX
LIZ IS INTAE EXTREME GROATIE BUCKIE HUNTING THESE DAYS.
SHE SAYS LUKKIN FUR THEM AT LOW TIDE NO LONGER REPRESENTS A BIG ENOUGH CHALLENGE.

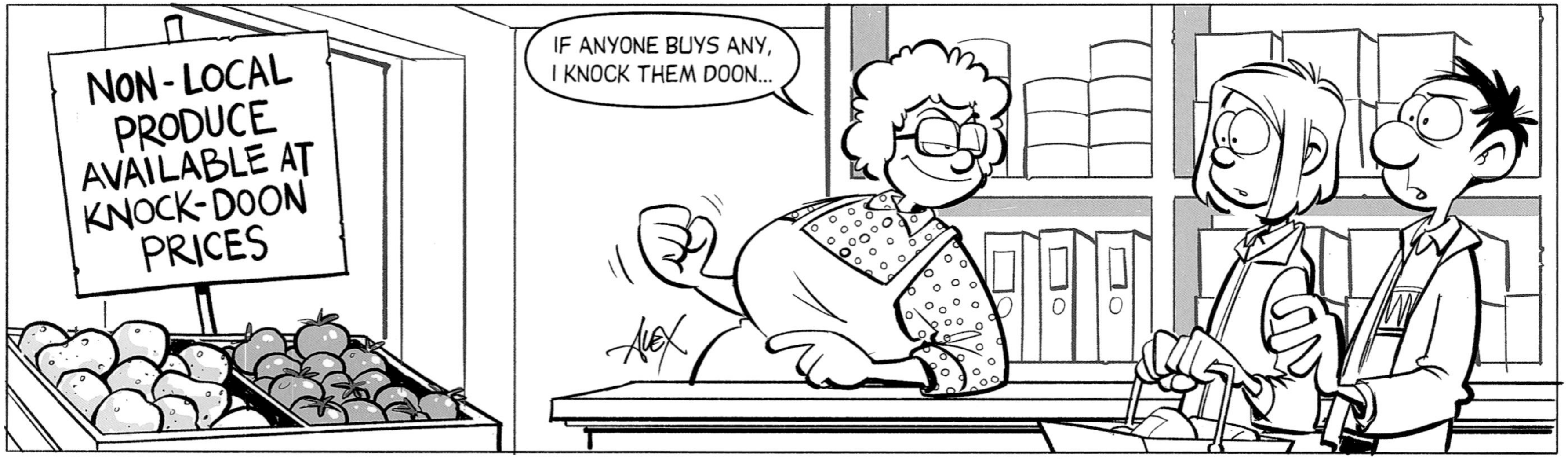
NON-LOCAL PRODUCE AVAILABLE AT KNOCK-DOON PRICES
IF ANYONE BUYS ANY, I KNOCK THEM DOON...
ALEX

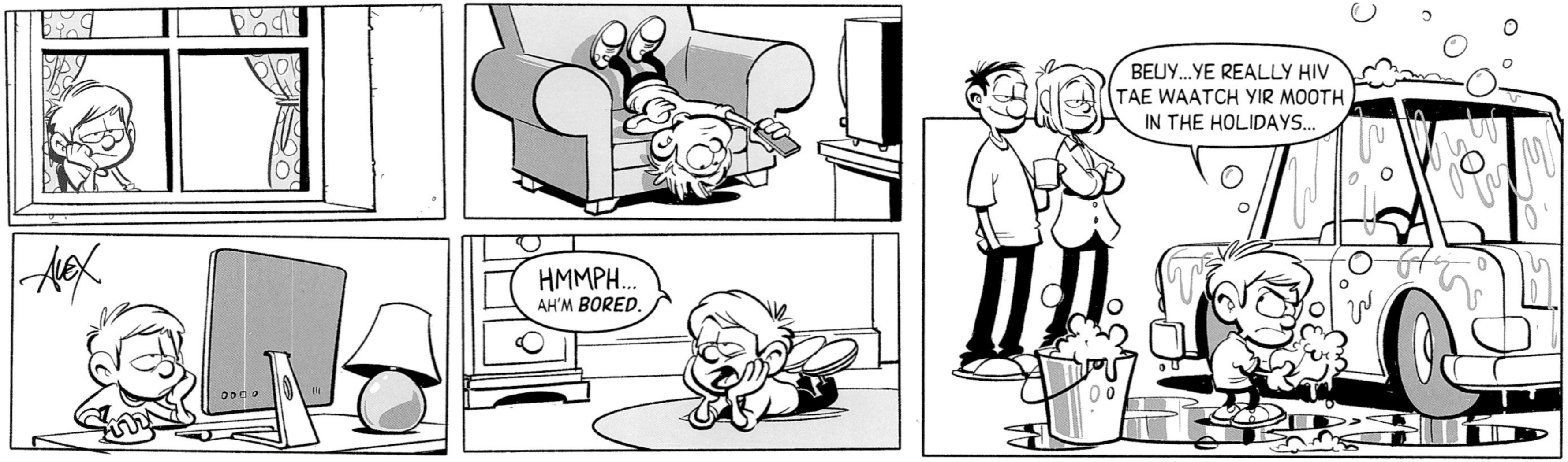
ALEX
HMMPH... AH'M BORED.
BEUY...YE REALLY HIV TAE WAATCH YIR MOOTH IN THE HOLIDAYS...

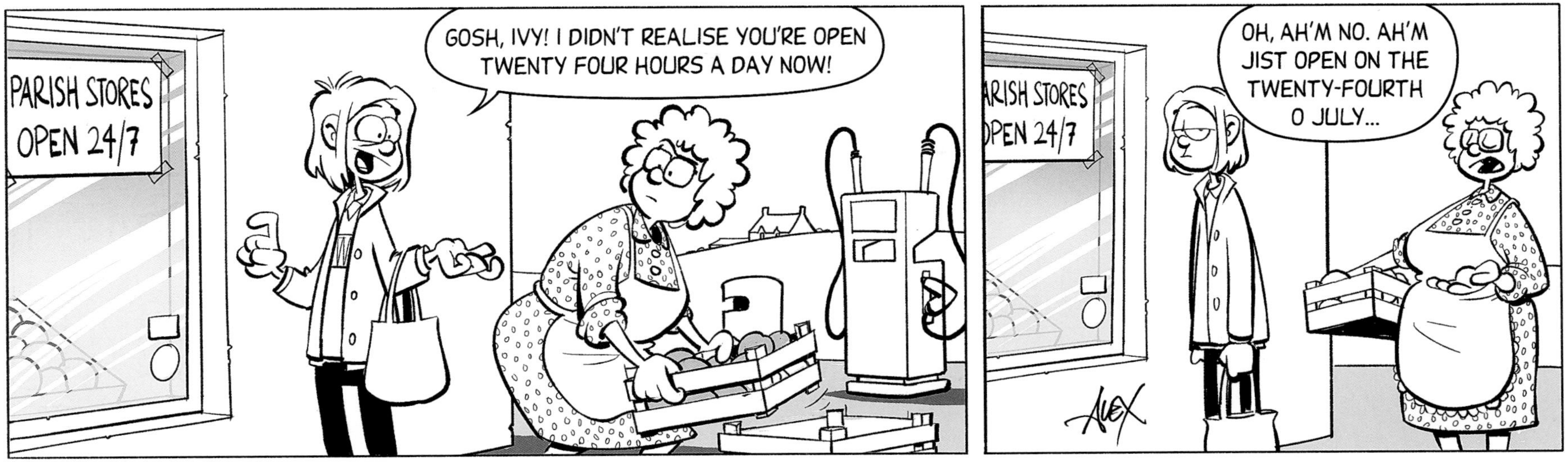
PARISH STORES
OPEN 24/7
GOSH, IVY! I DIDN'T REALISE YOU'RE OPEN TWENTY FOUR HOURS A DAY NOW!
PARISH STORES
OPEN 24/7
OH, AH'M NO. AH'M JIST OPEN ON THE TWENTY-FOURTH O JULY...
ALEX

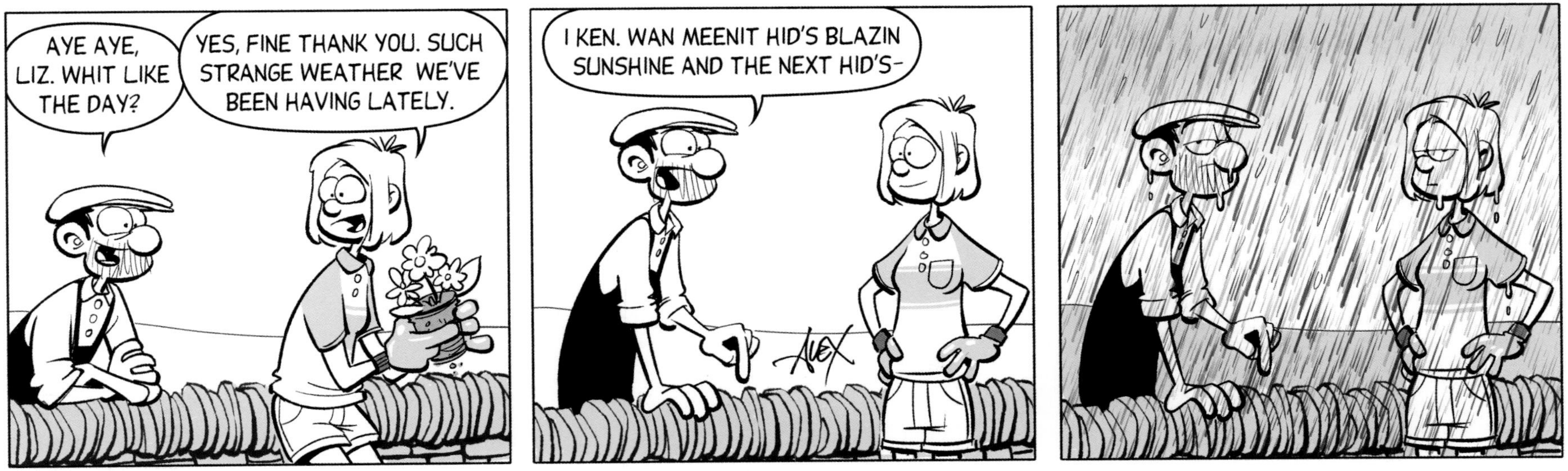
AYE AYE, LIZ. WHIT LIKE THE DAY?
YES, FINE THANK YOU. SUCH STRANGE WEATHER WE'VE BEEN HAVING LATELY.
I KEN. WAN MEENIT HID'S BLAZIN SUNSHINE AND THE NEXT HID'S-
ALEX

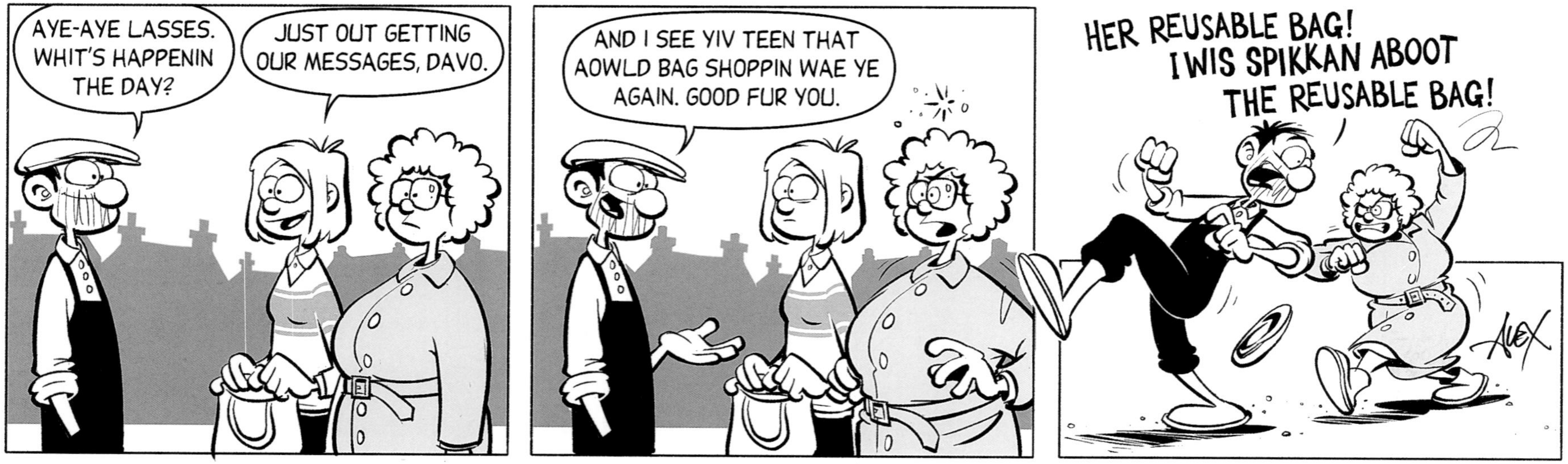
AYE-AYE LASSES. WHIT'S HAPPENIN THE DAY?
JUST OUT GETTING OUR MESSAGES, DAVO.
AND I SEE YIV TEEN THAT AOWLD BAG SHOPPIN WAE YE AGAIN. GOOD FUR YOU.
HER REUSABLE BAG! I WIS SPIKKAN ABOOT THE REUSABLE BAG!
ALEX

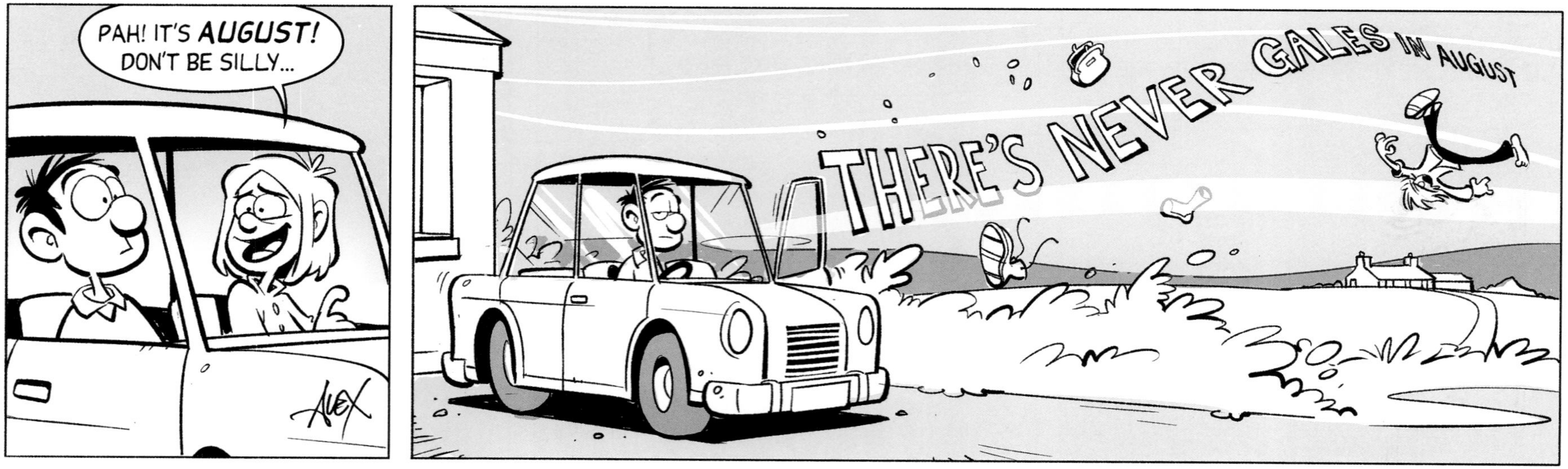
PAH! IT'S **AUGUST!** DON'T BE SILLY...
ALEX
THERE'S NEVER GALES IN AUGUST

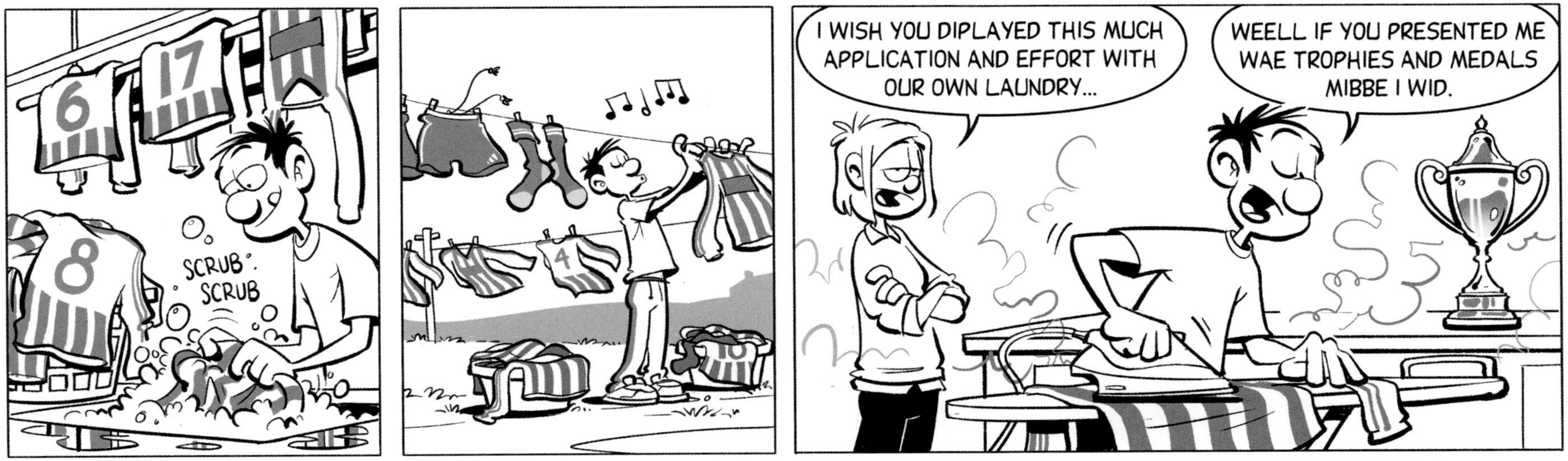
SCRUB
SCRUB
I WISH YOU DIPLAYED THIS MUCH APPLICATION AND EFFORT WITH OUR OWN LAUNDRY...
WEELL IF YOU PRESENTED ME WAE TROPHIES AND MEDALS MIBBE I WID.

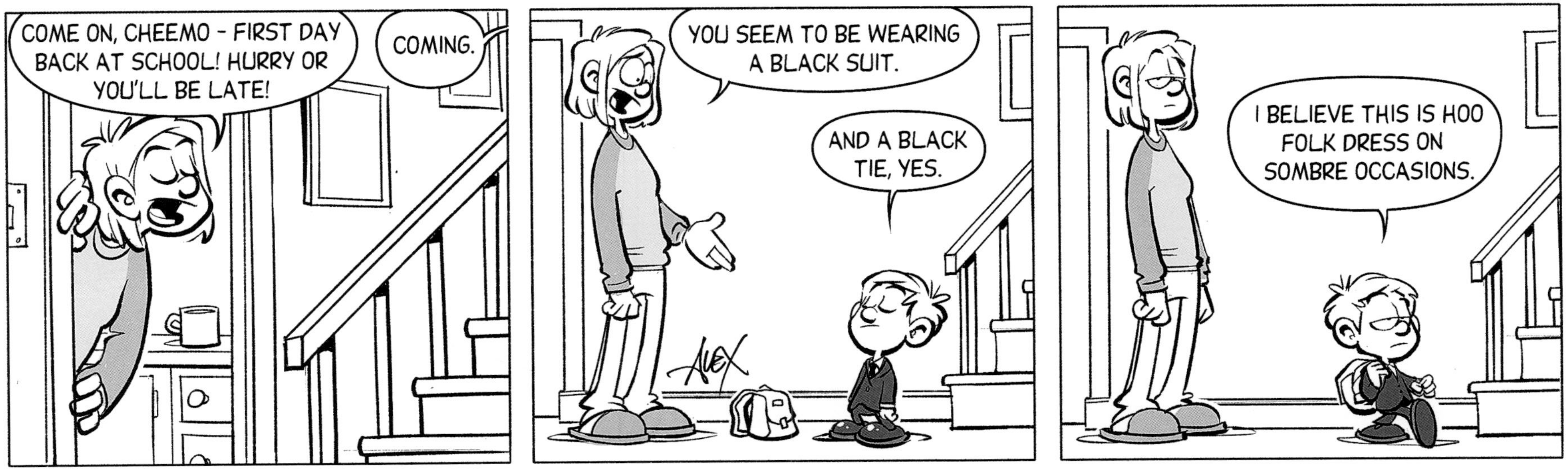
COME ON, CHEEMO – FIRST DAY BACK AT SCHOOL! HURRY OR YOU'LL BE LATE!
COMING.
YOU SEEM TO BE WEARING A BLACK SUIT.
AND A BLACK TIE, YES.
ALEX
I BELIEVE THIS IS HOO FOLK DRESS ON SOMBRE OCCASIONS.

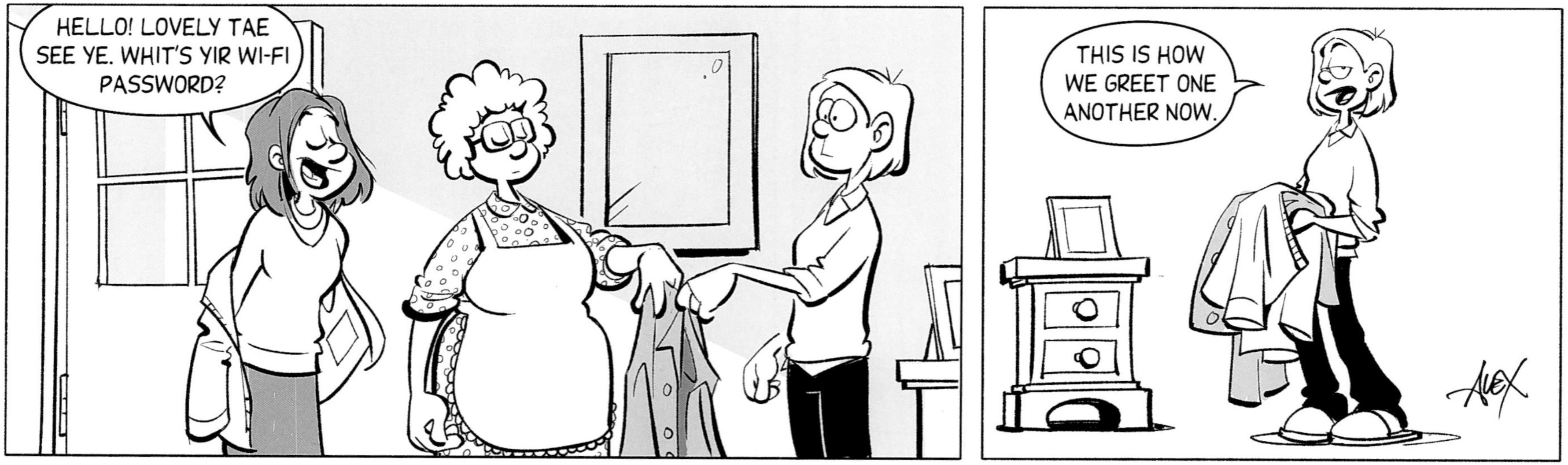
HELLO! LOVELY TAE SEE YE. WHIT'S YIR WI-FI PASSWORD?
THIS IS HOW WE GREET ONE ANOTHER NOW.
ALEX

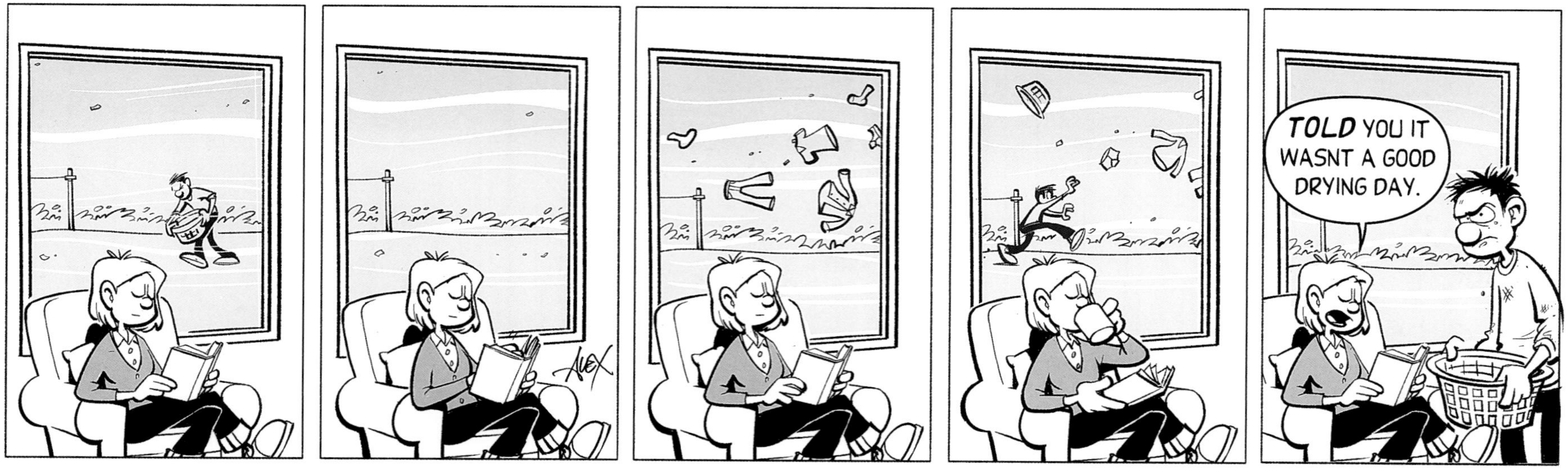
ALEX
**TOLD** YOU IT WASNT A GOOD DRYING DAY.

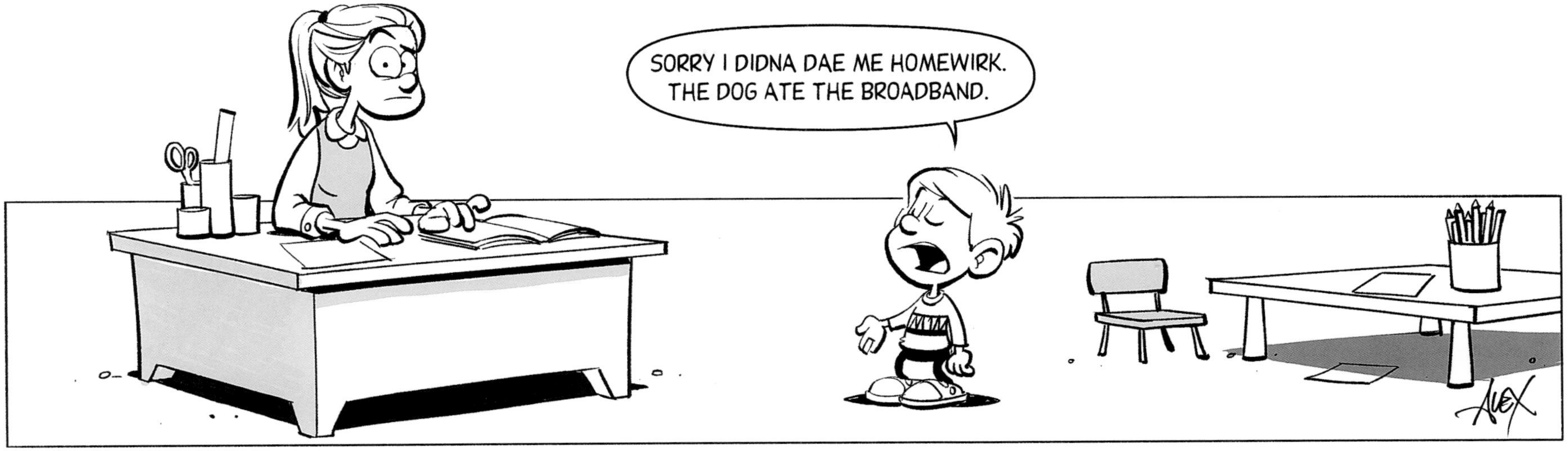
SORRY I DIDNA DAE ME HOMEWIRK. THE DOG ATE THE BROADBAND.
ALEX

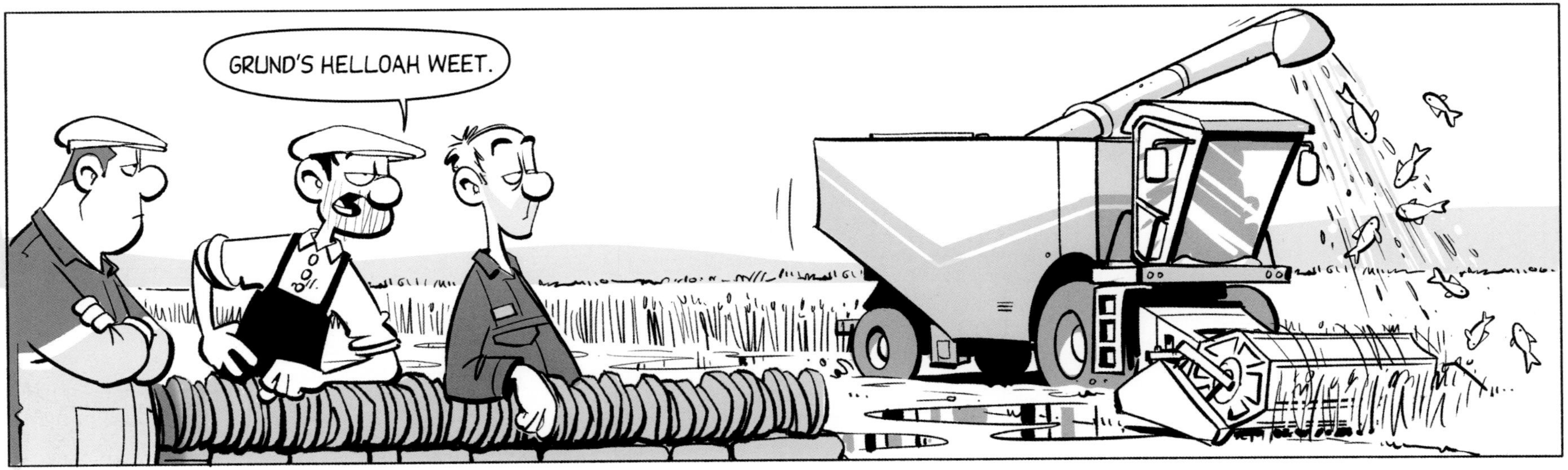
GRUND'S HELLOAH WEET.

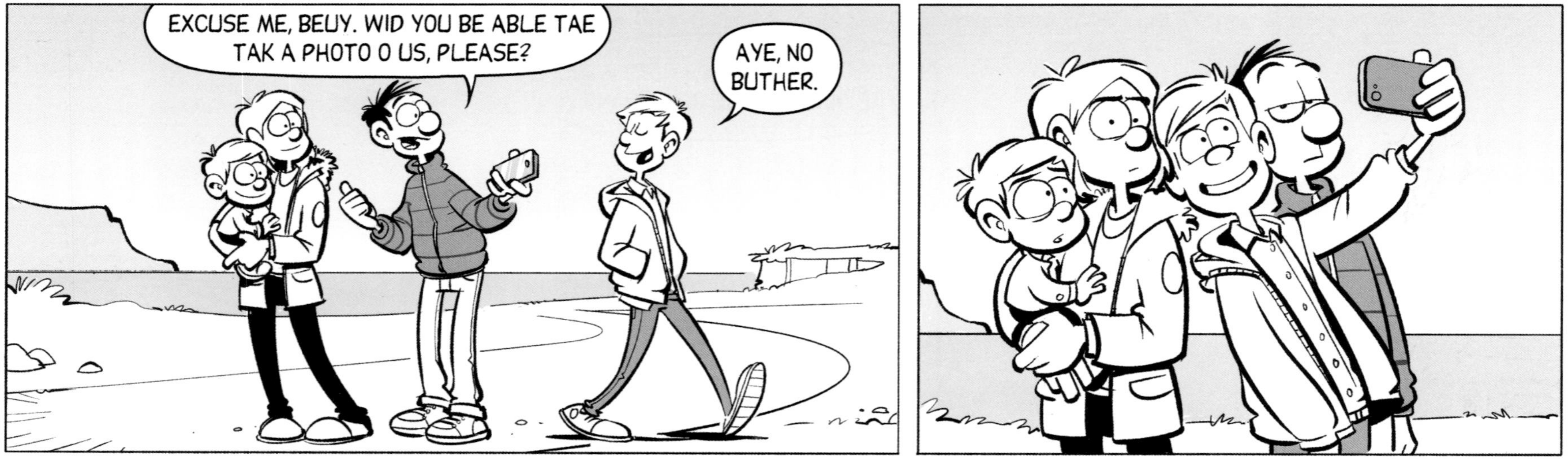
EXCUSE ME, BEUY. WID YOU BE ABLE TAE TAK A PHOTO O US, PLEASE?
AYE, NO BUTHER.

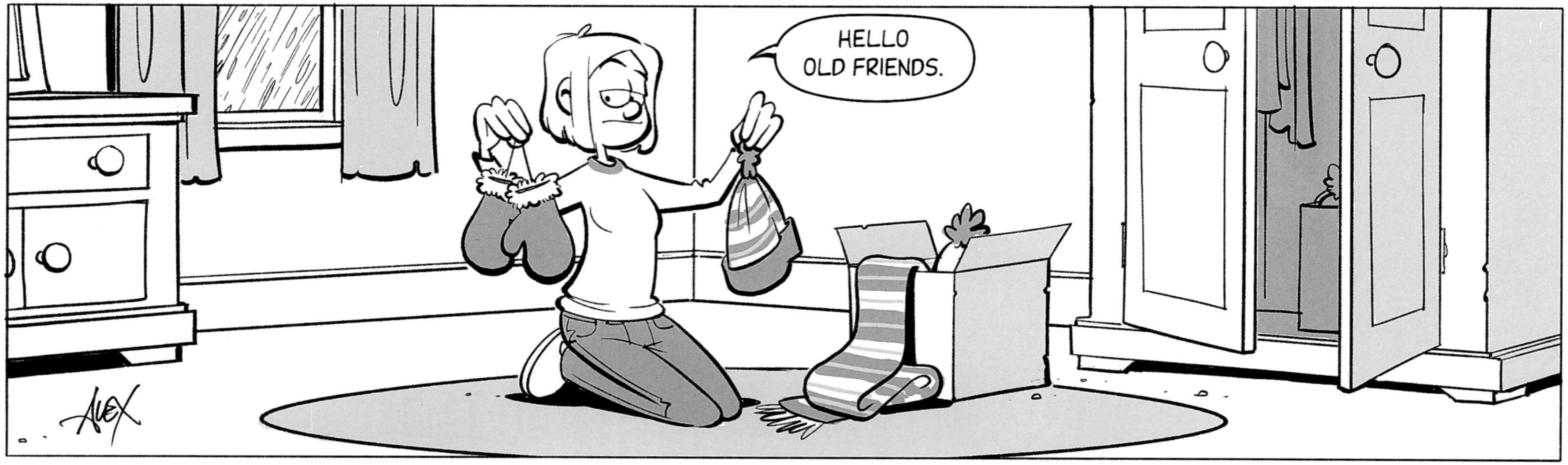
HELLO OLD FRIENDS.
ALEX

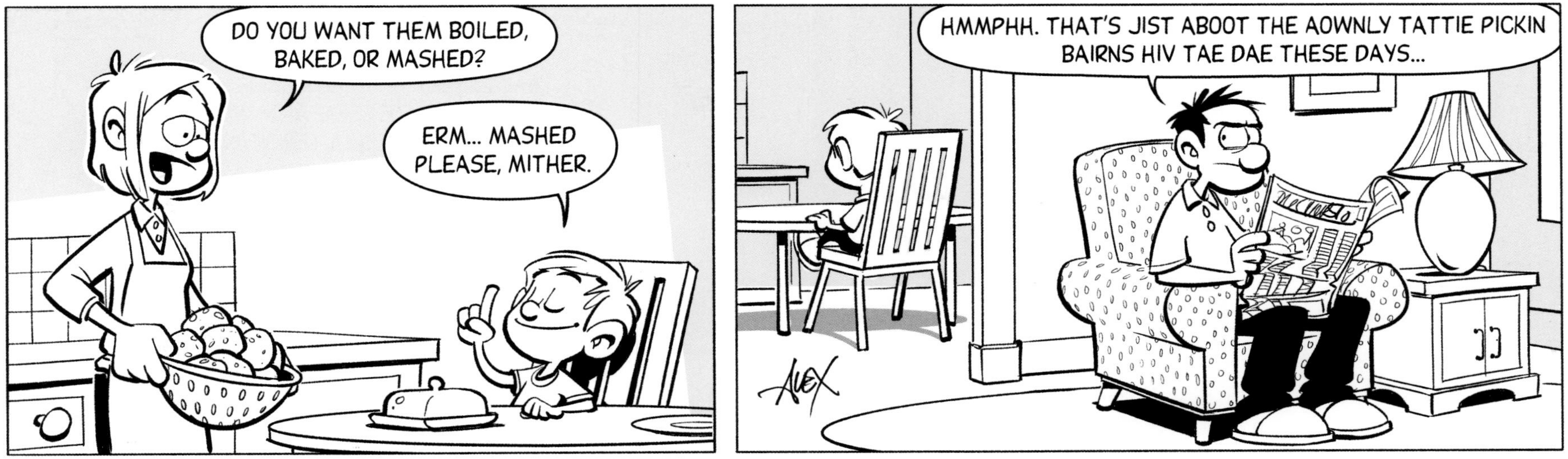
DO YOU WANT THEM BOILED, BAKED, OR MASHED?
ERM... MASHED PLEASE, MITHER.
HMMPHH. THAT'S JIST ABOOT THE AOWNLY TATTIE PICKIN BAIRNS HIV TAE DAE THESE DAYS...
ALEX

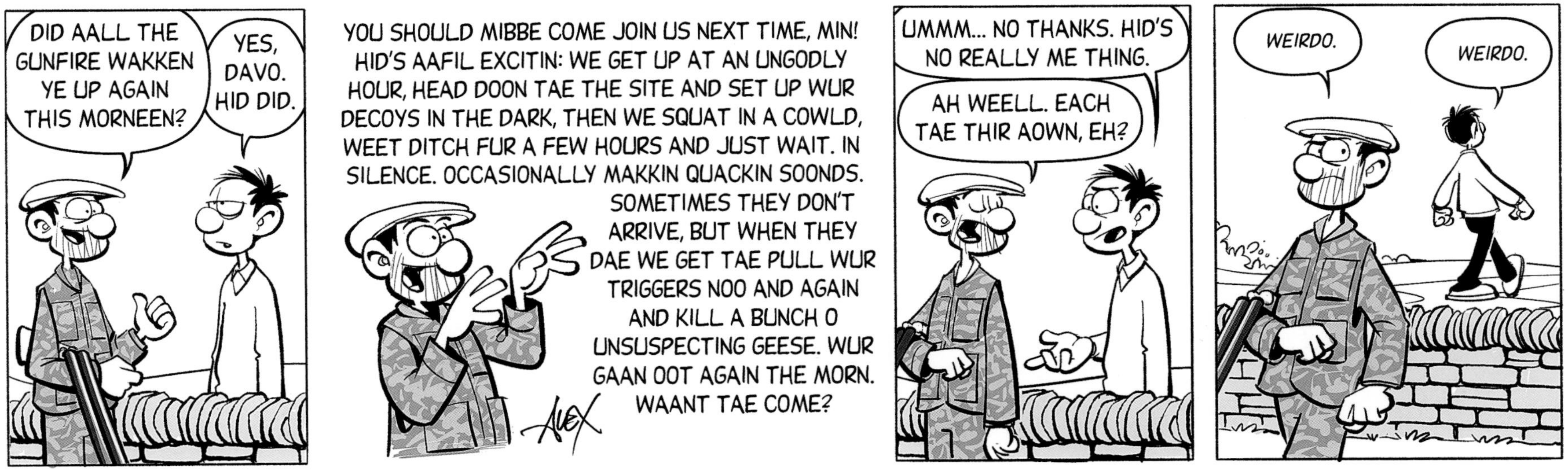
DID AALL THE GUNFIRE WAKKEN YE UP AGAIN THIS MORNEEN?
YES, DAVO. HID DID.
YOU SHOULD MIBBE COME JOIN US NEXT TIME, MIN! HID'S AAFIL EXCITIN: WE GET UP AT AN UNGODLY HOUR, HEAD DOON TAE THE SITE AND SET UP WUR DECOYS IN THE DARK, THEN WE SQUAT IN A COWLD, WEET DITCH FUR A FEW HOURS AND JUST WAIT. IN SILENCE. OCCASIONALLY MAKKIN QUACKIN SOONDS. SOMETIMES THEY DON'T ARRIVE, BUT WHEN THEY DAE WE GET TAE PULL WUR TRIGGERS NOO AND AGAIN AND KILL A BUNCH O UNSUSPECTING GEESE. WUR GAAN OOT AGAIN THE MORN. WAANT TAE COME?
ALEX
UMMM... NO THANKS. HID'S NO REALLY ME THING.
AH WEELL. EACH TAE THIR AOWN, EH?
WEIRDO.
WEIRDO.

MWA HA HAA!
AH'LL HIV YE KEN THAT UNDER AALL THESE EXTRA LAYERS THAT MITHER INSISTED I PIT OAN OOTSIDE, AH'M WEARIN AN UTTERLY TERRIFYIN ZOMBIE COSTUME.
ALEX

LIGHT, DAMN YOU!
SCRATCH
SKRITCH
SCRATCH
HURRY OAN FITHER! HID'S NO ROCKET SCIENCE!
ALEX

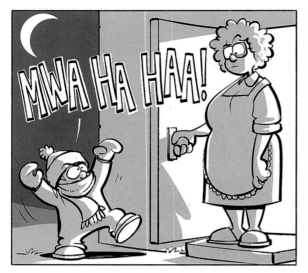

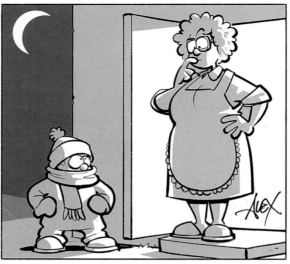

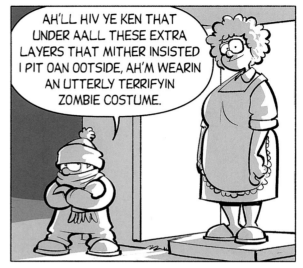

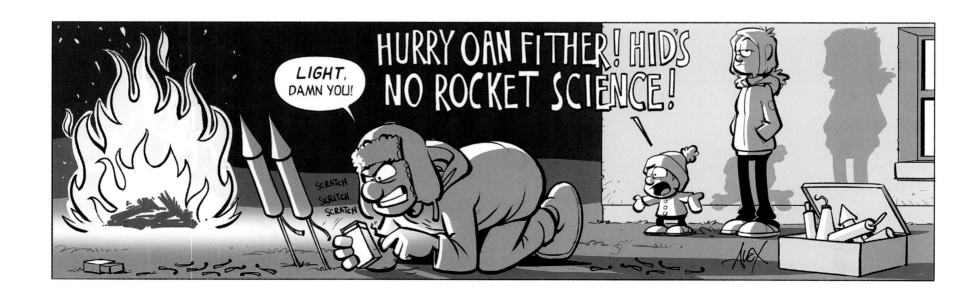

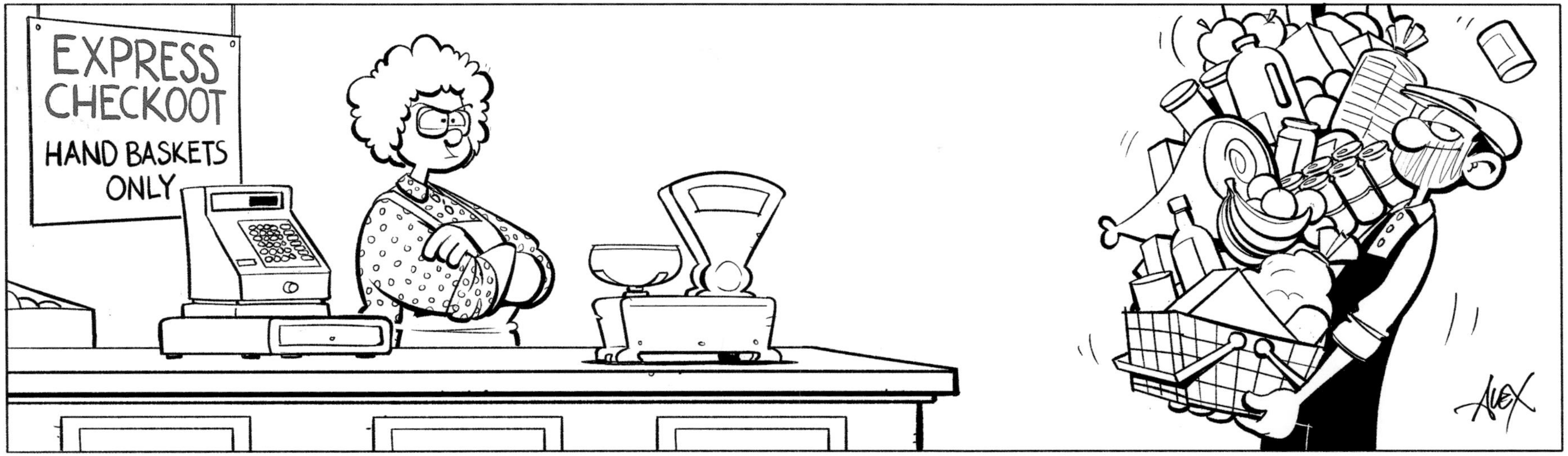
EXPRESS CHECKOOT
HAND BASKETS ONLY

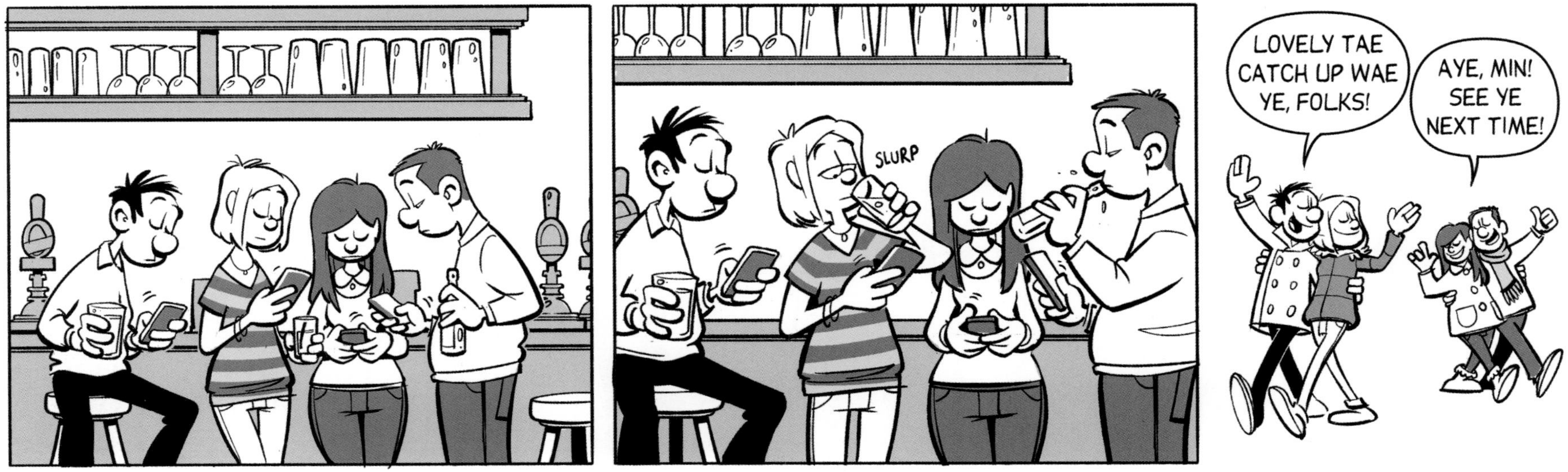
SLURP
LOVELY TAE CATCH UP WAE YE, FOLKS!
AYE, MIN! SEE YE NEXT TIME!

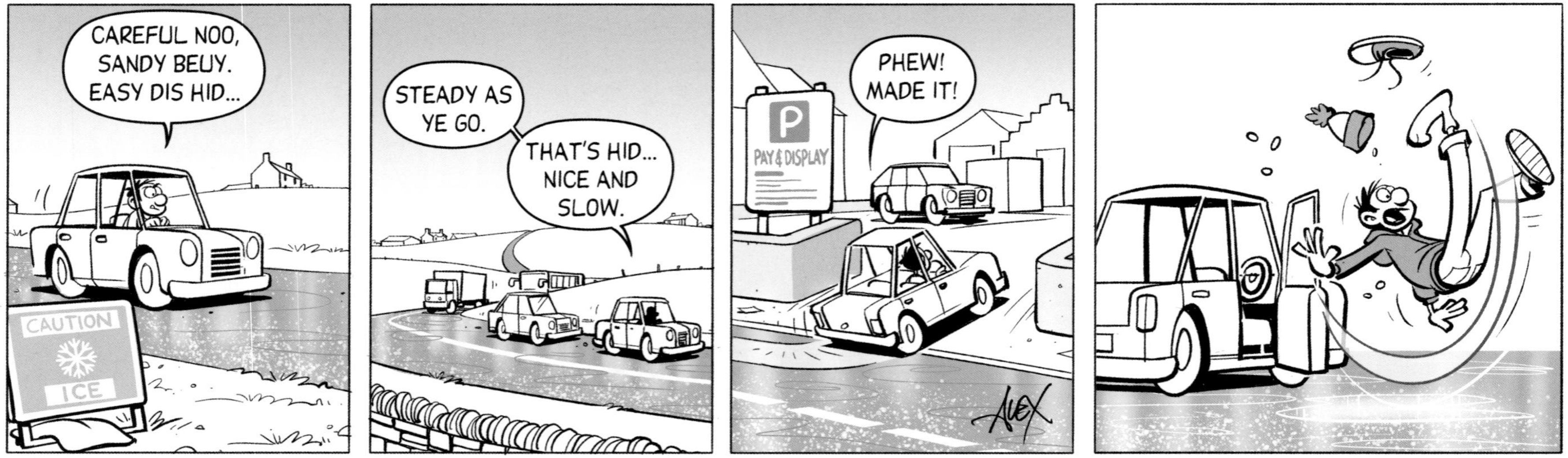
CAREFUL NOO, SANDY BEIJY. EASY DIS HID...
CAUTION
ICE
STEADY AS YE GO.
THAT'S HID... NICE AND SLOW.
P
PAY & DISPLAY
PHEW! MADE IT!
ALEX

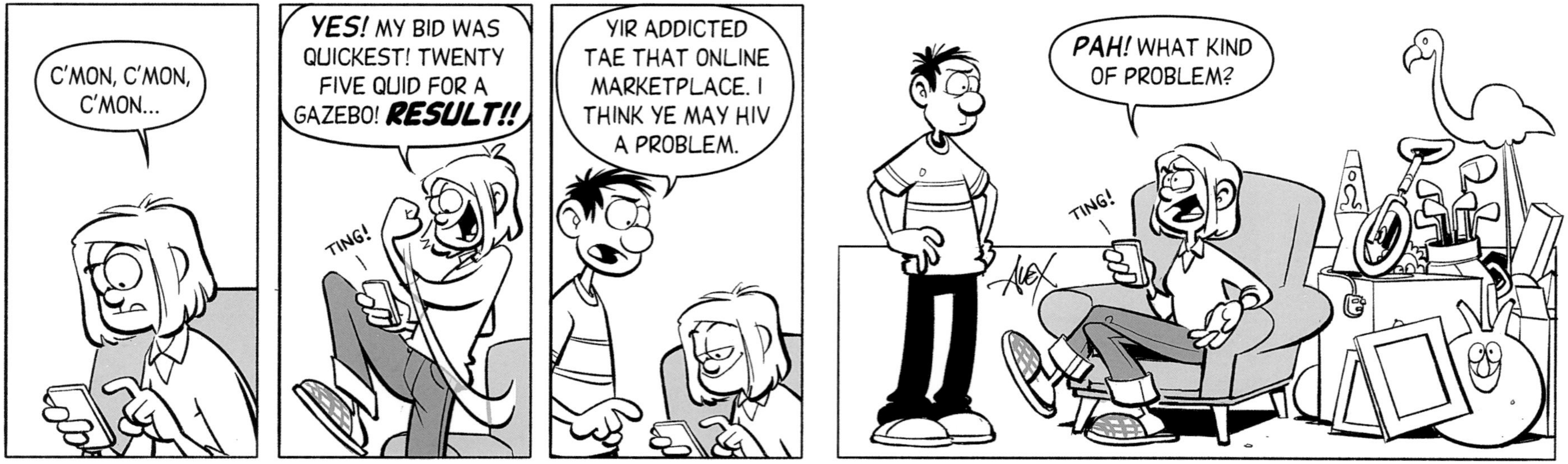
C'MON, C'MON, C'MON...
YES! MY BID WAS QUICKEST! TWENTY FIVE QUID FOR A GAZEBO! RESULT!!
TING!
YIR ADDICTED TAE THAT ONLINE MARKETPLACE. I THINK YE MAY HIV A PROBLEM.
PAH! WHAT KIND OF PROBLEM?
TING!
ALEX

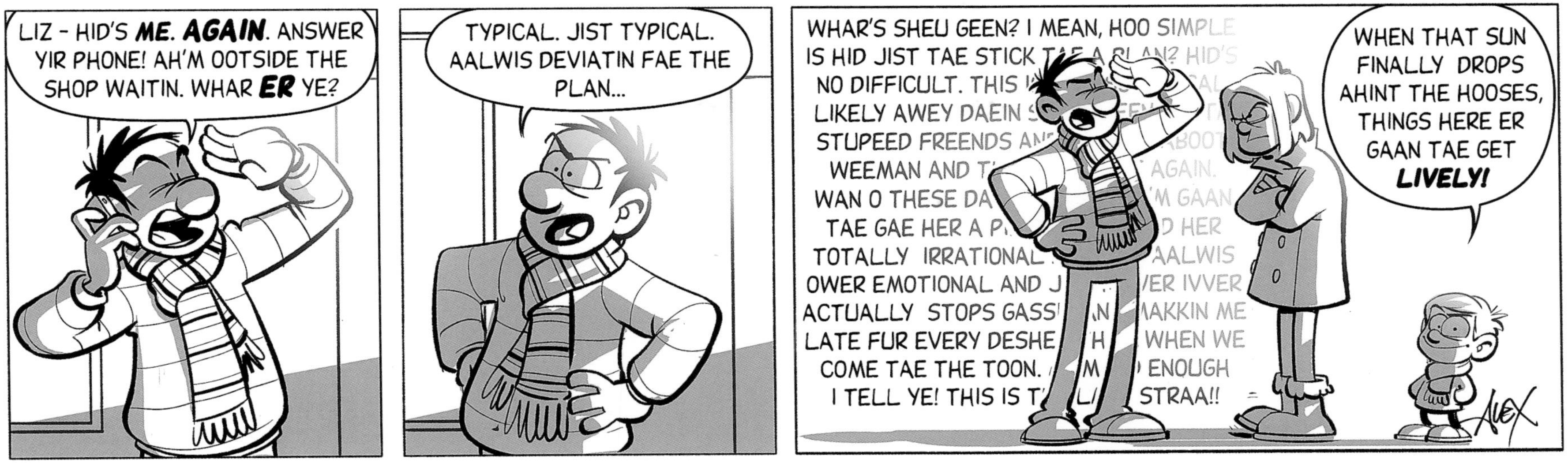
LIZ – HID'S **ME. AGAIN**. ANSWER YIR PHONE! AH'M OOTSIDE THE SHOP WAITIN. WHAR **ER** YE?
TYPICAL. JIST TYPICAL. AALWIS DEVIATIN FAE THE PLAN...
WHAR'S SHEU GEEN? I MEAN, HOO SIMPLE IS HID JIST TAE STICK TAE A PLAN? HID'S NO DIFFICULT. THIS
LIKELY AWEY DAEIN
STUPEED FREENDS AN ABOOT
WEEMAN AND AGAIN.
WAN O THESE DA M GAAN
TAE GAE HER A P D HER
TOTALLY IRRATIONAL AALWIS
OWER EMOTIONAL AND J VER IVVER
ACTUALLY STOPS GASS MAKKIN ME
LATE FUR EVERY DESHE WHEN WE
COME TAE THE TOON. ENOUGH
I TELL YE! THIS IS STRAA!!
WHEN THAT SUN FINALLY DROPS AHINT THE HOOSES, THINGS HERE ER GAAN TAE GET **LIVELY!**
ALEX

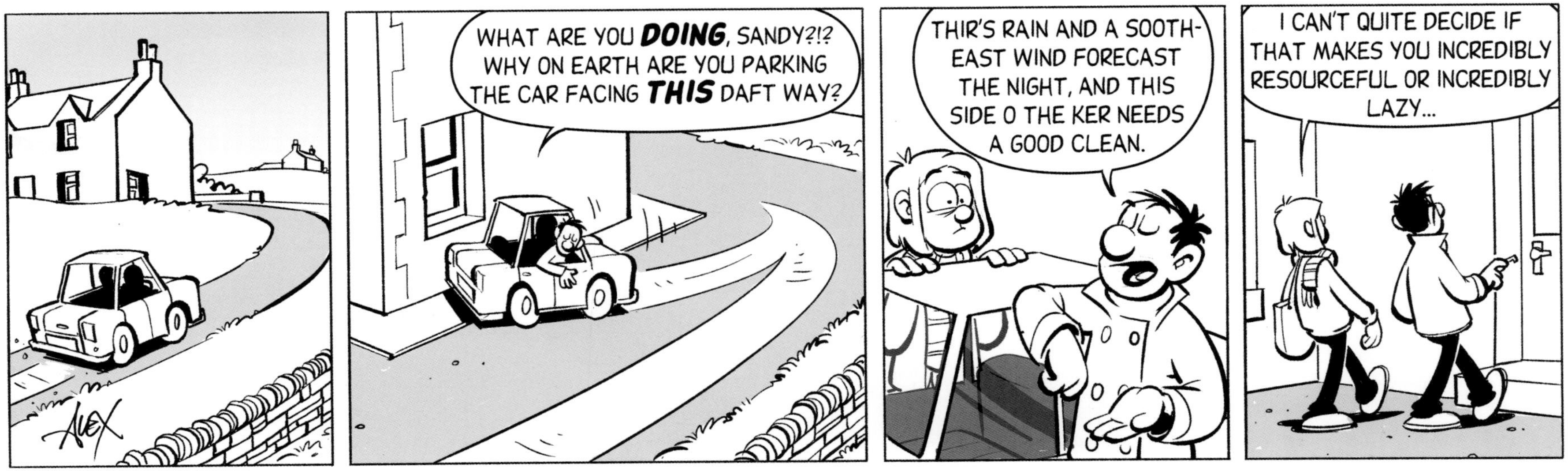
ALEX
WHAT ARE YOU **DOING**, SANDY?!? WHY ON EARTH ARE YOU PARKING THE CAR FACING **THIS** DAFT WAY?
THIR'S RAIN AND A SOOTH-EAST WIND FORECAST THE NIGHT, AND THIS SIDE O THE KER NEEDS A GOOD CLEAN.
I CAN'T QUITE DECIDE IF THAT MAKES YOU INCREDIBLY RESOURCEFUL OR INCREDIBLY LAZY...

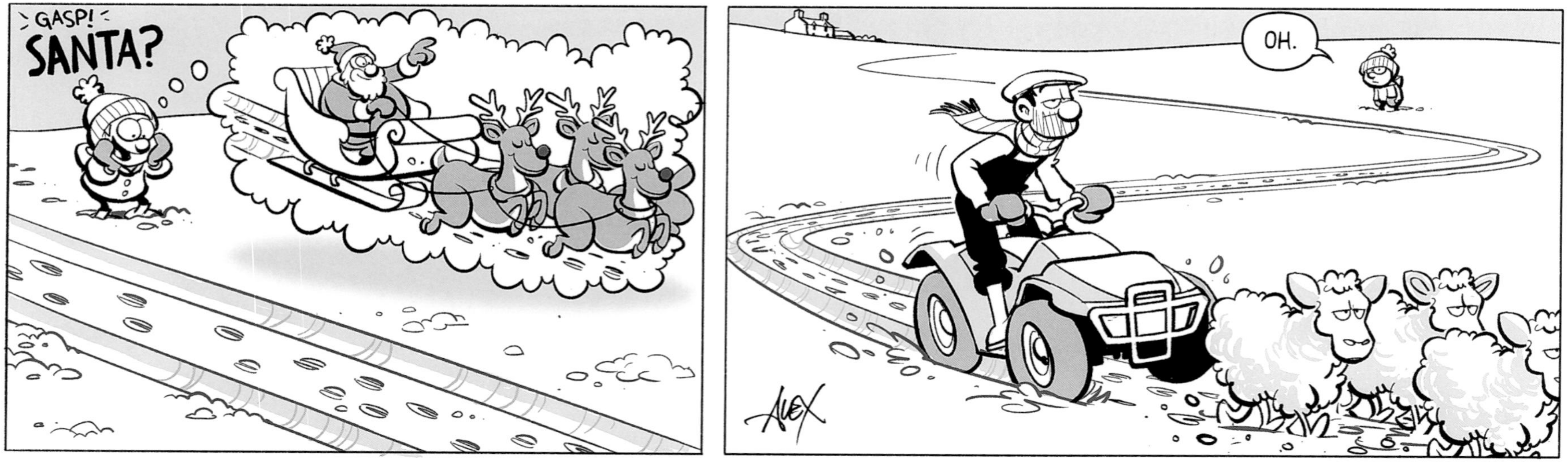
GASP!
SANTA?
OH.

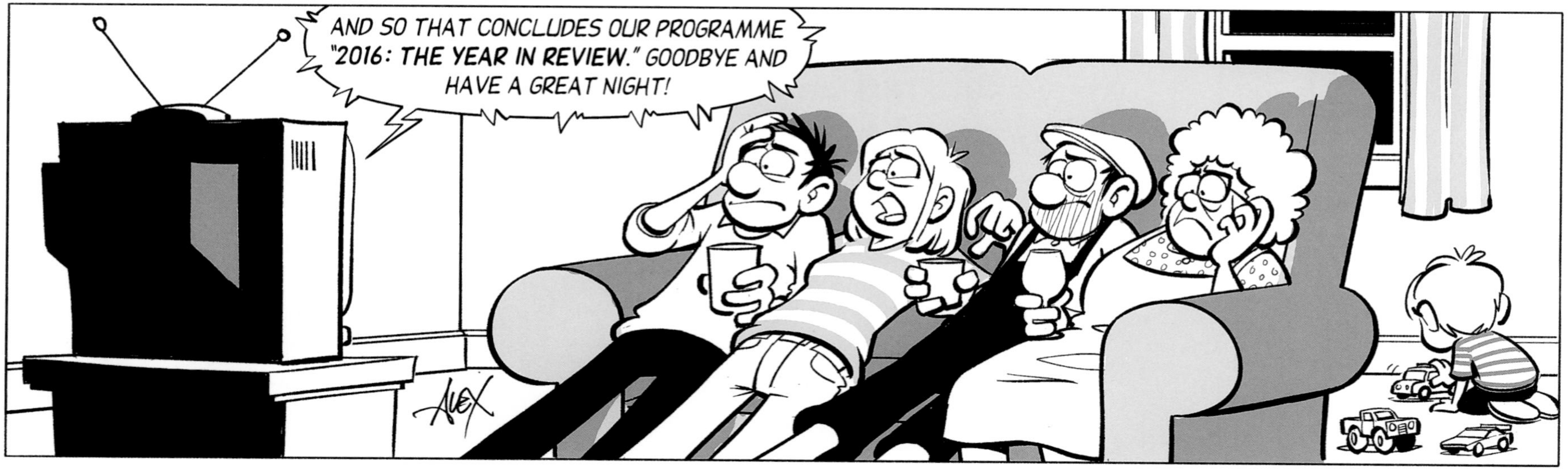
AND SO THAT CONCLUDES OUR PROGRAMME "2016: THE YEAR IN REVIEW." GOODBYE AND HAVE A GREAT NIGHT!

# 2017 CALENDAR

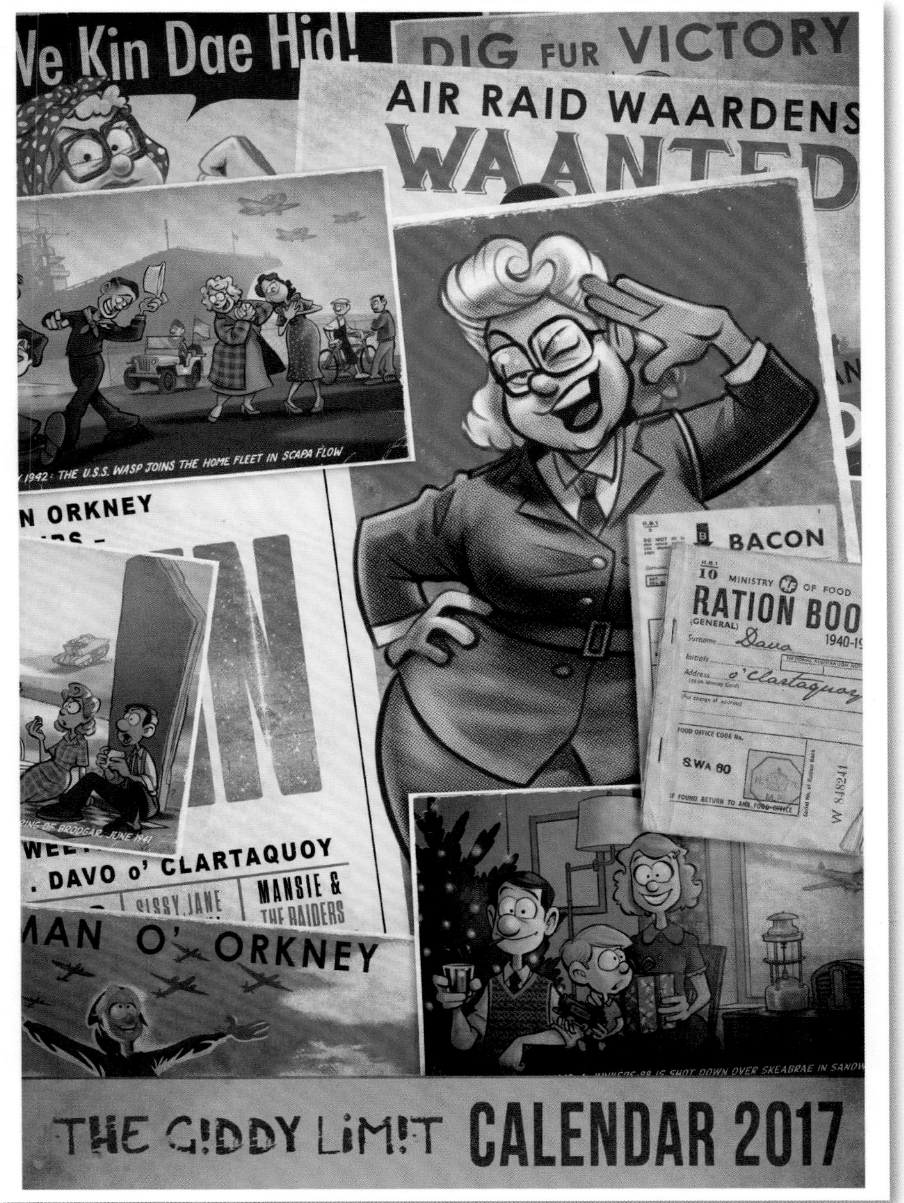
We Kin Dae Hid!
DIG FUR VICTORY
AIR RAID WAARDENS
WAANTED
1942: THE U.S.S. WASP JOINS THE HOME FLEET IN SCAPA FLOW
N ORKNEY
RING OF BRODGAR JUNE 1941
. DAVO o' CLARTAQUOY
SISSY JANE
MANSIE & THE RAIDERS
MAN O' ORKNEY
BACON
MINISTRY OF FOOD
RATION BOO
(GENERAL)
1940-1
S.WA 80
THE GIDDY LIMIT CALENDAR 2017

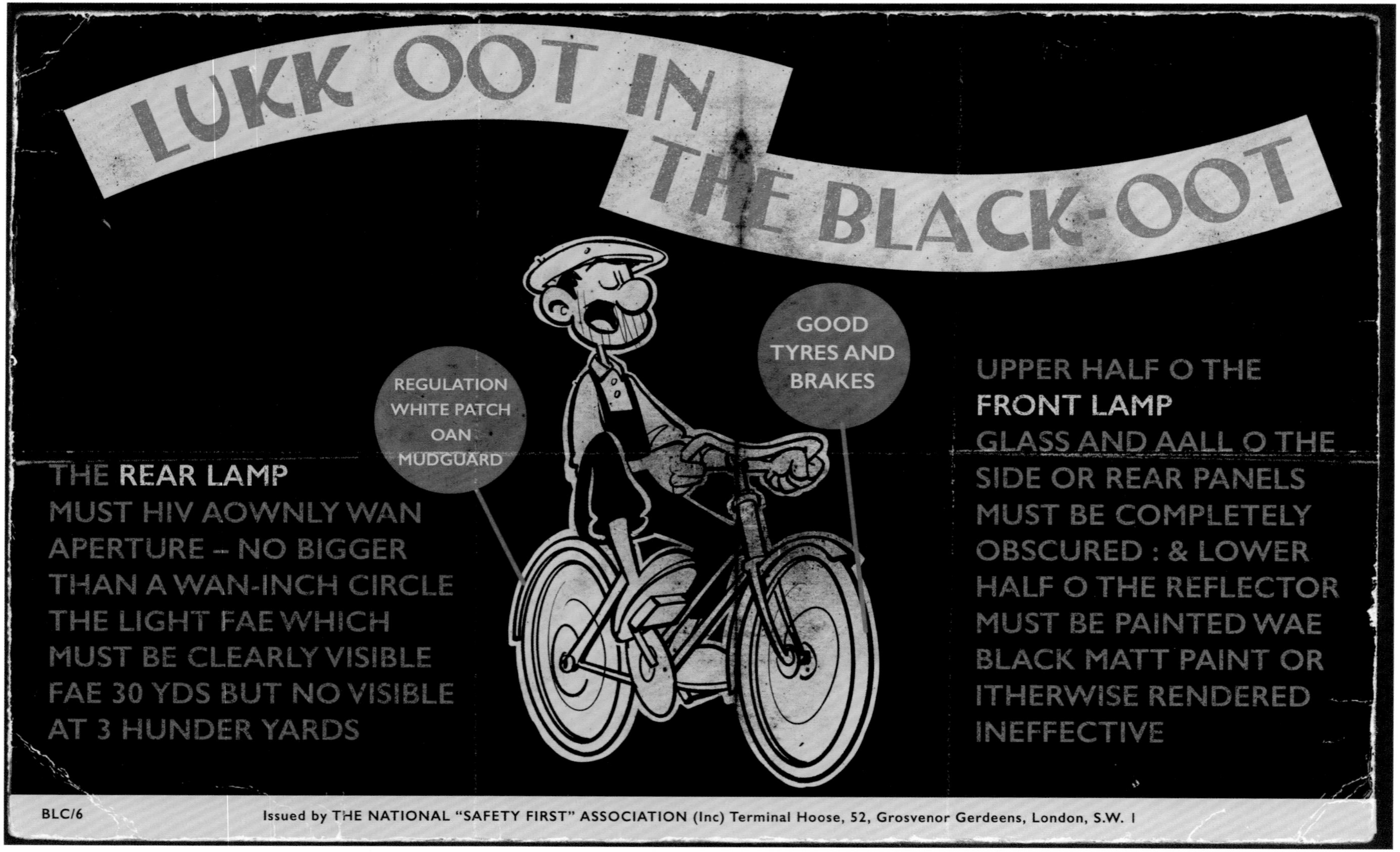

LUKK OOT IN THE BLACK-OOT
REGULATION WHITE PATCH OAN MUDGUARD
GOOD TYRES AND BRAKES
THE REAR LAMP MUST HIV AOWNLY WAN APERTURE – NO BIGGER THAN A WAN-INCH CIRCLE THE LIGHT FAE WHICH MUST BE CLEARLY VISIBLE FAE 30 YDS BUT NO VISIBLE AT 3 HUNDER YARDS
UPPER HALF O THE FRONT LAMP GLASS AND AALL O THE SIDE OR REAR PANELS MUST BE COMPLETELY OBSCURED : & LOWER HALF O THE REFLECTOR MUST BE PAINTED WAE BLACK MATT PAINT OR ITHERWISE RENDERED INEFFECTIVE
BLC/6
Issued by THE NATIONAL "SAFETY FIRST" ASSOCIATION (Inc) Terminal Hoose, 52, Grosvenor Gerdeens, London, S.W. 1

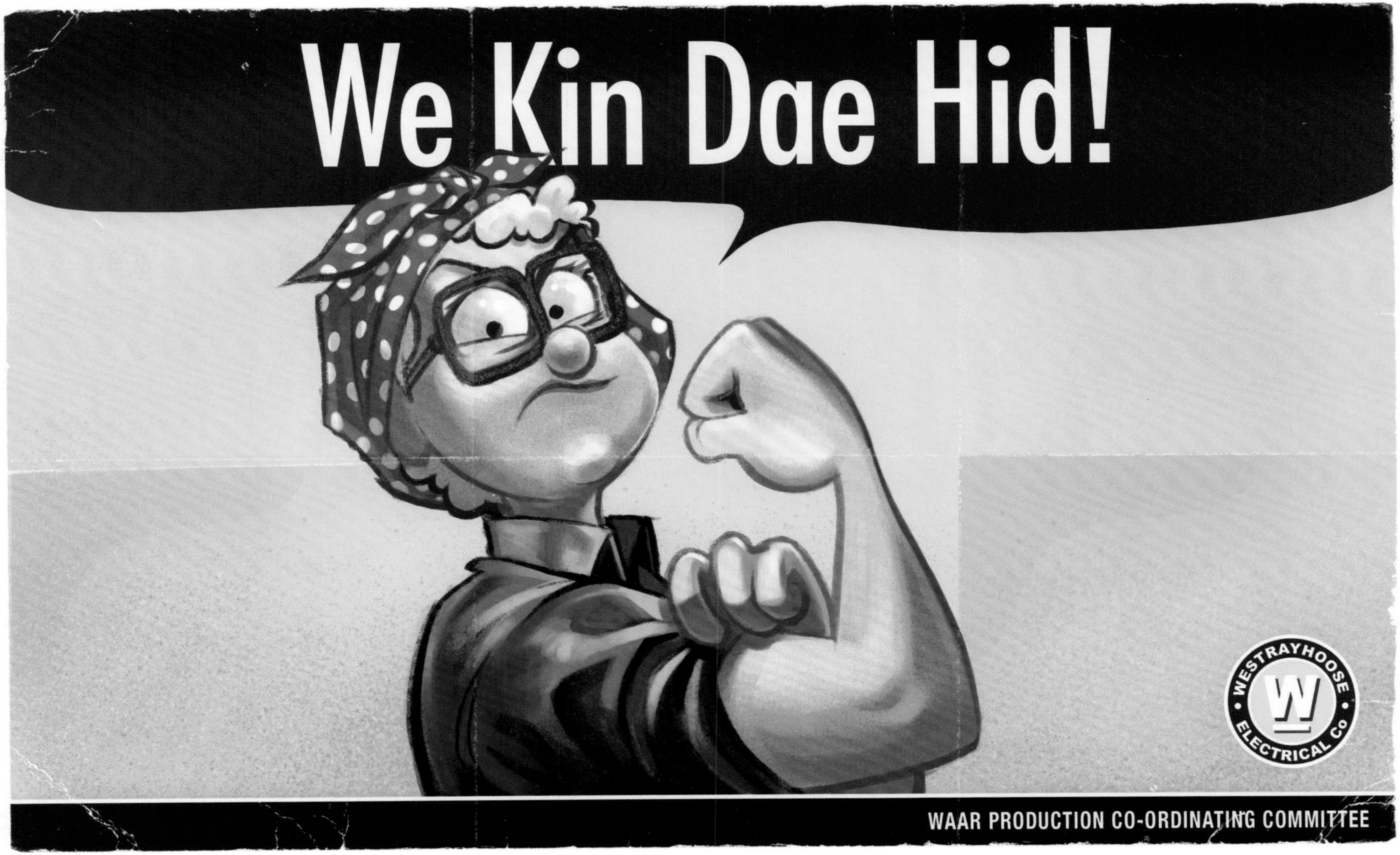
We Kin Dae Hid!
WESTRAYHOOSE
W
ELECTRICAL Co
WAAR PRODUCTION CO-ORDINATING COMMITTEE

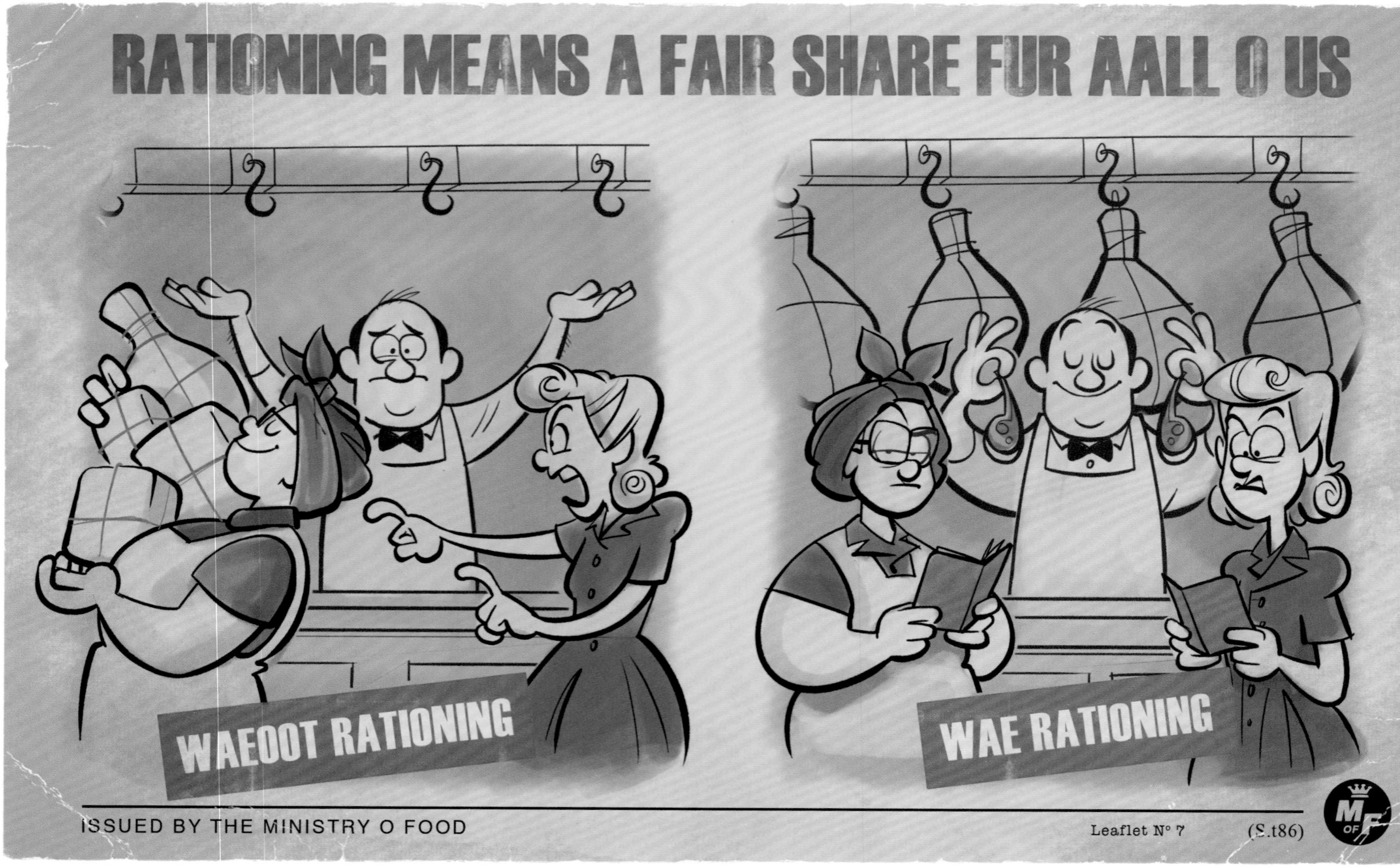
RATIONING MEANS A FAIR SHARE FUR AALL O US
WAEOOT RATIONING
WAE RATIONING
ISSUED BY THE MINISTRY O FOOD
Leaflet N° 7
(S.t86)

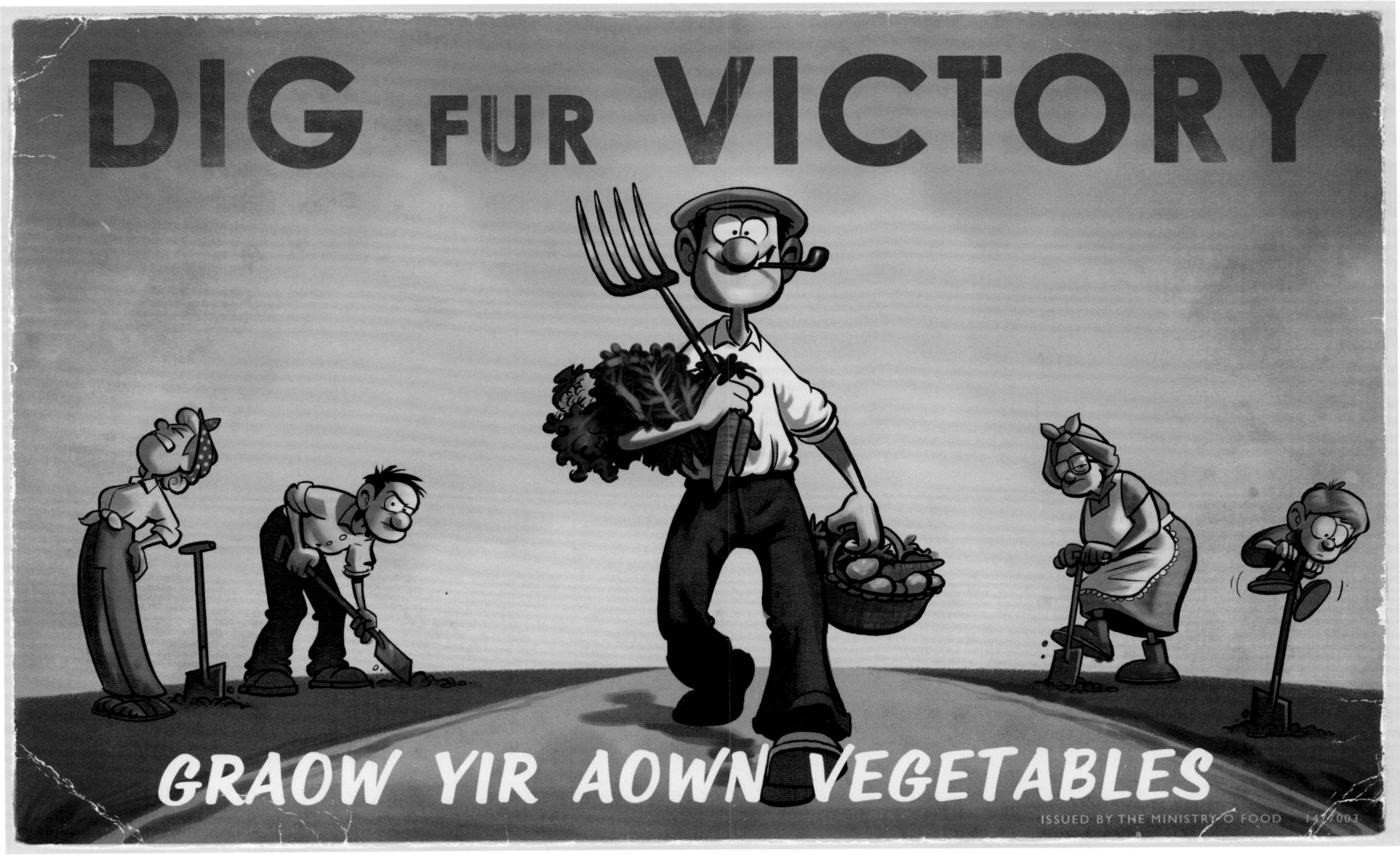
DIG FUR VICTORY
GRAOW YIR AOWN VEGETABLES
ISSUED BY THE MINISTRY O FOOD

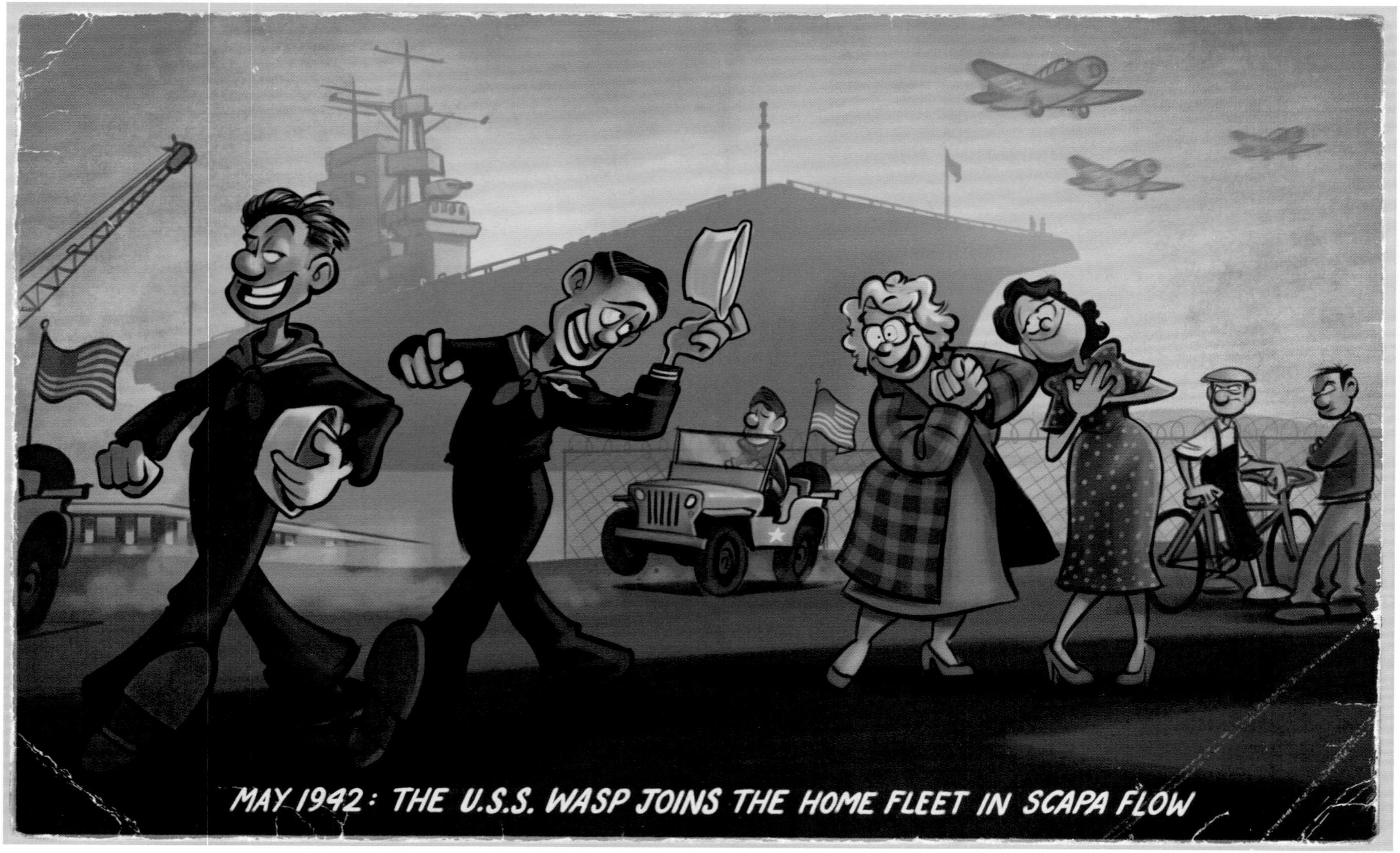
MAY 1942: THE U.S.S. WASP JOINS THE HOME FLEET IN SCAPA FLOW

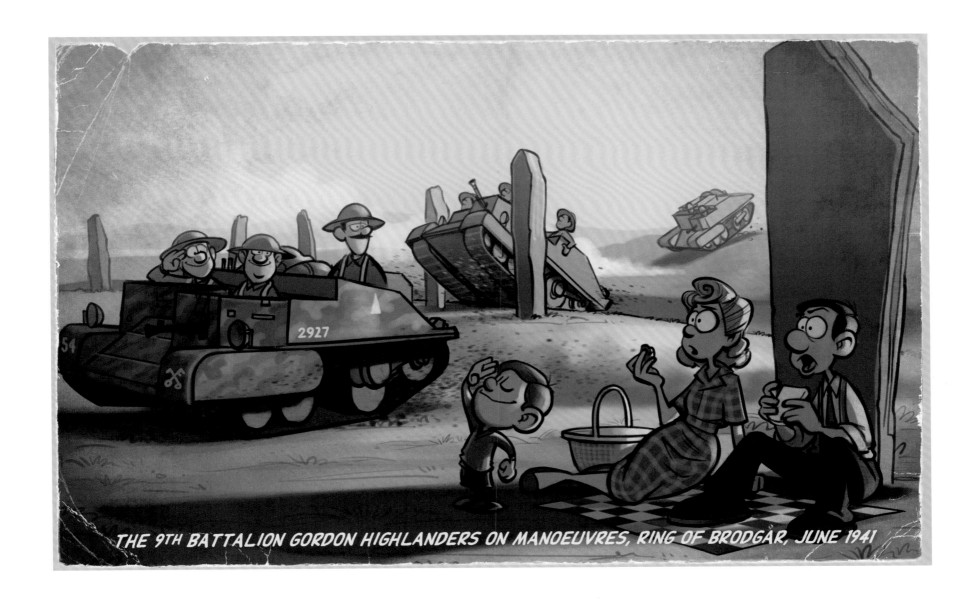

THE 9TH BATTALION GORDON HIGHLANDERS ON MANOEUVRES, RING OF BRODGAR, JUNE 1941

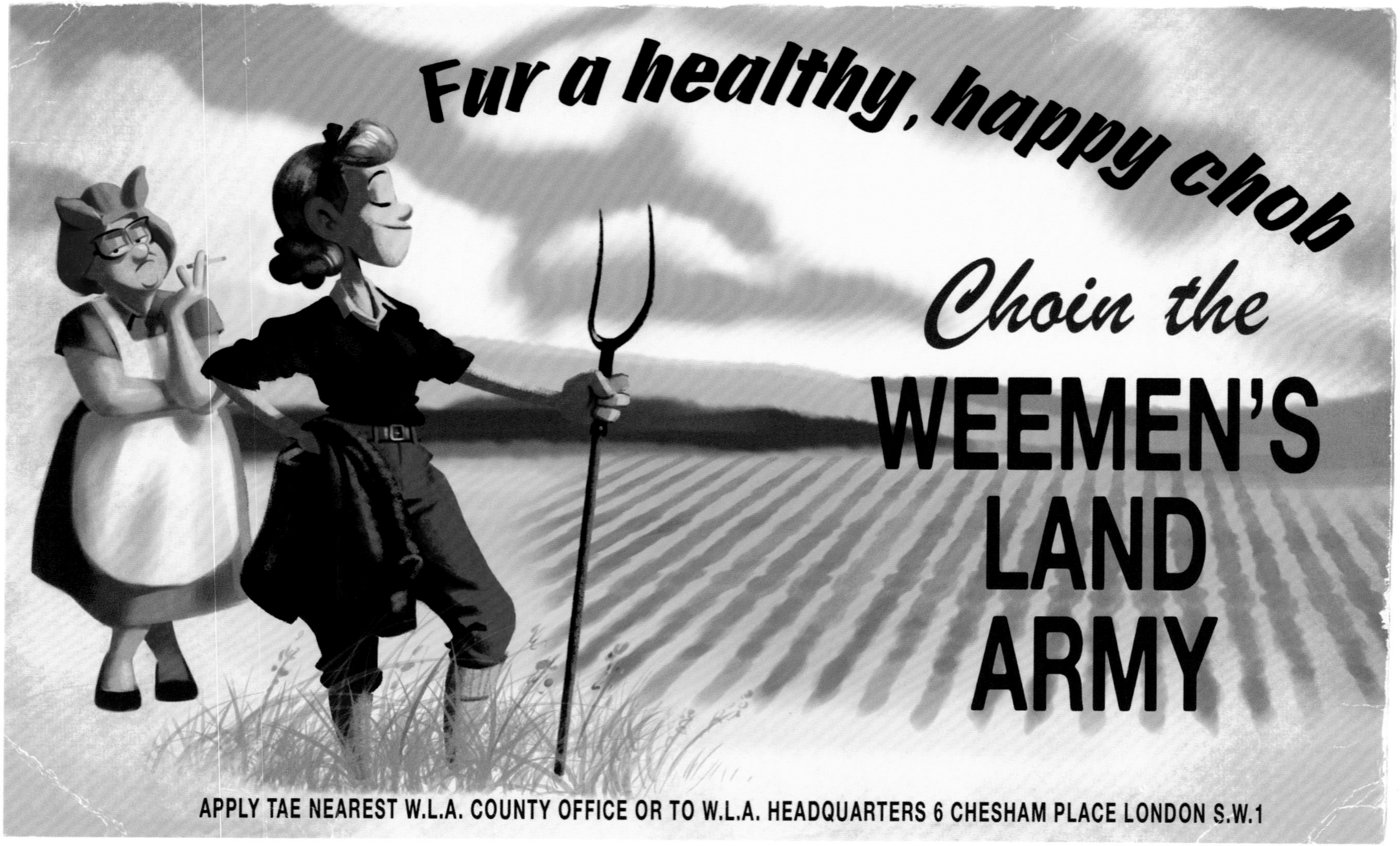
Fur a healthy, happy chob
Choin the
WEEMEN'S
LAND
ARMY
APPLY TAE NEAREST W.L.A. COUNTY OFFICE OR TO W.L.A. HEADQUARTERS 6 CHESHAM PLACE LONDON S.W.1

# GARRISON THEATRE

## CROCKNESS, HOY

**MONDAY, AUGUST 7th, 1944 AND WEEK**

| POPULAR PRICES 2/- 3/- 4/- 5/- | 2 MATINEES, Mon. & Wed. at 2.30 | TWICE NIGHTLY 6.20 8.40 |

### FIRST APPEARANCE IN ORKNEY
### INSINCERELY YOURS –

# IVY LYNN

## THE FORCES SWEETHEART

At the Piano . . . . . . . . . . . DAVO o' CLARTAQUOY

| JIMMOCK & THE HEIFERS | THE STENWICK BOYS | SISSY, JANE & MYRTYL | MANSIE & THE RAIDERS |

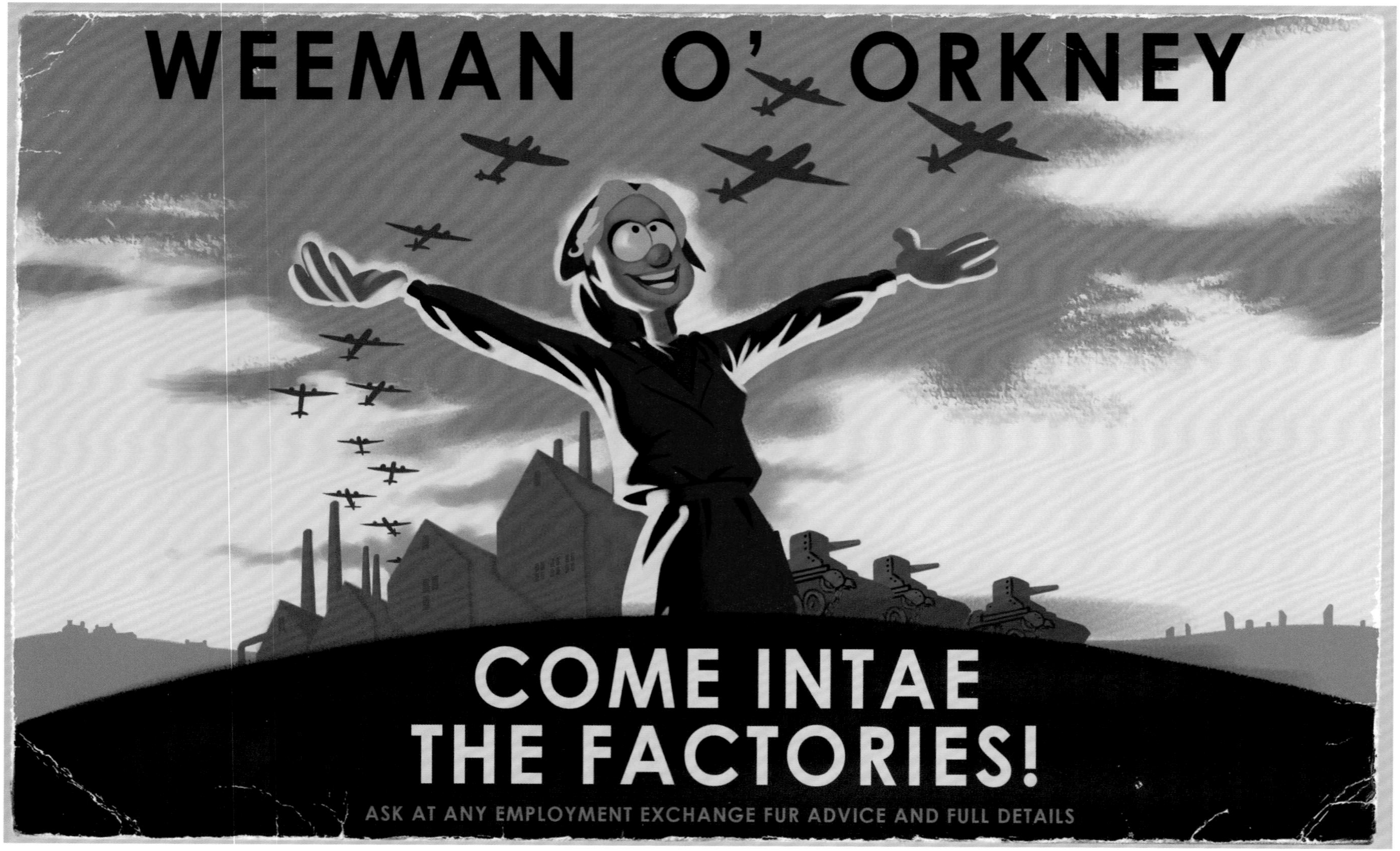
WEEMAN O' ORKNEY
COME INTAE THE FACTORIES!
ASK AT ANY EMPLOYMENT EXCHANGE FUR ADVICE AND FULL DETAILS

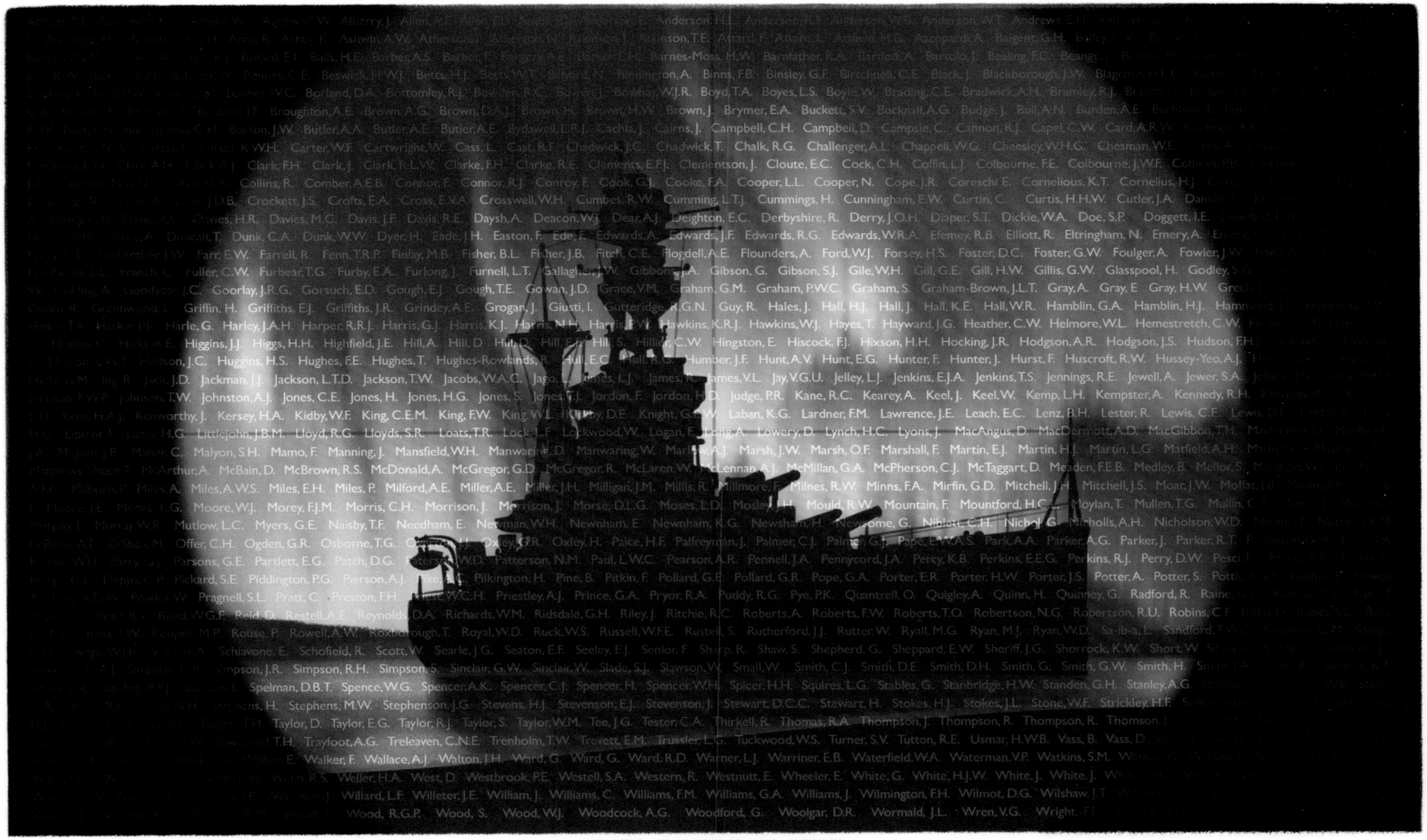
Anderson, H.L. Anderson, W.T. Andrews, E.H.
Atkinson, T.E. Attard, F. Attard, L. Attfield, H.G. Azzopardi, A. Baigent, G.H.
Sails, H.E. Barber, A.S. Barnes-Moss, H.W. Barnfather, R.A. Bartlett, A. Bartolo, J. Beating, F.C. Beangs
Binnington, A. Binns, F.B. Binsley, G.F. Birchnell, C.E. Black, J. Blackborough, J.W.
Bowhay, W.J.R. Boyd, T.A. Boyes, L.S. Boyle, W. Brading, C.E. Bradwick, A.H. Bramley, R.J.
Broughton, A.E. Brown, A.G. Brown, D.A.J. Brown, H. Brown, H.W. Brown, J. Brymer, E.A. Buckett, S.V. Bucknall, A.G. Budge, J. Bull, A.N. Burden, A.E.
Burton, J.W. Butler, A.A. Butler, A.E. Butler, A.E. Bydawell, L.R.J. Cachia, J. Cairns, J. Campbell, C.H. Campbell, D. Campsie, C. Cannon, R.J. Capel, C.W. Card, A.R.W.
Carter, W.F. Cartwright, W. Cass, L. Cast, R.T. Chadwick, J.C. Chadwick, T. Chalk, R.G. Challenger, A.L. Chappell, W.G. Cheesley, W.H.G. Chesman, W.L.
Clark, F.H. Clark, J. Clark, R.L.W. Clarke, F.H. Clarke, R.E. Clements, E.F.J. Clementson, J. Cloute, E.C. Cock, C.H. Coffin, L.J. Colbourne, F.E. Colbourne, J.W.F.
Collins, R. Comber, A.E.B. Connor, F. Connor, R.J. Conroy, F. Cook, G.J. Cooke, F.A. Cooper, L.L. Cooper, N. Cope, J.R. Coreschi, E. Cornelious, K.T. Cornelius, H.J.
Crockett, J.S. Crofts, E.A. Cross, E.V.A. Crosswell, W.H. Cumbes, R.W. Cumming, L.T.J. Cummings, H. Cunningham, E.W. Curtin, C. Curtis, H.H.W. Cutler, J.A.
Davies, H.R. Davies, M.C. Davis, J.F. Davis, R.E. Daysh, A. Deacon, W.J. Dear, A.J. Deighton, E.C. Derbyshire, R. Derry, J.O.H. Diaper, S.T. Dickie, W.A. Doe, S.P. Doggett, I.E.
Duncalf, T. Dunk, C.A. Dunk, W.W. Dyer, H. Eade, J.H. Easton, F. Ede, F. Edwards, A. Edwards, J.F. Edwards, R.G. Edwards, W.R.A. Efemey, R.B. Elliott, R. Eltringham, N. Emery, A.
Fairbrother, J.W. Farr, E.W. Farrell, R. Fenn, T.R.P. Finlay, M.B. Fisher, B.L. Fisher, J.B. Fitch, C.E. Flogdell, A.E. Flounders, A. Ford, W.J. Forsey, H.S. Foster, D.C. Foster, G.W. Foulger, A. Fowler, J.W.
French, C. Fuller, C.W. Furbear, T.G. Furby, E.A. Furlong, J. Furnell, L.T. Gallagher, J.W. Gibbons, J.A. Gibson, G. Gibson, S.J. Gile, W.H. Gill, G.E. Gill, H.W. Gillis, G.W. Glasspool, H. Godley
Goodyear, J.C. Goorlay, J.R.G. Gorsuch, E.D. Gough, E.J. Gough, T.E. Gowan, J.D. Grace, V.M. Graham, G.M. Graham, P.W.C. Graham, S. Graham-Brown, J.L.T. Gray, A. Gray, E. Gray, H.W.
Greenwood, L. Griffin, H. Griffiths, E.J. Griffiths, J.R. Grindey, A.E. Grogan, J. Giusti, I. Gutteridge, R.G.N. Guy, R. Hales, J. Hall, H.J. Hall, J. Hall, K.E. Hall, W.R. Hamblin, G.A. Hamblin, H.J.
Harle, G. Harley, J.A.H. Harper, R.R.J. Harris, G.J. Harris, K.J. Hawkins, K.R.J. Hawkins, W.J. Hayes, T. Hayward, J.G. Heather, C.W. Helmore, W.L. Hemestretch, C.W.
Higgins, J.J. Higgs, H.H. Highfield, J.E. Hill, A. Hill, D. Hingston, E. Hiscock, F.J. Hixson, H.H. Hocking, J.R. Hodgson, A.R. Hodgson, J.S. Hudson, F.H.
Hudson, J.C. Huggins, H.S. Hughes, F.E. Hughes, T. Hughes-Rowlands, R. Hull, E.C. Humber, J.F. Hunt, A.V. Hunt, E.G. Hunter, F. Hunter, J. Hurst, F. Huscroft, R.W. Hussey-Yeo, A.J.
Jackman, J.J. Jackson, L.T.D. Jackson, T.W. Jacobs, W.A.C. James, L.J. James, V.L. Jay, V.G.U. Jelley, L.J. Jenkins, E.J.A. Jenkins, T.S. Jennings, R.E. Jewell, A. Jewer, S.A.
Johnson, T.W. Johnston, A.J. Jones, C.E. Jones, H. Jones, H.G. Jones, S. Jones, T.J. Jordon, F. Jordon, H. Judge, P.R. Kane, R.C. Kearey, A. Keel, J. Keel, W. Kemp, L.H. Kempster, A. Kennedy, R.H.
Kenworthy, J. Kersey, H.A. Kidby, W.F. King, C.E.M. King, F.W. King, W.L. Kirby, D.E. Knight, G.W. Laban, K.G. Lardner, F.M. Lawrence, J.E. Leach, E.C. Lenz, B.H. Lester, R. Lewis, C.E.
Lister, H.G. Littlejohn, J.B.M. Lloyd, R.G. Lloyds, S.R. Loats, T.R. Lock, L.F. Lockwood, W. Logan, F. Long, A. Lowery, D. Lynch, H.C. Lyons, J. MacAngus, D. MacDermott, A.D. MacGibbon, T.H.
Mather, C. Malyon, S.H. Mamo, F. Manning, J. Mansfield, W.H. Manwaring, D. Manwaring, W. Marlow, A.J. Marsh, J.W. Marsh, O.F. Marshall, F. Martin, E.J. Martin, H.J. Martin, L.G. Matfield, A.H.
McArthur, A. McBain, D. McBrown, R.S. McDonald, A. McGregor, G.D. McGregor, R. McLaren, W. McLennan, A.J. McMillan, G.A. McPherson, C.J. McTaggart, D. Meaden, F.E.B. Medley, B. Mellor, S.
Miles, A. Miles, A.W.S. Miles, E.H. Miles, P. Milford, A.E. Miller, A.E. Miller, J.H. Milligan, J.M. Millis, R. Millmore, F. Milnes, R.W. Minns, F.A. Mirfin, G.D. Mitchell, J.H. Mitchell, J.S. Moar, J.W. Moffat, J.B.
Moore, J.E. Moore, L.G. Moore, W.J. Morey, F.J.M. Morris, C.H. Morrison, J. Morrison, J. Morse, D.L.G. Moses, L.D. Mosley, J.H. Mould, R.W. Mountain, F. Mountford, H.C. Moylan, T. Mullen, T.G.
Mutlow, L.C. Myers, G.E. Naisby, T.F. Needham, E. Newman, W.H. Newnham, E. Newnham, K.G. Newsham, H. Newsome, G. Niblett, C.H. Nichol, G. Nicholls, A.H. Nicholson, W.D.
Offer, C.H. Ogden, G.R. Osborne, T.G. Oxley, G.R. Oxley, H. Paice, H.F. Palfreyman, J. Palmer, C.J. Palmer, G.J. Pape, E.W.A.S. Park, A.A. Parker, A.G. Parker, J. Parker, R.T.
Parsons, G.E. Partlett, E.G. Patch, D.G. Patterson, W.D. Patterson, N.M. Paul, L.W.C. Pearson, A.R. Pennell, J.A. Pennycord, J.A. Percy, K.B. Perkins, E.E.G. Perkins, R.J. Perry, D.W.
Pickard, S.E. Piddington, P.G. Pierson, A.J. Pilkington, H. Pine, B. Pitkin, F. Pollard, G.E. Pollard, G.R. Pope, G.A. Porter, E.R. Porter, H.W. Porter, J.S. Potter, A. Potter, S.
Pragnell, S.L. Pratt, C. Preston, F.H. Priest, W.C.H. Priestley, A.J. Prince, G.A. Pryor, R.A. Puddy, R.G. Pye, P.K. Quantrell, O. Quigley, A. Quinn, H. Quinney, G. Radford, R.
Reid, D. Restell, A.E. Reynolds, D.A. Richards, W.M. Ridsdale, G.H. Riley, J. Ritchie, R.C. Roberts, A. Roberts, F.W. Roberts, T.O. Robertson, N.G. Robertson, R.U. Robins, C.F.
Rouse, P. Rowell, A.W. Roxborough, T. Royal, W.D. Ruck, W.S. Russell, W.F.E. Russell, S. Rutherford, J.J. Rutter, W. Ryall, M.G. Ryan, M.J. Ryan, W.D. Sandford
Schiavone, E. Schofield, R. Scott, W. Searle, J.G. Seaton, E.F. Seeley, E.J. Senior, F. Sharp, R. Shaw, S. Shepherd, G. Sheppard, E.W. Sheriff, J.G. Shorrock, K.W. Short, W.
Simpson, J.R. Simpson, R.H. Simpson, S. Sinclair, G.W. Sinclair, W. Slade, S.J. Slawson, W. Small, W. Smith, C.J. Smith, D.E. Smith, D.H. Smith, G. Smith, G.W. Smith, H.
Spelman, D.B.T. Spence, W.G. Spencer, A.K. Spencer, C.J. Spencer, H. Spencer, W.H. Spicer, H.H. Squires, L.G. Stables, G. Stanbridge, H.W. Standen, G.H. Stanley, A.G.
Stephens, H. Stephens, M.W. Stephenson, J.G. Stevens, H.J. Stevenson, E.J. Stevenson, J. Stewart, D.C.C. Stewart, H. Stokes, H.J. Stokes, J.L. Stone, W.F. Strickley, H.F.
Taylor, D. Taylor, E.G. Taylor, R.J. Taylor, S. Taylor, W.M. Tee, J.G. Tester, C.A. Thirkell, R. Thomas, R.A. Thompson, J. Thompson, R. Thompson, R. Thomson, J.
Trayfoot, A.G. Treleaven, C.N.E. Trenholm, T.W. Trevett, E.M. Trussler, L.G. Tuckwood, W.S. Turner, S.V. Tutton, R.E. Usmar, H.W.B. Vass, B. Vass, D.
Walker, F. Wallace, A.J. Walton, J.H. Ward, G. Ward, G. Ward, R.D. Warner, L.J. Warriner, E.B. Waterfield, W.A. Waterman, V.P. Watkins, S.M.
Weller, H.A. West, D. Westbrook, P.E. Westell, S.A. Western, R. Westnutt, E. Wheeler, E. White, G. White, H.J.W. White, J. White, J.
Willard, L.F. Willeter, J.E. William, J. Williams, C. Williams, F.M. Williams, G.A. Williams, J. Wilmington, F.H. Wilmot, D.G. Wilshaw, J.T.
Wood, R.G.P. Wood, S. Wood, W.J. Woodcock, A.G. Woodford, G. Woolgar, D.R. Wormald, J.L. Wren, V.G. Wright

14TH OCTOBER 1939

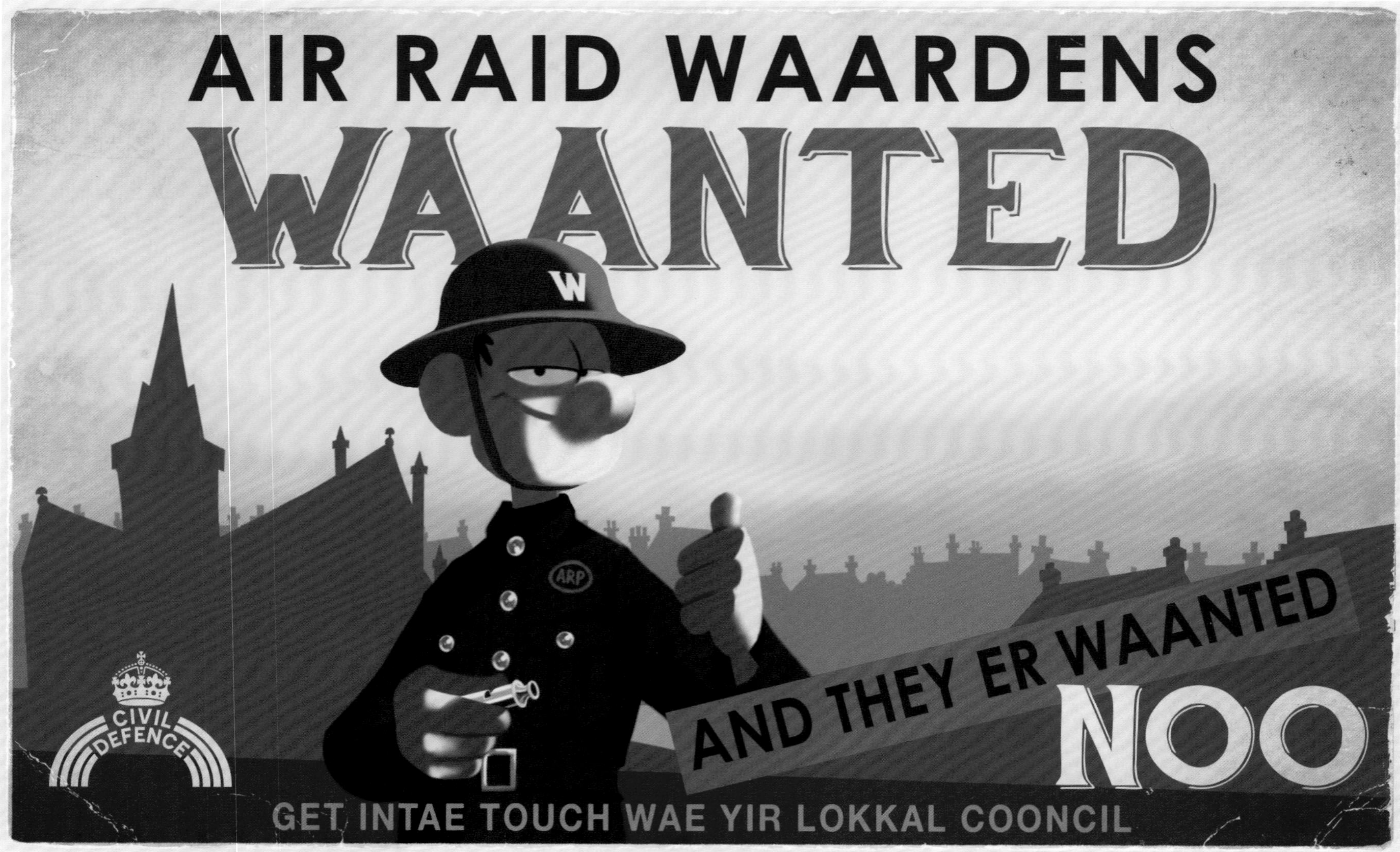
AIR RAID WAARDENS
WAANTED
W
ARP
AND THEY ER WAANTED
NOO
CIVIL DEFENCE
GET INTAE TOUCH WAE YIR LOKKAL COONCIL

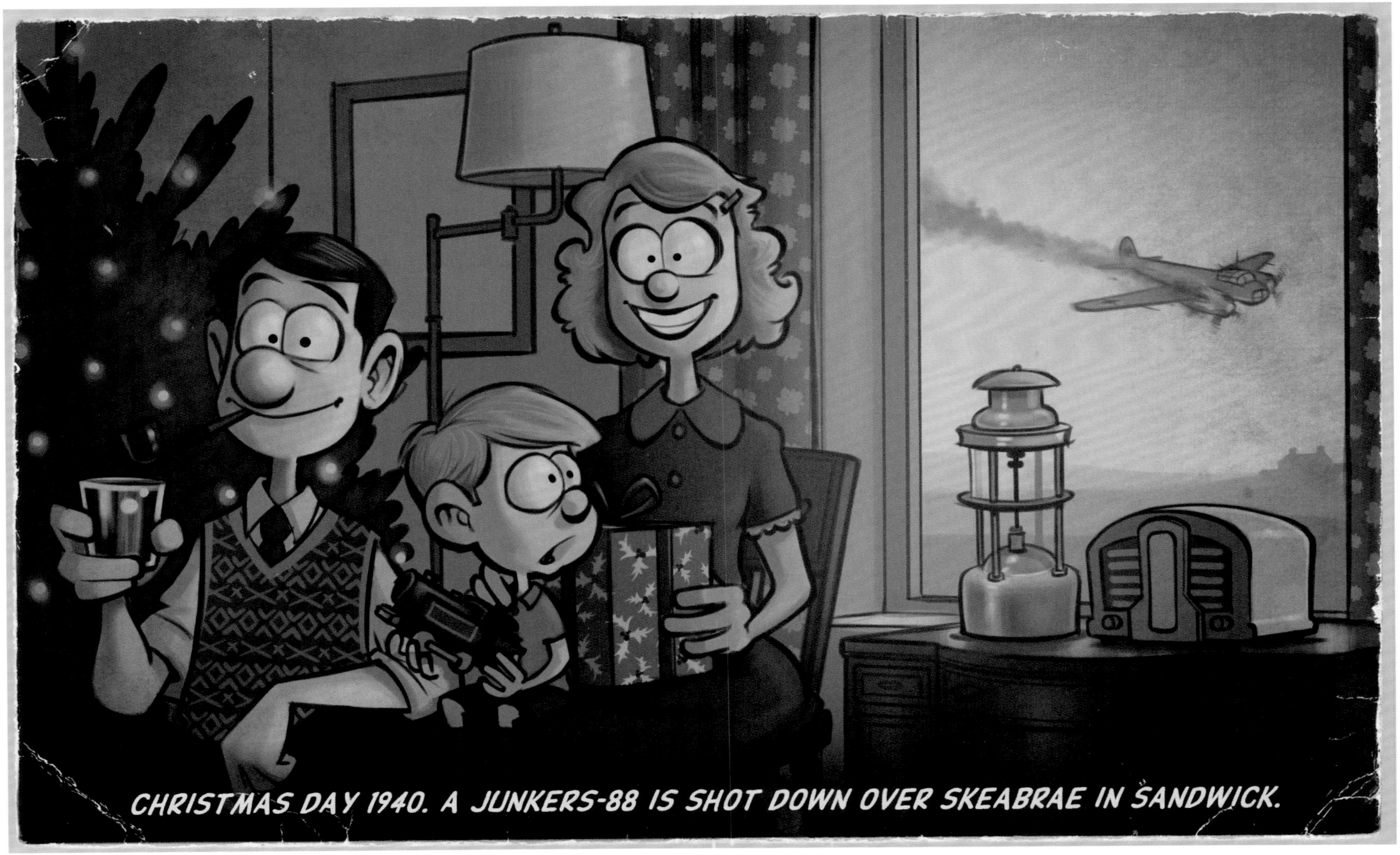
CHRISTMAS DAY 1940. A JUNKERS-88 IS SHOT DOWN OVER SKEABRAE IN SANDWICK.

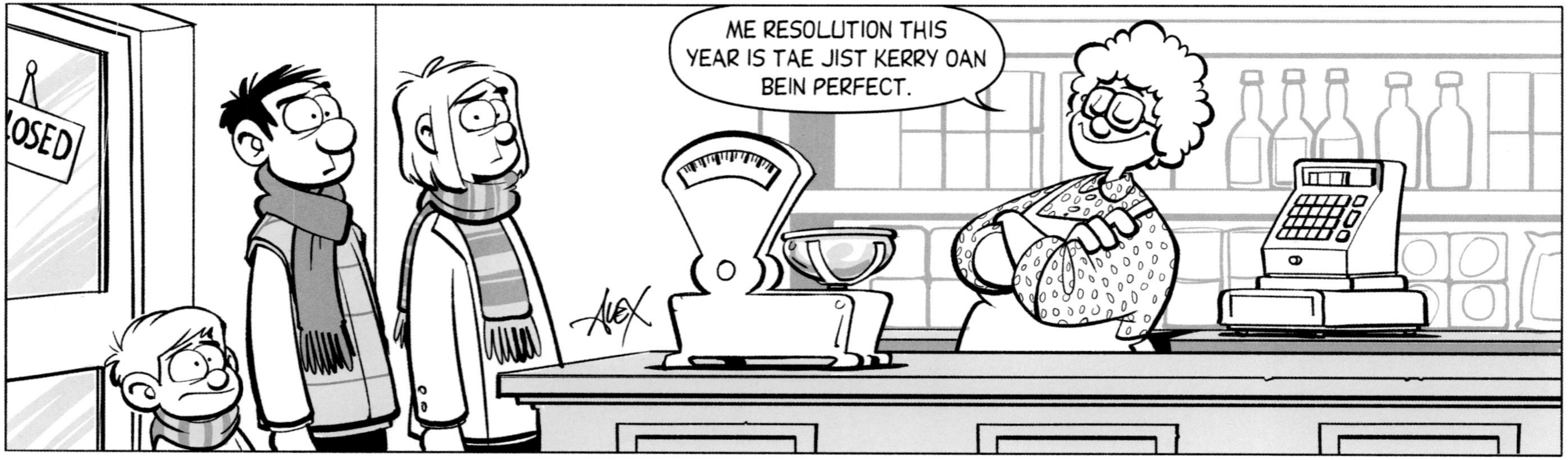
LOSED
ME RESOLUTION THIS YEAR IS TAE JIST KERRY OAN BEIN PERFECT.
ALEX

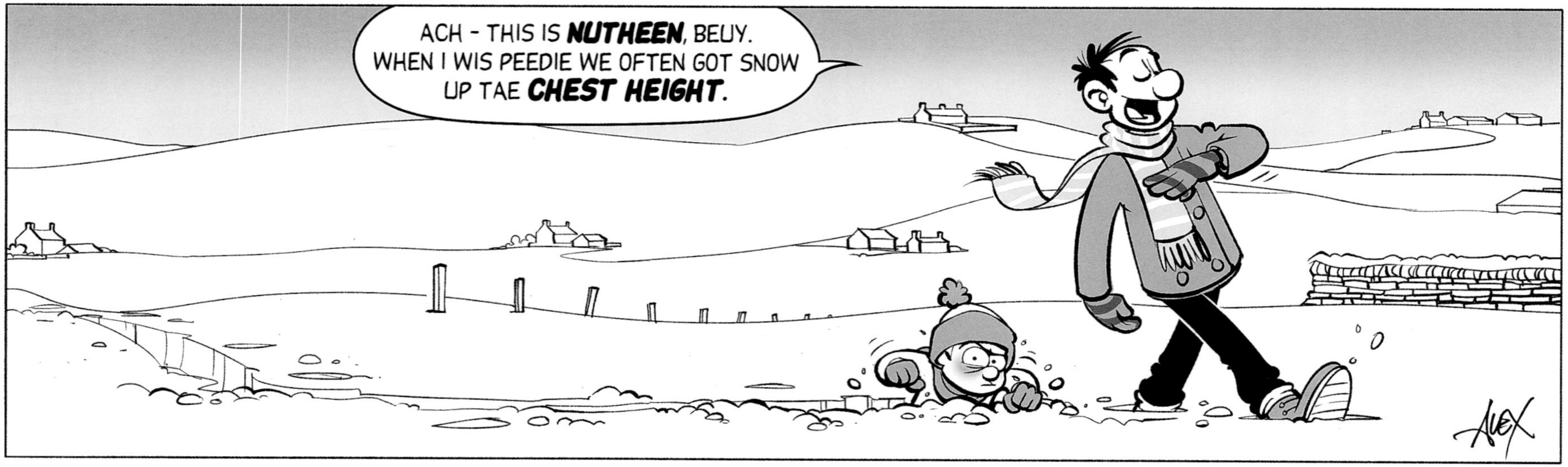
ACH - THIS IS NUTHEEN, BEUY. WHEN I WIS PEEDIE WE OFTEN GOT SNOW UP TAE CHEST HEIGHT.
ALEX

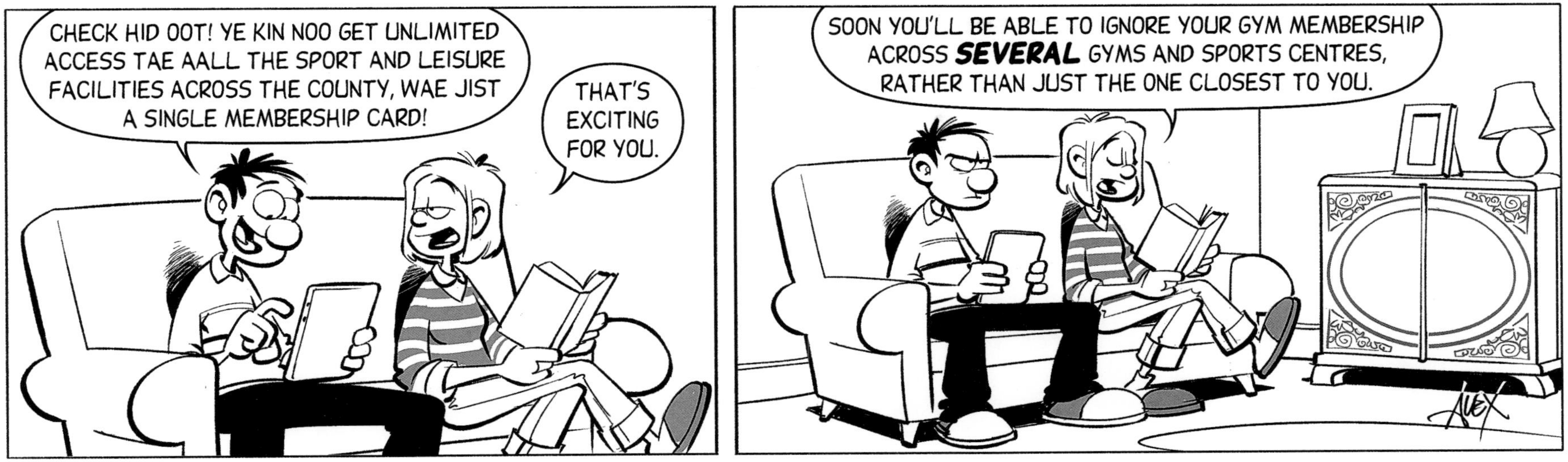
CHECK HID OOT! YE KIN NOO GET UNLIMITED ACCESS TAE AALL THE SPORT AND LEISURE FACILITIES ACROSS THE COUNTY, WAE JIST A SINGLE MEMBERSHIP CARD!
THAT'S EXCITING FOR YOU.
SOON YOU'LL BE ABLE TO IGNORE YOUR GYM MEMBERSHIP ACROSS **SEVERAL** GYMS AND SPORTS CENTRES, RATHER THAN JUST THE ONE CLOSEST TO YOU.
ALEX

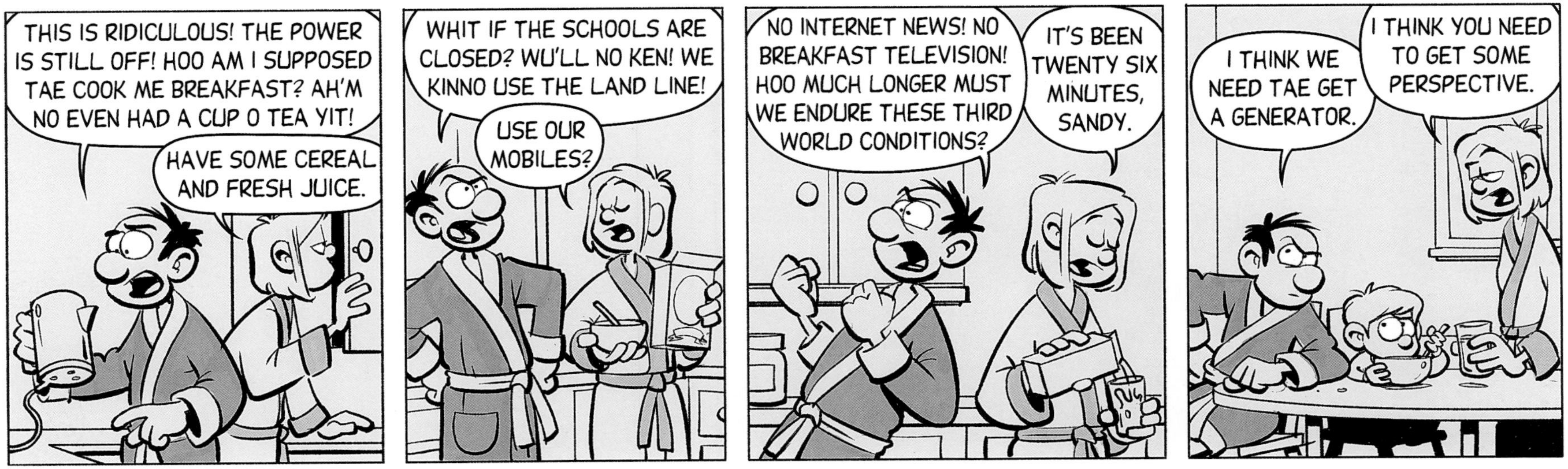
THIS IS RIDICULOUS! THE POWER IS STILL OFF! HOO AM I SUPPOSED TAE COOK ME BREAKFAST? AH'M NO EVEN HAD A CUP O TEA YIT!
HAVE SOME CEREAL AND FRESH JUICE.
WHIT IF THE SCHOOLS ARE CLOSED? WU'LL NO KEN! WE KINNO USE THE LAND LINE!
USE OUR MOBILES?
NO INTERNET NEWS! NO BREAKFAST TELEVISION! HOO MUCH LONGER MUST WE ENDURE THESE THIRD WORLD CONDITIONS?
IT'S BEEN TWENTY SIX MINUTES, SANDY.
I THINK WE NEED TAE GET A GENERATOR.
I THINK YOU NEED TO GET SOME PERSPECTIVE.

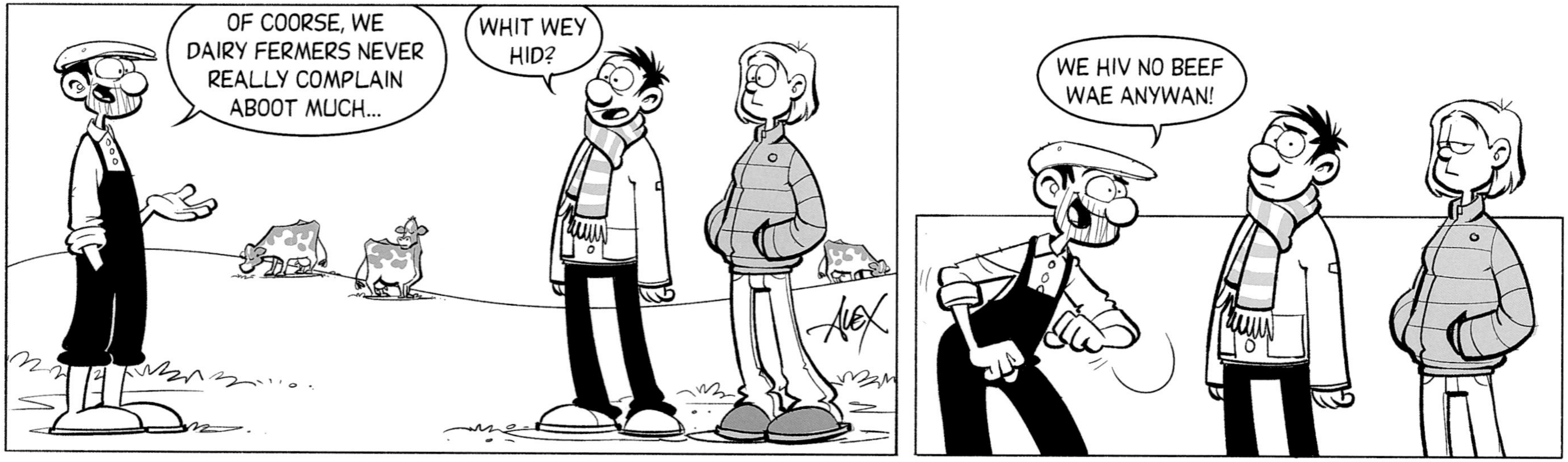
OF COORSE, WE DAIRY FERMERS NEVER REALLY COMPLAIN ABOOT MUCH...
WHIT WEY HID?
ALEX
WE HIV NO BEEF WAE ANYWAN!

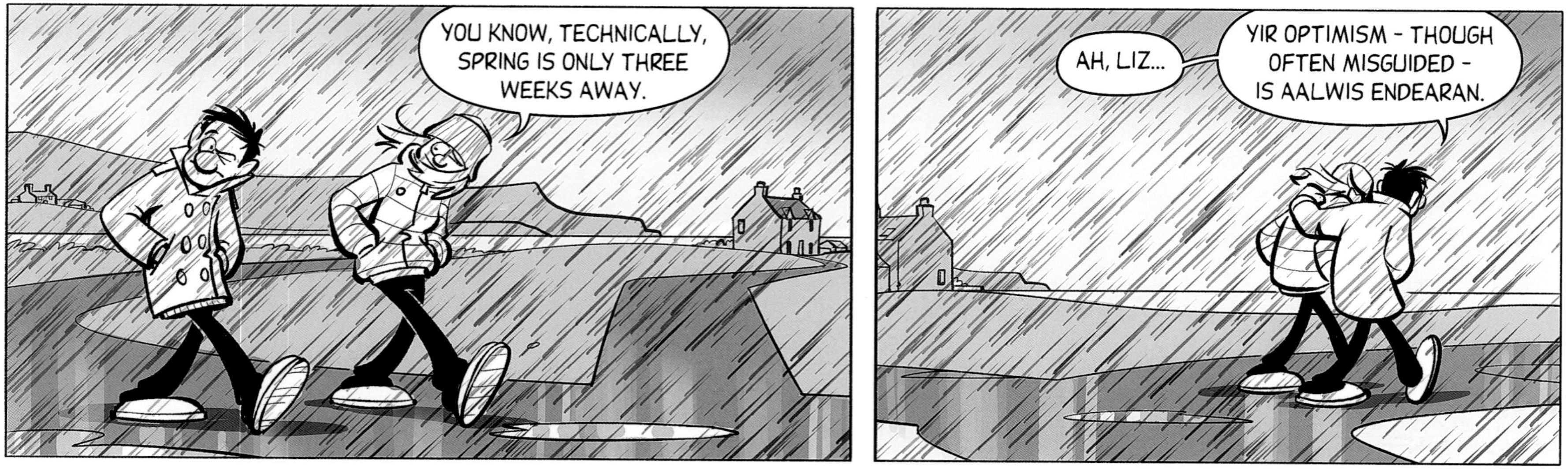
YOU KNOW, TECHNICALLY, SPRING IS ONLY THREE WEEKS AWAY.
AH, LIZ...
YIR OPTIMISM - THOUGH OFTEN MISGUIDED - IS AALWIS ENDEARAN.

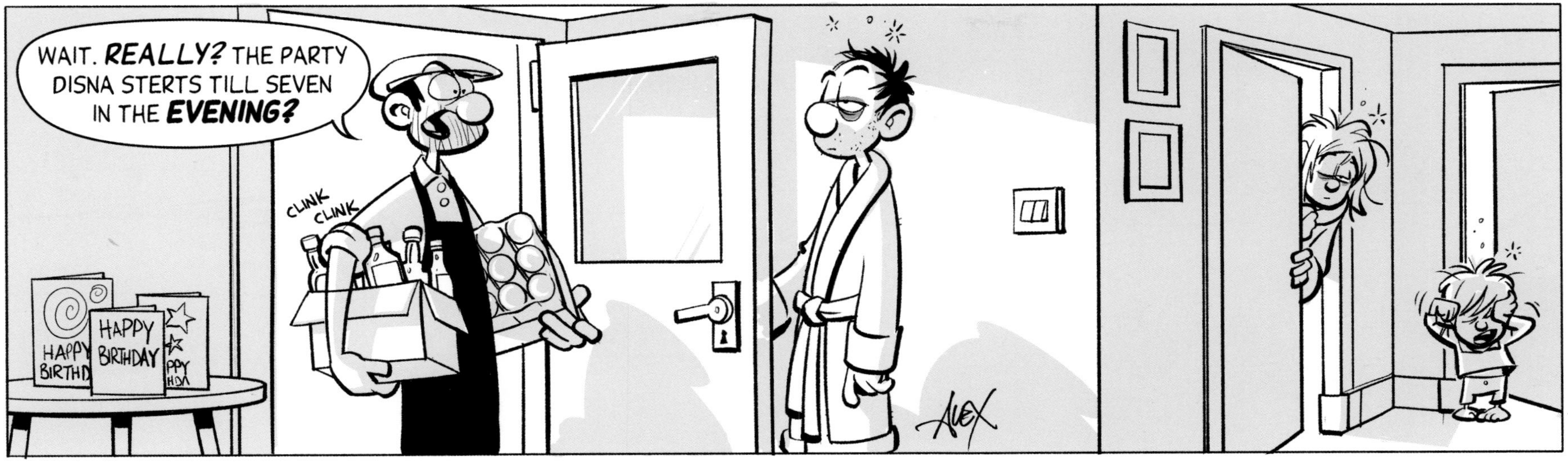
WAIT. REALLY? THE PARTY DISNA STERTS TILL SEVEN IN THE EVENING?
CLINK CLINK
HAPPY BIRTHDAY
HAPPY BIRTHDAY
ALEX

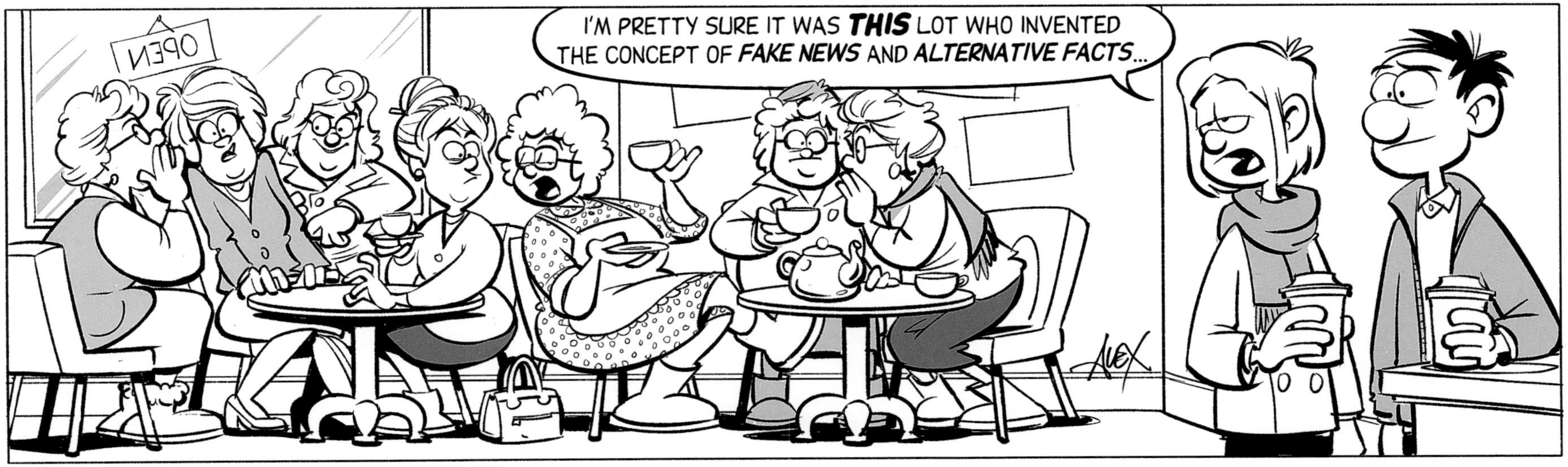
OPEN
I'M PRETTY SURE IT WAS THIS LOT WHO INVENTED THE CONCEPT OF FAKE NEWS AND ALTERNATIVE FACTS...
ALEX

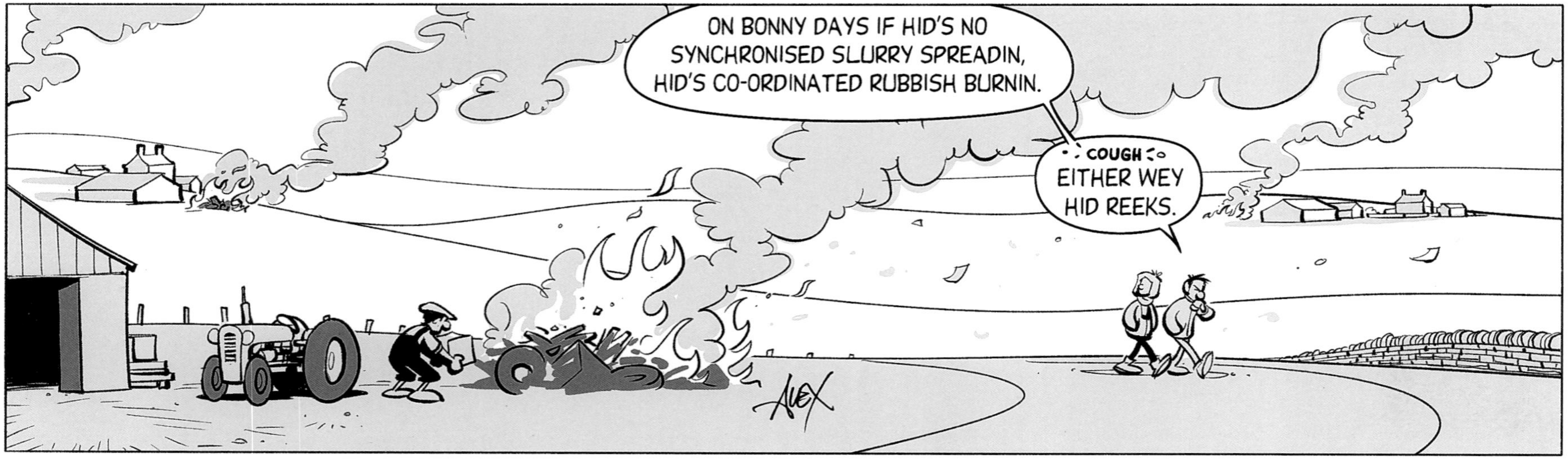
ON BONNY DAYS IF HID'S NO SYNCHRONISED SLURRY SPREADIN, HID'S CO-ORDINATED RUBBISH BURNIN.
COUGH
EITHER WEY HID REEKS.
ALEX

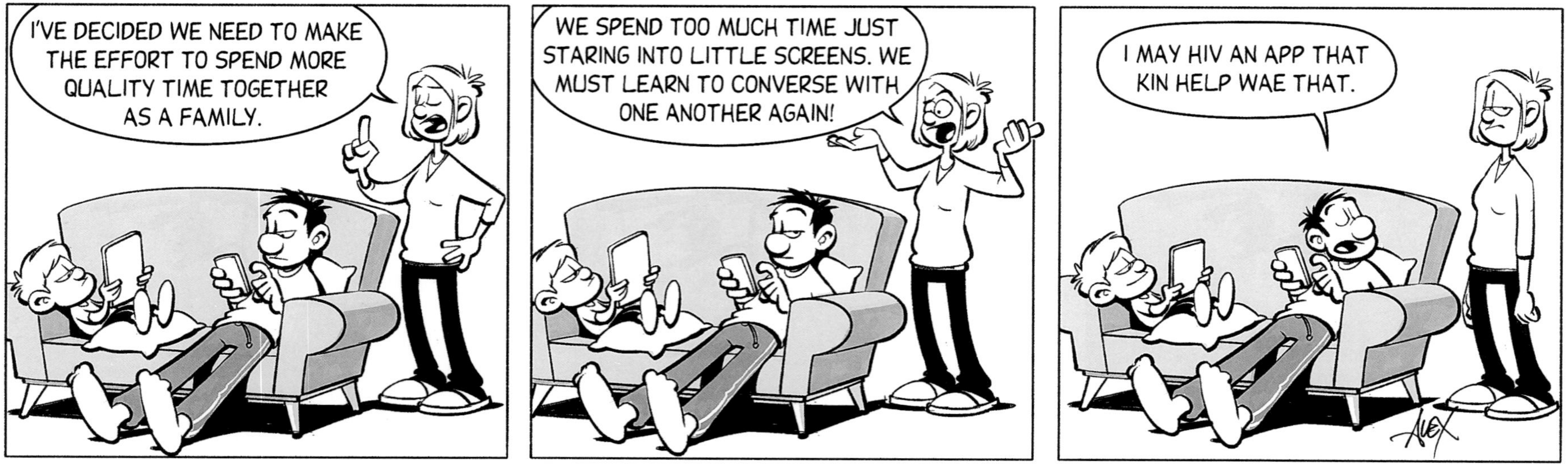
I'VE DECIDED WE NEED TO MAKE THE EFFORT TO SPEND MORE QUALITY TIME TOGETHER AS A FAMILY.
WE SPEND TOO MUCH TIME JUST STARING INTO LITTLE SCREENS. WE MUST LEARN TO CONVERSE WITH ONE ANOTHER AGAIN!
I MAY HIV AN APP THAT KIN HELP WAE THAT.
ALEX

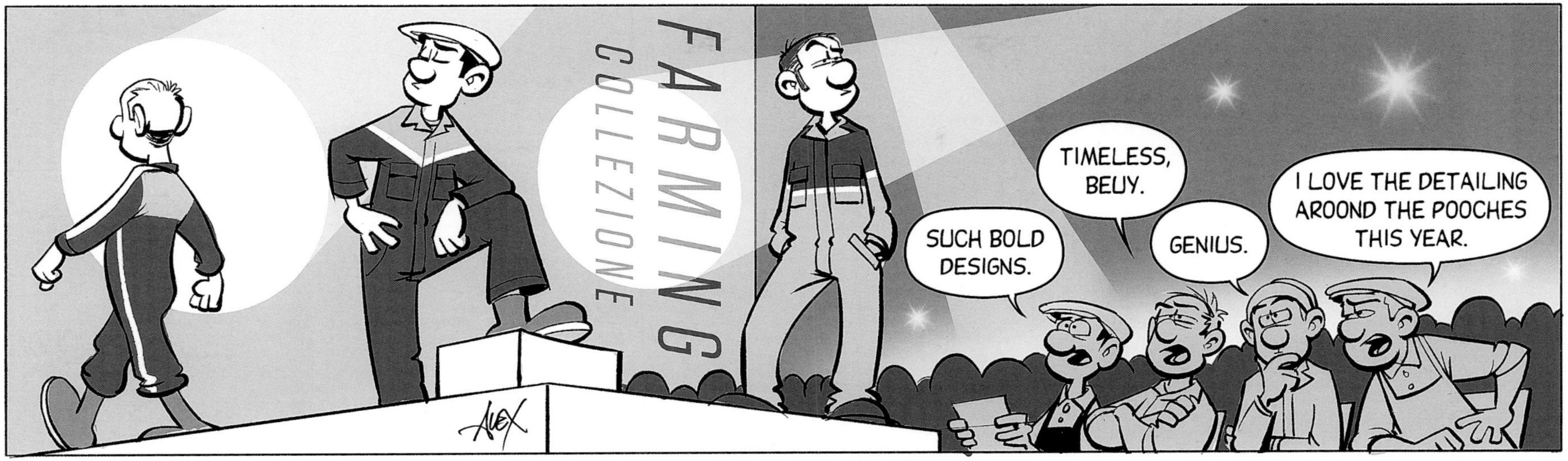
FARMING
COLLEZIONE
SUCH BOLD DESIGNS.
TIMELESS, BEUY.
GENIUS.
I LOVE THE DETAILING AROOND THE POOCHES THIS YEAR.

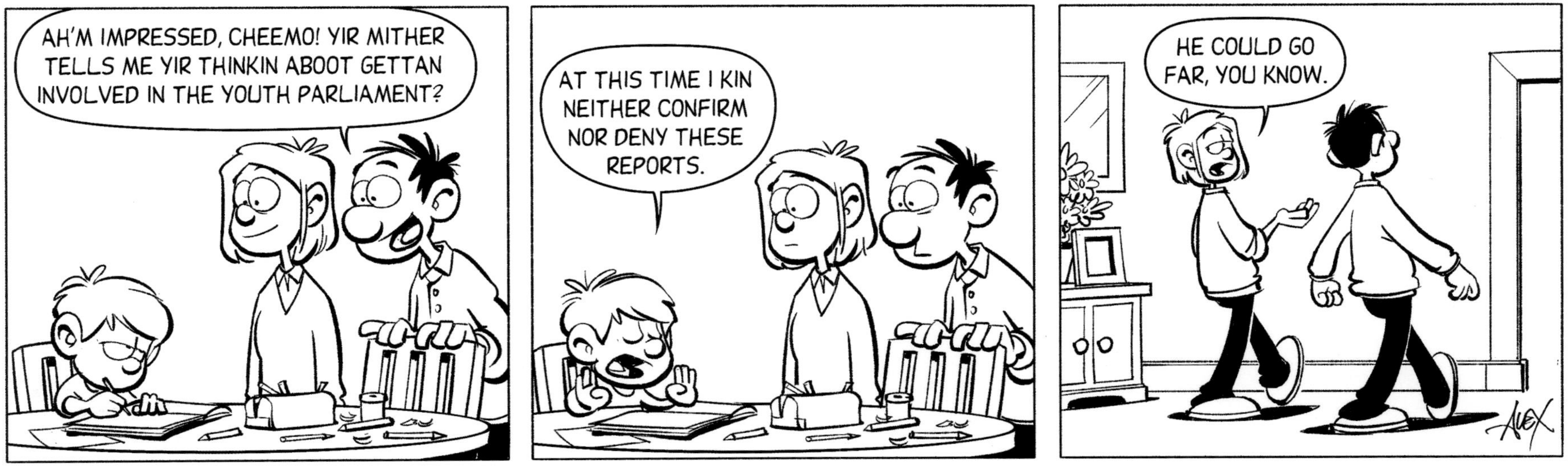
AH'M IMPRESSED, CHEEMO! YIR MITHER TELLS ME YIR THINKIN ABOOT GETTAN INVOLVED IN THE YOUTH PARLIAMENT?
AT THIS TIME I KIN NEITHER CONFIRM NOR DENY THESE REPORTS.
HE COULD GO FAR, YOU KNOW.

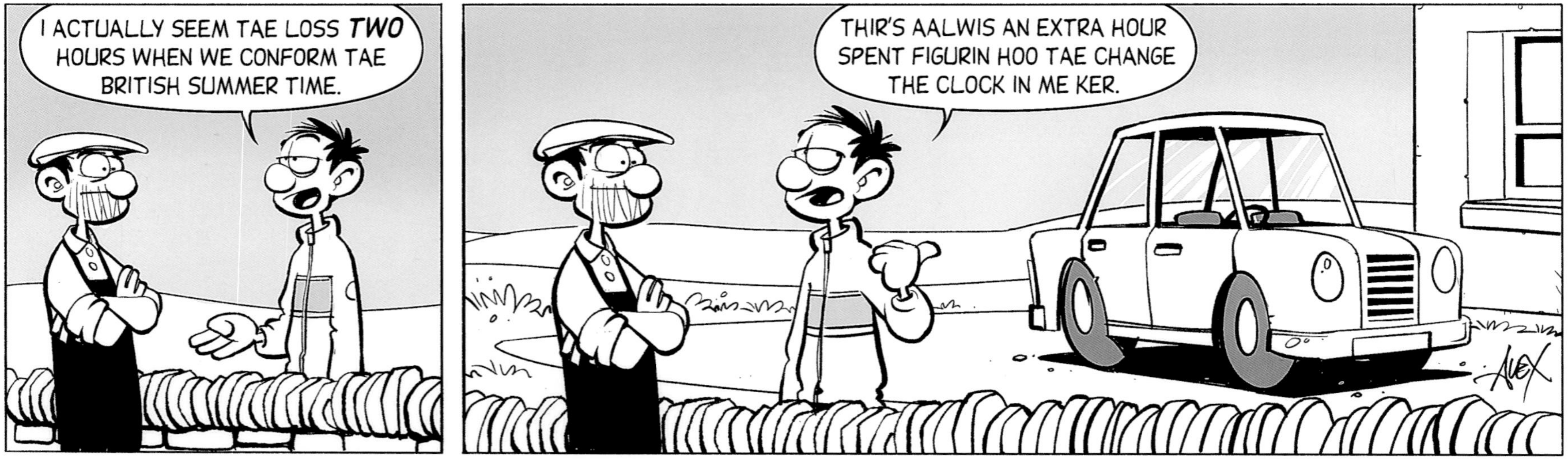
I ACTUALLY SEEM TAE LOSS **TWO** HOURS WHEN WE CONFORM TAE BRITISH SUMMER TIME.
THIR'S AALWIS AN EXTRA HOUR SPENT FIGURIN HOO TAE CHANGE THE CLOCK IN ME KER.
ALEX

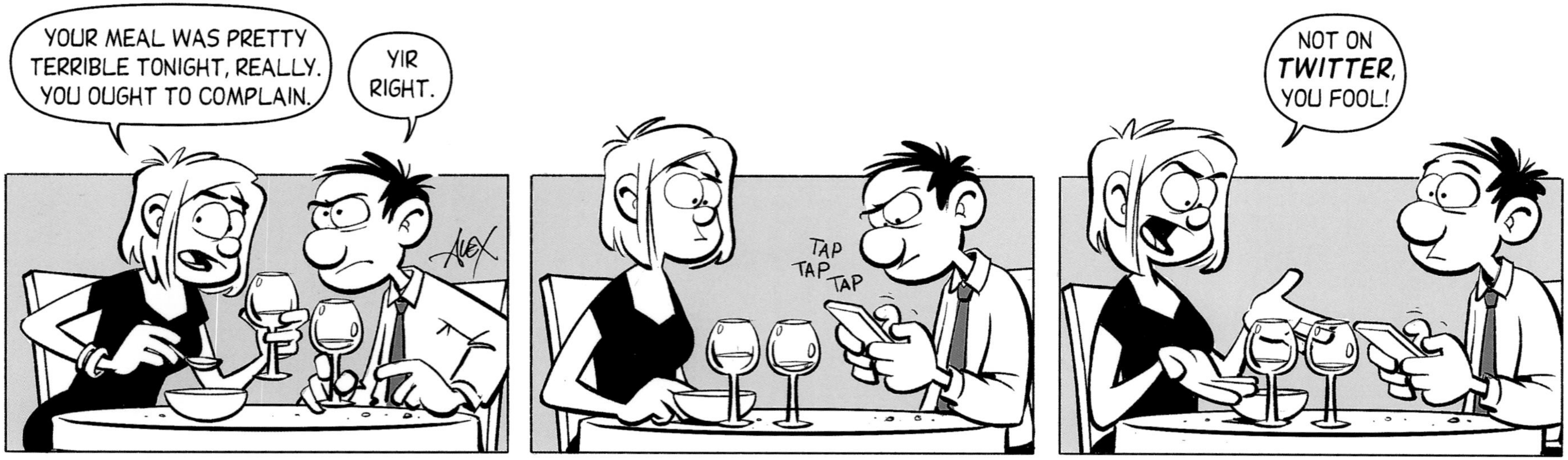
YOUR MEAL WAS PRETTY TERRIBLE TONIGHT, REALLY. YOU OUGHT TO COMPLAIN.
YIR RIGHT.
ALEX
TAP TAP TAP TAP
NOT ON **TWITTER**, YOU FOOL!

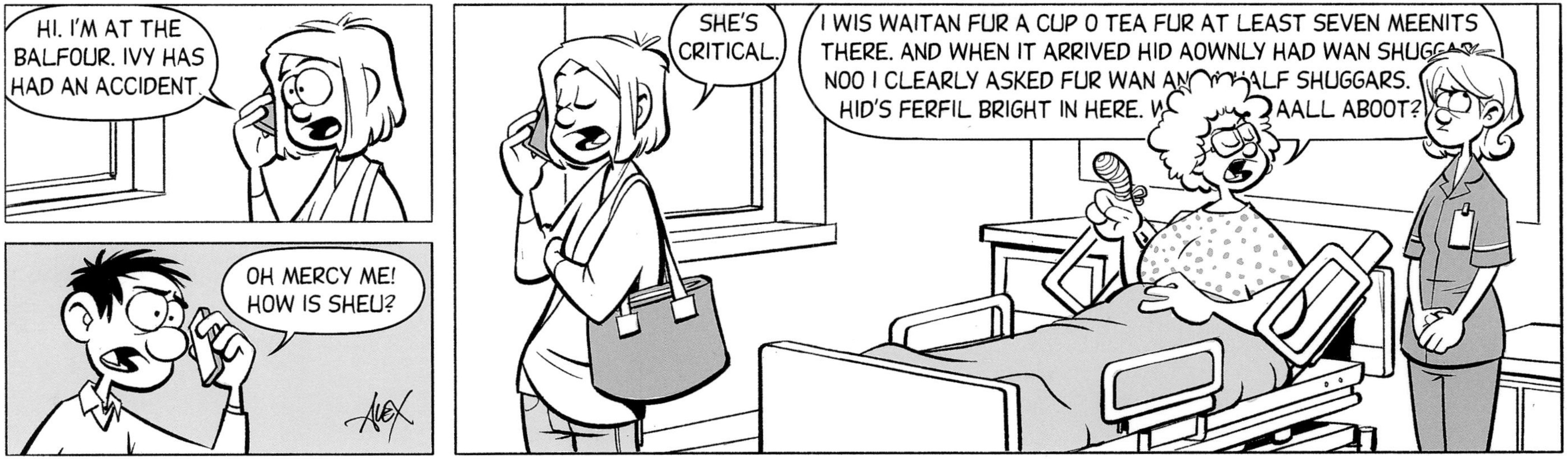
HI. I'M AT THE BALFOUR. IVY HAS HAD AN ACCIDENT.
OH MERCY ME! HOW IS SHEU?
SHE'S CRITICAL.
I WIS WAITAN FUR A CUP O TEA FUR AT LEAST SEVEN MEENITS THERE. AND WHEN IT ARRIVED HID AOWNLY HAD WAN
NOO I CLEARLY ASKED FUR WAN AN
SHUGGARS. HID'S FERFIL BRIGHT IN HERE.
AALL ABOOT?
ALEX

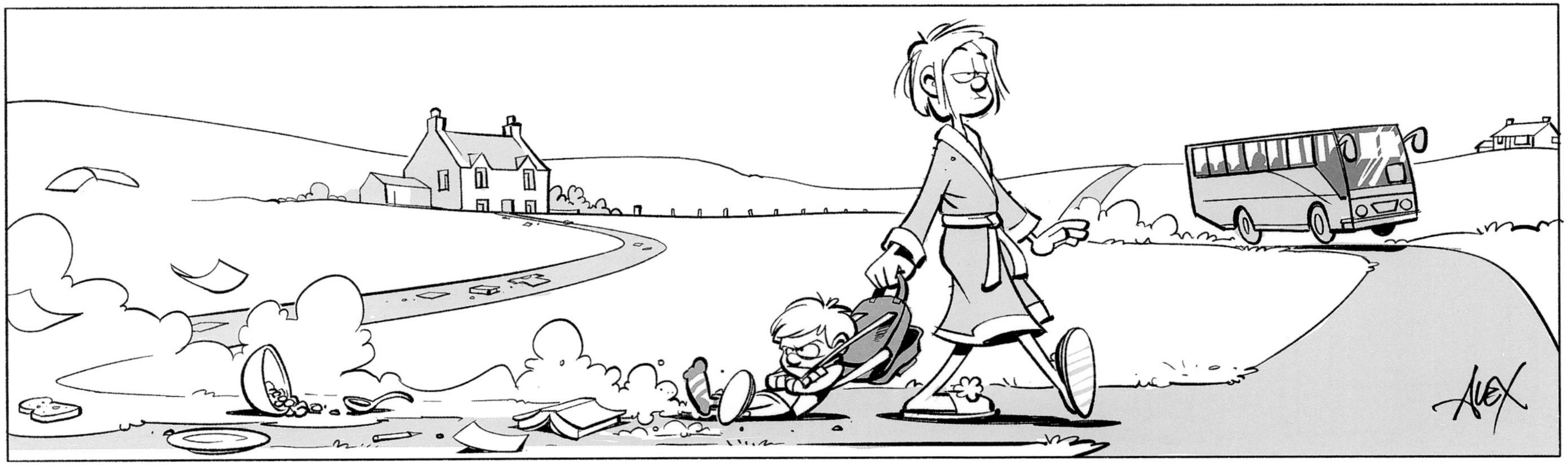
ALEX

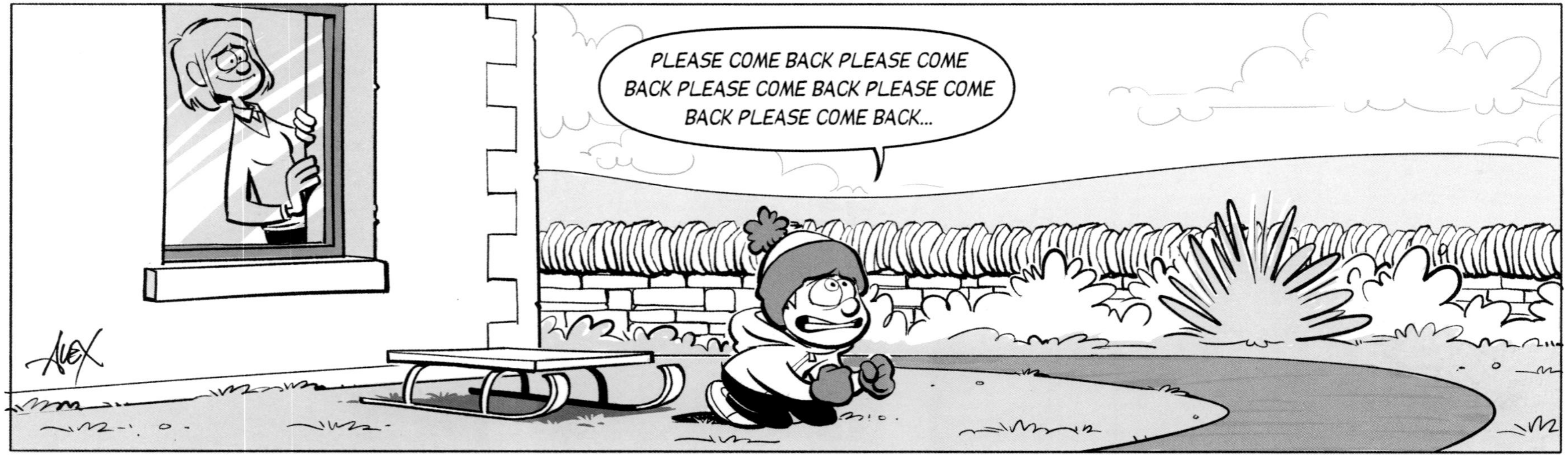
PLEASE COME BACK PLEASE COME BACK PLEASE COME BACK PLEASE COME BACK PLEASE COME BACK...
ALEX

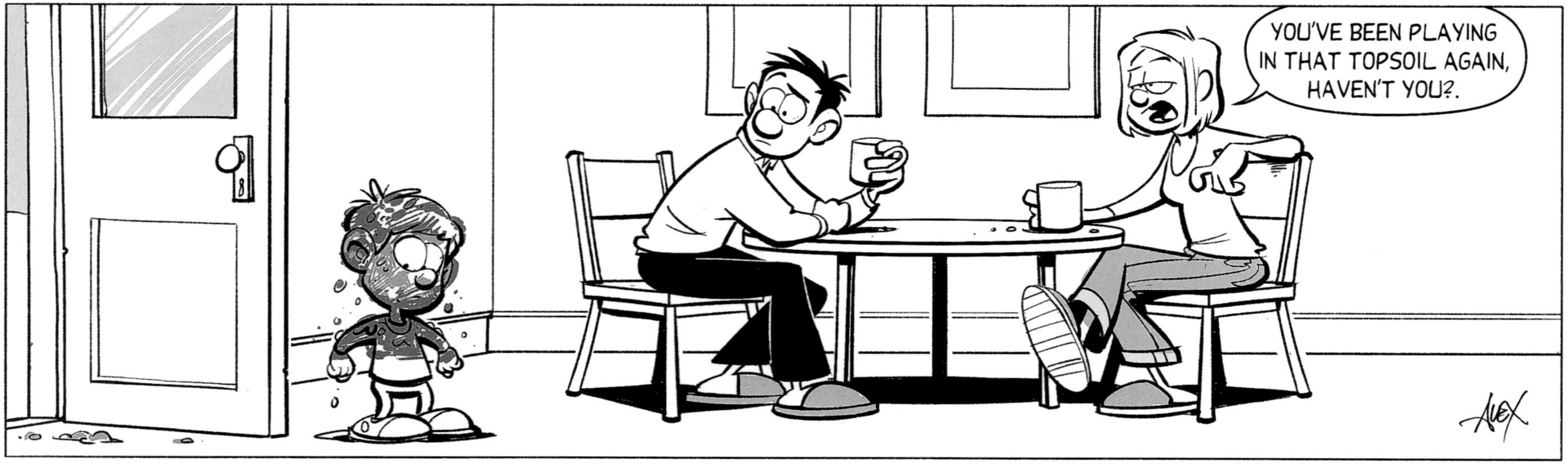
YOU'VE BEEN PLAYING IN THAT TOPSOIL AGAIN, HAVEN'T YOU?.
ALEX

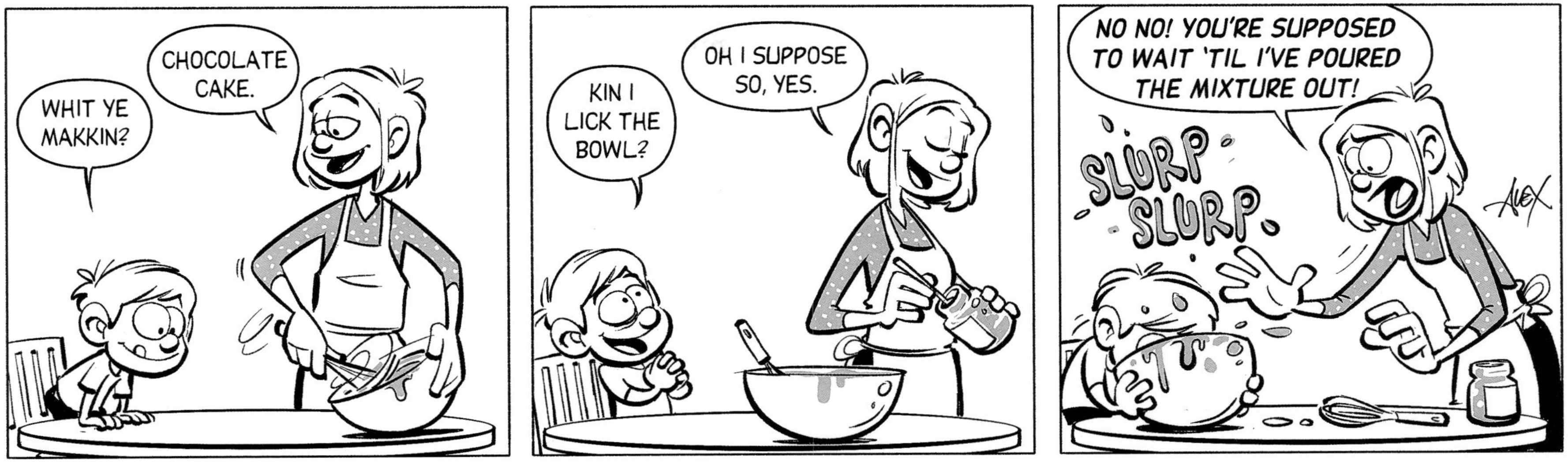
WHIT YE MAKKIN?
CHOCOLATE CAKE.
KIN I LICK THE BOWL?
OH I SUPPOSE SO, YES.
NO NO! YOU'RE SUPPOSED TO WAIT 'TIL I'VE POURED THE MIXTURE OUT!
SLURP SLURP
ALEX

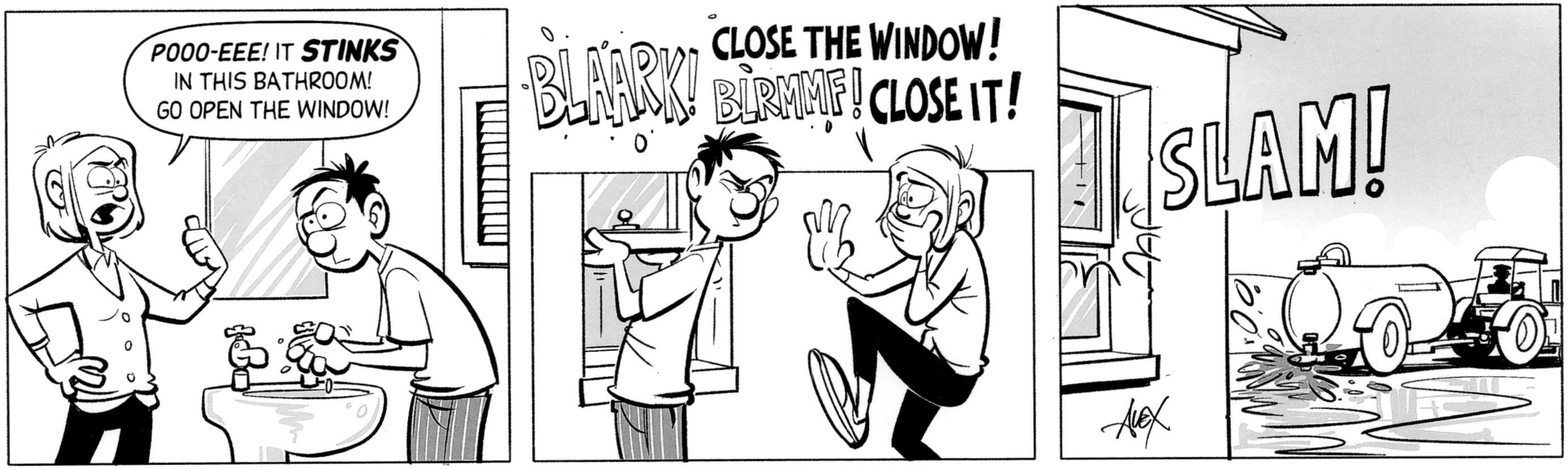
POOO-EEE! IT **STINKS** IN THIS BATHROOM! GO OPEN THE WINDOW!
BLAARK!
CLOSE THE WINDOW!
BLRMMF!
CLOSE IT!
SLAM!
ALEX

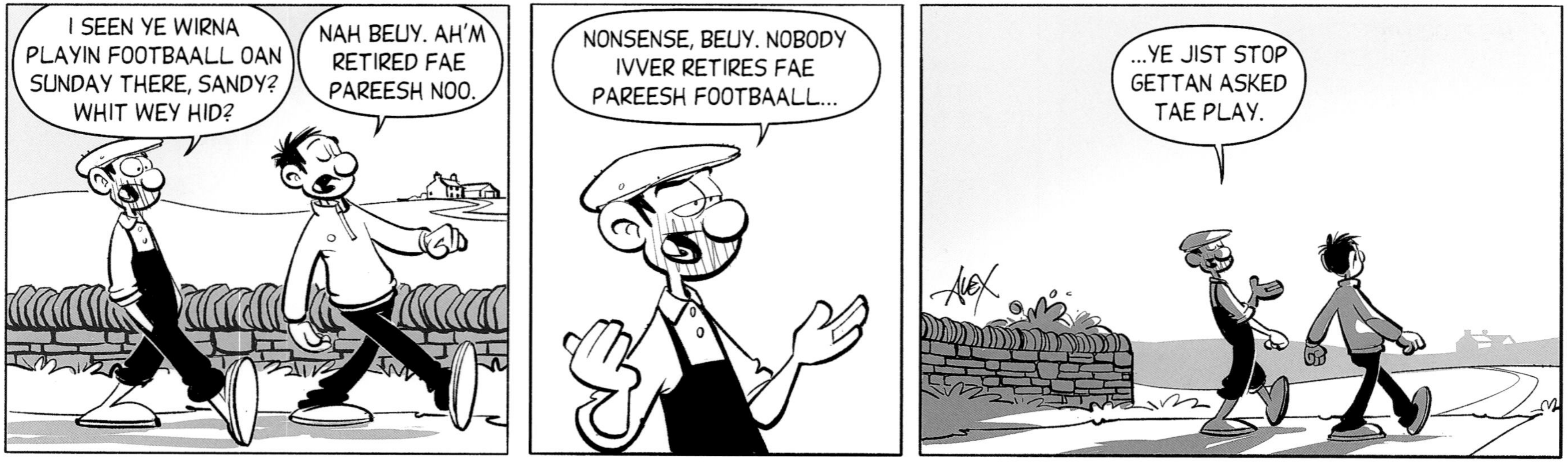
I SEEN YE WIRNA PLAYIN FOOTBAALL OAN SUNDAY THERE, SANDY? WHIT WEY HID?
NAH BEUY. AH'M RETIRED FAE PAREESH NOO.
NONSENSE, BEUY. NOBODY IVVER RETIRES FAE PAREESH FOOTBAALL...
...YE JIST STOP GETTAN ASKED TAE PLAY.
ALEX

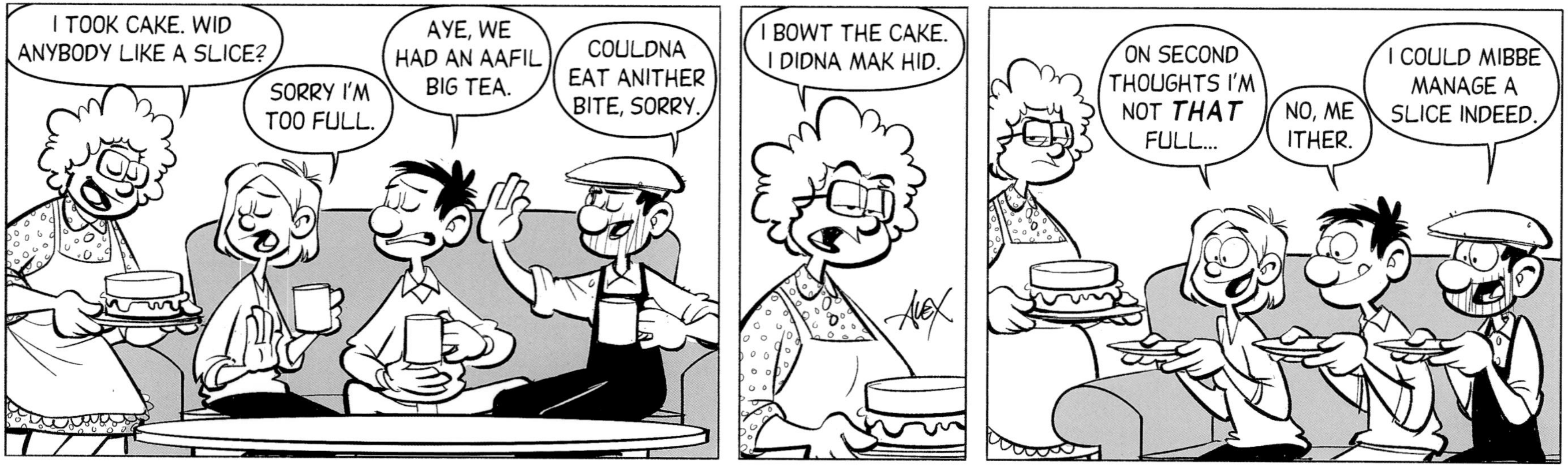
I TOOK CAKE. WID ANYBODY LIKE A SLICE?
SORRY I'M TOO FULL.
AYE, WE HAD AN AAFIL BIG TEA.
COULDNA EAT ANITHER BITE, SORRY.
I BOWT THE CAKE. I DIDNA MAK HID.
ALEX
ON SECOND THOUGHTS I'M NOT THAT FULL...
NO, ME ITHER.
I COULD MIBBE MANAGE A SLICE INDEED.

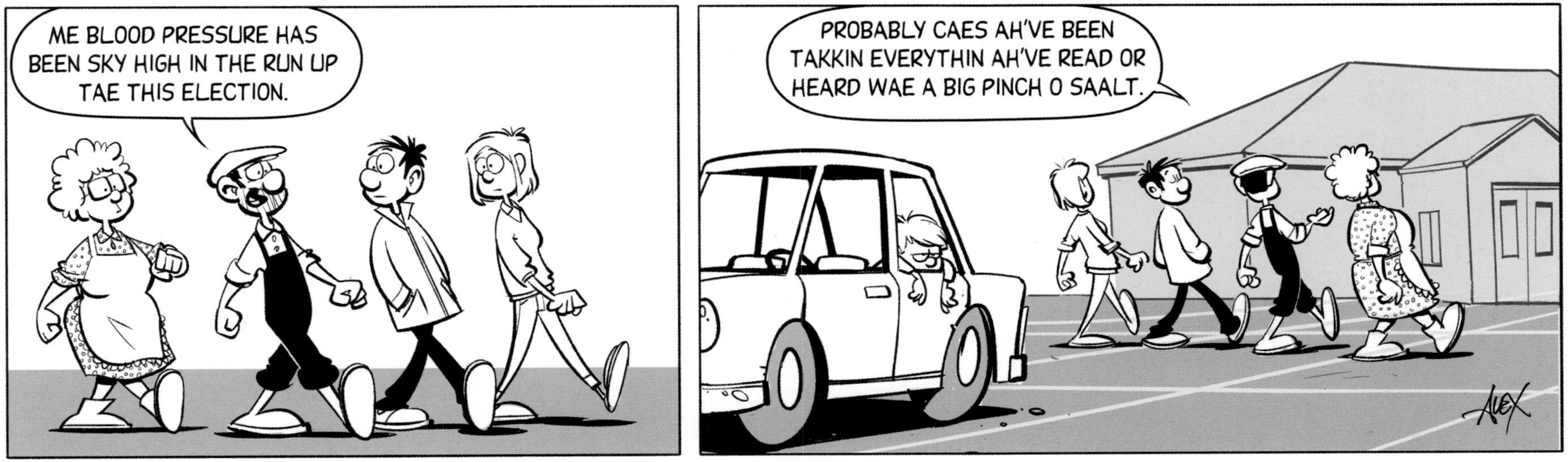
ME BLOOD PRESSURE HAS BEEN SKY HIGH IN THE RUN UP TAE THIS ELECTION.
PROBABLY CAES AH'VE BEEN TAKKIN EVERYTHIN AH'VE READ OR HEARD WAE A BIG PINCH O SAALT.

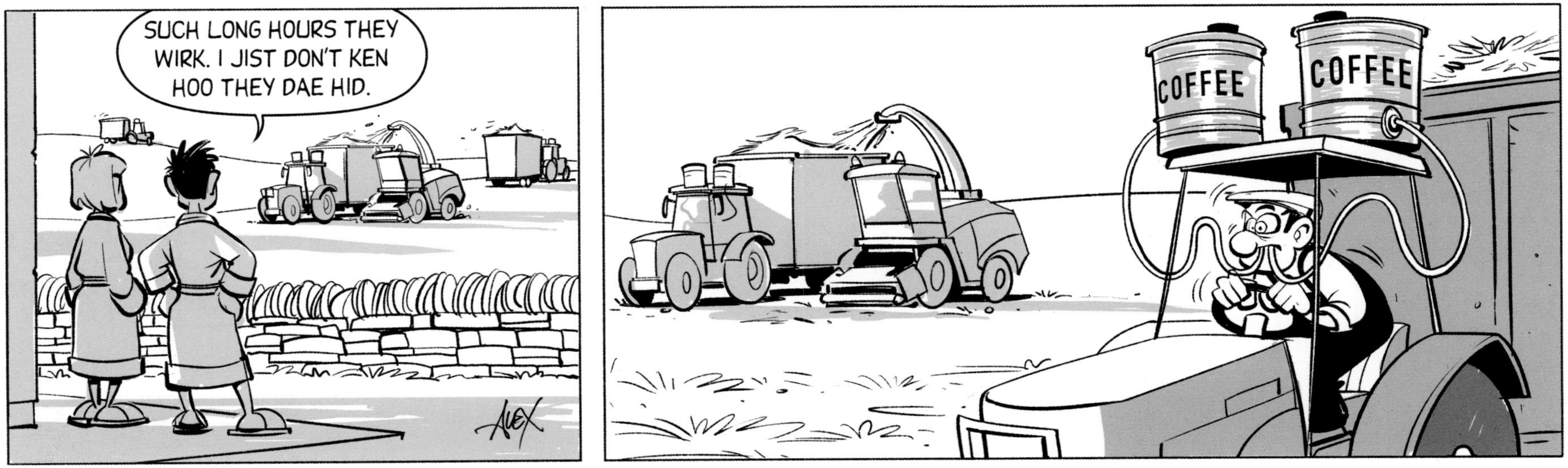
SUCH LONG HOURS THEY WIRK. I JIST DON'T KEN HOO THEY DAE HID.
COFFEE
COFFEE

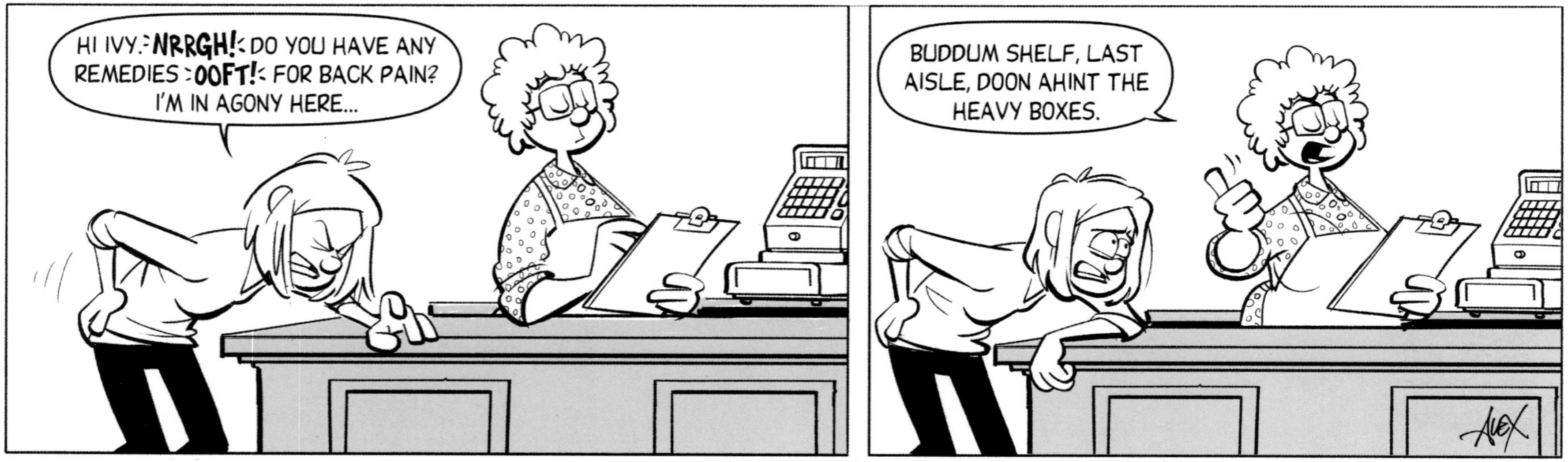
HI IVY. NRRGH! DO YOU HAVE ANY REMEDIES OOFT! FOR BACK PAIN? I'M IN AGONY HERE...
BUDDUM SHELF, LAST AISLE, DOON AHINT THE HEAVY BOXES.

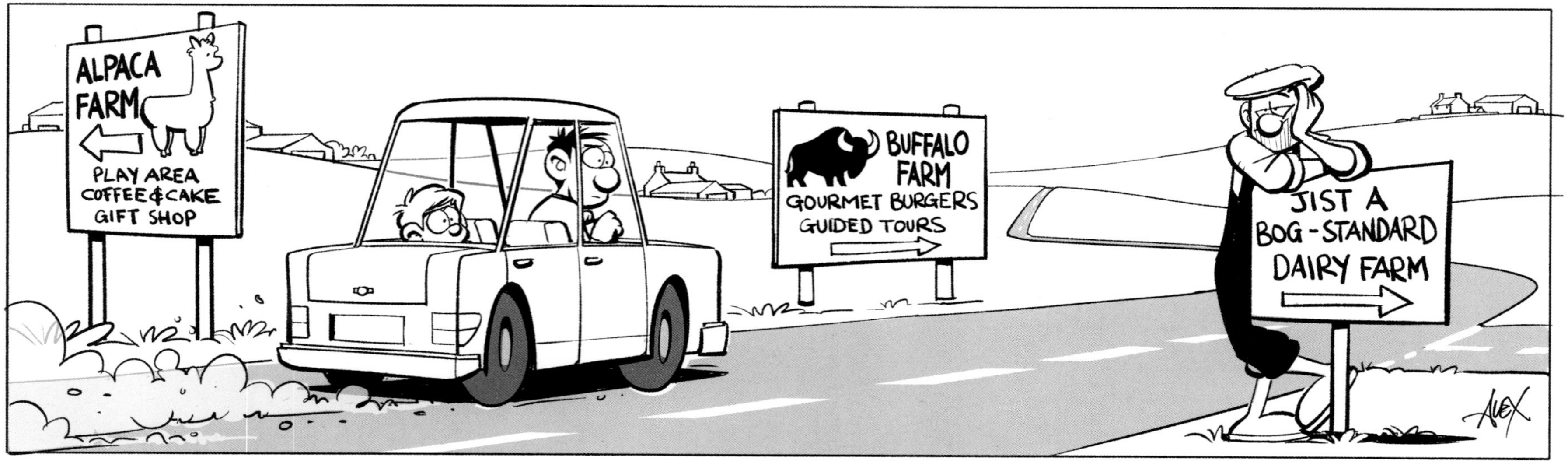
ALPACA FARM
PLAY AREA
COFFEE & CAKE
GIFT SHOP
BUFFALO FARM
GOURMET BURGERS
GUIDED TOURS
JIST A BOG-STANDARD DAIRY FARM

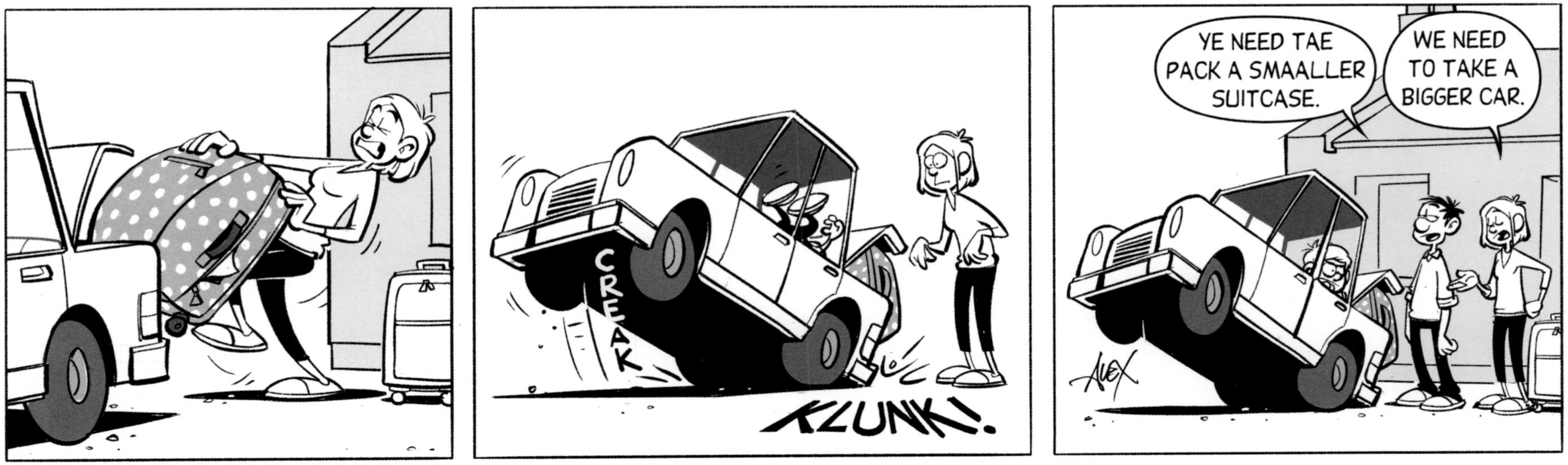
CREAK
KLUNK!
YE NEED TAE PACK A SMAALLER SUITCASE.
WE NEED TO TAKE A BIGGER CAR.
ALEX

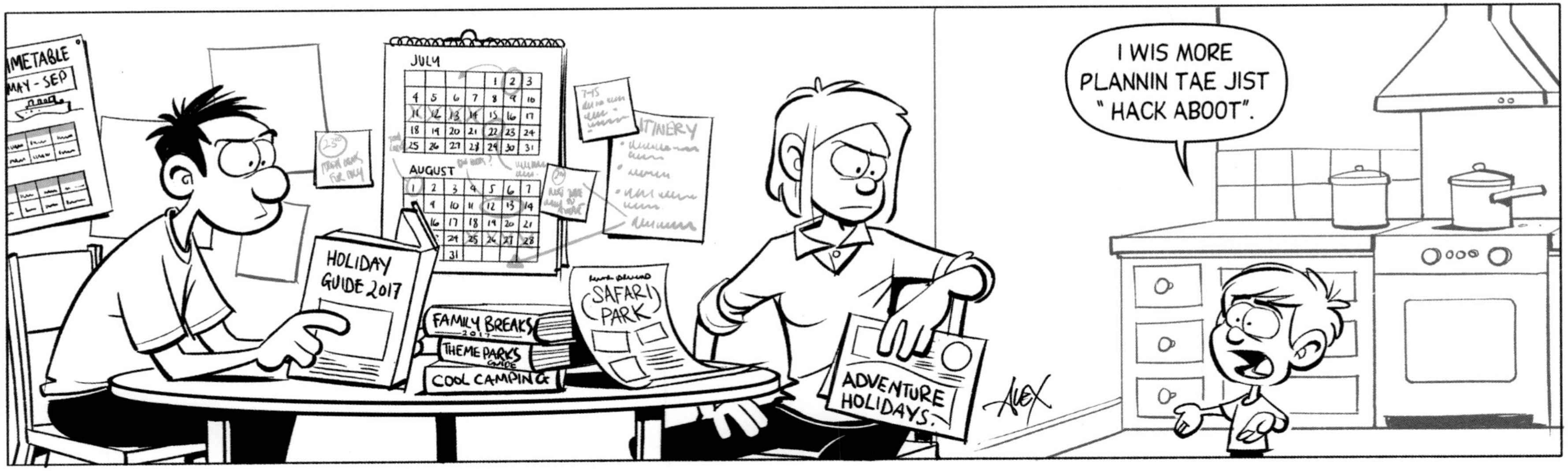
IMETABLE
MAY - SEP
JULY
AUGUST
ITINERY
HOLIDAY GUIDE 2017
FAMILY BREAKS 2017
THEME PARKS GUIDE
COOL CAMPING
SAFARI PARK
ADVENTURE HOLIDAYS
I WIS MORE PLANNIN TAE JIST "HACK ABOOT".
ALEX

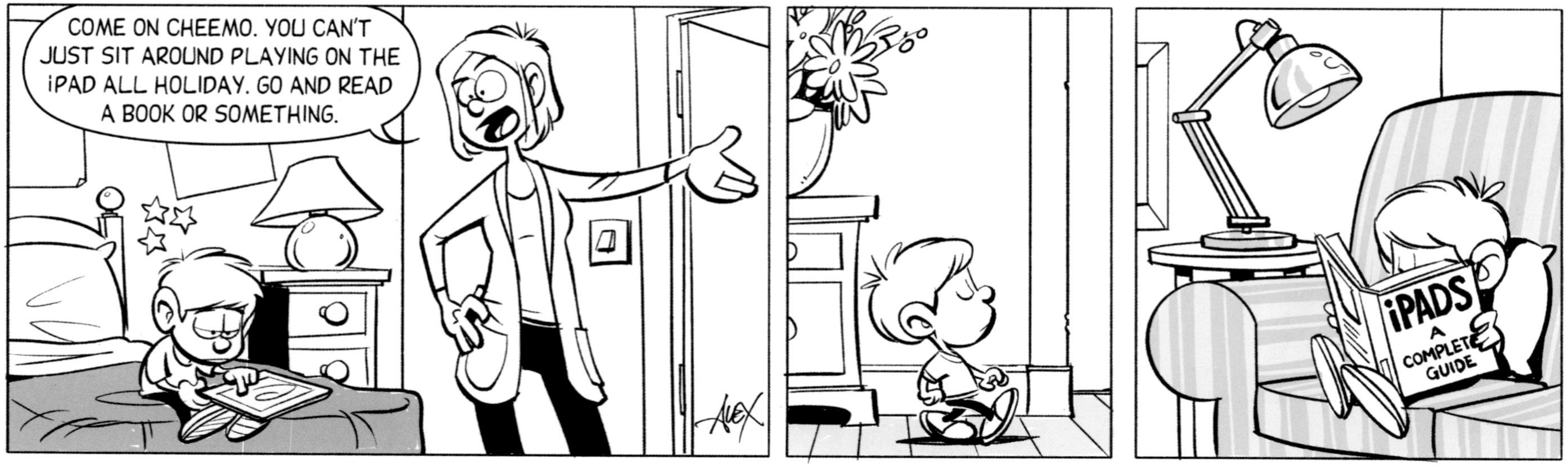
COME ON CHEEMO. YOU CAN'T JUST SIT AROUND PLAYING ON THE iPAD ALL HOLIDAY. GO AND READ A BOOK OR SOMETHING.
ALEX
iPADS
A COMPLETE GUIDE

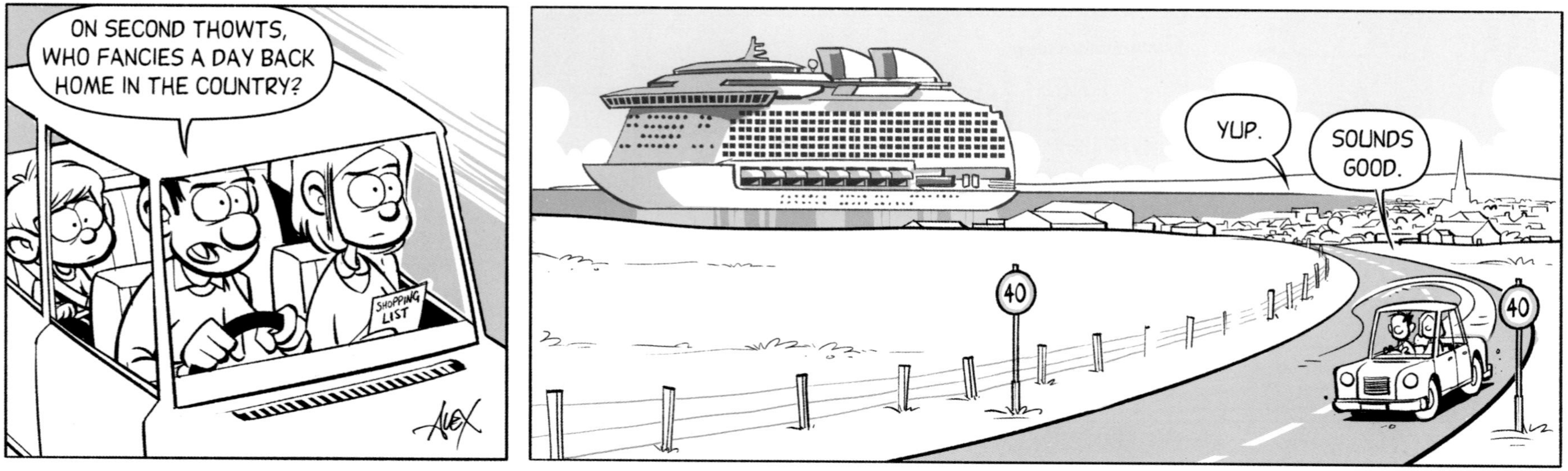
ON SECOND THOWTS, WHO FANCIES A DAY BACK HOME IN THE COUNTRY?
SHOPPING LIST
ALEX
YUP.
SOUNDS GOOD.
40
40

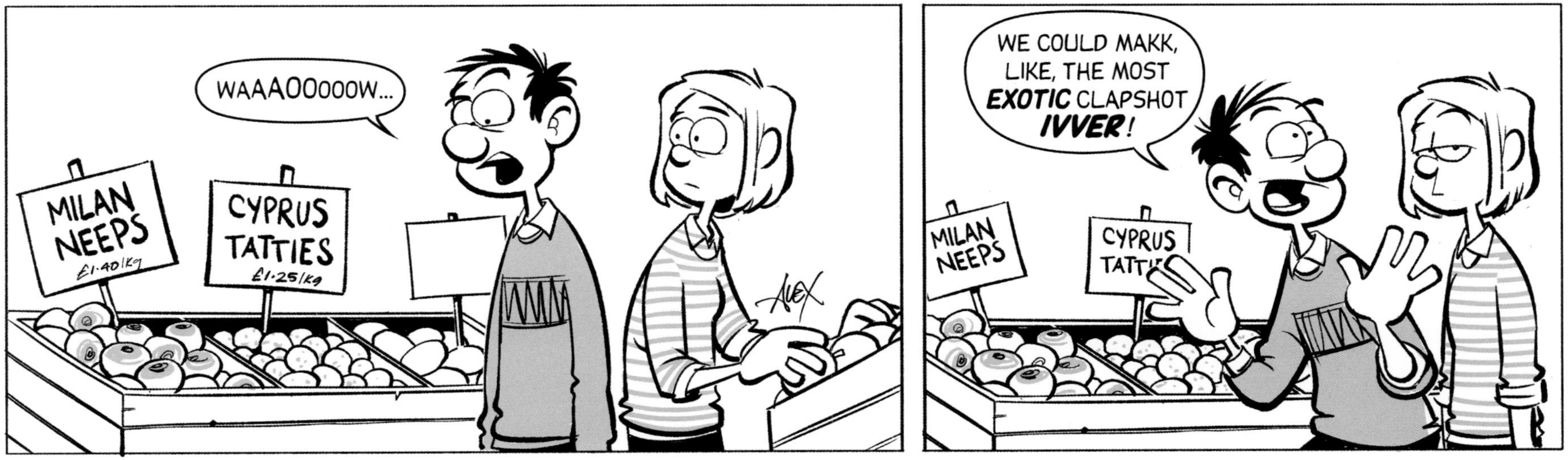
MILAN NEEPS £1·40/kg
CYPRUS TATTIES £1·25/kg
WAAAOOooow...
ALEX
WE COULD MAKK, LIKE, THE MOST **EXOTIC** CLAPSHOT **IVVER**!
MILAN NEEPS
CYPRUS

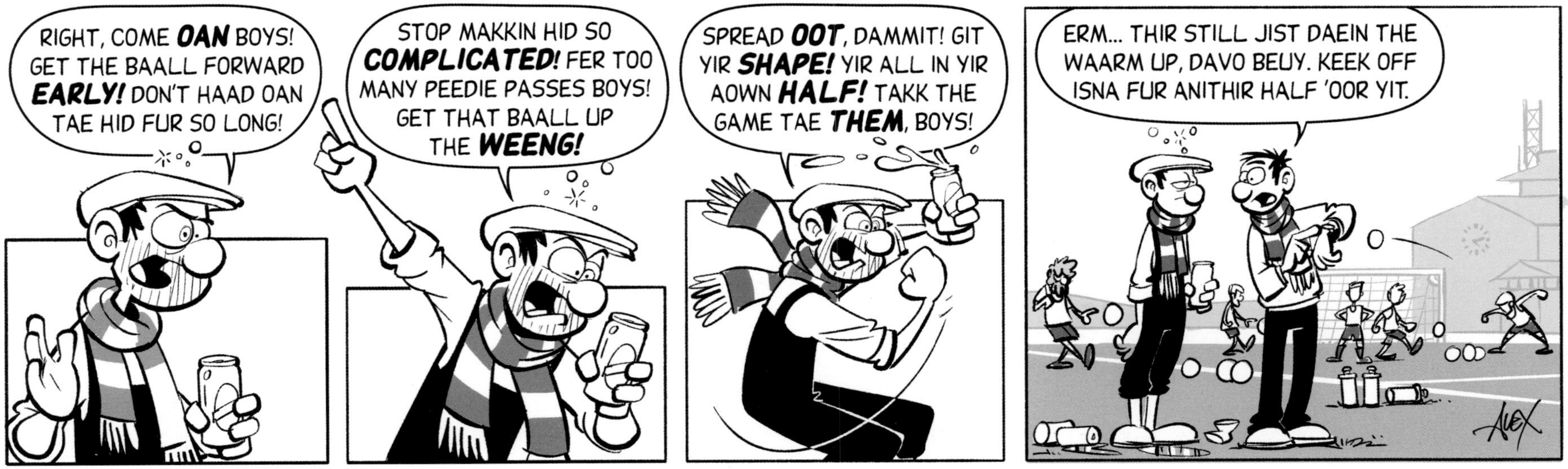
RIGHT, COME **OAN** BOYS! GET THE BAALL FORWARD **EARLY!** DON'T HAAD OAN TAE HID FUR SO LONG!
STOP MAKKIN HID SO **COMPLICATED!** FER TOO MANY PEEDIE PASSES BOYS! GET THAT BAALL UP THE **WEENG!**
SPREAD **OOT**, DAMMIT! GIT YIR **SHAPE!** YIR ALL IN YIR AOWN **HALF!** TAKK THE GAME TAE **THEM**, BOYS!
ERM... THIR STILL JIST DAEIN THE WAARM UP, DAVO BEUY. KEEK OFF ISNA FUR ANITHIR HALF 'OOR YIT.
ALEX

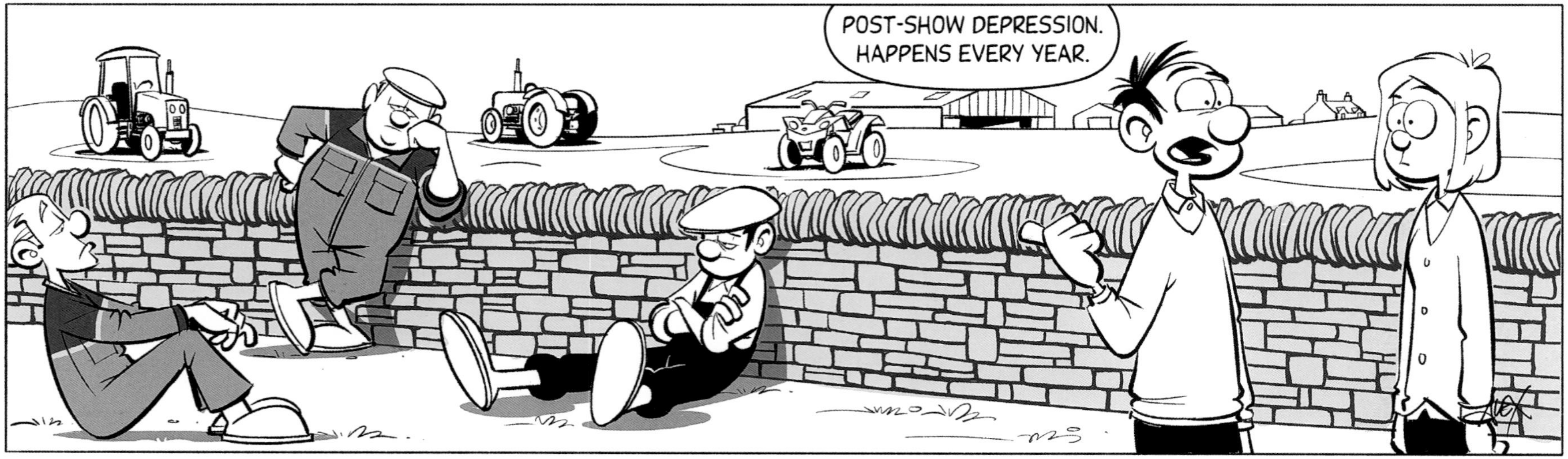
POST-SHOW DEPRESSION. HAPPENS EVERY YEAR.

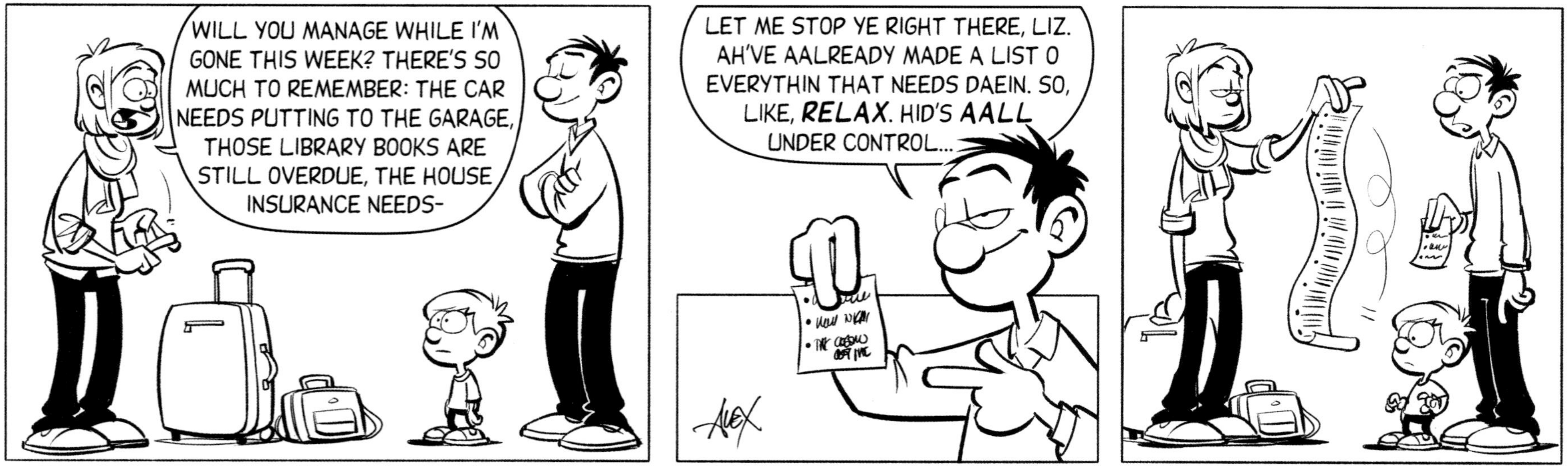
WILL YOU MANAGE WHILE I'M GONE THIS WEEK? THERE'S SO MUCH TO REMEMBER: THE CAR NEEDS PUTTING TO THE GARAGE, THOSE LIBRARY BOOKS ARE STILL OVERDUE, THE HOUSE INSURANCE NEEDS-
LET ME STOP YE RIGHT THERE, LIZ. AH'VE AALREADY MADE A LIST O EVERYTHIN THAT NEEDS DAEIN. SO, LIKE, **RELAX**. HID'S **AALL** UNDER CONTROL...

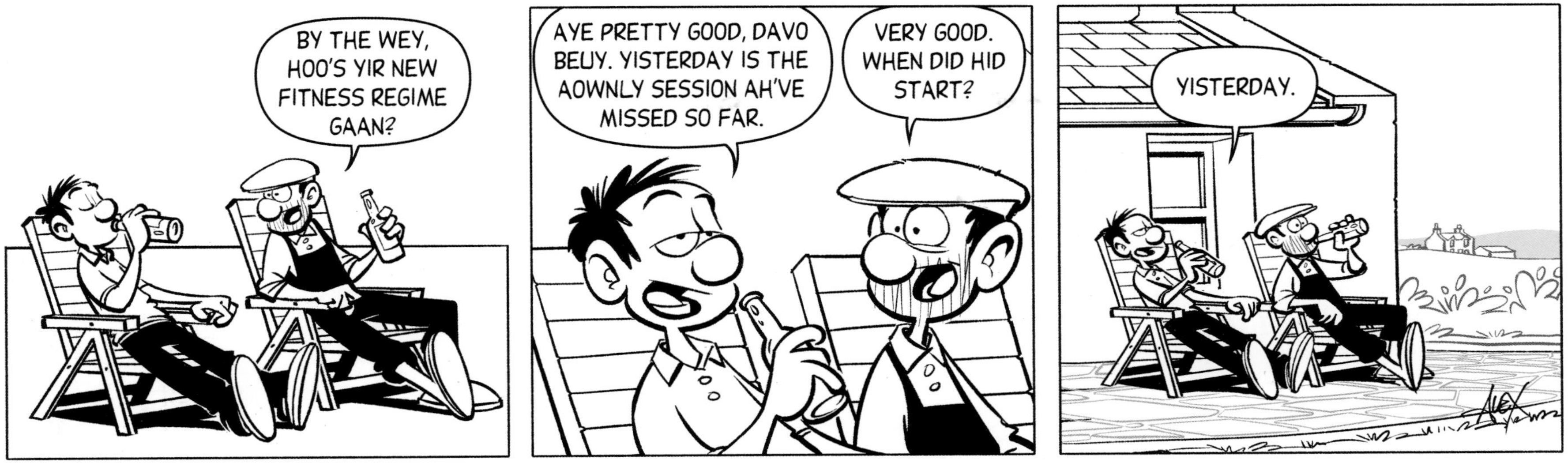
BY THE WEY, HOO'S YIR NEW FITNESS REGIME GAAN?
AYE PRETTY GOOD, DAVO BEUY. YISTERDAY IS THE AOWNLY SESSION AH'VE MISSED SO FAR.
VERY GOOD. WHEN DID HID START?
YISTERDAY.

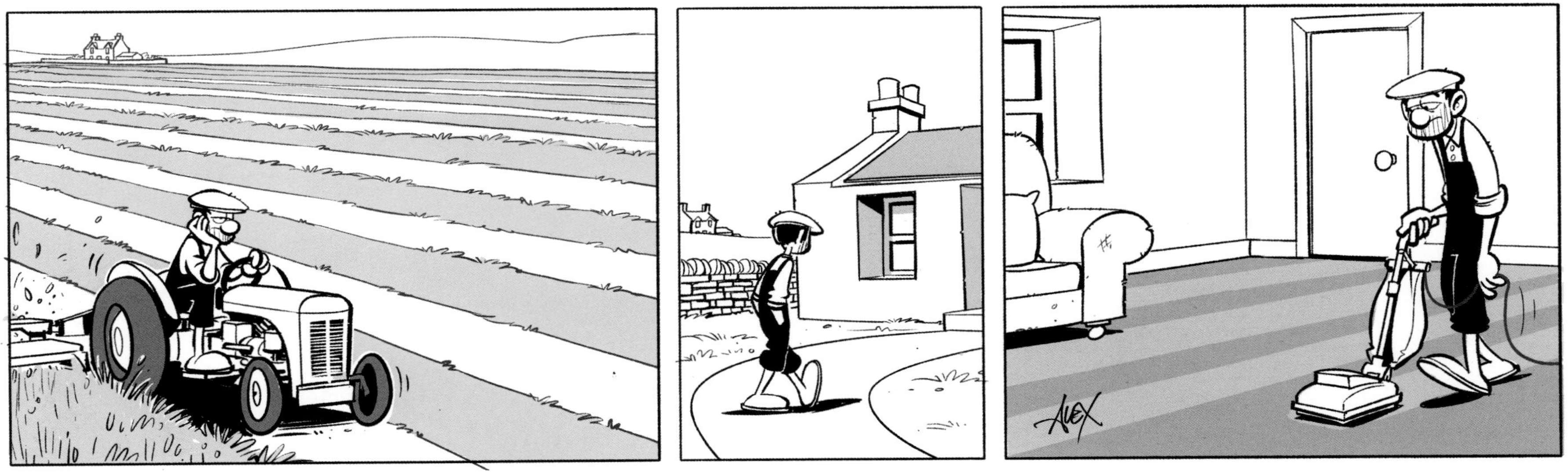

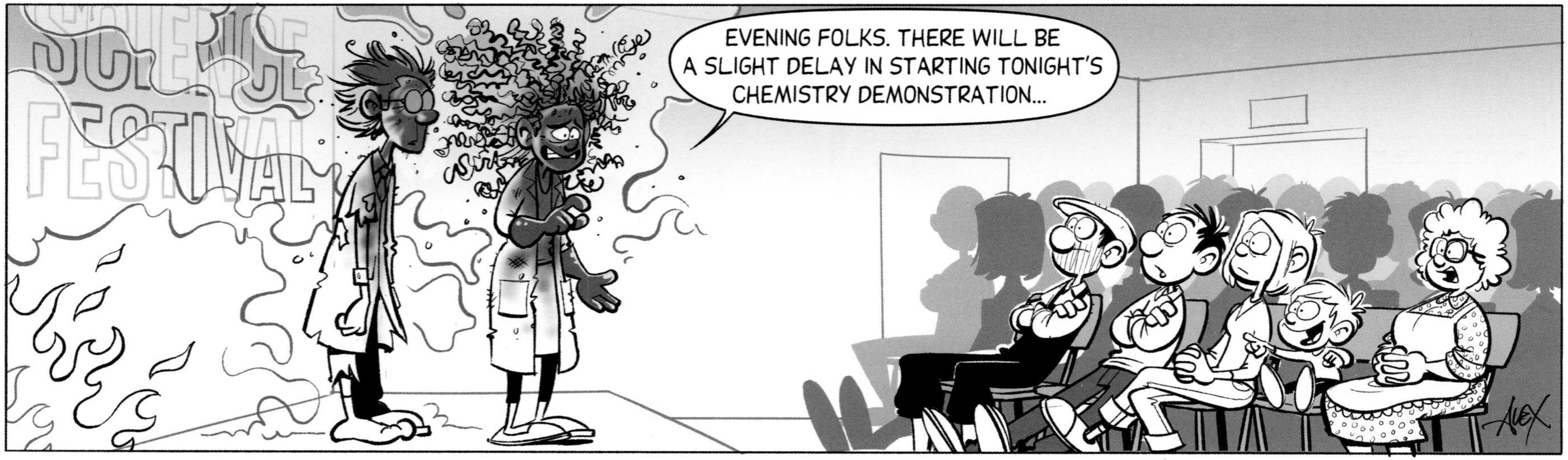
SCIENCE FESTIVAL
EVENING FOLKS. THERE WILL BE A SLIGHT DELAY IN STARTING TONIGHT'S CHEMISTRY DEMONSTRATION...
ALEX

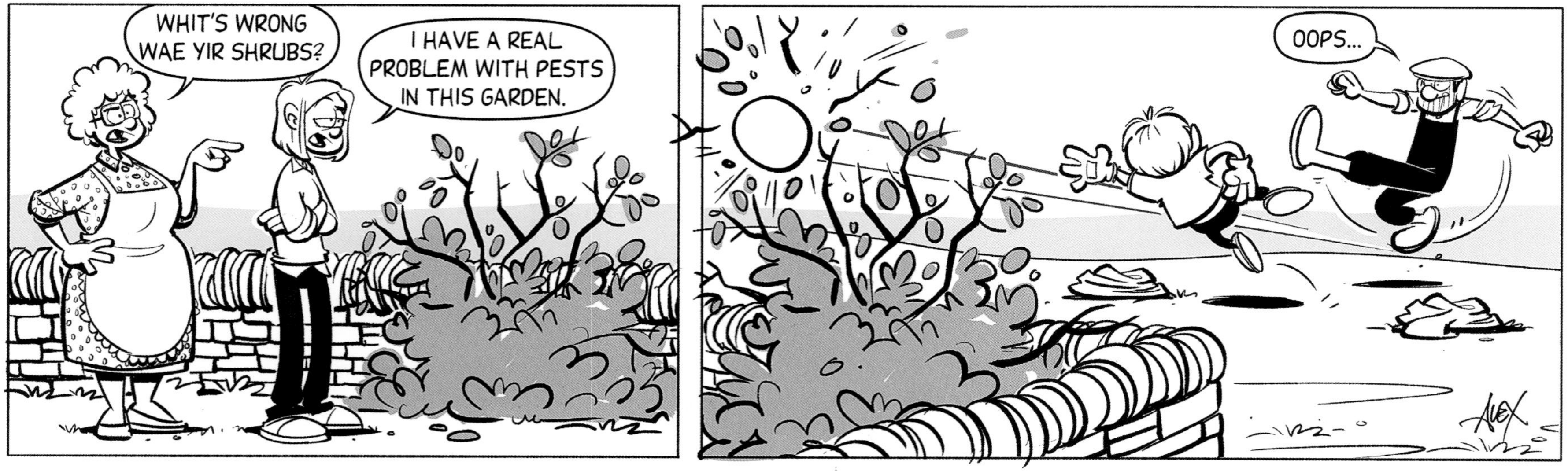
WHIT'S WRONG WAE YIR SHRUBS?
I HAVE A REAL PROBLEM WITH PESTS IN THIS GARDEN.
OOPS...
ALEX

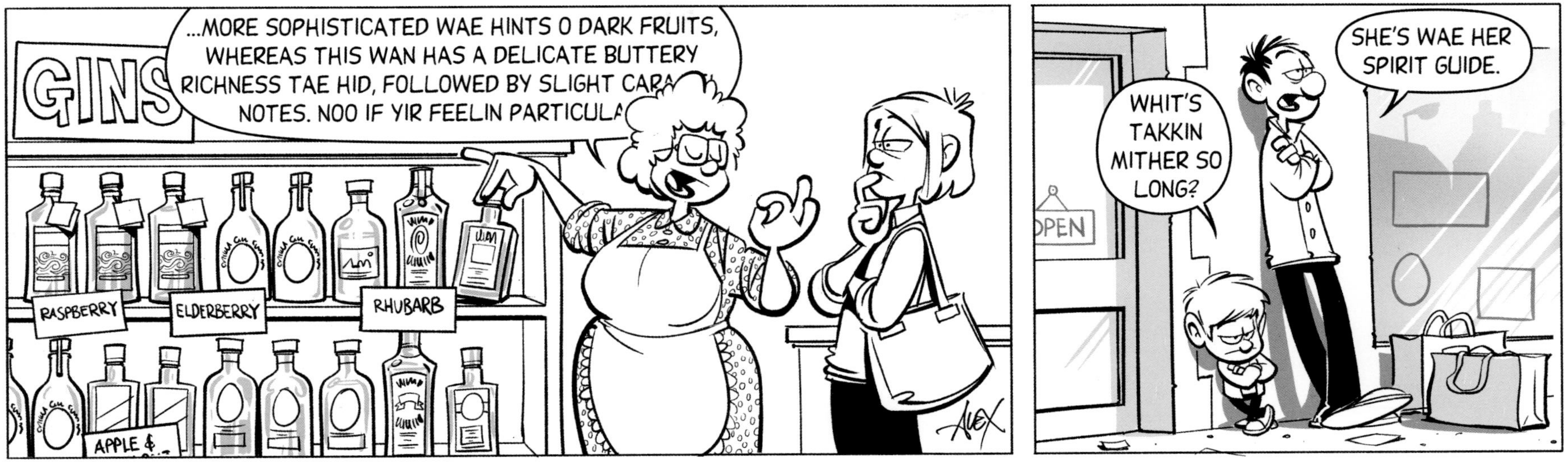
GINS
...MORE SOPHISTICATED WAE HINTS O DARK FRUITS, WHEREAS THIS WAN HAS A DELICATE BUTTERY RICHNESS TAE HID, FOLLOWED BY SLIGHT CARA NOTES. NOO IF YIR FEELIN PARTICULA
RASPBERRY
ELDERBERRY
RHUBARB
APPLE &
OPEN
WHIT'S TAKKIN MITHER SO LONG?
SHE'S WAE HER SPIRIT GUIDE.

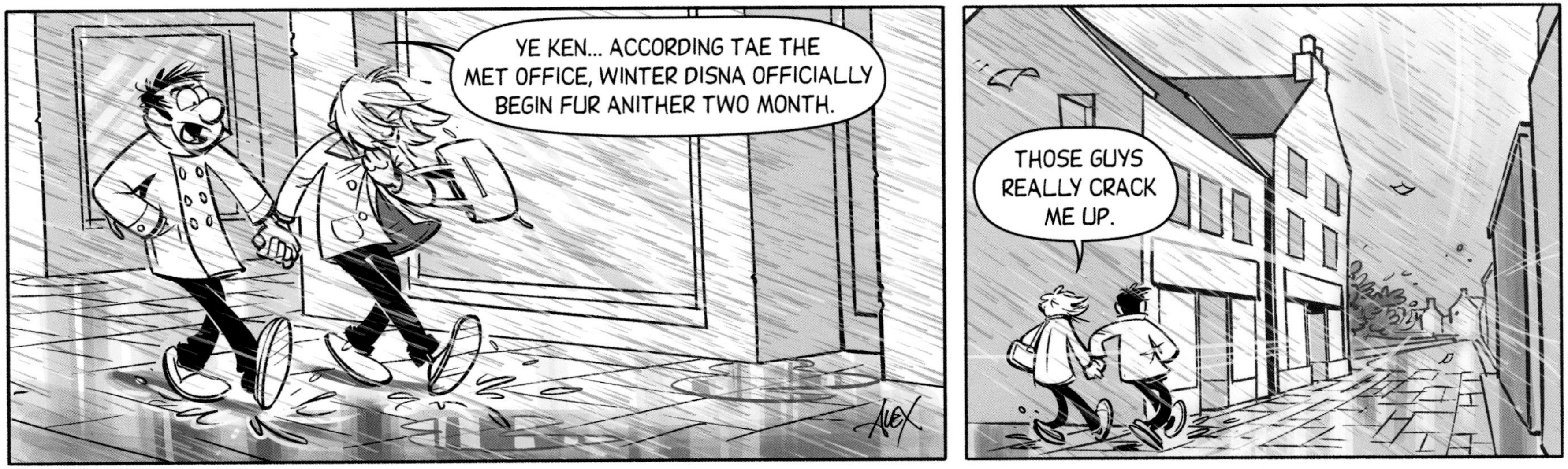
YE KEN... ACCORDING TAE THE MET OFFICE, WINTER DISNA OFFICIALLY BEGIN FUR ANITHER TWO MONTH.
THOSE GUYS REALLY CRACK ME UP.

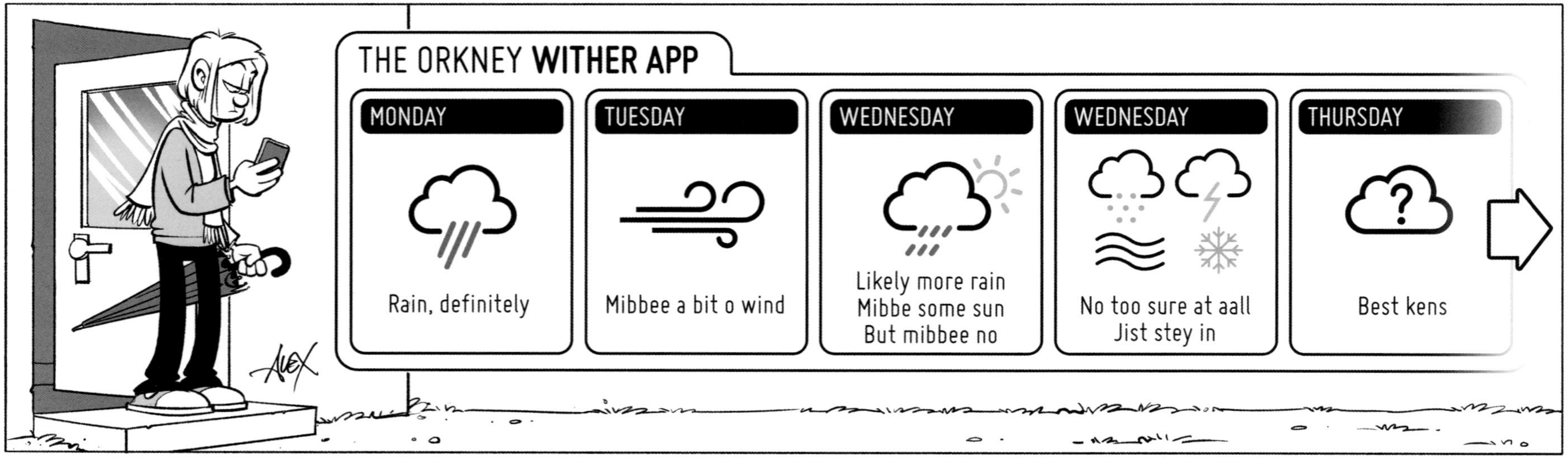
THE ORKNEY WITHER APP
MONDAY
Rain, definitely
TUESDAY
Mibbee a bit o wind
WEDNESDAY
Likely more rain
Mibbe some sun
But mibbee no
WEDNESDAY
No too sure at aall
Jist stey in
THURSDAY
Best kens
ALEX

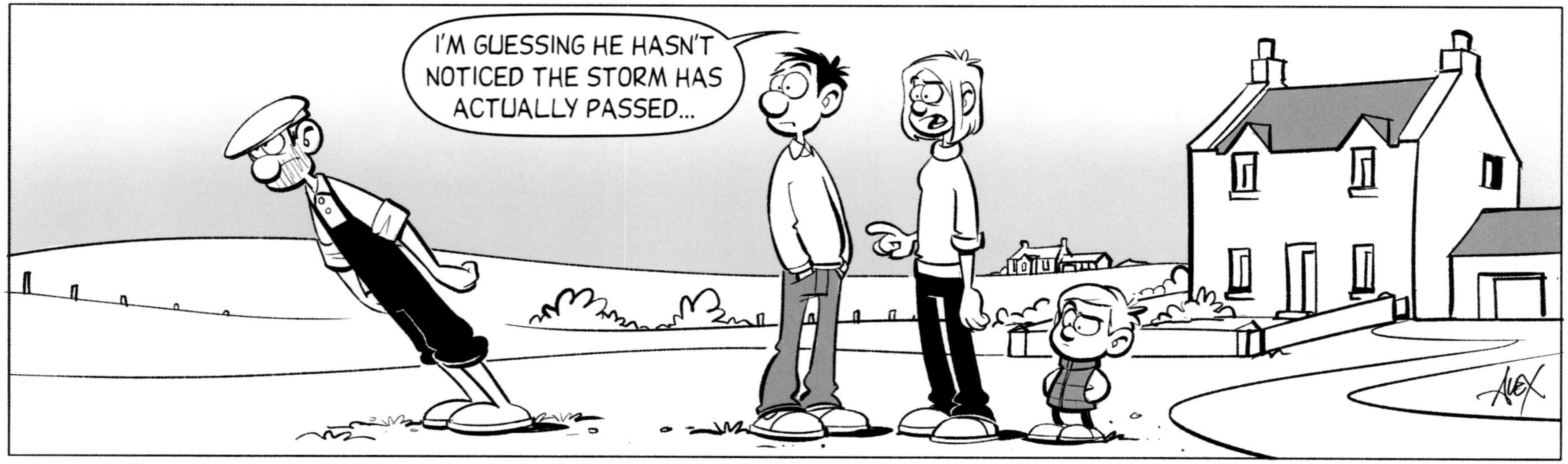
I'M GUESSING HE HASN'T NOTICED THE STORM HAS ACTUALLY PASSED...
ALEX

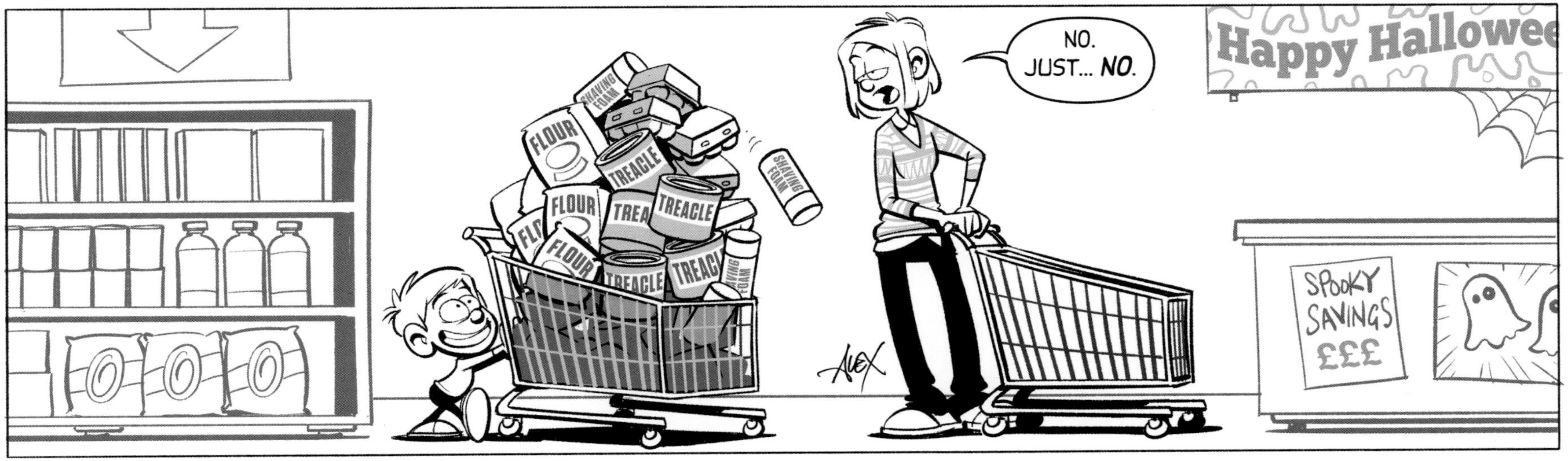
FLOUR
SHAVING FOAM
TREACLE
NO.
JUST... NO.
Happy Hallowee
SPOOKY SAVINGS £££
ALEX

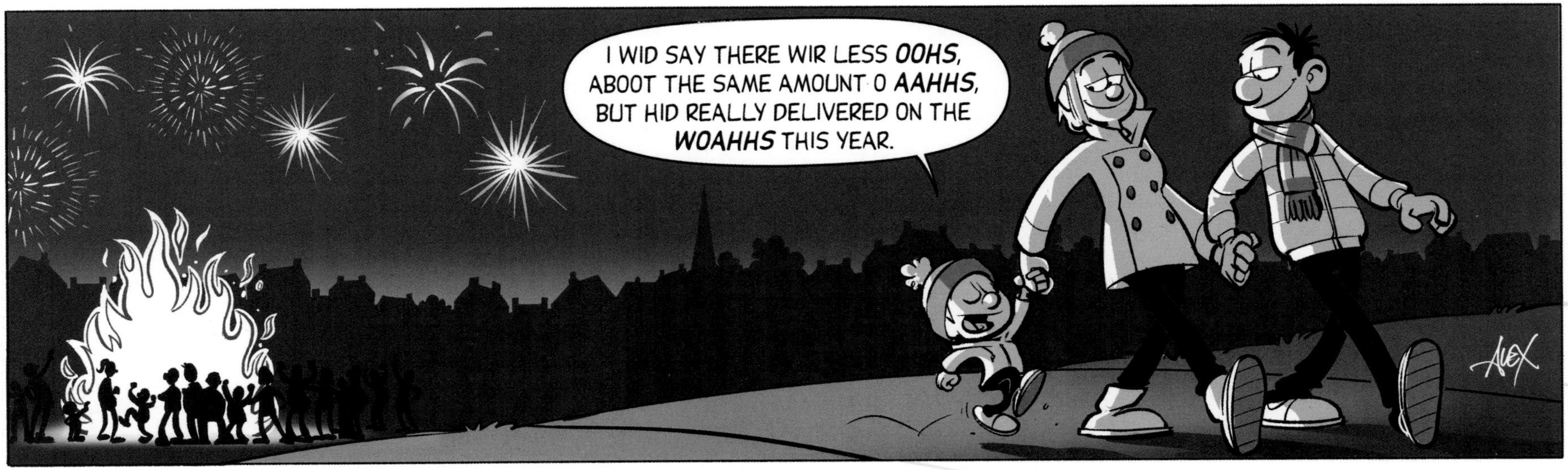
I WID SAY THERE WIR LESS OOHS, ABOOT THE SAME AMOUNT O AAHHS, BUT HID REALLY DELIVERED ON THE WOAHHS THIS YEAR.
ALEX

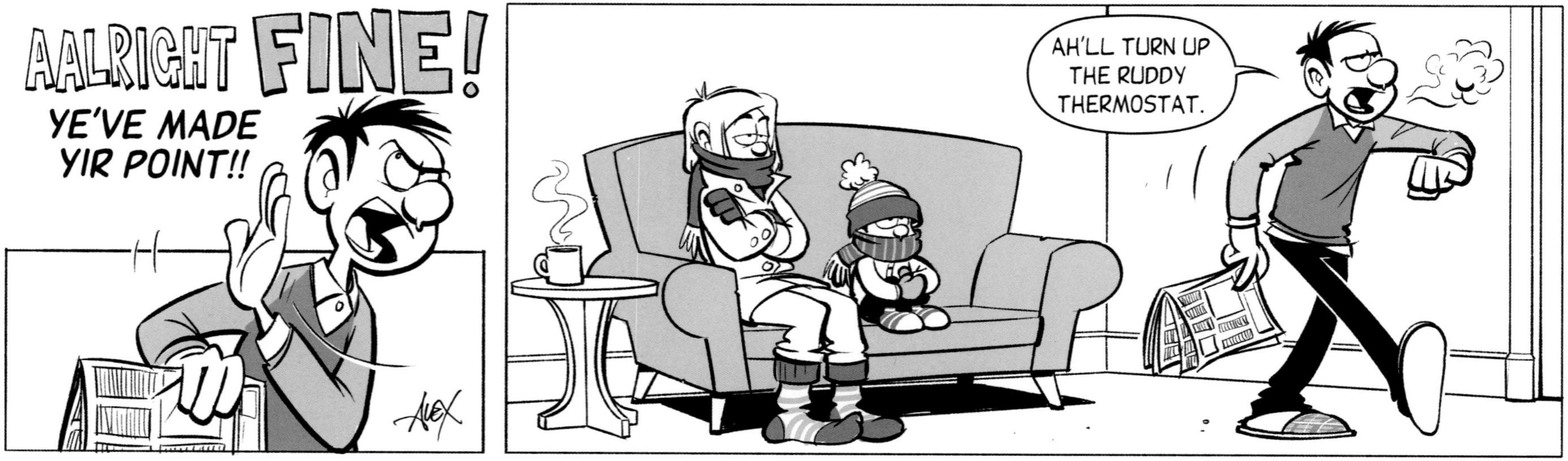
AALRIGHT FINE!
YE'VE MADE YIR POINT!!
AH'LL TURN UP THE RUDDY THERMOSTAT.
ALEX

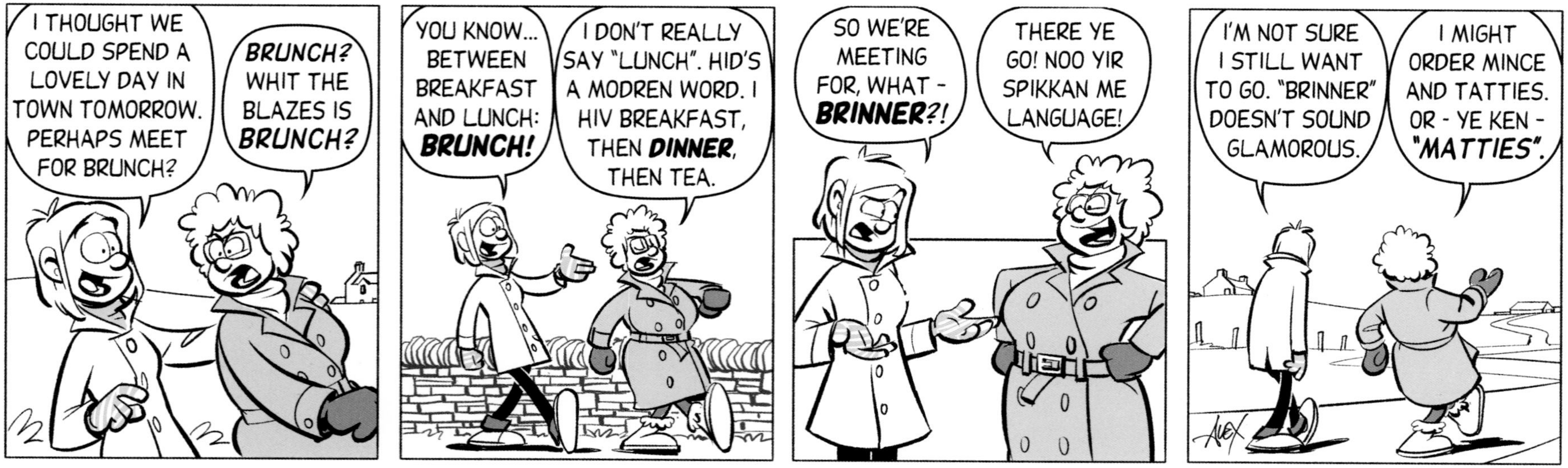
I THOUGHT WE COULD SPEND A LOVELY DAY IN TOWN TOMORROW. PERHAPS MEET FOR BRUNCH?
BRUNCH? WHIT THE BLAZES IS BRUNCH?
YOU KNOW... BETWEEN BREAKFAST AND LUNCH: BRUNCH!
I DON'T REALLY SAY "LUNCH". HID'S A MODREN WORD. I HIV BREAKFAST, THEN DINNER, THEN TEA.
SO WE'RE MEETING FOR, WHAT - BRINNER?!
THERE YE GO! NOO YIR SPIKKAN ME LANGUAGE!
I'M NOT SURE I STILL WANT TO GO. "BRINNER" DOESN'T SOUND GLAMOROUS.
I MIGHT ORDER MINCE AND TATTIES. OR - YE KEN - "MATTIES".
ALEX

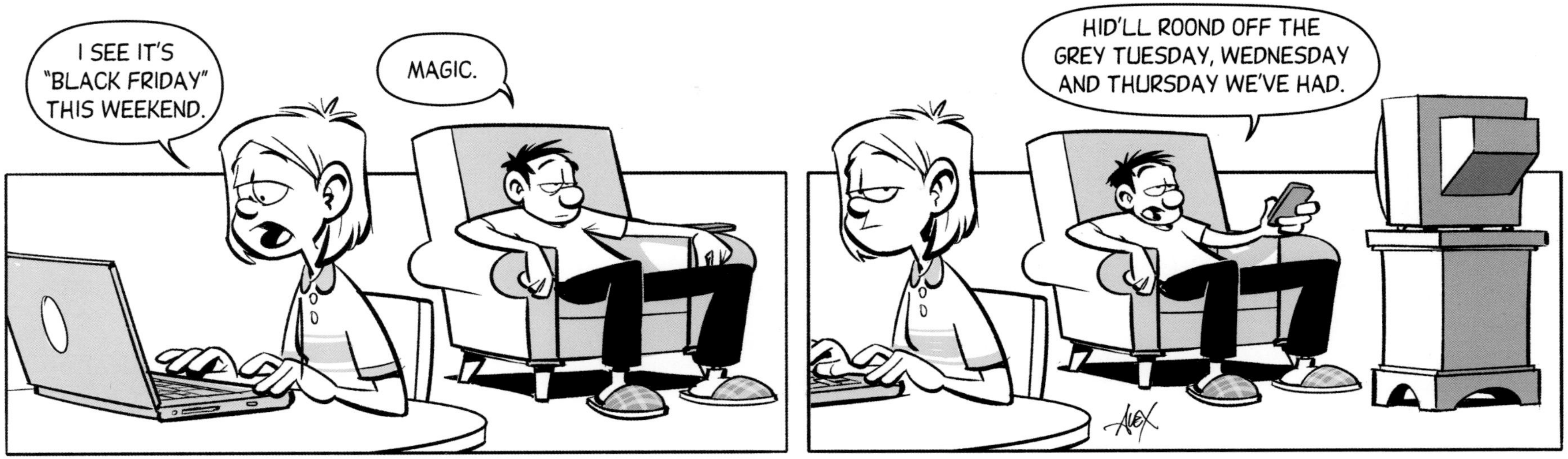
I SEE IT'S "BLACK FRIDAY" THIS WEEKEND.
MAGIC.
HID'LL ROOND OFF THE GREY TUESDAY, WEDNESDAY AND THURSDAY WE'VE HAD.
ALEX

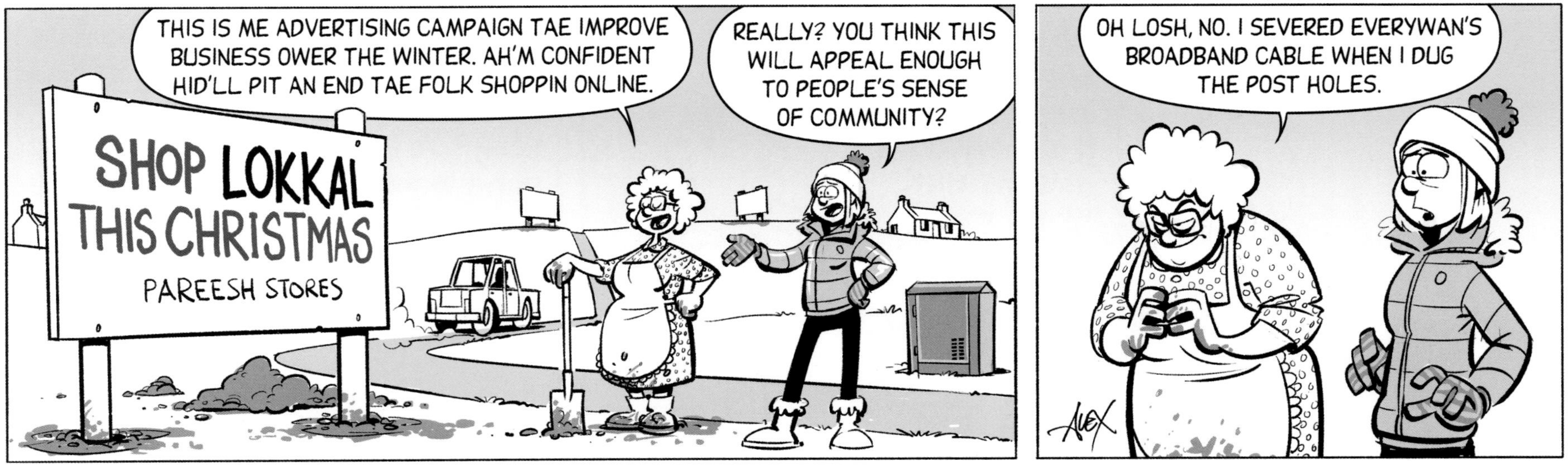
THIS IS ME ADVERTISING CAMPAIGN TAE IMPROVE BUSINESS OWER THE WINTER. AH'M CONFIDENT HID'LL PIT AN END TAE FOLK SHOPPIN ONLINE.
SHOP LOKKAL THIS CHRISTMAS
PAREESH STORES
REALLY? YOU THINK THIS WILL APPEAL ENOUGH TO PEOPLE'S SENSE OF COMMUNITY?
OH LOSH, NO. I SEVERED EVERYWAN'S BROADBAND CABLE WHEN I DUG THE POST HOLES.
ALEX

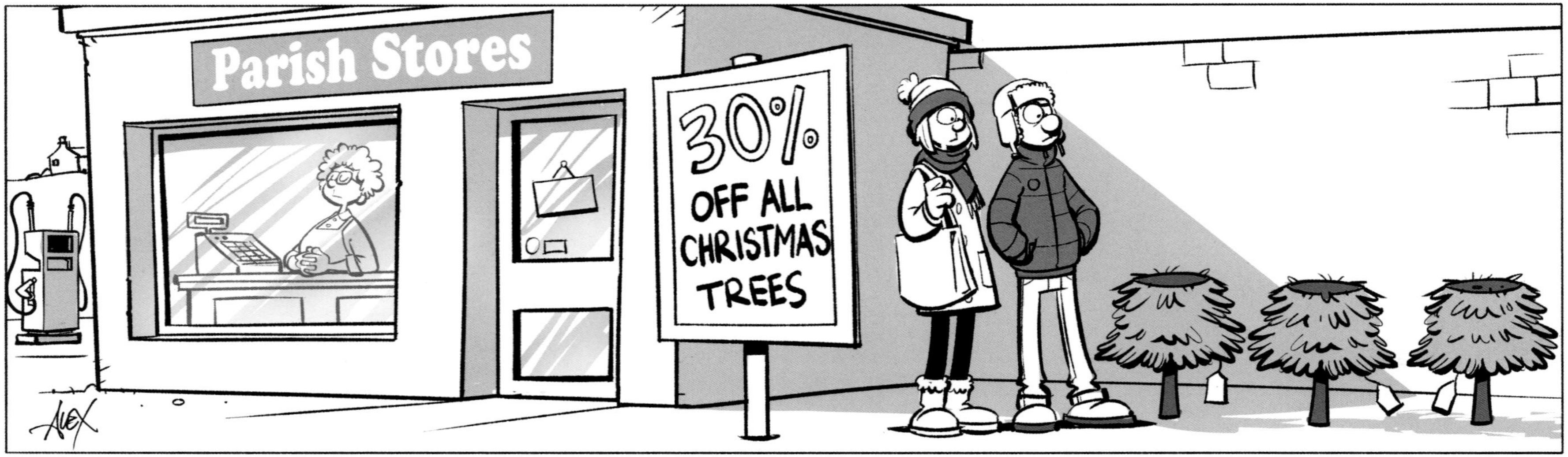
Parish Stores
30% OFF ALL CHRISTMAS TREES
ALEX

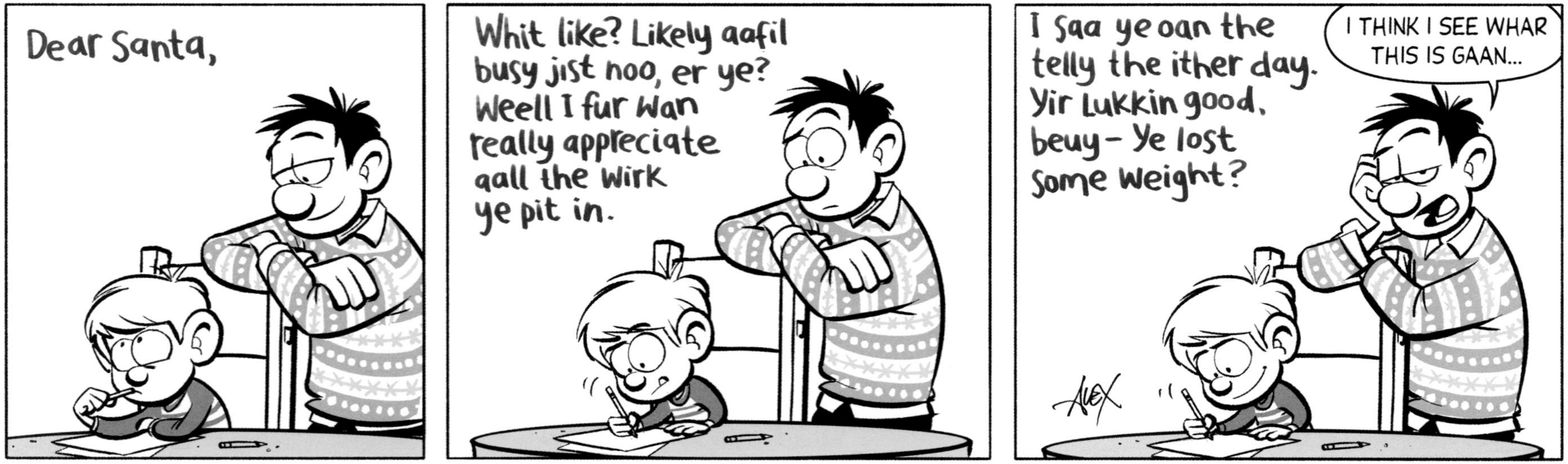
Dear Santa,
Whit like? Likely aafil busy jist noo, er ye? Weell I fur wan really appreciate aall the wirk ye pit in.
I saa ye oan the telly the ither day. Yir lukkin good, beuy - Ye lost some weight?
I THINK I SEE WHAR THIS IS GAAN...
ALEX

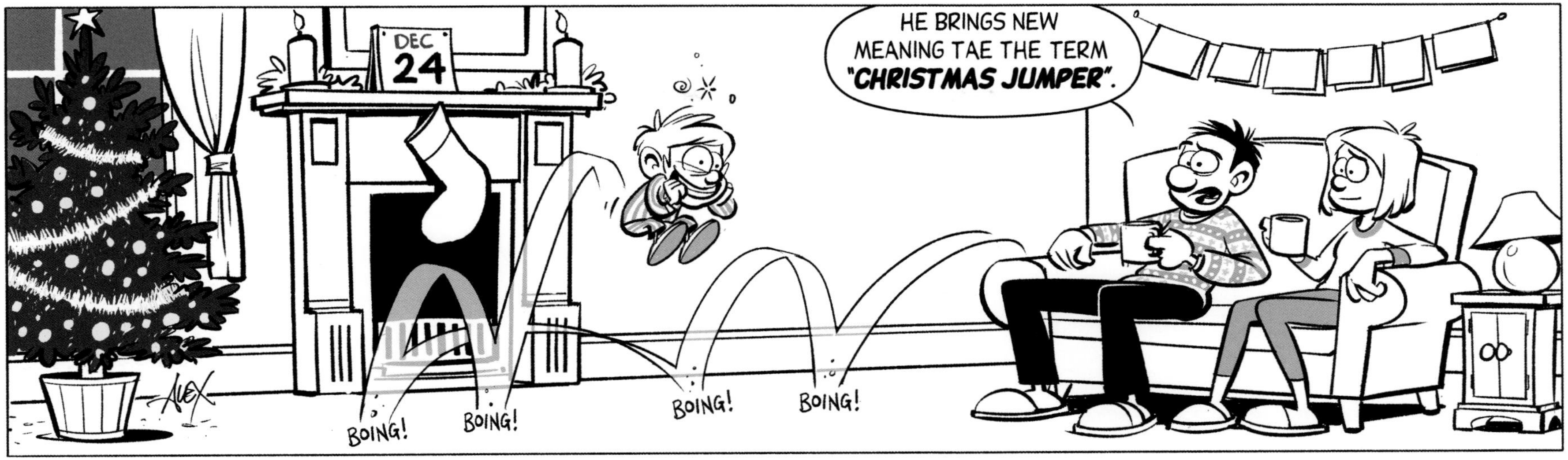
DEC
24
HE BRINGS NEW MEANING TAE THE TERM "CHRISTMAS JUMPER".
BOING!
BOING!
BOING!
BOING!
ALEX

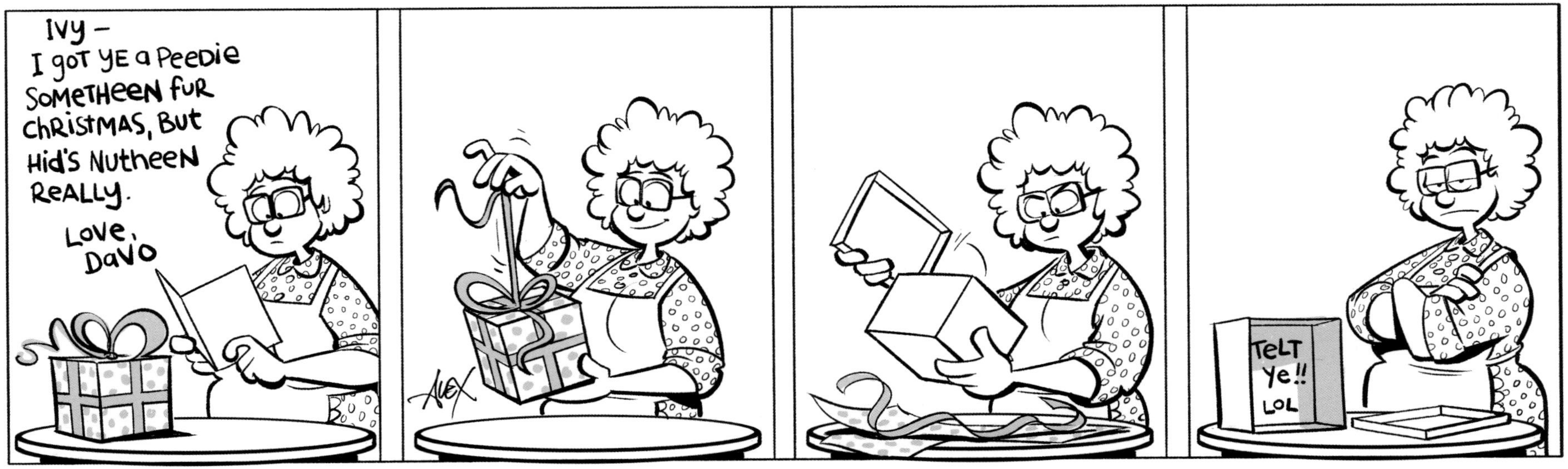
IVY –
I GOT YE A PEEDIE SOMETHEEN FUR CHRISTMAS, BUT HID'S NUTHEEN REALLY.
LOVE, DAVO
ALEX
TELT YE!! LOL

# 2018 CALENDAR

HINTS FOR HOLIDAYS
Orkney Edition 6D
WHAR TAE GO • WHIT TAE DAE • WHAR TAE STEY
900 PAGES PROFUSELY ILLUSTRATED
GIDDY AIRLINES
FASTEST AIR SERVICE
SANDAY
THE SUNSHINE ISLAND
SOOTH RONALDSAY FOR GOLF
HATSTON
18 MAY 1958
KIRKWALL
GRAND PRIX AUTOMOBILE
STROMNESS
LES ORCADES
ROUSAY
EGYPT OF THE NORTH
INGANESS BEACH
FOR
SEA BREEZES AND SUNSHINE
"LA SAINT OLA"
FLY THERE WITH GWA
HOLIDAYS ARE HAPPY DAYS
TANKERNESS & TOAB
DANDERS AROOND THE ORKNEY COAST
A NEW PUBLICATION
WESTRAY
THE BRACING NORTH ISLES RESORT
THE GIDDY LIMIT
Calendar 2018

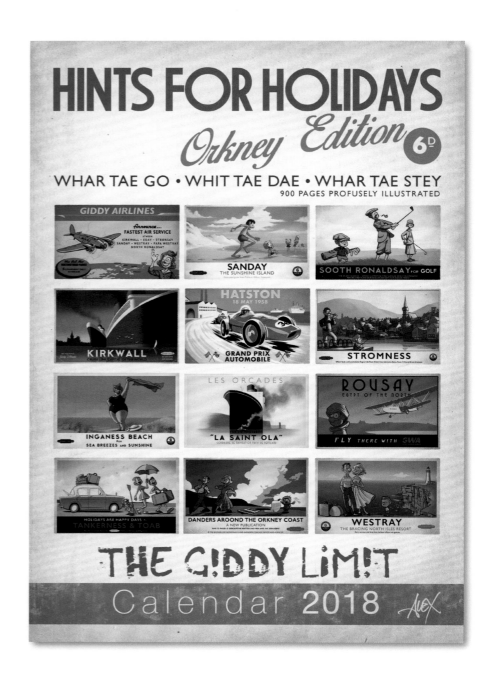

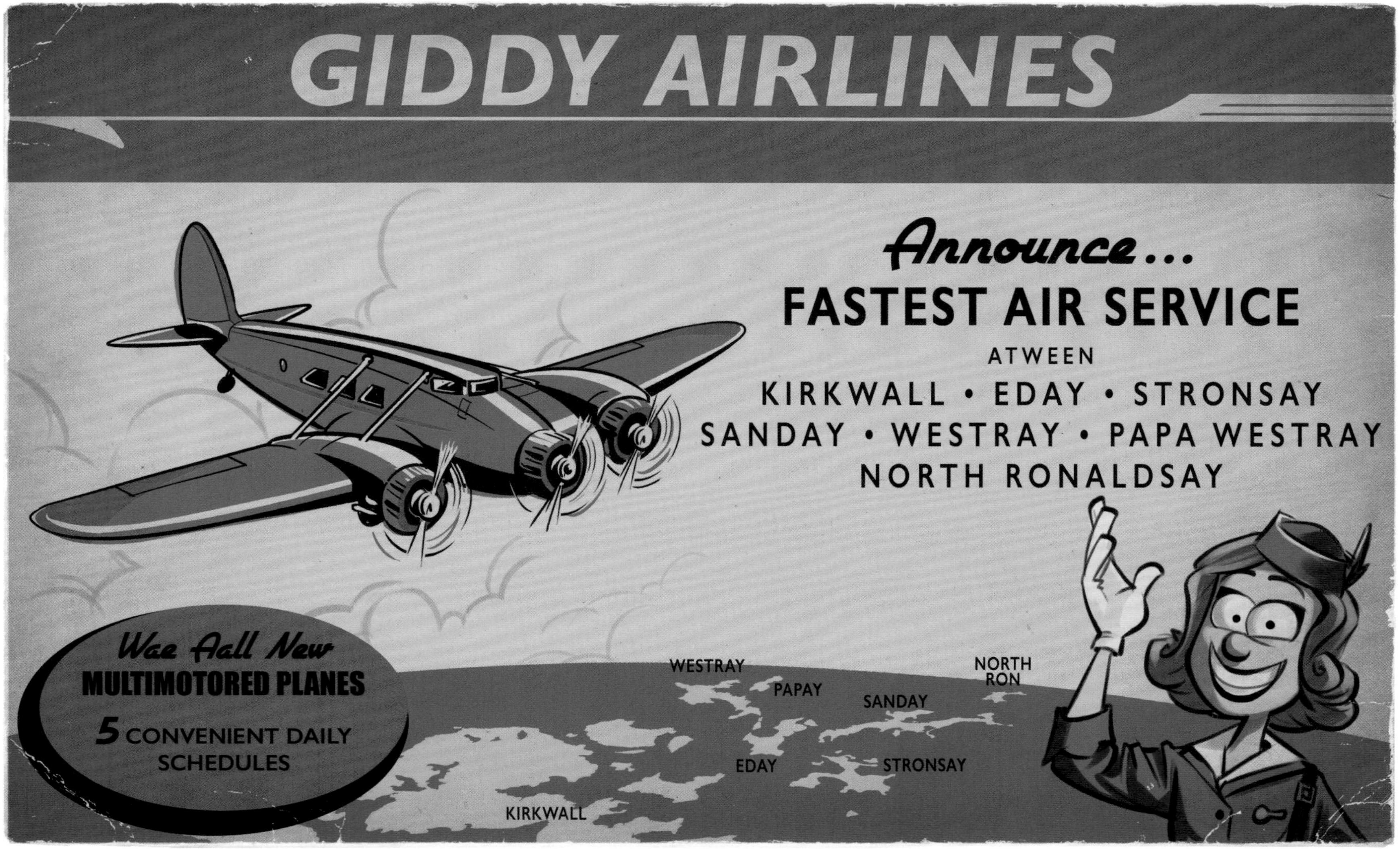
GIDDY AIRLINES
Announce...
FASTEST AIR SERVICE
ATWEEN
KIRKWALL • EDAY • STRONSAY
SANDAY • WESTRAY • PAPA WESTRAY
NORTH RONALDSAY
Wae Aall New
MULTIMOTORED PLANES
5 CONVENIENT DAILY SCHEDULES
WESTRAY
PAPAY
SANDAY
NORTH RON
EDAY
STRONSAY
KIRKWALL

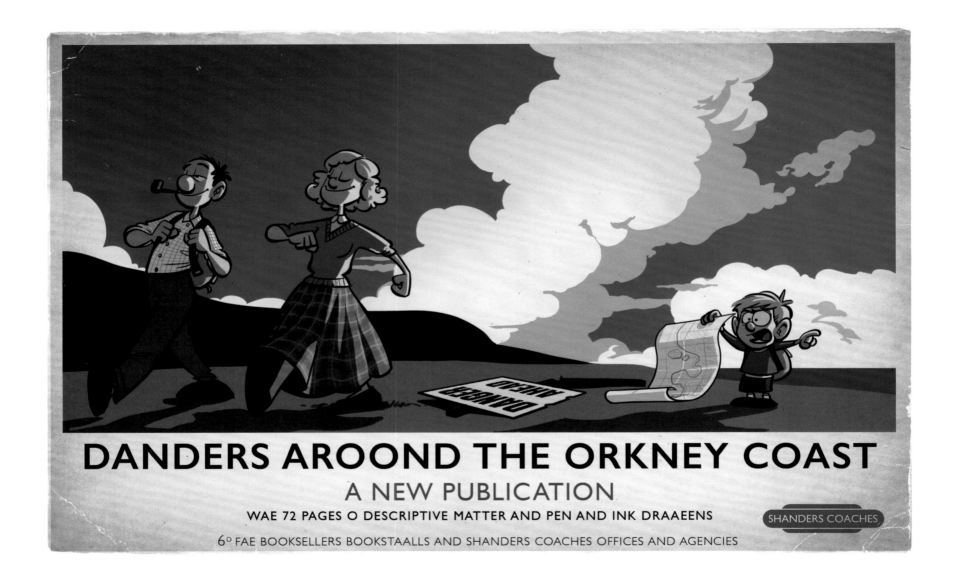

# DANDERS AROOND THE ORKNEY COAST

## A NEW PUBLICATION

**WAE 72 PAGES O DESCRIPTIVE MATTER AND PEN AND INK DRAAEENS**

SHANDERS COACHES

6ᴰ FAE BOOKSELLERS BOOKSTAALLS AND SHANDERS COACHES OFFICES AND AGENCIES

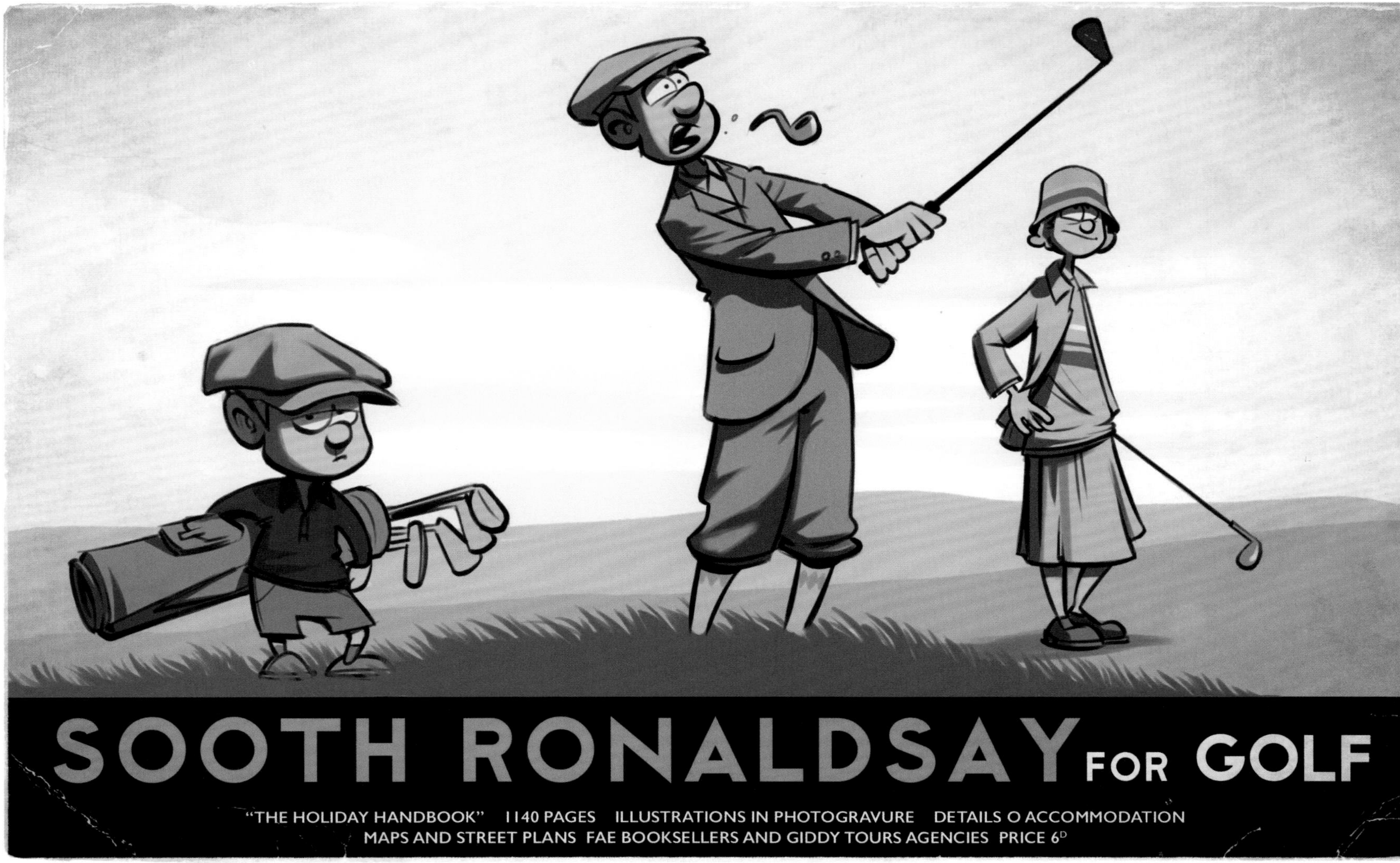
SOOTH RONALDSAY FOR GOLF
"THE HOLIDAY HANDBOOK" 1140 PAGES ILLUSTRATIONS IN PHOTOGRAVURE DETAILS O ACCOMMODATION
MAPS AND STREET PLANS FAE BOOKSELLERS AND GIDDY TOURS AGENCIES PRICE 6D

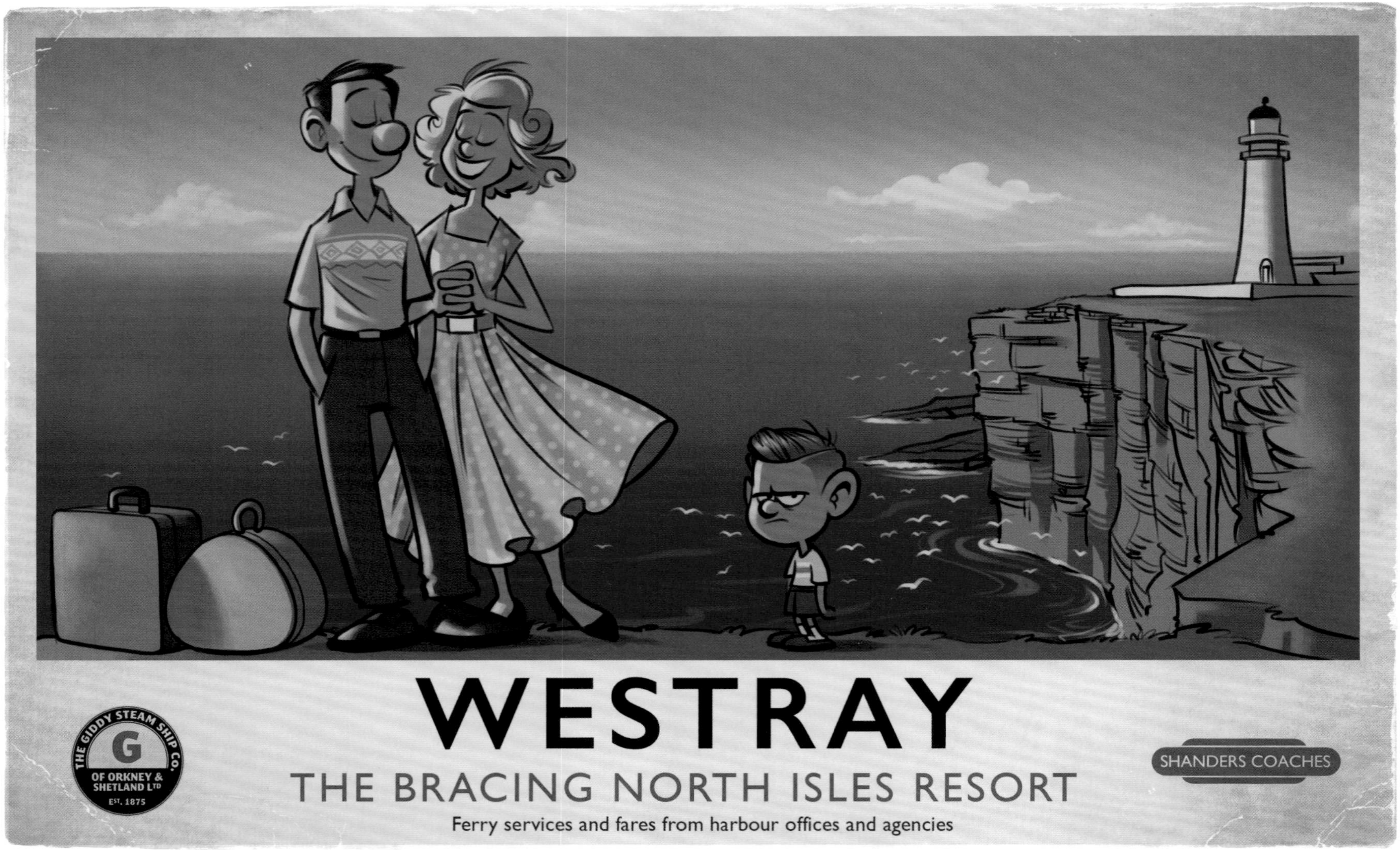
WESTRAY
THE BRACING NORTH ISLES RESORT
Ferry services and fares from harbour offices and agencies
THE GIDDY STEAM SHIP Co.
G
OF ORKNEY & SHETLAND LTD
EST. 1875
SHANDERS COACHES

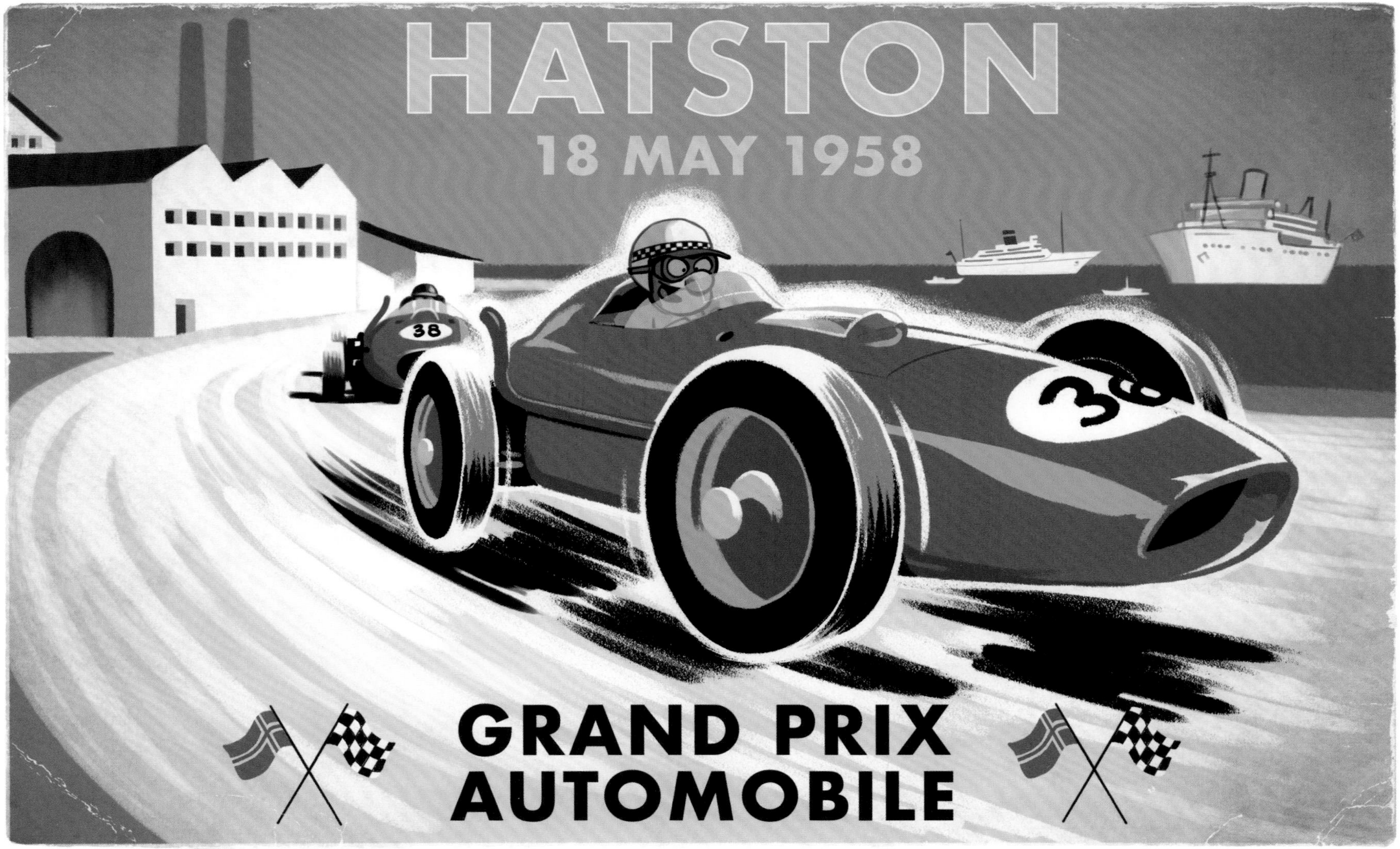
HATSTON
18 MAY 1958
38
38
GRAND PRIX
AUTOMOBILE

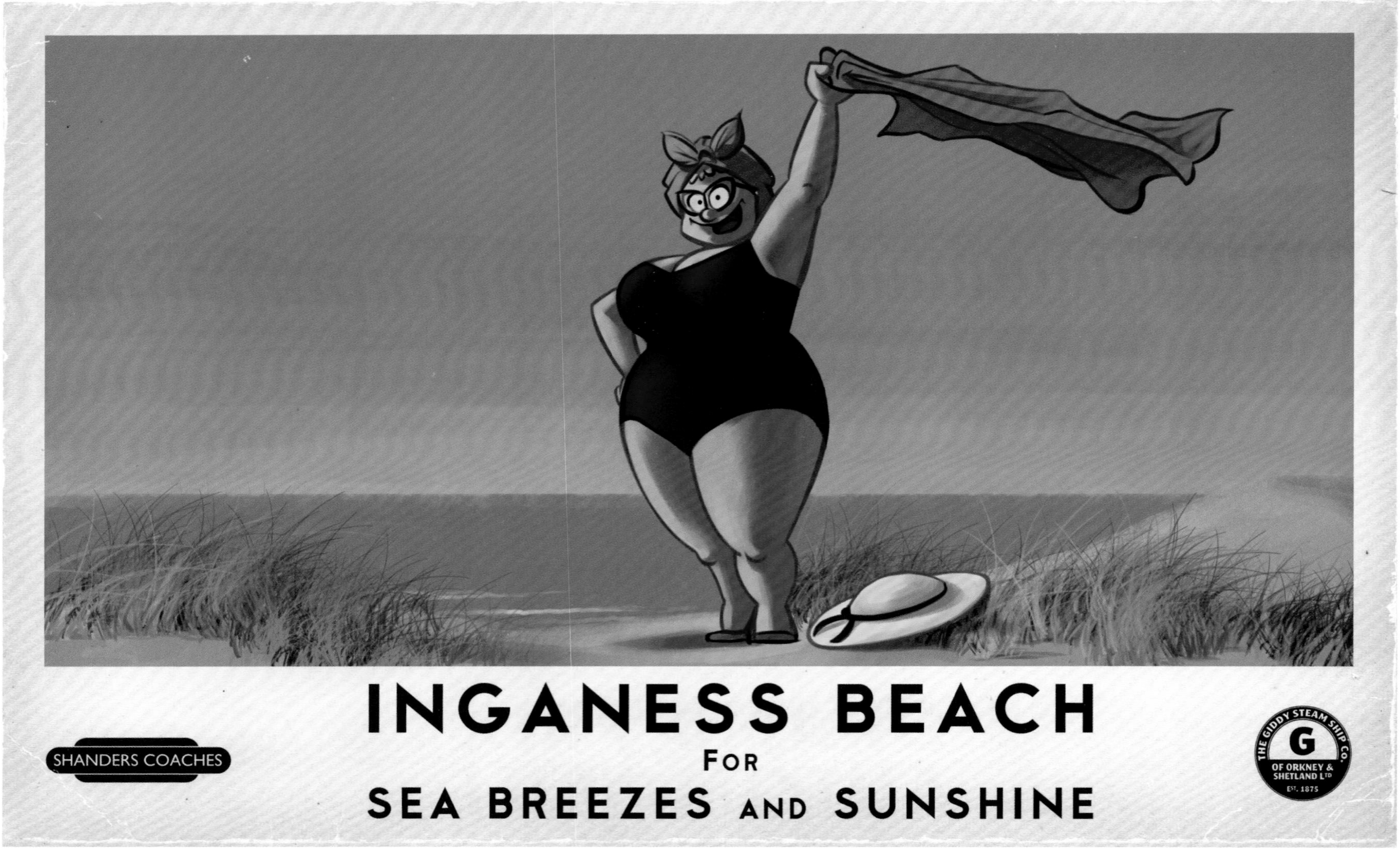

INGANESS BEACH
FOR
SEA BREEZES AND SUNSHINE
SHANDERS COACHES
THE GIDDY STEAM SHIP CO.
G
OF ORKNEY & SHETLAND LTD
EST. 1875

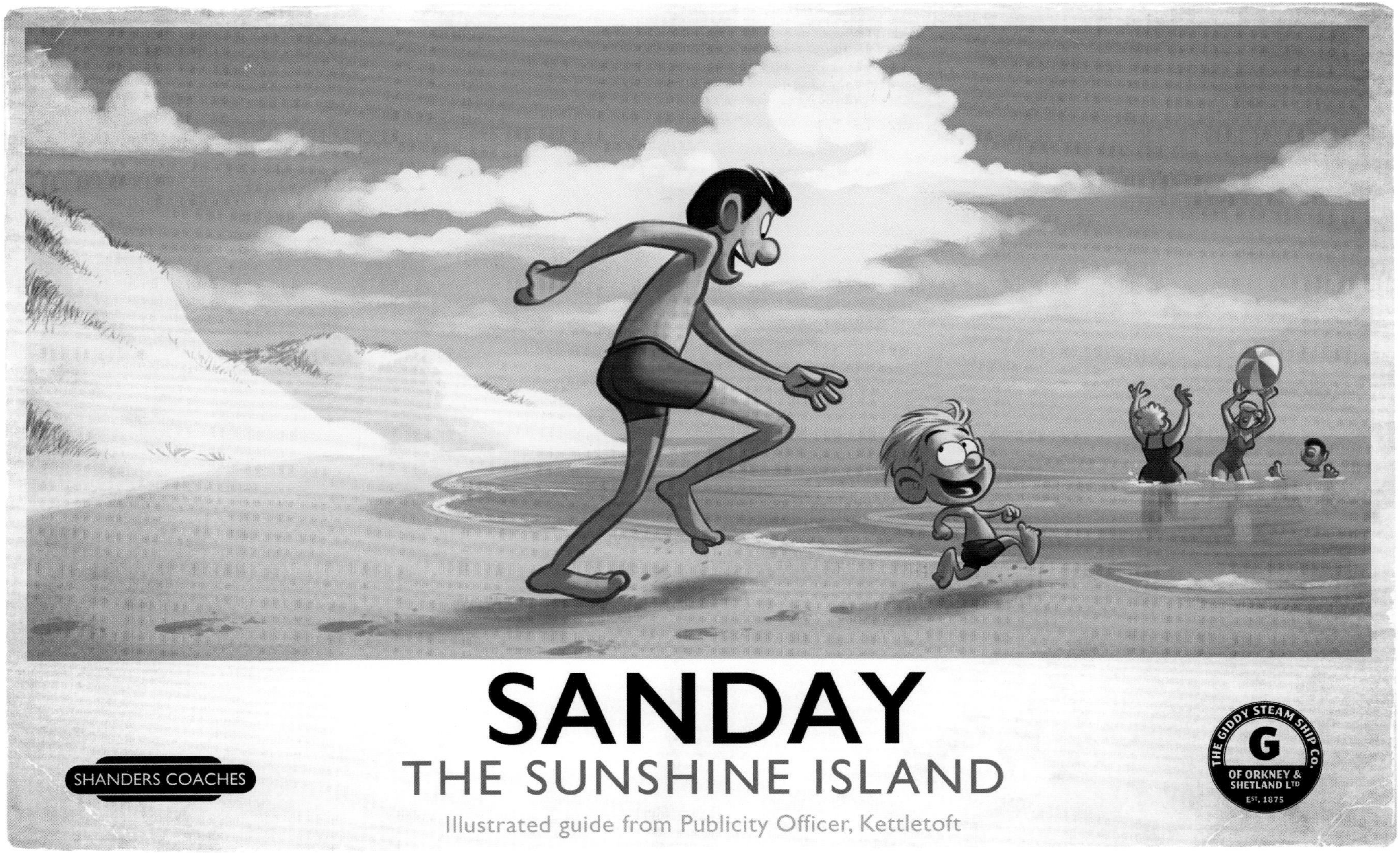
SANDAY
THE SUNSHINE ISLAND
Illustrated guide from Publicity Officer, Kettletoft
SHANDERS COACHES
THE GIDDY STEAM SHIP CO.
G
OF ORKNEY & SHETLAND LTD
EST. 1875

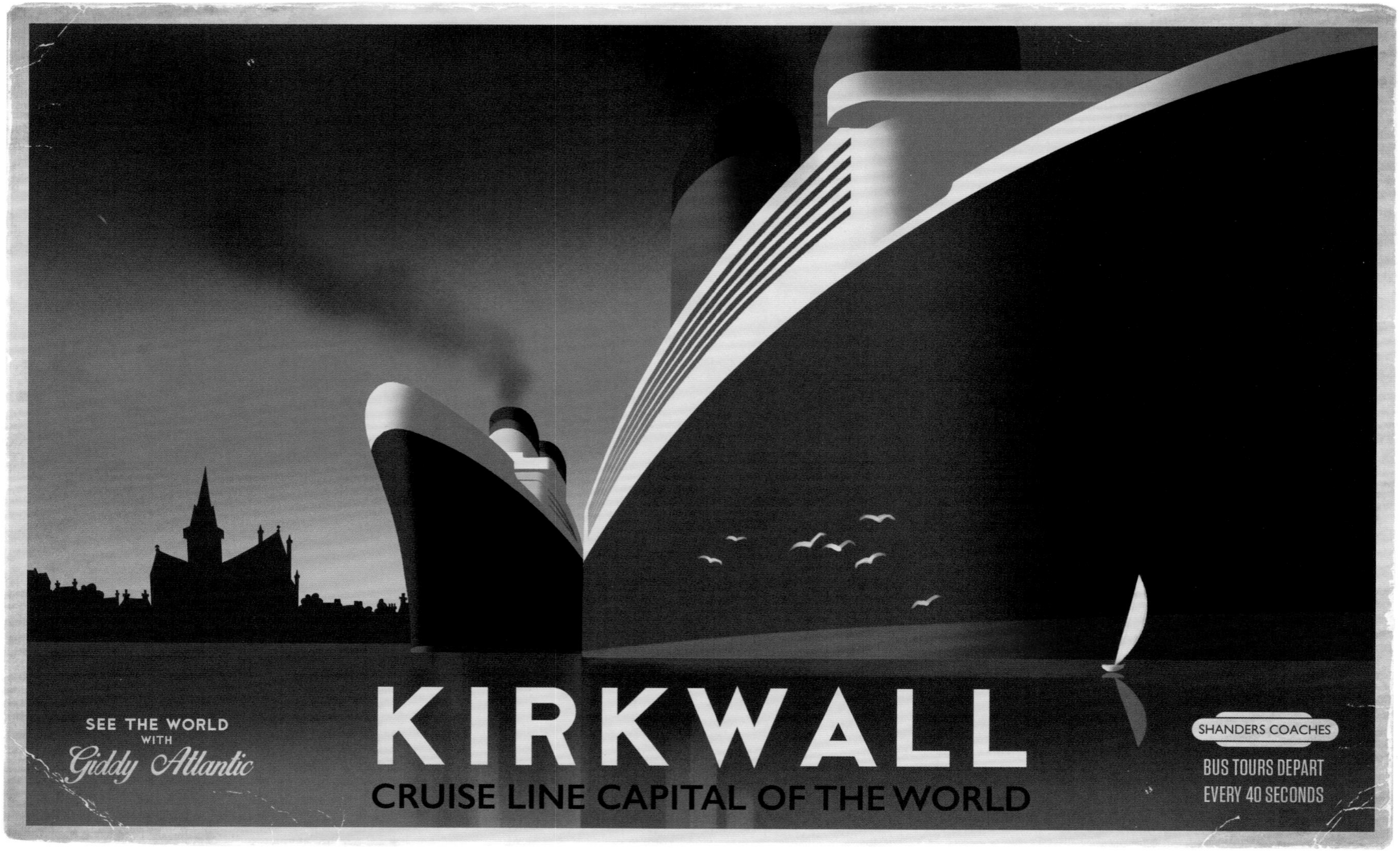
SEE THE WORLD
WITH
Giddy Atlantic
KIRKWALL
CRUISE LINE CAPITAL OF THE WORLD
SHANDERS COACHES
BUS TOURS DEPART
EVERY 40 SECONDS

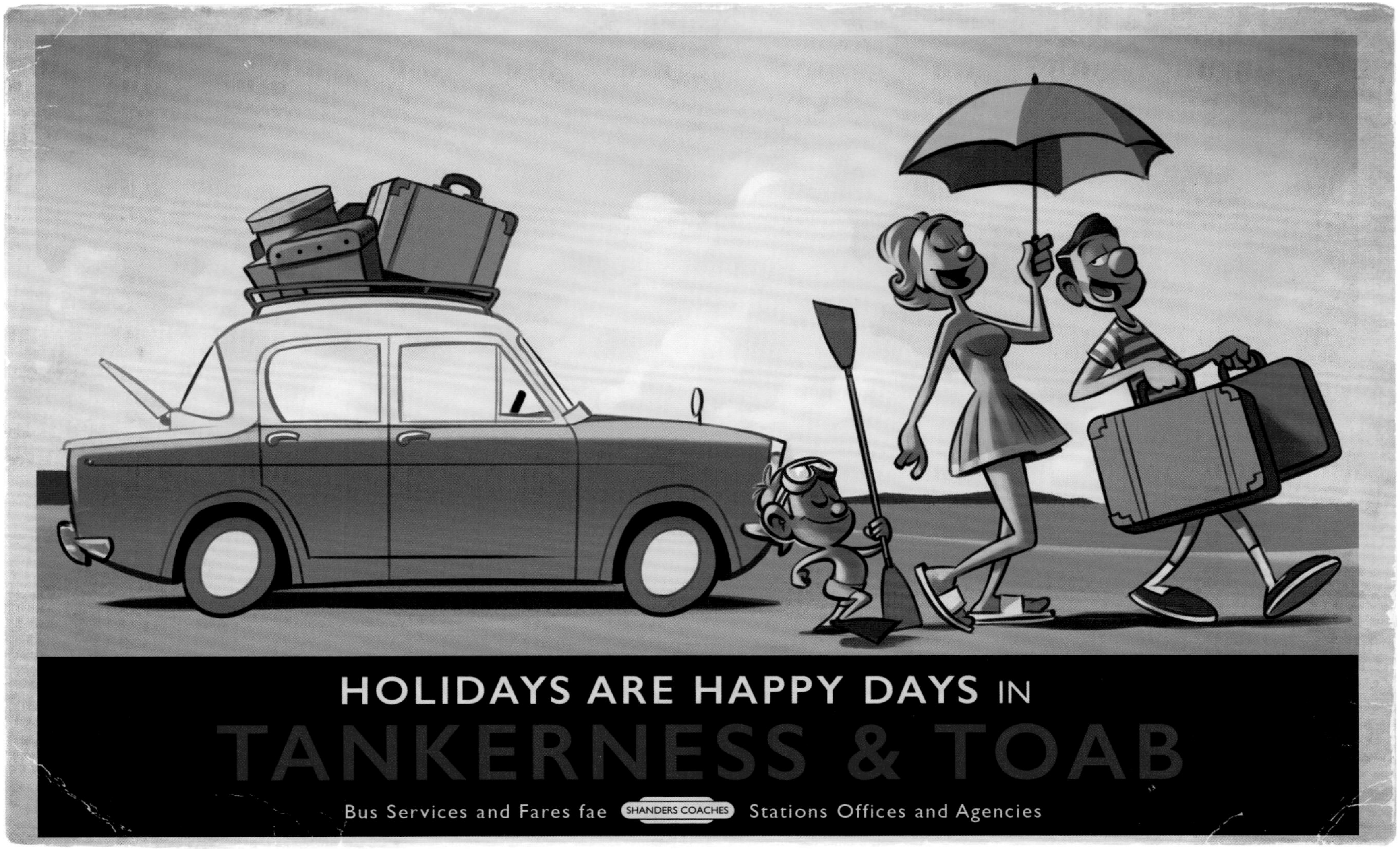
HOLIDAYS ARE HAPPY DAYS IN
TANKERNESS & TOAB
Bus Services and Fares fae
SHANDERS COACHES
Stations Offices and Agencies

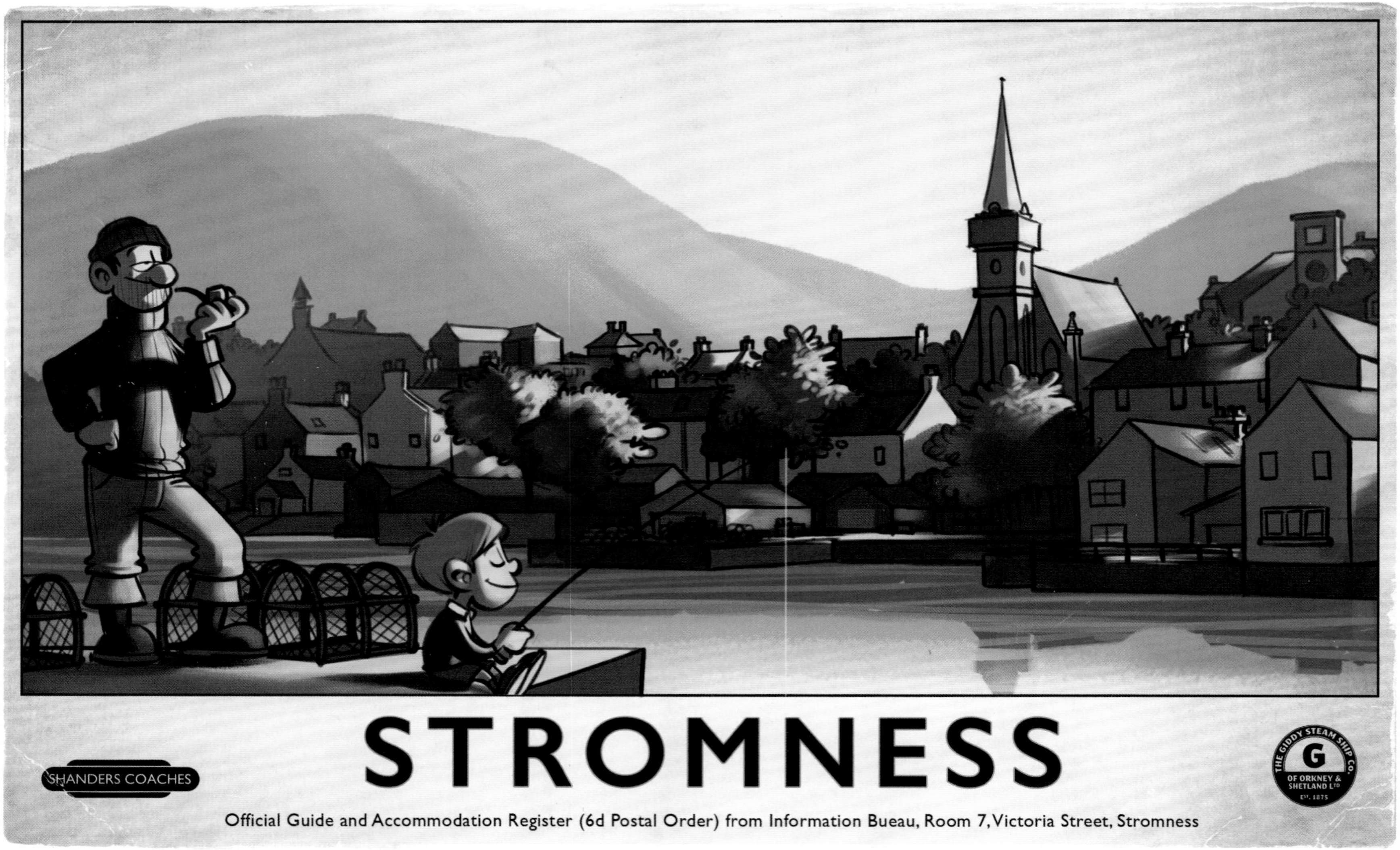

STROMNESS
SHANDERS COACHES
THE GIDDY STEAM SHIP CO.
G
OF ORKNEY & SHETLAND LTD
EST. 1875
Official Guide and Accommodation Register (6d Postal Order) from Information Bueau, Room 7, Victoria Street, Stromness

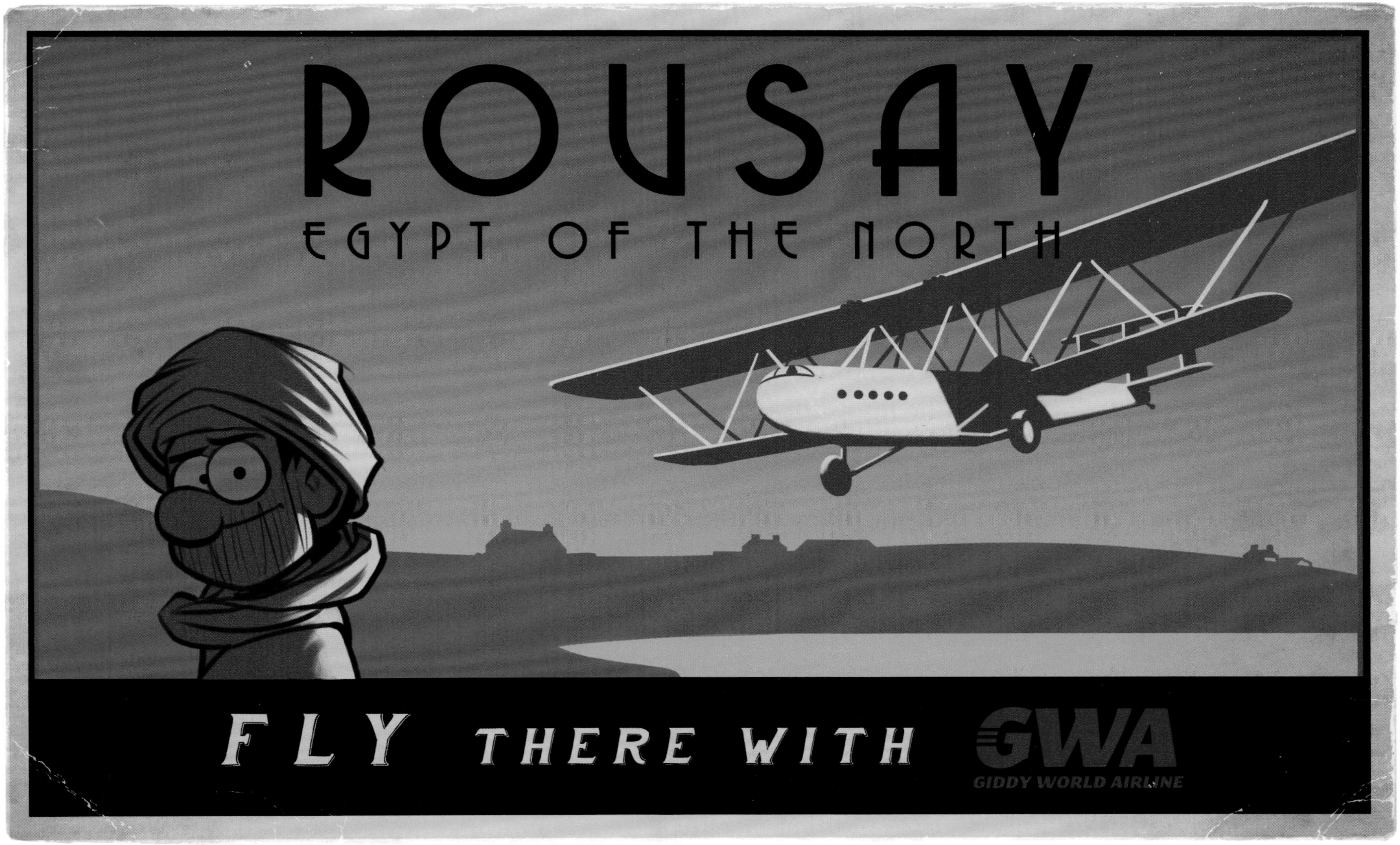
ROUSAY
EGYPT OF THE NORTH
FLY THERE WITH
GWA
GIDDY WORLD AIRLINE

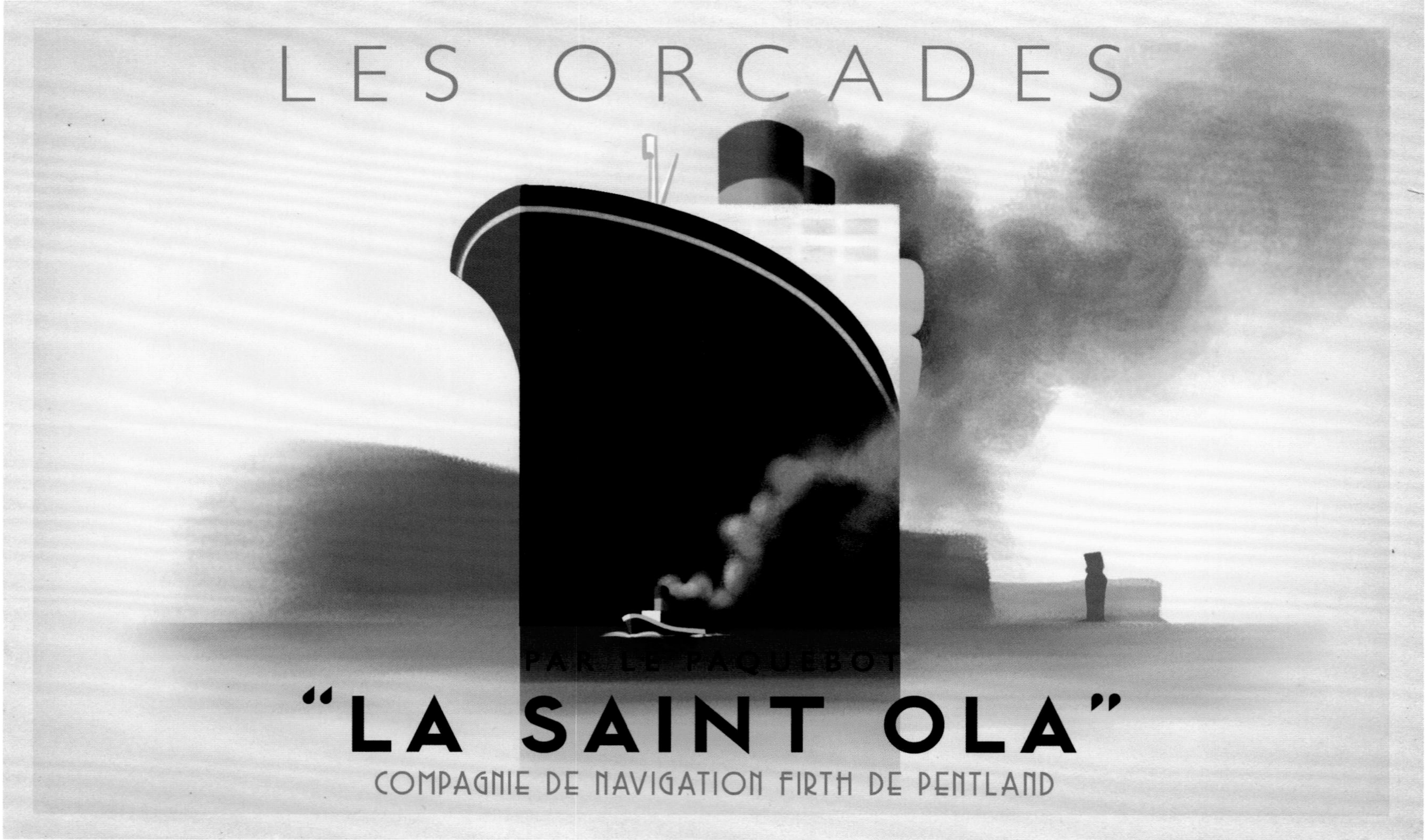
LES ORCADES
PAR LE PAQUEBOT
"LA SAINT OLA"
COMPAGNIE DE NAVIGATION FIRTH DE PENTLAND

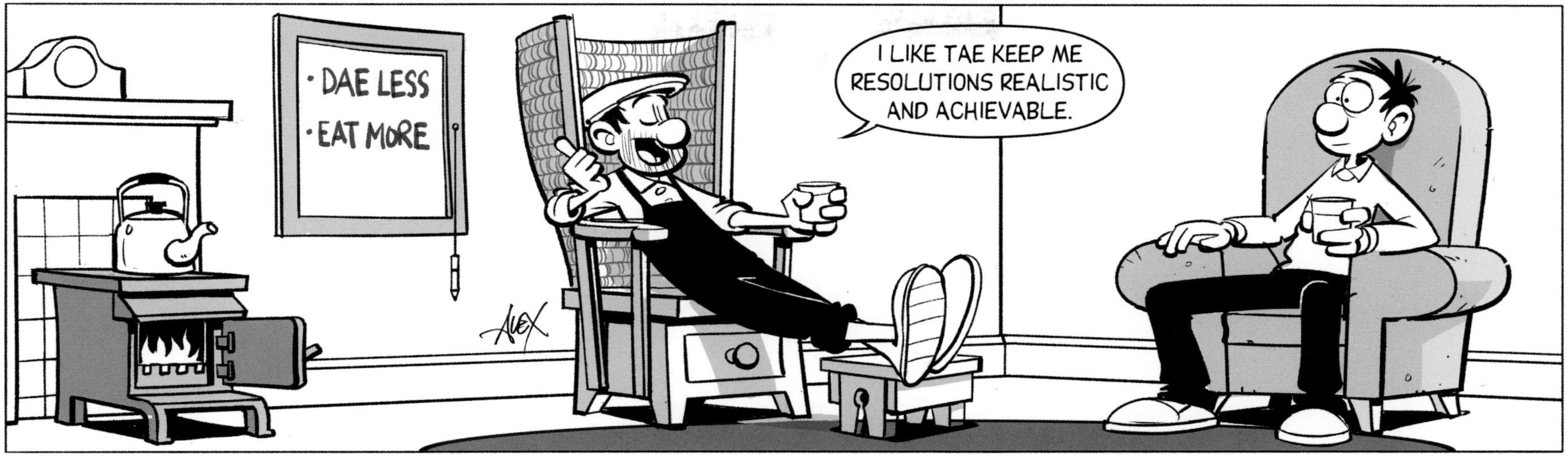

· DAE LESS
· EAT MORE
I LIKE TAE KEEP ME RESOLUTIONS REALISTIC AND ACHIEVABLE.
ALEX


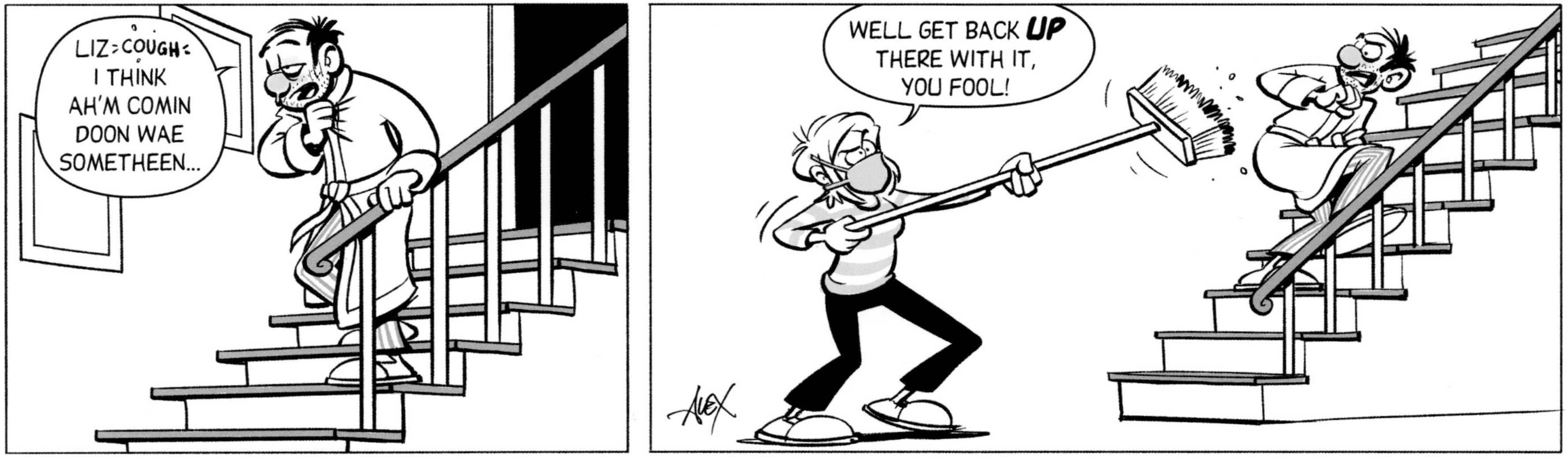

LIZ =COUGH= I THINK AH'M COMIN DOON WAE SOMETHEEN...
WELL GET BACK **UP** THERE WITH IT, YOU FOOL!
ALEX

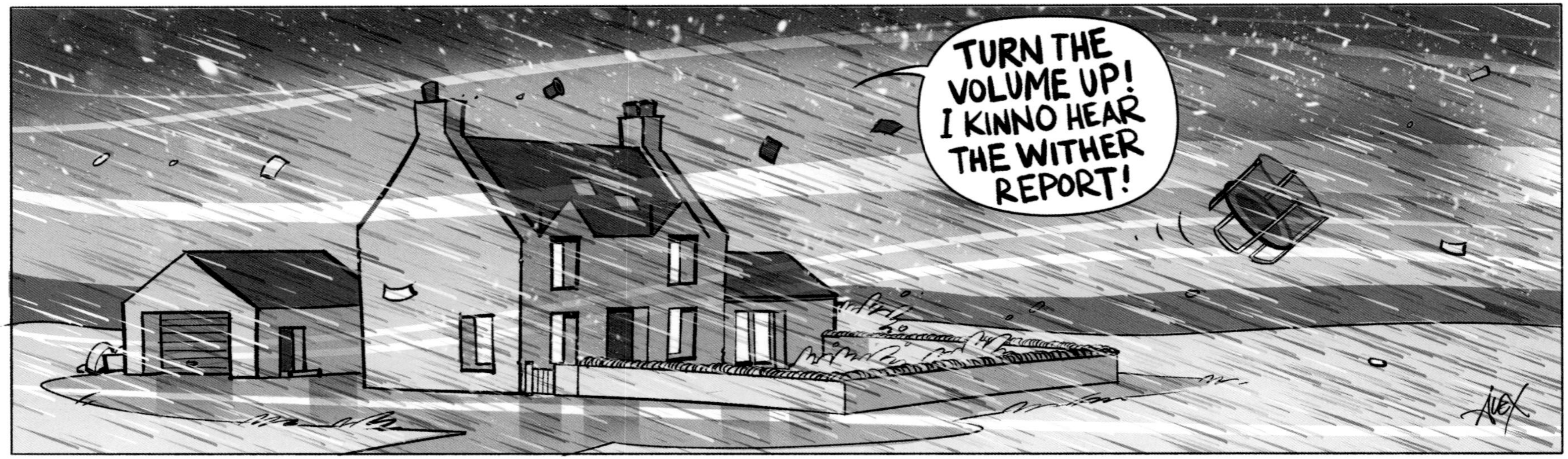
TURN THE VOLUME UP! I KINNO HEAR THE WITHER REPORT!

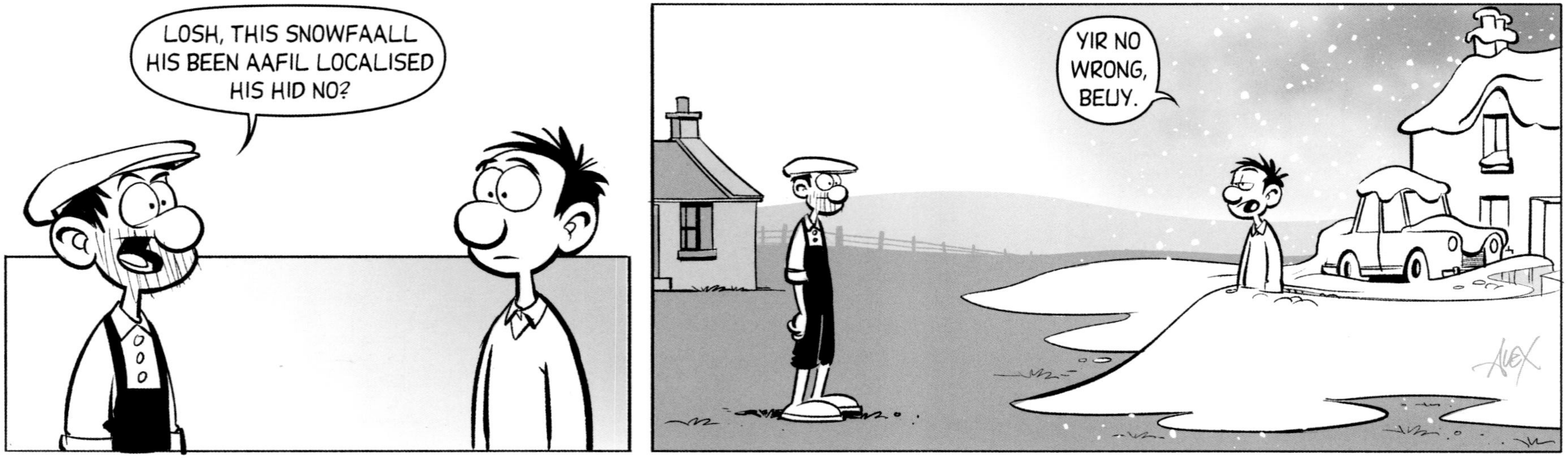
LOSH, THIS SNOWFAALL HIS BEEN AAFIL LOCALISED HIS HID NO?
YIR NO WRONG, BEUY.

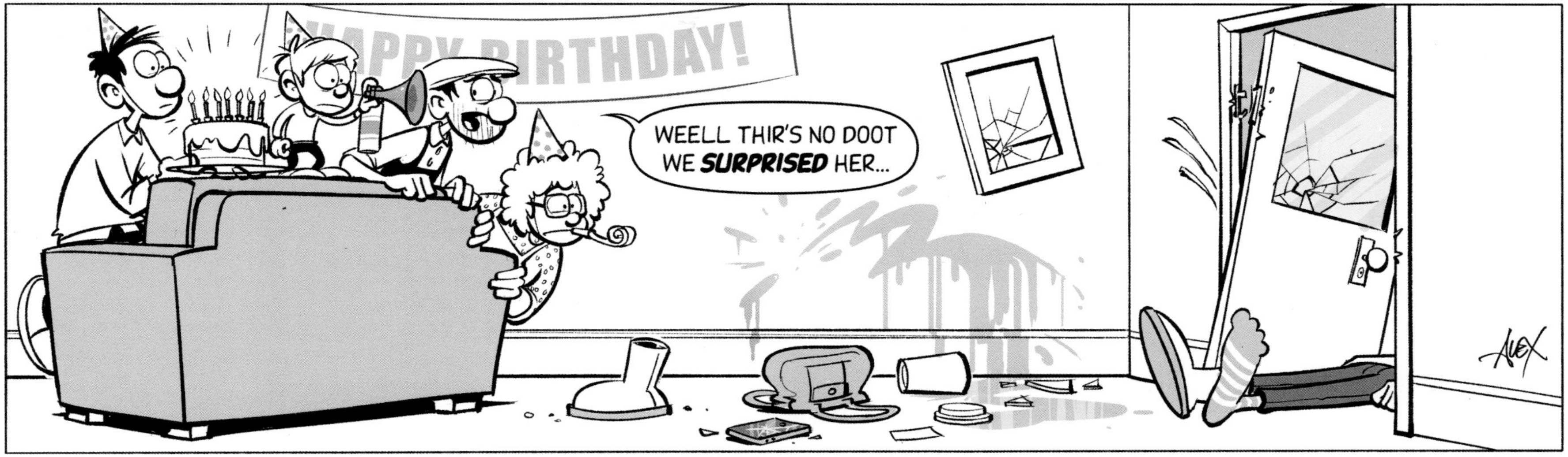
WEELL THIR'S NO DOOT WE **SURPRISED** HER...
ALEX

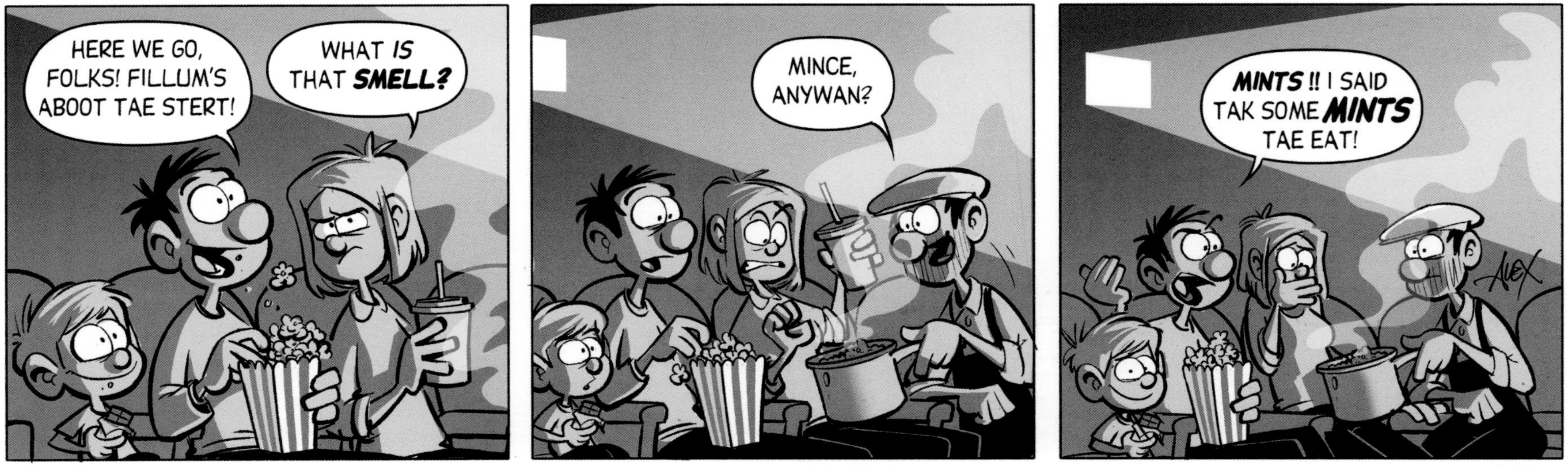
HERE WE GO, FOLKS! FILLUM'S ABOOT TAE STERT!
WHAT *IS* THAT **SMELL?**
MINCE, ANYWAN?
**MINTS**!! I SAID TAK SOME **MINTS** TAE EAT!
ALEX

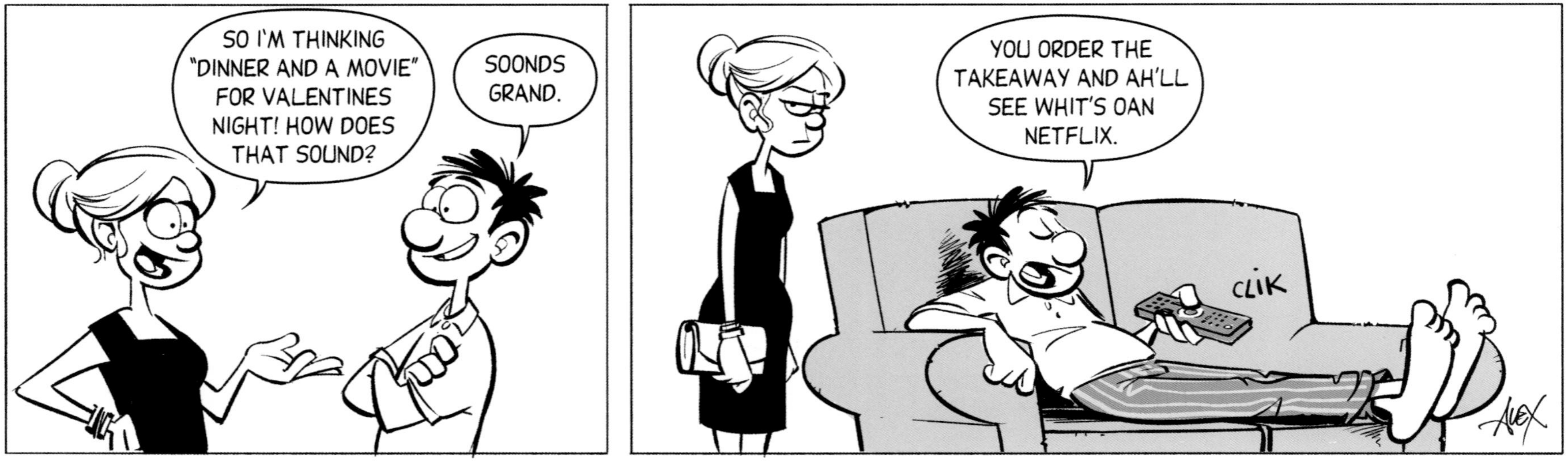
SO I'M THINKING "DINNER AND A MOVIE" FOR VALENTINES NIGHT! HOW DOES THAT SOUND?
SOONDS GRAND.
YOU ORDER THE TAKEAWAY AND AH'LL SEE WHIT'S OAN NETFLIX.
CLIK

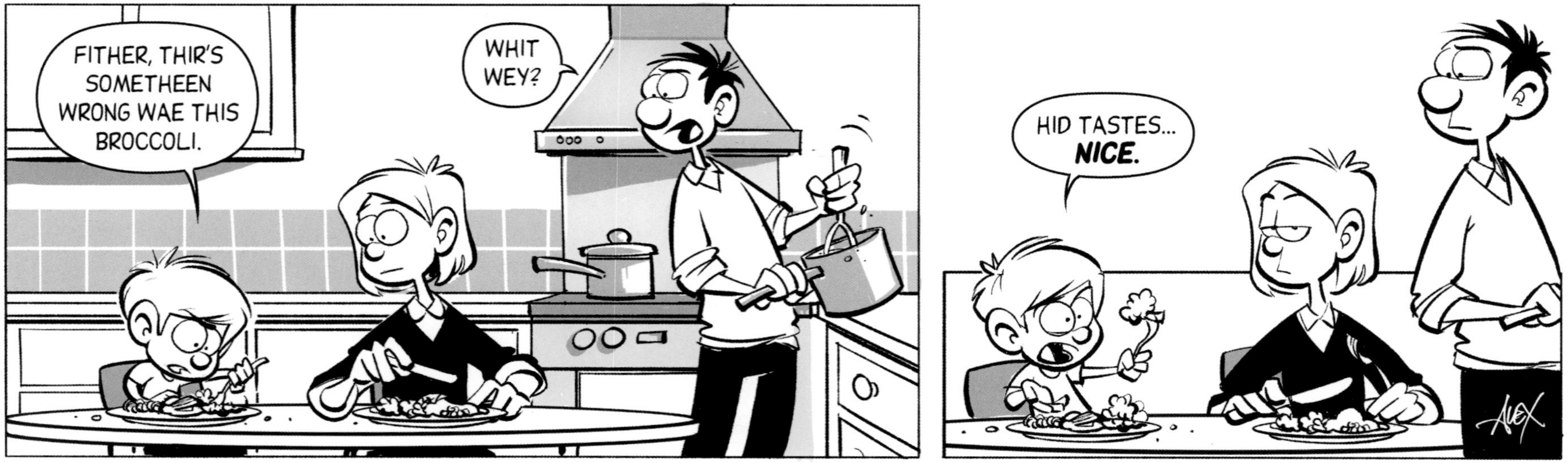
FITHER, THIR'S SOMETHEEN WRONG WAE THIS BROCCOLI.
WHIT WEY?
HID TASTES... **NICE.**

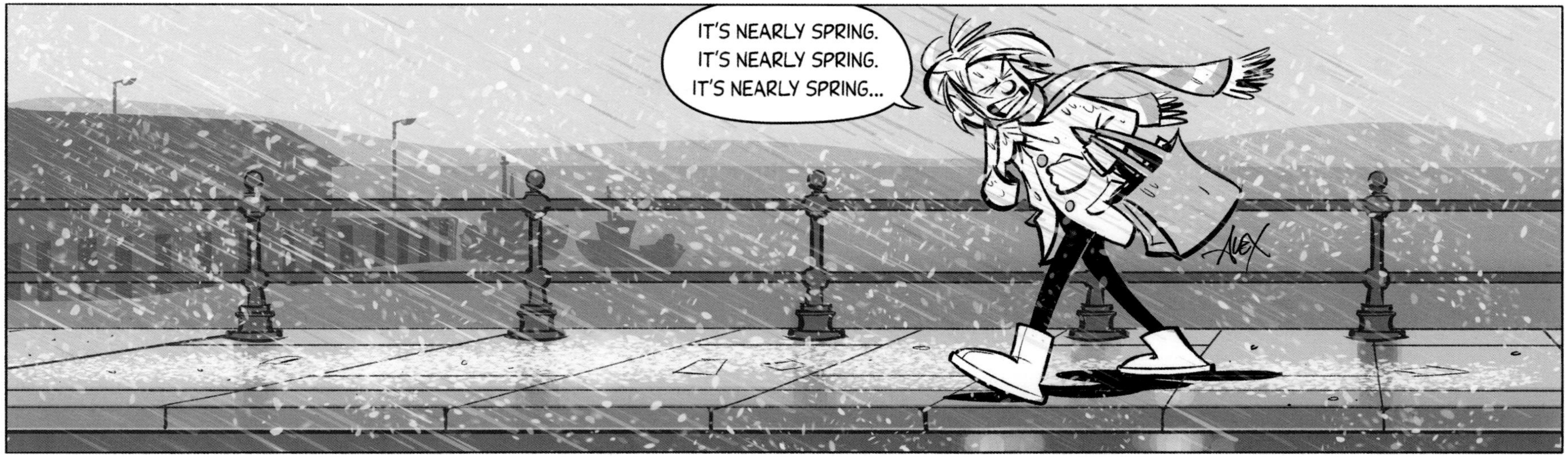
IT'S NEARLY SPRING.
IT'S NEARLY SPRING.
IT'S NEARLY SPRING...
ALEX

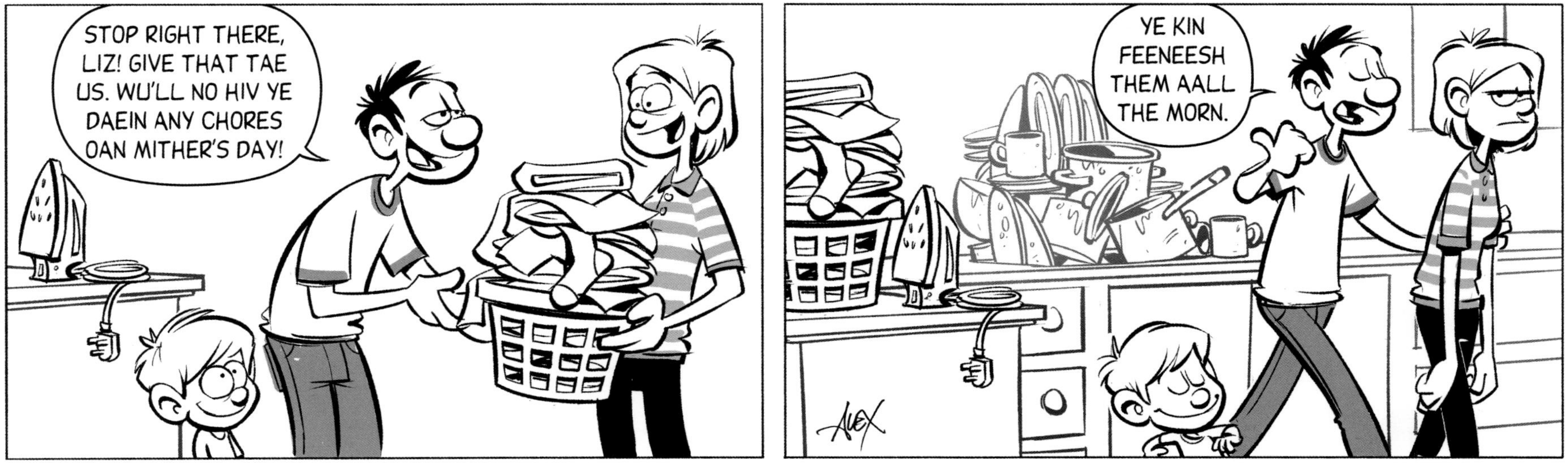
STOP RIGHT THERE, LIZ! GIVE THAT TAE US. WU'LL NO HIV YE DAEIN ANY CHORES OAN MITHER'S DAY!
YE KIN FEENEESH THEM AALL THE MORN.
ALEX

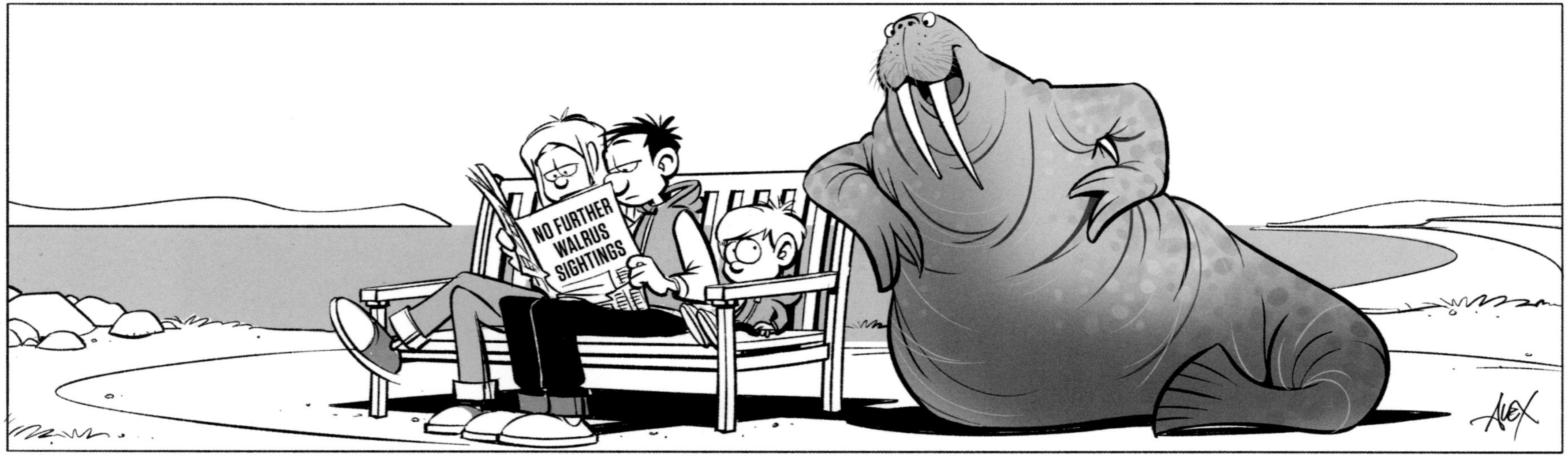
NO FURTHER WALRUS SIGHTINGS
ALEX

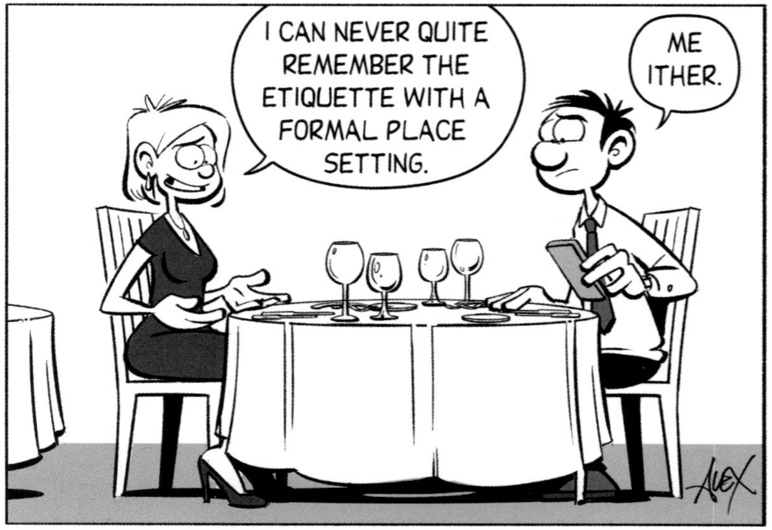
I CAN NEVER QUITE REMEMBER THE ETIQUETTE WITH A FORMAL PLACE SETTING.
ME ITHER.
ALEX

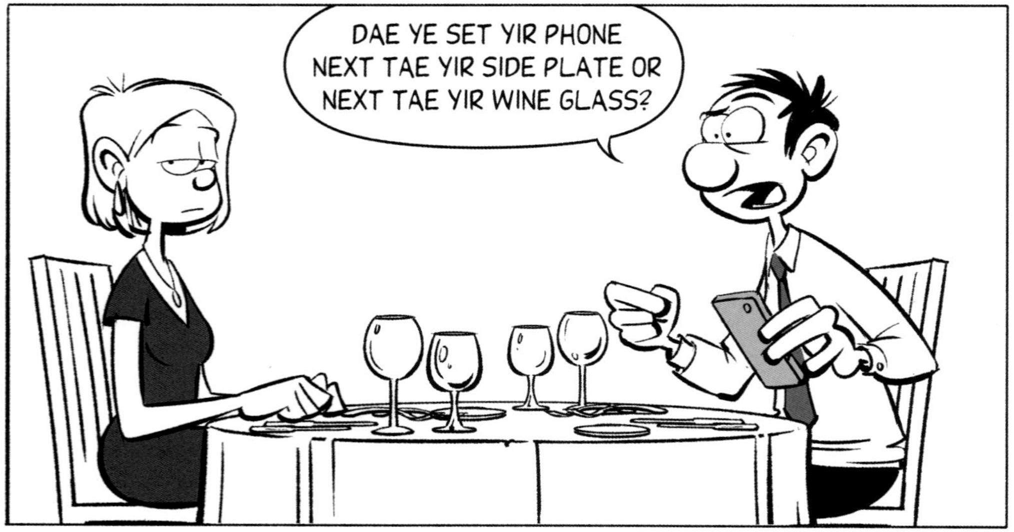
DAE YE SET YIR PHONE NEXT TAE YIR SIDE PLATE OR NEXT TAE YIR WINE GLASS?

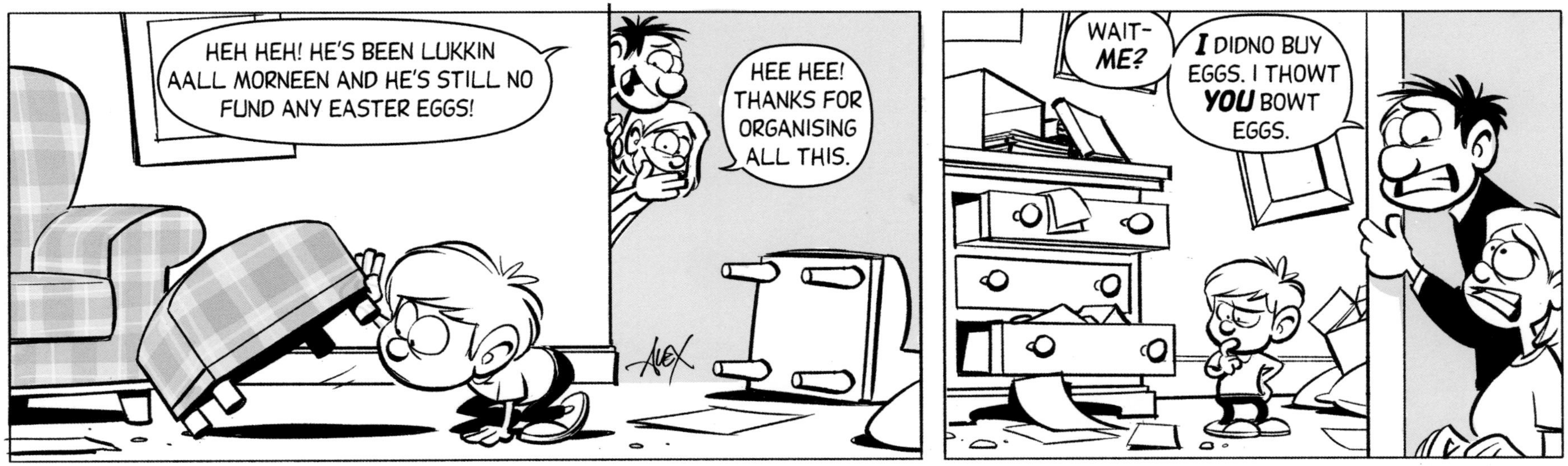
HEH HEH! HE'S BEEN LUKKIN AALL MORNEEN AND HE'S STILL NO FUND ANY EASTER EGGS!
HEE HEE! THANKS FOR ORGANISING ALL THIS.
WAIT- ME?
I DIDNO BUY EGGS. I THOWT YOU BOWT EGGS.

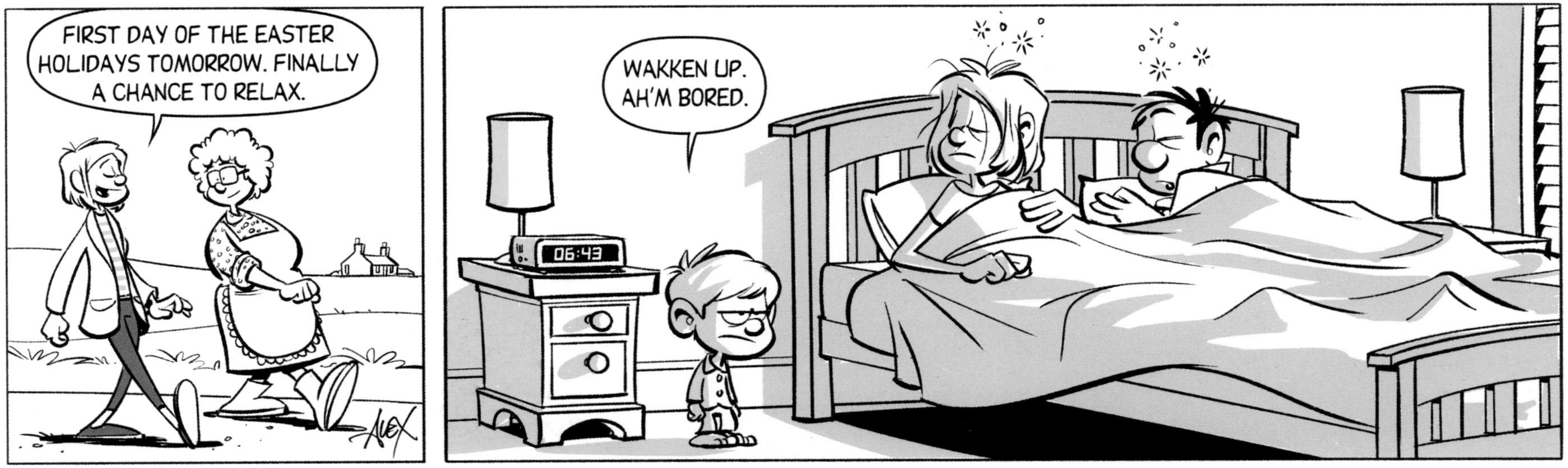
FIRST DAY OF THE EASTER HOLIDAYS TOMORROW. FINALLY A CHANCE TO RELAX.
WAKKEN UP. AH'M BORED.
06:43

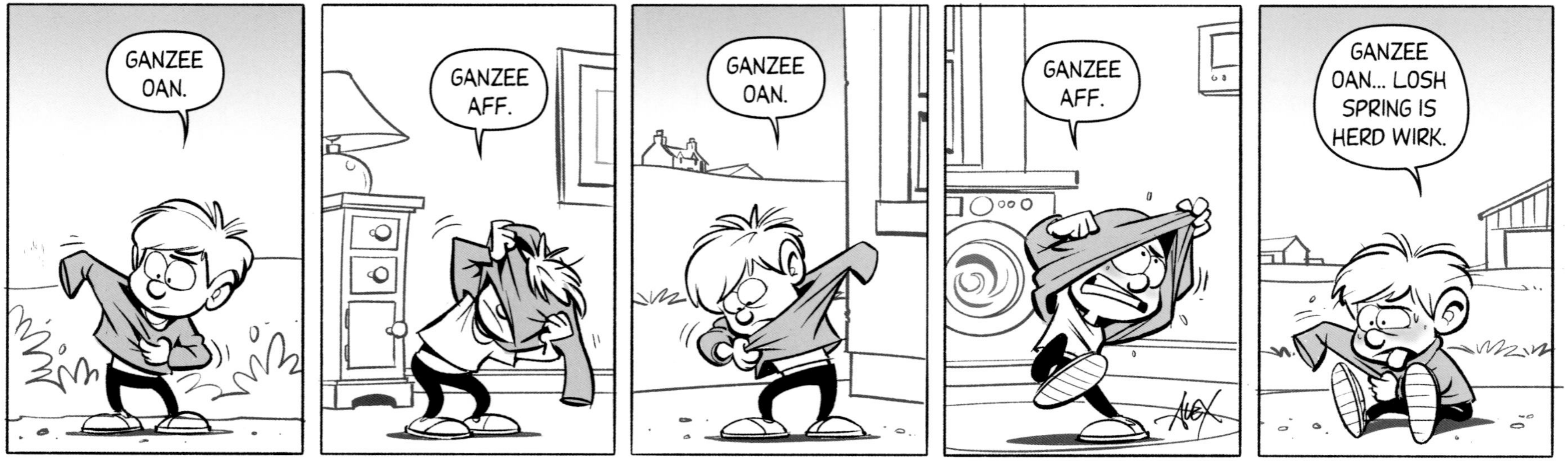
GANZEE OAN.
GANZEE AFF.
GANZEE OAN.
GANZEE AFF.
GANZEE OAN... LOSH SPRING IS HERD WIRK.

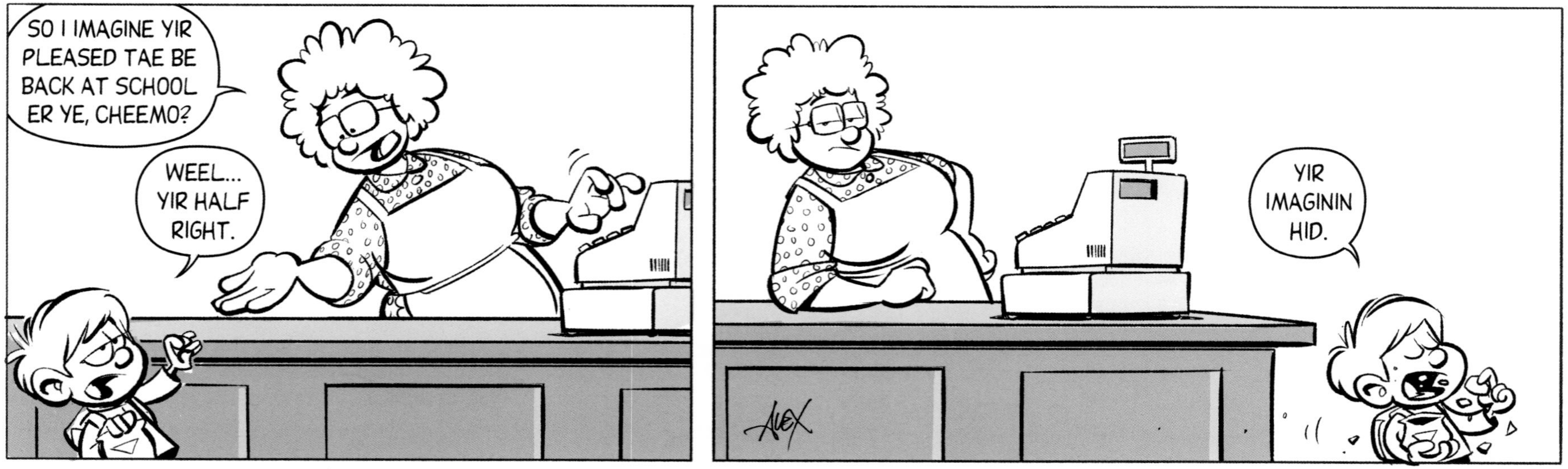
SO I IMAGINE YIR PLEASED TAE BE BACK AT SCHOOL ER YE, CHEEMO?
WEEL... YIR HALF RIGHT.
YIR IMAGININ HID.

I don't really.

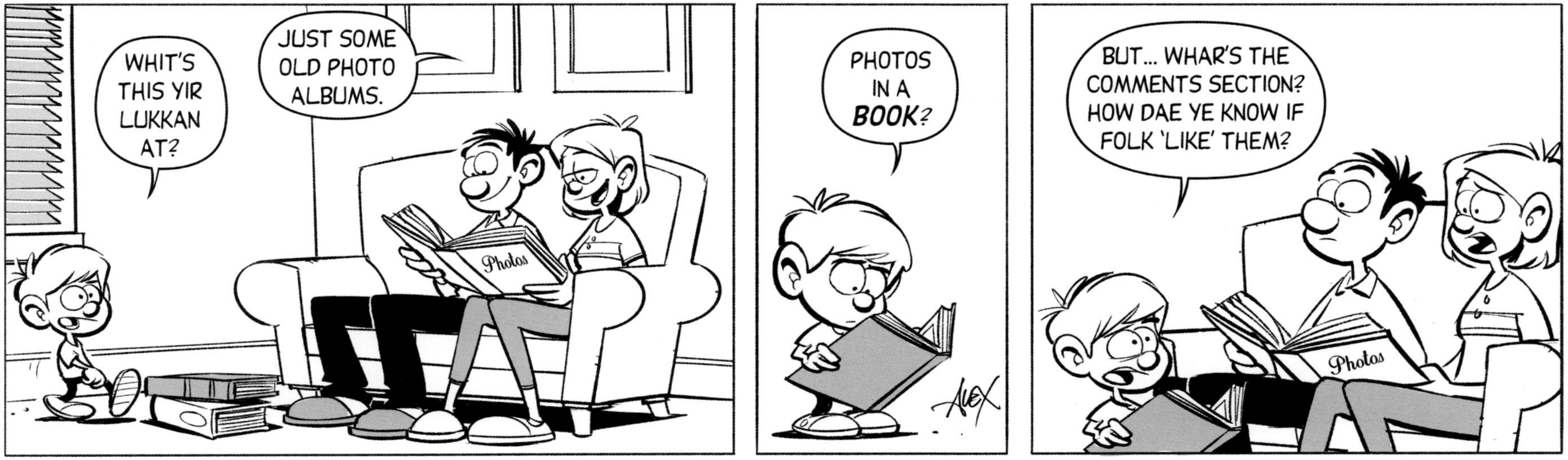
WHIT'S THIS YIR LUKKAN AT?
JUST SOME OLD PHOTO ALBUMS.
Photos
PHOTOS IN A BOOK?
ALEX
BUT... WHAR'S THE COMMENTS SECTION? HOW DAE YE KNOW IF FOLK 'LIKE' THEM?
Photos

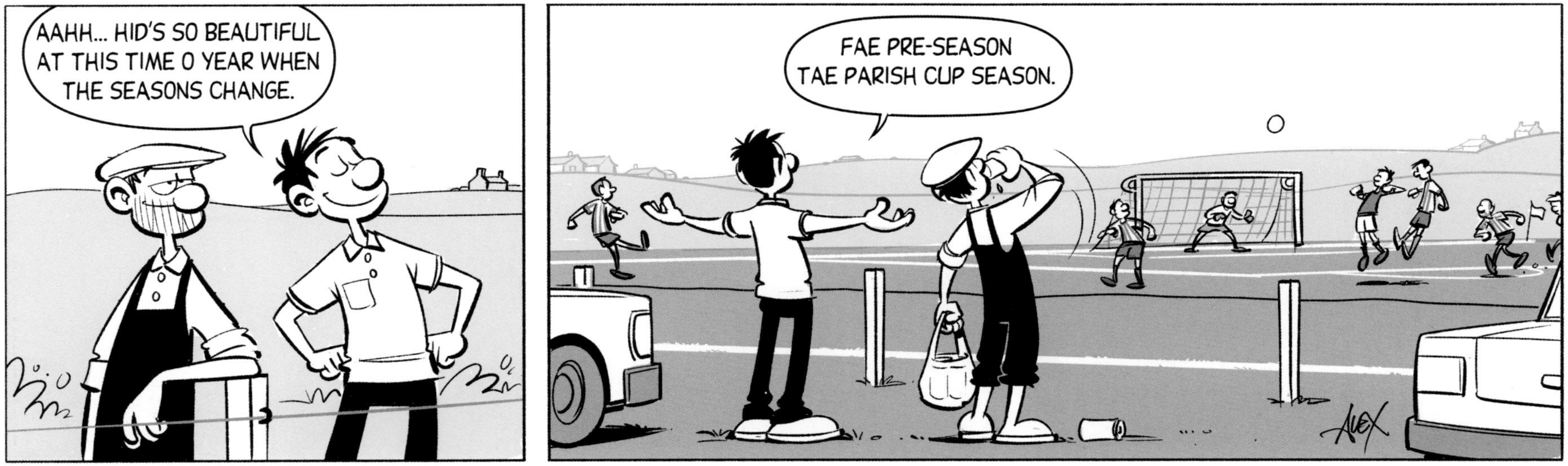
AAHH... HID'S SO BEAUTIFUL AT THIS TIME O YEAR WHEN THE SEASONS CHANGE.
FAE PRE-SEASON TAE PARISH CUP SEASON.
ALEX

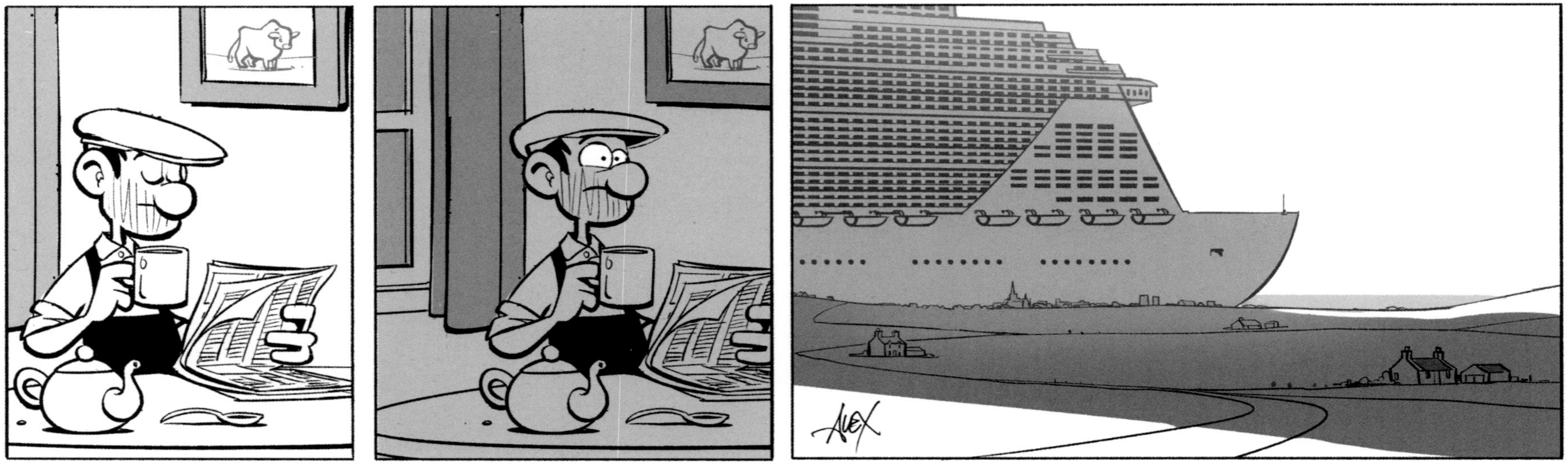

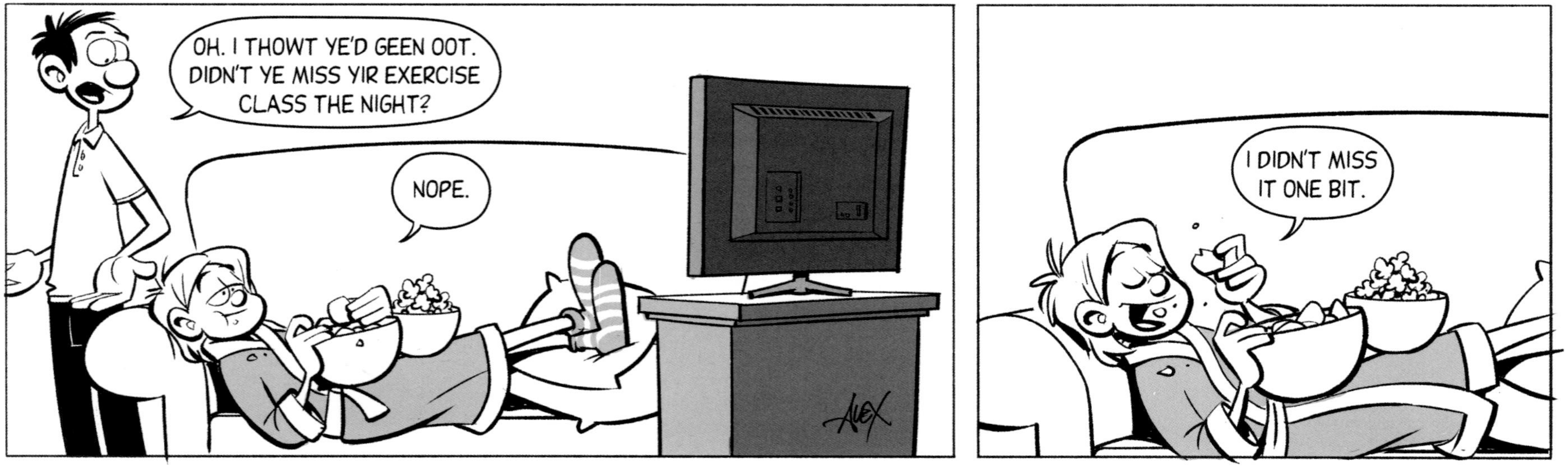
OH. I THOWT YE'D GEEN OOT. DIDN'T YE MISS YIR EXERCISE CLASS THE NIGHT?
NOPE.
I DIDN'T MISS IT ONE BIT.

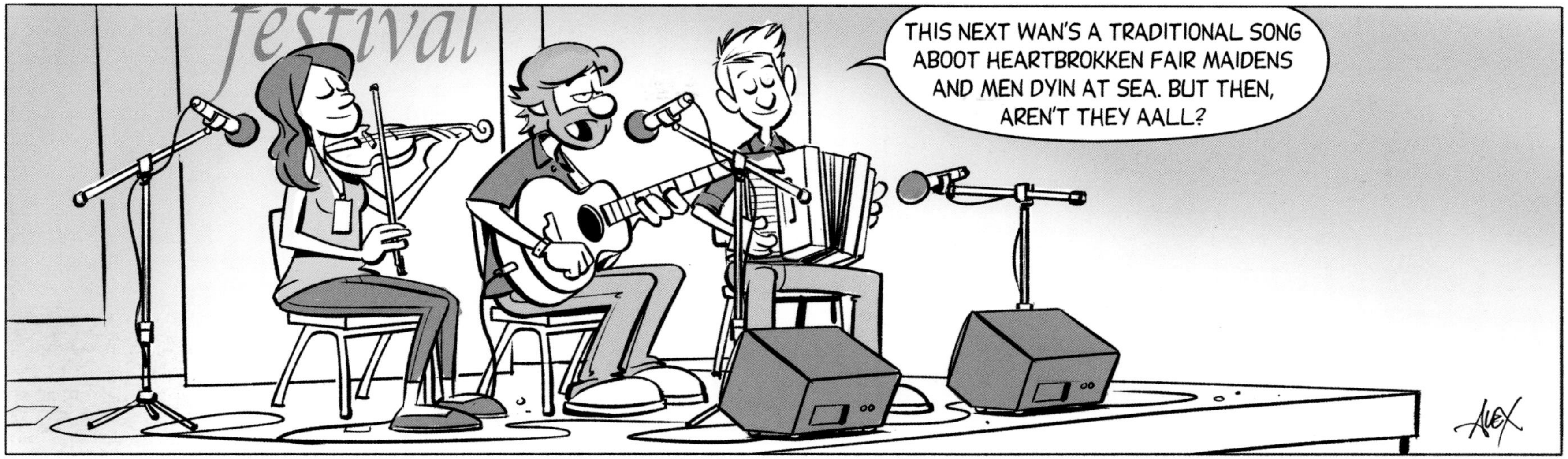
festival
THIS NEXT WAN'S A TRADITIONAL SONG ABOOT HEARTBROKKEN FAIR MAIDENS AND MEN DYIN AT SEA. BUT THEN, AREN'T THEY AALL?
ALEX

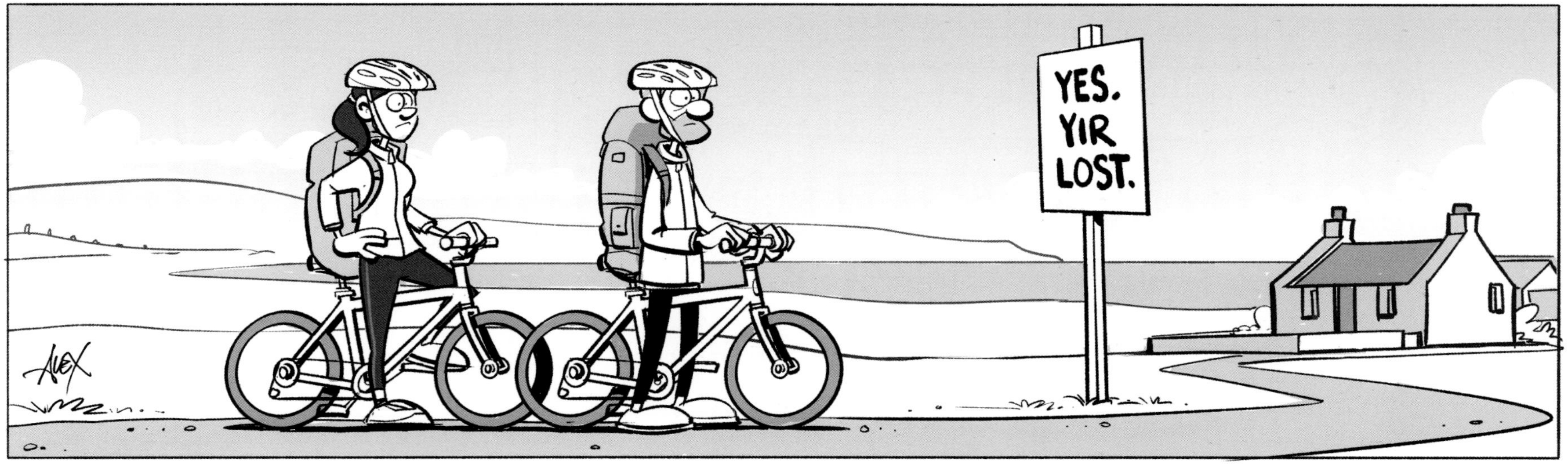
YES. YIR LOST.
ALEX

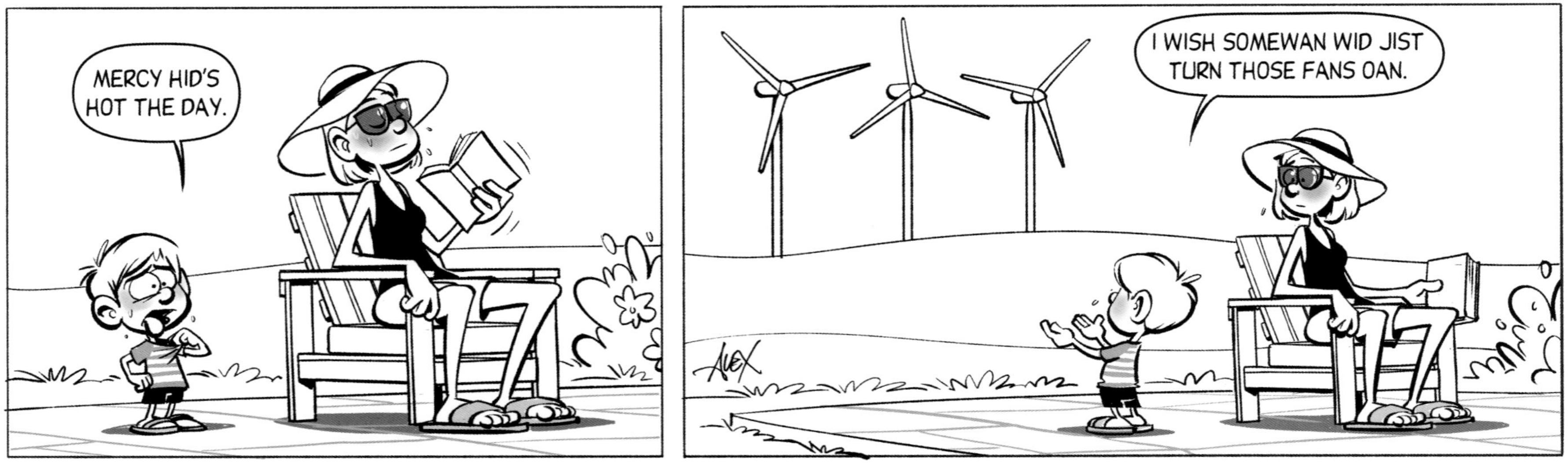
MERCY HID'S HOT THE DAY.
I WISH SOMEWAN WID JIST TURN THOSE FANS OAN.
ALEX

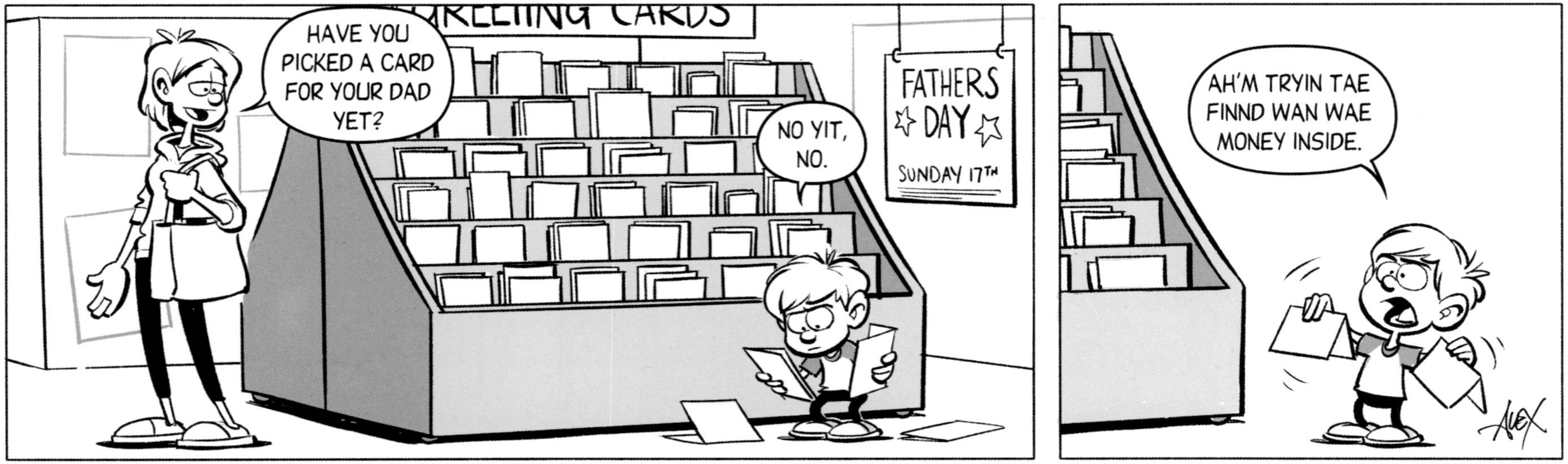
HAVE YOU PICKED A CARD FOR YOUR DAD YET?
NO YIT, NO.
FATHERS DAY
SUNDAY 17TH
AH'M TRYIN TAE FINND WAN WAE MONEY INSIDE.
ALEX

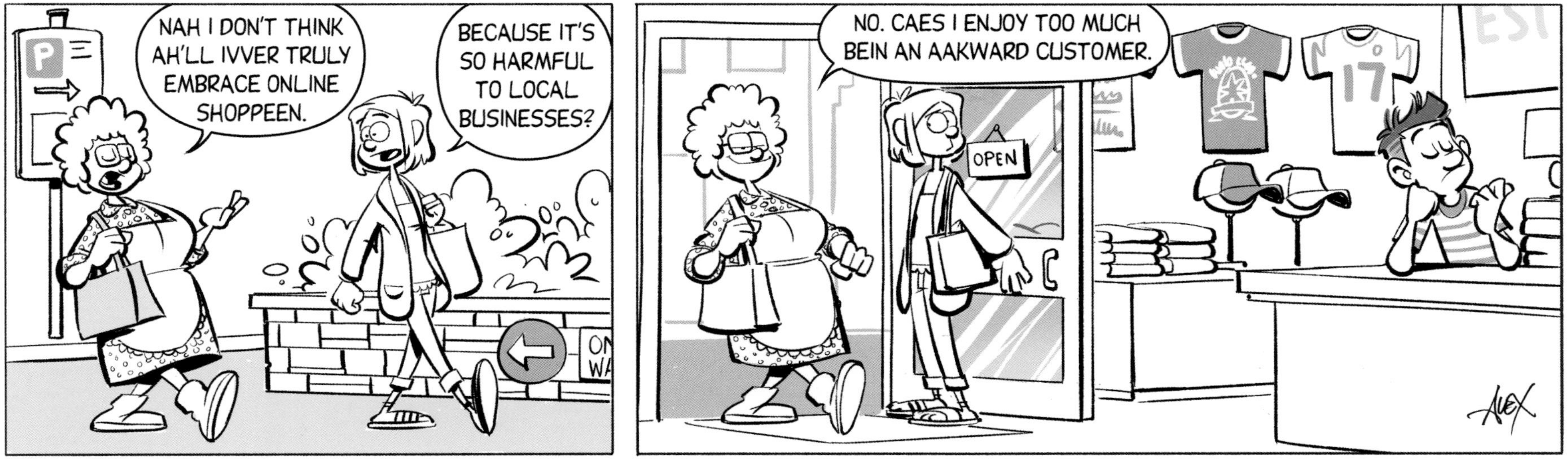
NAH I DON'T THINK AH'LL IVVER TRULY EMBRACE ONLINE SHOPPEEN.
BECAUSE IT'S SO HARMFUL TO LOCAL BUSINESSES?
NO. CAES I ENJOY TOO MUCH BEIN AN AAKWARD CUSTOMER.
OPEN

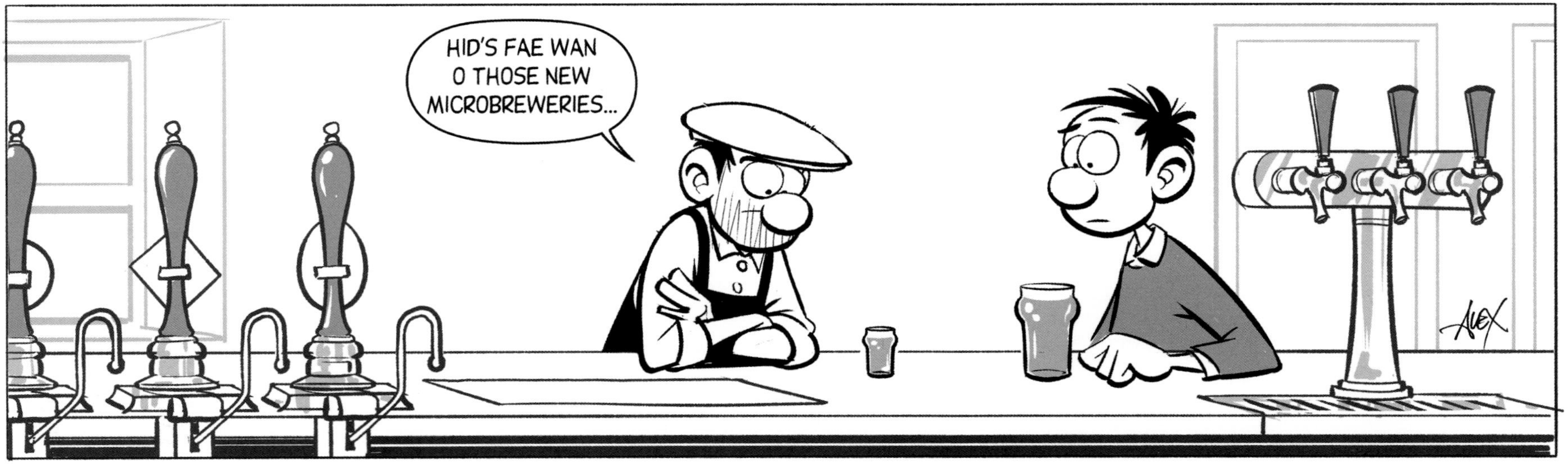
HID'S FAE WAN O THOSE NEW MICROBREWERIES...

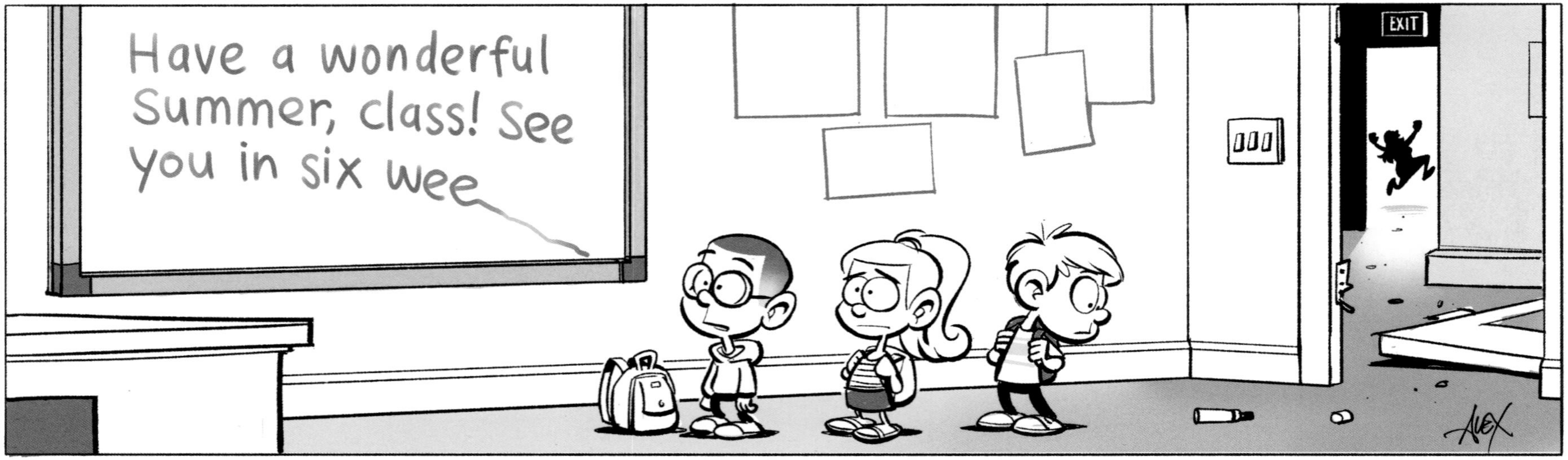
Have a wonderful Summer, class! See you in six wee
EXIT

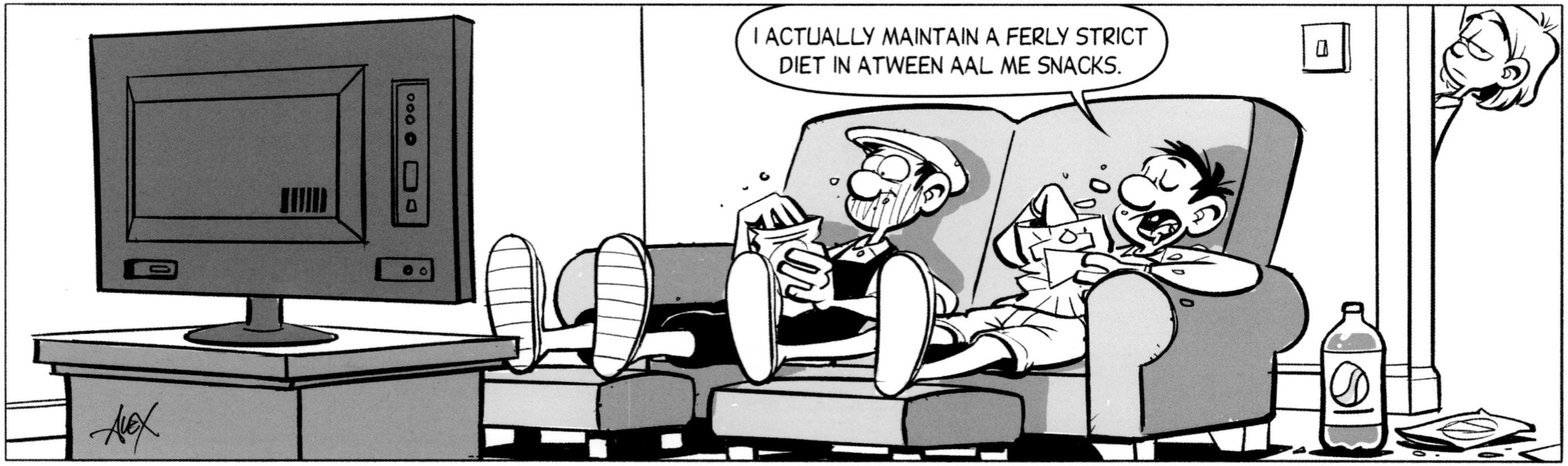
I ACTUALLY MAINTAIN A FERLY STRICT DIET IN ATWEEN AAL ME SNACKS.

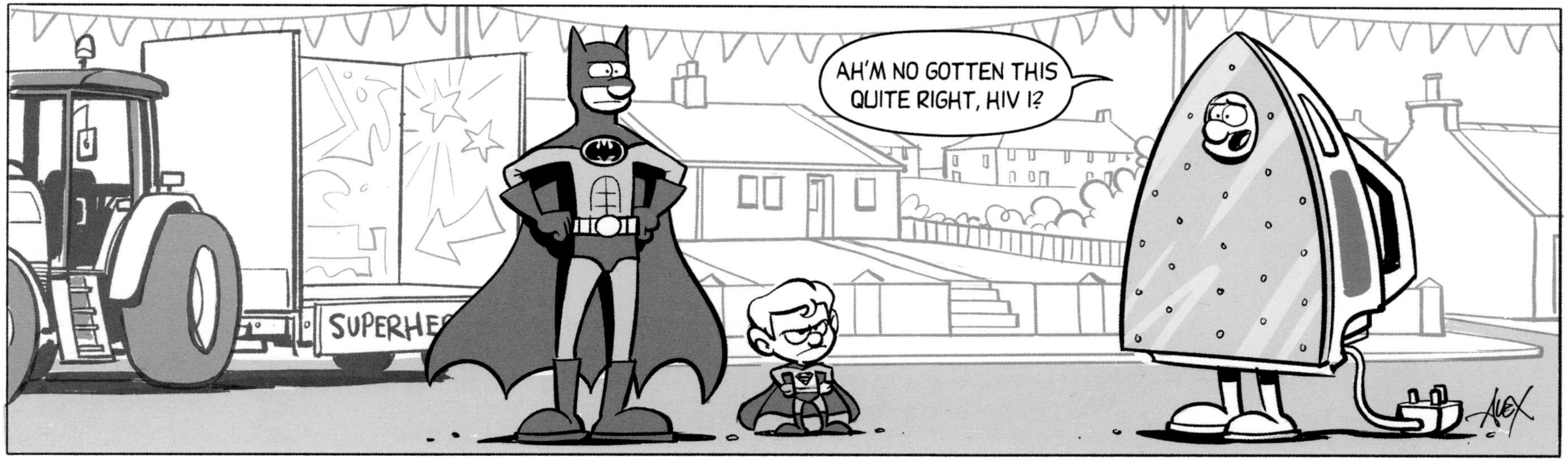
SUPERHE
AH'M NO GOTTEN THIS QUITE RIGHT, HIV I?
ALEX

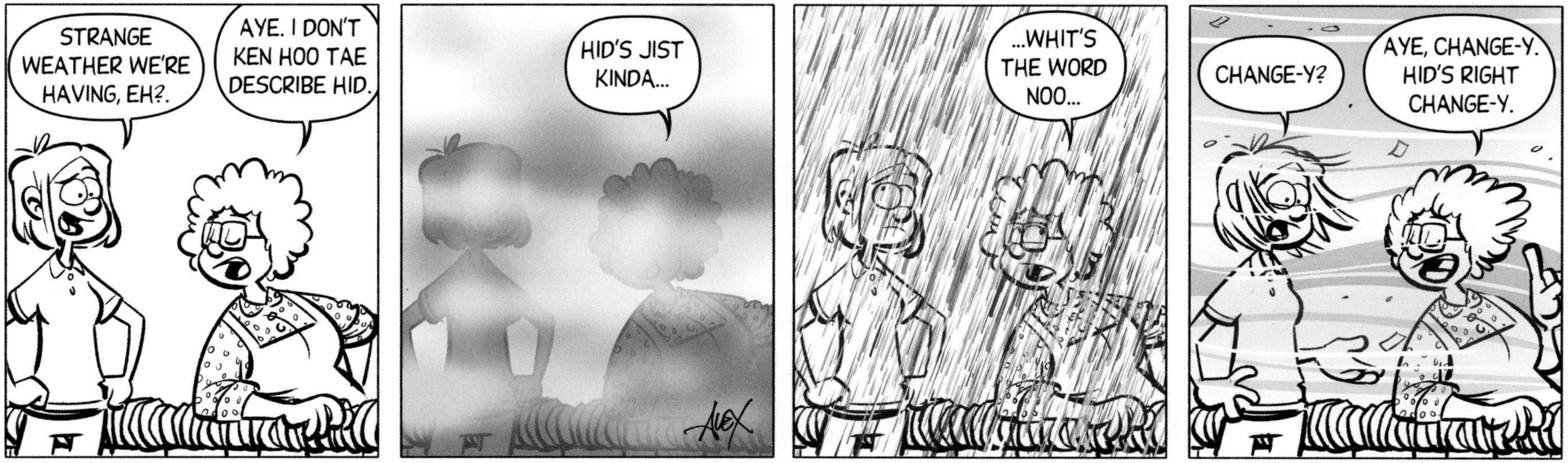
STRANGE WEATHER WE'RE HAVING, EH?.
AYE. I DON'T KEN HOO TAE DESCRIBE HID.
HID'S JIST KINDA...
ALEX
...WHIT'S THE WORD NOO...
CHANGE-Y?
AYE, CHANGE-Y. HID'S RIGHT CHANGE-Y.

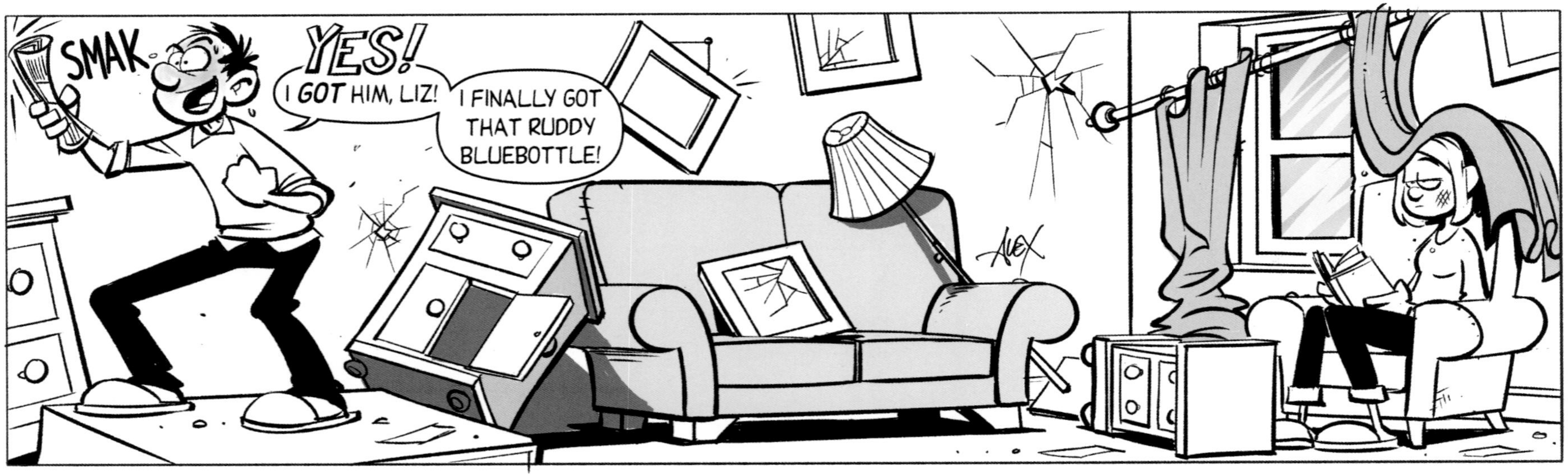
SMAK
YES!
I GOT HIM, LIZ!
I FINALLY GOT THAT RUDDY BLUEBOTTLE!
ALEX

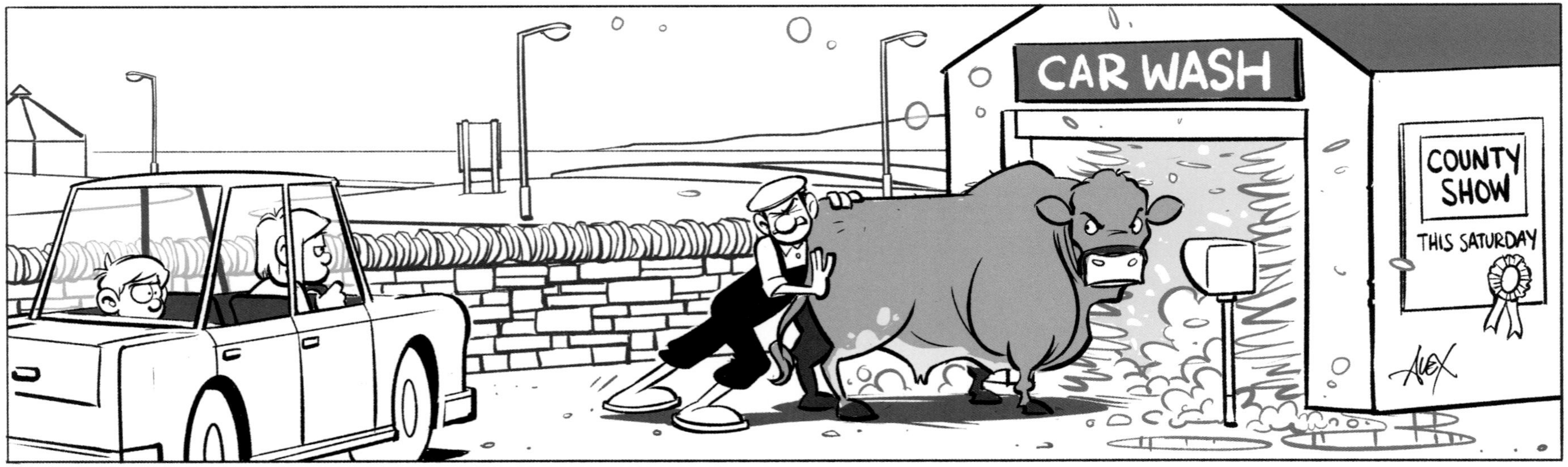
CAR WASH
COUNTY SHOW
THIS SATURDAY
ALEX

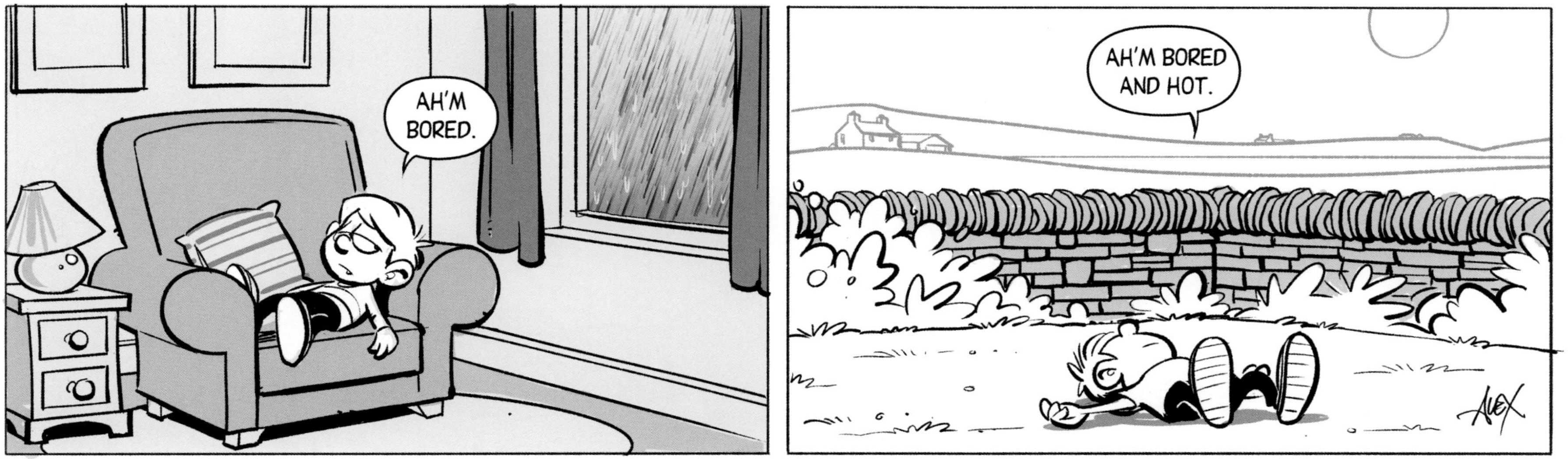
AH'M BORED.
AH'M BORED AND HOT.
ALEX

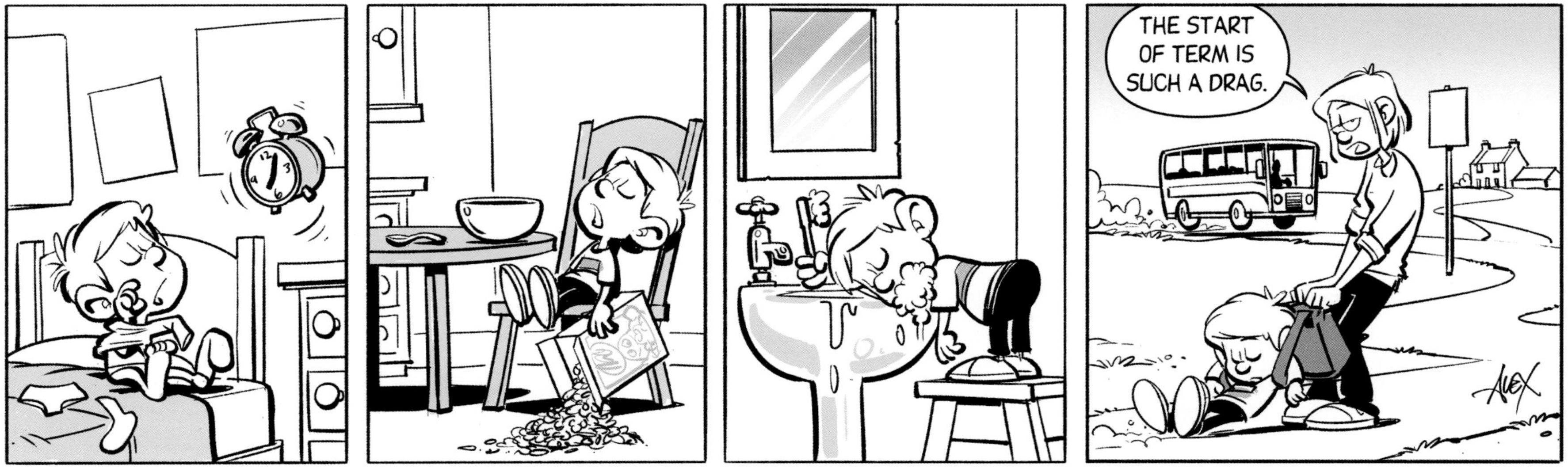
THE START OF TERM IS SUCH A DRAG.
ALEX

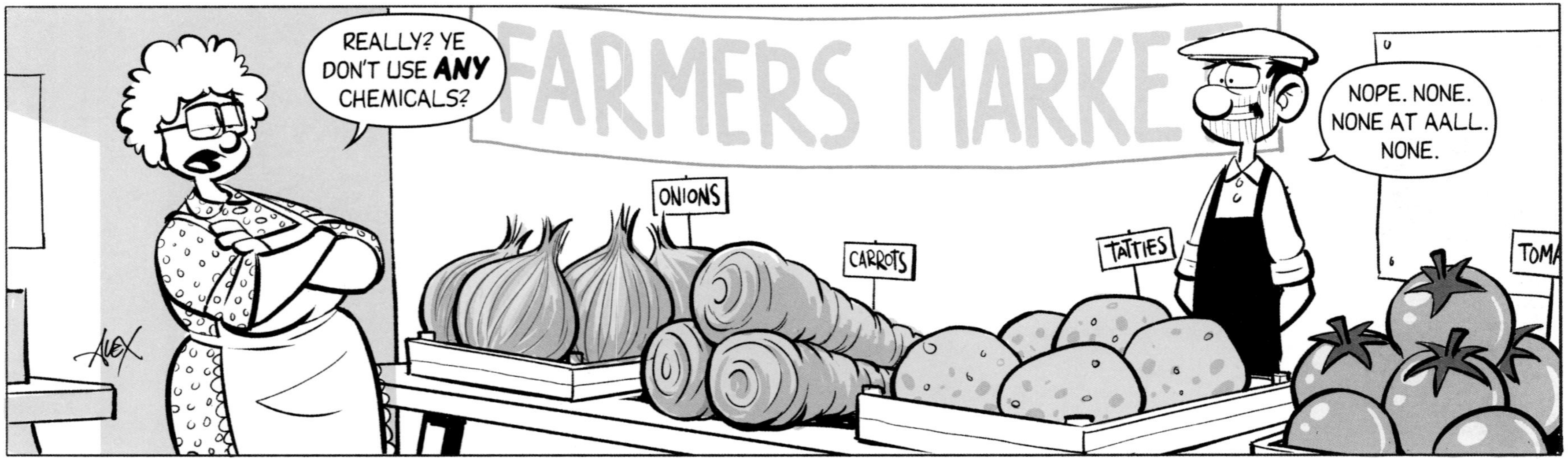
FARMERS MARKET
REALLY? YE DON'T USE **ANY** CHEMICALS?
NOPE. NONE. NONE AT AALL. NONE.
ONIONS
CARROTS
TATTIES
TOMA
ALEX

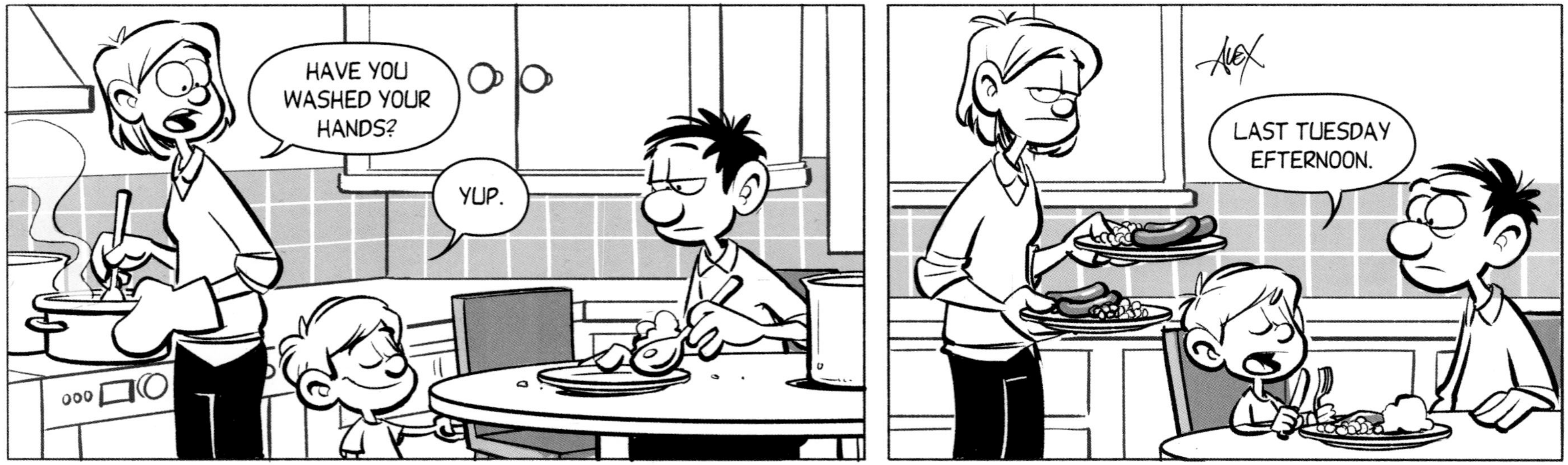
HAVE YOU WASHED YOUR HANDS?
YUP.
LAST TUESDAY EFTERNOON.
ALEX

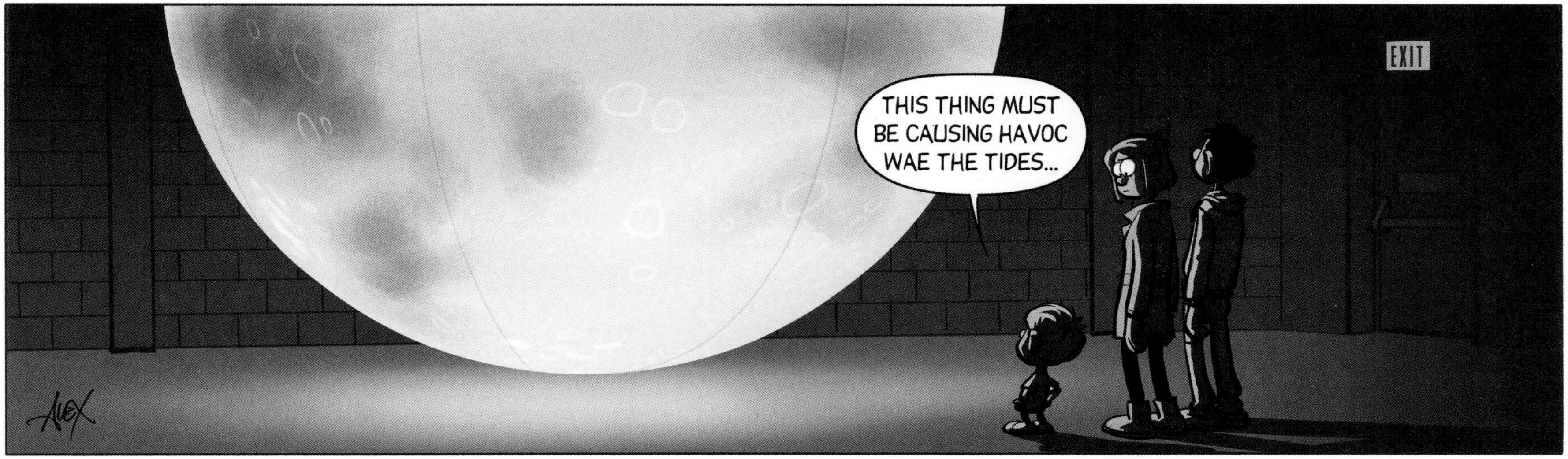
THIS THING MUST BE CAUSING HAVOC WAE THE TIDES...
EXIT
ALEX
Skyran Moon Exhibit

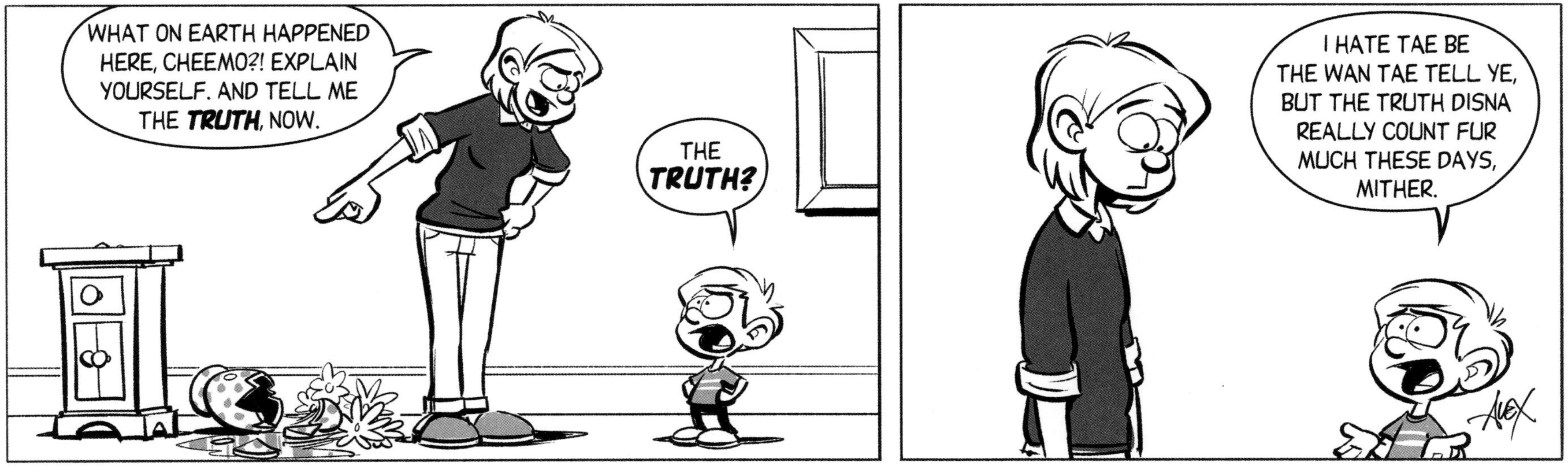
WHAT ON EARTH HAPPENED HERE, CHEEMO?! EXPLAIN YOURSELF. AND TELL ME THE **TRUTH**, NOW.
THE **TRUTH?**
I HATE TAE BE THE WAN TAE TELL YE, BUT THE TRUTH DISNA REALLY COUNT FUR MUCH THESE DAYS, MITHER.
ALEX

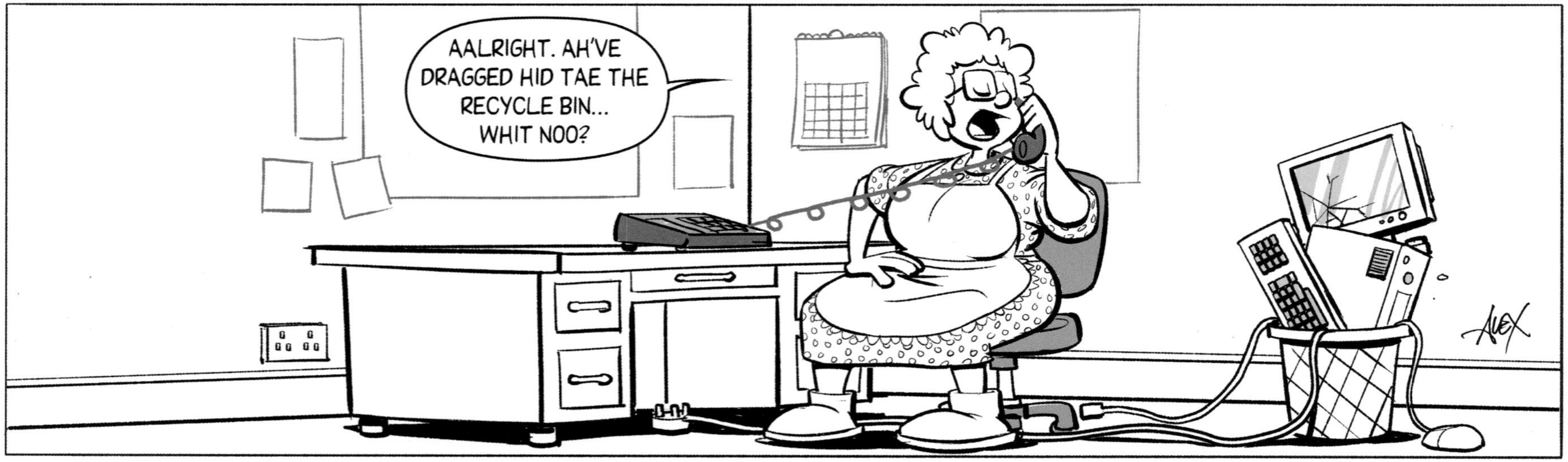
AALRIGHT. AH'VE DRAGGED HID TAE THE RECYCLE BIN... WHIT NOO?
ALEX

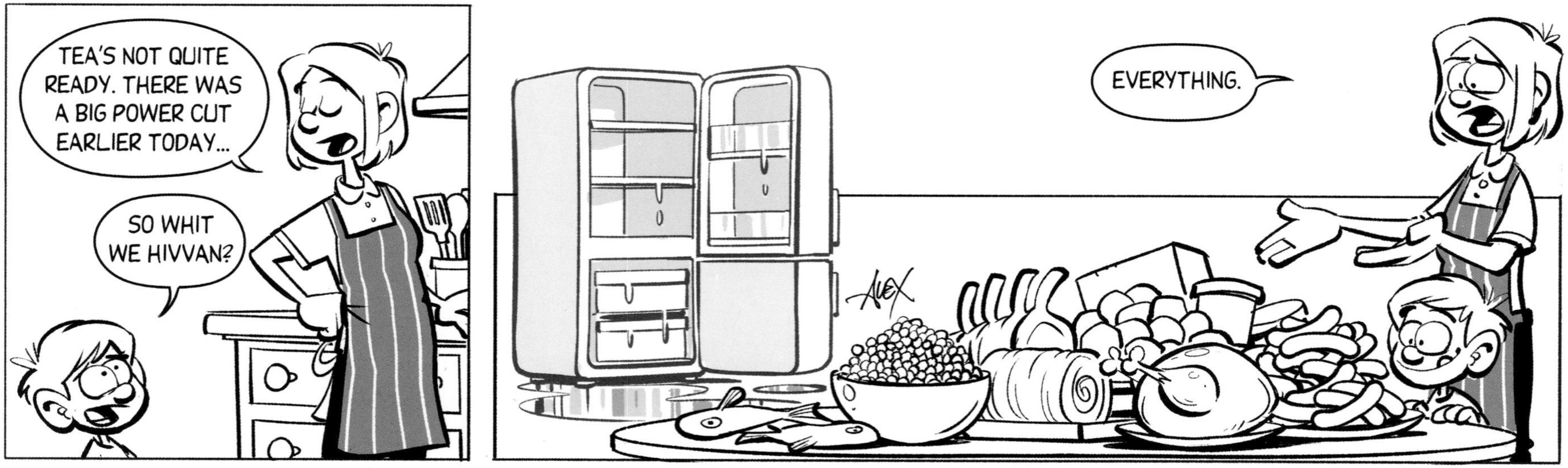
TEA'S NOT QUITE READY. THERE WAS A BIG POWER CUT EARLIER TODAY...
SO WHIT WE HIVVAN?
EVERYTHING.
ALEX

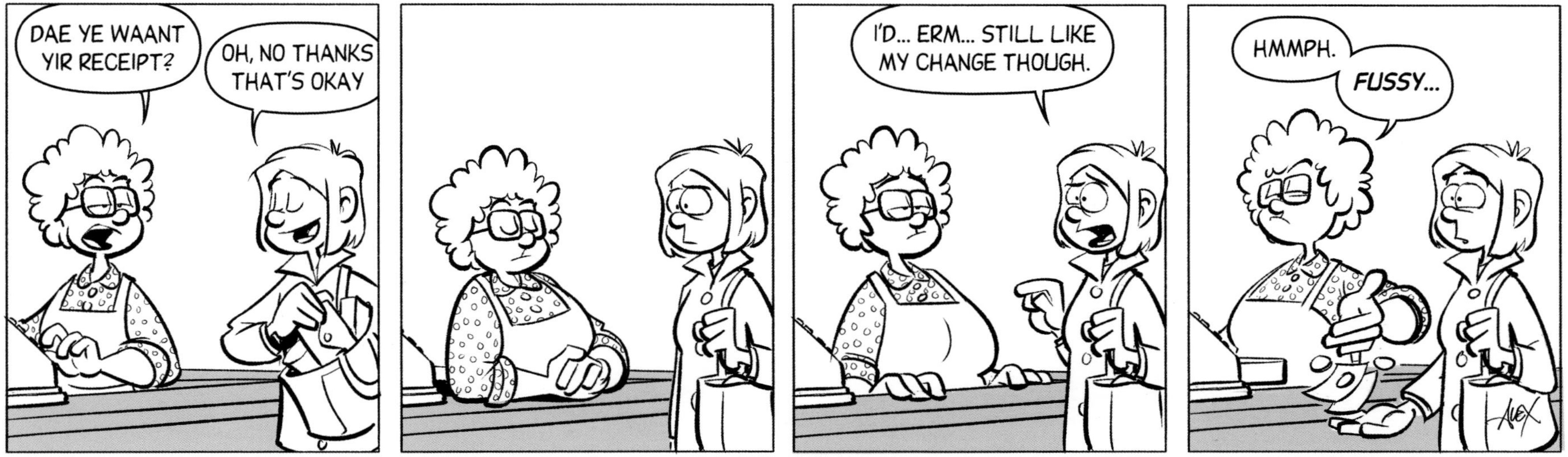
DAE YE WAANT YIR RECEIPT?
OH, NO THANKS THAT'S OKAY
I'D... ERM... STILL LIKE MY CHANGE THOUGH.
HMMPH.
FUSSY...
ALEX

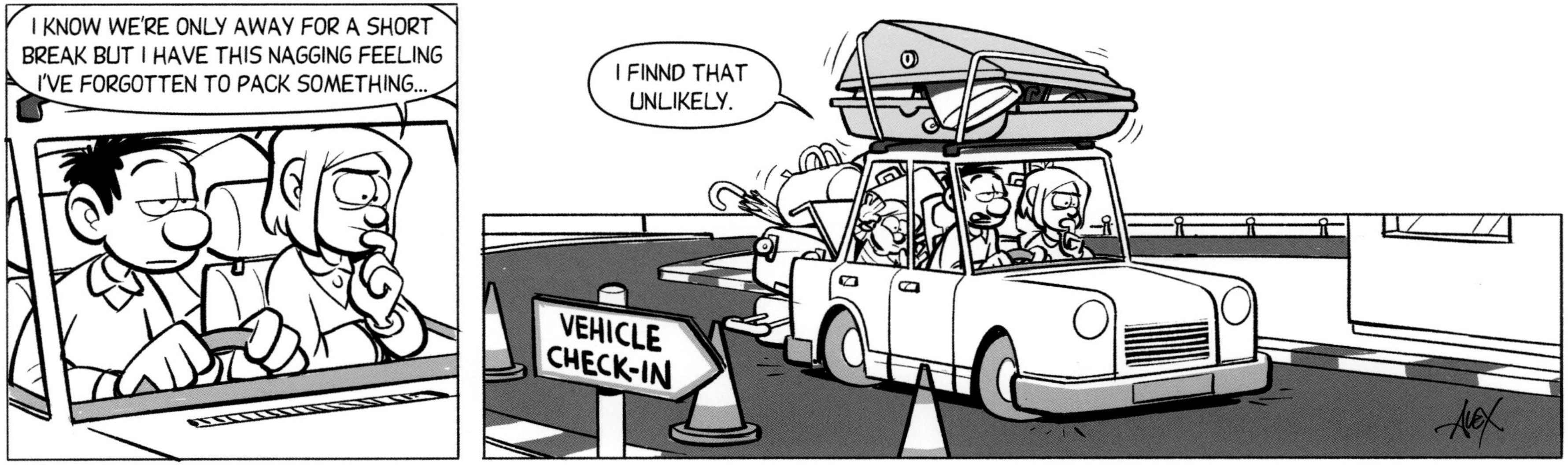
I KNOW WE'RE ONLY AWAY FOR A SHORT BREAK BUT I HAVE THIS NAGGING FEELING I'VE FORGOTTEN TO PACK SOMETHING...
I FINND THAT UNLIKELY.
VEHICLE CHECK-IN
ALEX

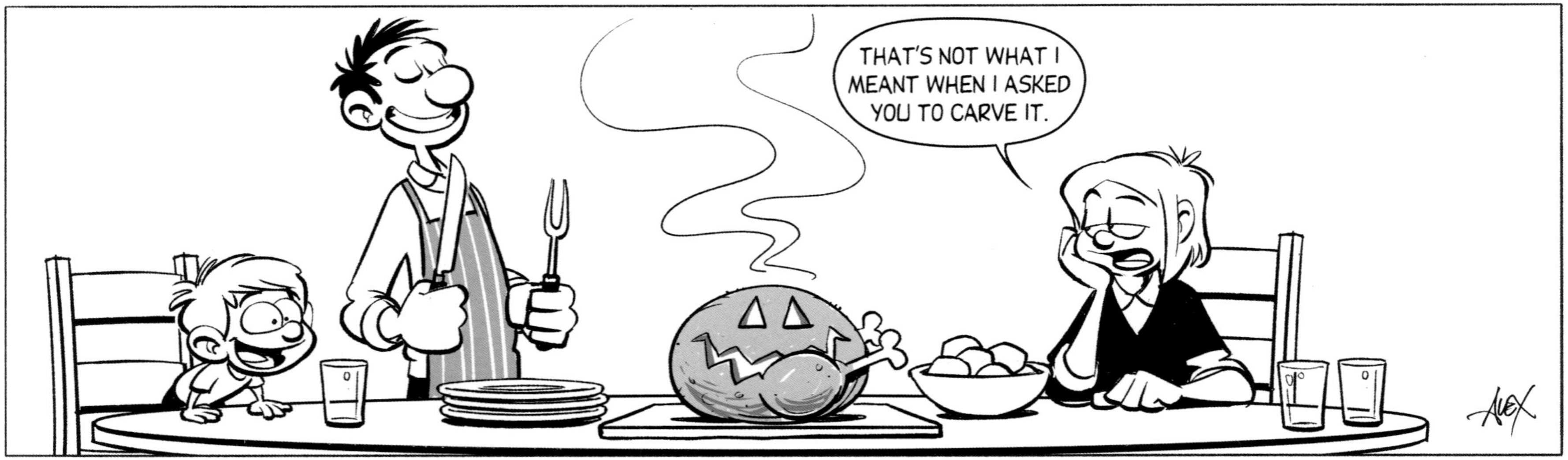
THAT'S NOT WHAT I MEANT WHEN I ASKED YOU TO CARVE IT.
ALEX

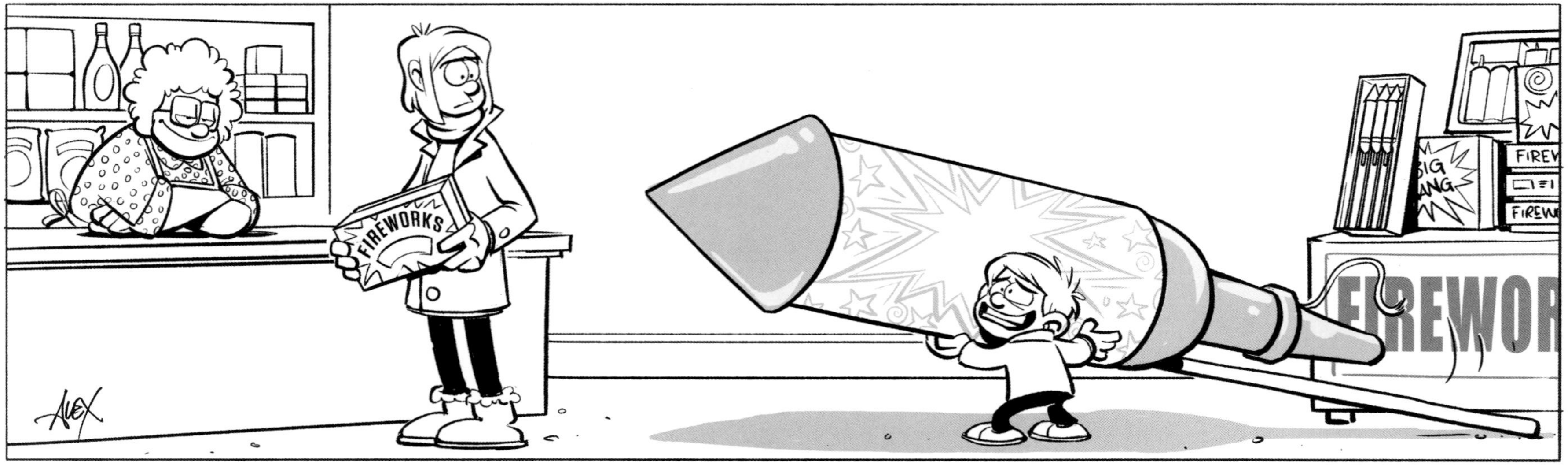
FIREWORKS
ALEX

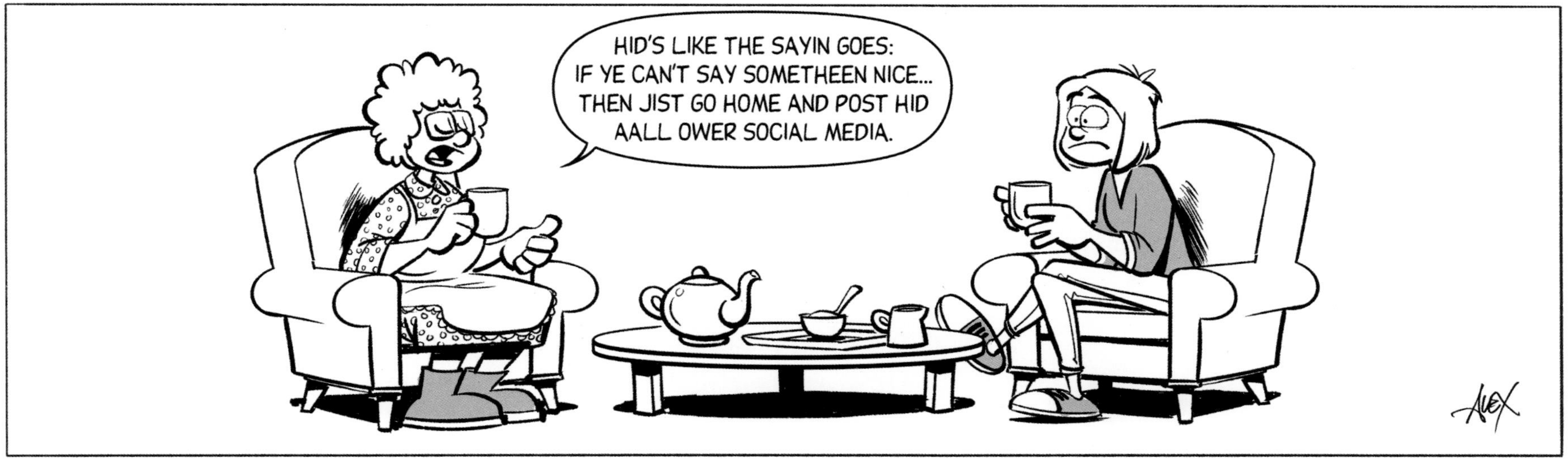
HID'S LIKE THE SAYIN GOES: IF YE CAN'T SAY SOMETHEEN NICE... THEN JIST GO HOME AND POST HID AALL OWER SOCIAL MEDIA.
ALEX

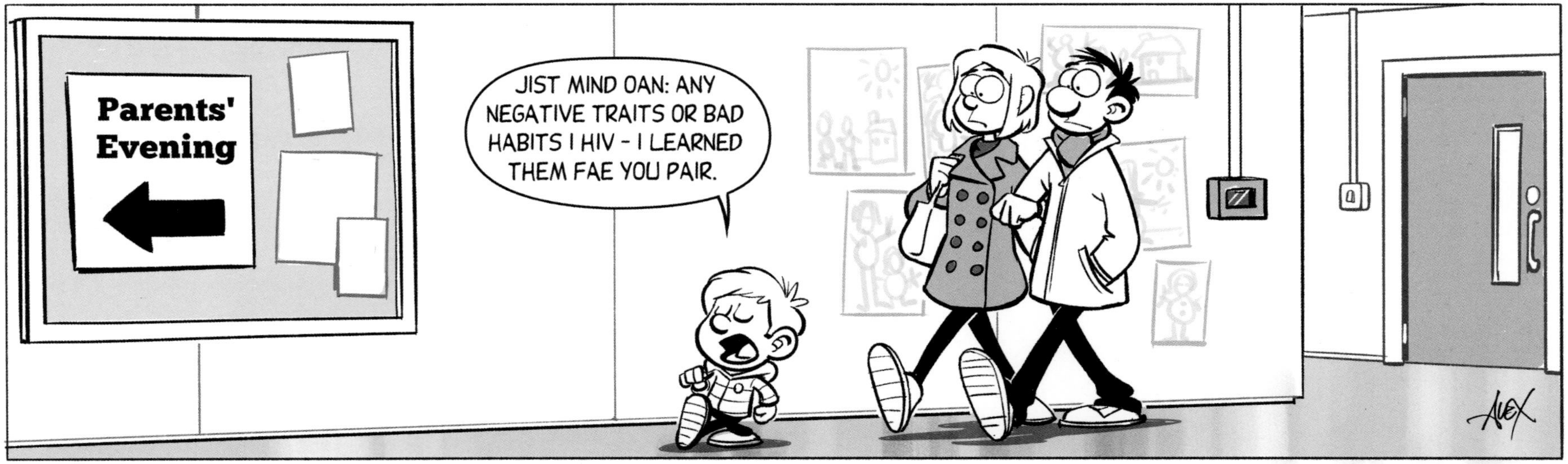
Parents' Evening
JIST MIND OAN: ANY NEGATIVE TRAITS OR BAD HABITS I HIV - I LEARNED THEM FAE YOU PAIR.
ALEX

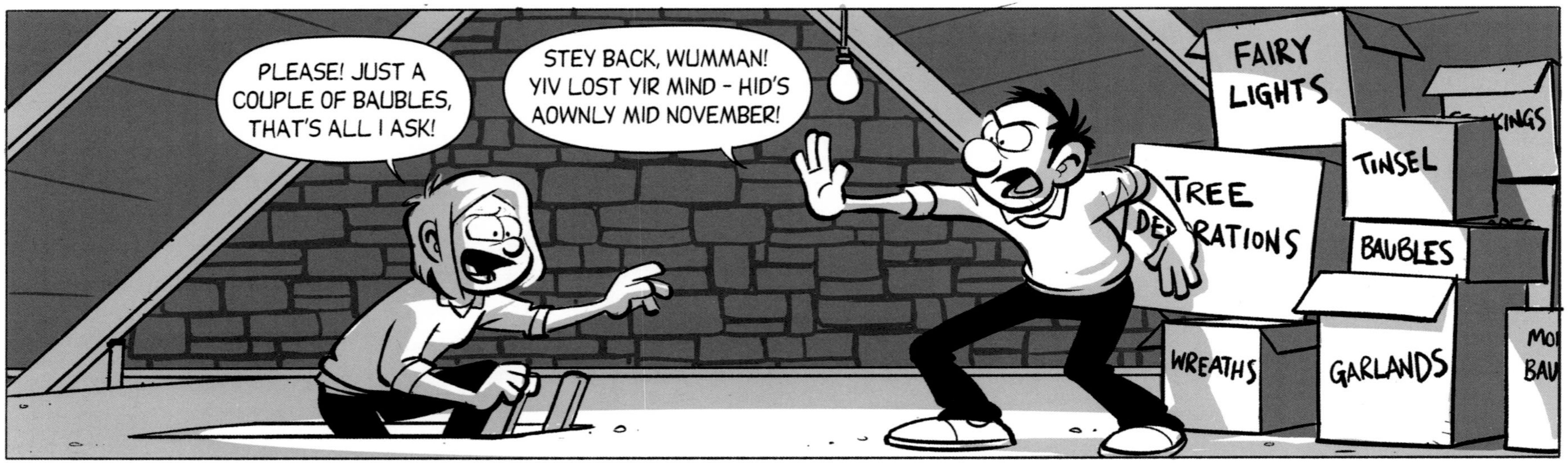
PLEASE! JUST A COUPLE OF BAUBLES, THAT'S ALL I ASK!
STEY BACK, WUMMAN! YIV LOST YIR MIND - HID'S AOWNLY MID NOVEMBER!
FAIRY LIGHTS
TINSEL
BAUBLES
WREATHS
GARLANDS

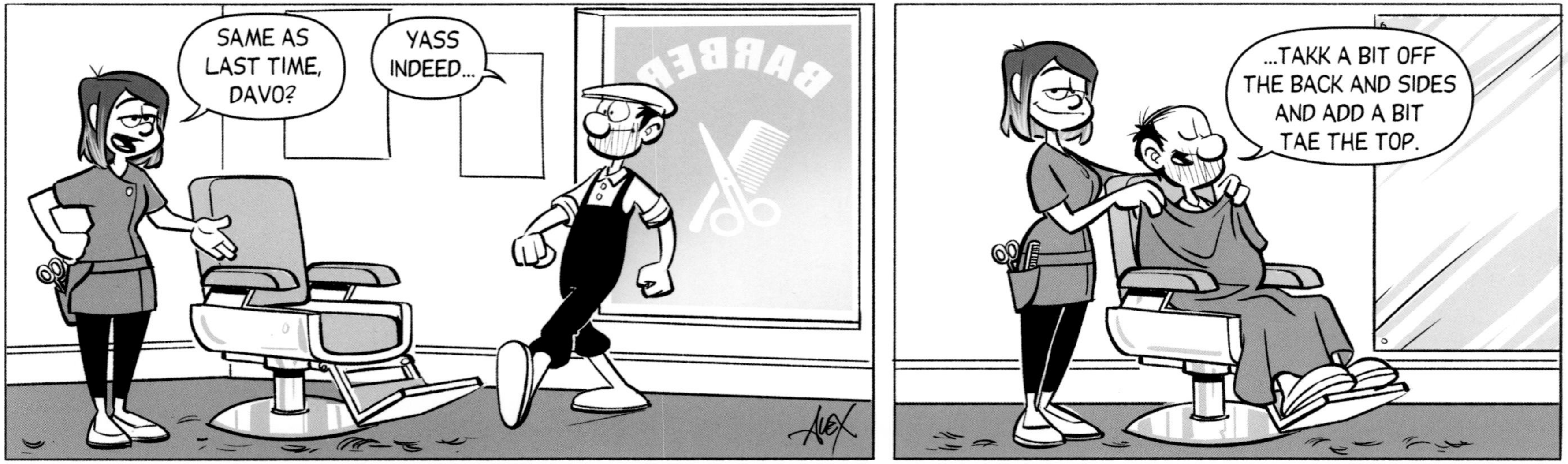
SAME AS LAST TIME, DAVO?
YASS INDEED...
...TAKK A BIT OFF THE BACK AND SIDES AND ADD A BIT TAE THE TOP.

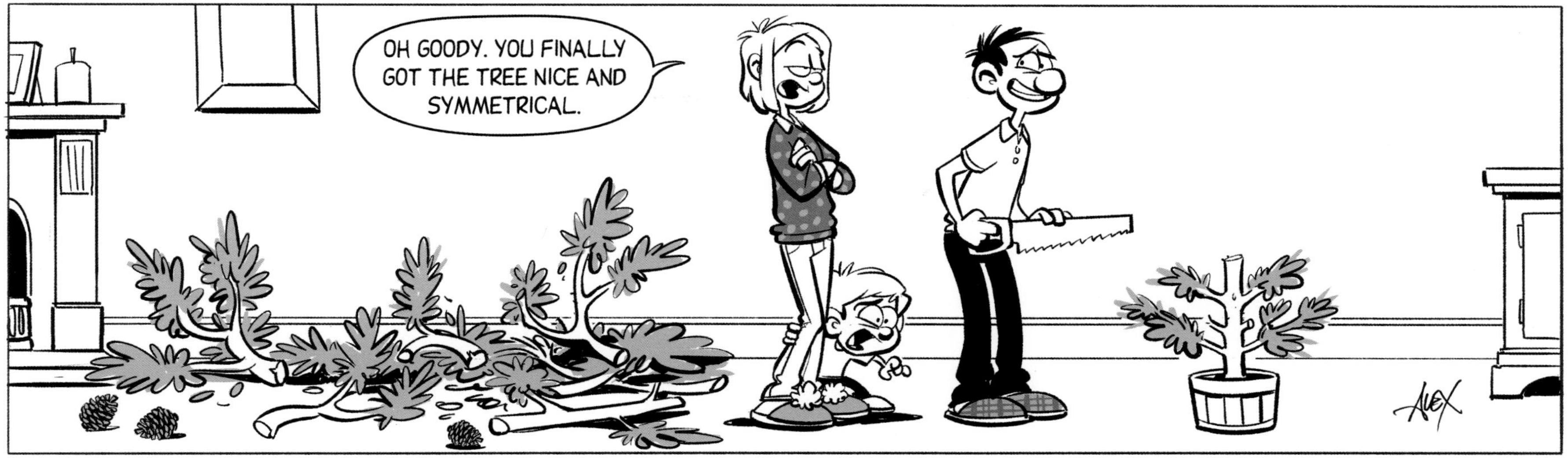
OH GOODY. YOU FINALLY GOT THE TREE NICE AND SYMMETRICAL.
ALEX

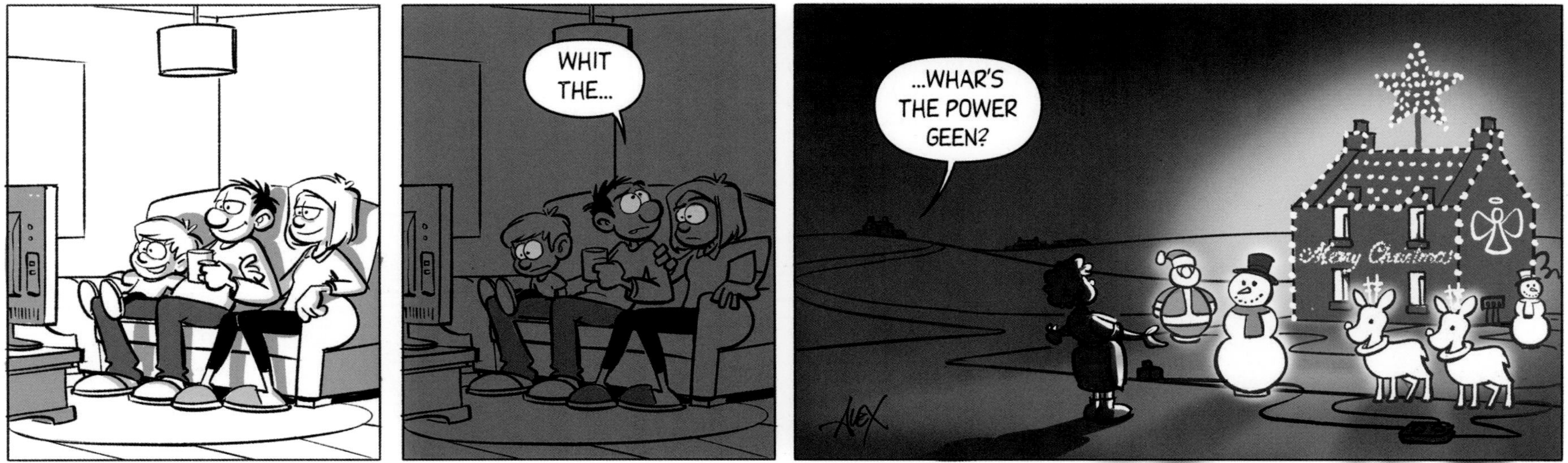
WHIT THE...
...WHAR'S THE POWER GEEN?
Merry Christmas
ALEX

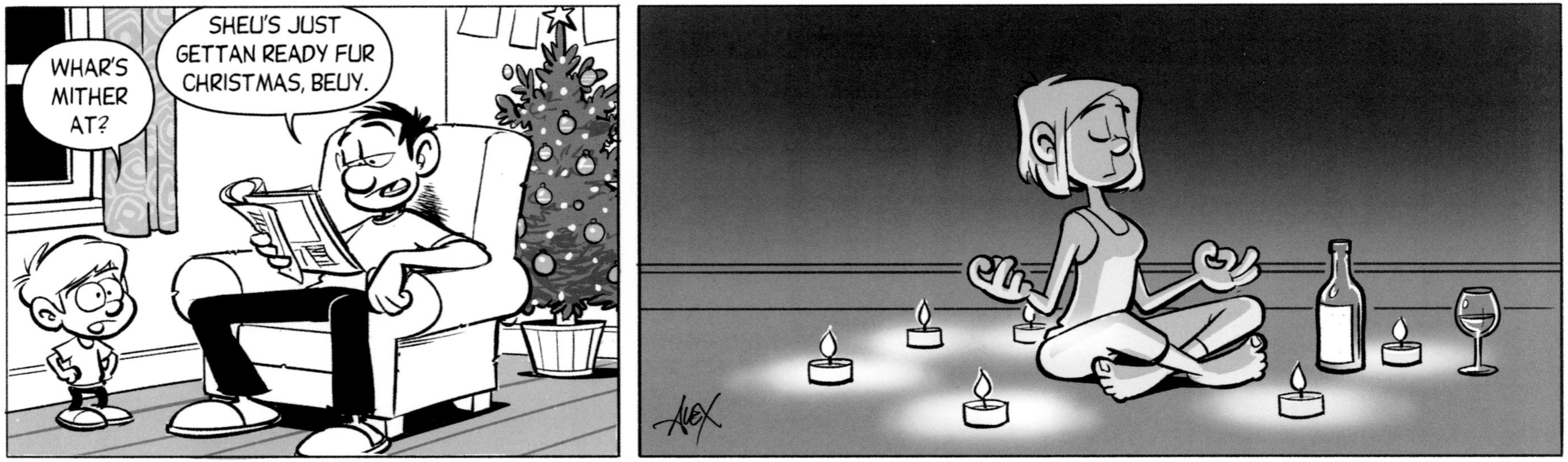
WHAR'S MITHER AT?
SHEU'S JUST GETTAN READY FUR CHRISTMAS, BEUY.
ALEX

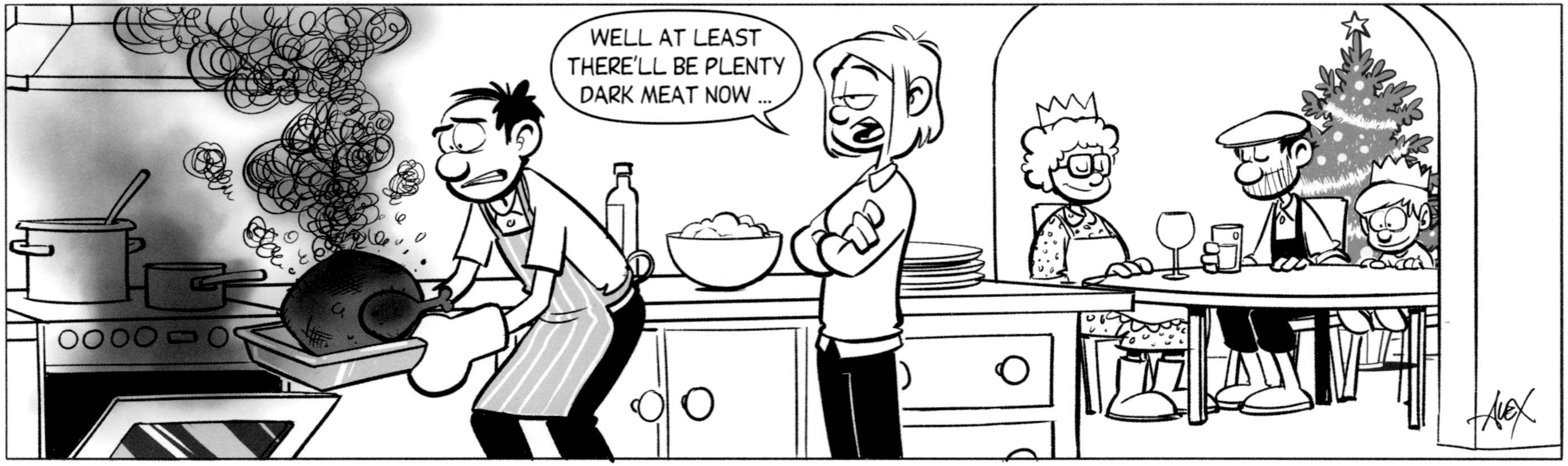
WELL AT LEAST THERE'LL BE PLENTY DARK MEAT NOW ...
ALEX

# 2019 CALENDAR

THE G!DDY LIM!T
DIS HOLLYWID
PLEEP FICTION
MINGIN' IN THE RAIN
ORKNEY's TECHNICOLOUR MUSICAL TREASURE!
JAAS
When Harray met Sanday...
WINDER WUMMAN
SILO
SANDWICK
OF NEW YORK
MY FAIR TAE MIDDIAN LADY
IVY HEPBURN · REX HARRAYSON
THE GREATEST COUNTY SHOWMAN
The Return o the Grett Adventure.
2019
Appointment Calendar
ALEX

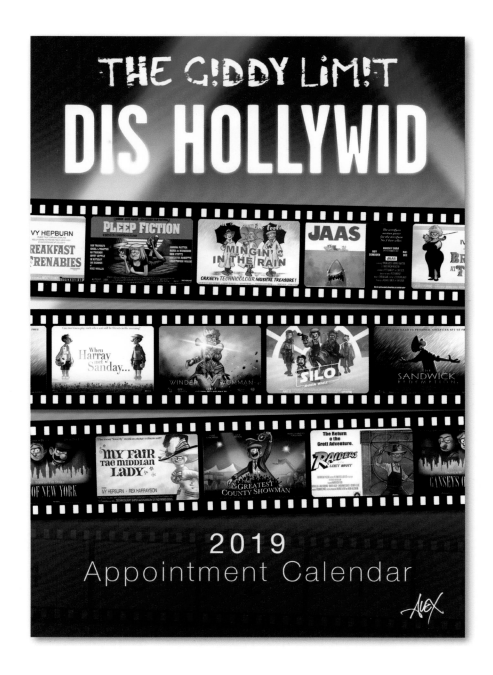

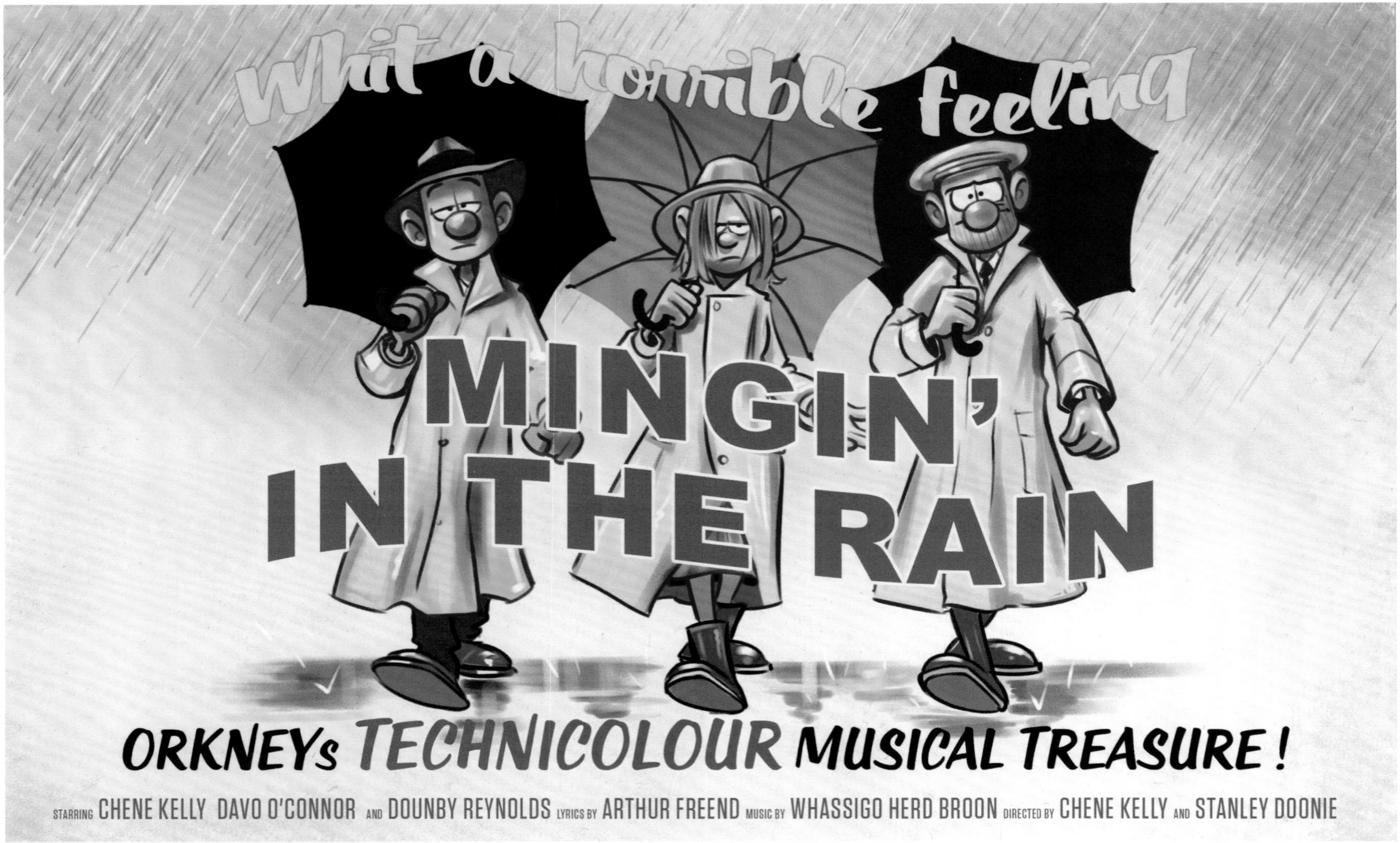
Whit a horrible feeling
MINGIN' IN THE RAIN
ORKNEYs TECHNICOLOUR MUSICAL TREASURE!
STARRING CHENE KELLY DAVO O'CONNOR AND DOUNBY REYNOLDS LYRICS BY ARTHUR FREEND MUSIC BY WHASSIGO HERD BROON DIRECTED BY CHENE KELLY AND STANLEY DOONIE

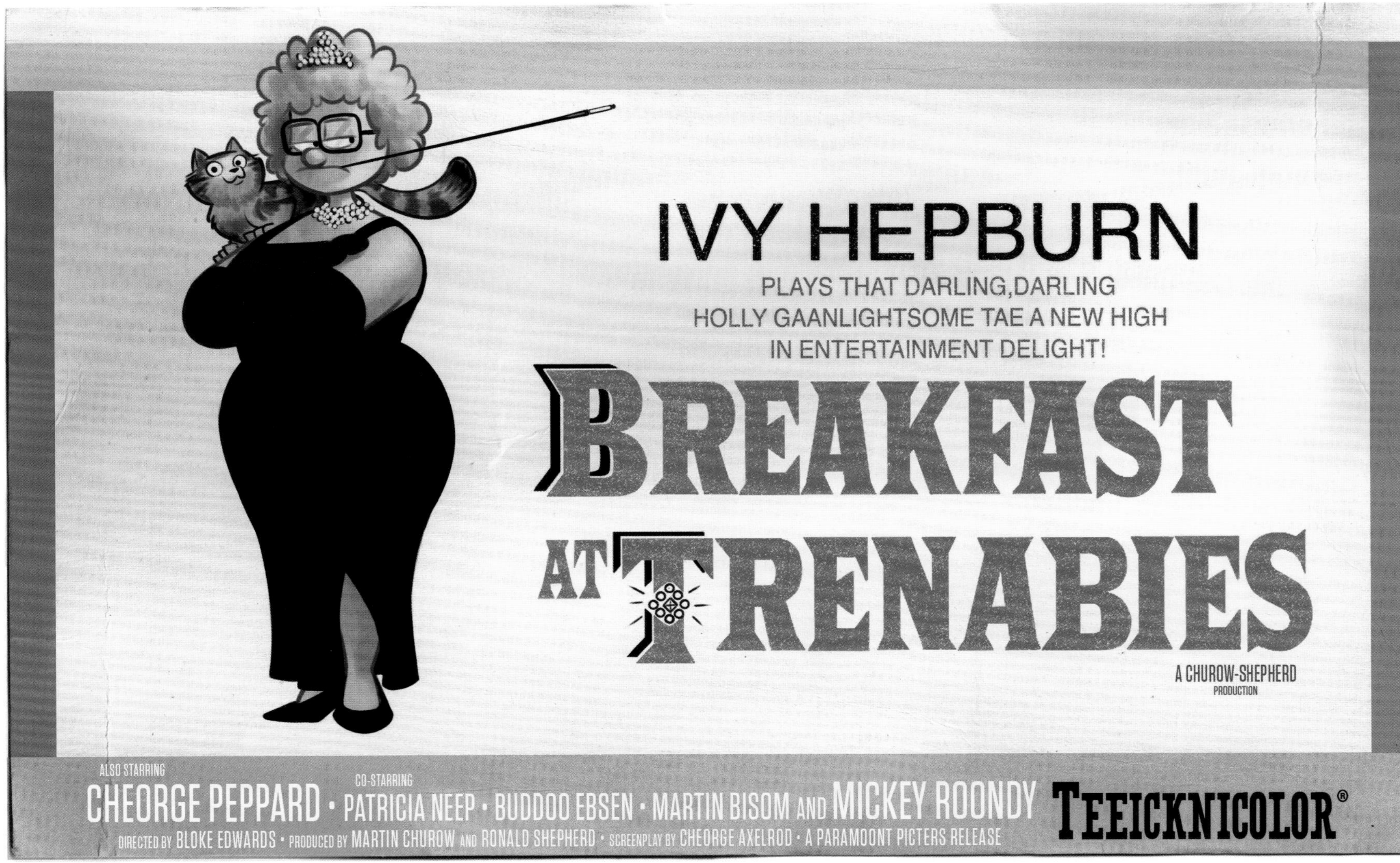
IVY HEPBURN
PLAYS THAT DARLING,DARLING
HOLLY GAANLIGHTSOME TAE A NEW HIGH
IN ENTERTAINMENT DELIGHT!
BREAKFAST
AT TRENABIES
A CHUROW-SHEPHERD
PRODUCTION
ALSO STARRING
CO-STARRING
CHEORGE PEPPARD · PATRICIA NEEP · BUDDOO EBSEN · MARTIN BISOM AND MICKEY ROONDY
TEEICKNICOLOR®
DIRECTED BY BLOKE EDWARDS · PRODUCED BY MARTIN CHUROW AND RONALD SHEPHERD · SCREENPLAY BY CHEORGE AXELROD · A PARAMOONT PICTERS RELEASE

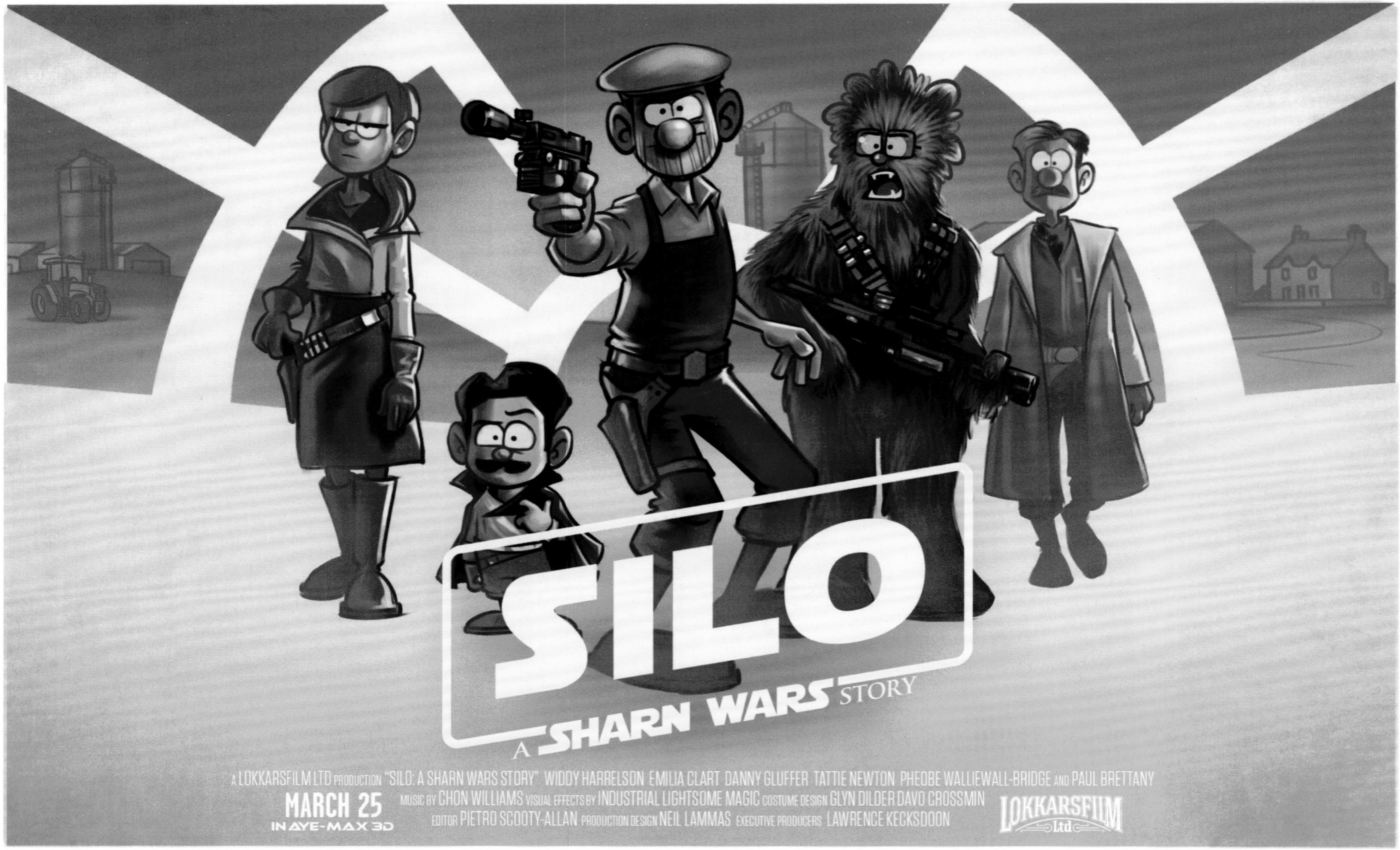
SILO
A SHARN WARS STORY
A LOKKARSFILM LTD PRODUCTION "SILO: A SHARN WARS STORY" WIDDY HARRELSON EMILIA CLART DANNY GLUFFER TATTIE NEWTON PHEOBE WALLIEWALL-BRIDGE AND PAUL BRETTANY
MARCH 25
IN AYE-MAX 3D
MUSIC BY CHON WILLIAMS VISUAL EFFECTS BY INDUSTRIAL LIGHTSOME MAGIC COSTUME DESIGN GLYN DILDER DAVO CROSSMIN
EDITOR PIETRO SCOOTY-ALLAN PRODUCTION DESIGN NEIL LAMMAS EXECUTIVE PRODUCERS LAWRENCE KECKSDOON
LOKKARSFILM Ltd

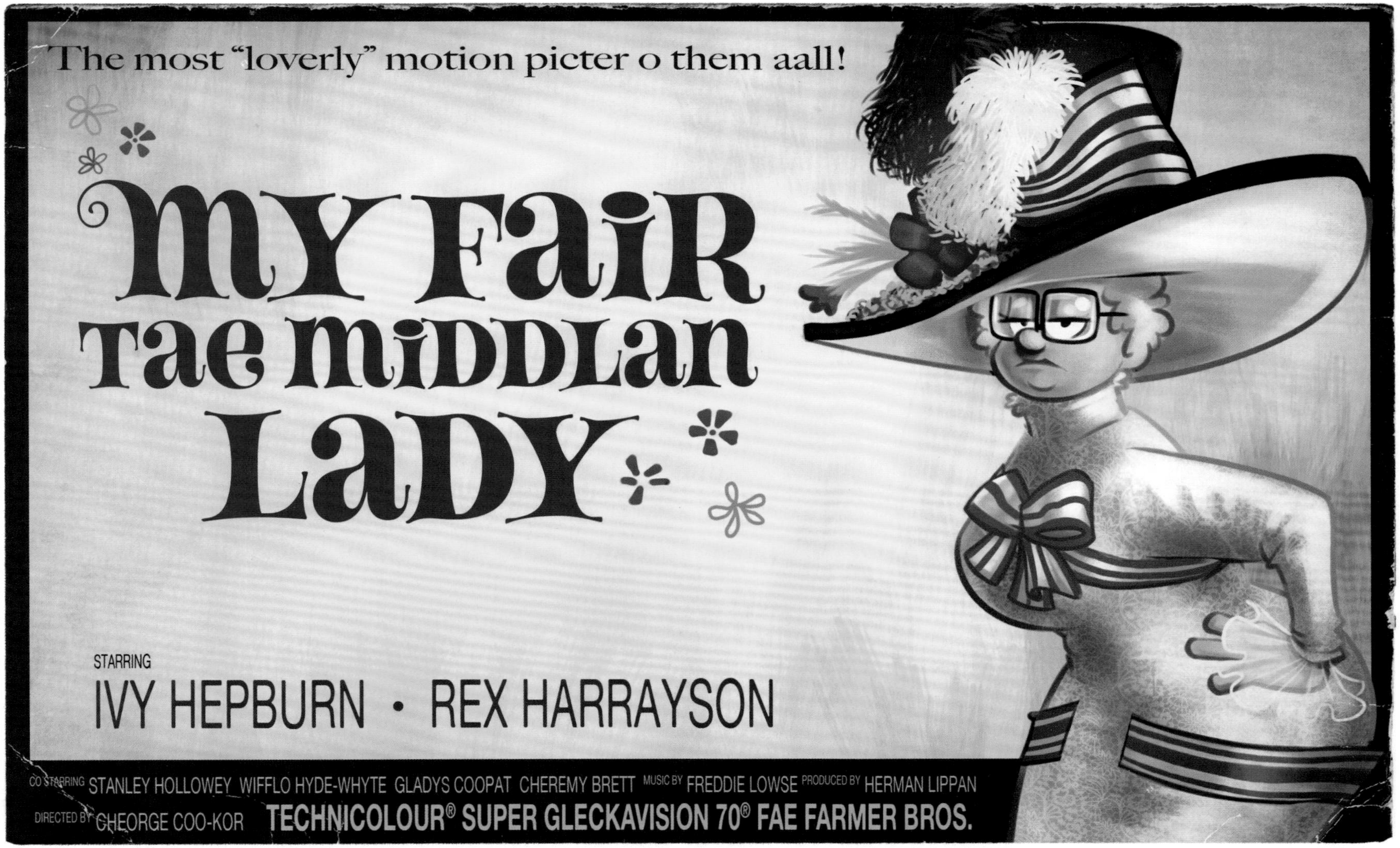

The most "loverly" motion picter o them aall!
MY FAIR TAE MIDDLAN LADY
STARRING
IVY HEPBURN • REX HARRAYSON
CO STARRING STANLEY HOLLOWEY WIFFLO HYDE-WHYTE GLADYS COOPAT CHEREMY BRETT MUSIC BY FREDDIE LOWSE PRODUCED BY HERMAN LIPPAN
DIRECTED BY CHEORGE COO-KOR TECHNICOLOUR® SUPER GLECKAVISION 70® FAE FARMER BROS.

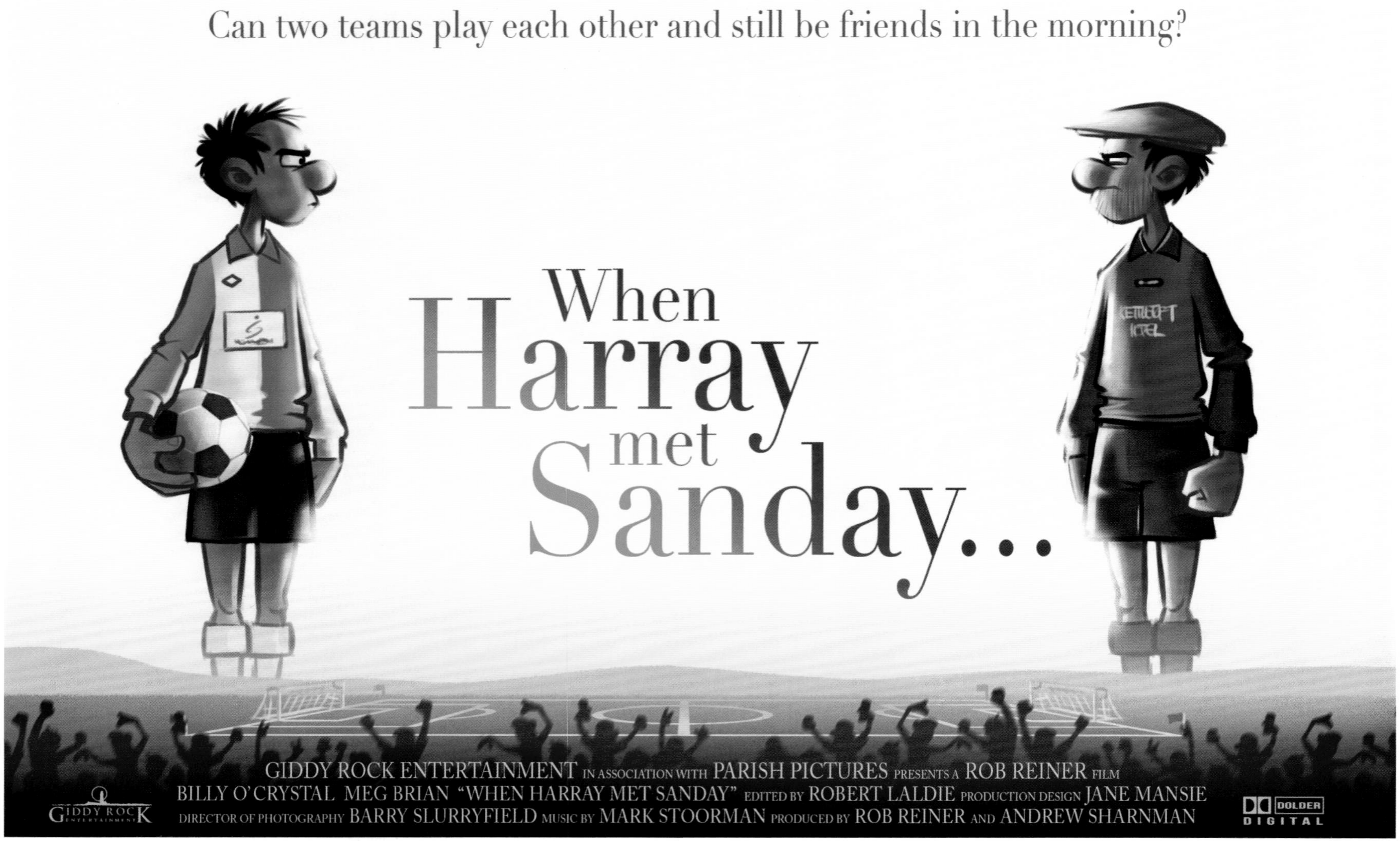
Can two teams play each other and still be friends in the morning?
When Harray met Sanday...
GIDDY ROCK ENTERTAINMENT IN ASSOCIATION WITH PARISH PICTURES PRESENTS A ROB REINER FILM
BILLY O'CRYSTAL MEG BRIAN "WHEN HARRAY MET SANDAY" EDITED BY ROBERT LALDIE PRODUCTION DESIGN JANE MANSIE
DIRECTOR OF PHOTOGRAPHY BARRY SLURRYFIELD MUSIC BY MARK STOORMAN PRODUCED BY ROB REINER AND ANDREW SHARNMAN
GIDDY ROCK
DOLDER DIGITAL

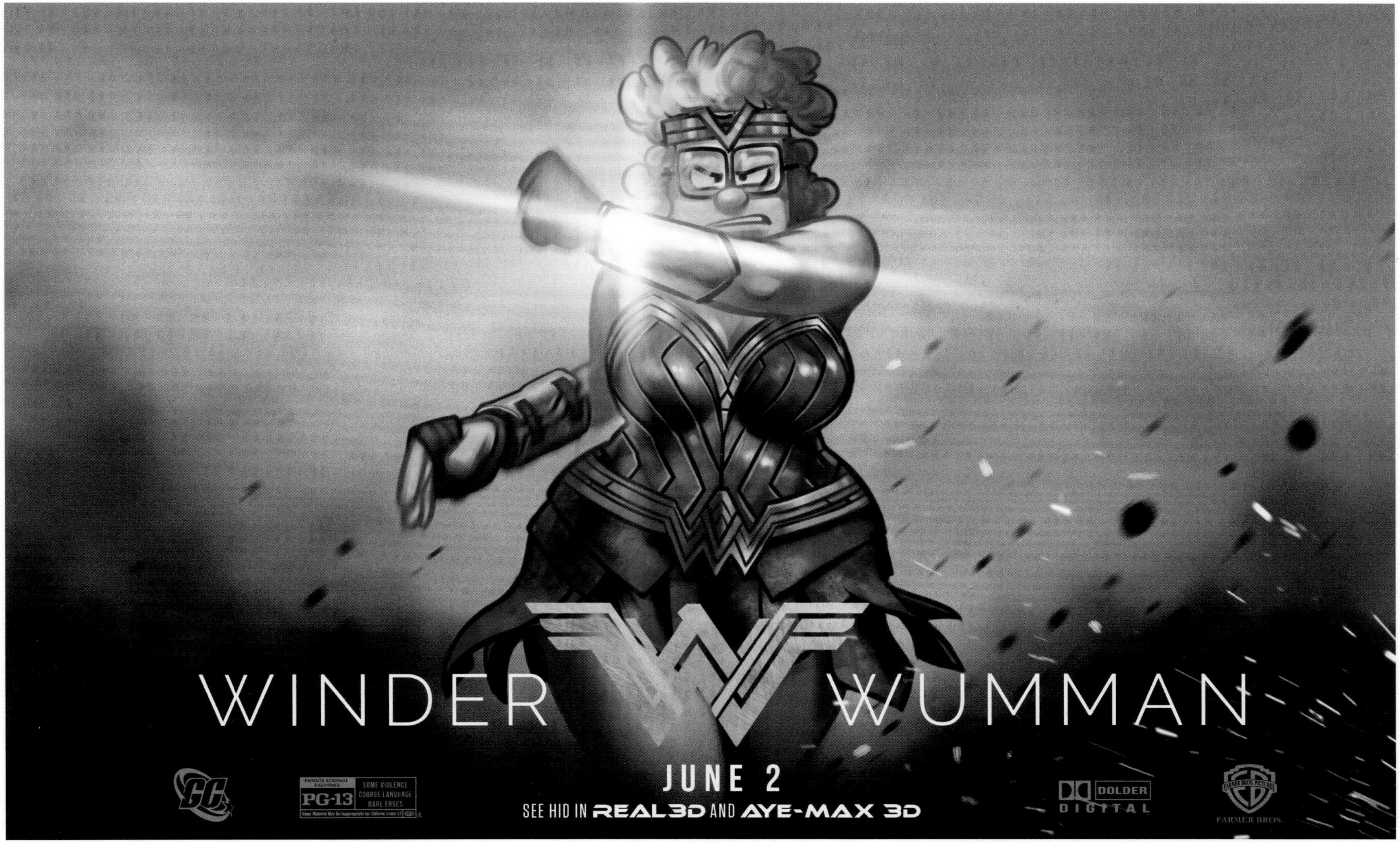
WINDER WUMMAN
PARENTS STRONGLY CAUTIONED
PG-13
SOME VIOLENCE
COORSE LANGUAGE
BARE ERSES
JUNE 2
SEE HID IN REAL3D AND AYE-MAX 3D
DOLDER DIGITAL
FARMER BROS.

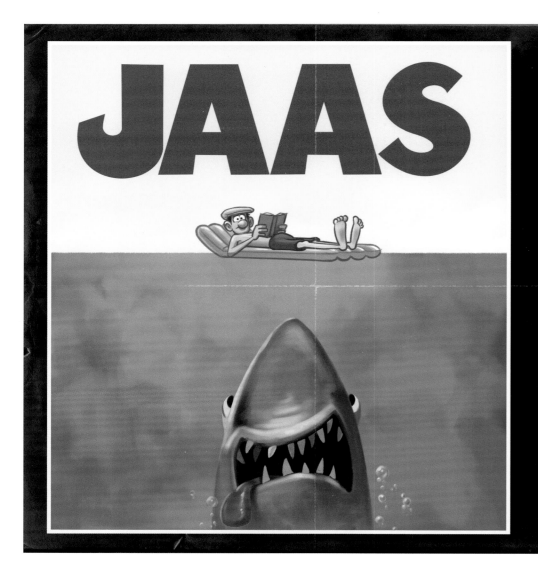

**The terrifyan motion picter fae the terrifyan No.1 best seller.**

**ROBERT SHAA**
(HE'S FAE STROMNESS, BEUY)

**HOY SCHEIDER**

**RICHARD DEULESS**

**JAAS**

Co-starring LORRAINE GANSEY · MURRAY HAMILTOON

A ZANUCK/BROON PRODUCTION

Screenplay by PETER BAINCHLEY and CARL GOLTIE

Based on the novel by PETER BAINCHLEY

Music by CHON WILLIAMS · Directed by STEVEN SPIELBRECK

Produced by RICHARD D ZANUCK and DAVO BROON

**May be parteecularly disturbing tae peedie bairns.**

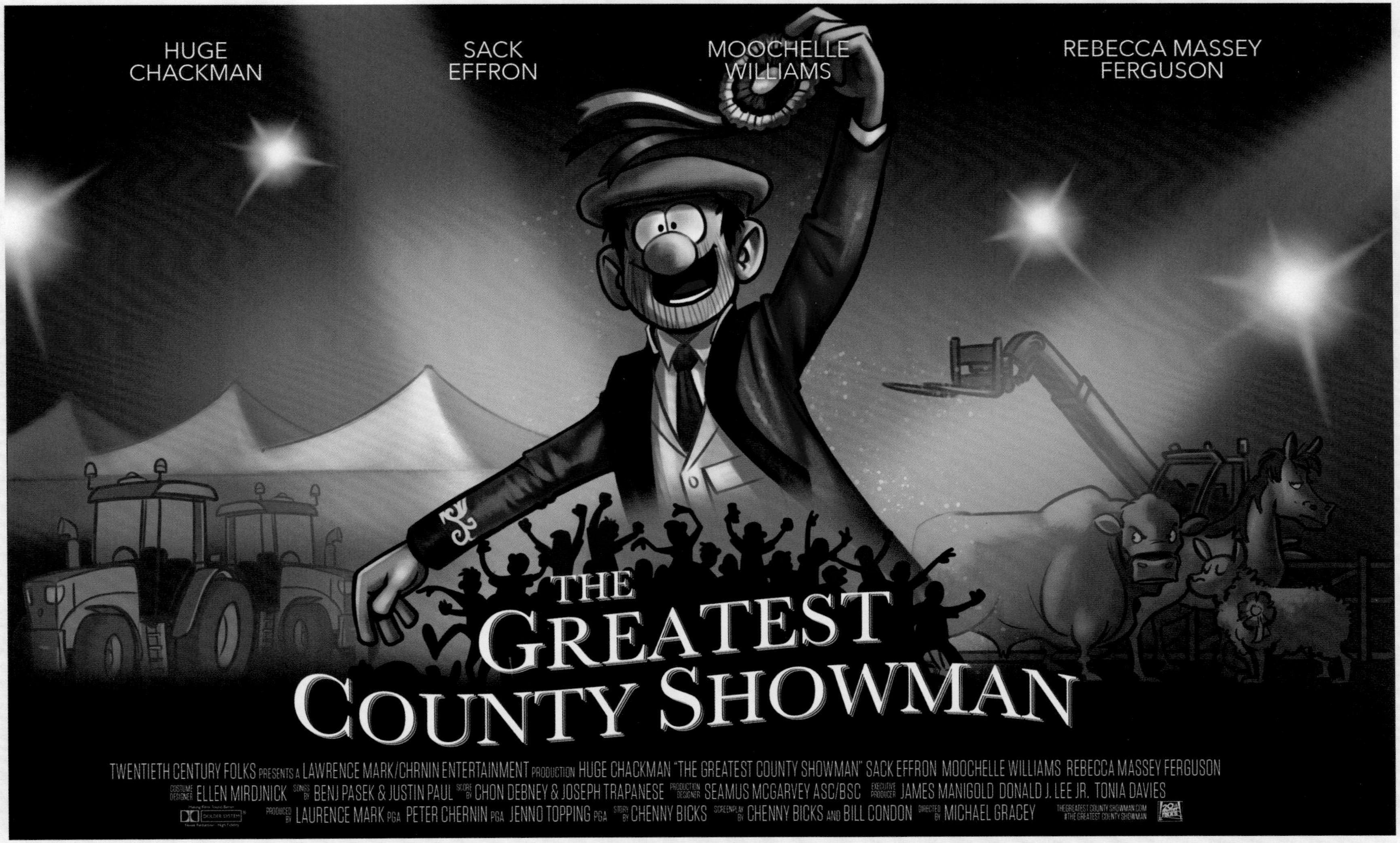

HUGE CHACKMAN
SACK EFFRON
MOOCHELLE WILLIAMS
REBECCA MASSEY FERGUSON
THE GREATEST COUNTY SHOWMAN
TWENTIETH CENTURY FOLKS PRESENTS A LAWRENCE MARK/CHRNIN ENTERTAINMENT PRODUCTION HUGE CHACKMAN "THE GREATEST COUNTY SHOWMAN" SACK EFFRON MOOCHELLE WILLIAMS REBECCA MASSEY FERGUSON
COSTUME DESIGNER ELLEN MIRDJNICK SONGS BY BENJ PASEK & JUSTIN PAUL SCORE BY CHON DEBNEY & JOSEPH TRAPANESE PRODUCTION DESIGNER SEAMUS MCGARVEY ASC/BSC EXECUTIVE PRODUCER JAMES MANIGOLD DONALD J. LEE JR. TONIA DAVIES
PRODUCED BY LAURENCE MARK PGA PETER CHERNIN PGA JENNO TOPPING PGA STORY BY CHENNY BICKS SCREENPLAY BY CHENNY BICKS AND BILL CONDON DIRECTED BY MICHAEL GRACEY
THEGREATESTCOUNTYSHOWMAN.COM
#THE GREATEST COUNTY SHOWMAN

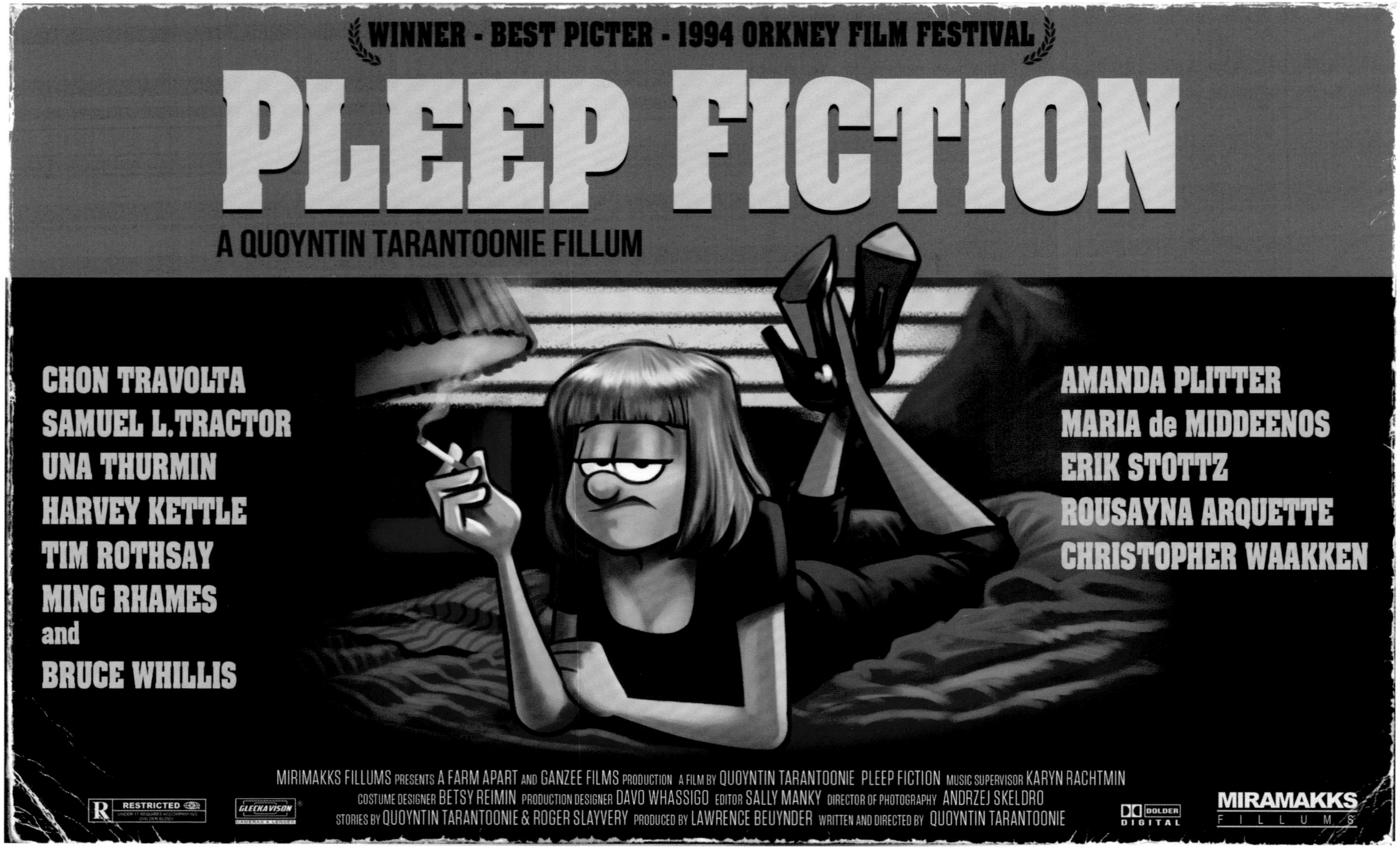
WINNER - BEST PICTER - 1994 ORKNEY FILM FESTIVAL
PLEEP FICTION
A QUOYNTIN TARANTOONIE FILLUM
CHON TRAVOLTA
SAMUEL L.TRACTOR
UNA THURMIN
HARVEY KETTLE
TIM ROTHSAY
MING RHAMES
and
BRUCE WHILLIS
AMANDA PLITTER
MARIA de MIDDEENOS
ERIK STOTTZ
ROUSAYNA ARQUETTE
CHRISTOPHER WAAKKEN
MIRIMAKKS FILLUMS PRESENTS A FARM APART AND GANZEE FILMS PRODUCTION A FILM BY QUOYNTIN TARANTOONIE PLEEP FICTION MUSIC SUPERVISOR KARYN RACHTMIN
COSTUME DESIGNER BETSY REIMIN PRODUCTION DESIGNER DAVO WHASSIGO EDITOR SALLY MANKY DIRECTOR OF PHOTOGRAPHY ANDRZEJ SKELDRO
STORIES BY QUOYNTIN TARANTOONIE & ROGER SLAYVERY PRODUCED BY LAWRENCE BEUYNDER WRITTEN AND DIRECTED BY QUOYNTIN TARANTOONIE
R RESTRICTED
GLECKAVISON
DOLDER DIGITAL
MIRAMAKKS FILLUMS

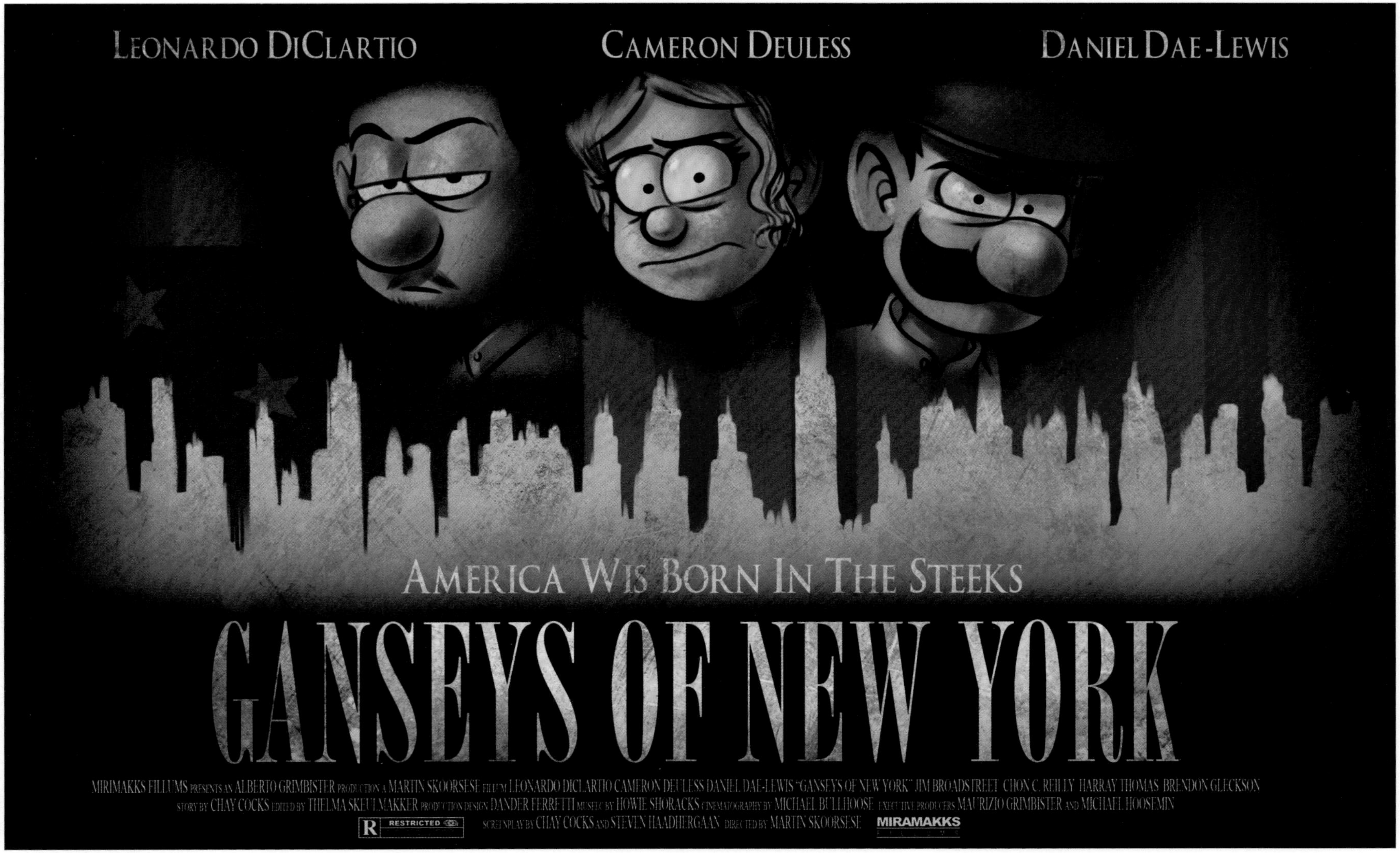
LEONARDO DICLARTIO
CAMERON DEULESS
DANIEL DAE-LEWIS
AMERICA WIS BORN IN THE STEEKS
GANSEYS OF NEW YORK
MIRIMAKKS FILLUMS PRESENTS AN ALBERTO GRIMBISTER PRODUCTION A MARTIN SKOORSESE FILLUM LEONARDO DICLARTIO CAMERON DEULESS DANIEL DAE-LEWIS "GANSEYS OF NEW YORK" JIM BROADSTREET CHON C. REILLY HARRAY THOMAS BRENDON GLECKSON
STORY BY CHAY COCKS EDITED BY THELMA SKEULMAKKER PRODUCTION DESIGN DANDER FERRETTI MUSEEC BY HOWIE SHORACKS CINEMATOGRAPHY BY MICHAEL BULLHOOSE EXECUTIVE PRODUCERS MAURIZIO GRIMBISTER AND MICHAEL HOOSEMIN
R RESTRICTED
SCREENPLAY BY CHAY COCKS AND STEVEN HAADHERGAAN DIRECTED BY MARTIN SKOORSESE
MIRAMAKKS

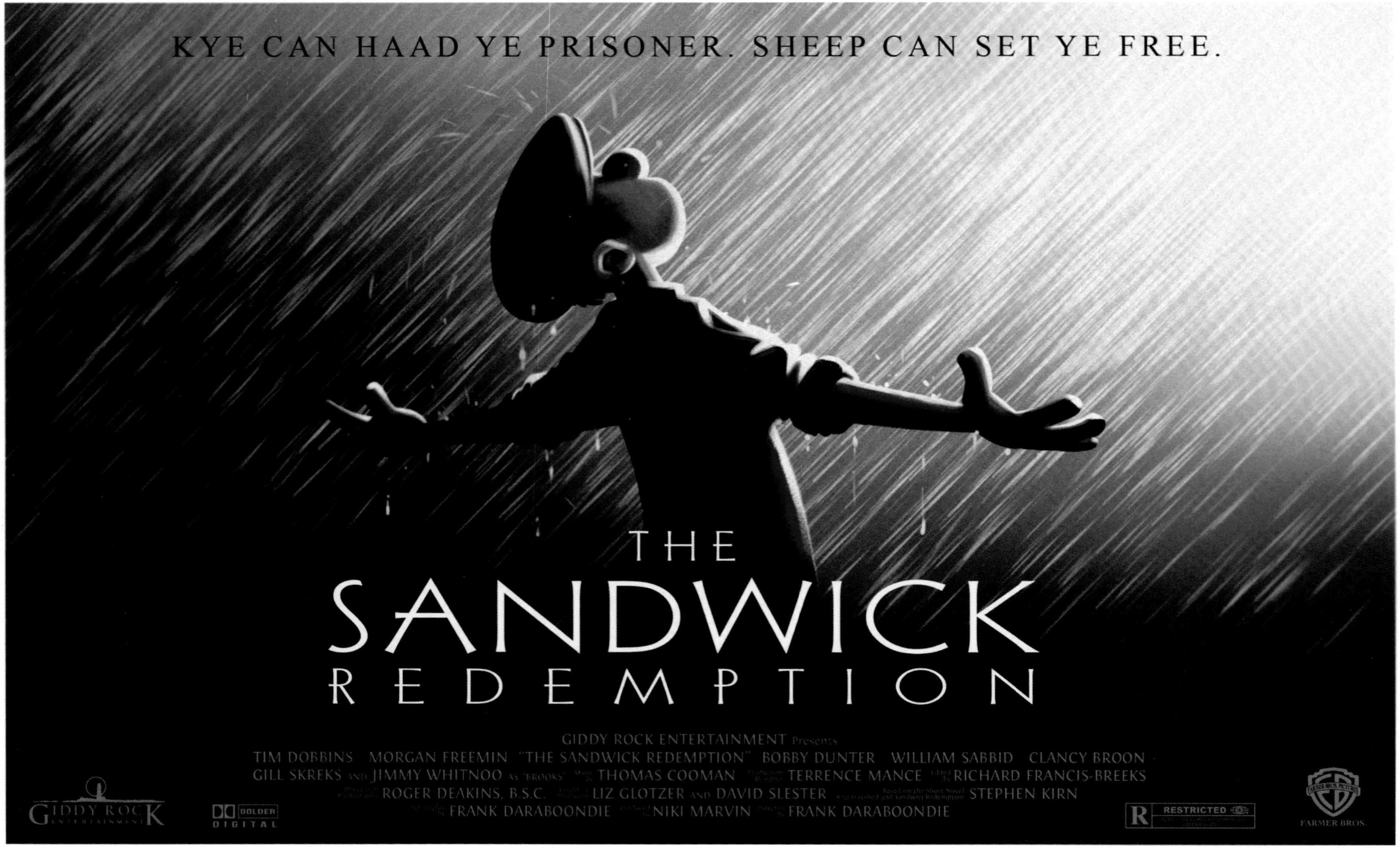

KYE CAN HAAD YE PRISONER. SHEEP CAN SET YE FREE.

THE
SANDWICK
REDEMPTION

GIDDY ROCK ENTERTAINMENT Presents

TIM DOBBINS    MORGAN FREEMIN  "THE SANDWICK REDEMPTION"  BOBBY DUNTER    WILLIAM SABBID    CLANCY BROON
GILL SKREKS AND JIMMY WHITNOO AS "BROOKS"  MUSIC THOMAS COOMAN  PRODUCTION TERRENCE MANCE  EDITOR RICHARD FRANCIS-BREEKS
CINEMATOGRAPHY ROGER DEAKINS, B.S.C.  EXECUTIVE LIZ GLOTZER AND DAVID SLESTER  BASED ON THE SHORT NOVEL BY STEPHEN KIRN
SCREENPLAY FRANK DARABOONDIE  PRODUCED NIKI MARVIN  DIRECTED FRANK DARABOONDIE

GIDDY ROCK
ENTERTAINMENT

DOLBY
DIGITAL

R RESTRICTED

FARMER BROS.

182

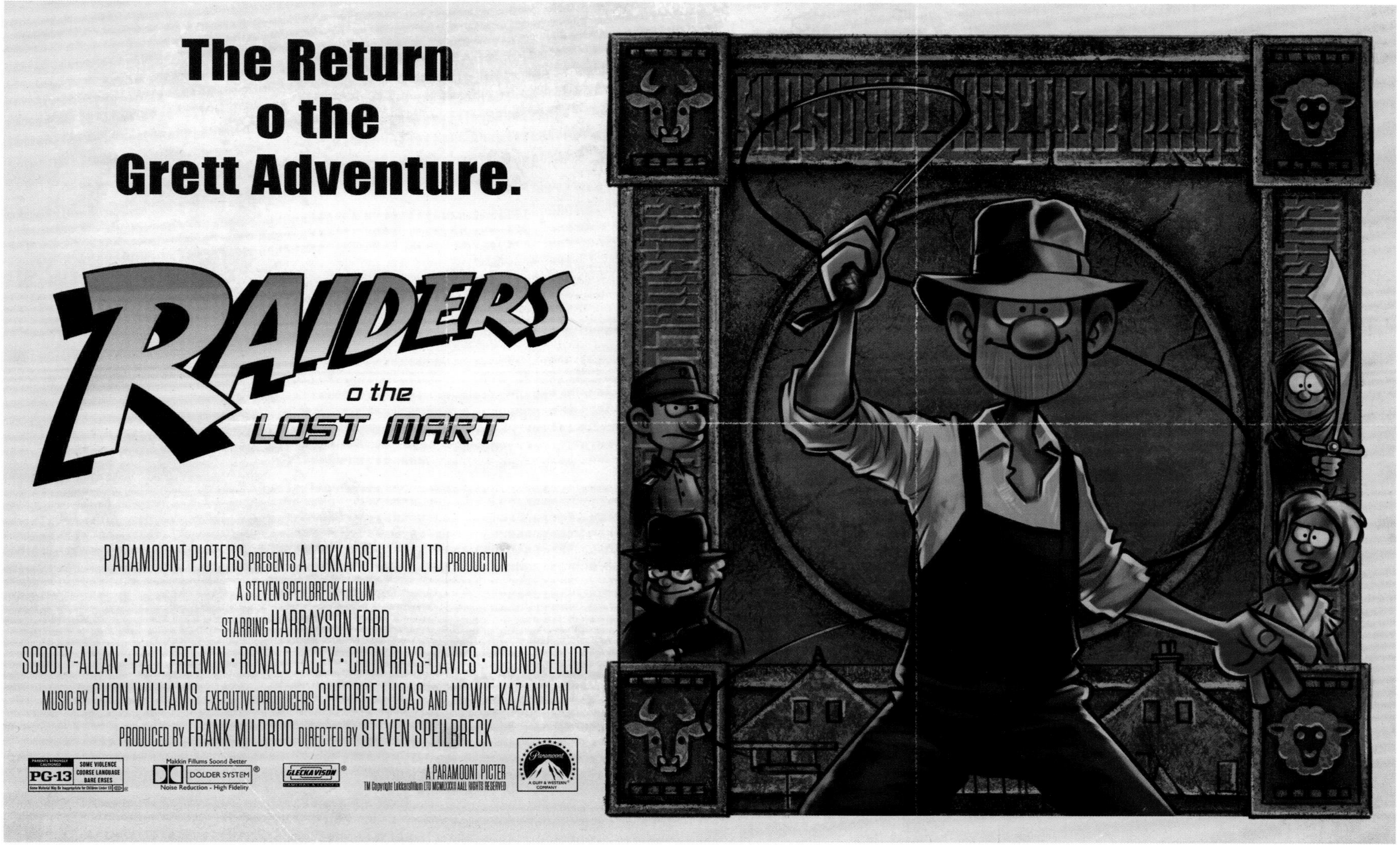
The Return
o the
Grett Adventure.
RAIDERS
o the
LOST MART
PARAMOONT PICTERS PRESENTS A LOKKARSFILLUM LTD PRODUCTION
A STEVEN SPEILBRECK FILLUM
STARRING HARRAYSON FORD
SCOOTY-ALLAN · PAUL FREEMIN · RONALD LACEY · CHON RHYS-DAVIES · DOUNBY ELLIOT
MUSIC BY CHON WILLIAMS EXECUTIVE PRODUCERS CHEORGE LUCAS AND HOWIE KAZANJIAN
PRODUCED BY FRANK MILDROO DIRECTED BY STEVEN SPEILBRECK
PARENTS STRONGLY CAUTIONED
PG-13
SOME VIOLENCE
COORSE LANGUAGE
BARE ERSES
Makkin Fillums Soond Better
DOLDER SYSTEM
Noise Reduction - High Fidelity
GLECKAVISON
A PARAMOONT PICTER
TM Copyright Lokkarsfillum LTD MCMLXXXII AALL RIGHTS RESERVED
Paramoont
A GUFF & WESTERN COMPANY

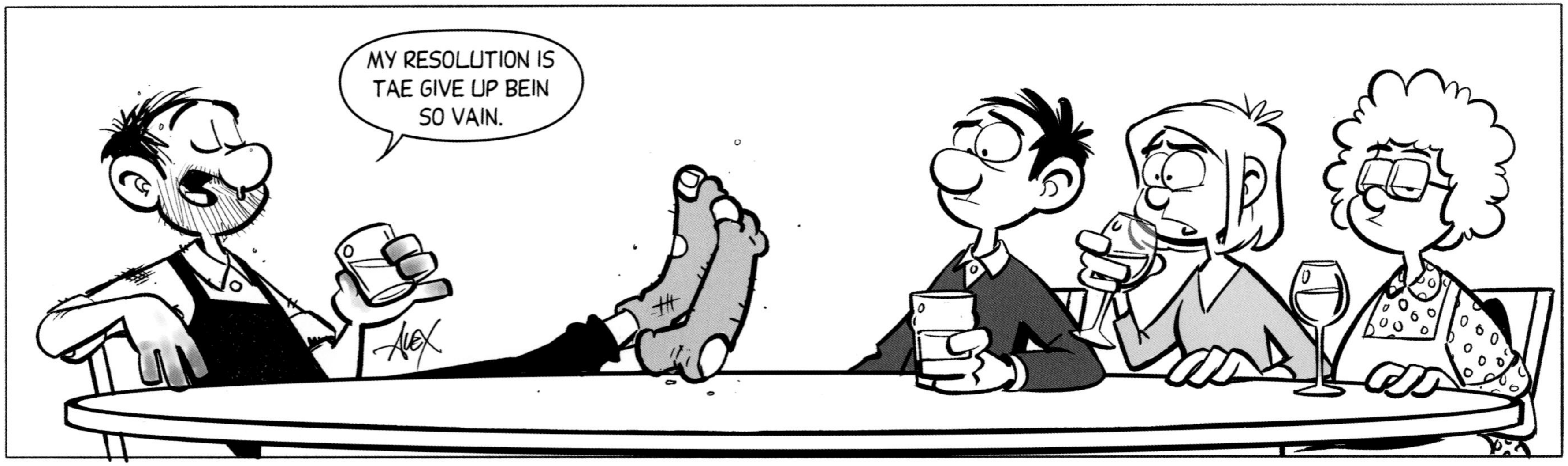
MY RESOLUTION IS TAE GIVE UP BEIN SO VAIN.

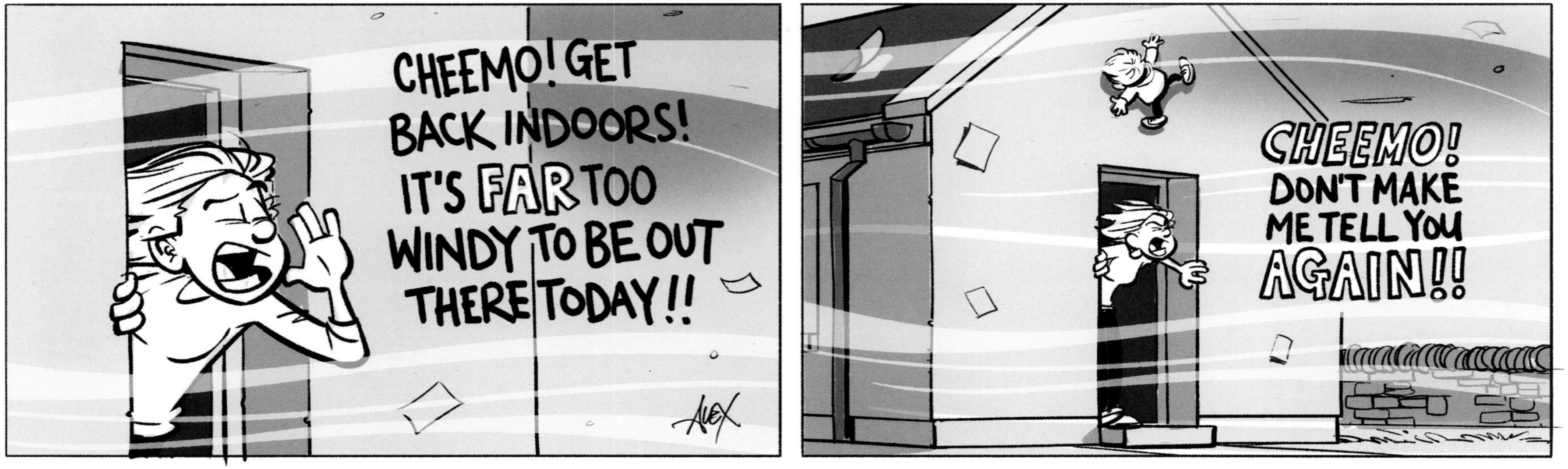
CHEEMO! GET BACK INDOORS! IT'S FAR TOO WINDY TO BE OUT THERE TODAY!!
CHEEMO! DON'T MAKE ME TELL YOU AGAIN!!

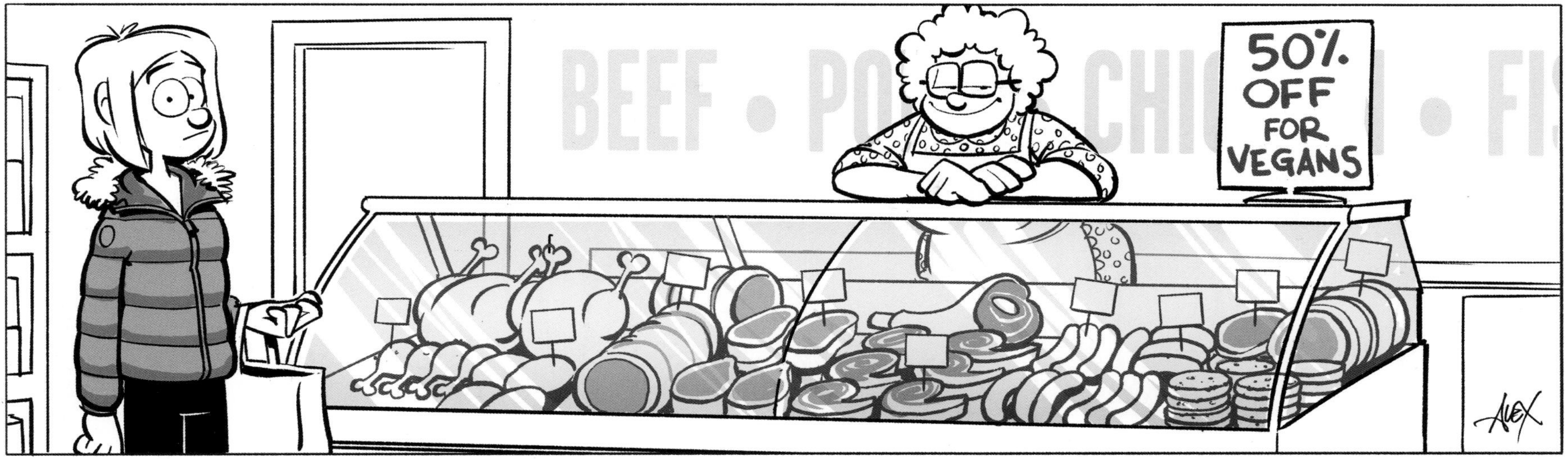
BEEF • PO CHIC • FIS
50% OFF FOR VEGANS
ALEX

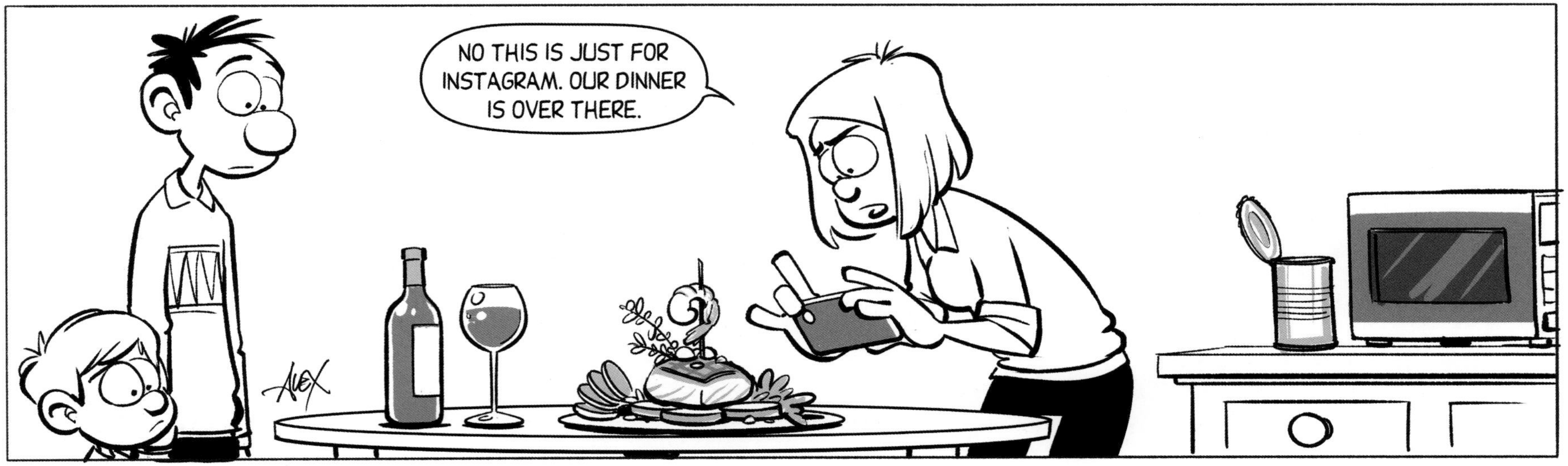
NO THIS IS JUST FOR INSTAGRAM. OUR DINNER IS OVER THERE.
ALEX

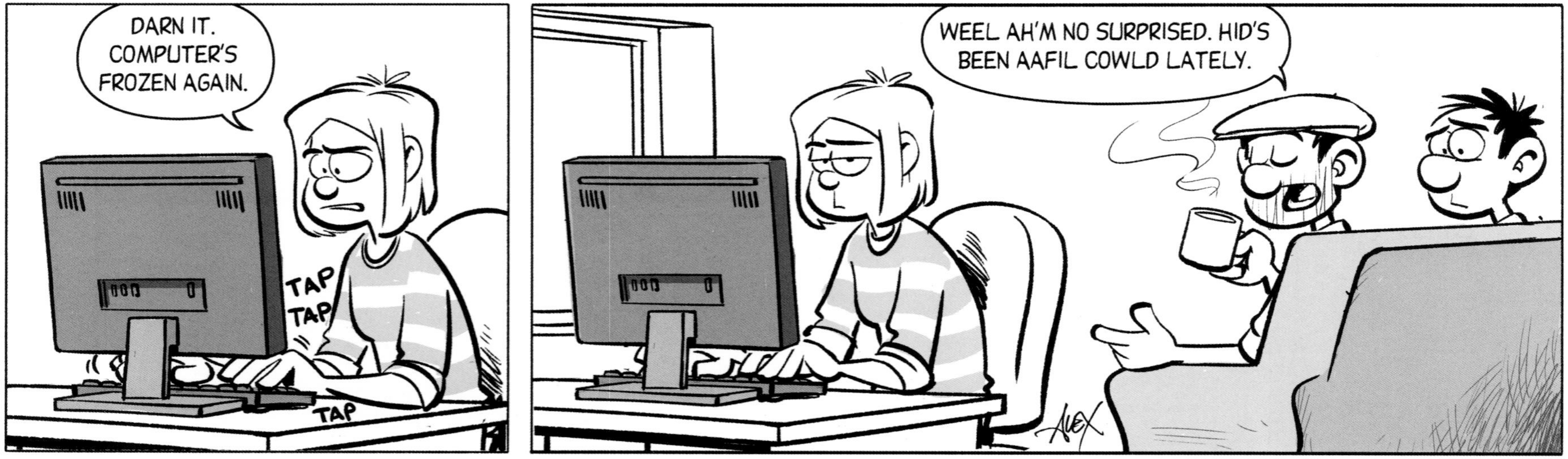
DARN IT. COMPUTER'S FROZEN AGAIN.
TAP TAP TAP
WEEL AH'M NO SURPRISED. HID'S BEEN AAFIL COWLD LATELY.
ALEX

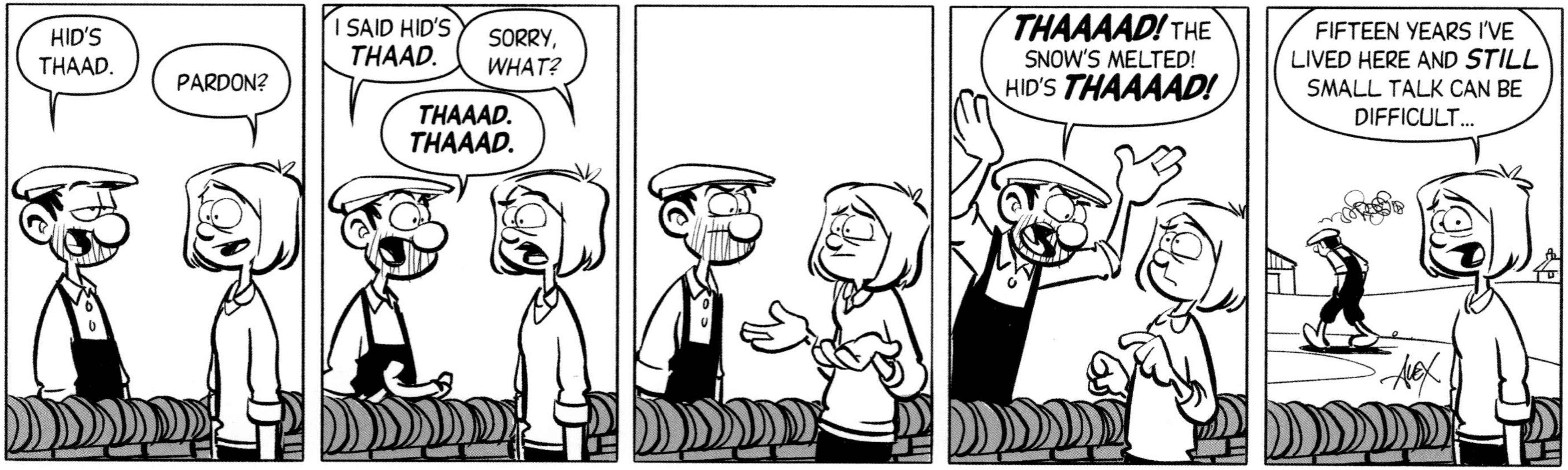
HID'S THAAD.
PARDON?
I SAID HID'S THAAD.
SORRY, WHAT?
THAAAD. THAAAD.
THAAAAD! THE SNOW'S MELTED! HID'S THAAAAD!
FIFTEEN YEARS I'VE LIVED HERE AND STILL SMALL TALK CAN BE DIFFICULT...
ALEX

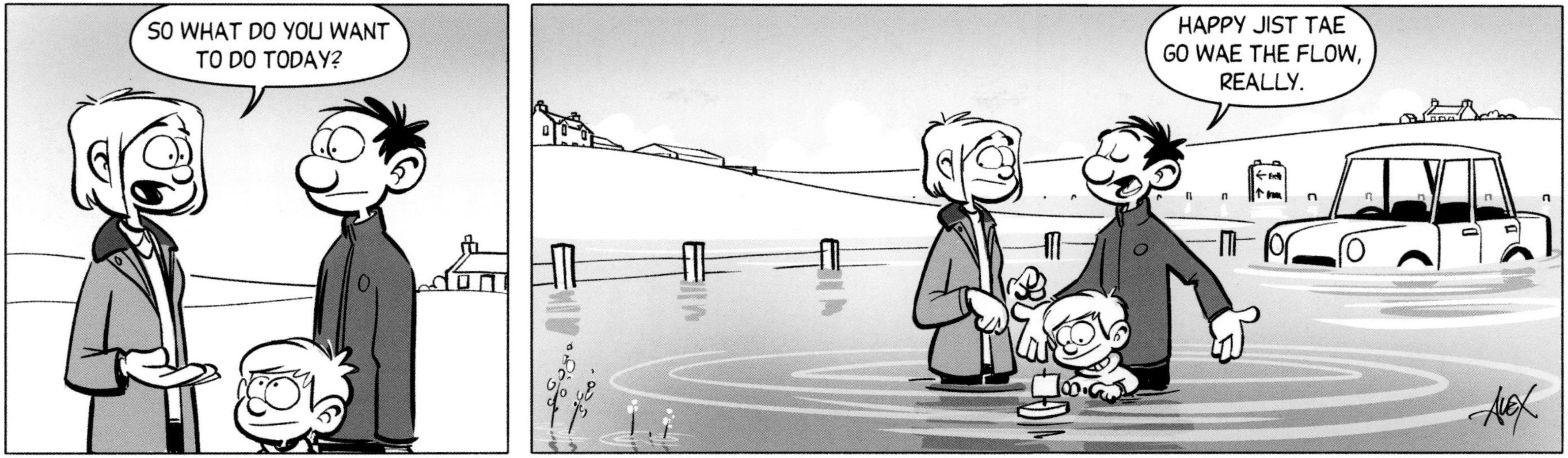
SO WHAT DO YOU WANT TO DO TODAY?
HAPPY JIST TAE GO WAE THE FLOW, REALLY.
ALEX

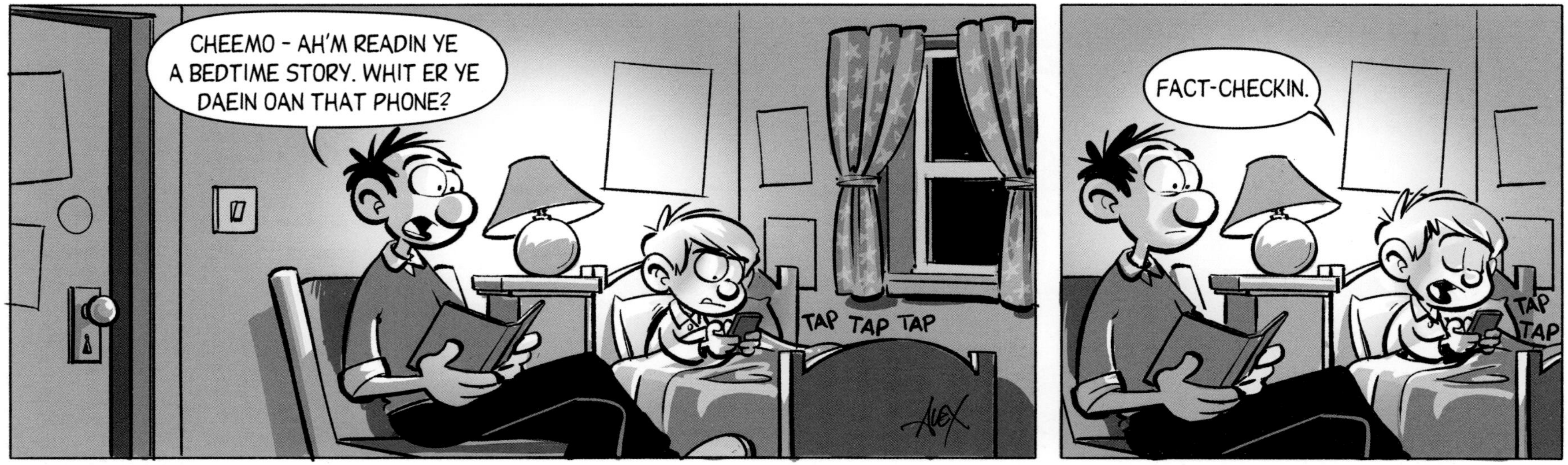
CHEEMO - AH'M READIN YE A BEDTIME STORY. WHIT ER YE DAEIN OAN THAT PHONE?
TAP TAP TAP
ALEX
FACT-CHECKIN.
TAP TAP

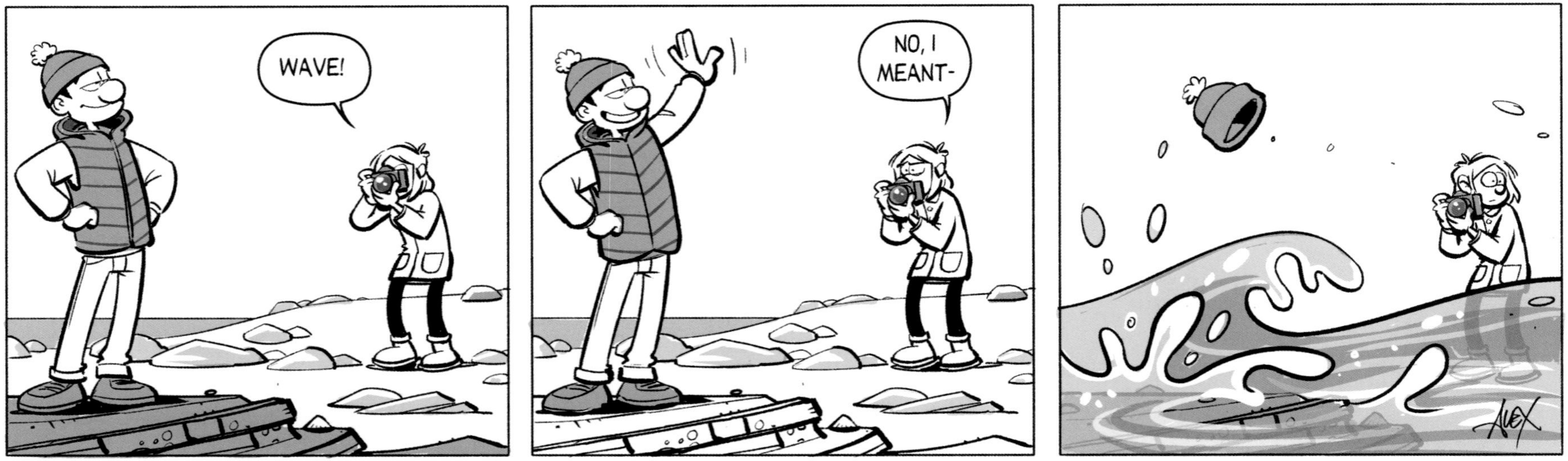
WAVE!
NO, I MEANT-
ALEX

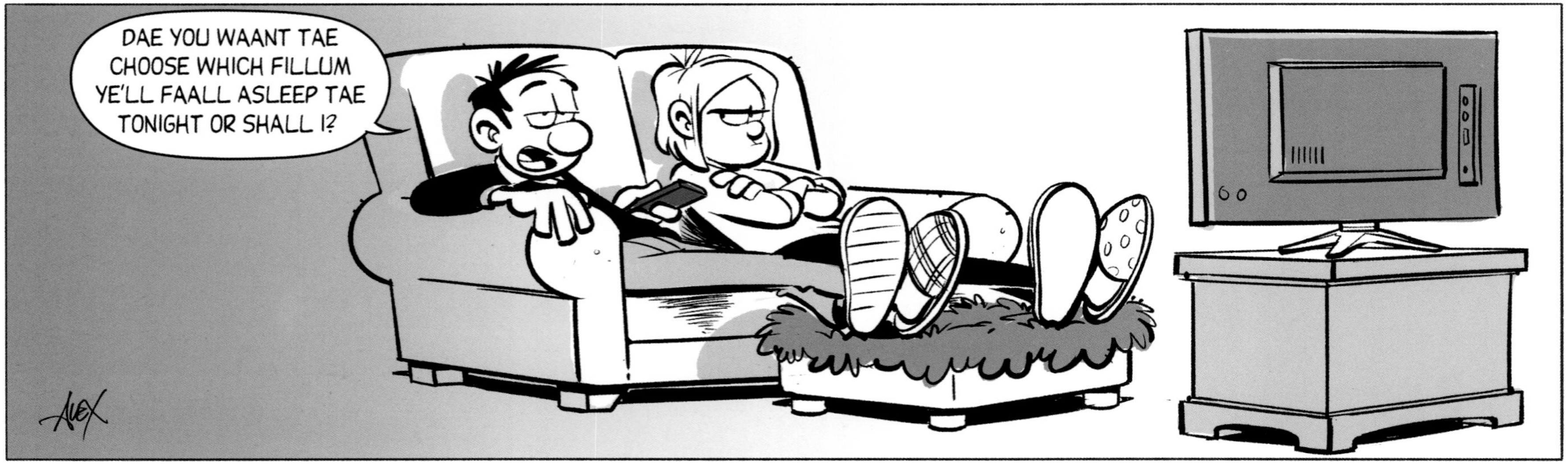
DAE YOU WAANT TAE CHOOSE WHICH FILLUM YE'LL FAALL ASLEEP TAE TONIGHT OR SHALL I?
ALEX

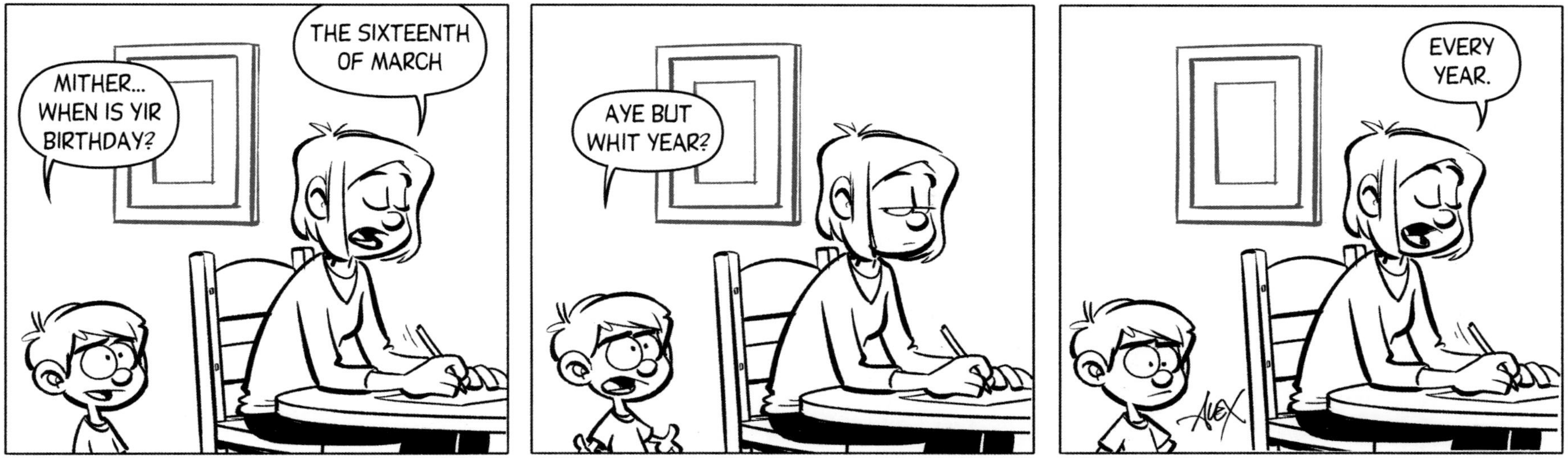
MITHER... WHEN IS YIR BIRTHDAY?
THE SIXTEENTH OF MARCH
AYE BUT WHIT YEAR?
EVERY YEAR.

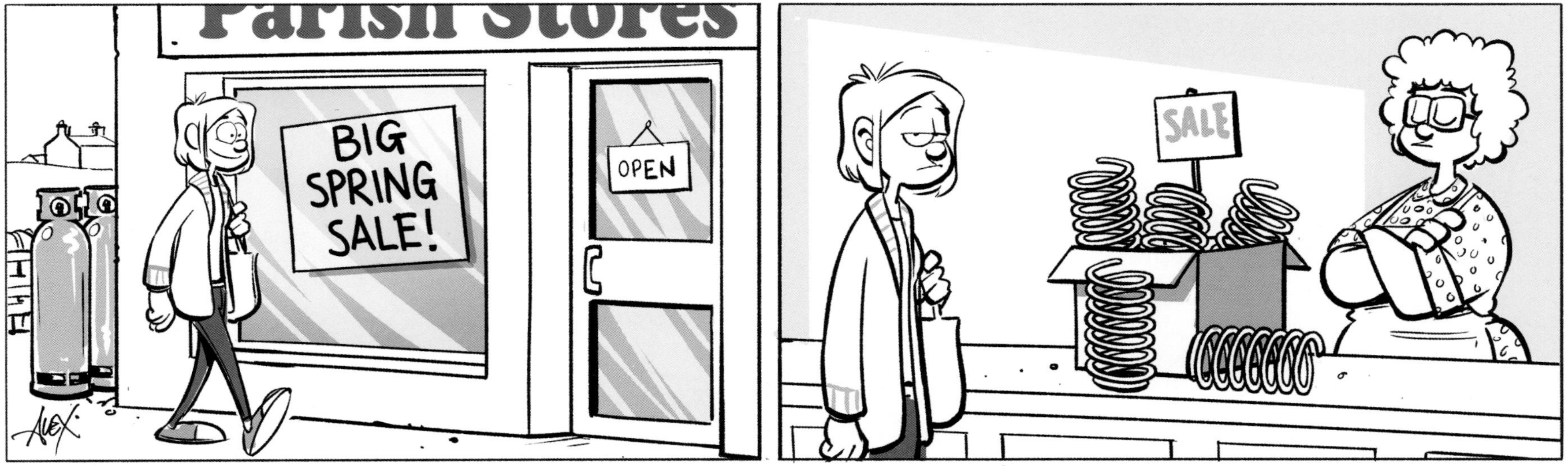
Parish Stores
BIG SPRING SALE!
OPEN
SALE

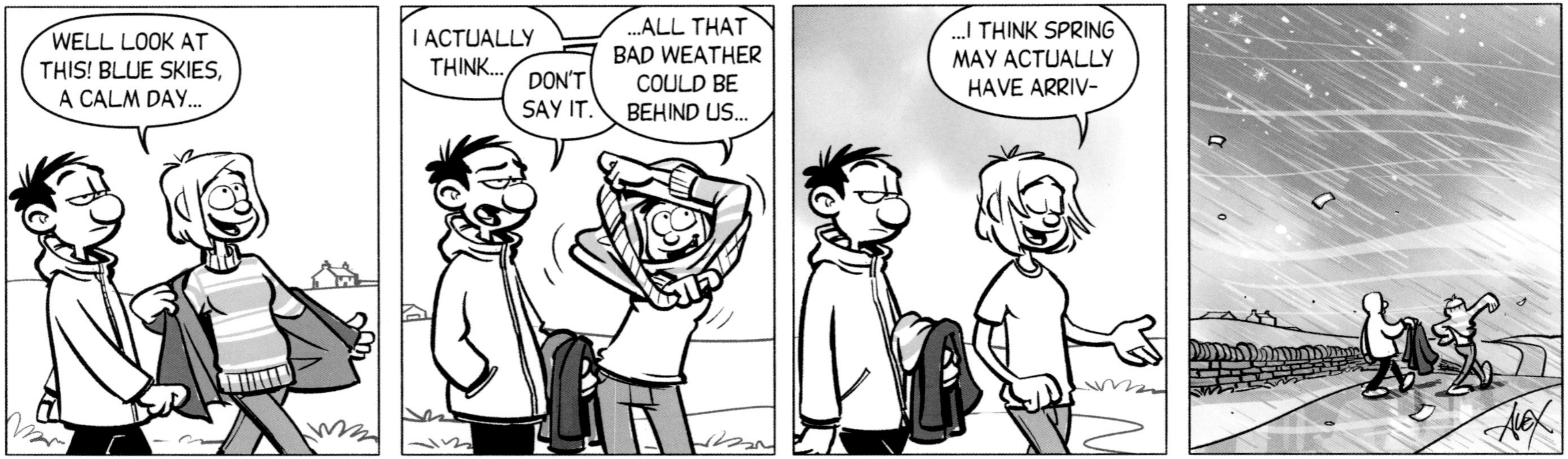
WELL LOOK AT THIS! BLUE SKIES, A CALM DAY...
I ACTUALLY THINK...
DON'T SAY IT.
...ALL THAT BAD WEATHER COULD BE BEHIND US...
...I THINK SPRING MAY ACTUALLY HAVE ARRIV-
ALEX

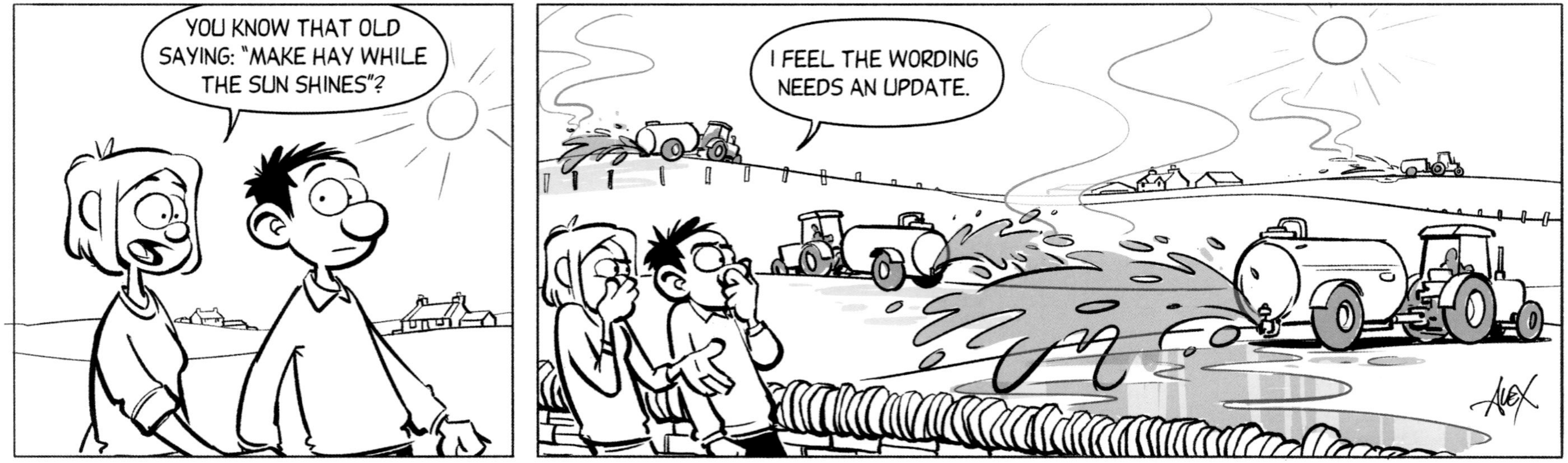
YOU KNOW THAT OLD SAYING: "MAKE HAY WHILE THE SUN SHINES"?
I FEEL THE WORDING NEEDS AN UPDATE.
ALEX

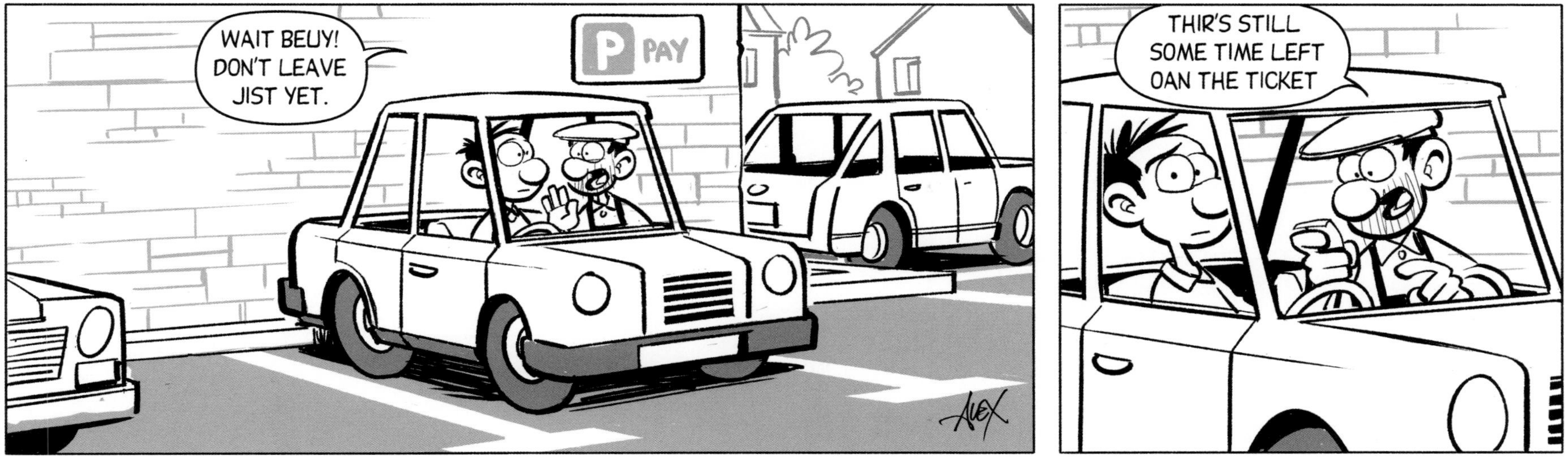
PAY
WAIT BEUY! DON'T LEAVE JIST YET.
THIR'S STILL SOME TIME LEFT OAN THE TICKET
ALEX

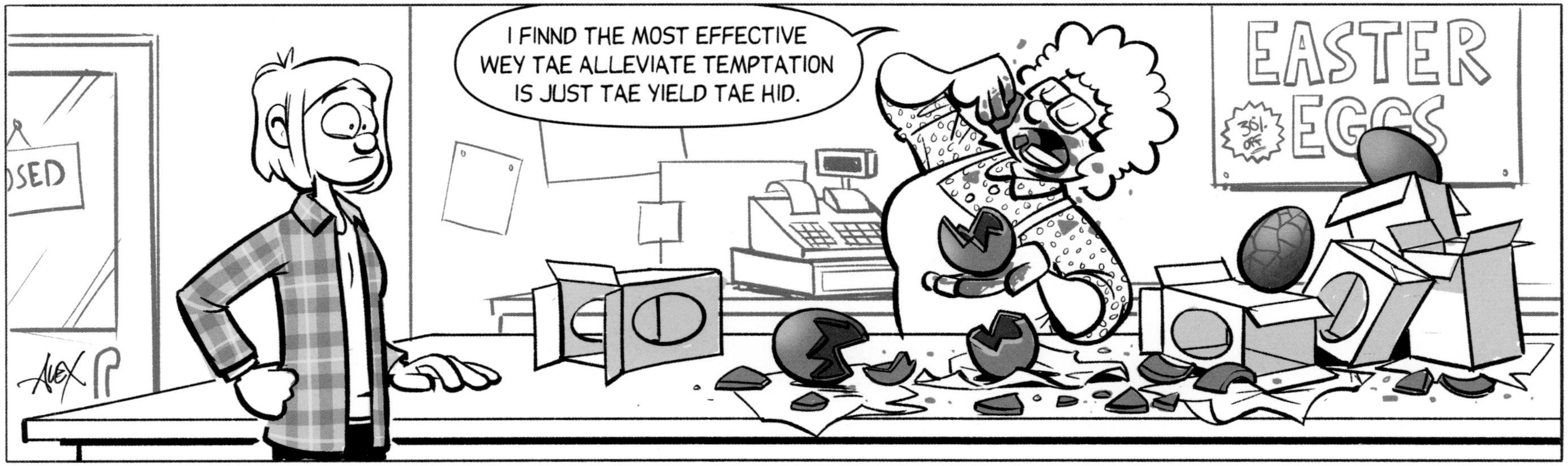
I FINND THE MOST EFFECTIVE WEY TAE ALLEVIATE TEMPTATION IS JUST TAE YIELD TAE HID.
EASTER EGGS
ALEX

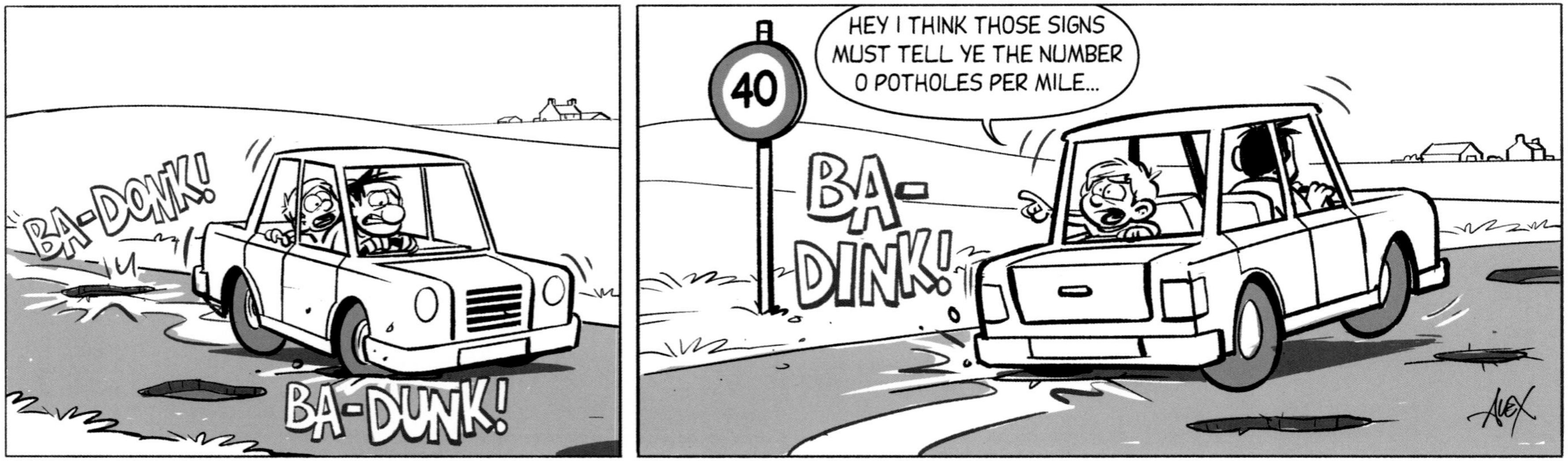
BA-DONK!
BA-DUNK!
40
HEY I THINK THOSE SIGNS MUST TELL YE THE NUMBER O POTHOLES PER MILE...
BA-DINK!
ALEX

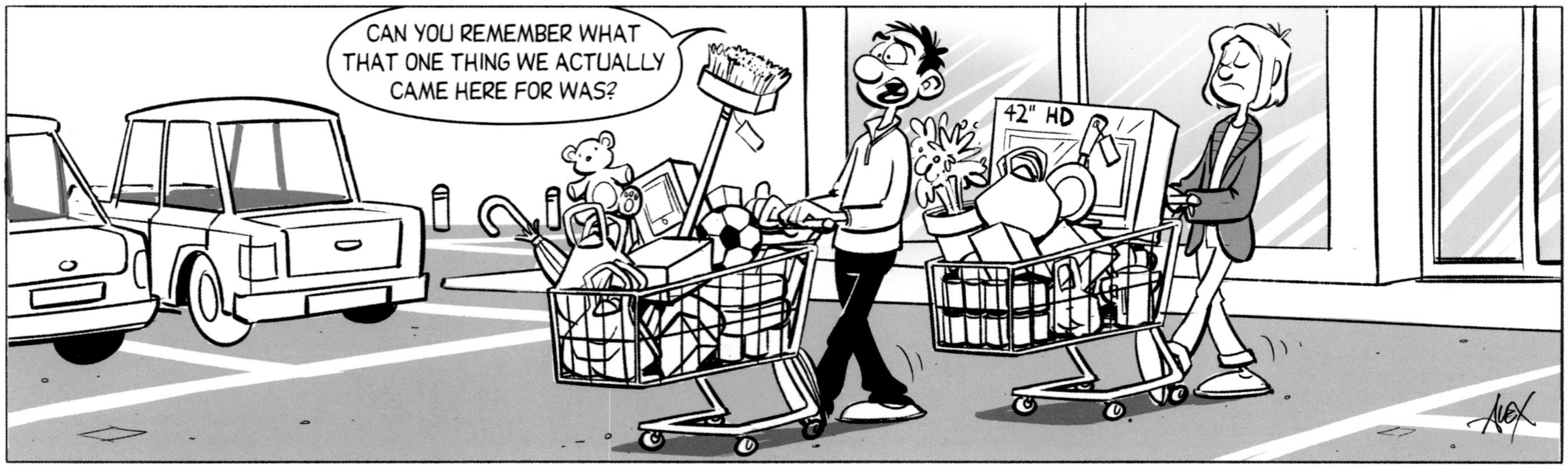
CAN YOU REMEMBER WHAT THAT ONE THING WE ACTUALLY CAME HERE FOR WAS?
42" HD
ALEX

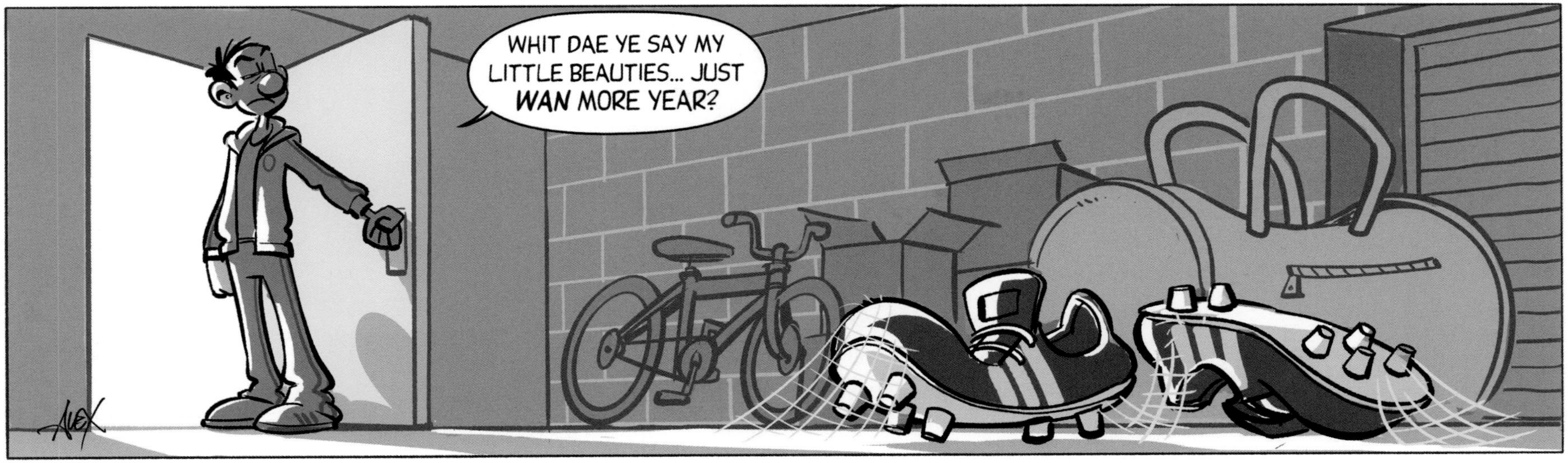
WHIT DAE YE SAY MY LITTLE BEAUTIES... JUST WAN MORE YEAR?

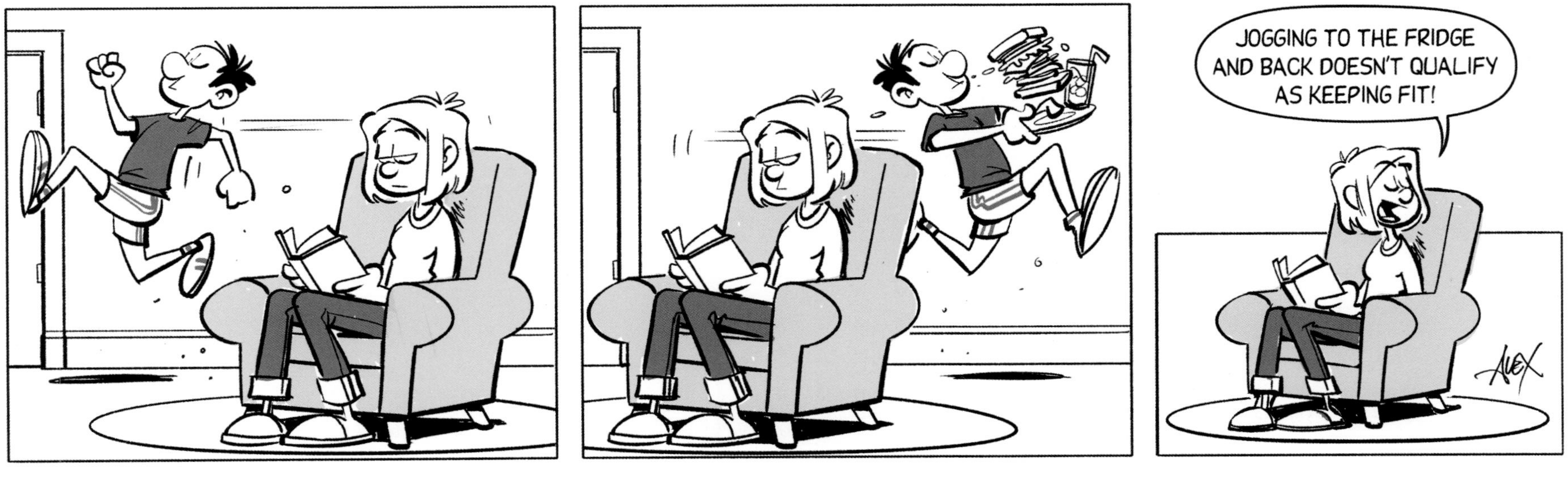
JOGGING TO THE FRIDGE AND BACK DOESN'T QUALIFY AS KEEPING FIT!

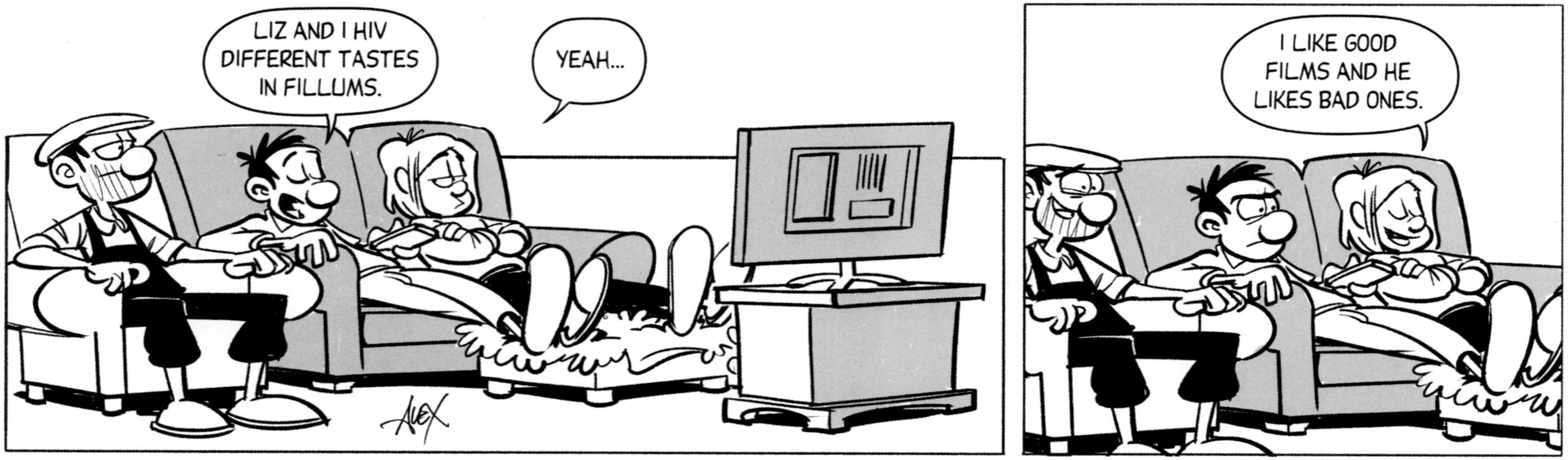
LIZ AND I HIV DIFFERENT TASTES IN FILLUMS.
YEAH...
I LIKE GOOD FILMS AND HE LIKES BAD ONES.
ALEX

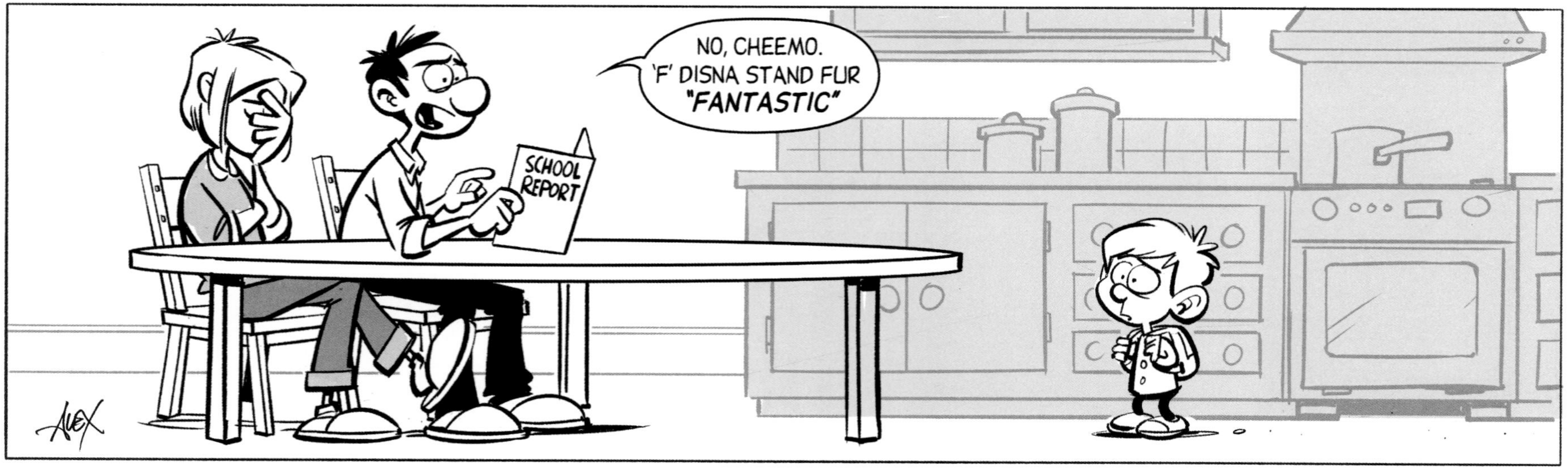
NO, CHEEMO. 'F' DISNA STAND FUR "FANTASTIC"
SCHOOL REPORT
ALEX

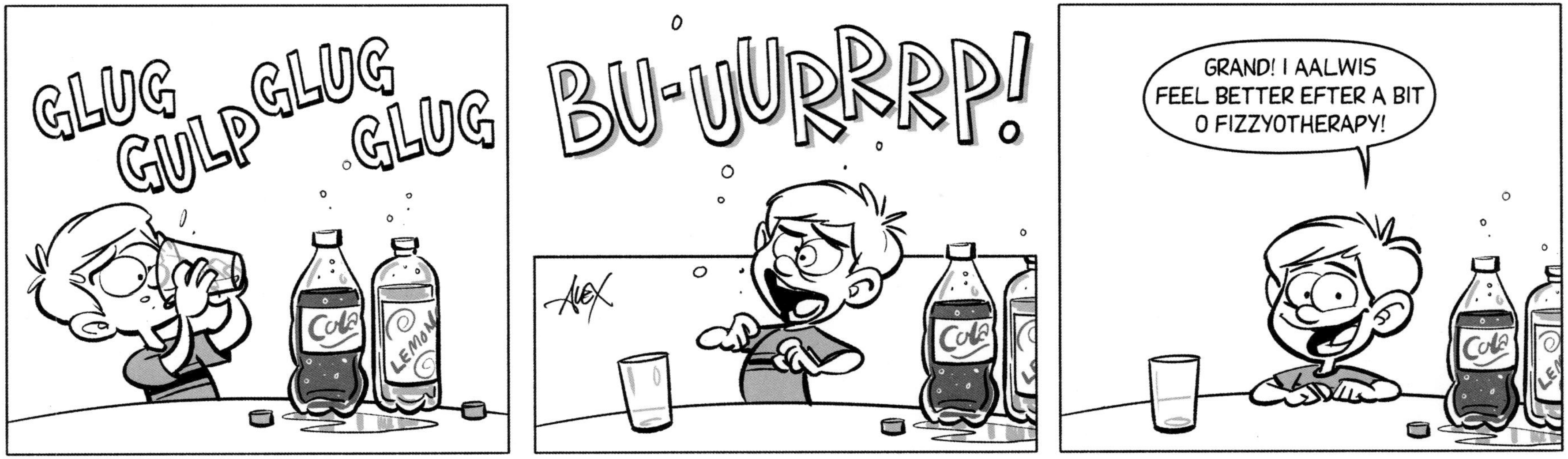
GLUG GULP GLUG GLUG GLUG
COLA
LEMON
BU-UURRRP!
ALEX
GRAND! I AALWIS FEEL BETTER EFTER A BIT O FIZZYOTHERAPY!

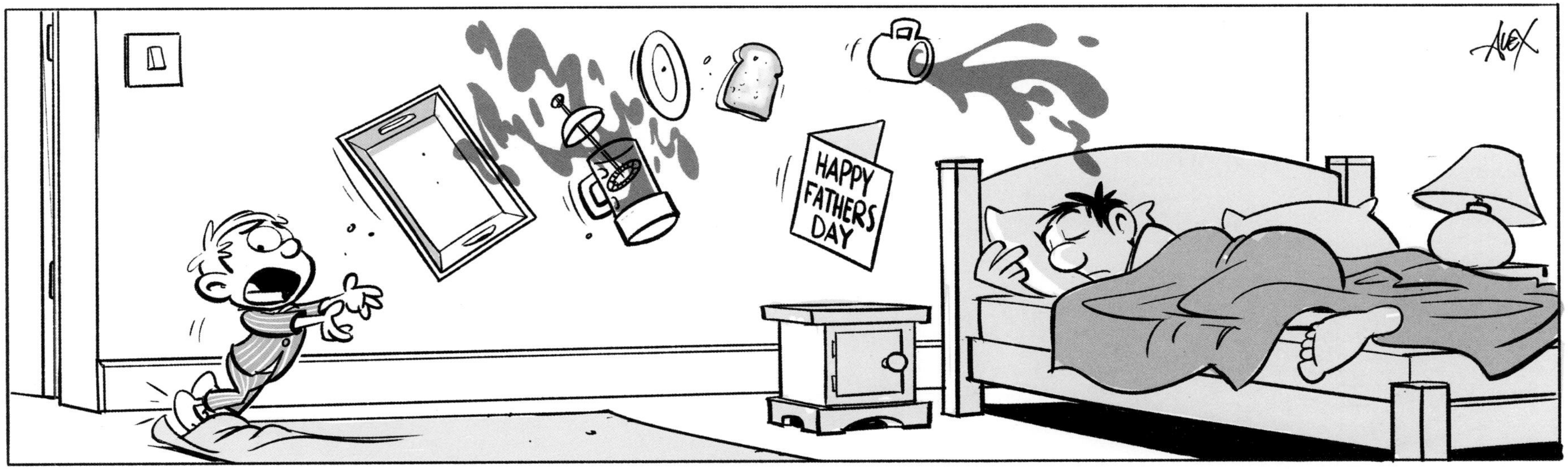
ALEX
HAPPY FATHERS DAY

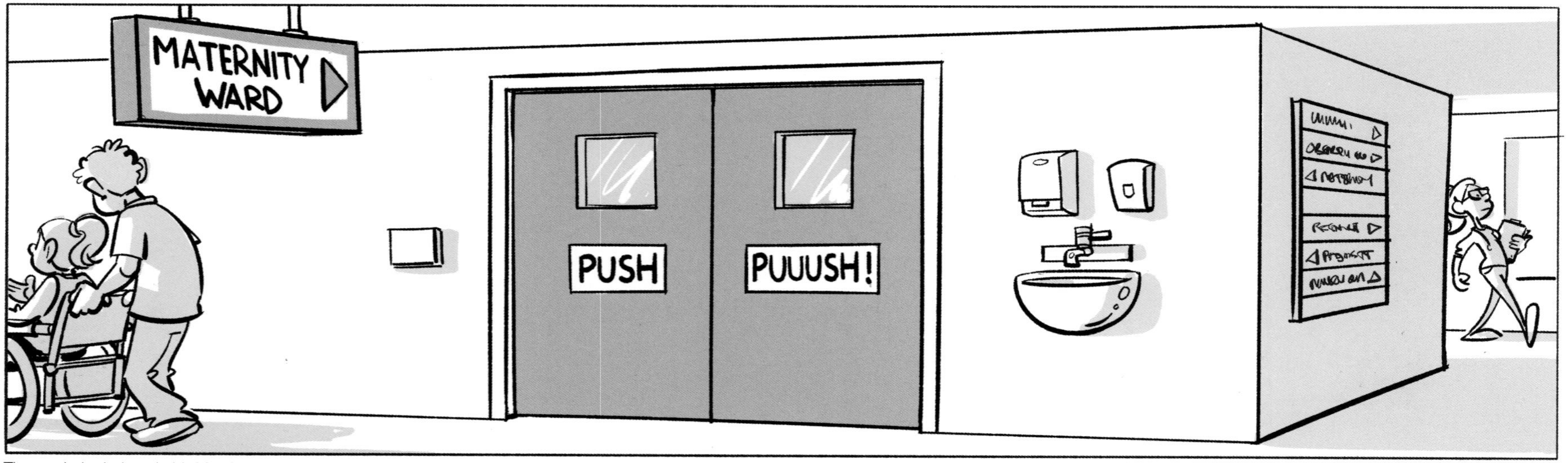
MATERNITY WARD
PUSH
PUUUSH!
The week the beloved old "Maty" closed.

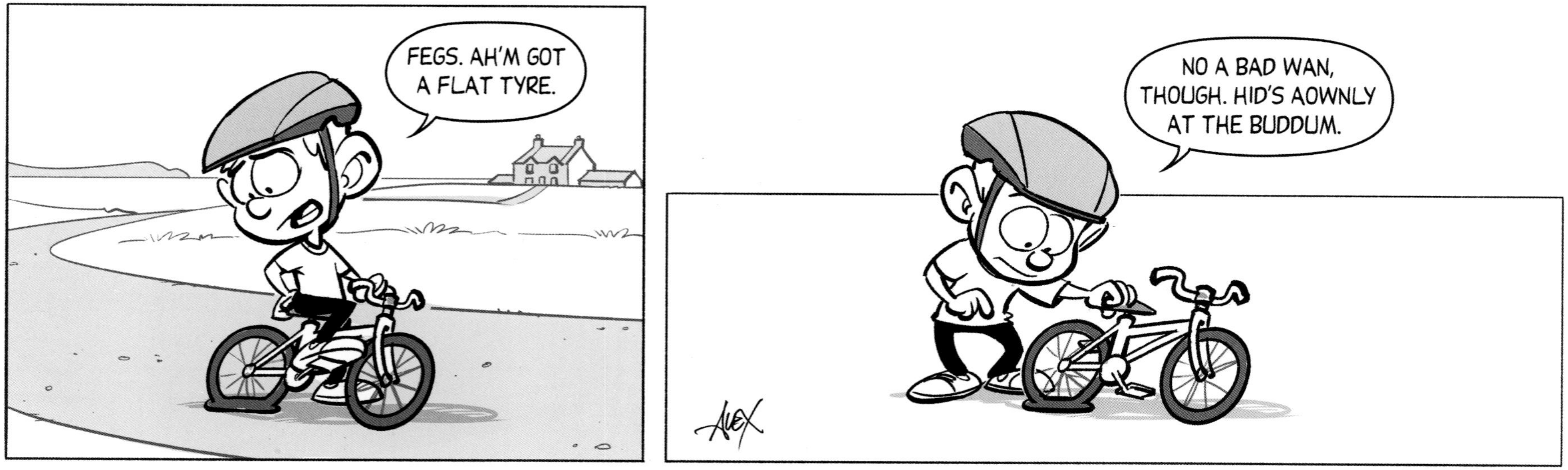
FEGS. AH'M GOT A FLAT TYRE.
NO A BAD WAN, THOUGH. HID'S AOWNLY AT THE BUDDUM.
ALEX

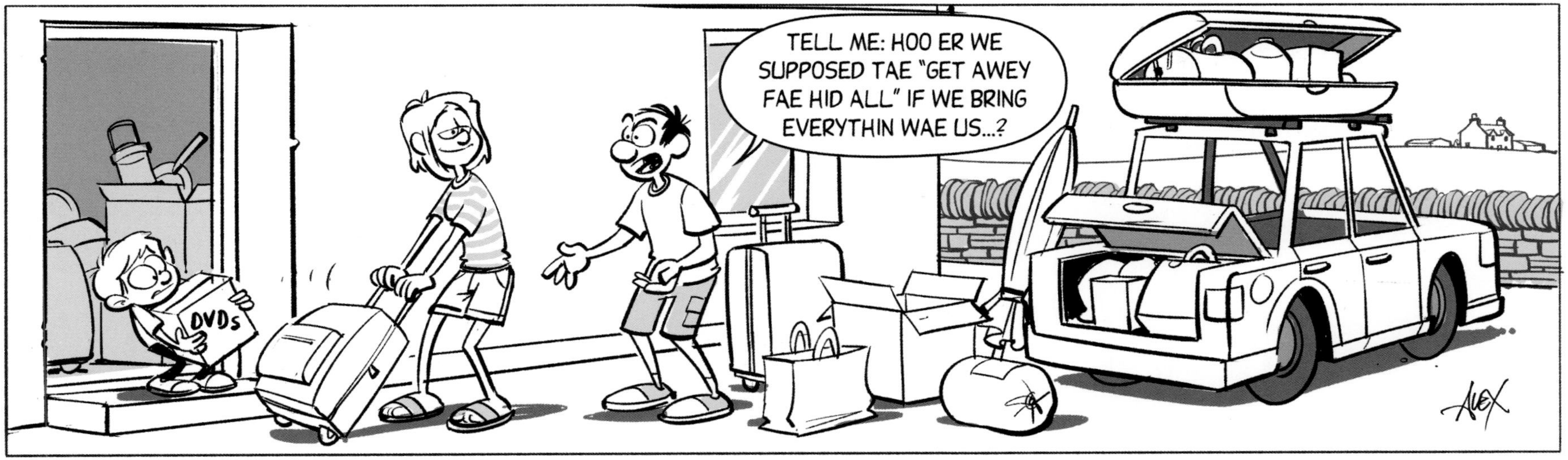
DVDs
TELL ME: HOO ER WE SUPPOSED TAE "GET AWEY FAE HID ALL" IF WE BRING EVERYTHIN WAE US...?

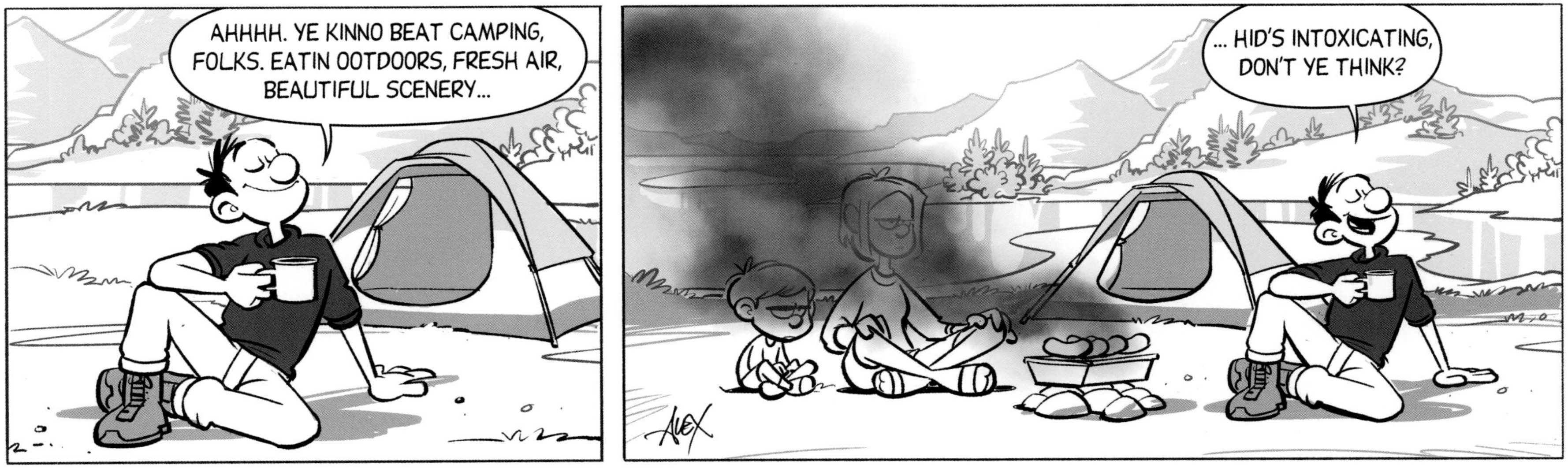
AHHHH. YE KINNO BEAT CAMPING, FOLKS. EATIN OOTDOORS, FRESH AIR, BEAUTIFUL SCENERY...
... HID'S INTOXICATING, DON'T YE THINK?

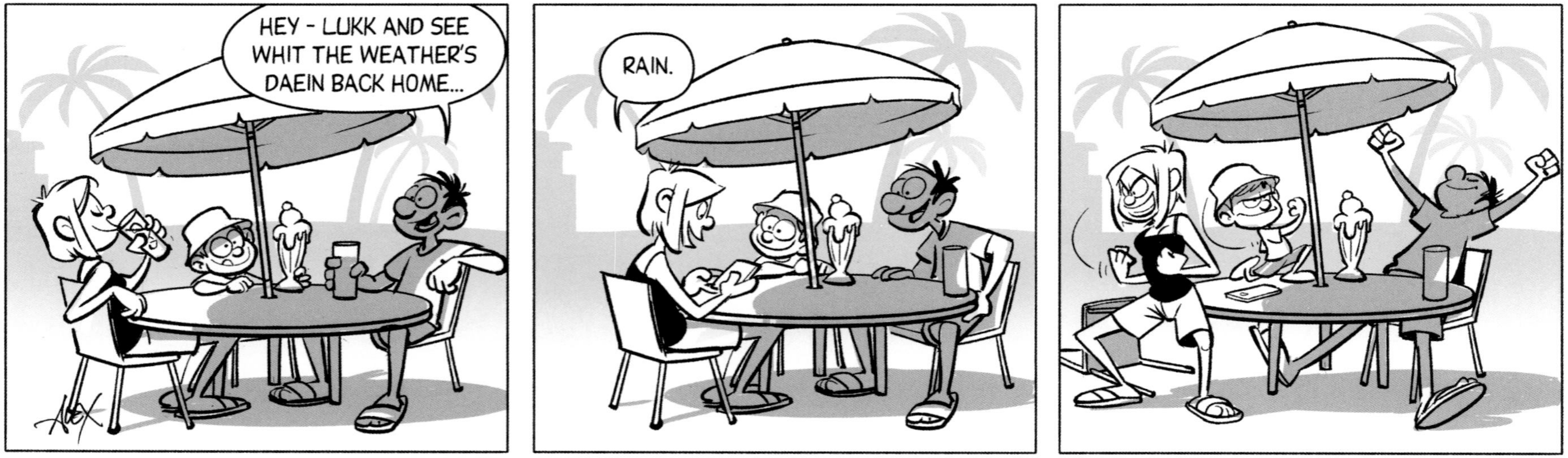
HEY - LUKK AND SEE WHIT THE WEATHER'S DAEIN BACK HOME...
RAIN.

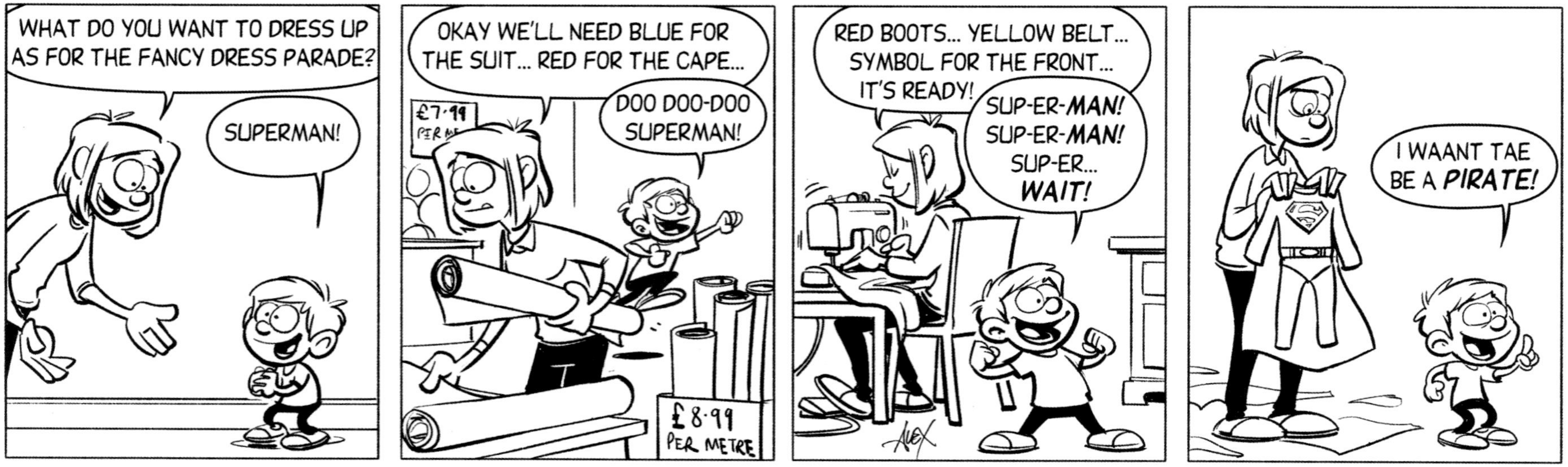
WHAT DO YOU WANT TO DRESS UP AS FOR THE FANCY DRESS PARADE?
SUPERMAN!
OKAY WE'LL NEED BLUE FOR THE SUIT... RED FOR THE CAPE...
DOO DOO-DOO SUPERMAN!
£8·99 PER METRE
RED BOOTS... YELLOW BELT... SYMBOL FOR THE FRONT... IT'S READY!
SUP-ER-MAN! SUP-ER-MAN! SUP-ER... WAIT!
I WAANT TAE BE A PIRATE!

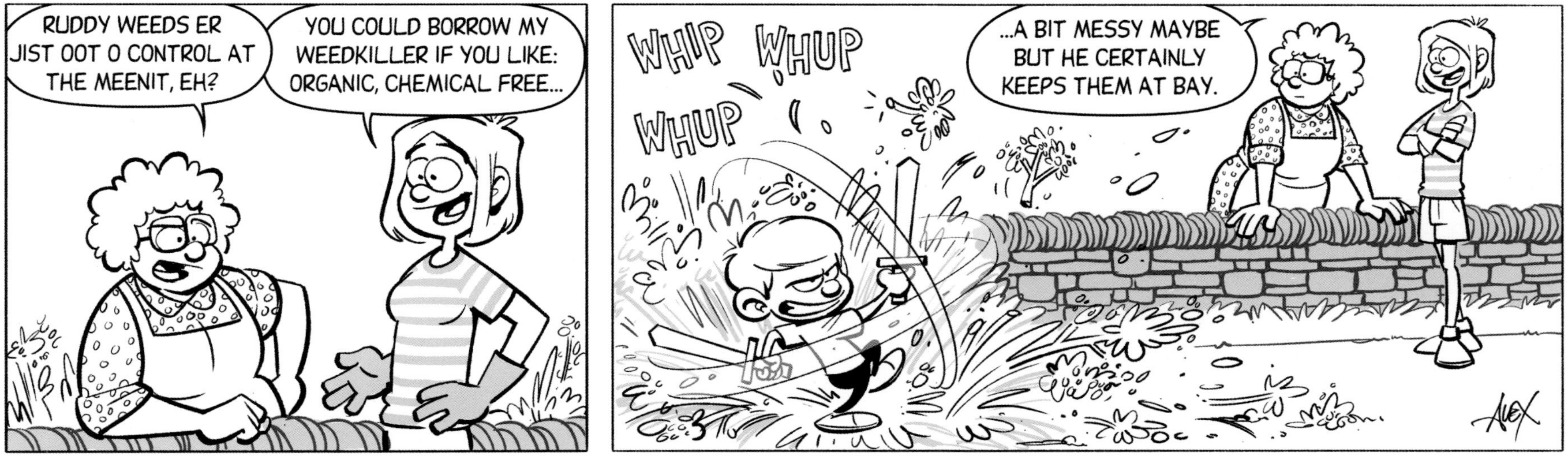
RUDDY WEEDS ER JIST OOT O CONTROL AT THE MEENIT, EH?
YOU COULD BORROW MY WEEDKILLER IF YOU LIKE: ORGANIC, CHEMICAL FREE...
WHIP WHUP WHUP
...A BIT MESSY MAYBE BUT HE CERTAINLY KEEPS THEM AT BAY.
ALEX

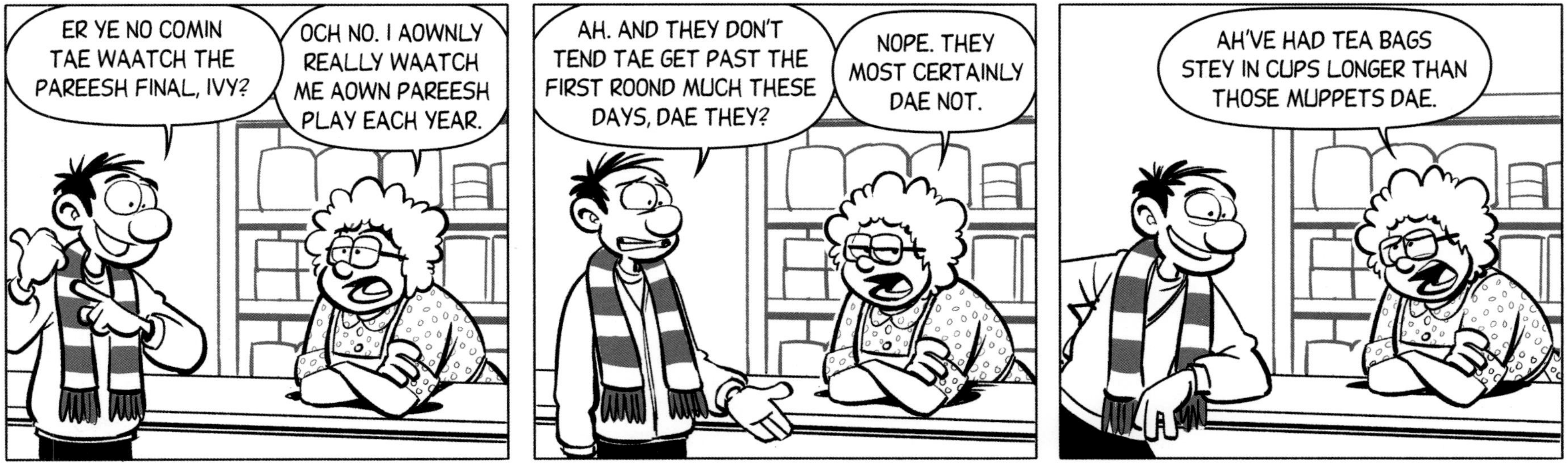
ER YE NO COMIN TAE WAATCH THE PAREESH FINAL, IVY?
OCH NO. I AOWNLY REALLY WAATCH ME AOWN PAREESH PLAY EACH YEAR.
AH. AND THEY DON'T TEND TAE GET PAST THE FIRST ROOND MUCH THESE DAYS, DAE THEY?
NOPE. THEY MOST CERTAINLY DAE NOT.
AH'VE HAD TEA BAGS STEY IN CUPS LONGER THAN THOSE MUPPETS DAE.

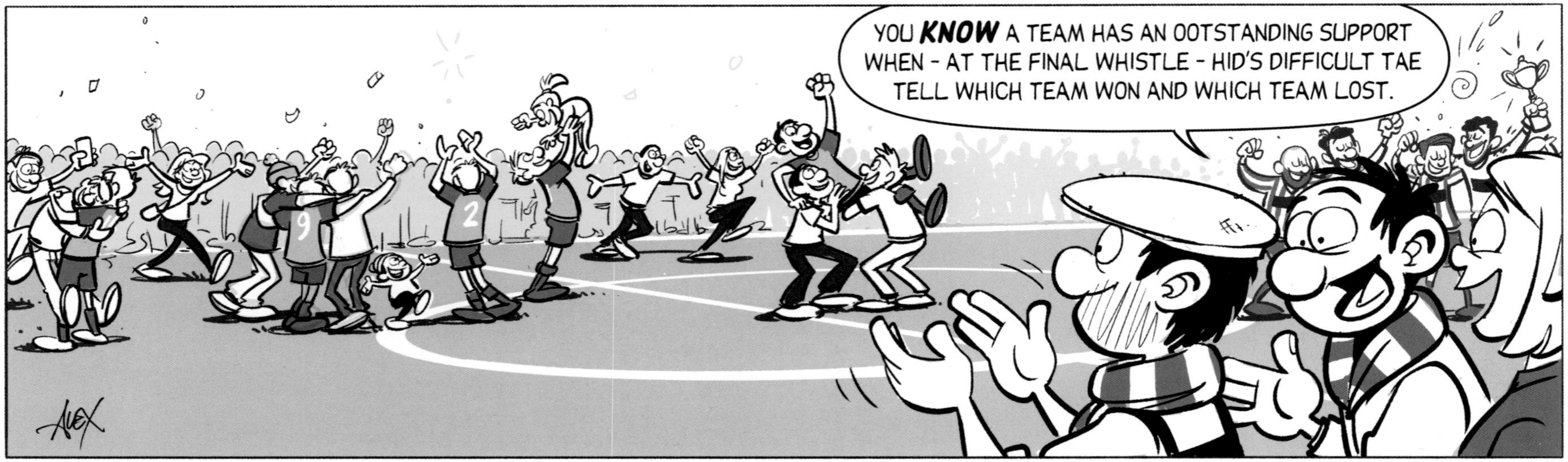
YOU KNOW A TEAM HAS AN OOTSTANDING SUPPORT WHEN - AT THE FINAL WHISTLE - HID'S DIFFICULT TAE TELL WHICH TEAM WON AND WHICH TEAM LOST.
ALEX

Stromness v Sanday Parish Cup Final 2019.

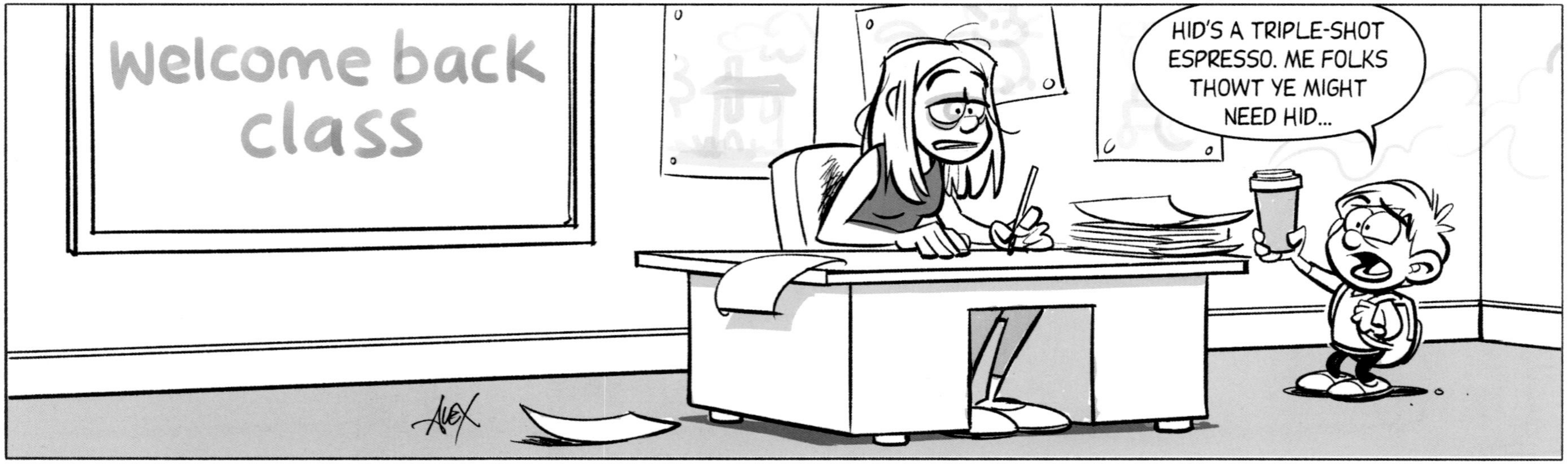
Welcome back class
HID'S A TRIPLE-SHOT ESPRESSO. ME FOLKS THOWT YE MIGHT NEED HID...
ALEX

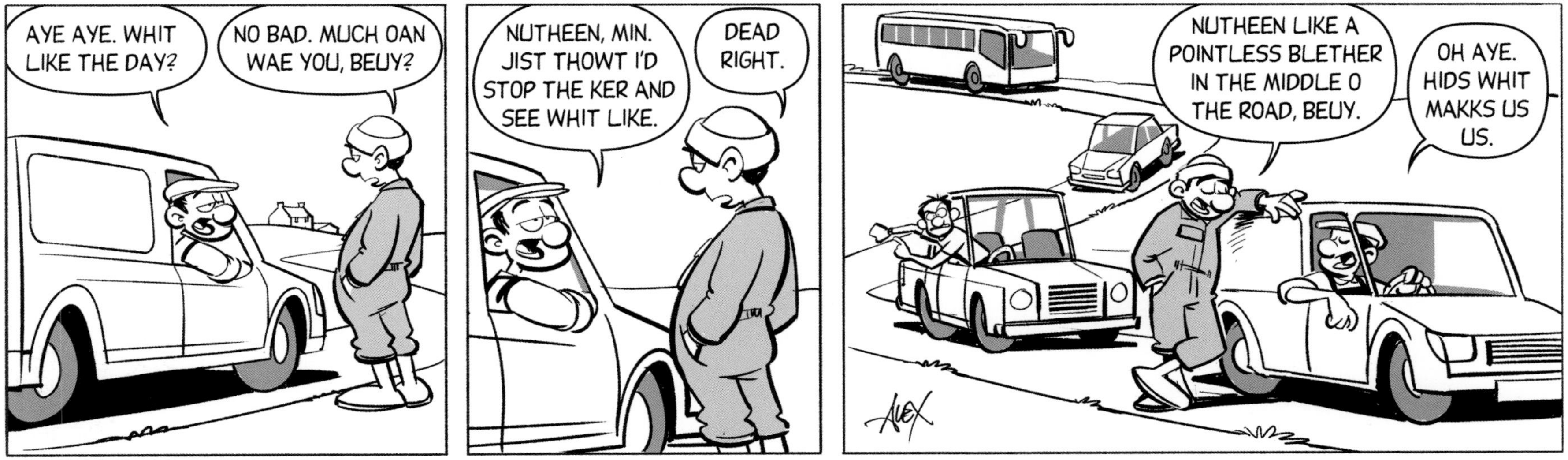
AYE AYE. WHIT LIKE THE DAY?
NO BAD. MUCH OAN WAE YOU, BEUY?
NUTHEEN, MIN. JIST THOWT I'D STOP THE KER AND SEE WHIT LIKE.
DEAD RIGHT.
NUTHEEN LIKE A POINTLESS BLETHER IN THE MIDDLE O THE ROAD, BEUY.
OH AYE. HIDS WHIT MAKKS US US.
ALEX

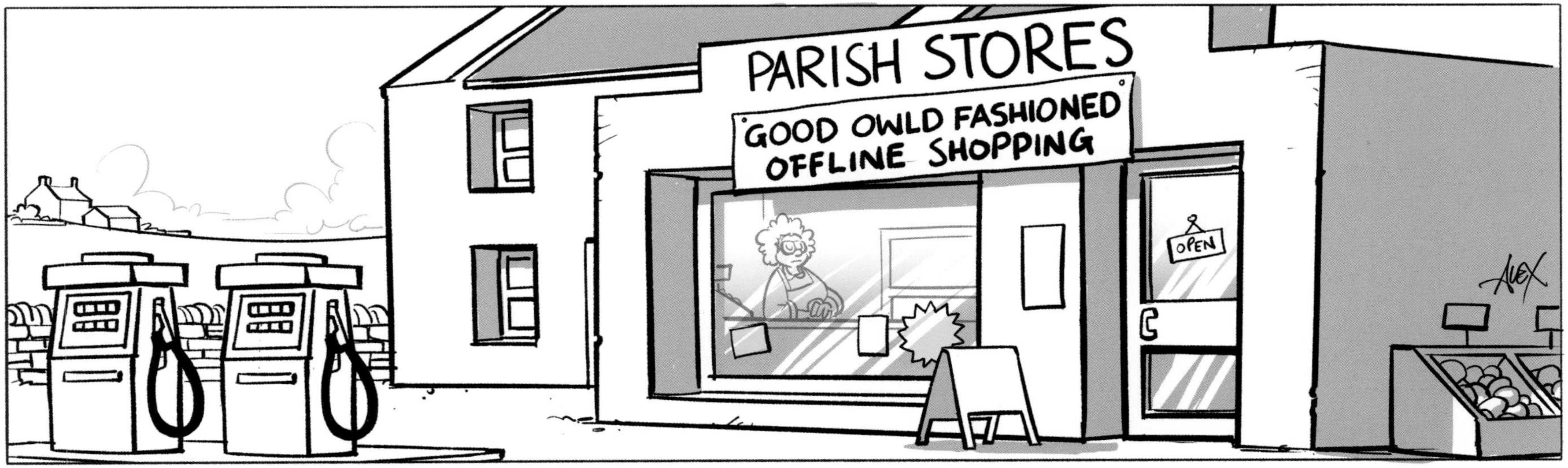
PARISH STORES
GOOD OWLD FASHIONED OFFLINE SHOPPING
OPEN
ALEX

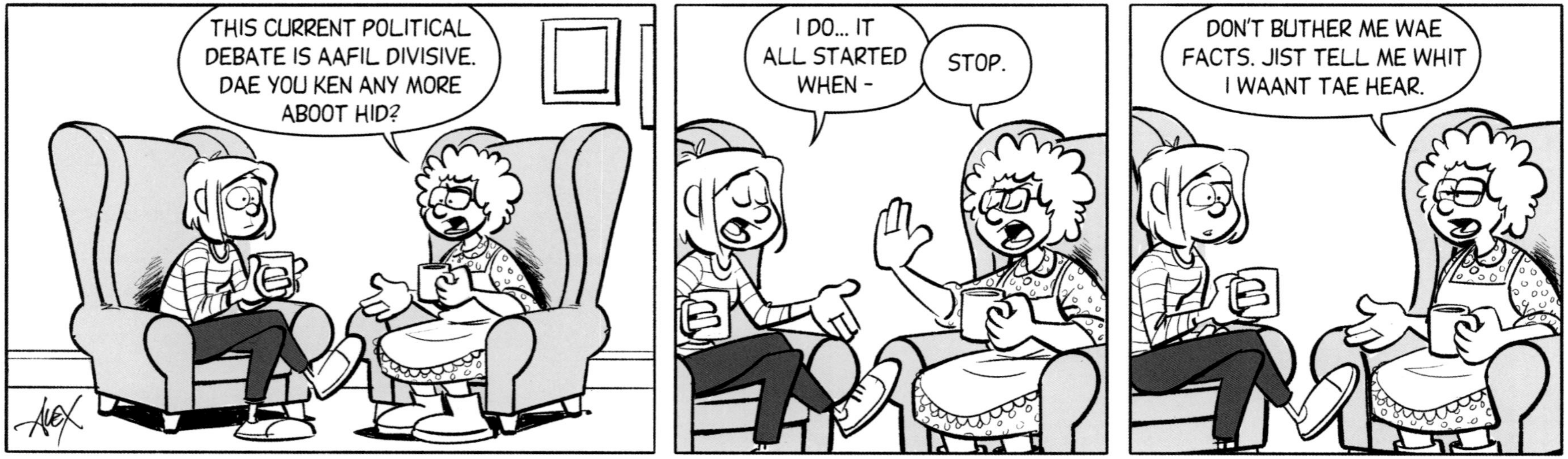
THIS CURRENT POLITICAL DEBATE IS AAFIL DIVISIVE. DAE YOU KEN ANY MORE ABOOT HID?
I DO... IT ALL STARTED WHEN -
STOP.
DON'T BUTHER ME WAE FACTS. JIST TELL ME WHIT I WAANT TAE HEAR.

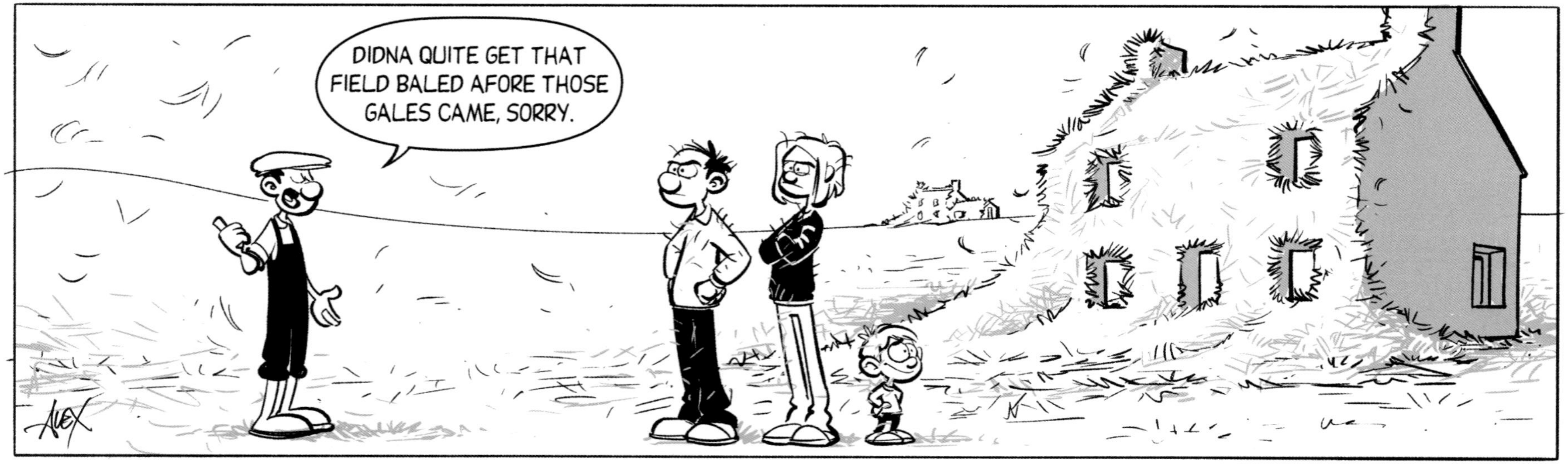
DIDNA QUITE GET THAT FIELD BALED AFORE THOSE GALES CAME, SORRY.

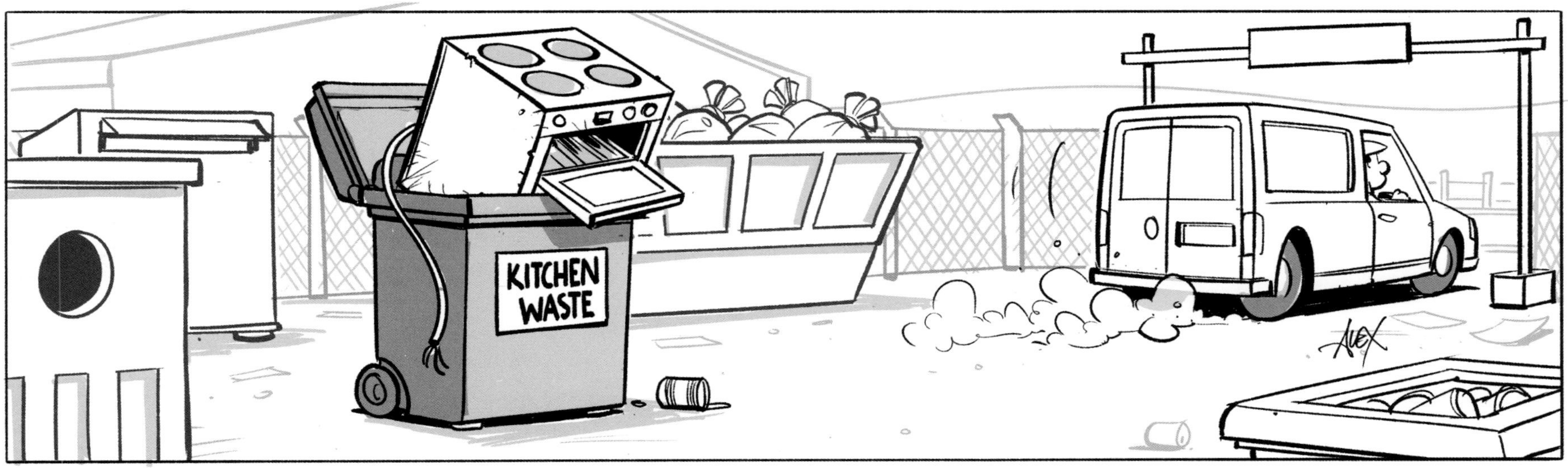
KITCHEN WASTE
ALEX

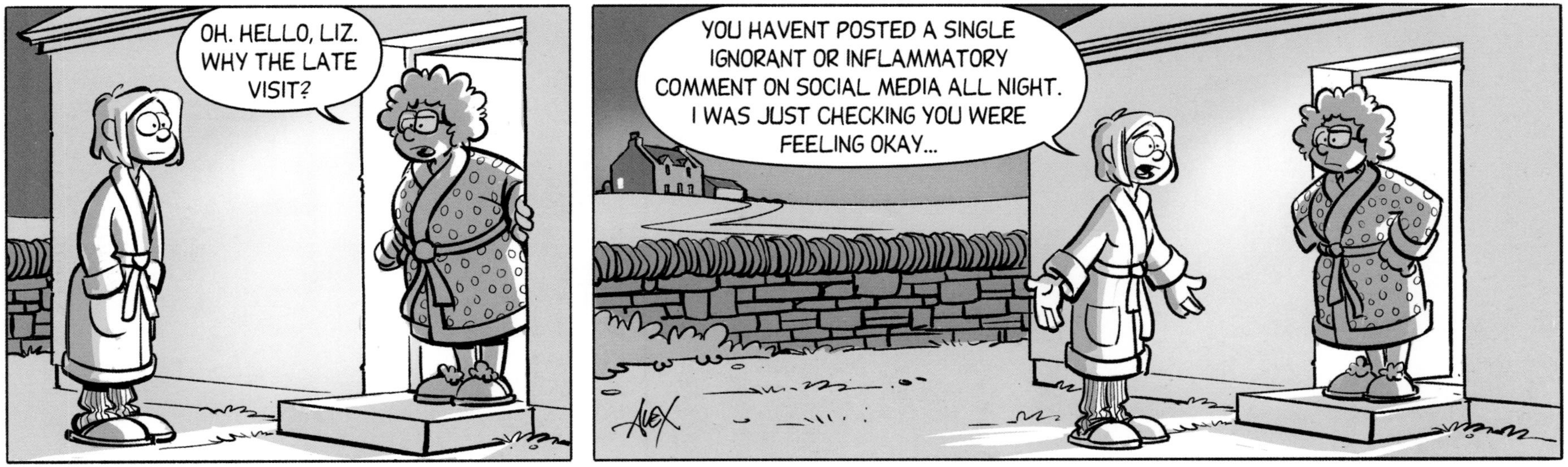
OH. HELLO, LIZ. WHY THE LATE VISIT?
YOU HAVENT POSTED A SINGLE IGNORANT OR INFLAMMATORY COMMENT ON SOCIAL MEDIA ALL NIGHT. I WAS JUST CHECKING YOU WERE FEELING OKAY...
ALEX

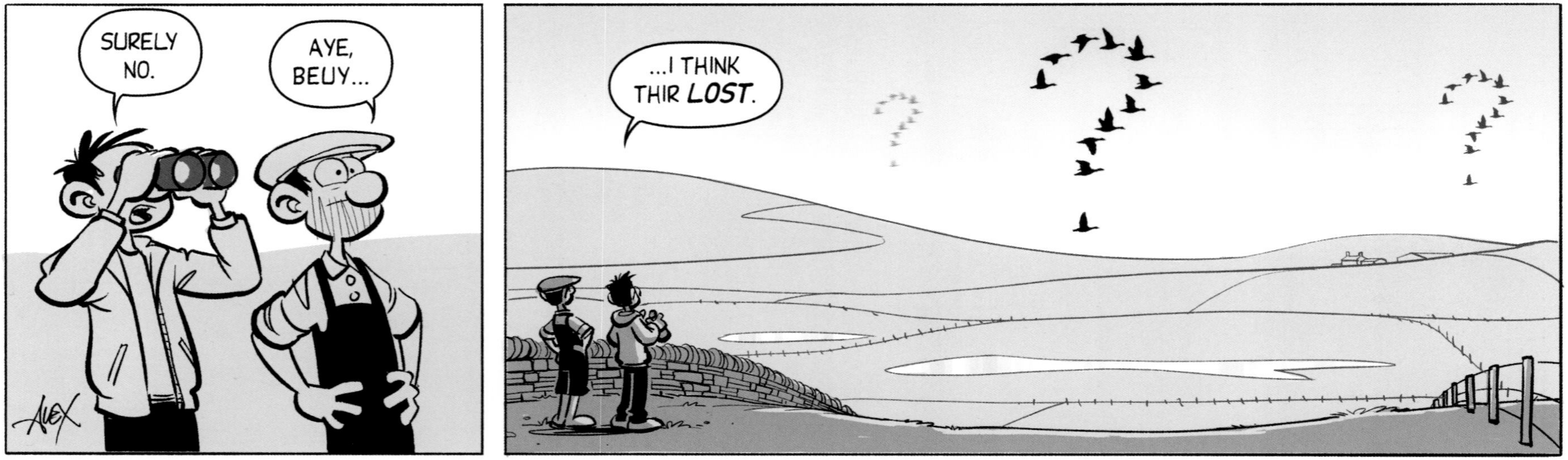
SURELY NO.
AYE, BEUY...
...I THINK THIR **LOST**.

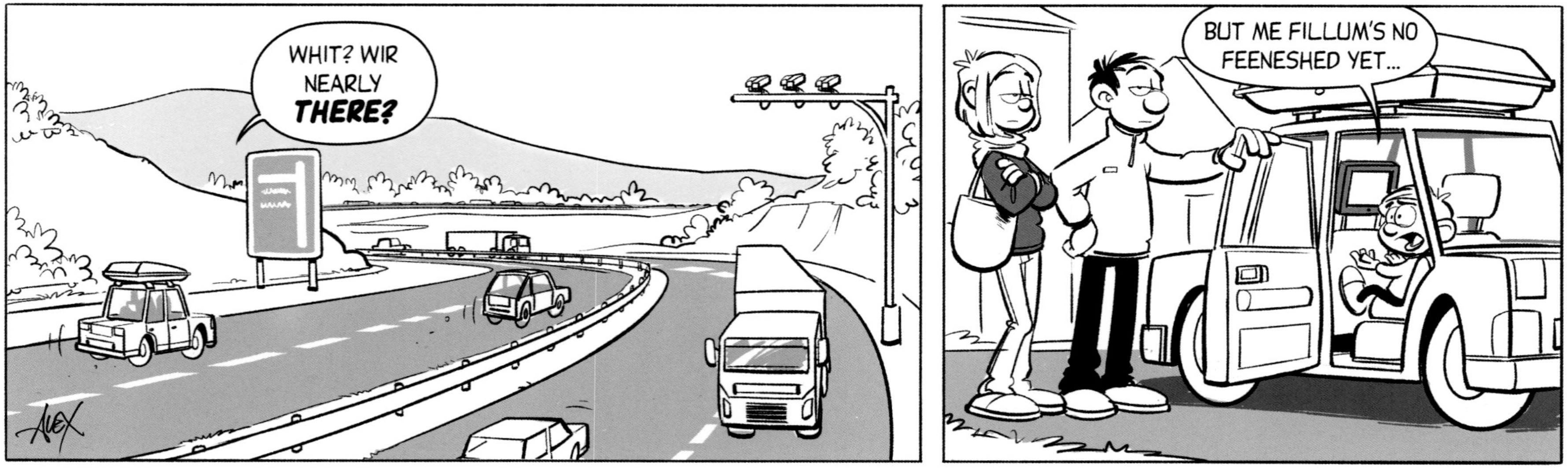
WHIT? WIR NEARLY **THERE?**
BUT ME FILLUM'S NO FEENESHED YET...

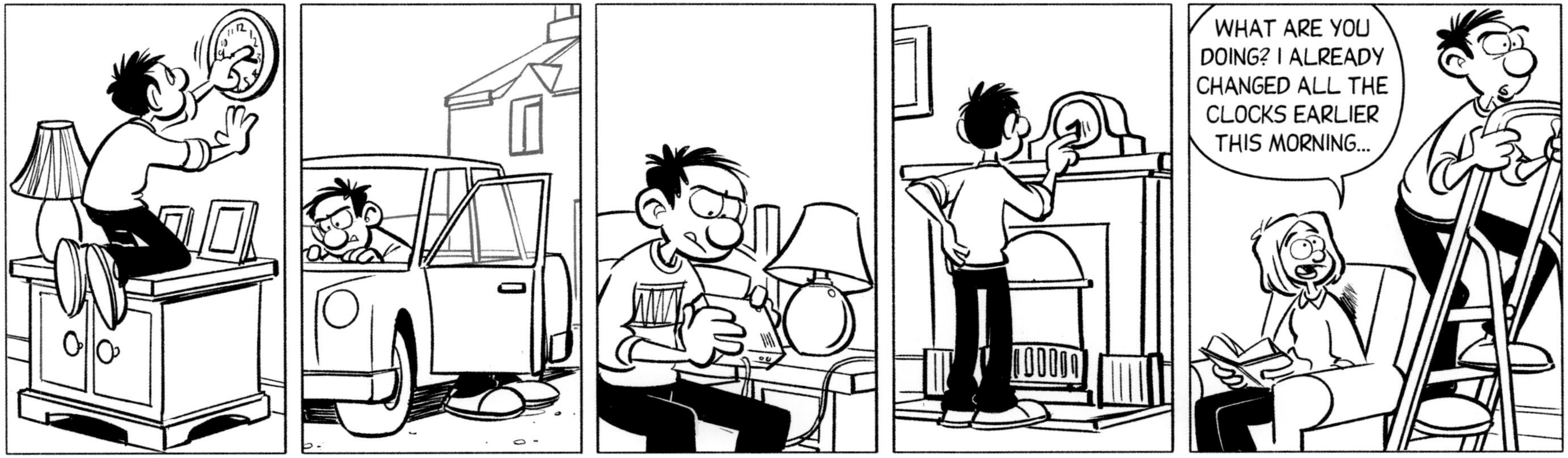
WHAT ARE YOU DOING? I ALREADY CHANGED ALL THE CLOCKS EARLIER THIS MORNING...

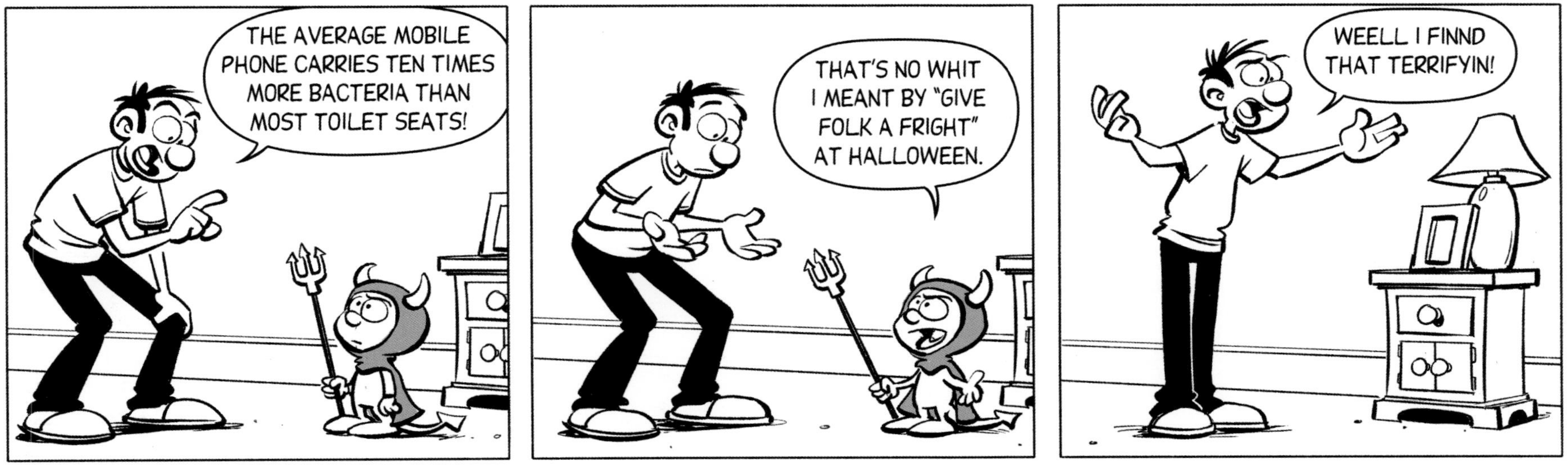
THE AVERAGE MOBILE PHONE CARRIES TEN TIMES MORE BACTERIA THAN MOST TOILET SEATS!
THAT'S NO WHIT I MEANT BY "GIVE FOLK A FRIGHT" AT HALLOWEEN.
WEELL I FINND THAT TERRIFYIN!

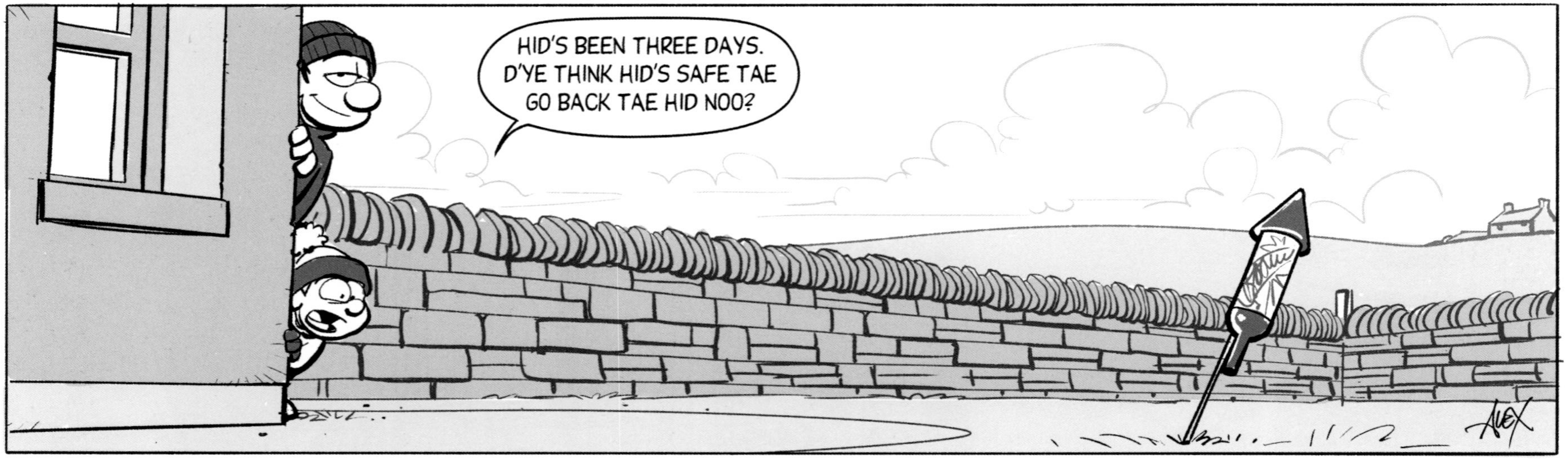
HID'S BEEN THREE DAYS. D'YE THINK HID'S SAFE TAE GO BACK TAE HID NOO?
ALEX

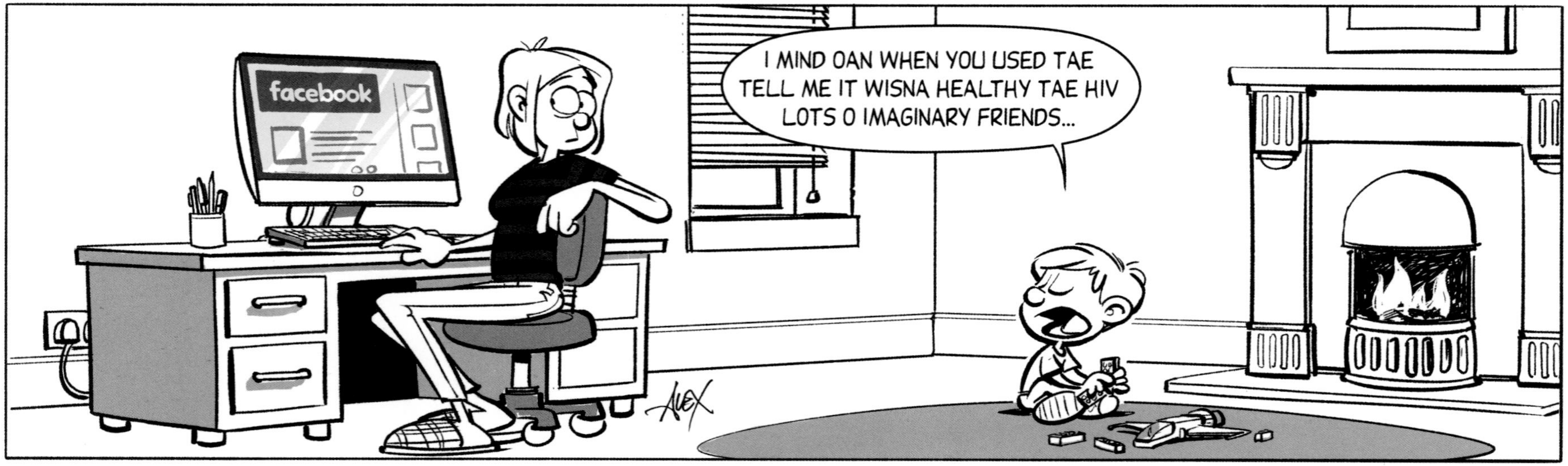
facebook
I MIND OAN WHEN YOU USED TAE TELL ME IT WISNA HEALTHY TAE HIV LOTS O IMAGINARY FRIENDS...
ALEX

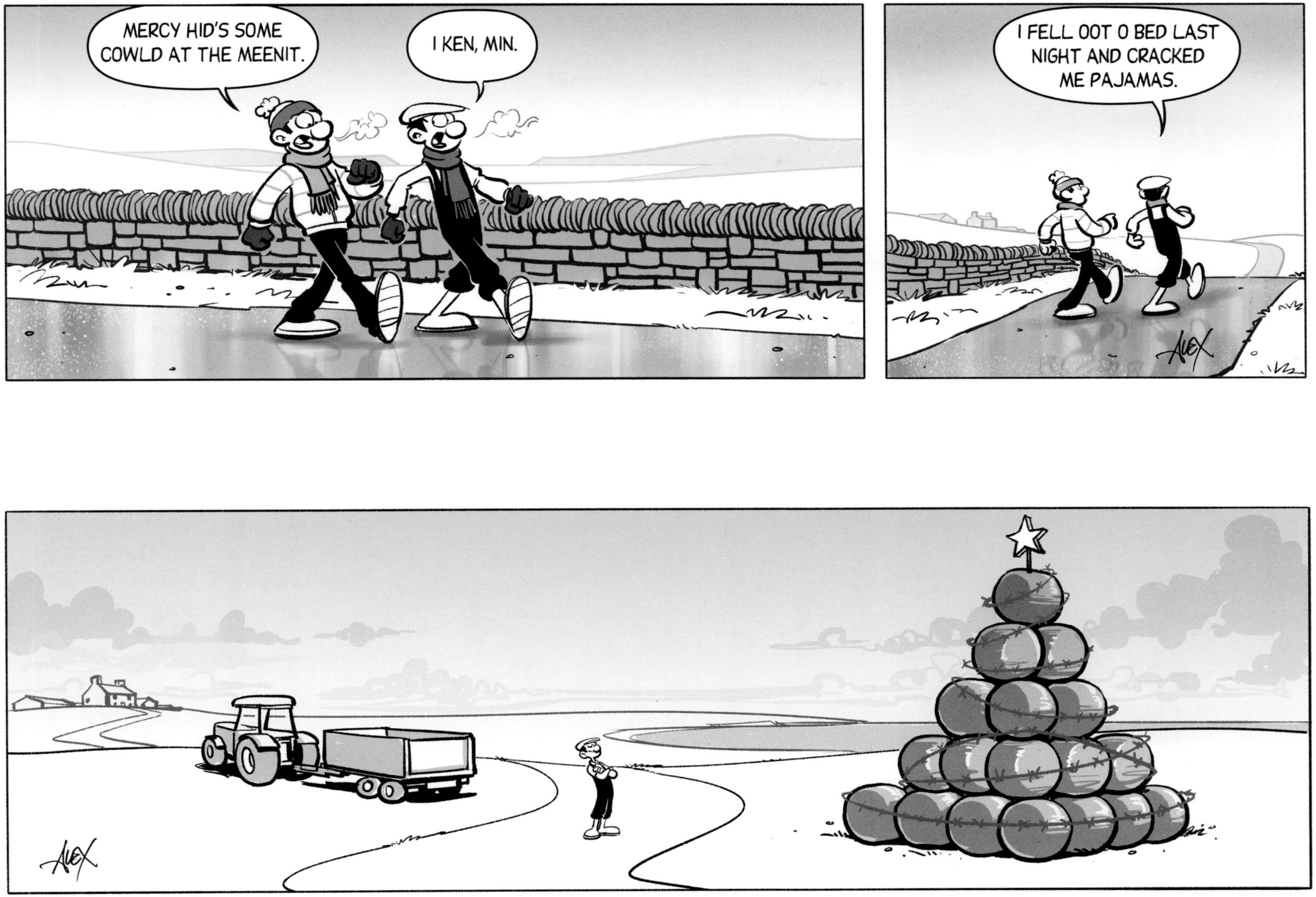
MERCY HID'S SOME COWLD AT THE MEENIT.
I KEN, MIN.
I FELL OOT O BED LAST NIGHT AND CRACKED ME PAJAMAS.
ALEX
ALEX

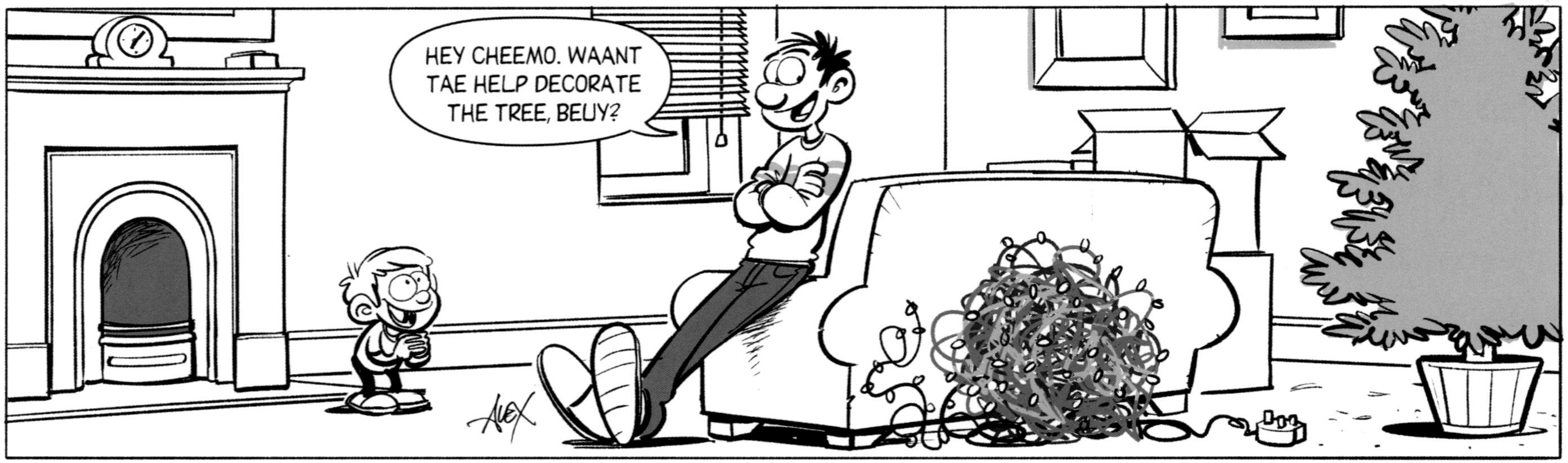
HEY CHEEMO. WAANT TAE HELP DECORATE THE TREE, BEUY?
ALEX

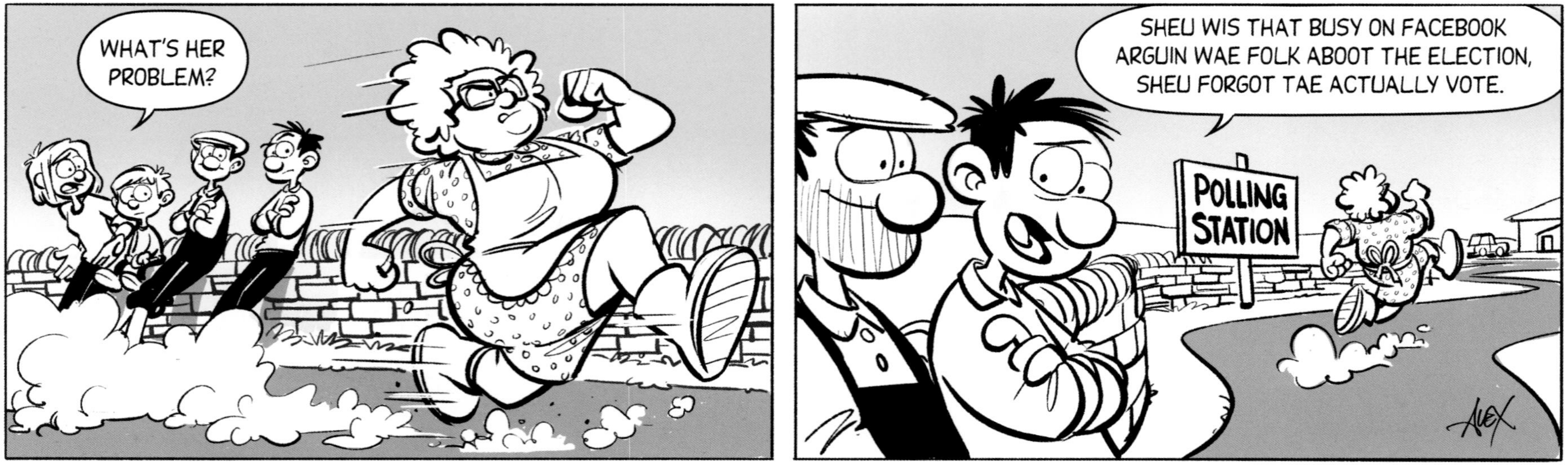
WHAT'S HER PROBLEM?
SHEU WIS THAT BUSY ON FACEBOOK ARGUIN WAE FOLK ABOOT THE ELECTION, SHEU FORGOT TAE ACTUALLY VOTE.
POLLING STATION
ALEX

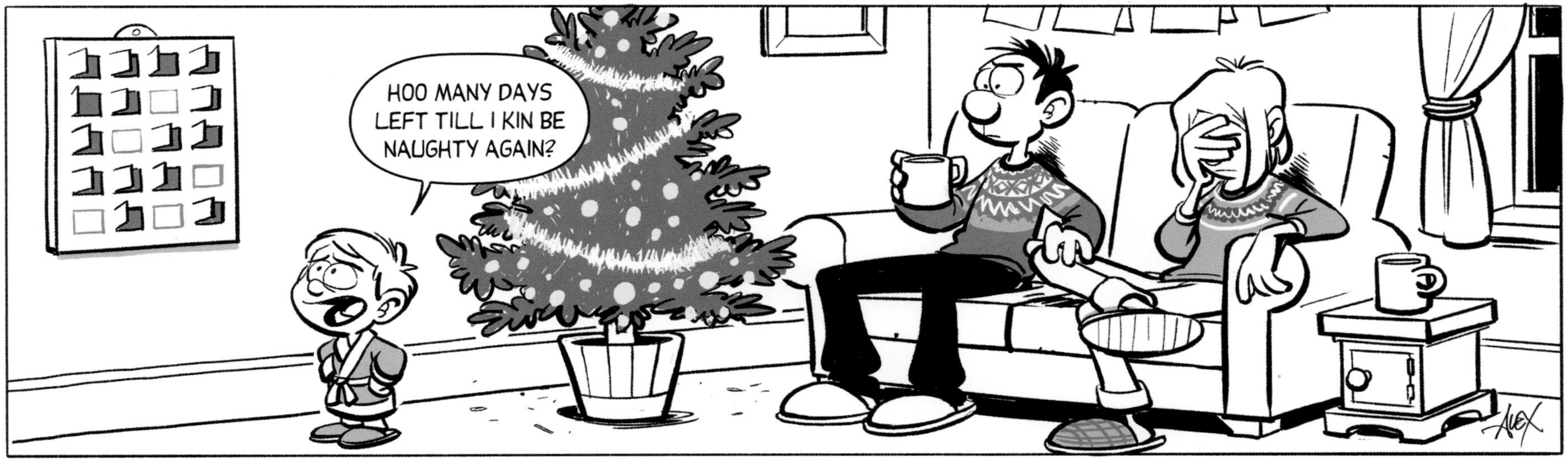
HOO MANY DAYS
LEFT TILL I KIN BE
NAUGHTY AGAIN?
ALEX

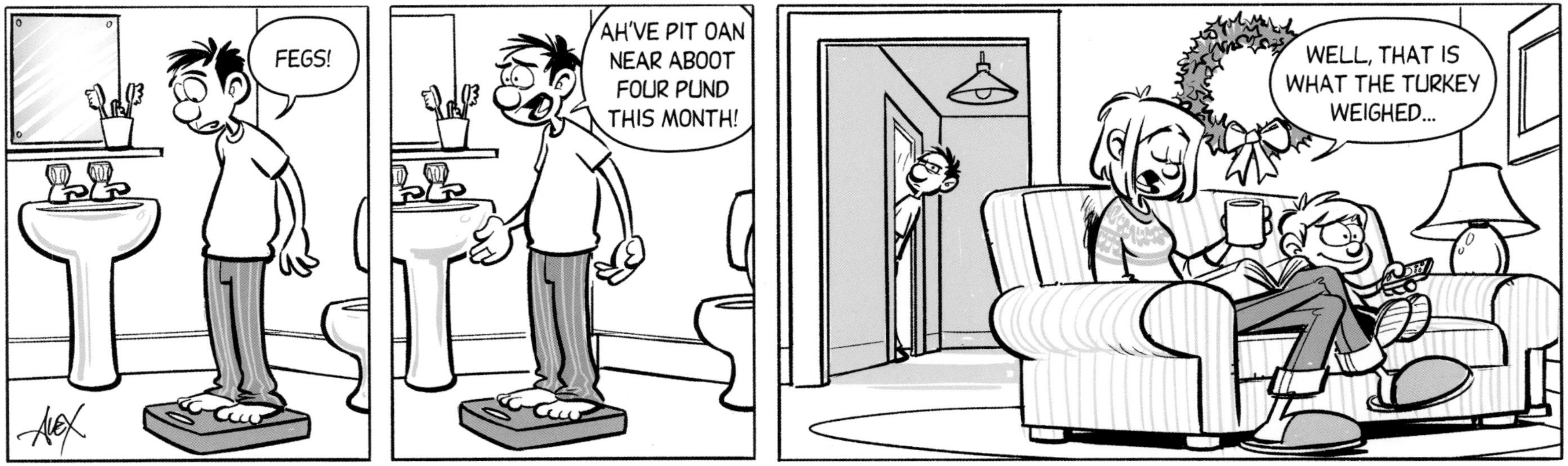
FEGS!
ALEX
AH'VE PIT OAN
NEAR ABOOT
FOUR PUND
THIS MONTH!
WELL, THAT IS
WHAT THE TURKEY
WEIGHED...

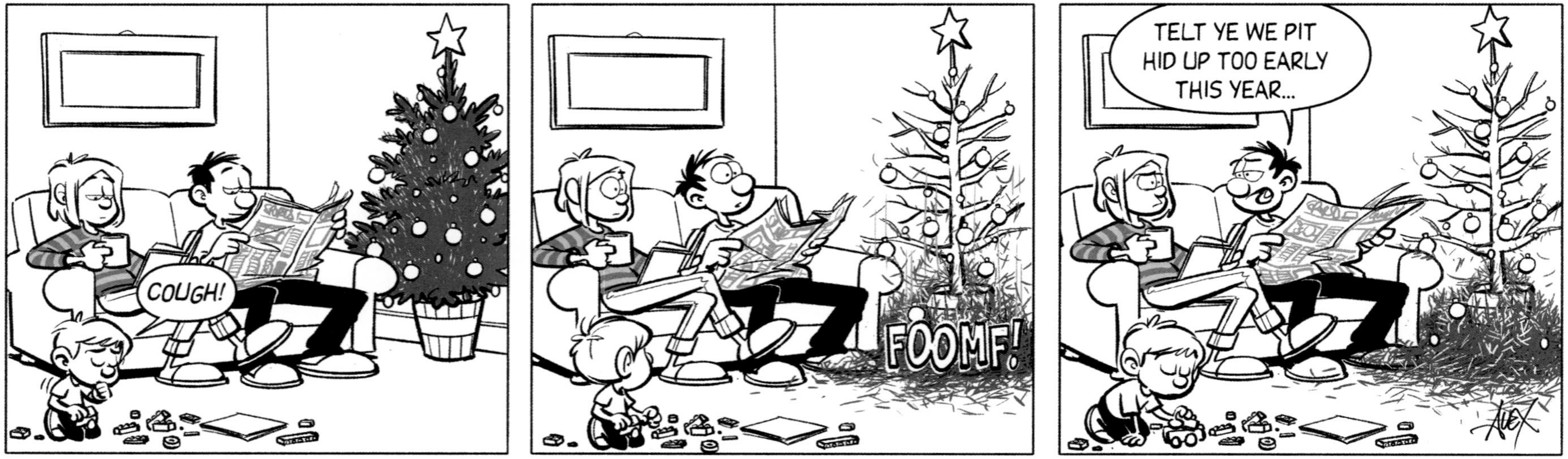
COUGH!
FOOMF!
TELT YE WE PIT HID UP TOO EARLY THIS YEAR...
ALEX

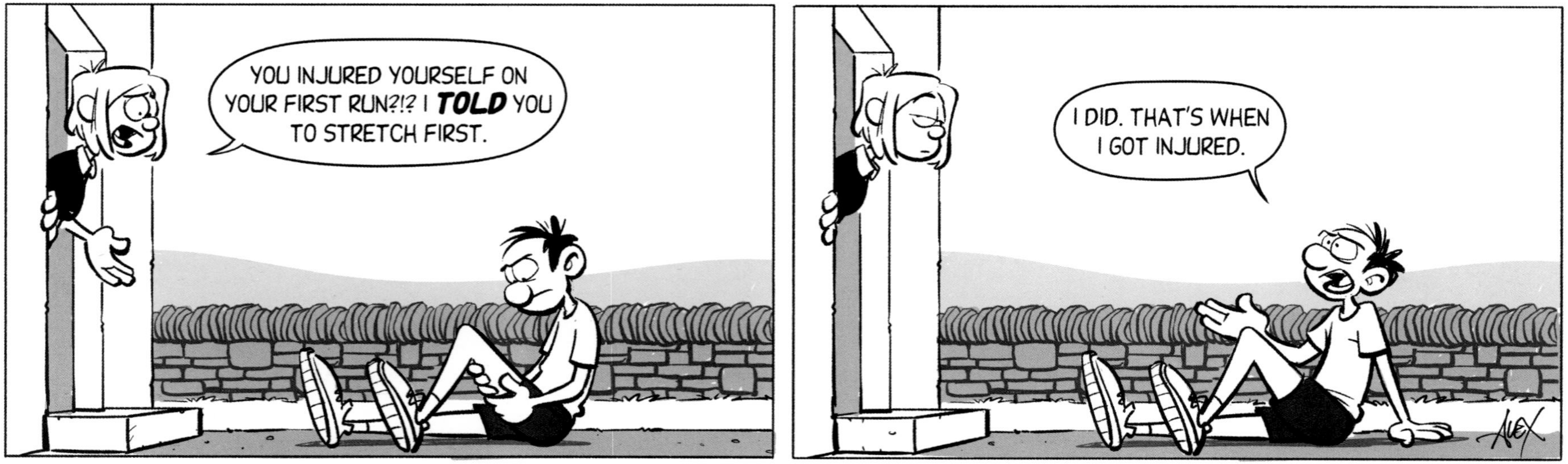
YOU INJURED YOURSELF ON YOUR FIRST RUN?!? I **TOLD** YOU TO STRETCH FIRST.
I DID. THAT'S WHEN I GOT INJURED.
ALEX

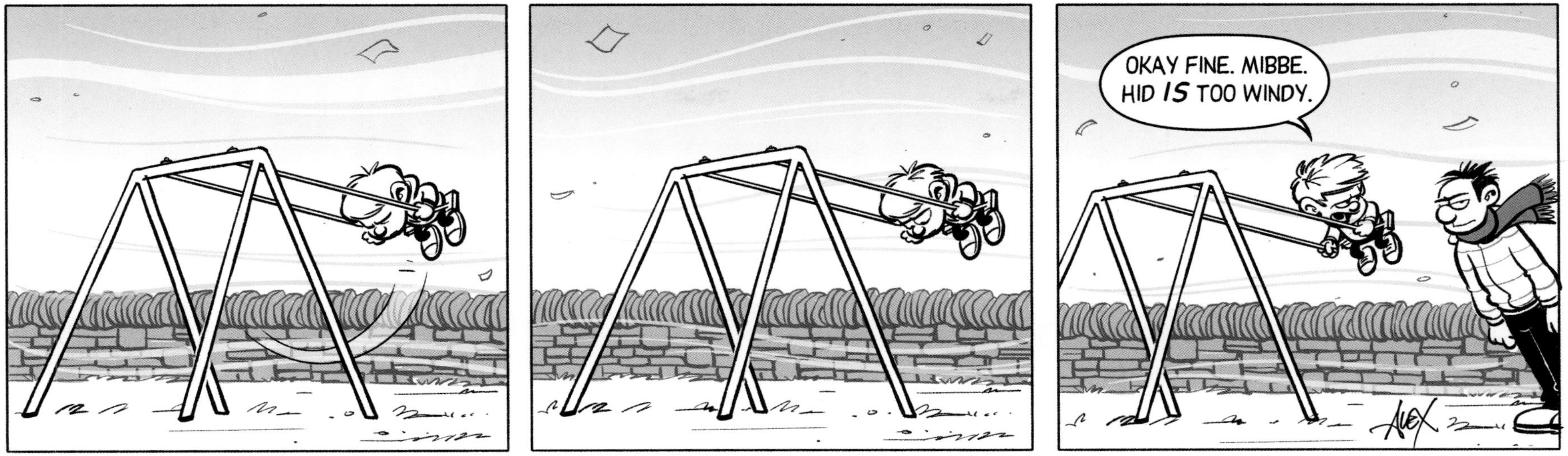
OKAY FINE. MIBBE.
HID IS TOO WINDY.
ALEX

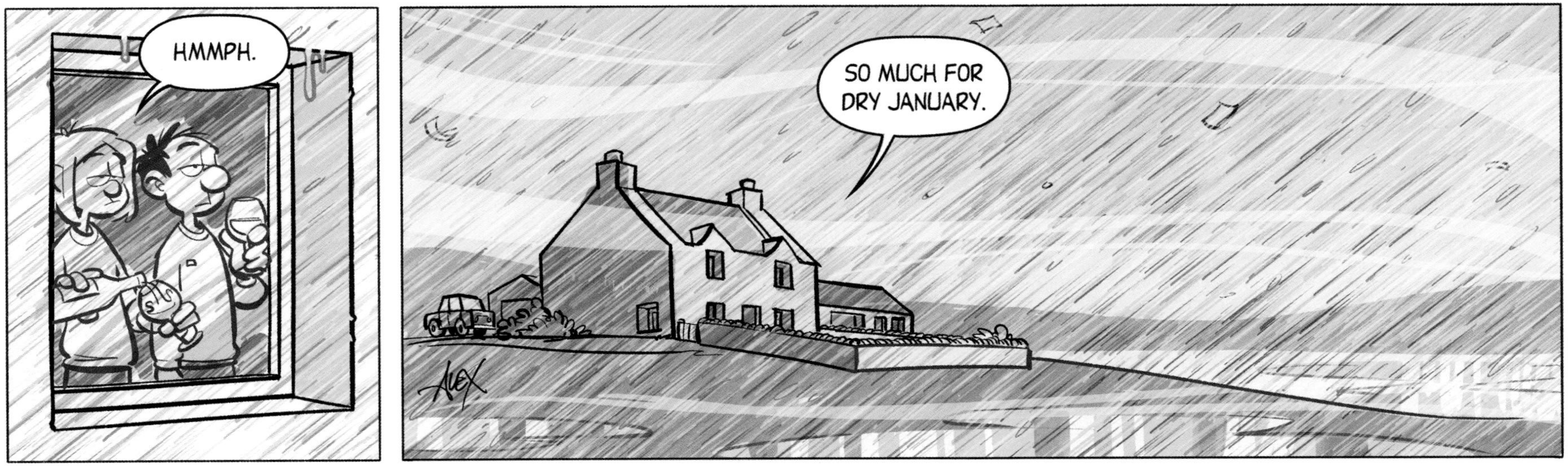
HMMPH.
SO MUCH FOR DRY JANUARY.
ALEX

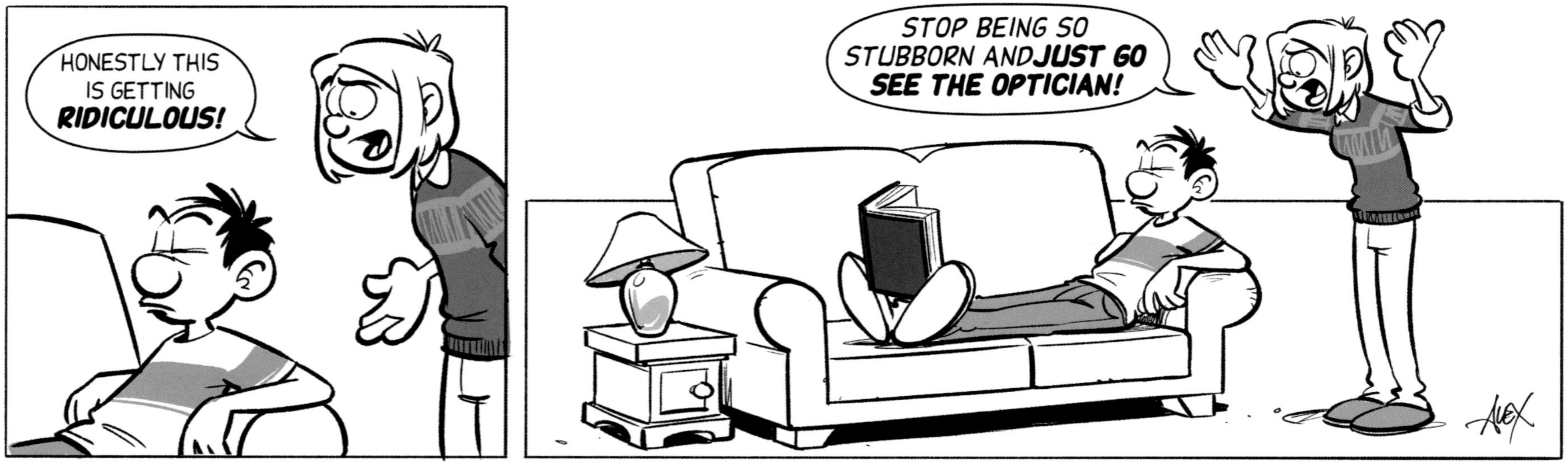
HONESTLY THIS IS GETTING **RIDICULOUS!**
STOP BEING SO STUBBORN AND **JUST GO SEE THE OPTICIAN!**
ALEX

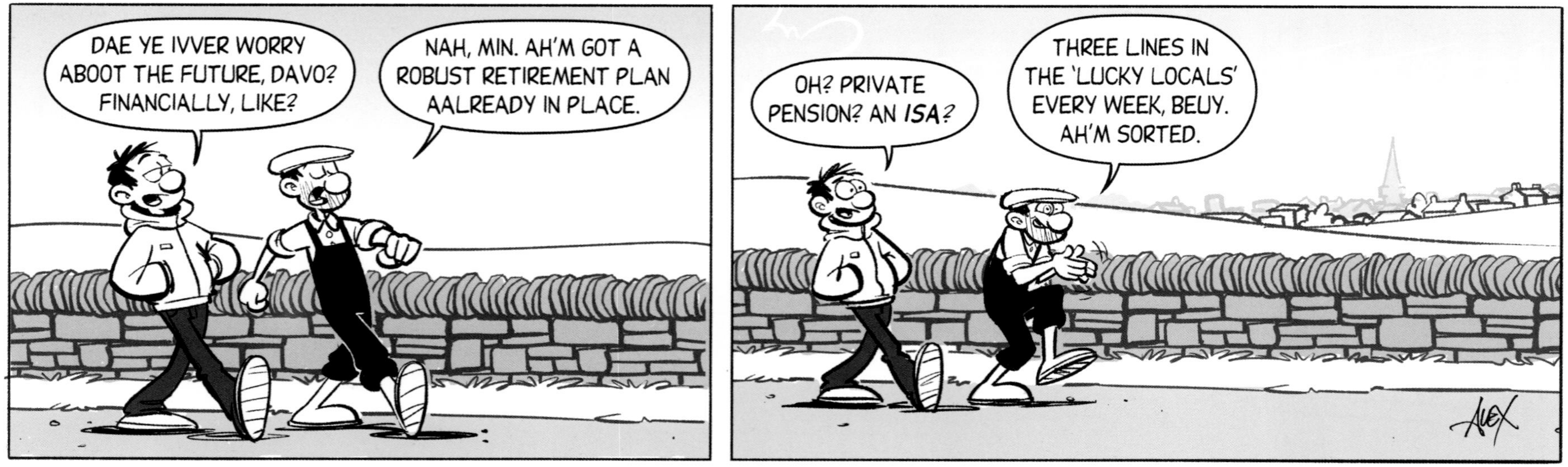
DAE YE IVVER WORRY ABOOT THE FUTURE, DAVO? FINANCIALLY, LIKE?
NAH, MIN. AH'M GOT A ROBUST RETIREMENT PLAN AALREADY IN PLACE.
OH? PRIVATE PENSION? AN *ISA*?
THREE LINES IN THE 'LUCKY LOCALS' EVERY WEEK, BEUY. AH'M SORTED.
ALEX

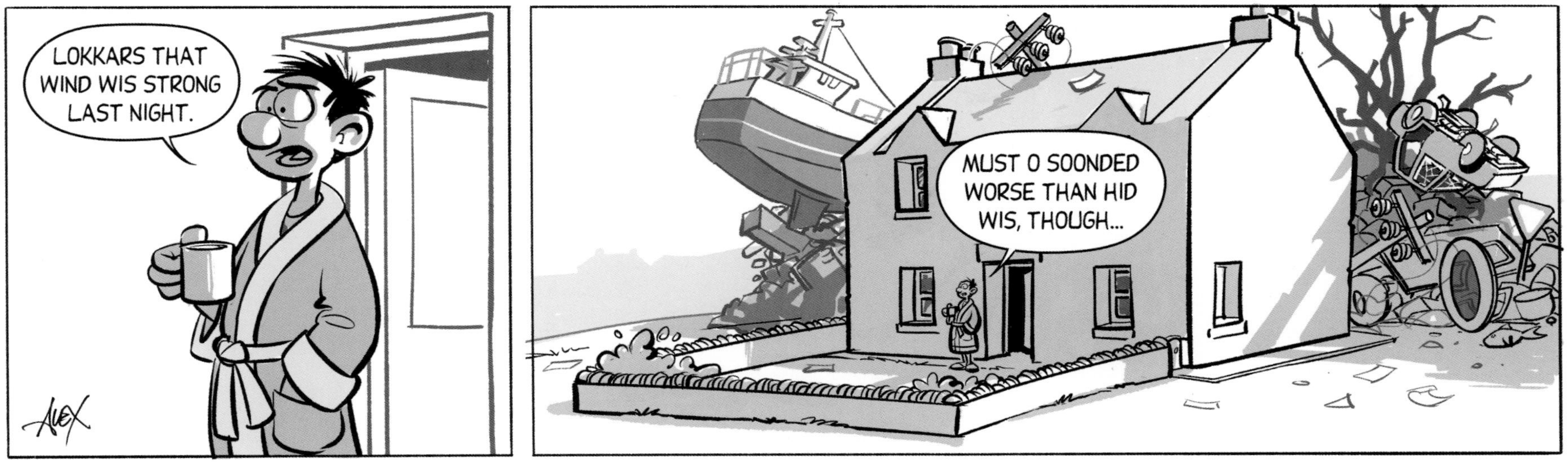
LOKKARS THAT WIND WIS STRONG LAST NIGHT.
MUST O SOONDED WORSE THAN HID WIS, THOUGH...

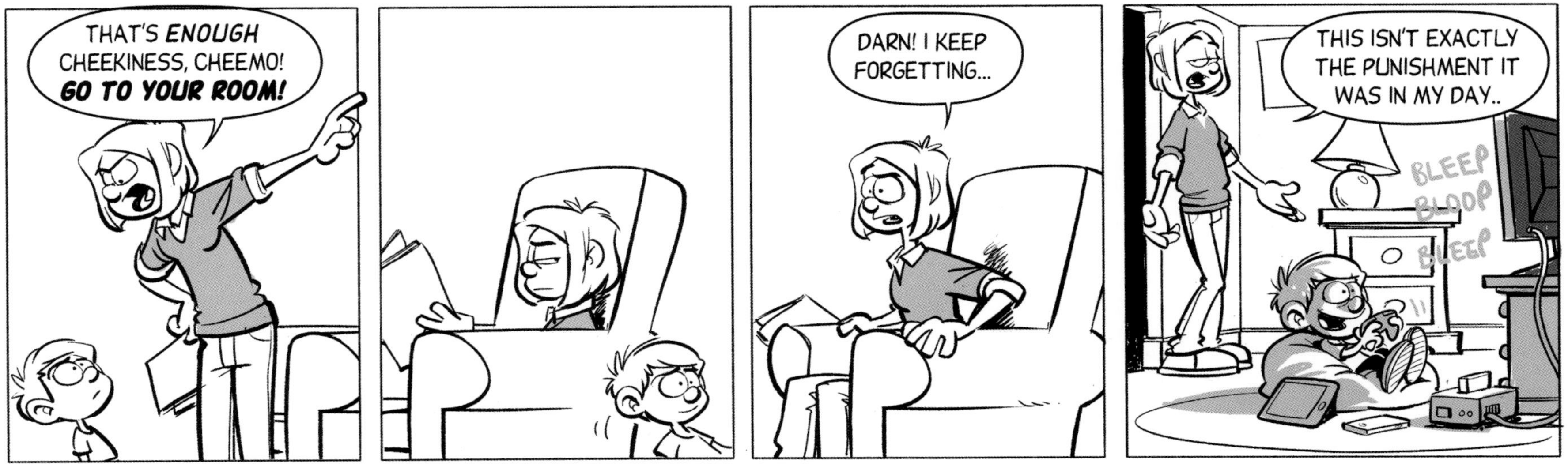
THAT'S ENOUGH CHEEKINESS, CHEEMO! GO TO YOUR ROOM!
DARN! I KEEP FORGETTING...
THIS ISN'T EXACTLY THE PUNISHMENT IT WAS IN MY DAY..
BLEEP BLOOP BLEEP

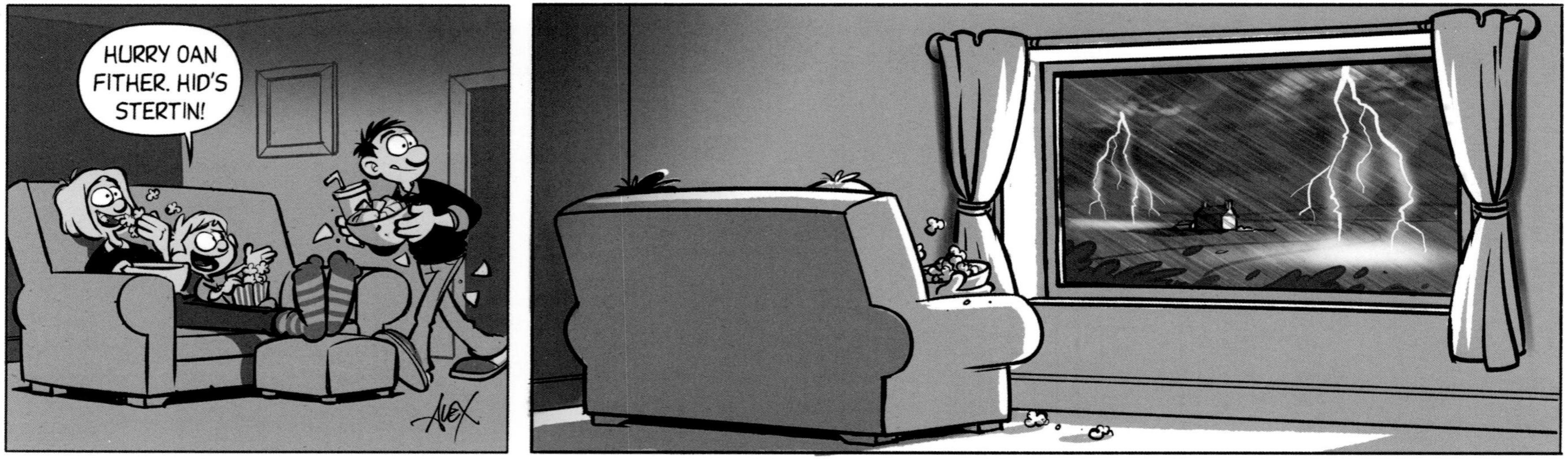
HURRY OAN FITHER. HID'S STERTIN!

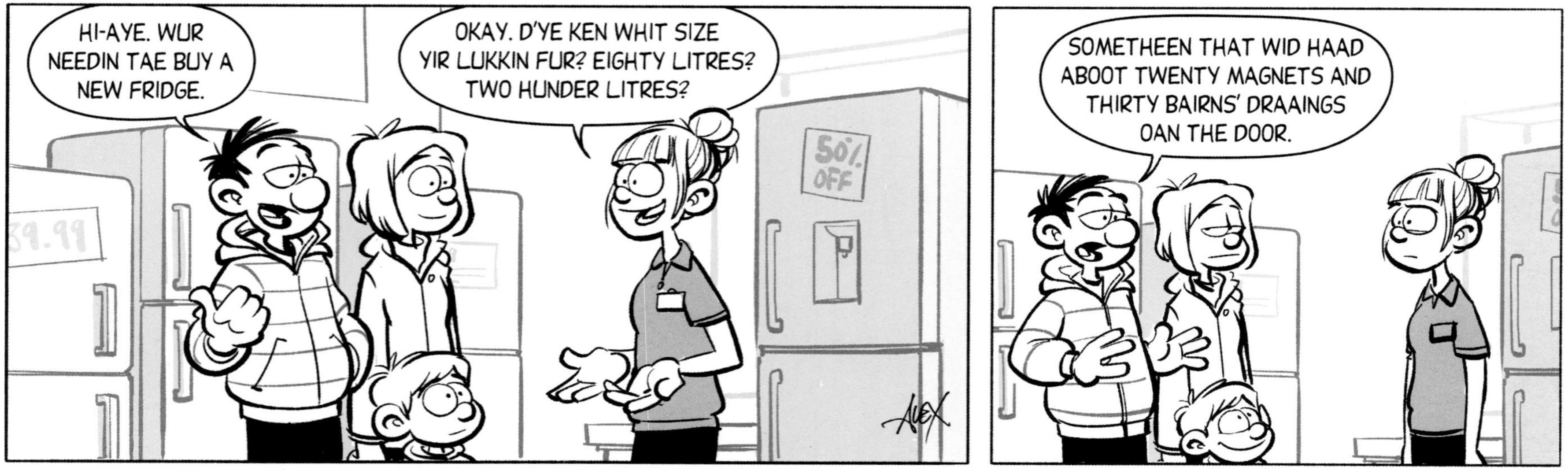
HI-AYE. WUR NEEDIN TAE BUY A NEW FRIDGE.
OKAY. D'YE KEN WHIT SIZE YIR LUKKIN FUR? EIGHTY LITRES? TWO HUNDER LITRES?
50% OFF
SOMETHEEN THAT WID HAAD ABOOT TWENTY MAGNETS AND THIRTY BAIRNS' DRAAINGS OAN THE DOOR.

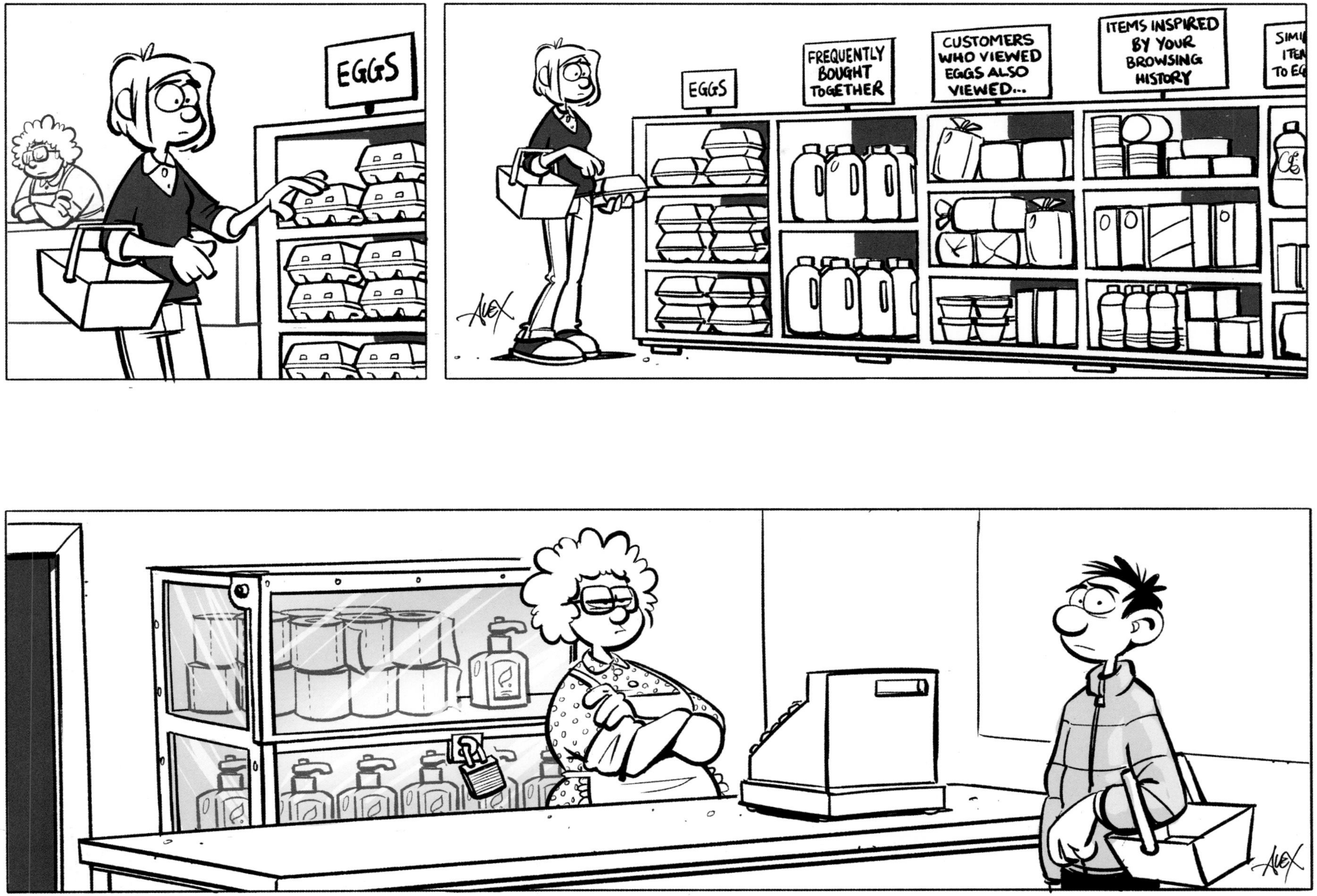
EGGS
EGGS
FREQUENTLY BOUGHT TOGETHER
CUSTOMERS WHO VIEWED EGGS ALSO VIEWED...
ITEMS INSPIRED BY YOUR BROWSING HISTORY

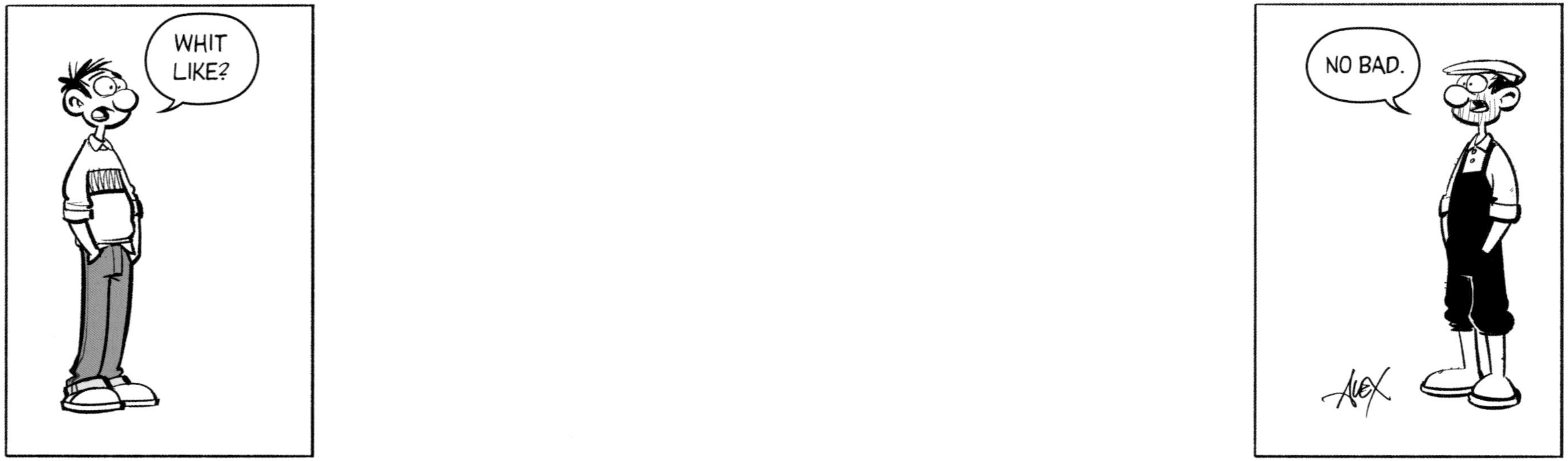
WHIT LIKE?
NO BAD.

Social Distancing, March 2020.

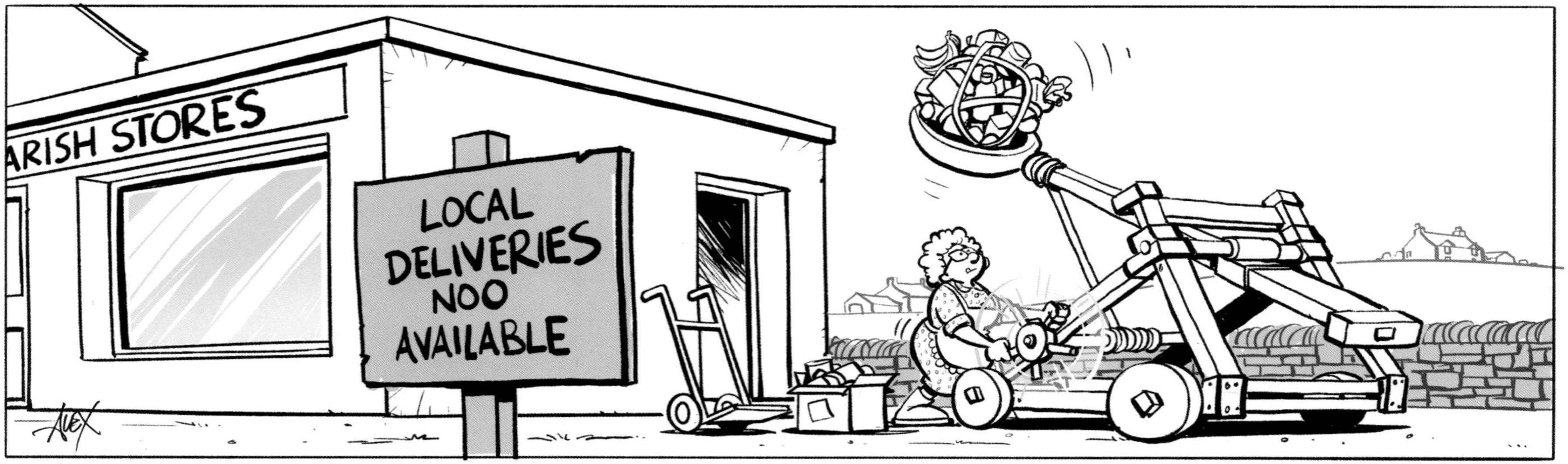
ARISH STORES
LOCAL DELIVERIES NOO AVAILABLE

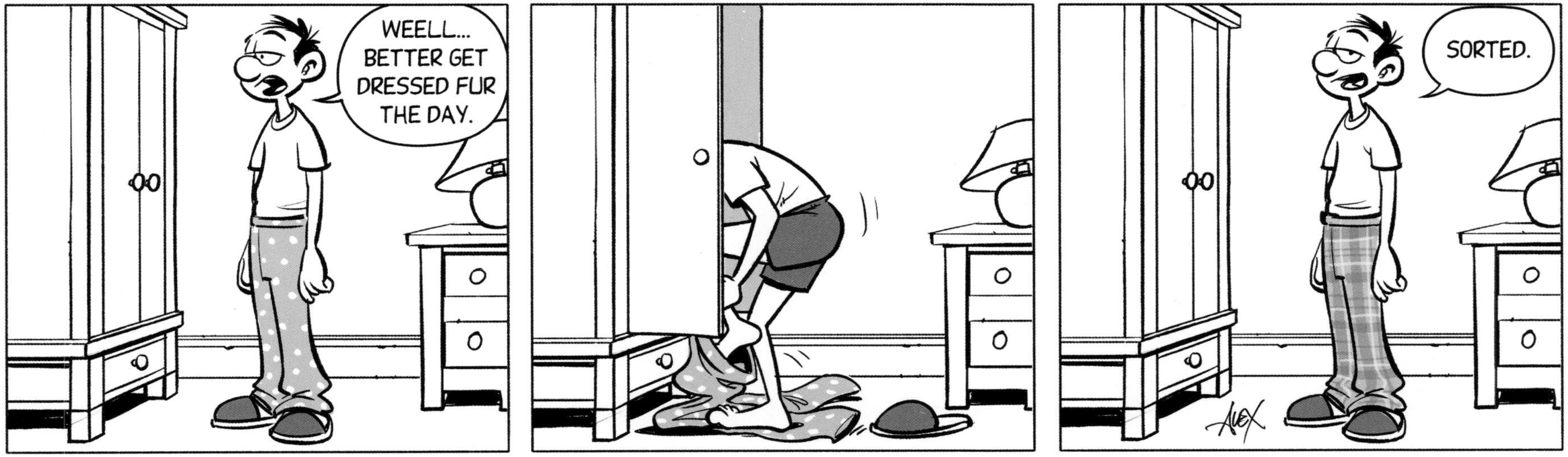
WEELL... BETTER GET DRESSED FUR THE DAY.
SORTED.
ALEX

# SUPPORT FOR HEROES POSTER

Coronavirus was dominating national headlines in late 2019, and by March 2020, Orkney had its first cases, and the imposition of national lockdown restrictions.

The community sprang into action to support the most vulnerable — those "shielding" or isolating at home. The heartwarming efforts of local people set the tone of those first few weeks of lockdown — and community spirit was further heartened by Orkney's "key workers" — those who continued to work, across essential sectors.

In April, The Orcadian joined forces with Alex, to create a front page that shone a light on, and paid tribute to those key workers.

The "split-screen" design, featuring people selflessly going about their business amid the crisis, took inspiration from the means of online communication we all had to adapt to quickly — online meetings with colleagues, family and friends. But it was also hugely inspired by the superheroes of the comic book world . . . only this time, the heroes were far from fictional works of art. Posties, refuse workers and NHS staff were among its stars, and as Alex said himself, we only wished we could fit more on the page!

The special "Supporting Orkney's Heroes" wrap newspaper cover hit shelves on Thursday, April 9, and within hours was a viral sensation on the internet.

Widely celebrated, it perfectly captured a historical moment in Orkney, and pledged the newspaper's support in style.

Later, 100 signed, limited edition poster prints of the page quickly sold out. The proceeds, totalling £2,000 were donated to Orkney Blide Trust, which promotes mental wellbeing — a worthy cause in such strange times.

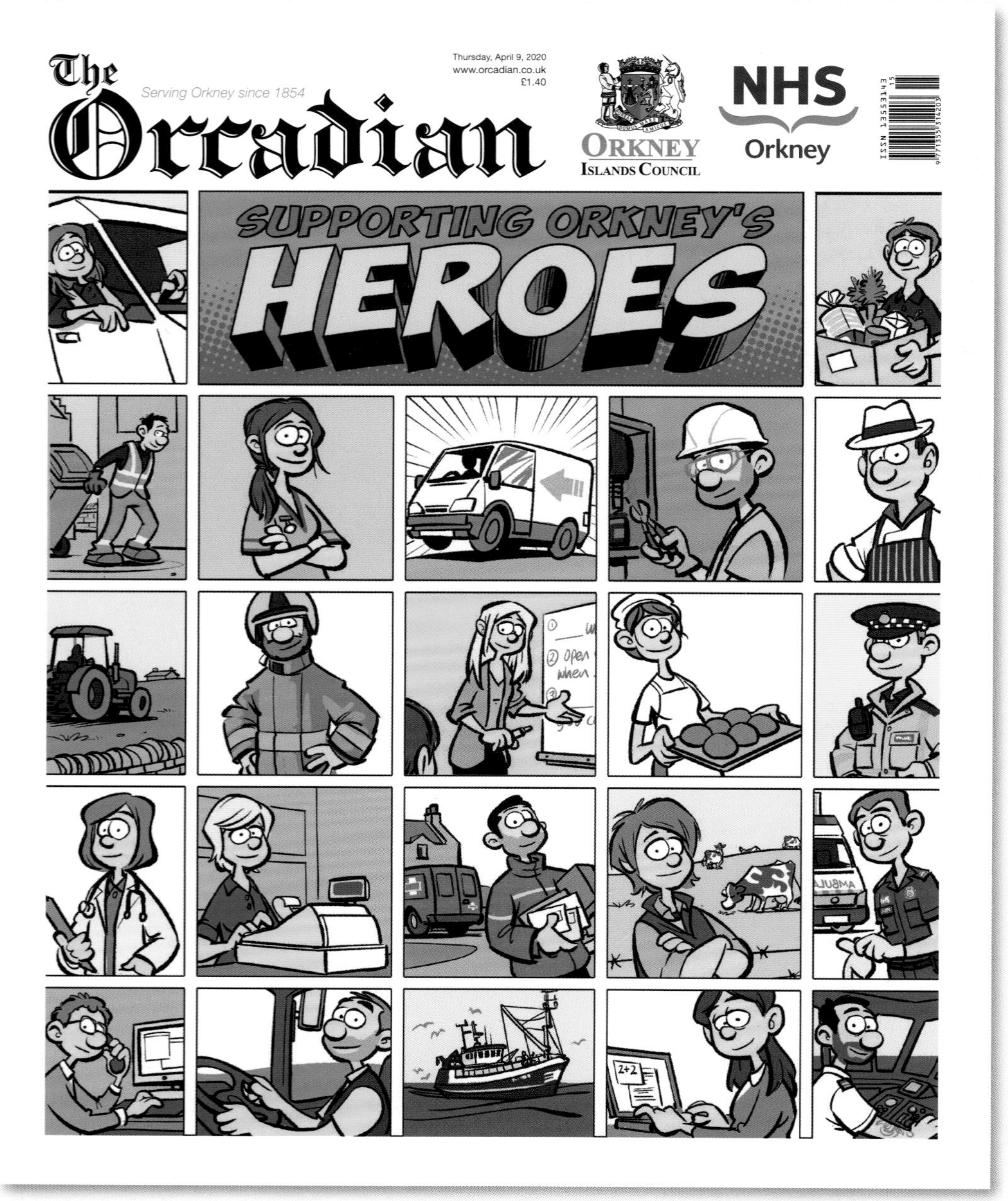
The Orcadian
Serving Orkney since 1854
Thursday, April 9, 2020
www.orcadian.co.uk
£1.40
ORKNEY
ISLANDS COUNCIL
NHS
Orkney
SUPPORTING ORKNEY'S
HEROES

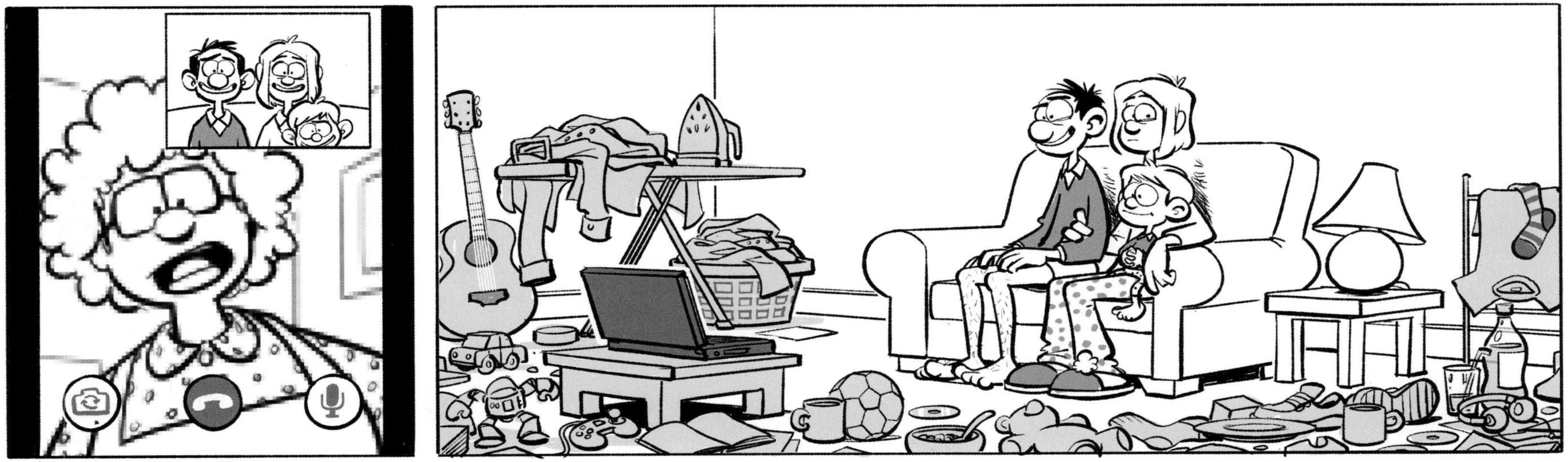

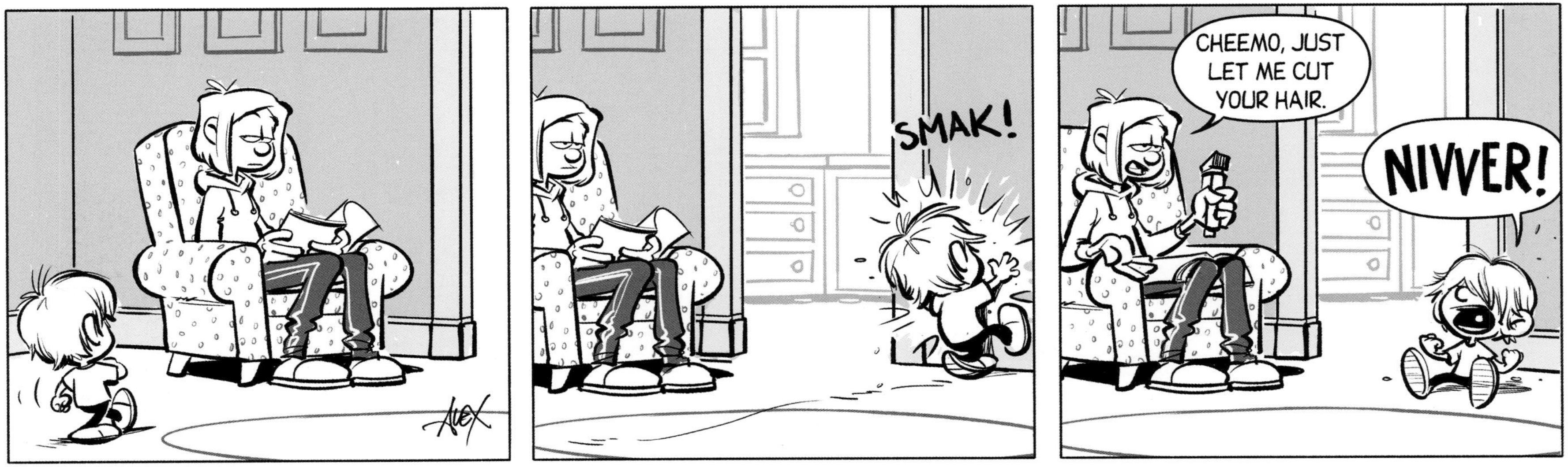
SMAK!
CHEEMO, JUST LET ME CUT YOUR HAIR.
NIVVER!

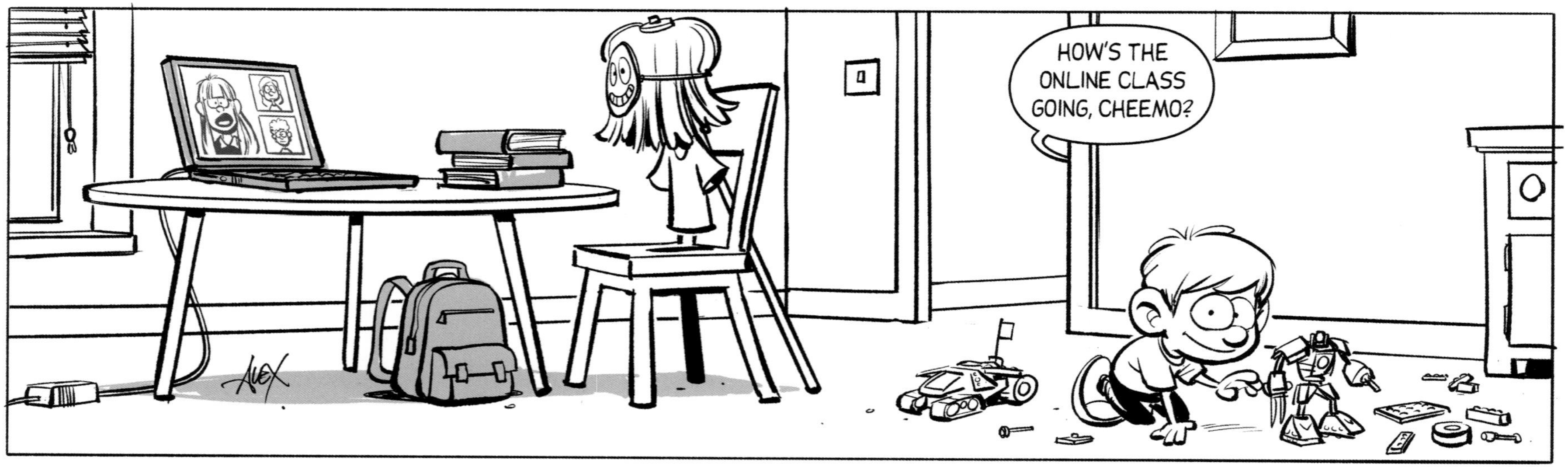
HOW'S THE ONLINE CLASS GOING, CHEEMO?
ALEX

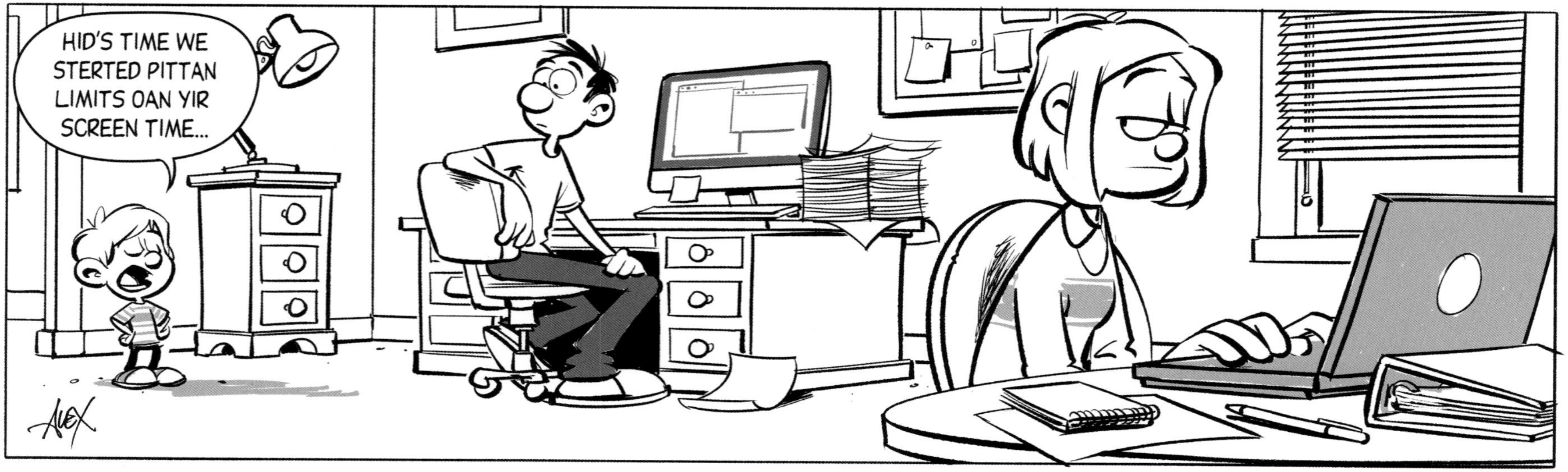
HID'S TIME WE STERTED PITTAN LIMITS OAN YIR SCREEN TIME...
ALEX

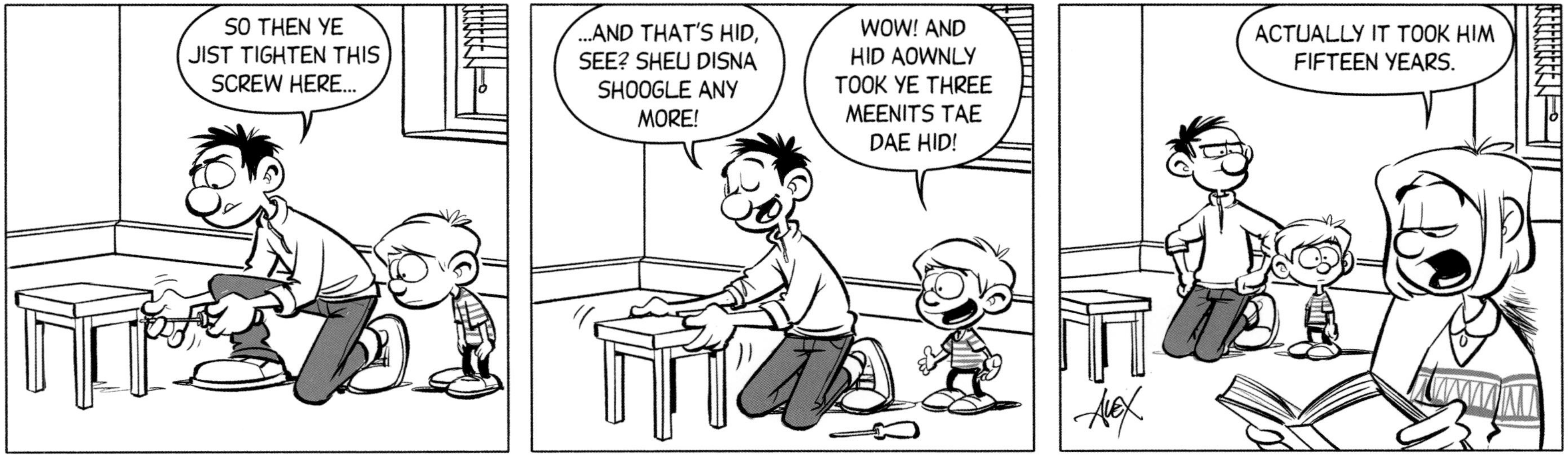
SO THEN YE JIST TIGHTEN THIS SCREW HERE...
...AND THAT'S HID, SEE? SHEU DISNA SHOOGLE ANY MORE!
WOW! AND HID AOWNLY TOOK YE THREE MEENITS TAE DAE HID!
ACTUALLY IT TOOK HIM FIFTEEN YEARS.
ALEX

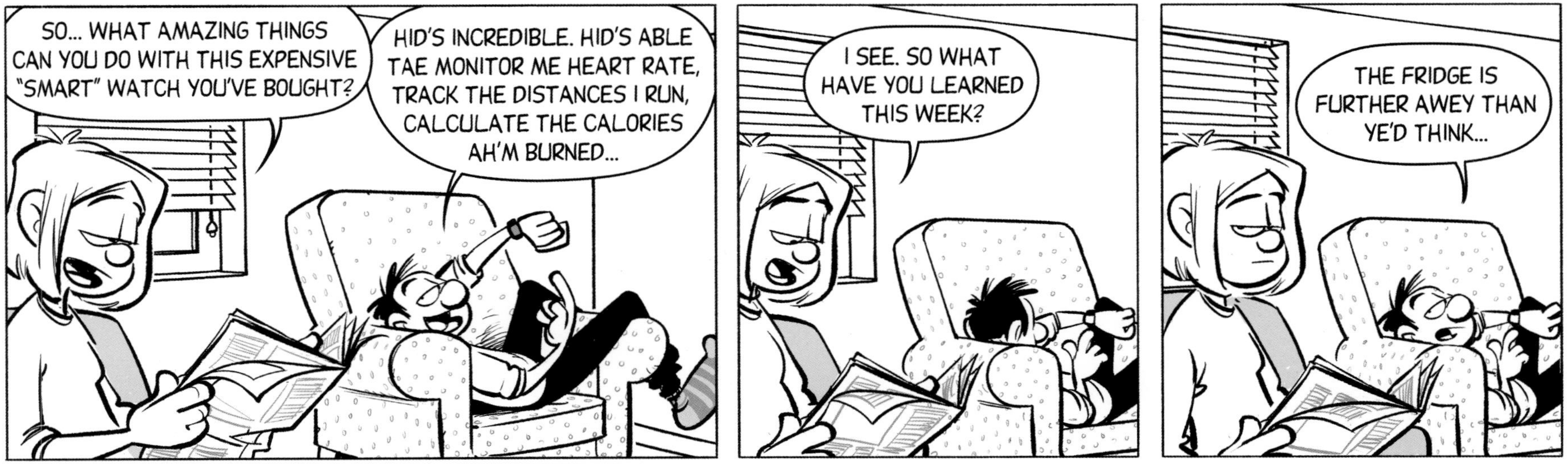
SO... WHAT AMAZING THINGS CAN YOU DO WITH THIS EXPENSIVE "SMART" WATCH YOU'VE BOUGHT?
HID'S INCREDIBLE. HID'S ABLE TAE MONITOR ME HEART RATE, TRACK THE DISTANCES I RUN, CALCULATE THE CALORIES AH'M BURNED...
I SEE. SO WHAT HAVE YOU LEARNED THIS WEEK?
THE FRIDGE IS FURTHER AWEY THAN YE'D THINK...

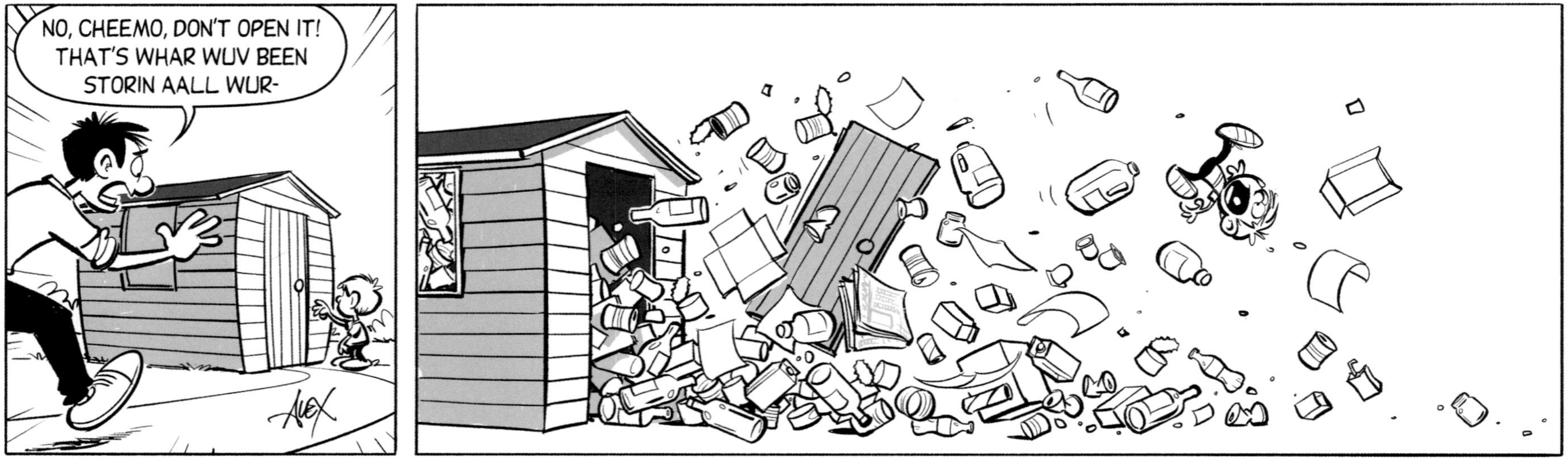
NO, CHEEMO, DON'T OPEN IT! THAT'S WHAR WUV BEEN STORIN AALL WUR-
ALEX

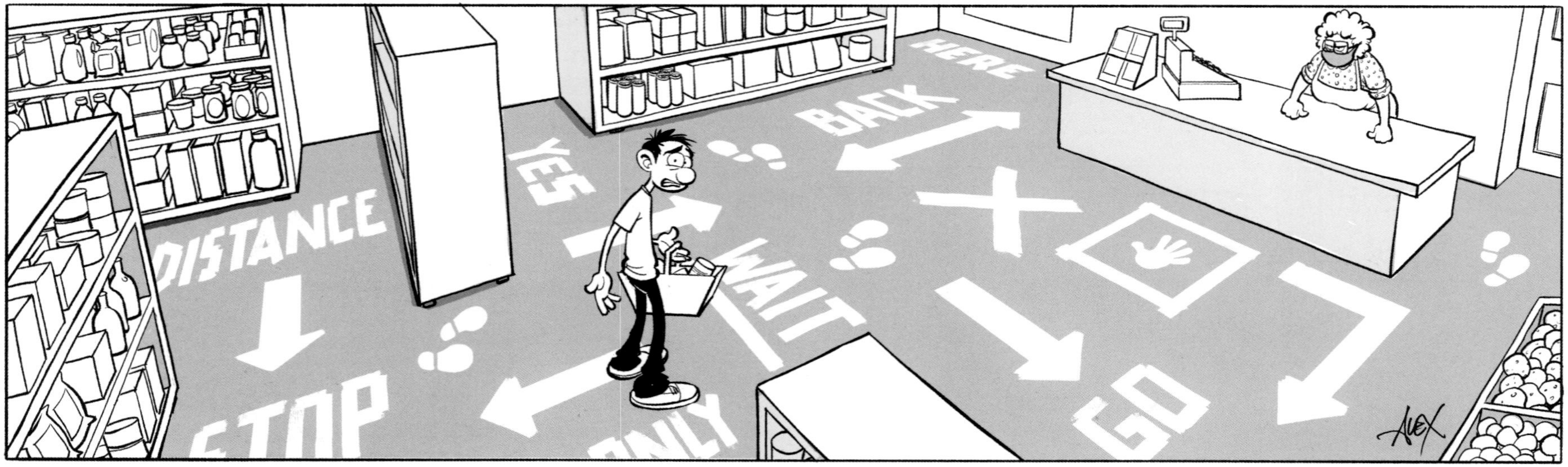
HERE
BACK
YES
DISTANCE
WAIT
STOP
ONLY
GO
ALEX

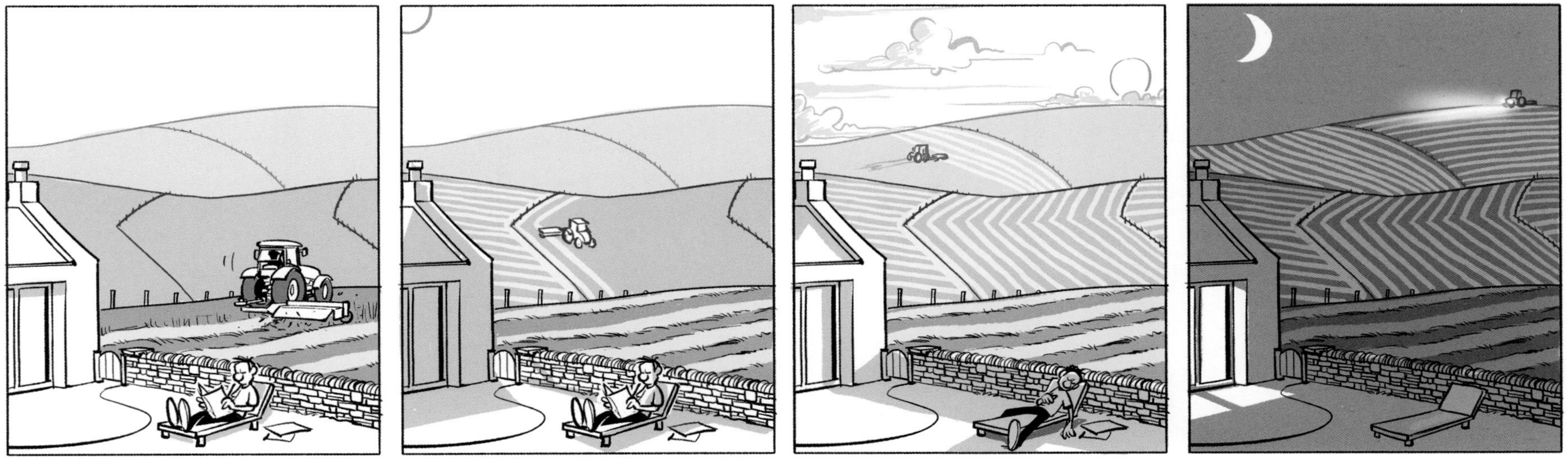

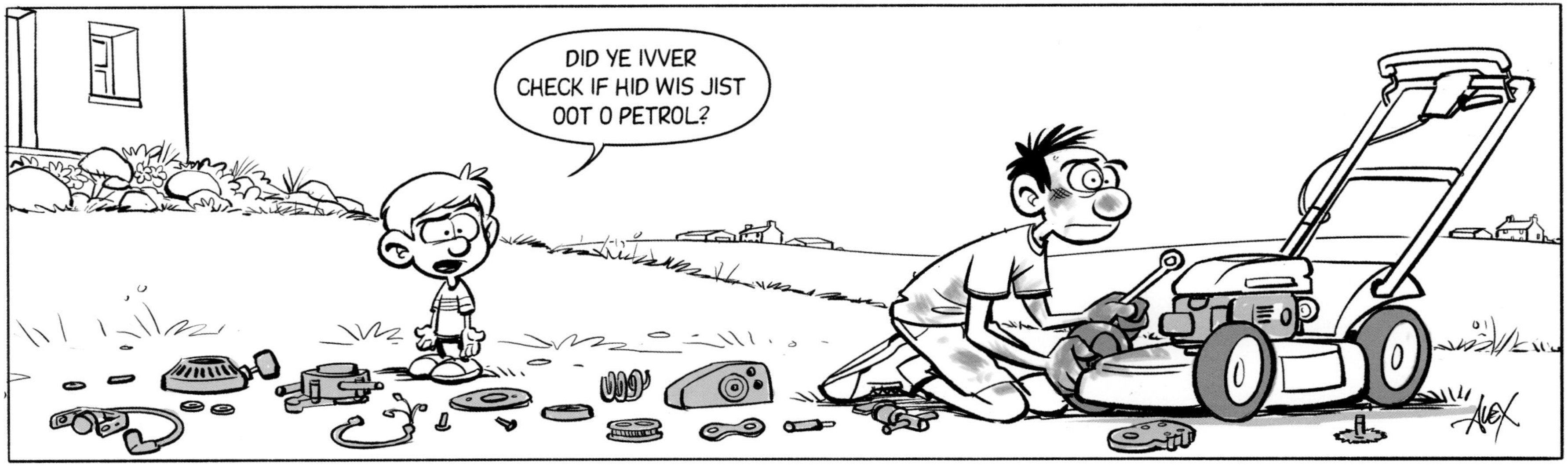
DID YE IVVER CHECK IF HID WIS JIST OOT O PETROL?
ALEX

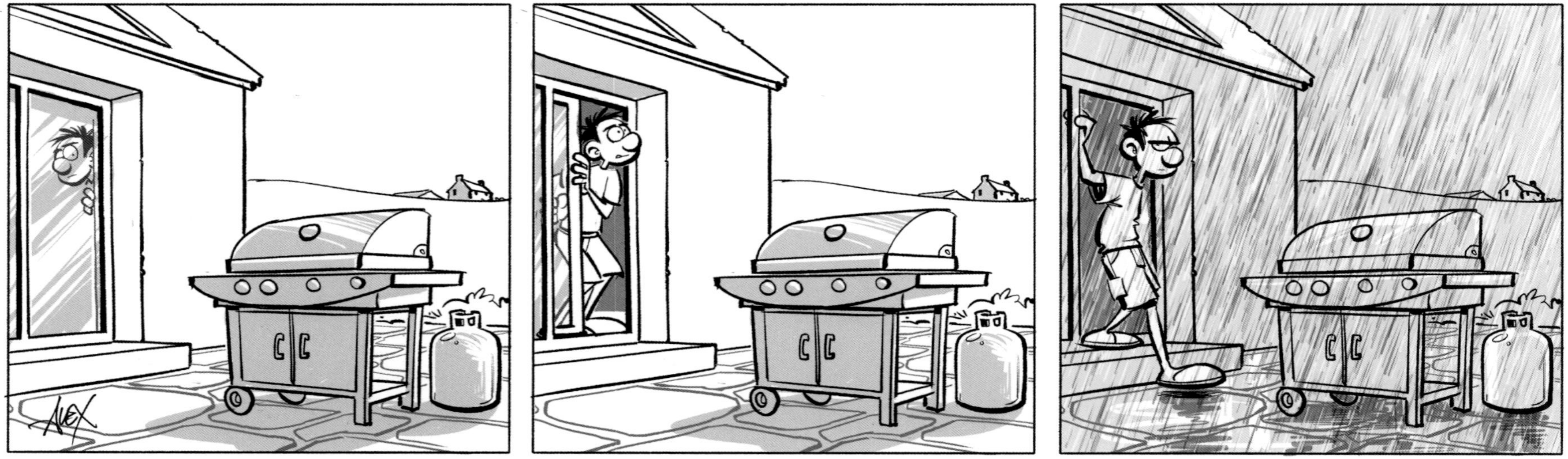
ALEX

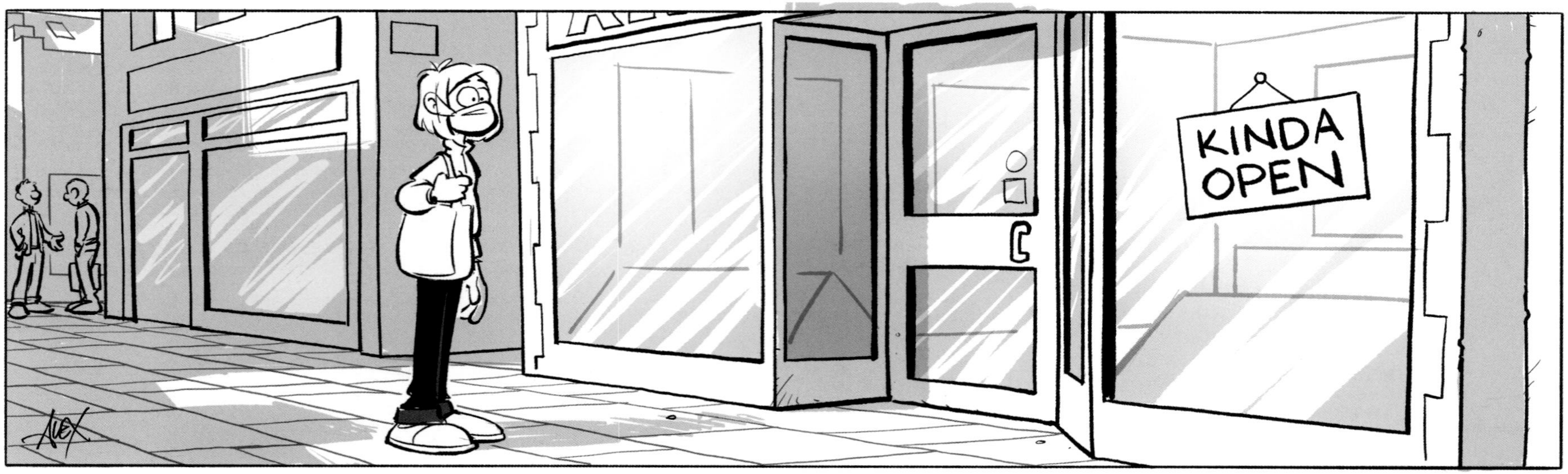
KINDA OPEN
ALEX

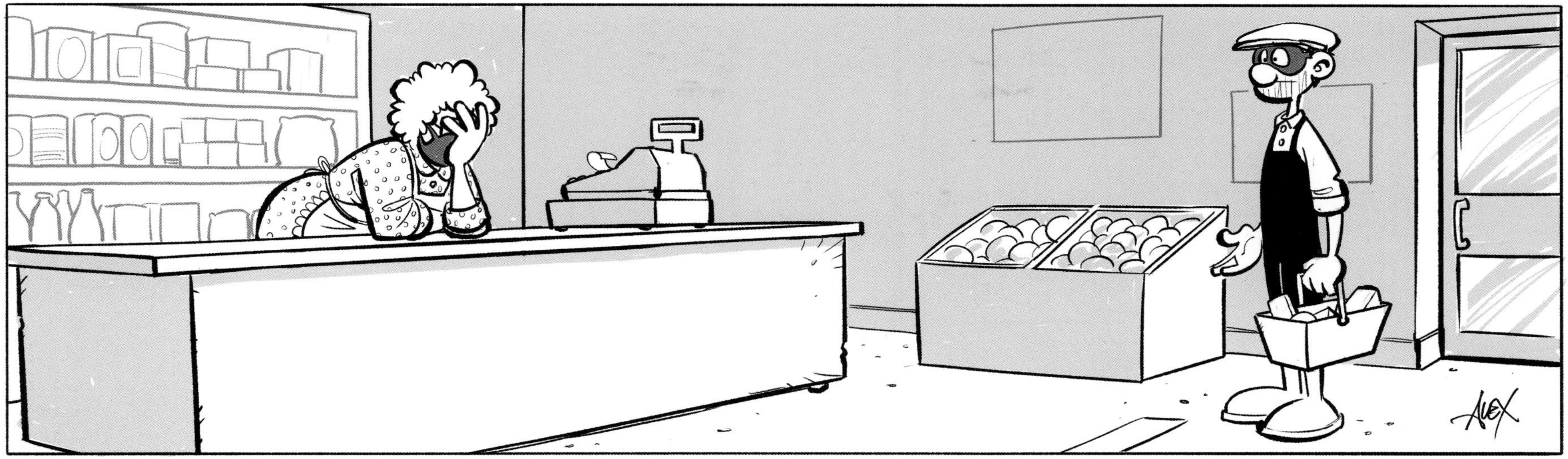

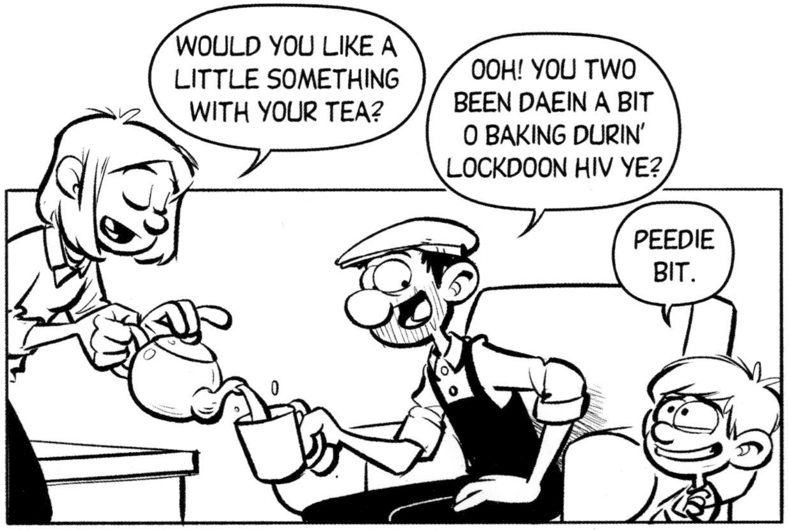
WOULD YOU LIKE A LITTLE SOMETHING WITH YOUR TEA?
OOH! YOU TWO BEEN DAEIN A BIT O BAKING DURIN' LOCKDOON HIV YE?
PEEDIE BIT.

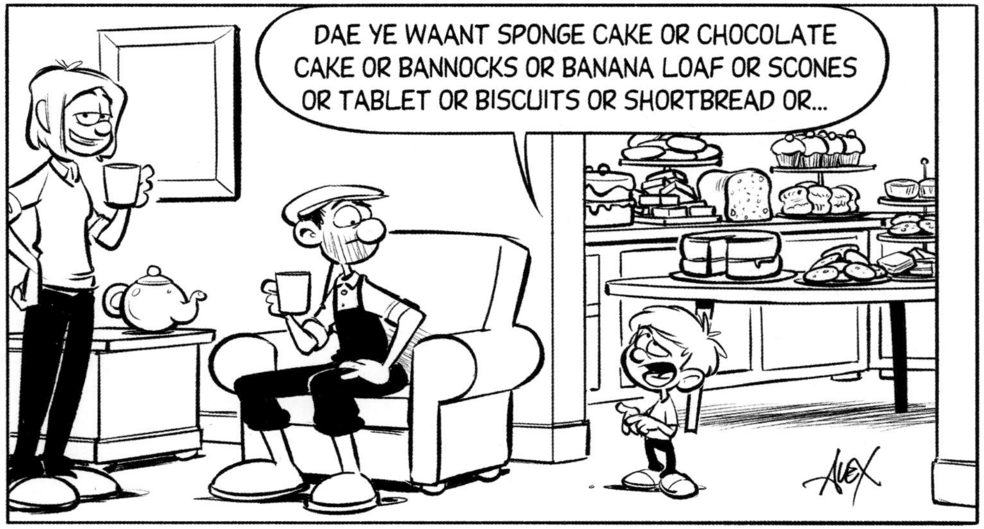
DAE YE WAANT SPONGE CAKE OR CHOCOLATE CAKE OR BANNOCKS OR BANANA LOAF OR SCONES OR TABLET OR BISCUITS OR SHORTBREAD OR...

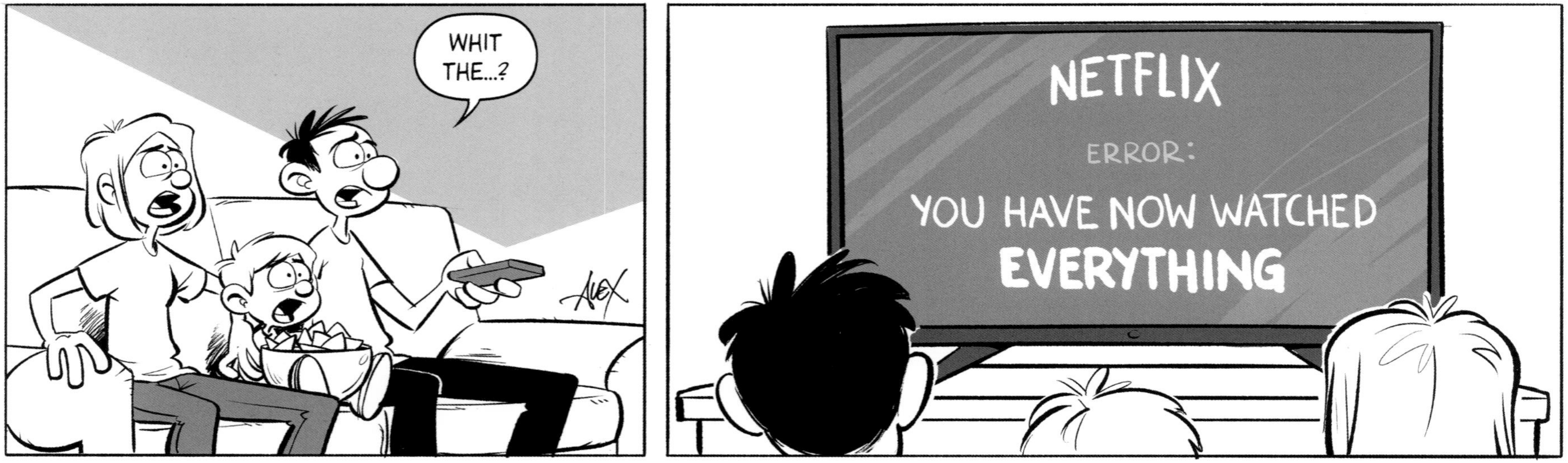
WHIT THE...?
NETFLIX
ERROR:
YOU HAVE NOW WATCHED
EVERYTHING

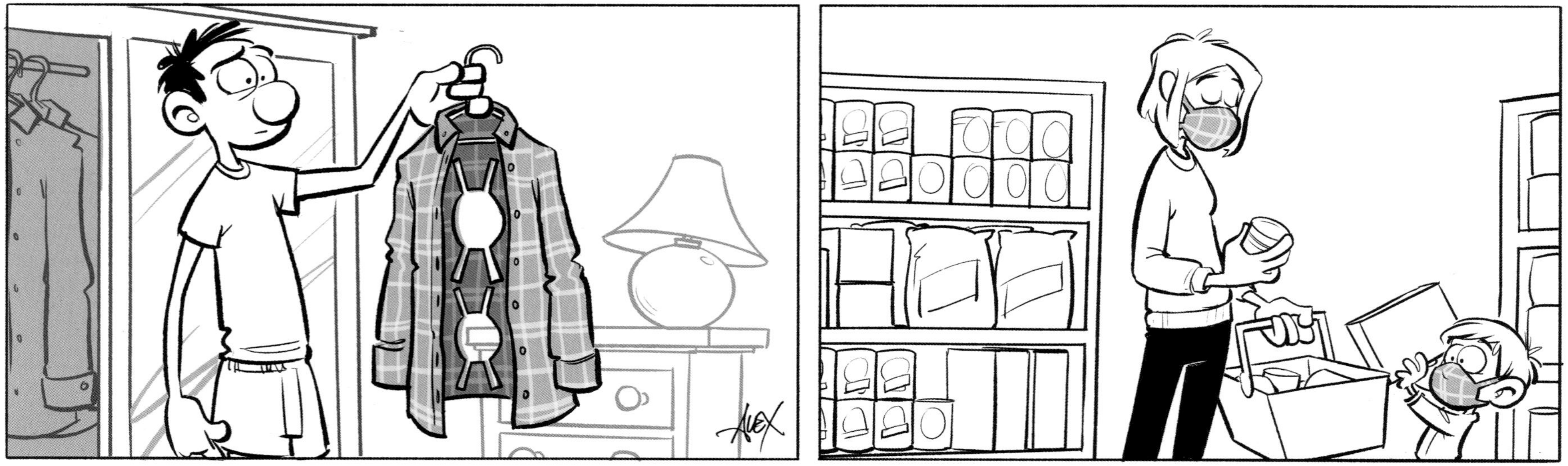

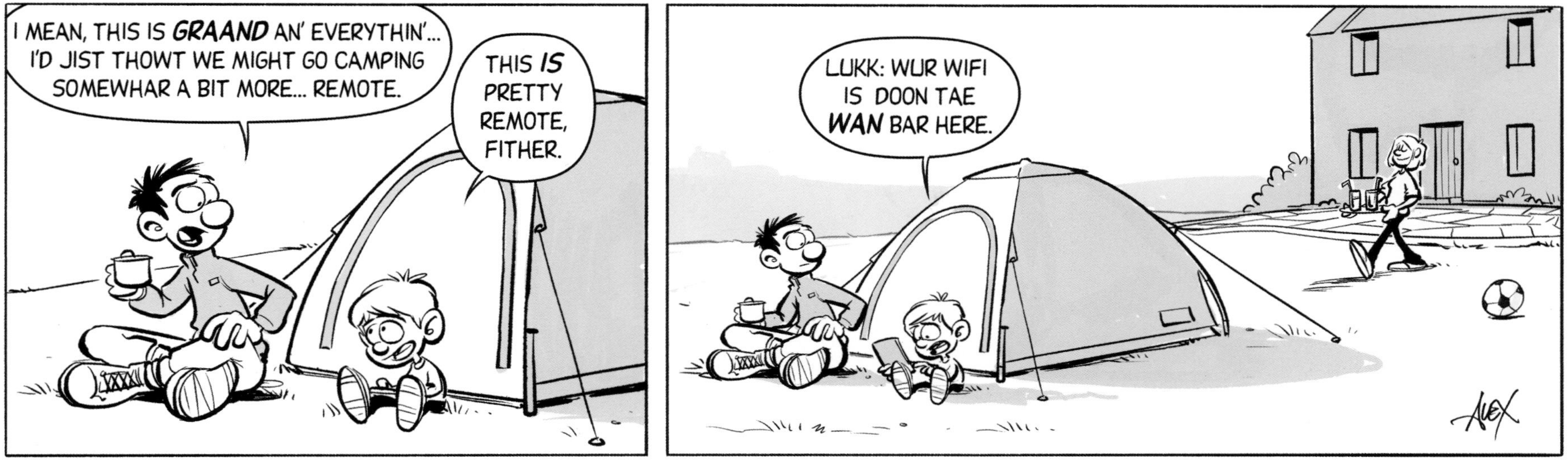
I MEAN, THIS IS **GRAAND** AN' EVERYTHIN'... I'D JIST THOWT WE MIGHT GO CAMPING SOMEWHAR A BIT MORE... REMOTE.
THIS ***IS*** PRETTY REMOTE, FITHER.
LUKK: WUR WIFI IS DOON TAE **WAN** BAR HERE.
ALEX

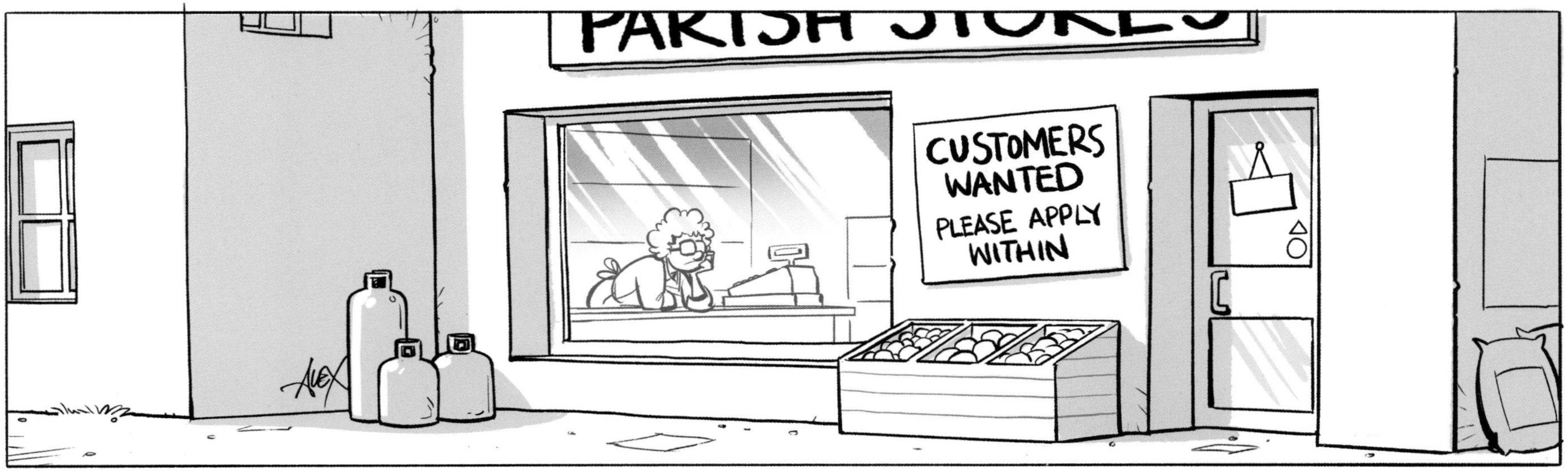
CUSTOMERS WANTED PLEASE APPLY WITHIN
ALEX

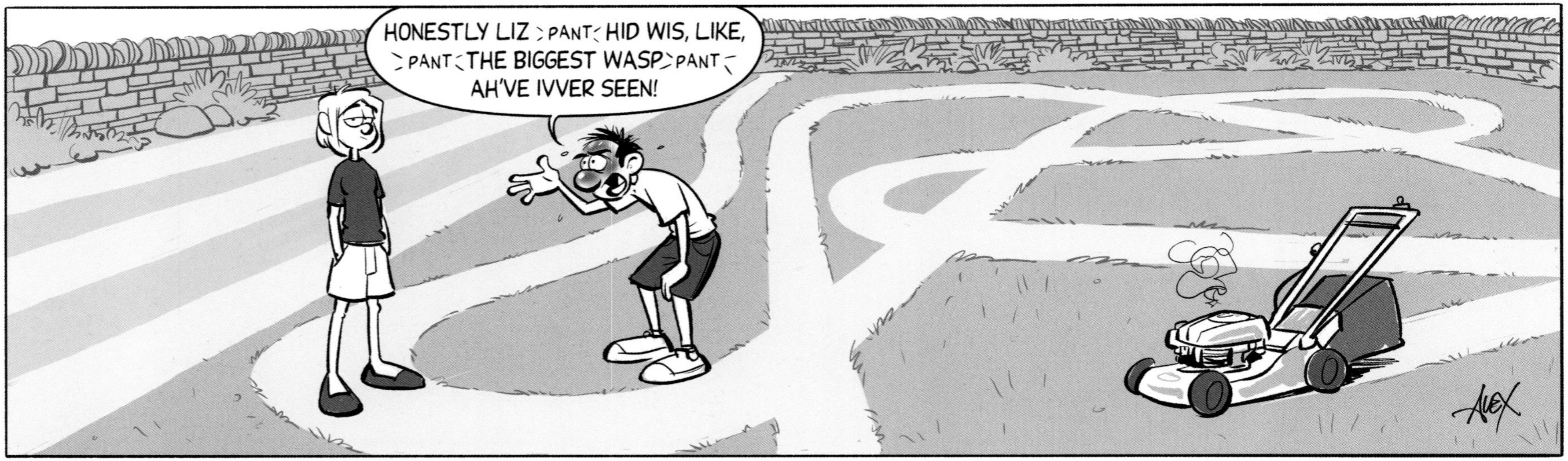
HONESTLY LIZ >PANT< HID WIS, LIKE, >PANT< THE BIGGEST WASP >PANT< AH'VE IVVER SEEN!
ALEX